AS WE SODOMIZE AMERICA

The Homosexual
Movement
and the
Decline of Morality
in America

AS WE SODOMIZE AMERICA

The Homosexual
Movement
and the
Decline of Morality
in America

O.R. Adams Jr.

WINEPRESS WP PUBLISHING

Packaged by WinePress Publishing, PO Box 428, Enumclaw, WA 98022. The views expressed or implied in this work do not necessarily reflect those of WinePress Publishing. Ultimate design, content, and editorial accuracy of this work are the responsibilities of the author.

Hardcover: ISBN 1-57921-278-6
Softcover: ISBN 1-57921-279-4
Library of Congress Catalog Card Number: 99-69337

ACKNOWLEDGMENTS

Grateful acknowledgment is made to my wife, Erika, who has given me moral support and help through the many years I have worked on this book—and suffered my irritations at some of the disgusting things about which I was writing; to my friend, John Perrine who helped me with proofreading and ideas; and to my secretary Cheran Mullins for her work and support.

Grateful acknowledgment is made to Peter LaBarbera, for his moral support and allowing the use of material from the Lambda Reports; to Dr. Paul Cameron for the material from him and his organization, the Family Research Institute; to Concerned Women for America; to members of Focus On The Family for the material furnished me; to Kevin Tebido and Colorado For Family Values for the voluminous material furnished; and to Tony Olmi, President, Lorenzo Espinosa, and other members of the New Mexico Christian Coalition for material furnished and their encouragement and ideas.

CONTENTS

INTRODUCTION

This book examines the homosexual movement as an integral part of the moral decline and disintegration of family values in this country which accompanied the political movement to the left since the 1960s. I also present possible ways we might move forward to regain the critically important values which supported the culture and society that made this a great country during the first two hundred years of its life, without losing the few improvements to our cultural ideas and principles that occurred since then.

A great deal of factual detail is included about the relevant things going on during the period covered, as disclosed by news items and articles. It is intended to show a coordinated slice of history during the period of time covered.

This book is written for the benefit of homosexuals as well as for those who are not.

By their movement and agenda, and by their "coming out" and promiscuity, homosexuals have done a terrible damage to themselves, and to innocent people who are not homosexuals. They introduced the deadly AIDS virus into this country and spread it among themselves and to innocent people. They contaminated blood supplies, sometimes intentionally, and were the cause of many completely innocent people dying of AIDS. Some were innocent children with hemophilia who had done nothing to deserve the terrible death inflicted upon them. I know of no other time in history when such devastation has been caused by such intentional vile and despicable acts. Yet, instead of being given the condemnation they deserve, they have been praised by our liberal news media and politicians.

Those who have acquired AIDS by their depraved acts have been treated as heroes. Those of us who have dared to say that such things are wrong are called bigots and homophobics. Laws are passed to protect homosexuals and those who have AIDS, at the expense of protecting the public from them. It has been difficult for persons who were raped or assaulted to even find out if the perpetrators had AIDS. These things are completely ridiculous. Many homosexuals have died of AIDS as a direct result of their vile and depraved acts, and many more will die because of such acts. As heinous as this activity has been, they plan something that is even more devastating.

In addition to destroying their own souls, they plan to destroy the very soul of this country by teaching us and our children that their depraved acts of sodomy are good and acceptable, and should even be "celebrated." When a country sinks to that level there is no lower that it can go. It will have reached the depth of depravity and corruption.

Since early Bible times, Sodom and Gomorrah have been considered by civilized societies to have been the ultimate of evil, degradation, and vile activities. In recent years we have videos of people engaging in acts, in public, in San Francisco, New York, and Washington, D.C., our nation's capital, that are more reprehensible than any described in the biblical accounts of Sodom and Gomorrah.

With the help of a gullible public, liberal news media, and those in the entertainment field who seem either to have no real knowledge of what they are endorsing, or have no real morals or courage, the homosexual movement has made great strides. Such words as "discrimination" and "bigot" have been misused to belittle and intimidate those who believe in Judaic-Christian principles. The media parrot the words made up by the homosexuals, for their propaganda purposes, such as "gay" and "homophobic".

Thirty years ago there was no definition of the word *gay* that fits the way it is now generally used. There was the definition, "wanton;

licentious; as, a gay-dog;" but that is not the way it is now applied to homosexuals, although that definition would be more appropriate than the way it is applied. Certainly the meaning usually intended by use of the word, gay, which is joyous and happy, has no application at all to the sick and destructive homosexual lifestyle that will be disclosed herein. Homophobic was not even in the dictionary, then. Homo means "man," and phobic means "fear." Homosexuals combined the two words and use it as a derogatory term in their propaganda for anyone who dares to still believe that the vile acts of sodomy are still wrong. The liberal media, entertainers, and others of the misinformed, dutifully and gullibly parrot the terms and use them in just the manner intended by the homosexuals.

They are going to teach us that black is white and white is black—and that right is wrong and wrong is right.

One of the words most effectively misused by the homosexuals and their supporters, has been the word, discrimination. It has been made to order for their purposes. This is because that ever since the beginning of the black civil rights movement, the people in this country have had it pounded into them that discrimination is wrong. An intelligent person is very discriminating as to a person he marries, works for, hires, associates with, or rents to, and has on his premises. Good moral character has always been an important factor, in considering all of these things. We will go into this issue in more detail later in Chapter 6, The Homosexual Agenda. The idea of non-discrimination has been so instilled into the American people that many of them have completely lost any ability to reason in this area.

Several years ago, while I was testifying before the New Mexico Legislature in opposition to a so-called "Gay Rights Bill," I was amazed to hear a conservative Republican legislator say, "I don't believe in discriminating against anyone, but I do not believe in giving these people any special rights because of any perceived sexual orientation." I was glad that the man's ultimate conclusion was correct, but I was disturbed by his illogical preface. I felt like saying: "Really, no matter how terrible the acts a person might engage in, you think that he should be looked upon and treated as a good decent person?"

On October 16, 1996, in the second debate of the Democrat and Republican presidential candidates, Robert Dole said essentially the same thing as the statement of the New Mexico state senator referred to above when asked what his position was on homosexual rights. He then made it worse by talking about how he supported the Americans With Disabilities Act, which, among other things, prohibits unreasonable discrimination against persons with disabilities. It is amazing that a person of his stature would have been so ill prepared and unknowledgeable on the subject. It is unthinkable that supposedly intelligent people cannot see the difference between a person's race or disability, and the vile and destructive acts of sodomy.

These are classic examples of the foolish thinking brought about in so many by the incessant anti-discrimination brain-washing to which we have been exposed for so many years.

The homosexuals immediately seized upon the idea, and quickly used it to their advantage. They were quick to usurp the ongoing civil rights movement as their own. And many blacks, mesmerized by the approach that they themselves had used so long, were quick to let them. The same is true of many in the Jewish community. However, there is one great difference. Since I began working against the homosexual movement, I have met a number of ex-homosexuals. I have never met an ex-black. A person is born in a certain race. Discriminating against a person for immoral and destructive conduct has no analogy at all to discriminating against a person because of his race.

In this book, I use the word *homosexual* to apply to both male and female persons who voluntarily engage in acts of sodomy. The word *sodomy* is used to define sexual acts between persons of the same sex.

Those working for the homosexual movement have had a well-laid-out plan as to their approach. They have been very successful. They talk about their mistreatment and how they are wrongfully discriminated against, but they do not want to go into the acts of sodomy in which they engage, and because of which they are classified as homosexuals. They fully realize how detrimental such knowledge and consideration of their acts would be to their agenda.

It is certainly amazing how members of the news media who cover homosexual issues avoid any discussion of what homosexual acts are —the acts by which homosexuals become homosexuals. This is exactly what the homosexual activists want, and what they have planned for us. The media fall right in line with the agenda. This is true even among many of the conservative columnists who write against parts of the movement.

As a young man I was a cowboy, I was in the armed forces for over three years during the Second World War, I was in combat overseas, I have been in a number of countries, and I was a federal law enforcement officer for over seven years. I have been an attorney since 1954, and in private practice since 1957. In the early days, I handled criminal cases when appointed by the courts, and after government legal aid came into existence, I was primarily a civil trial attorney. I thought that I knew a lot about people and a lot about life, but when I started studying about the acts of homosexuals, both men and women, I soon concluded that I had been rather naive. I would never have believed the utterly sick and filthy acts in which these people engage.

One cannot make a reasonable assessment as to whether or not homosexuality is a good, decent, and acceptable lifestyle without having a knowledge of the nature of the acts by which these people acquire their classification. I realize that even describing such things will turn the stomach of many decent people, but I consider it to be a necessary and critical part of this book.

For supposedly sane people to promote such things as an "acceptable alternative lifestyle" is depravity beyond my imagination. And for the news media, entertainers, and liberal politicians to knowingly support them is truly unbelievable. To what depth can a country sink? Besides the great moral destruction being done to our country, mortal moral and physical destruction is being done to the homosexuals. It is indeed a sad thing for one to gain his classification in life by the perverted sexual acts in which he engages.

One of the most destructive things that has happened as a result of the homosexual movement is the successful pressure brought on the American Psychiatric Association and the American Psychological Association which, primarily through intimidation, pushed them into regarding homosexuality as something that is normal, instead of a mental illness as it had been diagnosed during all of the time of the existence of these organizations, prior to this time. It is a sad moment in our history when medical diagnoses can be changed as a result of destructive politics. These organizations have abandoned a large segment of the population that is in dire need of their care.

A primary purpose of this book is to encourage homosexuals to leave this destructive way of life, and become decent human beings. There are those who will give them help, and many have been able to turn from homosexuality and become happy, productive, and satisfied as heterosexuals.

When the vile and sick acts of sodomy become acceptable, we will have lost the culture and decency that has been the backbone of our country.

It might be asked: Why has there been a concentration on the bad things going on in the country, and so little said about the good things? The answer is rather simple. It is not the good things that are ruining our country—it is the bad—and there has not been enough good to turn our country around from its hurtle toward destruction.

FORM AND STYLE USED

A number of authors use different, although acceptable, forms and styles. A comment on the uses in this book may be helpful. I have tried to be as accurate as possible in conveying factual information. I also try to give the source of facts that are not from my own personal knowledge, and to indicate the ideas of others. Information derived from a video tape will of course not have page references. Where information is obtained from a book or a writing, it will be indicated by quotations, or by references where exact quotes are not used, with page references, if from lengthy material. The references may pertain to several preceding sentences, or several preceding paragraphs.

My own ideas and comments will be indicated either by statements without references, or by putting my statements in parentheses where they are included with material being referred to. My statements placed within exact quotations will be only for the purpose of giving the substance of or an explanation of omitted material, or explaining words quoted (unless clearly indicated as my comments), and will be in brackets.

The common method of ellipses (...) indicates that material within a sentence quoted from has been omitted. Ellipses before a complete sentence quoted indicate that prior wording, immediately before that sentence, in the paragraph quoted from, was omitted. Ellipses followed by a space and a period (... .) indicate that source material within and at the end of a sentence has been omitted. A period, a space, and an ellipsis

(. ...) indicate that after the end of a full sentence quoted, subsequent material from the same paragraph of the source was omitted. When one or more paragraphs are left out of quotations, it will be indicated by an ellipsis of three asterisks (***) in the center of the page, after a paragraph, or in a paragraph.

Also, in many instances, a number of references to a particular subject, writing, book, or tape, are separated from material which is not about that particular subject or work by a series of dashes (-------------), in the center of the page.

CHAPTER 1

WHAT ARE HOMOSEXUAL ACTS?

W hat precisely do homosexuals do with one another, and how do those acts define their intentions toward the society in which they live? Listen to the voice of the aggressive homosexual agenda:

> This essay is *outré*, madness, a tragic cruel fantasy, an eruption of inner rage, on how the oppressed desperately dream of being the oppressor.
>
> We shall sodomize your sons, emblems of your feeble masculinity, of your shallow dreams and vulgar lies. We will seduce them in your schools, in your dormitories, in your gymnasiums, in your locker rooms, in your sports arenas, in your seminaries, in your youth groups, in your movie theater bathrooms, in your army bunkhouses, in your truck stops, in your all male clubs, in your houses of Congress, wherever men are with men together. Your sons will become our minions and do our bidding. They will be recast in our image. They will come to crave and adore us.
>
> Women you cry for your freedom. You say you are no longer satisfied with men; they make you unhappy. We connoisseurs of the masculine face, the masculine physique, shall take your men from you then. We will amuse them; we will embrace them when they weep. Women, you say you wish to live with each other instead of

men. Then go ahead and be with each other. We shall give your men pleasures they have never known because we are foremost men too and only one man knows how to truly please another man; only one man can understand with depth and feeling the mind and body of another man.

All laws banning homosexual activity will be revoked. Instead legislation shall be passed which engenders love between men.

All homosexuals must stand together as brothers; we must be united artistically, philosophically, socially, politically and financially. We will triumph only when we present a common face to the vicious heterosexual enemy.

If you dare to cry faggot, fairy, queer, at us, we will stab you in your cowardly hearts and defile your dead puny bodies.

We shall write poems of the love between men; we shall stage plays in which man openly caress man; we will make films about the love between heroic men which will replace the cheap, superficial, sentimental, insipid, juvenile, heterosexual infatuations presently dominating your cinema screens. We shall sculpt statues of beautiful young men, of bold athletes which will be placed in your parks, your squares, your plazas. The museums of the world will be filled only with the paintings of graceful, naked lads.

Our writers will make love between men fashionable and *de rigeur*, and we will succeed because we are adept at setting styles. We will eliminate heterosexual liaisons through usage of the devices of wit and ridicule which we are skilled in employing.

We will unmask the powerful homosexuals who masquerade as heterosexuals. You will be shocked and frightened when you learn that your presidents and their sons, your industrialists, your senators, your mayors, your generals, your athletes, your film stars, your television personalities, your civic leaders, your priests are not the safe, familiar bourgeois, heterosexual figures you assumed them to be. We are everywhere; we have infiltrated your ranks. Be careful when you speak of homosexuals because we are always among you; we may be sitting across the desk from you; we may be sleeping in the same bed with you.

There will be no compromises. We are not middle class weaklings. Highly intelligent, we are the natural aristocrats of the human race, and steely-minded aristocrats never settle for less. Those who oppose us will be exiled.

We shall raise vast, private armies, as Mishma did, to defeat you. We will conquer the world because warriors inspired by and banded together by homosexual love and honor are invincible as were the ancient Greek soldiers.

The family unit — spawning ground of lies, betrayals, mediocrity, hypocrisy and violence — will be abolished. The family unit, which only dampens imagination and curbs free will, must be eliminated. Perfect boys will be conceived and grown in the genetic laboratory. They will be bonded together in communal setting, under the control and instruction of homosexual savants.

All churches who condemn us will be closed. Our only gods are handsome young men. We adhere to a cult of beauty, moral and esthetic. All that is ugly and vulgar and banal will be annihilated. Since we are alienated from middle-class heterosexual conventions, we are free to live our lives according to the dictates of pure imagination. For us too much is not enough.

The exquisite society to emerge will be governed by an elite comprised of gay poets. One of the major requirements for a position of power in the new society will be indulgence in the Greek passion. Any man contaminated with heterosexual lust will be automatically barred from a position of influence. All males who insist on remaining stupidly heterosexual will be tried in homosexual courts of justice and will become invisible men.

We shall rewrite history, history filled and debased with your heterosexual lies and distortions. We shall portray the homosexuality of great leaders and thinkers who have shaped the world. We will demonstrate the homosexuality and intelligence and imagination are inextricably linked, and that homosexuality is a requirement for true nobility, true beauty in a man.

We will be victorious because we are filled with the ferocious bitterness of the oppressed who have been forced to play seemingly bit parts in your dumb, heterosexual shows throughout the ages. We too are capable of firing guns and manning the barricades of the ultimate revolution.

("For The Homoerotic Order," by Michael Swift ("Gay Revolutionary"), *Gay Community News* (Boston), Feb. 15-21, 1987; reprinted in *The Congressional Record*; reprinted in *The Colorado Model*, Colorado for Family Values, Colorado Springs, Co. 1993, pp. 5-9 to 5-10)

If the above sounds to you like Nazism and Fascism, then you are astute, because a large number of the ideas undoubtedly came from writings which inspired and played a part in the Hitler Nazi movement in Germany, as did the homosexuals involved in it. These things are documented in detail in the excellent book by Lively and Abrams, *The Pink Swastika,* Founders Publishing Corporation, Keizer, Oregon, 1995. That book should most certainly be read in detail by anyone who is interested in the long-standing history of the homosexual movement; and by anyone who may have been confused by recent false and misleading information being put out by those in the homosexual movement trying to convince the public that homosexuals were persecuted the same as the Jews by the Hitler regime. In truth, a large number of them were the persecutors, and were largely responsible for the atrocities against the Jews, and against the femmes group of homosexuals, as is detailed in *The Pink Swastika.* When referring to this book, a few of the very large number of references used will be included, as examples of some of the documentation used by the authors, and for further study by interested readers.

Getting back to The Homosexual Agenda diatribe, above, we might ask: Well, how could this possibly be accomplished? Perhaps a better question might be: How are large parts of it now being accomplished? We will go into this in detail in later chapters.

We will now examine the acts that the sick mind of the homosexual thinks are so great and beautiful.

BEHAVIOR WHICH CLASSIFIES HOMOSEXUALS

Homosexuals, their supporters, and much of the gullible part of the public, want to talk about homosexuality in the abstract. They want to talk about discrimination, mistreatment of homosexuals, "bigots," and "homophobics." Bigots are considered by that community to be anyone who thinks homosexuality is wrong or is not an acceptable "lifestyle." Homophobic is a word they made up to try to intimidate decent people who do not subscribe to their ideas. They do not want us to think about their homosexual acts, by which they are classified as homosexuals. This is the approach we see used, and it follows a plan that is set forth at length in "THE OVERHAULING OF STRAIGHT AMERICA—WAGING PEACE—PART TWO," by Marshall K. Kirk and Erastes Pill, *Guide Magazine,* November 1987, a large part of which was reprinted in The

Colorado Model, Colorado for Family Values, 1993, pages 5-11 to 5-19. One paragraph of the article states:

> And when we say TALK about homosexuality, we mean just that. In the early stages of any campaign to reach straight America, the masses should not be shocked and repelled by premature exposure to homosexual behavior itself. Instead, the imagery of sex should be downplayed and gay rights should be reduced to an abstract social question as much as possible. First let the camel get his nose inside the tent — and only later his unsightly derriere!

My approach to this problem is that it is impossible for one to make an informed decision about a matter without being informed. One cannot make an intelligent decision about that lifestyle without having knowledge of the acts that make up that homosexual lifestyle, and the acts by which these people become homosexuals.

The last thing an intelligent person should do is hide from or ignore the facts. If one is going to be for something, then the details should be known of the acts one is supporting. If a person is going to be against something, the precise nature of what one is opposing should be determined. General and vague statements about "rights" and "discrimination" are not meaningful, and can only lead to erroneous and often destructive conclusions.

This is an exhaustive list, but I feel it is vital to clearly document the medical and scientific sources of this information so that it cannot be construed as opinion or hyperbole. These are the facts that homosexuals wish to hide.

Although a large number of us have been uninformed and naive about the unbelievably vile acts in which homosexuals engage, my study has shown that a number of them are rather common knowledge in professional circles concerned with research in and treatment of the sickness of mind resulting in such activities. Six authorities have been chosen as reference sources for description of the homosexual acts listed below, and for the statistics relating to them. Not all of the references gave statistics in each of the categories, although all of the references referred to the acts.

One of the foremost researchers and writers in this country on homosexuality, its causes and effects, is Paul Cameron, Ph.D., a psychologist. Dr. Cameron is head of the Family Research Institute, which was located in Washington, D.C., and now is located in Colorado Springs, Colorado. In Appendix A of a book by Paul Cameron, Ph.D., *Exposing the AIDS Scandal,* Huntington House, Inc., Lafayette, La., 1988, are comprehensive statistics on some of the more common homosexual acts. References to these statistics will be: Cameron (1988). The references used by Dr. Cameron for Appendix A are:

Gebhard PH *The Kinsey Data*, NY: Saunders, 1979

Jay K & Young A *The Gay Report,* NY: Summit, 1979

Cameron P Sexual Orientation & STDs *Nebraska Med Journal*, 1985, 70, 292-99

Schecter MT Changes in sexual behaviour *Lancet*, 1984, 1, 1293

Jaffee HW National case-control study *Annals Internal Medicine*, 1983, 99, 145-51

Biggar RJ T-Lymphocyte ratios in Homosexual Men *JAMA*, 1984, 251, 1441-6

Quinn TC The Polymicrobial Origin of Intestinal Infection in Homosexual Men *New England J Med*, 1983, 309, 576-82

McKusick L AIDS and Sexual Behavior Reported by Gay Men in San Francisco Am J Public Hlth, 1985, 75, 493-6

Bell AP & Weinberg MS *Homosexualities,* NY: Simon & Schuster, 1978

Manligit GW Chronic immune stimulation by sperm alloantigens *JAMA*, 1984, 251, 237-48

Daling JR Sexual practices, STDs, and the incidence of anal cancer *New England J Med 1987, 317, 973-7*

Cameron P And coffee too International *Journal of the Addictions* 1982, 17, 569-74

Pine S *Back to Basics,* NY: Morrow, 1982, 211

Dr. Paul Cameron, Kirk Cameron, of Stanford University, and Kay Proctor of the University of Louisville, wrote the report, EFFECT OF HOMOSEXUALITY UPON PUBLIC HEALTH AND SOCIAL ORDER, published in *Psychological Reports*, 1989, 64, 1167-1179, on homosexual acts of both men and women, as well as perverse acts of heterosexuals. This was a comprehensive study, by questionnaire, and will be referred to as: Cameron, et al, (1989).

Similar statistics are disclosed in *The Gay Agenda*, by The Report, a VCR tape, published in 1992, which is an authoritative and comprehensive explanation of the homosexual movement, and homosexual activity. The narrators on the tape are David Llewellyn, President, Western Center for Law and Religious Freedom; Stanley Monteith, M.D., author of "AIDS, The Unnecessary Epidemic;" Joseph Nicolosi, Ph.D., a well known specialist in homosexuality, and author of "Reparative Therapy of Male Homosexuality," and many other publications; John Smid, an ex-homosexual, and Director of Love in Action, an organization which helps homosexuals who want to change to a decent way of life; and John Paulk, an ex-homosexual, and Administrator of Love in Action. Dr. Montieth gave the statistical references on homosexual acts. Reference is made as: *The Gay Agenda.*

Concerned Women for America published *The Homosexual Deception: Making Sin A Civil Right*, in 1991 and 1992. This is a comprehensive two part fifty-five page analysis of the homosexual agenda and the vile and destructive acts of homosexuals. It is exceptionally well documented with reputable studies and references. It is highly recommended reading for anyone interested in these issues. References will be to: Concerned Women for America (1991, 1992).

The fifth reference is a book by Lorraine Day, M. D., *AIDS—WHAT THE GOVERNMENT ISN'T TELLING YOU*, Rockford Press, Palm Desert Ca., 1991. Dr. Day, an internationally acclaimed orthopedic trauma surgeon and lecturer, was on the faculty of the University of California, San Francisco, for 15 years. She was Chief of Surgery at San Francisco General Hospital, and finally resigned because of the liberal, political, and false information being conveyed to the public, as well as those professionals at risk, by the federal and local governments, and by the hospitals and medical associations; and because of the dangers resulting from the way matters concerning AIDS were being handled. She relates how the secrecy and failure to disclose the identity of those with AIDS posed an extreme and deadly danger to those who treated them and to the public. Reference to her book will be: Day (1991).

Dr. Day did not give statistics or numbers for the homosexual acts listed below, but she did describe many of them and the dangers with which they were fraught.

Last but not least is an article, "Sodomy Laws," *The Colorado Model*, Colorado for Family Values, Colorado Springs, Co., 1993, pp. 3-6 to 3-11. The reference to this article in the statistics will be: CFV. This short six page article includes twenty-nine endnotes, many containing multiple references, which cover almost three large pages. It is exceptionally well researched and documented. The references for the part on acts of homosexual are:

"Murder, Violence and Homosexuality," Institute for the Scientific Investigation of Sexuality, 1987.

"What Homosexuals Do," Institute for the Scientific Investigation of Sexuality, 1987.

Jay, K. and Young, A., *The Gay Report*, (Summit, 1979), pp. 490-93, 553-96,563-4, 567.

Hart, J., "'Safe Sex' and the Presence of the Absence," *National Review*, May 8, 1987, p. 43.

Quinn, T. C., Stamm, W. E., et al, "The Polymicrobial Origin of Intestinal Infections in Homosexual Men," *New England Journal of Medicine*, 1983, 309 (10), pp. 576-582.

Bell, A. P. and Weinberg, M. S., *Homosexualities*, (Simon & Schuster, 1978).

Corey, L. and Holmes, K. K., "Sexual Transmission of Hepatitis A in Homosexual Men," *New England Journal of Medicine*, 1980, 302, pp. 435-438.

"Sexual Practices and Risk of Infection by the Human Immunodeficiency Virus," The San Francisco Men's Health Study, *Journal of American Medical Association,* 1987 (January 16), 257 (3), p. 323.

Stewart, S. A., *USA Today*, November 21, 1984.

McKusick, L., et al, "AIDS and Sexual Behavior Reported by Gay Men in San Francisco," *American Journal of Public Health*, 1985, 75, pp. 493-96.

Dr. Hunter Handsfield, Director of the Sexually Transmitted Disease Control Program in Seattle, Letter to the Editor, *American Journal of Public Health*, December 1985, 75, pp. 1449-1450.

Gebhard, P. H. and Johnson, A. B., *The Kinsey Data* (Saunders 1979)

Manligit, G. M. and Talpaz, M., et al, "Chronic Immune Stimulation by Sperm Allonantigens," *Journal of American Medical Association*, 1984, 251 (2), pp. 237-241.

U. S. Center for Disease Control Study (Atlanta, 1982) reported in Meridith, "The Gay Dilemma," *Psychology Today*, January 1984, p. 50.

Bell, A. P., Weinberg, M. S., and Hammersmith, S. K., *Sexual Prefer-ence*, (Indiana University Press, 1981).

Institute for the Scientific Investigation of Sexuality, "The Psychology of Homosexuality," ISIS, 1984.

White, M., *AIDS and The Positive Alternatives* (Marshal Pickering, 1987), pp. 73-75.

For the five references that gave statistics on particular acts, the percent of homosexuals that the studies show engaged in the respective acts are shown, and then a mean average of them is stated. If one of the authorities selected did not give statistics on a particular act, a line will be shown, and it will not be included in the average.

These first statistics apply to male homosexuals, but as we will later see, equally vile and heinous acts are committed by lesbians.

ORAL SEX (FELLATIO)		
Cameron, 1988:	"Almost all...."	—— %
Cameron, et al, 1989		100
The Gay Agenda		100
Concerned Women for America (1991, 1992)		——
CFV		——
AVERAGE		100 %

This act is one man taking into his mouth the penis of another man for the purpose of sexual stimulation and gratification, and is probably the most commonly known of all of the many homosexual acts.

Cameron states that homosexuals admit to swallowing semen about half of the time when engaging in this act, and explains the extreme danger involved. He says that they are "doing the next thing to con-suming raw human blood with all its attendant medical risks."

Concerned Women for America (1991, 1992) states (p. 12):

A study by McKusick, et al., of 655 San Francisco homosexuals ("AIDS and Sexual Behavior Reported by Homosexual Men in San Fran-cisco," *American Journal of Public Health*, December, 1985, 75, 493-496) reported that "knowledge of health guidelines was quite high, but this knowledge had no relation to sexual behavior." Only 24% of McKusick's sample claimed to have been "monogamous" during the past year. And of this 24%, 5% drank urine, 7% engaged in sex involving insertion of a fist in their rectums, 33% ingested feces, 53% swallowed semen, and 59% received semen in their rectums in the month just previous to the survey. ...

ANAL INTERCOURSE		
Cameron, 1988	80	%
Cameron, et al, 1989	93	
The Gay Agenda	93	
Concerned Women for America (1991, 1992)	——	
CFV	90	
AVERAGE	89	%

"The next most common homosexual act is rectal intercourse. It too is fraught with biological danger. ...Tearing or bruising of the anal wall (which is only one cell thick) ... is almost inevitable." (Cameron, 1988)

Dr. Monteith: "... the rectum was not built for intercourse. And so when you carry out anal intercourse, why you manage to tear the rectal mucosa, and you expand the sphincter in many instances. It is not a healthy activity and because as you tear the rectal mucosa, that there is such a high incidence of disease in these cases." (The Gay Agenda)

RIMMING		
Cameron, 1988	67	%
Cameron, et al, 1989	92	
The Gay Agenda	92	
Concerned Women for America (1991, 1992)	——	
CFV	90	
AVERAGE	85	%

"About two-thirds of homosexuals regularly use their tongues to explore the anuses of their sexual contacts and thus ingest biologically significant amounts of feces. While the human body has defenses against it, exposure to the fecal discharge of anyone (much less dozens of strangers) is patently unhealthful and unwise." (Cameron, 1988)

Dr. Monteith: "And then about 92% of homosexuals engage in something called 'rimming.' Rimming is simply licking in and around your partners anus and involves actually placing your tongue into the anus, and you couldn't do this without some ingestion of feces." (*The Gay Agenda*)

GOLDEN SHOWERS AND URINE SPORTS		
Cameron, 1988	30	%
Cameron, et al, 1989	29	
The Gay Agenda	29	
Concerned Women for America (1991, 1992)	25	
CFV	25	
AVERAGE	28	%

"About 30 percent of gays have 'showered' in the urine of others, and about 20 percent have drunk urine. Only about 15 percent of homosexuals regularly seek to be urinated on and about eight percent or nine percent regularly drink it. ..." (Cameron, 1988)

Dr. Monteith: "And then 29% engage in something called 'golden showers.' And what is a 'golden shower'? While a man lays on the ground, another man stands around him and urinates on him." (*The Gay Agenda*)

FISTING OR HANDBALLING		
Cameron, 1988	33	%
Cameron, et al, 1989	42	
The Gay Agenda	47	
Concerned Women for America (1991, 1992)	——	
CFV	41	
AVERAGE	41	%

"In 1983, well over a third of gays admitted to participating in fisting (inserting the hand and arm, sometimes up to the armpit, into the rectum of sex-partners). ...The rectum was not designed to accommodate the hand and arm. Thus many who engage in this behavior find their sphincter muscles weakened to such a degree that they can't control themselves. Given the various gay misuses of the rectum, it is hardly surprising that the latest review of rectal cancer implicated homosexual practices in a large fraction of recorded cases. ..." (Cameron, 1988)

Dr. Monteith: "Fisting involves about 47% of homosexuals. This "involves taking your fist and your arm and inserting it into a man's rectum, so he'd have sexual pleasure and you could have pleasure by inflicting this upon him." (*The Gay Agenda*)

SCAT—FUDGE SPORTS—MUD ROLLING	
Cameron, 1988	17 %
Cameron, et al, 1989	17
The Gay Agenda	17
Concerned Women for America (1991, 1992)	——
CFV	17
AVERAGE	17 %

"The latest national random survey found that 17 percent of gays admitted to having eaten and/or rubbed feces of partners. An additional 12 percent reported giving and receiving enemas as part of sexual pleasure." (Cameron, 1989)

Dr. Montieth states: "And then there's something called 'scat,' and about 17 percent of homosexuals engage in that. And that is actively eating human feces or rubbing human feces on your skin or rolling around on the floor in feces, something called 'mud rolling'." (*The Gay Agenda*)

Concerned Women for America, *The Homosexual Deception: Making sin a civil right*, 1991, 1992, at page 15, states:

A 1992 Study has reported that the proportion of homosexuals in London, England, who engage in "rimming" (oral stimulation of a partner's anus) has not declined since 1984 (Elford, J., et al, "Kaposi's Sarcoma and Insertive Rimming," *Lancet,* 1992:339: 938.27)

(Ingestion of feces during perverse "sexual" practices has recently been implicated in the transmission of an especially virulent form of cancer [Beral. V., et al, "Risk of Kaposi's Sarcoma and Sexual Practice Associated with Faecal Contact in Homosexual or Bisexual Men with AIDS," *Lancet,* 1992:339:632-35.28].)

"Toys" and Other Things

Of the five statistical references selected, only Cameron's 1988 publication included this subject in the study or report, and Dr. Cameron gave no statistics on the percentage of homosexuals engaging in such acts.

In the study referred to of Cameron, et al, 1989, it was reported that 19 percent of the bisexual men and 15 percent of the homosexual men engaged in sex with animals, but the details of the acts were not given.

"'Toy' is homosexual argot for various objects, including live animals, which are inserted into the rectum — sometimes bottles, carrots, lightbulbs or specially designed devices. The risk for contamination is considerable. More recently a small proportion of homosexuals do sex with animals — gerbils are commonly used." (Cameron, 1988)

"I recently heard about a rather famous male actor, you may have, too, for the story came over the wire, who had a dead gerbil removed from his rectum. That is not normal sexual behavior. That is not a 'variation' of lifestyle. It is 'depraved and self-abusive sex.'" (Day, 111)

These kind of acts are not only unbelievably vile, evil, and destructive to the people involved, but they are terribly cruel and inhumane to the animals upon which this cruelty is inflicted.

"It has been my observation during 15 years as a doctor in one of the world's most-frequented trauma hospitals that much of gay sex is of the harmful, sadistic and/or masochistic variety. Gays hurt each other. They also hurt themselves." (Day, 111)

The Gay Agenda commentators did not give details on this subject, but in the parade by homosexuals in San Francisco, many were shown with dildos, which is a term used by homosexuals for artificial penises and such sex devices.

Sadomasochism, Bondage, or Brutality		
Cameron, 1988	25	%
Cameron, et al, 1989	37	
The Gay Agenda	——	
Concerned Women for America (1991, 1992)	33	
CFV	33	
AVERAGE	32	%

Cameron (1988) states that about a quarter of homosexuals dabble in sadomasochism, where "lovers" are beaten or trussed up as a part of the sexual sport.

Cameron, et al, 1989, listed sadomasochism and bondage separately in their questionnaires and report, and gave the statistics as 37 percent and 32 percent, respectively.

The Gay Agenda video gave no statistics on this activity, but in the parade shown, such simulated acts were prevalent, as they were in videos of parades in New York and Washington, D.C., which will be referred to later.

A statement of Dr. Day regarding such acts as these was referred to, above. In addition she stated (pp. 111-112):

> One does not have to moralize about the rightness or wrongness of gay male sexual behavior. I don't believe that God singles out gay men for punishment. Nature imposes its own penalties. As a physician, I know very well that if we abuse our bodies we will get sick and possibly die.
>
> There are very serious health consequences to abusive and self-abusive sexual behavior. Gay males as a rule have been abusive to themselves and to their partners to a degree that is incomprehensible within the heterosexual world. Gay bathhouses have become the well-known dens of death from which AIDS has sprung like a specter straight out of hell.

The above classifications of homosexual acts are listed in the order that Cameron listed them in his book. He stated that he considered the order listed as important, because that generally is the order in which these acts are adopted. He states: "On average, gays report having their genitals manipulated by another male at about age 13. It takes about another two years before the first oral/genital contact (and it's almost always done first to the newcomer, reciprocity comes later). Around 16 or 17 is when the anus is used for sex; and it takes about another two years before the neophyte is using his mouth on the anus of others. By age 21 most gays have adopted most of these practices." He also notes that there are many individual exceptions. (Cameron, 1988)

The 1989 study by Cameron, et al, also shows the following percentages for male homosexuals:

Sex with animals	15 %
Threesomes, orgies, or group sex	88
Sex in gay bath	68
Sex in peep show or booth	50
Sex in public restrooms	66

If there are those who have any skepticism about whether or not "gays" really engage in the vile acts referred to above, I would refer them to *GAY SEX—A MANUAL FOR MEN WHO LOVE MEN*, by Jack Hart and illustrated by Bradley M. Cook, Alyson Publications, Inc., Boston, 1991, a 191 page book, including an index, filled with utterly sick and disgusting illustrations. The most amazing thing about it is that this country has lost its morality to the extent that such a thing could even be published and sent through the mail. All of the above are discussed as "natural acts," as well as sick and disgusting acts that are not included in the above statistics. It appears that there is nothing too vile and depraved for many who have sunk into homosexuality.

As to the regression into the various homosexual acts, as explained by Dr. Cameron, above, further light is shed on this by Kirk and Madsen, *After the Ball*, Penguin Books USA, Inc., New York, 1990, at pages 304-305:

> The course is much the same regarding sexual practices. When one is young and inexperienced, the tamest, most vanilla-flavored gay sex—mere cuddling and mutual masturbation—is more than enough

to do the trick: it's new, forbidden, 'dirty,' and exciting. As one gains experience, vanilla sex with one partner becomes familiar, tame, and boring, and loses its capacity to arouse. At first, the increasingly jaded gay man seeks novelty in partners, rather than practices, and becomes massively promiscuous; eventually, all bodies become boring, and only new practices will thrill. Two major avenues diverge in this yellow wood, two nerves upon which to press: that of raunch, and that of aggression.

The pursuit of sexual happiness via raunch—fetishism, water sports and coprophilia, and so forth—seeks, essentially, to restore erectile thrills by restoring the 'dirty,' hence forbidden, aspect of sex—thereby providing, as C. A. Tripp called it in *The Homosexual Matrix,* a new barrier of "resistance" to be overcome. Unfortunately, this, as with all attempts to sustain the *furor sexualis* of youth by sheer intensification of some peripheral aspect of the experience, is doomed to failure: mere amplification of 'dirtiness' results, finally, in mere wallowing in filth—which, however far the ante is upped, eventually fails to satisfy, or even to arouse. (Next stop, impotence.) Not all sleaze addicts choose to advertise the fact in newspapers, but those who do simultaneously entertain, turn the stomach, and demonstrate the futility of the endeavor better than anything we could invent. Consider the following personal ad:

> *Feet First* Ripe dirty nasty feet, Hot muscular smelly feet. Toe Jam. Uncut cheesy meat, Stink ... Heavy, funky male sweat. Who? Rex: unwashed, unshaven ... dude, ... 30's, ... hung, filthy, uncut, loaded with cheese, ripe pits sourballs, J/O games with nasty feet, pit sniffin' ... Get dirty and check out the pigpen ...

Aggressive sex is worse than a mere dead end: in extreme cases, it's dangerous. Typically, fast-lane gays who buy a (one-way) ticket on this express first get interested in bondage and discipline, then in sadomasochism in their thirties and forties; the really jaded run rapidly through the milder versions (and perversions) of this scene and graduate to whips, executioner's masks, and fist-fucking. So much does it take to stay excited. By the age of fifty, these unfortunates are in real trouble.

It should be added that not many reach the age of fifty anymore. Strangely enough, the book referred to above, *After The Ball,* was written by two well educated homosexuals, Marshall Kirk and Hunter Madsen.

Kirk is a Harvard graduate, a researcher in neuropsychiatry, a logician, and a poet. He now writes full time. Madsen received his doctorate in politics from Harvard, and he appears frequently on national media as an advocate for gay rights. The stated object of the book is to try to get the "gay" community to recognize the danger of its excesses and the harm to the "gay rights" cause by displaying these excesses to the public. "They then outline a boldly original battle plan for conquering bigotry by exploiting the news media." (From back cover of book.) The sad thing is that as intelligent as these two are, they still completely miss the boat. Their only real salvation is to leave the homosexual lifestyle.

Harvard University used to be one of our most respected universities, and still is considered so by some who remain on the far left of the political spectrum. *After the Ball,* supra, (pp. 309-310), in explaining some of the goings on at Harvard, accosting students in the men's room, passing obscene notes, invitations on the wall, and other homosexual sex displays, states:

> It apparently amazed a goodly number of others, as well—including staff and students who, less titillated than scandalized, left notes of their own ('Why can't a Harvard boy go to the john in this dump without being groped by a seedy queer?') in library suggestion boxes, taking violent exception to the ongoing lavatorial passion play—because reportedly, the Harvard Police, accompanied by maintenance personnel, eventually elbowed their way into the *dramatis personae.*
>
> Abruptly—and to the great dismay of those who need privacy to do their business—the *doors* disappeared from every toilet stall in the main Harvard Science Center men's room, and uniformed policemen were periodically observed patrolling the premises for perverts. Predictably, a protest— at once sardonically amused and annoyed—by one Scott Long appeared in the *Harvard Gay and Lesbian Newsletter* mocking the straight staff, students, and police who had whipped up a "tempest in a tearoom."
>
> Despite their high visibility, and attempts by authorities to squelch them, however, a coterie of gay men continues, daily and nightly, to perform the play before what is, all too often, an S.R.O. straight audience—in the men's rooms of Ivy League Colleges, and in the public lavatories, parks, and alleyways of every major city in the United States. Theirs is the wretchedest of all gay excesses.

Such men make no attempt to secure privacy for their intercourse, whether by locating a disused utility closet or waiting for a lull in the pedestrian traffic in and out of the lavatory; indeed, for many the dangerous possibility of being apprehended *entr'acte* is three fourths of the thrill. They masturbate at the urinals, wander totally naked up and down the length of the facility, and fellate one another in acrobatic positions in the open doorways of the stalls. When they ejaculate—and they do—on the seats, walls, or floors, they leave it there to congeal into a nasty, highly identifiable puddle. One can imagine the effect such a charming tableau has upon a young, sheltered, or uptight straight man, when he comes upon it suddenly and unexpectedly in a place in which he is accustomed to do his embarrassing but necessary business in peace and quiet.

After the Ball will be further discussed in Chapter 6, THE HOMO-SEXUAL AGENDA, in light of its stated purpose of promoting the "gay agenda."

The propensities and tendencies of so many in the "gay" community to engage in promiscuous, anonymous, and public sex shows severe mental and emotional problems that are in serious need of treatment, rather than promoting and promulgating these destructive tendencies. Yet the majority of them, instead of realizing this, think it is some kind of a civil right to do these things.

Washington Inquirer, November 19, 1993, at page 3, had this article:

Homos Want Public Sex

Queer Nation, the radical homosexual group, has condemned the U. S. Park Police for arresting persons for public sex on the P Street Beach, a grassy area alongside Rock Creek under the P Street Bridge, gateway into Georgetown. The group contends that the arrests are "an assault on the [homosexual] community by the government." The P Street Beach is in clear visual range of hundreds of pedestrians; it is also in close proximity to a junior high school — and to a plethora of homosexual bars. (*The Washington Blade, Nov., 12, 1993*)

S.F. Gay Newspaper Shows "Fisting"

The *San Francisco Bay Times*, one of the three leading homosexual newspapers in San Francisco, ran a photo of a man "fisting" another man in its December 29, 1994 issue.

The *Bay Times'* photo of a man's arm inside the bare buttocks of another accompanies a column by Lou Garou, who describes visiting a "private sex party" at a place called "Mack" on 10th Street in San Francisco. A caption under the "fisting" photo offers "Season's Greetings" from Rube and Lou, apparently the author.

Garou reports that Mack has a maze of rooms downstairs, some fitted with "glory holes"—gay slang for holes in the wall through which one man inserts his penis, which is then fellated by an anonymous man on the other side of the wall.

Upstairs, reports Garou, "There were perhaps six more men ... one of whom was getting fisted."

Garou writes that after watching the "fisting," he ventured to a "dark cubicle," reached out as a man wearing a L.A. Sheriff's Department uniform walked by," and orally sodomized the stranger.

Articles and photos with sadistic themes are common in the *Bay Times*, a biweekly newspaper, as are nudity and obscenities. One column in the same issue is titled, "[f—k—g] Donna Reed." (*Lambda Report*, April-June 1995)

It should be obvious to any sane and decent person that people who dwell on such things as the above - moreover engaging in them - are seriously sick of mind. It surely does not take a psychiatrist or psychologist to understand this, and when such professions cannot or do not recognize such emotional illness, then those professions are equally sick, and about at the end of any usefulness. They are becoming a detriment instead of an asset to society.

Let us consider the sick acts of Dr. Alfred Kinsey, who many have considered for years to be the world's greatest authority on sexuality. The following is from **Kinsey – A Homosexual!**, *Family Research Report*, Family Research Institute, Sept. - Oct. 1997, referring to an article (Jones, J.H., "Dr. Yes," *New Yorker*, August 25-Sept. 1, 1997, 98-113) by Dr. James H. Jones, who served on the scientific board of advisers of the Kinsey Institute for Sex Research:

According to Jones, Kinsey "was both a homosexual and, from childhood on, a masochist who, as he grew older, pursued an interest in extreme sexuality with increasing compulsiveness. His secret life was shared with a small circle of intimates, a few of whom became his sexual partners, sometimes in the name of 'research.' Remarkably, his activities did not prevent him from being a devoted husband and a caring, successful father. But they almost certainly did affect the objectivity and detachment of his work as a scientist; his celebrated findings, I now believe, may well have been skewed. From the very beginnings of his research into sexual behavior, the Americans who most persistently engaged Kinsey's attention were people who were either on the margins or beyond the pale; Homosexuals, sadomasochists, voyeurs, exhibitionists, pedophiles, transsexuals, transvestites, fetishists" (p. 101). ***

Kinsey was casually immodest. On a wasp-collecting trip a male assistant noted that Kinsey "would go naked if we were in a campground. He just plain didn't give a damn. Nor did he show any inhibitions about his bodily functions," said Homer Rainwater. ***

After interviewing an individual, "Y," Kinsey struck up a relationship which included sex with Kinsey, Kinsey's wife, and numerous others. "Y" related that he believed that Kinsey and his wife loved each other, but never or seldom had sex with each other. ***

"By the late nineteen-forties, ... [Kinsey's] risk-taking was becoming compulsive. If the press had got a hint of what was happening, his work and career would have been ruined. Kinsey compounded that risk by documenting, in his attic, many sexual acts on film. Not all of his colleagues and their spouses agreed to his request to be filmed. One staff wife later complained of the 'sickening pressure' she was under to have sex on film, saying that she felt that her husband's career at the institute depended on her acquiescence .... Clara was filmed masturbating and having sex with a staff member .... Homosexual men figured prominently in the filming sessions, and Kinsey's preference was for sadomasochists." ***

"According to William Dellenback, the institute's photographer, Kinsey was becoming overtly exhibitionist – to the point of having himself filmed, always from the chest down, while engaged in masochistic masturbation. The world's foremost expert on sexual behavior would insert an object such as a pipe cleaner or swizzle stick into his urethra, tie a rope around his scrotum, and then tug hard on the rope" (p. 113) ***

"Toward the end of his life, Kinsey's boundaries shifted again – to the point where he was apparently prepared to withhold moral disapproval of adult-child sexual contact. ... Wescott (a homosexual) remembered Kinsey's once telling him that of all the people he'd interviewed who had been molested as children, only a few felt that they had been personally harmed by the experience" (p. 113).

"One evening in August, 1954, Kinsey, dejected and bitter, stood in his offices in the basement of Wylie Hall looking up at some exposed pipes just below the ceiling. On this evening, he told a close friend, he threw a rope over the pipe, tied a knot around his scrotum and wrapped the other end around his hand. Then, he climbed onto a chair and jumped off." Shortly after this episode, Kinsey .... traveled to Peru to photograph a collection of erotic pottery. There Kinsey took to his bed, suffering from an infection in his pelvic region ... A physician friend ... labeled Kinsey's illness orchitis, pinpointing the testicles as the site of the infection." ***

Talk about a nit-wit whose whacked-out ideas dominate Hollywood and academia!

Things seem to only to get worse with time. *Human Events,* May 17, 1996, had a full page article on page 17 entitled, **Homosexuals Hold Aids-Benefit Orgy In Federal Building in Nation's Capital.** The article states in part:

> On April 13, an organization called "Friends Being Friends" hosted an event as part of what was supposed to be an AIDS benefit in the federally owned Andrew W. Mellon auditorium, in the Nation's Capital. What occurred, however, will more likely spread AIDS than alleviate it. Eyewitnesses to the proceedings observed numerous illegal activities, including nudity, sodomy, same-sex intercourse, drug dealing and drug use.
>
> ***
>
> The orgy at the Mellon Auditorium was one of several functions held as part of "Cherry Jubilee Weekend." ...The next morning, another Cherry Jubilee event, the "Farewell Brunch," was held in the Rayborn House Office Building, courtesy of openly gay Republican Rep. Steve Gunderson (R.-Wis.). Sponsors of the weekend included American Airlines, Snapple Beverages, Lite Beer, Starbucks Coffee, and Ben & Jerry's Ice Cream.
>
> This is not the first time the Mellon Auditorium has hosted a homosexual free-for-all. During the 1993 gay march on Washington, it was used for the "National S/S Leather Fetish Conference," featuring leather-clad "masters" and near-naked "submissives" in chains. It also

showcased graphic photos of anatomical feats too grotesque to mention in a family paper.

This public homosexual activity is not just limited to our major eastern and western cities. It is now a problem throughout the country. *Family Research Report*, Family Research Institute, October-November, 1995, had this article:

> *Omaha:* After police cleaned one park of homosexual activity by giving tickets for lewd conduct, gays have shifted to Elmwood Park. The city prosecutor noted that "It's just a continued amazement to me that this activity hasn't stopped or slowed down. It just moves.... This seems to increase the element of excitement or risk for some of these people ... arrests certainly haven't reduced the number of people willing to take the risk." (Omaha World-Herald 8/10/95)

On page 8 of the same Family Research Report is an article in Cameron's Corner (Dr. Paul Cameron):

Sex in Public Parks

A Lutheran minister and a Methodist district superintendent were just picked up in Omaha's parks for "indecent exposure/lewd conduct" ....

What's going on?

Why *do* gays have sex in parks?

According to Scott Giordano, writing in the August 1995 *Baltimore Alternative*, p. 21, 'This used to be my playground.'

Giordano said that as "gay men grow older, many turn to the park as a place to deal with their sexual repression. In virtually any big city, there not only lies [sic] an active gay night life, but also a public park where gay men congregate to participate in, or just watch anonymous sex."

There is no counterpart in heterosexuality for such wicked foolishness. From time to time a young couple may get carried away in a public place or even engage in public demonstrations of their passion. But nowhere in the world are public parks or public restrooms commandeered for heterosexual purposes.

As Giordano notes, "The fact is that public sex seems an ingrained part of gay male 'culture.' I confess to having done my share of cruising in the park, and I can speak from experience when I say that those men who cruise the parks are there for one reason only – to release sexual tension in any way possible. ..."

* * *

If anyone criticizes these fellows for ruining the park for anyone but themselves it's a result of "homophobia!" How convenient. "Homophobia" fits anyone or any institution that is not 100% for homosexuality.

Periodically, every gay paper runs a story about how gays are being discriminated against because they can't have public sex. Such a story invariably follows a roundup of gay malefactors by the police in one or two public parks. Further the police are usually there because a citizen complained – that her child was molested (usually in the men's room), or that as they were sitting down for a picnic, they had to watch men having sex just behind some bushes or right out in the open.

This kind of public sexual activity is largely due to many states and the District of Columbia either repealing or ignoring laws that made sodomy a criminal offense. This invited such activity. The results have been devastating.

The article of Concerned Women for America, supra, page 9, states:

Male homosexuals are 14 times more likely to have had syphilis than heterosexuals. They are eight times more likely to have had hepatitis A or B, and hundreds of times more likely to have had oral infection by STDs (sexually transmitted diseases) through penile contact. Homosexuals are thousands of times more likely than heterosexuals to have AIDS (Jaffe and Keewhan, et al., "National Case-Control Study of Kaposi's Sarcoma, etc. in Homosexual Men; Part 1, Epidemiologic Results," *Annals of Internal Medicine,* 1983, 99 (2), pp. 145–157).

Lesbians show similar patterns of high venereal disease incidence relative to the general population. Compared with heterosexual females, lesbians are 19 times more likely to have had syphilis and twice as likely to have had genital warts. They are four times more likely to have had scabies and seven times more likely to have had infection from vaginal contact. Lesbians are 29 times more likely to have had oral infection from vaginal contact, and 12 times more likely to have had oral infection from penile contact ("Medical aspects of Homosexuality," Institute for the Scientific Investigation of Sexuality, 1985,

Jaffe and Keewhan, et al, op. cit..) After passage of special homosexual advantage laws in San Francisco, the city saw a sharp increase in venereal diseases—up to 22 times the national average. By 1979, approximately 80% of the 75,000 people who visited San Francisco venereal disease clinics were homosexuals (*San Francisco Examiner*, April 23, 1979).

As you may have gathered from the above quotation, there appears to be little difference in the vile, despicable, and destructive acts engaged in by male homosexuals and those engaged in by female homosexuals (lesbians). The most definitive study I have found on the subject, which includes acts of lesbians, is the one, referenced above, by Cameron, et al, 1989. Also, in my thinking, I perceive little difference in bisexuals and homosexuals. They are both sex perverts, and both engage in homosexual acts. My studies indicate that there is little difference in the kinds of acts in which they engage, and in some instances the statistics are worse for the bisexuals than the homosexuals—especially as to the women.

The following are a few of the items from the tables in the study of Cameron, et al, 1989:

Acts of Females	Bisexual	Homosexual
Oral sex on female	90 %	96 %
Anal sex on female	28	48
Sadomasochism	21	8
Bondage	44	17
Fist in anus ("handballing")	33	8
Urination ("Golden showers")	17	——
Sex with animals	15	——
Threesomes, orgies, or group sex	71	25
Sex in public restroom	24	9

The study referred to above did not include vaginal "fisting" of females, but other material indicates that this is also a common practice with Lesbians.

"Sodomy Laws," CFV, supra, states, as to lesbians, that an eighth admit to sadomasochism , 8 percent admit to urinating on sexual partners, and 65 percent report having engaged in oral/anal sexual activity of inserting the tongue into or licking the anus. (This, of course, is besides the oral and anal sex referred to in the above tables, which is of the more common types of acts generally known to be engaged in by lesbians.)

Studies used by Concerned Women for America in THE HOMO-SEXUAL DECEPTION: MAKING SIN A CIVIL RIGHT, reflect that one-eighth of lesbians admit to practicing sadomasochism and 8 percent of them admit to engaging in "water sports" (urinating on their sexual partners). (p, 17) This publication further states:

> In a study previously referred to of "gay values" as reflected in 19 years' issues of the national homosexual magazine The Advocate, Dr. Judith Reisman found that: "gay-on-gay" violence is instigated in The Advocate as "'S&M,' 'spanking,' 'slaves wanted' etc.—and is largely endorsed by the prevailing 'gay' cultural values. Finding: roughly 13-22% of Advocate sex ads solicited or promised brutality, humiliation, 'gay-on-gay bashing' or other forms of sexual injury"...

Peter LaBarbera is one of the foremost writers and workers against the homosexual movement in the United States. He is the founder and editor of the Lambda Report, published in Washington, D.C. He should certainly be commended for his tireless and valuable work done in this area.

The following are excerpts from LaBarbera's June, 1994, Lambda Report:

> America's AIDS Czar has endorsed a New York City Youth AIDS conference in which literature claiming homosexual practices like "fisting" and anal intercourse are "safe" was made available to public school kids as young as age 12.
>
> Kristine Gebbie, President Clinton's National AIDS Policy Coordinator, was a featured speaker at the February 12 conference—which included such workshops as "Teaching about the wonderful world of latex" and "Dealing with homophobia." At the event, graphic gay sex pamphlets produced by the Gay Men's Health Crisis (GMHC), a New York AIDS group, were distributed from a literature table.

***

Approximately 175-200 youth attended the conference, entitled "Youth Teaching Youth about HIV/AIDS." The event ... featured the following seminars taught by homosexual activists:

- *"AIDS Activism," by Kate Barhart, founder of Youth Education life line (YELL), an offshoot of the homosexual extremist group ACT UP;*
- *"Understanding Homosexuality," by representatives of the Hetrick-Martin Institute, a gay outreach organization in New York City that oversees the Harvey Milk School, a city-backed public school for "gay" youth;*
- *Young Women & Sex: Information for Today," by another representative of Hetrick-Martin.*

...*New York Post* columnist Ray Kerrison blasted the AIDS conference and charged gay activists with recruiting youngsters into the homosexual lifestyle. ...

The GMHC "safer sex" pamphlets were first brought to the public's attention March 9 in another column by Kerrison who said conference organizers sought to "brainwash young people in sexual perversion while excluding parents from participation." In describing the "sleaze these people are dumping on innocent people," Kerrison noted the contents of the GMHC leaflets. The practice of "fisting" condoned in one brochure, he said, is not only luridly sadomasochistic, it is also physically dangerous, often causing internal injuries so severe that major corrective surgery is required.

***

New York City's public school system gave its backing to the youth AIDS conference, providing an office that organizers used to make preparations for the day-long event. The conference was advertised through fliers and posters placed in the city's public high schools. ...

***

...Several of the pamphlets were taken home from the event by a 15-year-old male student ....

One of the fliers, entitled "Rites of Passion, a Safer Sex Handbook for Lesbians," shows a woman's clenched fist next to the caption, "For safe penetration, use a slippery, lubed-up latex glove to enable one finger or a whole fist to safely rock her into a frenzy." On the cover is a nude woman, her navel and one breast pierced by earrings, grasping her genitals with her gloved hand.

In the brochure's glossary of terms, "fisting" is defined as: "insertion of an entire hand into someone's vagina or ass." Another photo in the brochure shows the pelvis of a naked woman, her legs spread apart, as a glove-covered clenched fist of another woman approaches her vagina.

Later the lesbian sex booklet advises:

When penetrating with other creative items such as cucumbers, course fruits, veggies, hairbrushes, poolcues, etc., be sure to dress them in condoms. Remember to use lube and wear gloves.

The pamphlet also shows a photo of various "dildos" and "buttplugs" behind the headline, "Sex Toys." "Buttplugs are designed for anal penetration ..." and advises:

Remember: assh—s are delicate. To reduce the risk of making small tears, make sure you use lots of lube.

***

This Lambda article also states that a Dr. Mary Davenport, an obstetrician and gynecologist, said that she is concerned that the frontal "fisting" described in the brochure could cause "trauma tears and lacerations" inside a woman's vagina, and that she was even more concerned about the anal fisting. It refers to a 1989 article in the *American Journal of Forensic Medicine and Pathology entitled "Vaginal 'Fisting' as a Cause of Death,"* reporting on the case of a young girl who died as a result of lacerations and extensive blood loss sustained when a man inserted a clenched hand and forearm into her vagina. The man was convicted of manslaughter. The article goes on to refer to statements of a Dr. Charles Papp, a colon and rectal surgeon in Lexington, Kentucky, about the extreme physical dangers of fisting. The Lambda article further states:

Dr. Papp said he has operated on people who had to have objects surgically removed from their rectum, presumably the result of sexual misadventures. He has removed objects ranging from vibrators to "a small shot put" from the rectums of unfortunate sexual experimenters. ...

***

The advocacy of "fisting" is part of a theme of sexual sadism that runs throughout the lesbian "Safer Sex Handbook" brochure. The following are listed under the heading "More Safer Sex":

slow, drop-by-drop hot wax
whipping/flogging
bondage

Under a section entitled, "Welts & Blisters," the flier advises, "Wear latex gloves and be sure to clean your canes, crops, whips, etc." Another section of the GMHC lesbian brochure, headlined "Blood Letting Sexual Activities," discusses cutting rituals" and anatomical "piercings." The text reads: "Whenever blood is present wear disposable latex gloves."

Under the subheading "Urine" in the "Water Sports" section, the lesbian flier tells readers:

You can enjoy golden showers [one person urinating on another] externally on unbroken skin, with a low risk of HIV transmission, although there are other possibilities of bacterial infection. Keep piss away from you eyes, and open cuts or sores on you body.

***

Another flier available at the conference that touched off public outcry is entitled "Listen Up. It is written in rap-style verse and tells its readers:

So, if you do men,
you can [f—], suck, eat ass,
whatever,
just do it safely.

Those are only a part of the vile acts included in the material given to the students. What it amounted to was an encouragement to engage in such acts, and a description of how to do them. The idea of such acts being done in a physically safe manner is completely ludicrous; and the mental and emotional harm that would be done to young people engaging in such things is truly immense.

It is unbelievable that a president of the United States, Bill Clinton, and his administration, would support such sick filthy conduct. But he and his administration have been promoting the acceptance of sodomy ever since he has been in office. We will go into more details of this later in the book. Our president has been a moving factor in dragging this country to its lowest depths of depravity.

We hear a lot these days about the "homosexual life-style." A more appropriate term would be "homosexual death-style."

Like the male homosexuals, the lesbians cannot seem to restrain themselves when they get together in parades or meetings. A further insight into their thinking and "morality" is given in an article about the 19th annual Michigan Womyn's Music Festival, that was reported to have attracted over 7,000 women, **"Nudity and Lots of 'PC' Characterize Lesbian 'Womyn's Festival,'"** by Leslie Carbone, *Lambda Report*, Jul. - Sept. 1995. A part of that article follows:

> The "festival" participants were clearly at war with the larger culture, and determined to flout its moral standards. At all public events, the great majority of women went topless, and many went nude below the waist as well. Camping areas were given bawdy names like "Amazon Acres" and "Bush Gardens," while the health care facility was called "The Womb." The menu was strictly vegetarian, personal needs were taken care of in "Porta Janes," and sundries like dental dams, latex gloves, lubricants and condoms could be purchased at the "Cuntree Store."
>
> The festival's entertainers pandered to this puerile delight in vulgarity. Poetry was read aloud by the "Salon of the Rainbow Clitoris." Music was played by "Tribe 8," who identified themselves as "San Francisco's own all-dyke, all-out, in-your-face, blade-brandishing, gang-castrating, dildo-swinging bullshit-detecting, aurally pornographic, Neanderthal-pervert band of patriarchy-smashing snatchlickers."
>
> What type of women would describe themselves in such crude angry terms? Perhaps the answer lies in the festival's need to provide such an abundance of abuse and recovery meetings. ...
>
> The more popular opiate, however, was sex. The atmosphere at the festival was charged with sexuality. Moans of ecstasy reverberated throughout the grounds, particularly in the camping areas. Sexual excitement was especially evident during the evening concerts, though only a minority engaged in public acts of intimacy. Volunteer security staff patrolled the camping sites at night, asking the louder lovers to be considerate of their neighbors trying to sleep.
>
> While lesbians are often portrayed as monogamous, promiscuity was rampant at the festival. Sex parties were common, and exhibitionism was everywhere. The pervasive nudity and lack of modesty added to the less than wholesome environment for the young girls

allowed into the main campground. Like their mothers, many of the girls went topless. ***

Although not all sex perverts are homosexuals, all homosexuals are sex perverts. It certainly is true that heterosexuals have engaged in some of the perverted acts referred to in this chapter, but the studies show that it certainly is not to the extent that homosexuals do. These acts are common-place with homosexuals.

In this book, a person is not considered a homosexual unless he or she engages in one or more of the acts described with one or more persons of the same sex. And some of them engage in a number of them, if not all of them.

Learning about the acts and thinking of homosexuals gives us a better insight into many things that are going on today. It was recently widely published that an art exhibit supported by our tax money, through the National Endowment for the Arts, caused quite a stir. Included was a photo by Robert Maplethorpe (now deceased of AIDS), who was supposed to have been a well-known "artistic" photographer. It was a photo of himself, with a bullwhip inserted in his naked rectum. Another was Andres Serrano's "Piss Christ," which was a photo of a Crucifix in a jar of urine. Because of this and other such displays, Senator Jesse Helms has been trying to get legislation passed that would stop the National Endowment for the Arts from getting tax money. So far he has not been successful, largely due to President Clinton and the Democrats.

The Washington Post, Sept. 10, 1993, carried an article about the complaints of the Christian Action Network about using our tax money for support of pornographic homosexual "art." Ann Steele, the NEA's acting chairman under the Clinton administration, reversed a decision made during the Bush administration, and granted $17,500 to an organization that had supported homosexual films, which were shown as part of the Sixth Annual Pittsburgh International Lesbian and Gay Film Festival held in October 1991. Examples of scenes in the films were a woman masturbating, two men performing oral sex in a bathtub, and a man licking the inside of a toilet bowl.

Family Alert, The Christian Action Network (CAN), September 1993, has a comprehensive article on an art exhibit it put together, which consisted of a large number of photographs of art being funded by the NEA, some of which were being shown at the time by the Whitney Museum and other organizations receiving NEA money. "The exhibit is exclusively 'art' which has been funded by The National Endowment for the Arts and Congress...." Two attempts to show the exhibit in the Capitol Building and then in the House Annex Building were shut down by Democratic members of Congress. Republican Rep. Philip Crane allowed CAN to show the exhibit of thirty-one pieces in his office. The following are examples of the "art" paid for by our tax dollars, as described by *Family Alert* and an article of *The Washington Times* (which included no date) included with the *Family Alert*:

- The two photos by Robert Maplethorpe and Andres Serrano, referred to above.
- A photo from a performance called *Meat Joy* in which a number of naked people wrestle around on the ground among dead chickens, raw fish, and sausages.
- A synthetic three foot mound of excrement.
- A picture from a movie entitled *A Spy* in which Jesus Christ is depicted with naked women's breasts.
- A photo from a movie entitled *Skull____*, in which one man tries to insert his head into another man's rectum.
- A dismembered sculpture of two women having oral sex.

The *Family Alert* article also explains that the exhibit included photos by photographer Joel-Peter Witkin, who had received four NEA grants for his work, totaling over $50,000. "Mr. Witkin works with gruesome, grotesque, masochistic, and anti-religious genre. He was described by *Vanity Fair* magazine as 'the most outrageous photographer at work today, far more provocative than Robert Maplethorpe at his kinkiest.'" The article further states:

> Included in the Witkin collections was his 1982 photo (perhaps his most famous and expensive) *Le Baiser* (The Kiss). In preparing for this photo, Mr. Witkin employed a pathologist to sever the head vertically in half of an unclaimed body at the morgue. The two halves of the same head were then turned together so that the dead man could be photographed kissing himself. It is reported that a relative of

the dead man saw the photo and complained to Mr. Witkin who was then forced to destroy the photo negative.

Other of Witkin's photos include *Woman Castrating a Man,* and *Arm_____,* which shows a man with his arm inserted into another man's rectum. His photography highlights the use of models with severed genitalia, arms and limbs. He also makes use of dead fetuses, which his models hold in many of the photos. Mr. Witkin is also fond of religious imagery whereby he incorporates various depictions of Christ with hermaphrodites, as a naked woman, and naked on the cross. He also has a photo of crucified monkeys on either side of a male human.

The Phyllis Schafly Report, October 1993, also shows the extreme sickness and depravity of Witkin, and gives classic examples of the depravity that our liberal media and the NEA have reached.

In a book of his photographs published in 1985, Witkin wrote an afterword in which he issued a plea for models to contact him about having their pictures taken. He didn't want just any models. Here are his peculiar specifications, written in his own words:

"A partial listing of my interests: physical prodigies of all kinds, pinheads, dwarfs, giants, hunchbacks, pre-op transsexuals, bearded women, active or retired side show performers, contortionists (erotic), women with one breast (center), twins joined at the foreheads, twins sharing the same arm or leg, living Cyclopes, people with tails, horns, wings, fins, claws, reversed feet or hands, elephantine limbs, etc. All people with unusually large genitals. Sex masters and slaves. Human skeletons and human pin cushions. People with complete rubber wardrobes. Geeks. Private collections of instruments of torture, romance, of human, animal and alien parts. All manner of visual perversions. A young blonde girl with two faces. Any living myth. Anyone bearing the wounds of Christ."

The April issue of the magazine *Vanity Fair* featured a glowing article about Witkin. The author was apparently star-struck with Witkin's perversions and preoccupation with morbidity, praising his "quixotic sense of his divine mission" and calling him "Saint Joel-Peter of Kodak." *Vanity Fair* even gave its readers a preview photo of one of Witkin's latest creations, which will be featured in an upcoming exhibition: the head of a man, with a section of skull removed, converted into a vase with flowers stuck into it.

Not only are we being taught that wrong is right and right is wrong; that sodomy is good and acceptable, and that believing in the Bible's condemnation of it is bigotry; but we are being taught that the vilest of grotesque depictions is wonderful art, worthy of support by the NEA. And with our tax dollars.

Time and space will not allow a full coverage of the homosexual trash and filth that has been put out, mainly for the benefit of sexual perverts, and contributed to by our tax money through the NEA. It continues. Dr. James Kennedy, of Coral Ridge Ministries, in a news letter dated March 22, 1995, states:

> Since Ms. Alexander (Actress Jane Alexander, appointed head of the NEA a few months earlier) promised arts funding would be "more in tune with the American public" (Chronicle 1/18/95), she has overseen the distribution of taxpayer's money to a shocking assortment of "artists," including:
>
> - Tim Miller, who used previous NEA grant money to "disrobe and sexually stimulate himself on stage (and among the audience)" in a presentation called "My Queer Body."
> - Kitchen Theater, which used previous NEA grant money to pay an "actress" to "invite the audience to examine the inside of her genitalia with a flashlight."
> - Bruce Nauman, whose exhibit is described by the Washington Times as 60 pieces of not only video, holography, and other components, but also "pornography, more pornography and perversion." (The exhibition includes clowns whose genitals light up, profane four-letter words presented in neon lights, scenes of abuse, torture, violence, and still more.)
> - Walker Art Center in Minneapolis, where one "performer" carved designs into another man's back, "soaked up the blood with paper towels, and then tossed the blood-soaked towels over the heads of his audience."

Washington Inquirer, 1-10-97:

> ... Rep. Peter Hoekstra (R.-Mich.) blasted the (NEA) last week for giving more than $100,000 to a New York video and film distributor that specializes in flicks with lesbian themes. According to *The*

Washington Times, Hoekstra penned a six-page letter to NEA chief Jane Alexander, saying that the video output of the group, Women Make Movies (WMM), "has the appearance of a veritable taxpayer funded peep show." *** Among the titles listed in the film catalog are: "Ten Cents a Dance," which contains bathroom sex and two women discussing their mutual attraction; "Sex Fish," which portrays a "furious montage of oral sex, public restroom cruising and ... well ... tropical fish," says the catalog; and "Coming Home," which talks of the "sexy fun of trying to fit a lesbian couple in a bathtub." ***

A key speaker in *The Gay Agenda* video, supra, was Joseph Nicolosi, Ph.D., author of "Reparative Therapy of Male Homosexuality," (Jason Aronson, 1991), and other publications. He is a specialist in the treatment of male homosexuals. In the video, Dr. Nicolosi states:

> Gay subculture is built around sexuality, so gay theater is about sex. Gay poetry is erotic poetry. Gay art is erotic art. Eroticism is a fiber of the gay culture. If you look at a very glossy polished magazine, a gay magazine, let's say, and on it's cover, it's a very sophisticated cover, and the first two or three articles will be a very intellectual, sociological, or political discussion about the gay movement and then if you go in the back, you'll see all these ads and all these 900 numbers and that's where the money is. That's where the whole economy of the gay movement is.

In my opinion, it would be very difficult for a decent person, who has not been exposed to or studied the homosexual culture, to really fathom the filthy acts and ideas which seems to permeate their thinking. Consider the utter sickness of mind described in the parts quoted below from the article, "**Homosexual Artist Strips Naked In Taxpayer-Funded D.C. Act**," *Lambda Report*, Jul. - Sep. 1995:

> Tim Miller, a homosexual actor and activist whose sexually-laden stage acts receive taxpayer funding through the National Endowment for the Arts, gave more "homoerotic" performances in August in which he stripped naked and talked crudely about his sexual encounters with other men.
>
> Miller's act, "Naked Breath," was the featured show at the Woolly Mammoth Theater in Washington, D.C.—an avant-garde playhouse

that itself received $11,000 in federal NEA monies in 1994. **LR** editor Peter LaBarbera attended a performance August 19.

Miller opens the act by asking a man in the audience to "breath on my dick." Twice in the show he bares his genitalia, including one scene in which he pulls his pants and underwear to his ankles and receives a ritualistic sponge bath from a pre-selected man in the audience. Miller also mixes the pornographic with the blasphemous, such as when in the course of describing one of his homosexual encounters, he talks about dragging his male lover's St. Peter medallion through the semen he had just released on the man's chest.

Although sympathetic press accounts reported Miller's act was toned down from previous works like "My Queer Body" (in which he roams nude into the audience), "Naked Breath" is rife with graphic "homosex" talk. At one point in the act, Miller shouts over and over how he and one boyfriend "LOVE TO [F—] EACH OTHER."

In 1994, Miller was awarded $9,375 by the embattled federal arts agency to support his solo theater acts. The NEA grant signed by chairman and actress Jane Alexander states that the money—approved for the period April 1994 to April 1996—supports "activities which contribute to your creative development and artistic growth and may include research, travel for theater-related purposes . . . ." ***

... Miller, whose Los Angeles based homosexual theater company Highways received about $15,000 in NEA money last year—is also a theater professor at UCLA. ***

It is disgusting that a citizen's money is taken away by forced taxation and given by our government to support repulsive sacrilegious filth such as that related above.

At the risk of embarrassment that I was having such things sent to me, I had several copies of homosexual publications sent to my office, and obtained a catalog from which various things could be ordered. I found almost nothing in them that was not related to perverted sex. The language and pictures are so exceedingly vile and degrading that I will not torture the readers with explicit descriptions of much of it. My research indicates that Dr. Nicolosi's description of homosexual "art" and "literature" was indeed charitable.

Some of the magazines were *wilde*, published in San Francisco, and primarily for homosexual men. The ones I received were published in 1995. They were all slick nice looking magazines from the outside, and completely full of filth on the inside. There were pictures of numerous naked men, many with "piercing" and "jewelry" inserted in their penises and other body parts. There were photos of men in bed together and in all imaginable positions. There were advertisements of places to go to have sex. In the May/June issue there was a full-page advertisement on several places to go in New York at night, with crude descriptions and implications on what could be done there. In this issue there was a full-page color picture of over twenty men and women who all appeared to be stark naked, except for some jewelry and eyeglasses, grouped closely together and with some in vulgar positions. The caption for the picture of this group was: "Our willing subjects came together in Boston at OutWrite, the bi-annual conference for queer writers. These revealing writers hail from Florida, Connecticut, Colorado, Georgia, Wisconsin, Massachusetts, New York and California. Together, they have quite a body of work."

I examined several publications of *Steam*, a quarterly published in San Francisco. Again, I found nothing but oral and pictorial homosexual pornography. An example was an article entitled "MY FAVORITE GLORYHOLE - In the Temple of Brotherly Love," at page 348, in the Autumn, 1995, issue of Steam. "Gloryhole" is a term common to homosexuals meaning a hole in the partition between two stalls in a restroom through which two men, one in each of the adjoining stalls, engage in acts of sodomy, both anal and oral. The "Temple" referred to was Temple University. The writer named six "glory" holes with their exact locations, where he engaged in such acts. Two on Temple University campuses, one at Strawbridge and Clothier (a store, I suppose), two in parks, and one in an open area where he committed such acts in the bushes in the daytime, preying on high school boys in the area, and apparently on any man that came along. Graphic descriptions were given of the acts, along with a very graphic drawing. He states that in this open area, in one evening, he had sex with six drunk high school boys and ten men. The back of this issue includes a graphic poem about sodomy of all kinds "in restrooms at rest-stops, libraries, universities, parks, bus stations." The two issues of Steam averaged over 300 pages each, and they amount to pure filth.

"Sexplorers - the guide to doing it on the road," published by PDA Press, Inc., 1995, San Francisco, Ca., is a 96 page booklet of names and addresses of places for homosexuals to have sex, in various cities and towns, in all 50 states and Washington, D.C., and a large number of foreign countries. The places listed are bathhouses, clubs, bookstores, video stores, colleges, universities, parks, etc., and even includes places like public restrooms in an airport, with "gloryholes."

I examined a catalog named "Voyages," published in 1994, which listed every kind of sex device I have heard of in studying this trash, and then some, plus a large number of videos and magazines. It listed all kinds of dildos and penis-shaped vibrators, with harnesses to hold them, whips, various things to insert in rectums, chains, handcuffs, leather harnesses, and other items for all kinds of sex perverts, although a large part of these things appeared that they would have been for lesbians.

All of these publications I have named were ordered and received in the mail. Thirty years ago, selling such things would have been a criminal offense in all states that I know about, and sending them through the mail would have been a federal crime. A country that now openly allows such things is at the lowest ebb of morality. It appears that there is now nothing that is too dirty and filthy to be allowed, and in fact even promoted by many of our federal agencies since Bill Clinton became president. Some of the blame must also be placed on decisions of liberals in the United States Supreme Court.

The reader should not get the impression that all of the writing and art of homosexuals, is trash and filth, even in modern times. This just seems to be the general modern day tenor of writing and art done by homosexuals for homosexuals.

I have read stories by Oscar Wilde before I knew he was a homosexual. The ones I read were certainly weird, but, to me, they wouldn't have identified him as a homosexual. I have read poetry of Walt Whitman, and I never knew he was a homosexual until I began studying about homosexuality. However, these two wrote back at a time when such trashy filth as was described above would have been completely unacceptable by the public, and would in fact have been illegal. I wonder what their writings would have been like today.

Even today, it cannot be said that everything written in homosexual publications is morally unacceptable, although the general theme of the writings certainly is. I understand that The Advocate is the most prominent news magazine for "gays" and lesbians. Certainly there are articles in the magazine that are thoughtful, well written, and not tainted with eroticism. There are pictures and advertisements that are not pornographic. I am sure that there are other such publications. But, even in *The Advocate*, it seems that there is a compulsion to cross the line into things that are unacceptable to decent society. For example, *The Advocate*, June 25, 1996, issue, and a number of other 1996 issues, had pictures of two naked men indecently embracing each other, advertising a book, Love Between Men. Most, if not all, of the issues I looked at had pictures of naked and almost naked men together, in connection with articles and in a large number of advertisements. And about all of the "thoughtful" non-pornographic articles are a general promotion of the homosexual agenda; that is the acceptance by society of homosexuality as a good and decent lifestyle.

The Advocate, April 30, 1996, had an article about San Francisco Mayor Willie Brown officiating a mass same-sex wedding. Pictures of pairs of men and a pair of women are shown kissing.

The Advocate, ibid., had an article, "Star '96," about a star, Anthony Rapp, in the "musical sensation," "Rent." The article states in part:

> Anthony Rapp wants to win a Tony award. He knows snagging Broadway's highest honor could do wonders for his career, but he has another, more political reason for wanting to hear his name called when the awards are given out this year. "Think of the visibility." he says excitedly, picturing the ceremony in his head. "Millions of people watching me lean over and kiss the man I'm seeing—on the lips. That's a great image that I'd want to leave people with."
>
> Rapp had better start practicing his kiss now, because when Tony nominations are announced in May, he seems a contender. ...
>
> ***
>
> Rapp also says he prefers using the word *queer* instead of *gay* to describe his sexuality. "I think, primarily, I am homosexual—politically, socially, and sexually," he says. "But I say 'queer' because I've had girlfriends and boyfriends. And I still really enjoy sex with women. To me, *queer* means that you have the potential to love someone of the same sex, but maybe not exclusively." In fact, he adds, his ultimate fantasy is to be with a man *and* a woman in "some sort of crazy *wedding Banquet* kind of family."

When substantial numbers of our people come to admire people like Anthony Rapp, and like the popular rock singer, Michael Jackson, our society has hit an all-time low. One distinguished writer and jurist, Judge Robert Bork, in his great book, *Slouching Towards Gomorrah*, (Harper Collins Publishers, Inc., New York, 1996), wonders if we have gone so far that our country is irredeemably on its way to self destruction.

The following describes things in *The Gay Agenda* video, cited above.

This video starts out with a riot incident in California, on September 29, 1991, after Governor Pete Wilson vetoed a "Gay Rights Bill," which would have granted special minority rights for homosexuals. Homosexuals are shouting, blowing whistles, breaking windows, setting buildings on fire, and confronting the police. They are displaying signs such as "Fuck you, Pete." One sign says "Queer Holy War." This is all being done in public in the presence of the police

Many of them are dressed in "drag," and many are displaying generally obscene appearances.

Their battle cry was "We're here, we're queer." Their noise and whistle blowing is deafening.

Llewellyn states that the object is to try to change the morals of the country; and that they are trying to commence this through legislation. They have a program to indoctrinate children in schools with the idea that there is nothing wrong with homosexuality.

The tape shows a parade in San Francisco. It is unbelievable that such a vile and base display could go on in this country in public. Since Bible times, Sodom and Gomorrah have been considered the ultimate examples of depravity. But, as explained in Chapter 3, there is nothing described in the Biblical accounts of Sodom and Gomorrah that is as evil and filthy as what was shown being done in the daytime, in public, before the police, in this parade and on the streets. There were also children in the parade.

Both men and women are involved and it is full of displays of gross nudity and partial nudity, such as bare-breasted women. Both men and women are acting out homosexual sex acts. The scenes are indescribably loathsome, offensive, and disgusting.

One man has a bare behind, and a leather harness on that extended around his waist and between his legs, and had on some kind of a red dildo which appears to be a penis sticking out in front of him. Men are dressed up as and heavily painted up as women, acting out sex acts with others.

There were displays of various kinds of sadomasochism. Some of them were in harnesses and chains of different kinds, with collars around their necks, crawling on their hands and knees, and being led by chains by their "masters," who were in leather shirts and clothing. One man was striking another man, who was in chains, with a whip.

One man appears to be marching stark naked, except for a strap around his waist and what appears to be a yellow condom on his erect penis.

Nude and almost naked men are lying on the sidewalk and pavement and appear to be engaging in oral sexual intercourse.

Many participants are leading their little children with them through these activities. They appear proud to have them taking part in it.

A huge sign is displayed stating "GOD IS GAY."

This kind of thing goes on and on—like Dante's *Inferno*.

The following is the substance of a part of what the narrators had to say regarding homosexual acts:

> The majority of homosexuality, especially male, is centered around anonymous sexual encounters. Relationships with long term partners are very rare – very rare. Most people don't even know that these activities are taking place and if they knew they'd be extremely shocked, because they're going on right under their noses. (Paulk)
>
> Some of the places, for example, could be public parks in a big city, where there are secluded areas, homosexuals will meet and cruise one another and go behind a clump of bushes and have an encounter. This is very, very common with the people that I knew. Also, they go to public restrooms such as highway road stop rests, they go to restrooms in malls and have sex. There even used to be a joke in New York City about shopping bag day. You'd take a shopping bag and go into a restroom and close the door and stand in the shopping bag and someone else would sit on the stool and so you'd think only one person was in there, because the feet were obscured by the shopping bag. (Paulk)
>
> Another location that's probably the most prevalent place is called a "bath house." And I know when the AIDS scare became really

prevalent a lot of the bath houses in larger cities like New York City, San Francisco, and Los Angeles supposedly closed, but I know for a fact that as recently as just this year, I know people were going to bath houses. They basically have nothing to do with taking a bath at all. You usually pay about $12.00 to get a little membership card, you go into a locker room and check your clothes, and you walk around with as many as one or two hundred other people. They have a series of private rooms with doors or large rooms with mats on the floor, or bunks and things like this. Most of the rooms are either pitch black or very dimly lit. And, for example, just orgies go on in there, people will walk in there and have sex with multiple partners, and they have no idea who they're having sex with. I know this for a fact. (Paulk)

I went into the gay lifestyle right out of high school when I was eighteen, was in that for two years. I was constantly trying to fill some kind of void that was there. I was doing anything I could do to fill it, primarily through sexual encounters and temporary relationships that did not last, and I just found that after two years that I needed something to boost my sagging self-esteem. So I became a female impersonator. Solely out of the need for attention and affirmation. I was worshipped by people in the lifestyle, but after four years I would go home and the loneliness was even worse. The depression became worse, because I was getting all this attention at the bar in shows that I would do and when I would go home I was still alone, still looking for somebody. (Paulk)

(The video showed photographs of John Paulk dressed up and made up as a woman, and he indeed looked like an attractive young lady. However, he was able to overcome that lifestyle and on July 19, 1992, he was married to a woman and apparently was still happily married when the video was made.)

When a number of homosexuals get together, they seem unable to restrain themselves, and they show their true colors. They gather to convince the public of their decency and the justice of their causes, and they do the opposite. They are their own worst enemies in this regard, and seem to have the same suicidal complexes that were displayed in infecting large numbers of their members with AIDS. Their only salvation, politically, is that the news media sanitizes and misinforms the public as to what they do. Several videos are referred to in this book, and on each of them the most vile and despicable acts imaginable are shown taking place in public, before the police, and before children. Yet little of it was shown to us by the national news media, which deliberately ignored the worst things that went on.

The introduction in *The Gay Agenda—The March on Washington, The Report, 1993,* a VCR tape, correctly states:

> They were coming to the nation's capital to proclaim to the American public that they are an oppressed people, denied equal opportunities. Announced as being the largest demonstration ever for the rights of homosexuals, activists hope to bring together over a million gays and lesbians from across the nation in a dramatic display of political unity. Timing of the event was critical as the government moved toward its showdown over the issue of gays in the military. Public awareness of the strength and conviction of the gay community was perceived as essential in winning congressional support for the gay agenda. It was time to show the nation that homosexuals are a respectable segment of this land of diversity. As time goes on and the role of the news media turns from reporting gay issues to promoting them, it comes as no surprise that the news services nationwide portrayed the event as a gathering of fair minded serious citizens. Marching to the beat of gay activism a sympathetic press characterized the event as a festive celebration and joyous, peaceful affair.

The scenes on the tape were in public, in our nation's capital. The noise and whistling was similar to the rioting going on when Governor Wilson vetoed the "Gays Rights Bill" in California, except that I observed no fires and large destruction.

There were obscenities and signs displayed which were similar to the gay parade in San Francisco—this one may have been worse in that regard.

There was an extremely obscene Drag Queen show at the Washington Monument.

The signs and obscenities were continual. One large sign on the back of a T-shirt on a man stated: "BUTT-FUCKING IS FUN" and under that was "QUEER NATION." Another large sign being displayed and carried high was : "SUCK COCK FOR JESUS." Others: "CHRIST LOVES QUEERS," "I SUCK DICK," "EAT PUSSY NOT COWS."

An Asian woman displays a large sign: "SUCK MY QUEER ASIAN PUSSY."

Simulated, or real sex acts were prevalent.

A large group of shaved head individuals ("skinheads") were singing and shouting: "JESUS SUCKS A MEAN DICK."

There were children present and participating in the parades.

When a nation promotes and tolerates such things as this, and particularly in our nation's capital, our morality has sunk into the depths of Hell.

CFV Report, June, 1993, "What the Media Didn't Show You–Sado-Masochists Hold 'S/M-Fetish' Conference as Part of Gay March on Washington–'Fisting' display inside a federal building!" by Peter LaBarbera, describes various things on sale in the Mellon Auditorium, including leather cat-O'-nine-tail whips, chained and leather hoods, handcuffs, canes, and other assorted implements used by such people. A Baltimore company calling itself "Stocks and Bonds" sold stockades and body racks (to which people are strapped with legs and arms outstretched, to receive punishment). Various kinds of electric shocking and torture devices were displayed. The article further states:

> In the back of the room, near the display for Drummer magazine, men were engaged in periodic floggings of one another's buttocks in a kind of public exhibition of S/M techniques. As a crowd looked on approvingly, one man — using a cat-o'-nine-tails — would whip the rear end of the other who was bent over submissively, grasping his own ankles. After several hard lashes, the flogger would reach over and comfort the one who had just received his "punishment" — kissing and petting him. Such is the bizarre world of "leather" sex, which, according to Gay Sex author Jack Hart, is quite popular among homosexuals.
>
> At the rear of the auditorium, on a pulled-down projector screen, was the graphic photograph of a seated man in shirt-and-tie engaged in "fisting" a naked man standing beside him. I had read and heard

about the grotesque gay practice of "fisting" before, but seeing an actual photo of it was perhaps the most revolting experience of my life. For this I can thank the "Kinky Art Slide Show."

***

As I left, I paused to ask a man draped in leather if I could take his picture. He responded: "Do you want me or my master?" He proceeded to inform me that he was a "slave" who lived under a 25-year contract with his master. In the lexicon of S/M, that means he had willfully renounced his rights and submitted himself as a sex slave to obey the orders of his dominant partner, as laid out in an official "slave contract." (A sample copy of such a contract can be found in _The Lesbian S/M Safety Manual._) Strange, indeed. But like much in the gay movement, it was true.

***

Interestingly, one item on the "leatherman's" political agenda is to pressure the American Psychiatric Association (APA) to change its official definitions of sadism, masochism, and sadomasochism from being considered a "disorder." Twenty years ago, gay activists succeeded in pressuring the APA to remove homosexuality from its list of disorders.

Moreover, open S/M advocate Bill Hileman was one of 11 homosexual activists who attended an unprecedented meeting with President Clinton on April 16. (1993)

We certainly can be thankful that all of our country is not yet quite as bad as Washington, D.C., particularly since Clinton became president.

Dan Schrader is a well known homosexual activist in Albuquerque. He registered the following complaint to the editor of the _Albuquerque Tribune_, September 29, 1994:

In 1987, I danced nude in a Washington, D.C., gay nightclub. Only blocks from the U. S. Capitol, and my nude dancing was legal.

***

Why can a man walk legally down Central with his loaded gun in plain view, but I cannot walk legally (go) down Central with my penis in plain view? Are loaded guns less dangerous, less frightening and more socially acceptable than penises?

Then we have the Stonewall Celebration in New York. Scenes and comments on this one are on the VCR, *STONEWALL — 25 YEARS OF DECEPTION,* The Report, 1994. The introduction states:

> Sunday, June 26, 1994, the Twenty-Fifth Anniversary of the Stonewall Inn Riots which were touched off when police raided a gay bar in New York's Greenwich Village. The media reported on parades commemorating the event with glowing coverage. Viewers across the country were exhorted to look upon Stonewall as a glorious milestone in the evolution of human rights. Reporters set aside the customary rules against editorializing and took a clearly pro-homosexual position on the controversy of so-called gay liberation. Why is the media's portrayal of gay activism so consistently positive? Why are any concerns about the homosexual movement dismissed as bigotry? And why does the media downplay or eliminate aspects of gay events that might paint a more balanced picture?

The film shows various demonstrations, noise, and gyrations similar to the ones described on the previous tapes on the San Francisco and Washington parades and demonstrations, except, again, there was no rioting, setting fires, and breaking of windows as there was in the part of the San Francisco tape relating to the riot after Governor Wilson's veto.

There was a scene of a very oddly dressed man who appeared to be playing with his penis with a condom on it in public. A large number of men were stark naked, fondling and kissing one another. Topless lesbians were interspersed throughout the parade.

Then there are scenes from the Gay Pride Parade the next day in San Francisco.

One float had a woman with a dildo on, simulating sexual intercourse with another woman whose back was to her. There are a large number of naked men parading around showing off their penises, apparently trying to keep them as erect as possible.

A commentator on the video states:

> Gay historian, Martin Duberman, in his book, *Stonewall,* admits that homosexual activists, at the time of the riot, described the Stonewall Inn as a haven for "chicken hawks," adult males who coveted underage boys, a real dive, an awful sleazy place, where the purveying

of drugs and young flesh went on. So this is hardly the beginning of a noble civil rights movement. And this is a far cry from Rosa Parks being forced to sit at the back of a bus. The media's cheer-leading coverage of the anniversary of the riots, failed to point out that the Stonewall Inn was an unlicensed bar and the police periodically raided the establishment, not because they had nothing better to do than to harass homosexuals, but because the bar was known for illegal activities. To this day, the Stonewall Bar, a Mecca for gays around the world, has its seedy side.

***

Coinciding with the week of the Stonewall celebration were the Gay Games, a kind of "Olympics" for gay athletes. ...

***

In its zeal to paint only the most positive picture, the media also failed to point out that not just so-called sexual orientation, but sexuality was very much part of the week of the Gay Games and the Stonewall celebration. Visitors' guides contained page after page of ads and listings appealing to those looking for sexual encounters.

***

In honor of the Gay Games, Attorney General Janet Reno, with a special ten day waiver, lifted the restrictions against HIV infected aliens entering the country. Given the potential dangers, what conclusions must we draw from the gay community's insistence on promoting environments in which unrestrained sexuality is clearly encouraged?

***

There were two Stonewall parades. One starting at the United Nations, and one starting at the Stonewall Bar. The second parade was illegal, yet the police, rather than preventing the parade from proceeding, escorted the marchers up Fifth Avenue....

This second parade was by the North American Man/Boy Love Association (NAMBLA) and I believe that it was the worst that I have seen on any of the three tapes referred to. There were children present, and they were escorted by the New York police under orders of Mayor Rudolph Giuliani. He marched in front of the other parade that began at the United Nations.

Peter LaBarbera is one of the foremost writers in the country on the homosexual movement. He was founder and is the Editor of the Lambda Report. He was also one of the many commentators on the Stonewall tape. The August 1994, issue of the *Lambda Report* states that when asked why they did not do something about the nude men, several policemen said that they were under orders to do nothing.

A narrator also states:

> Attendance at the main "Stonewall" parade was estimated by police at 90,000 – a fraction of the million predicted by homosexual organizers. The low turnout was reminiscent of last year's "March on Washington," in which inflated gay estimates also proved unfounded.

Family Research Institute, Inc., *Medical Consequences of What Homosexuals Do*, 1992, states:

> 6,714 obituaries from 16 U.S. homosexual journals over the past 12 years were compared to a large sample of obituaries from regular newspapers. The obituaries from the regular newspapers were similar to U.S. averages for longevity: the median age of death of married men was 75 and 80% of them died old (age 65 or older). For unmarried or divorced men the median age of death was 57 and 32% of them died old. Married women averaged age 79 at death; 85% died old. Unmarried and divorced women averaged age 71 and 60% of them died old.
>
> The median age of death for homosexuals, however, was virtually the same nationwide — and, overall, less than 2% survived to old age. If AIDS was the cause of death, the median age was 39. For the 829 gays who died of something other than AIDS, the median age of death was 42 and 9% died old. The 140 lesbians had a median age of death of 45 and 23% died old.
>
> 2.9% of gays died violently. They were 116 times more apt to be murdered; 24 times more apt to commit suicide; and had a traffic-accident death-rate 18 times the rate of comparably aged white males. Heart attacks, cancer and liver failure were exceptionally common. Twenty percent of lesbians died of murder, suicide, or accident — a rate 512 times higher than that of white females aged 25-44. The age distributions of samples of homosexuals in the scientific literature from 1858 to 1992 suggests a similarly shortened lifespan.

In the nineteen seventies, when many state legislatures gave in to the pressures of the homosexual lobbies and began repealing state laws making sodomy a crime, they openly invited the death and destruction which has subsequently taken place. The result was great and mortal harm to the country as a whole, and to many innocent people – but the greatest death and destruction was visited upon the homosexuals themselves. The homosexual activists bear the direct responsibility for this calamity.

PROMISCUITY

The promiscuity of homosexuals is also unbelievable to those uninformed on the subject. We have touched on this, above, and in addition to the material under this subheading, there will be more later in this chapter, under the subheading, "Spreading the AIDS Virus."

The object of the book, *After The Ball*, by Kirk and Madsen, supra, was previously explained. Although the authors are completely misguided, in that they are still promoting homosexuality in the book, I do consider it to be the most thoughtful and well written of any current writing by homosexuals I have read. Although they are preaching to homosexuals to clean up their act, to try to help their agenda to gain public acceptance, even they seem compelled to use vile and profane language. Nevertheless, the book gives us valuable insight into the homosexual "lifestyle." In commenting on the promiscuity of homosexuals, and attempts by many "gays" to have more permanent relationships, they state (p. 330):

> ... Sooner or later, the roving penis rears its ugly head.
> ... And no matter how happy a gay man may be with his lover, he's likely eventually, to go dowsing for dick.
> ... the cheating ratio of 'married' gay males, given enough time, approaches 100%. ...
> Many gay lovers, bowing to the inevitable, agree to an 'open relationship,' for which there are as many sets of ground rules as there are couples. ...

Cameron (1988), in Appendix A, refers to a diary study for his statistics on the average number of partners per year for gays, and the nature of the acts committed. He tabulates that on the average, in one year, they: fellated 106 different men, and swallowed fifty of their seminal discharges; experienced seventy-two penile penetrations of the anus; and ingested the fecal material of twenty-three different men. "Many of these encounters involved activities in which the partners neither knew one another nor exchanged words, and occurred in restrooms, bathhouses, and other public places."

Dr. Monteith states in the *The Gay Agenda* video:

> Studies show that male homosexuals average between 20 and 106 partners every year. The average homosexual has 300 to 500 partners in his lifetime. Thirty-seven percent engage in sadomasochism, at least 28% have engaged in sodomy with more than a thousand men. Compared to heterosexuals, male homosexuals are 8 times more likely to have had hepatitis, 14 times more likely to have had syphilis, and 5,000 times more likely to have contracted AIDS.

Concerned Women for America, The Homosexual Deception: Making Sin A Civil Right, supra, pp. 14-16, states:

> AIDS research released in 1982 by the U.S. Center For Disease Control reported that the typical homosexual interviewed claimed to have had over 500 different sexual partners in a lifetime. Considered by themselves, the AIDS victims in this study averaged more than 1,100 lifetime sexual partners. Some reported as many as 20,000. A psychologist we interviewed tells of counseling a homosexual clergyman who claimed more than 900 sexual partners to date.
>
> In perhaps the most thorough study of homosexual behavior ever undertaken, published by the Kinsey Institute in Bell and Weinberg's book, *Homosexualities, a Study of Diversity Among Men and Women* (New York, Simon and Schuster, 1978, pp. 308-309), we learn that:
> * 43% of white male homosexuals estimated they had sex with 500 or more different partners. 75% had 100 or more. 28% (the largest subcategory) reported more than 1000 partners.
> * 79% said more than half their partners were strangers.
> * 70% said more than half their sexual partners were men with whom they had sex only once.

* * *

(Incidentally, evidence exists of high levels of lesbian promiscuity, which correlates with previously-mentioned high disease-incidence statistics among lesbians. Jay and Young's *Gay Report* [op. cit., p. 5] revealed that 38% of lesbians surveyed had between 11 and more than 300 lifetime sexual partners – far beyond the norm for heterosexual women. In *Homosexualities,* op. cit., Bell and Weinberg reported that 41% of white lesbians admitted to having between 10 and 500 sexual partners.)

"Sodomy Laws," CFV, supra, p. 3-7, as to male homosexuals, states:

The detrimental consequences of this behavior is exploded when the amount of sexual partners with whom homosexuals copulate are examined. Most homosexual exchange occurs between strangers, 70 percent admitting that they had had sex only once with over half of their partners. Homosexuals average somewhere between 20 and 106 different partners per year. The average homosexual has had 300 to 500 partners during a lifetime. Twenty-eight percent of homosexuals have had sodomy with 1000 or more partners, 70 percent with 50 or more partners, and only 2 percent have had what could be described as monogamous or semi-monogamous relationships. Of these monogamous relationships, however, still 5 percent drank urine, 7 percent incorporated fisting, 33 percent ingested feces, 53 percent swallowed semen, and 59 percent received sperm up their rectum during the previous month of study. Still other studies indicate that "monogamy" for homosexuals lasts between 9 and 60 months. (Citations were omitted from this material, but were given above for the CFV statistical information.)

The physical danger, danger of disease, and emotional harm of this kind of behavior is obviously enormous.

RELATIONS WITH YOUTH

Lamenting the indiscretions of what they consider some of the greats of the "gays" throughout history, Kirk and Madsen write:

When you find a given failing even in a community's best and brightest, you suspect its overwhelming prevalence among the great unwashed. In this context, it's noteworthy that Alan Turing, Oscar Wilde, and perhaps Leonardo da Vinci—each, in his own time and unique vein, among the most brilliant minds the gay community ever produced—*all* embroiled themselves in serious legal trouble by carrying on indiscreetly with young men. Da Vinci stood trial; Wilde was imprisoned, destroying his personality and career; Turing chemically castrated by order of the court, killed himself.

Arguably, each of these great men knew the law of his time, had ample scope to conduct his affairs in the same discretion and privacy employed by lesser mortals, and, having a first-rate mind, must have known, on some level, that flaunting his 'deviation' in the public's face was an ideal way of losing his reputation, career, and even life. Yet, for the sake of what, we cannot fathom, each man threw caution—and with it everything else—to the winds.

It's remarkable that these geniuses—the very cream of the human crop—could fail so devastatingly to see their world as it really was, and to exercise minimal restraint. In our view, their failure argues wishful thinking. Some might call it 'the courage of the individual to stand alone against oppression,' but, judging actions by the practical criterion of their consequences, it looks awfully foolish.

And on the clay feet of their betters, more humble gays continue to bumble along. (*After The Ball*, p. 345)

It is odd that Kirk and Madsen omitted Walt Whitman from their listing of the great homosexuals in history. The following is an excerpt from the *Family Research Report*, January-February, 1996:

Walt Whitman Was A Teacher

Although he is celebrated today as a gay poet, Walt Whitman began his career as a teacher. In 1841 he was denounced from the pulpit, tarred, feathered and run out of town on a rail for sexual involvement with his male students. (Reynolds, D. C., [1995], *Walt Whitman's America: a cultural biography*, New York: Knoph.) ...

"Sodomy Laws," CFV, supra, p. 3-6, states:

One survey by two homosexual authors found that 73 percent of homosexuals had at some time had sex with boys 16-19 years old or younger. (Jay and Young, supra, p. 275) It is no wonder that one of the stated objectives of the National Gay Task Force is to remove "age of consent" laws from state statutes, permitting voluntary sex with minors. (1972 Gay Rights Platform, drawn up at the national Coalition of Gay Organizations convention [Chicago, 1972]. Rueda, D. T., *The Homosexual Network* [Devin Adair, 1982.])

Protecting our young people from homosexuals is an exceedingly serious problem in our society. It is a problem in which we have sadly failed, and if the homosexual activists had their way, there would be no protection.

Child Molestation and Homosexuality, Family Research Institute, Inc., 1993, is a report covering over twenty surveys by professionals and other reputable organizations. Included were four surveys on advances and assaults by teachers on students in their care. This report ends with the following:

Proportionality: The Key

Study after nationwide study has yielded estimates of male homosexuality that range between 1% and 3%. The proportion of lesbians in these studies is almost always lower, usually about half that of gays. So, overall, perhaps 2% of adults regularly indulge in homosexuality. Yet they account for between 20% to 40% of all molestations of children.

... Investigation of those suffering severe chronic mental illness implicates child molestation as a primary cause (45% of Bigras *et al's* patients were homosexually abused).

If 2% of the population is responsible for 20% to 40% of something as socially and personally troubling as child molestation, then something must be desperately wrong with that 2%. Not every homosexual is a child molester. But enough gays do molest children so that the risk of a homosexual molesting a child is 10 to 20 times greater than that of a heterosexual.

Goals of the Gay Movement

The gay movement is forthright about seeking to legitimize child-adult homosexual sex. In 1987, *The Journal of Homosexuality,* the scholarly organ of the gay rights movement, published "Pedophilia and the Gay Movement." Author Theo Sandfort detailed homosexual efforts to end "oppression towards pedophilia." In 1980 the largest Dutch gay organization (the COC) "adopted the position that the liberation of pedophilia must be viewed as a gay issue... [and that] ages of consent should therefore be abolished ... by acknowledging the affinity between homosexuality and pedophilia, the COC has quite possibly made it easier for homosexual adults to become more sensitive to erotic desires of younger members of their sex, therefore broadening gay identity." In 1990 COC achieved a significant victory: lowering the age of consent for homosexual sex in Holland to 12 (unless the parents object, in which case it goes up to 15). In the U. S. and Canada, the *North American Man-Boy Love Association*, marches proudly in many gay pride parades with the stated goal of removing the barriers to man-boy sex. Note the phrases *"oppression* towards pedophilia" and *"liberation* of pedophilia." It is clear that those who advocate the legalization of sex between adults and children intend to argue that such conduct is a "civil right," deserving of the same legal protections afforded to other minorities. A large proportion of Americans regard that argument as a mere pretext to giving "sexual predators" free reign to take advantage of vulnerable children.

Conclusion

Not only is the gay rights movement upfront in its desire to legitimize sex with children, but whether indexed by population reports of molestation, pedophile convictions, or teacher-pupil assaults, there is a strong, disproportionate association between child molestations and homosexuality. Ann Landers' claim that homosexuals molest children at no higher rate than heterosexuals do is untrue. The assertion by gay leaders and the American Psychological Association that a homosexual is less likely than a heterosexual to molest children is patently false. (Citations omitted)

There is no reasonable excuse for a person in her position making such a statement as that attributed to Ann Landers. It is for the obvious purpose of promoting the homosexual movement. The American Psychological Organization should now be considered less than a pseudo-scientific organization, for the positions it has taken and the statements it has made. They probably back up their argument by pointing out that more child molestations are by heterosexuals than by homosexuals. But they have to know the fallacy of not comparing the population statistics, as explained above in the report by Family Research Institute, Inc.

Concerned Women for America, *The Homosexual Deception: Making Sin A Civil Right*, supra, pp. 5-7. states:

> ... Child molestation is regarded in every state as a criminal offense.
>
> Yet it is common knowledge that homosexuals are notorious practitioners of sex with minors. *The Gay Report* (Summit Books, 1979, p. 275), a survey of homosexual attitudes and behavior by Jay and Young, two *homosexual* researchers, revealed that 73% of homosexuals surveyed had at some time had sex with boys 16-19 years of age or younger.
>
> J. C. Coleman, in *Abnormal Psychology and Modern Life* (1964) lists early homosexual experience as the main cause of homosexuality. He found that more than 50% of adult homosexuals had been seduced by older homosexuals before the age of 14. (pp. 5-6)
>
> ***
>
> A survey in *The British Journal of Sexual Medicine* (April 1987) reported the mean age of homosexuals' first sexual encounters with other males as 15 years and one month. Homosexuals are, statistically, about 18 times more likely to engage in sexual practices with minors than heterosexuals. Crime statistics reveal that about 31% of children younger than 13 who claim to have been molested by men were homosexually assaulted. ("Child Molestation and Homosexuality," Institute for the Scientific Investigation of Sexuality, 1987. See also *Psychological Reports,* 1986, #58, pp. 327-337, which reveals that homosexuals, [while representing perhaps 2% of the population] perpetrate more than one-third of all reported child molestations.)
>
> A nationwide investigation of child molestation in the Boy Scouts of America (see *Insight* magazine, June 17, 1991) reported 1,151 complaints by Boy Scouts of abuse by Scout leaders in the past 19 years, in all 50 States and the District of Columbia. This makes, the article stated, "sex abuse more common in Scouting than accidental deaths and serious injuries.... In that time, at least 416 men have been arrested or banned from Scouting for molesting boys in their care." The Boy Scouts have spent literally millions of dollars in litigation related to this abuse.

Dr. Monteith states:

> The carefully kept secret in America today is the young man's health study which was recently carried out in San Francisco, and

actually released in 1992. It was carried out by the Department of Public Health where they got young boys just entering the homosexual lifestyle. They actively recruited them out of our homes, out of our schools today. And those young boys, aged 15 to 19, who have had all the education in the world, who've been told over and over again the dangers of homosexual practices and have been indoctrinated in "safe sex," and of that group, 10 to 12% are already HIV positive, 26% are Hepatitis B positive, and those who have HIV disease are going to die. (*The Gay Agenda*)

Llewellyn states:

Homosexuals have a long history of focusing on youth. The North American Man/Boy Love Association has worked for two decades to abolish age consent laws, so that adult males could legally solicit sex from boys. (*The Gay Agenda*)

Dr. Nicolosi states:

Let's consider the adolescent, the thirteen-, fourteen-, or fifteen-year-old kid who thinks he is homosexual. Now to think one is homosexual or to feel homosexual feelings in adolescence is very natural. It happens very, very frequently by many people who eventually become heterosexual. But there are programs, counseling programs around the country, in California it's called Project 10, but there are many such programs around the country which are pro-gay. And so you get a 15-year-old kid who goes to his pro-gay counselor, and the counselor may well be homosexual, and the kid says, "Well, I have these homosexual thoughts or feeling or behaviors." Now the counselor can say, "Well, welcome to the gay community, you're one of us," which is what I'm concerned about. (*The Gay Agenda*, supra)

Concerned Women for America, *The Homosexual Deception: Making Sin a Civil Right,* supra, pp. 6-8, states:

Knowing that between one fourth and one third of child molestations involve man-boy contact, homosexual extremists are now conveniently attempting to claim that male molesters of boys should not be considered homosexuals. However, a recent Canadian study of male child molesters revealed the following: (1) 30% of the offenders studied admitted to having engaged in homosexual acts with adults; and (2) 91% of molesters of non-familial boys admitted to no lifetime sexual contact other than homosexual—i.e., their sexual orientation was clearly homosexual (Marshall, W. L., et. al., \"Early onset and deviant sexuality in child molesters.\" (*Journal of Interpersonal Violence,* 1991, 6, 323-336).

Among homosexual activists themselves, a heated debate rages over whether the homosexual community should include among their ranks homosexuals who have sex with the young. In a typical editorial favoring inclusion that appeared recently in the homosexual newspaper *Bay Area Reporter* (Feb. 13, 1992, p. 6), one Bradley Rose said:

> ...What is a pedophile? A pedophile is not a rapist or murderer, or a devil, but a person who loves... As a gay child, I would have welcomed sexual relations with males, of adult age as well as my own...
>
> Gay liberation is stuck in backwaters as long as gay children are denied their sexuality and as long as parents are allowed to push their gay children into the roles of hetero adults... Most of the heteros just don't know how to give gay-affirming support to their children (the homosexual ones as well as the non-gay ones). Let's give them a hand.

Similarly, support for "gay men who love boys" is found in a recent editorial in the *San Francisco Sentinel,* another homosexual newspaper. In fact, the editorial states that "the love between men and boys is the foundation of homosexuality" ("No Place for Homo Homophobia," March 26, 1992).

***

Dr. Judith Reisman, President of The Institute for Media Education, has released a not-yet-published study titled "A Content Analysis of *The Advocate* [a national homosexual magazine] 1972-1991" speaking to the issue. *The Advocate* is generally recognized as a "mainstream" publication on the homosexual subculture. Reisman argues persuasively that *The Advocate* closely reflects national "gay culture" and homosexual "community values."...

Among Reisman's findings: " 'Boys,' 'chicken' [a common homosexual term for underage young sexual partners] and 'teens' are solicited and displayed sexually in *The Advocate* is encouraged by prevailing gay cultural values. Finding: 10-20% of *Advocate* ads sexually solicit boys/teens within a larger pool of 58% prostitution ads. Up to 23% of sex customers wanted 'hairless' or smooth bodies while 38% used youth cues ('boys,' 'youth,' 'son') to recruit boy lovers".... .

***

It should come as no surprise, then, that homosexual extremist manifestos such as "The 1972 Gay Rights Platform" have consistently called upon governments to: (1) "Repeal all state laws prohibiting private sexual acts involving consenting persons [i.e., not consenting adults]"; and for (2) "Repeal of all laws governing the age of sexual consent." (In 1991, under considerable lobbying pressure by, among others, homosexual activists and their liberal supporters, the state of New Jersey significantly lowered the age of consent in laws relating to sexual behavior within its sovereignty.)

The subject of the next chapter is causes of and cures for homosexuality. However, because of its relation to homosexual acts, it will be touched on here.

What Causes Homosexual Desire and Can It Be Changed?, Family Research Institute, 1992:

There is evidence that homosexuality, like drug uses, is "handed down" from older individuals. The first homosexual encounter is usually initiated by the older person. In separate studies 60%, 64%, and 61% of the respondents claimed that their first partner was someone older who initiated the sexual experience.

How this happens is suggested by a nationwide random study from Britain: 35% of boys and 9% of girls said they were approached for sex by adult homosexuals. Whether for attention, curiosity, or by force, 2% of the boys and 1% of the girls succumbed. In the U. S., 37% of males and 9% of females reported having been approached for homosexual sex (65% of those doing the inviting were older). Likewise, a study of over 400 London teenagers reported that "for the boys, their first homosexual experience was very likely with someone older: half the boys' first partners were 20 or older; for girls it was 43 percent." A quarter of homosexuals have admitted to sex with children and underaged teens, suggesting that homosexuality is introduced to youngsters the same way other behaviors are learned – by experience. (References omitted)

Whether it is because the homosexual movement is gaining in momentum, or for whatever reason, it appears that homosexual molestation of the young is on the increase. Family Research Report, Jan.-Feb. 1996, contains an article on child molestation, which included a comprehensive search of newspaper articles by two computer internet searches. One used *FirstSearch* to search the 25 largest national and regional newspapers for the last six years (1989-1995, inclusive), the other was a *Newsbank* microfiche survey of the 200 largest newspapers for the last five years (1990-1995). The following is stated about these two searches:

> When they molested, homosexuals accounted for proportionally more child victims than heterosexuals did. On *FirstSearch's* sample of 25 of the nation's largest newspapers, homosexuals/bisexuals accounted for 61% of the 564 victims logged for the last 6 years. The *Newsbank* sample reported that homosexuals accounted for 747 (85%), bisexuals for 86 (10%), and heterosexuals for 51 (6%) of the 884 victims (if the article said "boys," "girls," or "many," we counted their number as 2, so our estimates are conservative).

There is no question that young people should be protected from practicing homosexuals, and by this I mean any homosexuals currently engaging in homosexual acts. I do not mean ex-homosexuals who have managed to be cured of their sickness and have completely left the destructive lifestyle. Many such people as the latter have become upstanding citizens, and some are among our most important workers against the homosexual agenda because they fully realize the dangers.

CFV Report, Colorado for Family Values, June 1995, states:

> One Gay man summed up the truth in *The Advocate*, America's largest gay news magazine. "How many gay men, I wonder, would have missed out on a valuable, liberating experience—one that initiated them into their sexuality—if it weren't for so-called molestation?" (Carl Maves, "Getting Over It," *The Advocate*, 5 May 1992, p. 85)
>
> Realizing the incredible public relations disaster pedophilia represents to their cause, homosexual leaders have consistently tried to keep the subject "out of sight" of middle America and to play down their historical association with child abuse.

... Among those protesting this hypocrisy was long-time gay activist David Thorstad, who complained that pedophilia was being swept under the rug by the gay rights movement which " . . . seeks to sanitize the image of homosexuality to facilitate its entrance into the social mainstream." (Man-Boy Love and the American Gay Movement, *The Journal of Homosexuality*, 1990, vol. 20, pp. 251-252) Thorstad— former president of the New York City Gay Activists Alliance, founding member of the Coalition for Lesbian and Gay Rights, founding member of NAMBLA, and author of a book about the early homosexual activist movement—has written such bold statements as, "Man-boy love has been a player in gay liberation since the mid-nineteenth century ... it lies close to the roots of gay liberation ... In all cultures and in all historical periods, men and youths have been getting it on, because they are naturally attracted to each other." (David Thorstad, "The Death of Gay Liberation?", *NAMBLA Bulletin*, June 1994, vol. 14, no. 4, pp. 8-9)

(My comment: It indeed takes a sick mind to want to take sexual advantage of young lads, who have a natural affinity and often a hero worship for older men—men who should be teaching them principles of morality and leadership, such as is done by a good scoutmaster, school teacher, Sunday school teacher, minister, or priest, to whom their care is intrusted.)

"The Overhauling of Straight America," the landmark playbook for homosexual strategy, makes it quite clear why such statements threaten the movement's political goals. "NAMBLA must play no part in such a campaign. Suspected child molesters will never look like victims." Later, it cautions: "The masses must not be repulsed by premature exposure to homosexual behavior itself." (Kirk and Pill, "The Overhauling of Straight America," *Guide*, November, 1987, pp. 14-24)

Evidence showing that pedophilia is in fact a common part of the homosexual lifestyle is staggering. Ironically, much of it comes from homosexuals themselves.

Psycho-sexual researcher, Dr. Judith Reisman analyzed the contents of *The Advocate* between the years 1972 and 1991. Roughly 10-20% of ads since 1972 have both subtly and blatantly, solicited child/teen boy entrapment. (Judith Reisman, *A Content Analysis of* The Advocate, unpublished manuscript, p. 18)

Faced with these statistics, homosexual activists are now trying to deflect the discussion by claiming that male molesters of boys should not be considered homosexuals at all. But a recent study of Canadians imprisoned for pedophilia reveals the truth: 30% of the offenders studied admitted to having engaged in homosexual acts as adults, and 91% of molesters of non-famial boys admitted to no lifetime sexual contact *other* than homosexual. In other words, their sexual preference was clearly homosexual. (W. L. Marshall, et al, "Early onset and deviant sexuality in child molesters," *Journal of Interpersonal Violence*, 1991, vol. 6, pp. 323-336)

. . .The journal *Psychological Reports* revealed that homosexuals, while representing perhaps 2% of the population, perpetrate more than one-third of all reported child molestations. (*Psychological Reports*, 1986, vol. 58, pp. 327-337)

Sex researchers Masters and Johnson describe the process of establishing "homophile orientations" as follows: "In most cases, homophile interests developed in the early to mid-teens . . . Recruitment usually was accomplished by an older male, frequently in his twenties, but occasionally men in their thirties were the initiators . . . the teenager was left with the concept that whether or not he continued as an active homosexual, he would always be homophile-oriented. (C. Masters and O. Johnson, *Human Sexual Inadequacy*, [Boston: Little, Brown and Co. 1979], p. 180)

An article in the *St. Louis Post-Dispatch*, 2-20-94, states:

Michael A. Euer, a grade school principal and Boy Scout leader whose work with children brought him much acclaim, has been convicted on 10 charges of sexually abusing three boys in his care.

For many years, Euer was the East Prairie, Mo., version of small-town hero; Kiwanis president, award-winning scout volunteer, church leader, committee member. He was known for commitment to youth that went far beyond the classroom.

Now he is known also for cruelly victimizing some of his young charges. Euer had been indicted on 35 charges, involving 12 boys. The prosecutor said that charges were dropped involving nine of the boys to reduce the size of the case. This abuse had apparently been going on for as long as 23 years, and some cases were too old to prosecute, the article said.

The part of the diatribe at the beginning of this chapter of "Michael Swift" saying "we will sodomize your sons" is no idle threat. It continually and frequently happens. The following is an article about a homosexual molester who almost got his just deserts.

Child rapist gets 30 years

An Albuquerque man was given the maximum sentence today for raping a 3-year-old boy in an abandoned East Central motel

Brian James Lucero, 26, was sentenced to 30 years imprisonment on a combination of three charges: 18 years for criminal sexual penetration, nine years for kidnapping and three years for child abuse.

"I don't think the defendant could be trusted to make a rational decision ever again. I can't put him back on the street where this could happen to another member of society," District Court Judge W.C. "Woody" Smith said.

Lucero was found guilty in November of raping the boy April 24, 1992. The boy had been riding his bicycle near his home when he was abducted and taken to the abandoned Villa Inn Motel when a neighbor heard him screaming.

The neighbor rescued the boy and beat Lucero with a 2-by-4 board. (*The Albuquerque Tribune*, 1-27-93)

Homosexual molestation of young people is terrible and devastating to them. It is unbelievable that many homosexuals, and many of their supporters in the fields of psychiatry and psychology, see nothing wrong with it. The abuse is widespread, and the effect on the young victims is heart rendering.

In the *Albuquerque Journal*, 6-20-97, was an article about the well-known hockey player, Sheldon Kennedy, with the Boston Bruins. A coach, Graham James, was given a three-and-a-half-year jail sentence in Canada after pleading guilty to two counts of abuse against Kennedy and another unnamed player. Fortunately, Kennedy finally had the courage to disclose the matter and get something done about it. He was first victimized when he was fourteen, and the article tells of the trauma, nightmares, and feelings of guilt he suffered. The following is an excerpt from the first part of the article:

BOSTON – The letters came in thick, heavy piles, about a thousand a week at first. There have been too many letters for Sheldon Kennedy to count, but never so many that he'll become inured to the horrifying tales they tell. He knows their stories all too well because he lived them

From teen-agers to 50-year-olds, the letter writers reveal their darkest secrets. Like Kennedy, who in January disclosed he had been sexually abused by his junior hockey coach more than 300 times over a 10-year period, they also had been violated by someone they trusted. Their lives were clouded by an anger they couldn't understand, their self-esteem shattered by shame. Unable to voice the unmentionable, they suffered in silence until Kennedy gave them the courage to speak. ***

Although he's gratified his disclosure made it easier for other victims to confront their past, his frankness created new problems. That's because with every well-intentioned expression of sympathy he receives and every interview he does, he relives his nightmares. ***

"They just know you're in such a scared position. You absolutely have no clue about what to do. A lot of people probably think, 'Why don't you just kick him or run away?' but you can't. You're vulnerable." ***

In the *Albuquerque Journal*, 3-8-98, was and article about Dr. David Sylvester LaMure, a pathologist in Roswell, New Mexico, who was convicted of sexually molesting boys, and was sentenced to eighteen years in prison. He admitted to having sex with 76 boys under the age of eighteen. He said he met the boys "in gay bars, on the street and in other places." A federal magistrate recommended that the defendant be released from jail or get a new trial, because his attorney based his strategy on the erroneous belief that the legal age of consent was lower than it was at the time of the offenses.

From two Albuquerque daily newspapers, the *Albuquerque Journal*, and the *Albuquerque Tribune*, for the years 1992 through 1996, just in ordinary reading of the newspapers, over 40 articles were found on homosexual attacks and abuse of boys. Of course, some were repeat articles about the same incident or offender. None of this group involved Catholic priests, who will be considered separately. We will consider just a few of the many incidents.

An article of November 3, 1993, reported 27 year old Ricky Gilbert pleading guilty to molesting two eight-year-old boys in Alamogordo, N. M. Gilbert was on parole at the time for a Georgia conviction for molesting young boys.

There were several articles in the first half of 1996 about a molester, Dan McQuay, who was up for release from a Texas prison, and decided he wanted to be castrated. He was quoted as saying: "I got away with molesting over 240 children before getting caught for molesting just one little boy."

There were two articles in March 1992 about the arrest of Ed Savitz, a fifty-year-old vice president of a Philadelphia actuarial firm, who had molestation charges filed against him. The article stated that Savitz had AIDS. "This defendant may have been engaged for several years in both oral and anal sexual contact with as many as several hundred males." Charges were "involuntary deviate sexual intercourse, sexual abuse of children, indecent assault and corrupting the morals of a minor." Such things as pornographic photos of minors, and paying young boys "for their underwear and socks, and for sexual contact" were related in the article.

In *The Albuquerque Tribune* an article of November 29, 1994, stated that police in Northern Ireland had uncovered a sex ring that involved more than 100 children, the youngest being three years old. Most of the children were boys ages eight to twelve. Three men were in custody awaiting trial. "The abuses described in the children's statements include rape, sodomy and group sex."

It would appear that many homosexuals have been extremely clever in concealing their molestation over long periods of time. A September 14, 1995, front page headline article in *The Albuquerque Tribune* was about a Gallup, N. M., former high-school principal, Charles Edwin Johnson, who was charged with 402 criminal counts of sexually abusing ten male students from 1980 to 1981. We need to keep in mind that the case had not yet been tried and proved. However, we also need to keep in mind that in the cases that are proved, there are undoubtedly a large number of molestations that never come to light. Also, there are surely a large number of homosexual child abusers who are never charged at all.

An article on an unrelated case was in the *Albuquerque Journal* of October 16, 1995, about another former Gallup school principal, Fred David Johnson, who was sentenced to twenty-eight years in prison for the kidnapping and abuse of an eleven-year-old boy. Items found by the police in Johnson's apartment included "sexually oriented reading material and numerous photographs." According to the judge, another thing found was a manual written by Johnson on "how to molest children and get away with it." Strangely enough, the article stated that Johnson was playing with the boy's feet and sucking his toes. A later *Albuquerque Journal* article, November 11, 1995, related that the manual said that the author had "performed sexual acts on young boys during more than 25 years as a teacher." The article said that Johnson had molested dozens of children. The prosecutor said that Johnson was convicted previously in U. S. District Court in New Mexico in 1984 of criminal sexual penetration of a minor and went to prison. The manual says that the "kinds of ... boys to exploit are students, Boy Scouts, choir boys, altar boys, athletes and studious boys who are completely unaware of life itself."

In June, 1996, there were various articles and television news items about the Southern Baptist Church Convention voting to boycott Disneyland because the organization granted "family" benefits to homosexuals, and because of indecent films being made and shown by Disney, including homosexual films. An *Albuquerque Journal* article of October 26, 1995, is about Victor Salva, director of the movie, "Powder," made for Disney Co. A man who had previously been a victim of Salva, stated that Salva had oral sex with him in 1987 when, as a twelve-year-old, he appeared in the director's low-budget film "Clownhouse." Salva, 37, who videotaped the act, refused comment. In 1988 he pleaded guilty to five counts of child sex abuse. He served fifteen months in jail and completed parole in 1992.

Most of the articles for the five-year period referred to were about charges against and convictions of homosexuals for multiple acts against numerous boys, many under the age of twelve, and included use of pornographic photos, video tapes, and other depraved, strange and abhorrent acts.

An opinion was handed down by the New Mexico Court of Appeals on December 21, 1992, *State v. Lamure*, which shows us how heinous homosexual perversion can be. The court affirmed the conviction of the defendant, a pathologist. He was convicted of five counts of criminal sexual contact with a minor, two counts of criminal sexual penetration, and one count of extortion, all involving one adolescent victim. There was a pretrial hearing on excluding evidence of prior acts involving a number of adolescent males, including the defendant's two sons. The defendant ended up withdrawing his objections to this evidence, relying on the opinion of a psychologist, Dr. Dougher, who specialized in treating sex offenders. Dr. Dougher testified that the defendant was a homosexual pedophile, which caused him to be sexually attracted to male adolescents. He also testified that it was his opinion that the defendant's claim of a non-coercive relationship with the victim was more consistent than the victim's claim of a coercive relationship.

An article in the *Albuquerque Journal*, July 9, 1995, previously in the Chicago Tribune, was entitled, "Victim of Prison Rape Devotes Life to Battle." It was about Stephen Donaldson, who formed the organization, Stop Prison Rape. Donaldson estimates that more than 300,000 inmates are abused each year in our nation's prisons. The article states that a 1982 study found a 14 percent sexual assault rate in one California prison, a 1984 study reported that 28 percent of the inmates in six New York state prisons had been the target of sexual aggression at least once, and that a 1994 study found that 22 percent of male inmates at three Nebraska prisons reported they had been pressured or forced into sexual contacts. Only 29 percent of the Nebraska inmates said that they reported the incidents of sexual assault to the prison staff.

The following is from an article, "6 Accused in Waco Sex Ring. *Albuquerque Journal*, 12-2-97:

> WACO, Texas — Bellmead police believe they have uncovered a ring of men who have seduced teen-age boys with money and drugs, then sexually assaulted them.
>
> ... six men have been arrested for their alleged involvement in multiple sexual assaults on juveniles in the Waco area over the last two-years.
>
> Seven boys between the ages of 14 and 17 have been identified as victims, according to the newspaper.
>
> "There's a lot more victims that we don't know of," said Detective Thomas Noble of the Bellmead Police Department, north of Waco.

In the last several years there have been reports of innumerable Roman Catholic priests and brothers, in the U.S. and other countries, who have had homosexual relations with altar boys and other young boys under their care or influence. This has been widely reported in the news media, and there have been so many that I do not know if anyone has tried to count them; but I know that these homosexual acts against boys by priests would number in the hundreds, and possibly thousands. It has truly been unbelievable, and although many of the settlements of lawsuits have been kept secret, I am sure that the church and its insurance companies have been forced to pay out many millions of dollars. I have about 145 clippings from Albuquerque's two main newspapers, covering an approximate four-year period from 1993 to 1996, on homosexual abuse of boys and young men by priests, and I am sure that this was far from all of them. There have also been several national television shows and news articles on the problem. A few of the incidents will be discussed to try to give the readers some idea of these horrible and unnatural crimes committed against humanity and individuals.

It would appear that once a person sinks into the life of sodomy there is no bottom to the depths of their depravity. Homosexuality is a terrible sickness of mind that should never be accepted, condoned or encouraged, either by law or by "tolerance."

An article, "Faith, death and betrayal," *U. S. News & World Report*, March 11, 1996, is about one example. "The Busam family placed a retarded son, Joey, in the care of Catholic brothers. Now he is dead of AIDS." The article states:

- One brother kept a 6-foot boa constrictor at the facility. Helplessly retarded men said he ordered them to drop their pants and bend over, then placed something by their anus. "Feel my snake?" the brother asked. Was it the snake or the man's penis? Prosecutors were never sure.

- In a drunken stupor, night after night another brother roamed the facility while the retarded men slept. According to a court affidavit, the brother slid into the beds of some men and molested them. In a letter to Ohio authorities, one retarded man wrote: The brothers "use me for a girl. They force me to do it. I am a human being. ..."

The description of Joey's death of AIDS is indeed heartbreaking:

... He mumbled a few words to his mother, Claire. At 85 pounds, Joey was frail, well below his normal weight of 135. Beneath the covers, his arms and legs were matchstick thin. Scars and lesions covered his body. Morphine dulled the pain. By early morning the following day, Joey's breathing became labored. A little before midnight, he swallowed twice, and then the life went out of his blue eyes.

Things such as this reinforce my Christian beliefs. Joey did nothing to deserve the terrible things that happened to him; and his torturers may or may not get their just deserts on this earth. But I have an abiding faith that Joey will sometime and in some way be compensated for the pain he had to bear; and that his torturers will get what they have coming to them. Things will be properly evened out. These are the teachings of the New Testament. Two and two always makes four. Otherwise, there is no real balance in life.

Another monster, ex-priest James Porter, age fifty-eight, was sentenced to eighteen years in prison in December, 1993, after pleading guilty to forty-one counts of child molesting and sexual assaults. Twenty-two of his victims told of the pain and embarrassment they endured. He was charged with molesting dozens of children and young men, including four New Mexico altar boys. The news article, of what victims (now grown) related in court, stated:

> "I want you to know, James Porter, that you may have forgotten me and my face and my name, but I will never forget what you did to me," John Vigorito told the court.
>
> Daniel Lyons told how Porter raped him, and "when I would scream, he would put his hand over my mouth so no one could hear. Today, I am heard."
>
> Victims told of nightmares, depression, drug and alcohol addictions and at least four attempted suicides.
>
> "As I look at the faces of my fellow survivors, I see the pain we suffered. There is no punishment imaginable that can erase our pain," said John Warburton. (*Albuquerque Journal*, December 7, 1993)

The Albuquerque Tribune, September 9, 1993, had an article about Thomas Perea, then thirty-six years old, suing a seventy-six-year-old retired Roman Catholic priest, Delbert Blong, in Colorado. Perea said that Blong controlled him for twenty-one years, commencing when Perea was fifteen, and that Blong gave him AIDS. Perea said Blong abused him even after he became an adult and consented to sex. Perea said Blong had four other lovers, two of whom died of AIDS and two of whom have HIV. How the mind of a homosexual like Blong works is a mystery to me. He admitted the relationship and blamed everything on Perea, a mere child when it started. Were it not so horribly tragic, one statement attributed to Blong about the affair would have been downright comical:

> ... Blong said Wednesday on NBC's "Today" show: "When a 13-year-old takes off his clothes and sits in your lap, what can you do?"

The puzzling fact that a person would go on television and say such things reminds me of the unexplainable things done by homosexuals, in public, and in the parades, as previously related.

"For more than two decades, Roman Catholic priests sexually abused boys aged 7 to 16 at a boarding school in a Santa Barbara (California) seminary, a panel organized by a Franciscan order concluded." (*The Albuquerque Journal*, 12-1-93)

"The 17 young men who accused former priest Jason Sigler of sexually abusing them when they were children settled their lawsuits with Sigler on Monday for $13 million, according to their lawyer, Bruce Pasternack." (*The Albuquerque Journal*, 11-30-93) This was another New Mexico case.

These depressing articles from court cases, both civil and criminal, against homosexual priests go on and on. "Priest-sociologist Andrew Greeley says sex abuse of minors by Roman Catholic clergy is widespread in the United States, involving between 2,000 and 4,000 priests and more than 100,000 victims." (*The Albuquerque Tribune*, 3-25-93)

An article by Richard Silva, a journalist, "**Priest's abuse rapes soul of his victim**," *The Albuquerque Tribune*, January 27, 1994, aptly sums up the terrible damage done to a young person when he or she goes to a person for help about homosexuality, or possible homosexual feelings, and the person to whom he or she goes for help is a homosexual who proceeds to take advantage of that person. This is particularly true when the troubled person is seeking help from a religious source. The article was about a personal friend of Silva, who long after the experiences still suffered from "a poverty of self-confidence and self-esteem" from "undergoing a deep psychological trauma," which "would be too much for most people to bear." He had then born the burden of the abuse he had received for two decades. He read about a priest who had been charged with sexual abuse, and said, "It's about time they caught him, and I hope he rots in jail." The young man was in his twenties and had just gotten out of the military service. He seemed to have a problem about his sexual preference which deeply troubled him. He was in deep spiritual and emotional distress, and went to this priest for help. The priest seduced him. To make matters worse, and when he would have been in even more severe emotional distress, he went to another priest, and was again homosexually seduced. Silva states:

> I don't wish to confuse this with pedophilia. Our friend was not a child. He was not overpowered by someone stronger. But he was a Catholic whose soul was in distress, and he was exploited by those with whom we have entrusted the secrets of our innermost demons.
>
> Furthermore, had he received proper counseling and not been exploited, it is possible that he might have chosen heterosexuality.
>
> ***
>
> The raw pain I heard in my friend's sobs that night told me his soul was tormented. And if this priest is brought to justice, I can't help but hope, as does my friend, that he rots in jail, saving others from becoming his victims.
>
> God help us from the venom that these priests have brought upon us.

It appears that one homosexual priest and his victims may have gotten some justice. An Associated Press article, "Priest Gets Life Term in Child Assaults," *Albuquerque Journal*, 4-2-98, states:

> DALLAS – Suspended Roman Catholic priest Rudolph "Rudy" Kos was sentenced Wednesday to the maximum of life in prison for sexually assaulting altar boys ... .
>
> Kos, 52, was convicted Saturday on three counts of aggravated sexual assault and was sentenced to life imprisonment on each. The same jury also convicted him of one count of indecency with a child for which he was sentenced to 20 years in prison.

Kos was sentenced to 20-year terms on each of three other charges to which he pleaded guilty at the start of the trial. He also must pay $10,000 in fines for each of the seven counts.

Four victims told police they were molested about 1,350 times over five years.

Under parole guidelines in effect at the time the crimes were committed, Kos will be eligible to seek parole in 15 years. ...

Last year allegations against him led to a record $119.6 million civil judgment against Kos and the Catholic Diocese of Dallas. Witnesses testified during an 11-week trial that Kos sexually abused boys from 1981 to 1992 at three Dallas area churches. ***

On ABC News, May 9, 1996, there was a story saying that the largest child pornography ring in history had been broken up and that a number of people had been arrested. It was stated that the leads developed when one of the men involved in it was prosecuted for sexually molesting a thirteen-year-old boy. The news also showed a Republican senator stating that the U.S. Attorneys had been lax in prosecuting these types of cases, because homosexuals were involved. Another person, apparently speaking for the Clinton administration, denied this laxness. It was surprising that ABC gave as much information as was given, because the liberal news media are in a habit of sanitizing such things, and striving to make homosexuals as acceptable to the public as possible. I saw articles about this in two Albuquerque newspapers, and neither made any mention of the homosexual involvement. This certainly appears to be sanitizing of the news for the purpose of protecting the homosexual community from derogatory information about homosexuals. Fortunately, there are a few conservative publications from which we can get more of the truth. An article about this incident in the *Christian American*, Christian Coalition, July/August 1996, states:

Most people applauded when the U.S. Postal Service shut down one of the largest child pornography rings in U. S. history. But shortly after the case came to light, a Postal Service inspector complained on national television that U.S. Attorney Janet Napolitano refused to cooperate with the sting.

"They didn't like the fact that all of these people were interested in sex with young boys. They believed that we were targeting homosexual males," Karen Casset of the Postal Service told a reporter on ABC's 20/20.

Napolitano was quick to deny the charge.

"It's just not true – flat wrong," she said.

The postal investigators went around Napolitano and worked with local prosecutors to obtain a warrant to search the home of James Norman Moore. They found a large amount of child pornography and arrested Moore.

"He stated to me that he had been sexually active with young boys all of his adult life," Casset said. "He admitted to in excess of 200 victims."

So who is Napolitano?

She was appointed a U.S. Attorney by President Clinton in 1993, shortly after Attorney General Janet Reno (also appointed by Clinton) fired all 93 sitting U. S. Attorneys. Napolitano came to the office with no experience as a prosecutor.

What qualified her for the job?

She had been a member of the Democratic National Committee and was the first woman to hold the number-two post in the Arizona Democratic Party. She also managed a few state Senate races and worked on Clinton's campaign in Arizona.

But, perhaps most importantly, Napolitano was one of the attorneys who represented Anita Hill during Supreme Court Justice Clarence Thomas' 1991 nomination hearing.

HOMOSEXUALS IN THE MILITARY

At various places in this book, the push by the Clinton administration for homosexuals in the military, and the opposition of those in the military, of congress, and of the people, have been explored. The primary purpose of taking up the subject in this chapter is to show the nature of homosexual acts in the military, and the apparent inability of the homosexual mind to discern what is right and what is wrong.

When William Jefferson Clinton took office as president in 1993, he immediately commenced a two-pronged assault on the military.

He at once tried to open the services to homosexuals, by executive order; and he began trying to get women mixed in with men in the military—in training and in combat situations—and even having men's and women's quarters in the same barracks.

There was immediate and strong opposition to removing the bar to homosexuals in the military from the people and from Congress. Opposition to the president's feminist thrust was slower and less effective.

It has now been well established in recent years that the close mixing of men and women in military services results in impermissible sexual acts, including sexual relations between unmarried service members, fraternization, pregnancies of unmarried women, assaults and rape. It is much more so when homosexuals get into the services, because they are in the barracks, the showers, and restrooms with the men and women with whom they wish to have sexual relations. Adding to this is the fact that those with natural sensibilities and instincts tend to violently react to homosexual advances—particularly men. This has led to the death of some homosexuals, and severe beatings of others, as shown by the studies referred to below.

The dissension between Congress and the administration over allowing homosexuals into the military led to various studies on the effect of homosexuals in the military in prior years. A few homosexuals, by deceit, had always been able to get into the military, so there was information about the problems caused. And, considering the few that had been able to infiltrate the services, the problems were indeed serious.

The Gay Nineties – What the Empirical Evidence Reveals About Homosexuality, by Dr. Paul Cameron, Adroit Press, Franklin, Tenn., 1993, is another fine writing by one of the foremost experts on homosexuals and the homosexual movement. His book contains two full chapters on homosexuals in the military: Chapter 4, "Military Retreat;" and Chapter 5, "An Empirical View of Gays in the Military." The following contains information from these chapters, along with my own comments.

I consider this information important from several aspects. It shows the promiscuity of homosexuals and their apparent inability to control their perversion—even in the military—and it gives us further insight into to the terribly depraved acts of homosexuality.

In considering the case studies presented, we should keep in mind that, because they were legally barred, there were very few homosexuals in the service—when compared to their percentages in the general population. Because the services attempted to bar homosexuals, and because sodomy was a criminal offense, there is no way the services could accurately estimate the number of homosexuals who gained admittance. I do know that in my more than three years of active duty during World War II, I never personally knew one person that was identified as a homosexual, nor of one homosexual incident. Yet the studies show that there were many heinous and foul acts committed by homosexuals in the service—both women and men.

In other parts of this book information will be presented about the opposition to homosexuals in the military, and the reasons for the opposition. I would like to point out here that because of the control of the administration, and because the Democrats were in control of Congress in the first term of the Clinton administration, many of the studies were biased and slanted in favor of the homosexual agenda.

The strategy of the General Accounting Office, which was supposed to be conducting a study of the effect of homosexuals in the military, was to rely on information from organizations that were already known to favor homosexuals in the military, such as the ACLU (which had a Gay and Lesbian Task Force), the American Psychiatric Association, the American Psychological Association, and the American Medical Association. (p. 160)

Fortunately, there were some reputable and empirical studies made that bolstered and supported the continued opposition of Congress to open homosexuals in the military. Two of these studies are of primary importance, because they contain information on actual acts committed by some who were able to deceive the military in gaining admission to the services.

There were also recent news reports on incidents relevant to the question. The following are two such incidents referred to in *The Gay Nineties*, (pp. 180-181):

In September of 1992, fourteen soldiers from Ft. Hood were discharged from the service after they were videotaped engaging in homosexual acts in a public restroom. Nine were separated under "other than honorable conditions." Three received "general discharges," and therefore may receive benefits. Two received honorable discharges after a hearing revealed "mitigating circumstances." Small wonder that with the consequences so light, there should be *fourteen* involved in this particular incident, which resulted in charges ranging from indecent exposure to sodomy. (*New York Native*, October 12, 1992, p. 14)

In June of 1993, the press reluctantly and curtly reported the conviction of two sailors in Jacksonville, Florida. Both had raped shipmates, one aboard a U.S. naval vessel, the other while ashore. (New York Times, June 7, 1993)

One interesting thing which I have observed and commented on many times in this book is that the mind of a person advanced in homosexuality seems to lose the ability to even determine or distinguish what is right and wrong—and what is vile and degrading from what is good and decent.

Dr. Cameron, in *The Gay Nineties*, gives us one more good example of this homosexual phenomenon of lack of logic and understanding. Homosexual Congressman Gerry Studds and Mary Ann Humphrey worked to promote the allowing of homosexuals in the military. (As explained later in this book, Studds was censured for his relations with a seventeen-year-old male congressional page.) Mary Ann Humphrey was forced to resign as a captain in the Reserve because of her lesbianism. Studds promoted a book— *My Country, My Right to Serve: Experiences of Gay Men and Women in the Military, Word War II to the Present*, Harper Collins, New York, 1990—edited by Ms. Humphrey, containing a collection of testimonials by homosexuals who had gotten into the military. The following are two examples of the many incidents in that book:

> *A 52-year-old male said that he had always fantasized about enlisting in the Army in order to engage in homosexual acts and lied about his predilections in order to gain entry. About American society he is quoted as saying: "From what I have ascertained, our culture says you can do anything you like as long as you don't get caught. (p. 7) (He subsequently died of AIDS.) ***
>
> A female, 57 years of age, lied about her lesbianism in order to enlist: "But, by God, when I got into basic, I thought I had been trans-

ferred to hog heaven! No damn kidding! Lordy!" (p. 11) [*The Gay Nineties*, pp. 189-191]

This and other examples Dr. Cameron relates from the Studds and Humphrey book distinctly show the fallacious reasoning of homosexuals. Never should such people be allowed in the close proximity of decent young people in the service. To think that such people will not prey upon the young men and women, and violate the code of military conduct, is indeed absurd. But then people like Studds and Humphrey seem to see nothing at all wrong with this—this is what they want. Perhaps Gerry Studds felt that he was in "hog heaven" when he was around the page boys in Congress.

Speaking generally of the incidents disclosed in the Humphrey book, Dr. Cameron observes:

> *** It was obvious from these accounts that homosexuals, rebels by definition, find themselves doubly challenged in the Armed Forces. The rules and constraints they so despise are infinitely more authoritarian in the military than in civilian life and the consequences of disobeying them far more devastating. ...
>
> A second problem revealed in the Humphrey book was to be found in the compulsive sexuality of homosexuals. It is abundantly clear from these narratives that the great majority of homosexuals find abstinence impossible. Indeed, many obviously seek military service because of the sexual opportunities it affords. These people have no intention of obeying the Uniform Code of Military Justice, or else they soon discover that obedience is impossible or too difficult to consider seriously. They seem driven to engage in illicit conduct despite the severe penalties imposed. *** (pp. 197-198)

However, as detrimental as the accounts given in the Humphrey–Studds book were to their own argument for homosexuals in the military, they still seemed to realize that there needed to be omissions of important homosexual conduct in order to make the accounts somewhat less revolting. Cameron explains that in this regard the book omitted any accounts of sex with children or violent rape. (p. 212) In my opinion this could only have been done to give a deceitful and slanted argument in behalf of homosexuals.

As to the omissions from the Humphrey book, Dr. Cameron makes the further statement:

> So the case histories offered in this book provided the "best possible scenario" for homosexual service in the Armed Forces. 130 homosexuals were interviewed. Only 42 were chosen—28 men and 14 women. Make no mistake about it: this was a book with an agenda. Yet to many normal, objective readers, the 42 interviews provided dramatic and conclusive proof that homosexuality and military service are incompatible. (p. 190)

Other more accurate and definitive studies were made on the question of the effects of homosexuals in the military.

In late 1992, after the election of Clinton, Family Research Institute (FRI), then in Washington D.C., headed by Dr. Paul Cameron, conducted the most comprehensive survey of information of homosexuals in the military of which I have had any knowledge. The survey included 654 respondents who had served in the military or were currently serving; two random mail samplings totaling 25,000 questionnaires; and hand delivered anonymous questionnaire to 83 officers and enlisted personnel currently serving at accessible bases. "These three surveys, though different in methodology and size of sample, yielded 2,457 respondents with remarkably similar attitudes and experiences." The following is a summary analysis of 245 reported incidents (pp. 199-201):

- Respondents reported three murders, two of them "fraggings."
- Fifty-three incidents (or 22 percent) included beatings.
- Nineteen incidents (or 8 percent) involved homosexual rape.
- Fifty-six (or 23 percent) involved molesting a sleeping or drunken comrade.
- Fifty-four (or 22 percent) involved "fraternization"—that is, a superior engaging in sexual relations with a subordinate.
- Fifty-one (or 21 percent) involved a "pass"—i.e., a sexual approach, either verbal or physical.
- Nine (or 4 percent) involved children.
- Six of the incidents (or two percent) took place in showers.
- Two of the incidents involved transvestites.

- One service member was knifed, another was pushed in front of a car, two were thrown out of windows, and yet another was hurled down a flight of stairs.

The survey resulted in information over a period of many years. Several of the homosexual acts included in the many testimonials gathered in the FRI study are given for the purpose of showing the pitiful sickness of homosexuality (pp. 203-208):

- 1938: "I was with a S/Sgt [staff sergeant]. He said he had to pee so we stopped and I started to join him. Immediately he clamped his mouth on my penis and told me that he would bite it off unless I discharged into him. I was afraid and 18 and just avoided him from then on." ***
- 1957: "I noticed my clerk (a blue-eyed blonde) began to smell rank of sweat and seemed nervous and inattentive after 3 days on the job after transfer in. . . . I had another female clerk who I knew talk to her—but it took her 5 weeks on the job to [tell me] of her 1st day at Barlsdale female barracks and being raped in the shower. Yes, I helped her and worked with base authorities to trap her lesbian barracks chief and female officers to be put out of service . . . many others came forward after we caught them." ***
- 1955: (Tripler Army Hospital, Honolulu) "Gay hospitalman, in a ring including ships cook on my ship, took a 10 year old sick male child and performed oral sex on him. This was the same ward our children would be patients in while we were at sea with no communications (I was a submariner)."
- 1965: (Storeroom aboard ship) One E, was unable to extract a bottle from his rectum, which led to a medical evacuation problem." ***
- 1952: (Dharam, Saudi Arabia) "While anal sodomy was performed the lower individual suffocated (his head being in a pillow)." ***

Another important study was made which should have been highly accurate because of the source and nature of the information obtained.

Under orders from the Office of the Assistant Secretary of Defense, Col. Richard H. Black investigated homosexual acts in the Army, and compiled a list of 102 punitive separations from the Army during the fiscal years 1989 through 1992 that involved court-martialed cases.

(p. 211) Cameron estimates that this number would have been about one-seventh of the total homosexuals discharged (based on figures on the number discharged for a 1989-90 period compiled by the General Accounting Office). Unless serious violations of public order were involved, commanders usually got them out with honorable or general discharges, without specifying homosexuality, as a matter of expedience—just to get them out of the service. (p. 211) Col. Black gave his synopses of the cases with specific case numbers, which are shown is parentheses. Most of them were summarized in *The Gay Nineties*. The ones set forth below were selected to show further incidents exemplifying the utter sickness of homosexuality and the acts engaged in by such people (pp. 212-222):

- (57) (child molestation) A private first-class, who was AWOL, kept the two male children of his sister's friend. The boys were 10 and 7. While babysitting he anally sodomized both boys. He also had both boys put their penises into his anus. Anal sodomy occurred ten times over these months. [2 victims]
- (58) A staff sergeant, divorced from his wife, brought their children to his home on post at Fort Knox, Kentucky. There he took his six-year old son into his bed and had the boy masturbate him to ejaculation. [Guilty, 1 victim]
- (59) (child molestation) A staff sergeant fondled the genitals of his son and placed his penis in his son's mouth while the boy slept. [Guilty, 1 victim]
- (32) (child molestation) A specialist first class admitted that he engaged in sex with his own sons and had engaged in sex with boys in other countries for money. He also said he had used his rank to gain homosexual favors from junior soldiers. He committed indecent acts with his 13-year-old nephew and had sex with his 14-year-old adopted Korean son. [Guilty, 3 victims]
- (33) (Boy Scout Master) A sergeant, while a Boy Scoutmaster at Fort Hood, Texas, committed oral and anal sodomy on Boy Scouts aged 9 to 12 years. He used leather straps, dog collars, a dildo, and a dildo attached to the end of a policeman's night stick in the performance of these acts. The sergeant videotaped these acts, which lasted between 30 and 50 minutes. Among the acts: anal sodomy of a male child while he screamed: "Oh God, please stop. You're hurting me. Please, please, stop." The sergeant stuck his

penis into this boy's rectum six times in a ten minute period, telling the boy to "Relax." [9 victims] ***

- (16) (rape) A private was in his barracks room in Germany, drinking and watching videos with two other privates. A specialist was
down the hall in another room watching a pornographic video
that showed scenes of anal intercourse. The private continued
drinking and fell asleep. The other privates left the room. The
specialist returned to the room and began anally sodomizing the
unconscious private. The private awoke and "froze" in shock and
fear, whereupon the specialist attempted to insert his penis into
the private's mouth. The private screamed and then began crying
and cowering in the corner of the room. His screams led other
soldiers to the room. . . . [Guilty, 1 victim] ***

- (98) (rape) A staff sergeant, on three separate occasions asked
three different subordinates to "suck your dick." This sergeant
also molested sleeping soldiers and exposed himself to civilians.
[Guilty, 4 victims]

SPREADING THE AIDS VIRUS

A Time of Aids - The Zero Factor, is a sixty-minute color video produced by Films for the Humanities, Inc., in 1993, and was shown on
public television. It is an excellent history of the spread of the AIDS
virus, its commencement in this country, and traces it back to Gaeton
Dugas, referred to as Patient Zero, who introduced it and spread it widely
in this country by his typical promiscuous homosexual activity.

The description on the VCR tape states:

> This program takes us from the bath houses of San Francisco,
> New York, and Los Angeles to Fire Island. We meet the physicians
> who first saw the symptoms of Kaposi's sarcoma and pneumonia in
> their gay patients; we meet men whose friends have died of AIDS and
> who themselves have AIDS now; we meet a woman from CDC (Cen-
> ter for Disease Control) who did her own check on patient histories
> and discovered that all had one thing in common: Gaeton Dugas or
> Patient Zero.

The following is a summary of the substance of the film, including quotes from the narrators, a number of whom were homosexuals.

The events go back to 1979, when the medical community was searching desperately for the causes of the many deaths and infections among homosexuals, which was later determined to be AIDS. It is the story of a deadly disease – now turned into a plague.

Laws which made sodomy a crime were being repealed. Homosexuals were rejoicing. They were "coming out of the closet" and showing their true colors of depraved sexual acts and promiscuity.

The film then shows parades and pictures of homosexuals in their activity. The scenes were filthy and disgusting, and it is amazing that people in this country would engage in such acts in public, or that they would be allowed to. The scenes were similar to those on the tapes, *The Gay Agenda, The March on Washington,* and *Stonewall.*

Speaking of Fire Island, one homosexual stated:

> ...All of us had grown up, being told everything we thought and wanted was evil and sick, and suddenly there is this island of beautiful, intelligent and incredibly sexy men, all available to each other 24 hours a day. It was truly the linchpin of our sexual liberation and sexual oppressiveness.

Various speakers, taking turns:

> I felt part of the most extraordinary sexual experiment in human history. I honestly believe that never before in human history had so many men had so much sex with so many other men who were having sex.
>
> ***
>
> Fire Island in New York was a small coastal community that exploded with party-loving vacationers during the summer months. It became the Mecca of gay liberation.
>
> ***
>
> Jerry Rosenbaum was a Wall Street stock broker with a six-figure income. At work, in his gray suit, no one knew he was gay. On Fire Island, he could shed his disguise and be himself.
>
> ***

...People came in from everywhere to find out why we really liked Fire Island. It was seductive. It was intoxicating. And the glue that held it all together was sex, drugs and rock 'n roll. That was our story.

* * *

It was a brief bit of time that was about to end. It was a sexual smorgasbord like the world had never seen and a very heady experience from a liberation point of view, very thrilling to be among all those beautiful men and it was a very short time before that all came crashing to an end. Just as we had discovered it and tasted it, it took this very sinister historical turn.

* * *

The tape then goes back to the mid-seventies and describes how the AIDS symptoms and related diseases were showing up to an epidemic degree among the homosexuals, especially in San Francisco, and describes the search to find what it was and what was causing it. The search started out in the bathhouses of San Francisco. The researchers describe the goings on in the bathhouses in the Castro District of San Francisco, and vile sexual behavior going on among great numbers of people.

Various speakers:

Michael Callin was 20 when he left home. In the small Ohio town he grew up in, homosexuality was viewed as immoral. His new lifestyle in the big city soon brought its first mild inconvenience, a case of gonorrhea.

* * *

I was still so very much a small town boy from the Midwest, I felt unclean, and I just felt really creepy. But all of my friends said, "Oh, please, the clap, no problem, you just get your shot and go back out. It's a risk you take, it's not a big deal, it's not fatal." By the end of my sexual career in 1980, every single time I had sex I got something. So at the age of 26, I had to face the fact that I'd had sex with about 3,000 men, and I'd had Hepatitis A, Hepatitis B, Hepatitis non A, Hepatitis non B, herpes, Simplex 1 & 2, shigella and amebic histolytica, giardia, syphilis, gonorrhea, non-specific urethritis, C & V, E. B. V., venereal warts, ...

The effects of this disease on the homosexuals is depressing to look at, with sores in various places on their skin, and their faces, and other body parts. A lot of these things were just considered as cancerous sores. It was then explained how the disease was tied to the breakdown of the immune system. Originally the disease was found only in "gay" men. It is then described how the homosexuals were flying around the world and it then broke out in Denmark and in various other European countries. The first case in Britain was contracted from a man in San Francisco.

(A British commentator refers to people as homophobics who were concerned about being around the people who had the disease. He obviously had already very foolishly accepted the political propaganda of the "Gay" movement. Any decent person with any sanity would have been afraid of being around them. No one knew then, and because of the political intrusion into the problem, we still don't know all of the ways that the disease may be contracted. Grown people as well as children have contracted the disease in ways that have not yet been determined or explained. The politics of AIDS and the homosexual movement are a shame and a disgrace to the country. Prior to our country contracting this political sickness, venereal diseases were reported and traced. Reasonable precautions were taken to prevent the spread. This has never been done with AIDS and homosexuals.)

As explained by the video, the investigators did trace the beginning of the disease in this country to Gaeton Dugas, a Canadian Airline steward, who traveled extensively. He gave the disease to a large number of men in this country and probably to a lot of men in other countries, too. "His job took him all over the United States, as well as the rest of the world."

The video describes the ingenious methods used by various doctors over the country to trace the AIDS cases, and the cooperation between them and the patients. (Much of this was done before they actually knew what the virus was and that it was incurable by current medical science. This was before it became so politicized by the homosexual activists and their liberal supporters. Under today's conditions, with the legally imposed secrecy, they probably could not have traced AIDS to the source in this country.)

One of the investigators located Dugas and sent word to him that an interview was requested. Two months later he showed up and was interviewed by the research team. The investigator described him as, "one of the most handsome, seductive individuals I've ever known." Dugas visited the CDC headquarters in Atlanta, and was able to give them the names of seventy-three different people that he had sexual contacts with in the past five years. He had Kaposi's sarcoma (which was undoubtedly AIDS related). The investigators set out to track them down. Dugas had contact with a group at Fire Island who had first become ill with the AIDS virus. He was involved with nine AIDS patients in the Los Angeles area. They linked him to cases throughout the world. Altogether they linked him to forty surviving AIDS patients. Although Dugas was warned and the investigators tried to stop him, he refused to change his "lifestyle." He continued to visit the bathhouses and such places. He said: "Nobody is going to stop me, its my civil right." (From the evidence, this man is just one of many who had the same attitude. They knowingly and intentionally exposed many individuals over the country to this deadly disease. Yet our liberal news media have never criticized them nor blamed them for the awful plague they inflicted on this country. Instead, many were held up as some kind of heroes. Such absurd thinking is common of the liberal media, even today.)

A narrator on the film makes the statement that doctors were hesitant to let people know about this disease, because they did not want to cause "homophobia." (It is difficult to believe that the politics were taking hold this early, in the beginning of the 1980s, and that people who had the duty to protect others could take such an utterly stupid attitude.)

One of the narrators who had advocated warning people makes the statement in the video:

> The main message ... a gay men's health crisis, was not given out at all, it was to spread information, which they refused to do, because to tell gay people to stop having sex or "to cool it," was such a controversial thing in those days, that no organization was prepared to make that statement. And I became a pariah, basically, for making that statement. And for many years, people wouldn't talk to me. I was thrown off the board at GMAC, because I said these things.

The film then describes how "gays" spread the virus to others, how they were giving blood, and how drug users and needle users (many of whom were homosexual) sold their blood. It describes how the AIDS virus was spread to hemophiliacs, and to other innocent people by blood transfusions of tainted blood.

Never before in our history was a dangerous plague or epidemic of this nature handled in such disregard for the citizens of this country. Death and destruction has been visited on many innocent people, including innocent children, because of the intentional acts and disregard by the homosexual activists, and by the gutless government officials and members of the medical community.

Dr. Lorraine Day, *AIDS - WHAT THE GOVERNMENT ISN'T TELL-ING YOU,* supra, explains in Chapters 2 and 3, how she unsuccessfully tried to keep the medical community in San Francisco from taking contaminated blood from members of the homosexual community, and the sharp criticism and abuse she incurred. Blood drives were organized and directed by homosexuals. Blood drives with such names as "Arm in Arm" and "The Harvey Milk Club" blood drive. Harvey Milk was a well-known San Francisco homosexual activist. Blood drives were held in the Castro District in San Francisco, and "gays" were invited to "come to the party" and bring their partners. "The Castro district in San Francisco has the highest per capita rate of AIDS-infected individuals of any place in the nation." (p. 30)

(We would have to divorce ourselves from common sense to believe that there were not many "gays," knowing they had AIDS, intentionally giving blood with the purpose of contaminating the blood supply and spreading it to innocent people. They could not all have been so stupid as not to know the effect of what they were doing.)

Dr. Day states (pp. 64-66):

When the Senate investigators several years ago were sent to investigate the safety of the blood supply at the Irwin Memorial Blood

Bank, they also came to talk to me. I told them of my futile struggle to stop the blood drives in an area where AIDS was prevalent.

One of the investigators said to me: "Gay terrorism was involved."

According to this official, Irwin Memorial received a threat that if the Castro district was excluded from the blood drives, *there would be a concerted effort on the part of disaffected gays to contaminate the Irwin Memorial blood supply with AIDS on purpose.*

When I think back on all the furor of that summer, this explanation makes a lot of sense to me. What doesn't make much sense is that the government did nothing, after knowing what had occurred. What makes even less sense is that Irwin Memorial caved in. Those two incidents show that we are polarizing. When it comes to AIDS, both sides are willing to let violence speak. Resorting to violence is not a novel idea.

As long ago as 1983, Robert Schwab, former president of the Texas Human Rights Foundation and a homosexual activist dying of AIDS, had this to bestow on the rest of the world:

> There has come the idea that if research money (for AIDS) is not forthcoming at a certain level by a certain date, all gay males should give blood.... What ever action is required to get national attention is valid. If that includes blood terrorism, so be it.
>
> *Dallas Gay News,* May 20, 1983

There have been ugly threats like distant thunder, verbally as well as in print. Often the homosexuals' attitudes have been, "I am going to die anyway. I might as well take somebody with me."

It was not a pretty picture.

Dr. Day, at page 73, states:

> From 1978 through 1985, virtually all hemophiliacs who required the clotting factor were infected (with AIDS) through blood bank inventory blood and now face certain death.

Dr. Day explains on page 74 that the type of transfusion referred to is of a particular kind for which it takes many donors to make one routine transfusion.

Dr. Day, at page 106, quotes passages from Kirk and Madsen, supra, (pp. 292-293):

> Many gays reject morality, offering any one of a variety of reasons, rational and emotional, for doing so. But there's a simpler darker reason why so many gays choose to live without morality: as ideologies go, amorality is damned convenient. And the mortal enemy of that convenience is the value judgment.
>
> It quickly became clear to us that urban gays assumed a general consensus to the effect that everyone has the right to behave just as he pleases ... Everyone was to decide what was "right for him" – in effect, to make up the rules as he went along. In fact, they boiled down to a single axiom: I can do whatever I want and you can go to perdition....
>
> We found that in the gay press this doctrine had hardened into stone. The more outrageous the behavior, the more it was to be seen as "celebrating our unique sensibility and culture": the less ethically defensible, the less one was to feel entitled to speak out against it, lest one be accused of attempting to resurrect that bugbear, "traditional morality."

For her writing, Dr. Day had an adviser, who was a homosexual, and had come to San Francisco in 1961. He describes over a dozen bathhouses in San Francisco. Included were such names as "The Handball Express," "The Hothouse," and "Animals." "Some rooms were equipped with exotic equipment such as stockades, sling harnesses, mirrors, shackles, etc. There was much fisting in the bathhouses. "They virtually all had venereal diseases or had had venereal diseases and had thereby weakened certain mucous tissues." He describes how some of the showers were equipped with plastic hoses for them to stick up their rectum. "Every perversion imaginable was done in the gay community." (pp. 117-120)

Dr. Day states:

> The deadly virus, sad to say, has made little difference in sexual practices in the homosexual community. AIDS spreads because, as in the past, so now, gay male sex is still the old variety: sadistic, masochistic, promiscuous, hedonistic, contemptuous, anonymous, and unhygienic in the extreme. I see the result in the emergency room.

The "disease" in additional numbers of gays becoming infected, a "fact" so often referred to in media coast-to-coast, is a spurious one: if most gays are already infected, there will be "fewer" new infections. (p. 130)

**

It is proper to note the similarity between the AIDS epidemic and war. Already there have been more deaths from AIDS than from the entire Vietnam conflict. (p. 265)

It is beyond the imagination of a decent person that a group of people could be so sick and depraved that they would visit such unseemly and terrible destruction on themselves, and on innocent men, women, and children. Now they would teach us and our children that this is an "acceptable alternative lifestyle." They even want living in sodomy to be blessed as the sacred sacrament of marriage.

The Homosexual Deception: Making Sin a Civil Right, supra, p. 10:

On October 15th, 1990, the Colorado Department of Health, Tom Vernon, director, issued data that implicated homosexual behavior in approximately 85% of the 1,500 AIDS cases reported in Colorado as of the end of September 1990. 85.2% of these cases have occurred in the metropolitan Denver area alone.

One study demonstrates that 6,349 Americans who contracted AIDS from contaminated blood as of 1992 received this from homosexuals. Most women in California who contracted AIDS through heterosexual activity were infected by bisexual men. (Chu, et al., "AIDS in Bisexual Men in the U. S.," *American Journal of Public Health,* 1992:82:220-224).

It also appears that even the Red Cross and other blood bank groups succumbed to the "gay" politics, and also to greed, and became a party to the destruction. Who knows which affected them the most – the politics or the money? But the tragedy visited on innocent people in this country appears to have been, to a large extent, knowingly and willfully done, and is a crime and a disgrace to our country. Also, the long cover-up of the matter is a disgrace to this country and the national media.

An Associated Press article, in the *Albuquerque Journal*, May 5, 1994, stated:

> WASHINGTON — The American Red Cross and other blood-bank groups refused to adopt a screening test in 1983, publicly contending there was no hard evidence people could get AIDS from transfusions. But internal documents show that Red Cross officials acknowledged that the disease could be transmitted through blood.
>
> The nation's three major blood collectors – the Red Cross, the American Association of Blood Banks and the Council of Community Blood Centers – said in a public statement on Jan. 13, 1983:
>
> "The presently available medical and scientific evidence that AIDS can be spread by blood components remains incomplete. ...We do not advise routine implementation of any laboratory screening program for AIDS by the blood banks at this time."
>
> The groups refused to adopt the test for hepatitis B, a surrogate test that Centers for Disease Control said could have been in place by March 1982. The AIDS or HIV test had yet to be developed.
>
> The groups maintained that the test was too expensive and that there was no hard evidence that people could get AIDS from transfusions, despite CDC officials' assertions that the disease posed a serious threat to the blood supply.
>
> Privately, however, officials of the Red Cross believed AIDS could be transmitted through the blood, according to internal documents obtained by The Associated Press.
>
> ***
>
> The CDC estimates that 6,567 Americans have developed AIDS from transfusions since 1981. Only 29 of those cases were caused by transfusions received after March 1985, when blood banks voluntarily began using a new HIV, or Human Immmunodeficiency Virus, was discovered as the cause of AIDS in 1984.

The article goes on to give the argument of Paul Cumming, former Red Cross planning and marketing manager, that, "Given the same information, the same environment at the time, I don't see that we made any mistakes." However, this does not square with the information in their files at the time, and with Cumming's own internal memo of Feb. 5, 1983. The Associated Press article states:

> Paul Cumming ... wrote in an internal memo: "The available evidence strongly suggests that AIDS is transmissible" through blood.

What "environment" was Cumming talking about? The evidence presented by Dr. Day strongly indicates that the "environment" would primarily have been "gay" politics and pressure. Please note that the Associated Press article was dated May 15, 1994. Why did it take so long to get this information out to the public? Dr. Day presented it to the media in the 1980's, and all she got was severe criticism from both television and newspapers, and was referred to as homophobic. In her book, published in 1991, some three years before the AP article, she calls the severe criticism she got for revealing the information, and the "Gay" political propaganda about the dangers of the disease as "AIDSSpeak." (See Chapters 2 and 3, Day, 1991)

Consider the following facts derived from Dr. Day's book, *AIDS—WHAT THE GOVERNMENT ISN'T TELLING YOU*, 1991, (PP. 74-80):

- In 1978, it was determined that AIDS was a deadly blood-borne disease.
- In 1982, both the Federal Drug Administration (FDA) and the Centers for Disease Control (CDC) knew that blood transfusions could transmit the AIDS virus.
- Virtually all of the diagnosed cases of AIDS were in homosexual men, at that time.
- There was a test available at the time that could have detected 80% of the homosexual blood donors by testing for the anti-hepatitis B core antibody, which that percentage of "gay" males had because of their sexual practices.
- Both the CDC and the FDA informed the blood banks that they could eliminate 80% of the AIDS virus from their blood supply by the use of this surrogate test for the anti-hepatitis B core antibody.
- The CDC could have demanded and the FDA could have enforced the use of the test, but they chose not to.
- The blood banks chose to ignore the requests and the warnings, and refused to use the recommended test.

- For three years the blood banks accepted contaminated blood, 80% of which could have been eliminated by the testing.
- Because of these procedures, virtually all of the hemophiliacs in the country who needed a particular clotting factor transfusions were infected with the AIDS virus.

I am very dubious about the part of the Associated Press release, referred to above that states: "Only 29 of those cases were caused by transfusions received after March 1985, when blood banks voluntarily began using a new HIV test." I believe that this may be a false statement that continues to mislead the public about the danger of taking blood from homosexuals. Of course, all people who acquired AIDS from blood transfusions were not hemophiliacs. On page 74 of Dr. Day's book, supra, is a graph taken from the *Stockton Record*, April 15, 1990, which appears to have come from the Gannett News Service, and shows the source: Centers forDisease Control. It is entitled: "Hemophiliacs Stricken By AIDS." It contains the statement: "An estimated 20,000 Americans have hemophilia, and 55% of them are believed to be infected with the AIDS virus. ..."

However, a distinction must have been made between those who were infected with the virus and full-blown AIDS cases, as is often done. The graph shows new cases and deaths from 1981 through 1989, and the totals for the period were shown as 1,316 new cases and 837 deaths for the period. (As noted, above, the blood banks began using the AIDS test in March, 1985.) Of the 1,316 new cases, only 228 new cases are shown for the period 1981 through 1985, whereas 1,088 are shown for the period from 1986 to 1989. This does not square at all with part of the Associated Press report, referred to above, as to only 29 cases of AIDS from blood transfusions since March 1985. I certainly do not believe that there is any evidence to support the idea that 1,088 hemophiliacs got full-blown AIDS from 1986 to 1989, and that 29 or less were all that came from blood transfusions. It is also a puzzle to me how anyone could say with any certainty that people who had blood transfusions, and later developed AIDS, did not get the virus from a blood transfusion.

There is also another important fact to consider. Dr. Day explains on page 30 that there is no commercially available test for the AIDS virus itself, and that the tests used by the blood banks tested only for the antibody to AIDS, and that it usually takes at least three months and it sometimes takes as long as three years for an infected person to develop the antibodies. Because of this "negative window," the AIDS tests are far from reliable for the protection of the blood supply. This negative window Dr. Day speaks of was well known to the public and to the officials in San Francisco. Dr. Day states at page 48:

> ...In June of 1989, the *San Francisco Chronicle* reported the findings first documented in the *New England Journal of Medicine* on page 1458:
>
> > The AIDS virus may lurk undetected for as long as three years in the blood cells of some infected men, even though standard antibody tests indicate that the men are uninfected....

The article then explains that the research was done in Los Angeles, and gives further details. Dr. Day (p. 49) also details a UPI release in the summer of 1988 that gave details and statistics on the danger of the "negative window."

Considering the well-known information about AIDS and the testing for it, it was indeed criminal for homosexuals to insist on the "right" to give blood in these blood drives to which Dr. Day strenuously objected, and for which she was abused by the officials and the news media, and it was criminal for the blood banks to hold blood drives in the Castro district, which was a homosexual stronghold.

The above statistics on spreading AIDS to innocent people shows a horrible injustice that was not necessary. Let us consider a specific example of the kind of pain and suffering wrought, keeping in mind that this is only one among thousands:

The Albuquerque Tribune (Associated Press) 10-16-90:

> MONTPELIER, VT. — A 3-year-old girl whose father committed suicide rather than watch his family be ravaged by AIDS has died of the disease, a month after her mother.
>
> The death of Angela Folsom on Sunday left just one survivor in the family of Jennifer Folsom, who made her battle with AIDS public this summer to show the disease can strike the traditional family in rural America.

Jennifer Folsom's husband, Doug Folsom, committed suicide in June. His wife said he was unable to bear watching the disease destroy the family.

Angela had never learned how to walk and moved in with her grandparents after her mother died Sept. 3.

"She was just worn down," said Fred Kenney, her uncle. "A lot of it was the transition of losing her mother and moving to another home."

Jennifer Folsom believed she contracted the disease through a blood transfusion during an emergency appendectomy in 1979. That was before blood supplies were tested for the virus.

She was diagnosed with the disease in 1988, and tests later found that Angela also had AIDS. Another daughter, 5-year-old Nicolette, has not tested positive for the virus and is the sole surviving member of the family.

Kenney said Nicolette, who attended her mother's funeral, is living with her grandparents but may move in with an aunt and cousin.

He said an art therapist visits Nicolette twice weekly. The girl once drew a picture of the sky with a rope hanging down to the house. She told her mother it was God sending a rope for Angela.

But shortly after her father's suicide, Nicolette amended the caption, saying, "It was for Daddy."

Even in 1979, this need not have happened. Dr. Day (ibid.) pointed out that it was known in 1978 that AIDS was a "deadly blood-borne disease." Homosexuals spread the disease and contaminated the blood supplies, and homosexual politics caused such things as this horrible destruction to the Folsom family. Never before in our history was such a deadly disease dealt with in the cavalier way that has been used with the AIDS disease. With much less deadly diseases, in the past, forced detection has been used, sources and possible victims were traced. Forced treatment and isolation was used, and even quarantines. No homosexual who has contributed to this destruction is an admired hero to any sensible person. And, contrary to the way the media plays it up, there is nothing whatsoever heroic about a person dying with AIDS who contracted it by his or her own vile and depraved conduct. This is true whether or not such person is a well-known celebrity being glamorized by the liberal media. What they have done is reprehensible and destructive to themselves, and many of them undoubtedly infected others with their deadly disease. And, as has been shown, it was often intentionally done — the very height of depravity. We should keep this in mind when we read the newspaper articles about these great "heroes" with AIDS.

N.Y. sex clubs re-emerge despite AIDS

NEW YORK – Several years after New York City health officials cracked down on commercial sex establishments in an effort to fight AIDS, new sex businesses are proliferating once again.

This time around city officials appear to be taking a more conciliatory approach. They are reaching out more to the sex clubs and seeking their cooperation in monitoring themselves rather than forcing further closings.

They say the clubs, which offer patrons anonymous sex with multiple partners, can actually help reduce the spread of the virus if their patrons can be steered to practice safer sex. ***

The clubs range from bathhouses and bars to movie houses and bookstores where patrons pay an entrance fee to have sex in open areas and closed rooms. *** (*The Albuquerque Tribune*, 3-8-93)

The following was an article in the *Washington Inquirer*, Nov. 26, 1993:

Homosexual Suicide Club?

Homosexual men in the Washington area have found a new way to risk infection with deadly AIDS: a so-called "massage club" where as many as a hundred persons an evening gather for what a weekly newspaper called "largely overt" sex, often unprotected. Details were published in The City Paper on Sept. 24. "When the towel-clad men touch each other," the paper reported, "they're angling for sex, mostly unsafe sex." Although the "more sensible guest" might stick to safe sex, "what a bore! Why not a three-, four-, or moresome .... with an audience in the wings?" The club is flourishing, The City Paper said, because of the "striking-down of the District's sodomy law." The reporter wrote, "All of these men, whether too young to be sensible or too old to care, could be giving their lives to be here." Admission is $7. (The City Paper, Sept. 24, 1993; also ads in The Washington Blade, autumn issues, 1993)

This is going on in Washington, D.C., our nation's capital, under President Clinton, who has supported the homosexual agenda from the moment he came into office. It is sickening to see the pictures he has made of Hillary and himself, coming out of church on Sunday, with him carrying the Bible. How could anything be more hypocritical?

Family Research Institute, *Medical Consequences of What Homosexuals Do* 1993, states:

> Homosexuals rode into the dawn of sexual freedom and returned with a plague that gives every indication of destroying most of them. Those who treat AIDS patients are at great risk, not only from HIV infection, which as of 1992 involved over 100 health care workers, but also from TB and new strains of other diseases. Those who are housed with AIDS patients are at risk. Dr. Max Essex, chair of the Harvard AIDS Institute, warned congress in 1992 that "AIDS has already lead to other kinds of dangerous epidemics.... If AIDS is not eliminated, other new lethal microbes will emerge, and neither safe sex nor drug free practices will prevent them." At least 8 and perhaps as many as 30 patients had been infected with HIV by health care workers as of 1992.
>
> The typical sexual practices of homosexuals are a medical horror story — imagine exchanging saliva, feces, semen and/or blood with dozens of different men each year. Imagine drinking urine, ingesting feces and experiencing rectal trauma on a regular basis. Often drunk, high, and/or in an orgy setting. Further, many of them occur in extremely unsanitary places (bathrooms, dirty peep shows), or, because homosexuals travel so frequently, in other parts of the world.
>
> Every year, a quarter or more of homosexuals visit another country. Fresh American germs get taken to Europe, Africa and Asia. Foreign homosexuals regularly visit the U. S. and participate in this biological swapmeet.

MURDER AND BRUTALITY

The sickness of homosexuality shows up in more than the private sex acts of homosexuals. They often show excesses in such things as exhibiting themselves, brutality in their sex acts, as previously explained, and in extreme cruelty such as atrocities and mass murder, as subsequently detailed.

"Sodomy Laws,", CFV, supra, p. 3-6, states:

> Out of all of the mass murders in the U.S. over the past 17 years, homosexuals killed at least 68 percent of the victims, were implicated in at least 41 percent of the sets of crimes, committed 70 percent of the 10 worst murder sets, and were involved in five of the eight murder sets perpetrated by two or more people. ("Murder, Violence and Homosexuality," supra; cf. Allen, C., *A Textbook of Psychological Disorders*, 2nd ed. (Oxford University Press, 1969) and de River, J. P., *The Sexual Criminal,* 2nd ed. C. C. Thomas, 1956)
>
> "Violence and Homosexuality," *Family Research Report*, Family Research Institute, Washington, D. C., 1993, states that "excessive violence is naturally associated with other forms of social pathology."

The Pink Swastika, supra, pp. 174-176, refers to an editorial in *The New York Times*, January 21, 1984, for the statement that "many of the most violent multiple murders have been committed by homosexual males." It also refers to *Debating the "Gay Rights" Issue*, Brooks, Oregon, Oregon Citizens Alliance, 1993, p. 97, for the statement: "eight of the top ten serial killers in the United States were homosexuals ... and that homosexuals were responsible for 68% of all mass murders. *The Pink Swastika*, pp. 174-176, referring to Clowes, p. 96, gives the following as a list of the nine leading homosexual serial killers, eight of which were in the top ten most prolific killers as of 1992:

> Donald Harvey: 37 Murders ... [a] nurse's aide [who] was convicted of 37 murders in Kentucky and Ohio. Psychologists testified that "Harvey said he was a homosexual." *The New York Times, August 20, and August 17th 1991 ...*
> John Wayne Gacy: 33 Murders ... [a] professed homosexual ... who killed 33 young men and boys and buried them in his basement. *The New York Times, February 22, 1980.*
> Patrick Wayne Kearney: 32 Murders ... "an acknowledged homosexual" and "... perpetrator of the 'homosexual trash bag murders.' " *The New York Times, July 27, 1977.*

<u>Bruce Davis</u>: 28 Murders ...killed 28 young men and boys after having sex with them. *The New York Times, January 21, 1984*

<u>Corll, Henley and Brooks</u> (error in spelling of names is corrected): 27 Murders. Dean Corll, Elmer Wayne Henley, and David Owen Brooks were members of a Texas homosexual torture/murder ring that captured and mutilated 27 young men *The New York Times, July 27, 1972.*

<u>Juan Corona</u>: 25 Murders ... an admitted homosexual, killed 25 male migrant workers. *The New York Times, October 4, 1972.*

<u>Jeffrey Dahmer</u>: 17 Murders ... a convicted child molester and practicing and admitted homosexual lured 17 young men and boys to his apartment, had sex with them, then killed them and dismembered them. He ate parts of his victims bodies ... Dahmer was active in "gay rights" organizations and had participated in "gay pride" parades. *Michael C. Buelow. "Police Believe Suspect Killed 17." The Oregonian, July 26, 1991, pages A1 and A24. Also: "Relative in Dahmer Case Sues." USA Today, August 6, 1991, page 3A. Also October 1991 Focus on the Family letter.*

<u>Stephen Kraft</u>: 16 Murders ... killed at least 16 young men after drugging, sodomizing and torturing. *Robert L. Mauro. "The Nation's Leading Serial Killers." The Wanderer, October 31, 1991.*

<u>William Bonin</u>: 14 Murders ... tortured and killed 14 young men ... had sex with his victims before and after they died. *Robert L. Mauro. "The Nations Leading Serial Killers." The Wanderer, October 31, 1991.*

"Violence and Homosexuality," (The FRI report, supra), listed the first six murderers listed above by *The Pink Swastika*, stating that they were the top six U.S. male serial killers, and that they were all "gay." This FRI report also stated:

Although the total number of victims dispatched by a given killer is often in doubt, (e.g., homosexual Henry Lucas claimed that he killed 350), it appears that the modern world record for serial killing is held by a Russian homosexual, Andrei Chikatilo, who was convicted in 1992 of raping, murdering and eating parts of at least 21 boys, 17 women and 14 girls. The pathology of eating one's sexual victims also characterized Milwaukee's Jeffrey Dahmer in 1992. He not only killed 17 young men and boys, but cooked and ate their body parts.

Consideration of the above, particularly from a statistical standpoint, leaves no doubt in the validity of the above statement referred to in the FRI report that violence is naturally associated with other forms of social pathology. This report, *Violence and Homosexuality*, supra, also states:

> Lesbian Aileen Wuornos laid claim in 1992 to "worst female killer" with at least 7 middle aged male victims. She singlehandedly topped the lesbian nurse team of Catherine Wood and Gwen Graham, who had killed 6 convalescent patients in Grand Rapids, Michigan.
>
> The association between serial murder and homosexuality isn't recent. Two gays compete for the spot of "world's worst murderer." During the Nazi rein of terror, Auschwitz executioner Ludwig Tiene strangled, crushed, and gnawed boys and young men to death while he raped them. Though his grand total is uncertain, he often murdered as many as 100 a day. Gilles de Rais (BlueBeard) brutally destroyed the lives of 800 boys. Each lad was lured to his home, bathed and fed. Just as the poor boy thought "this is my lucky day," he was raped, then killed by being ripped or cut apart and either burned or eaten.
>
> A study of 518 sexually-tinged mass murders in the U.S. from 1966 to 1983 determined that 350 (68%) of the victims were killed by those who practiced homosexuality and that 19 (44%) of the 43 murderers were bisexuals or homosexuals.

Considering that homosexuals constitute approximately 2 percent of the population, these statistics are indeed high. As to the mass murders, homosexuals killed thirty-four times as many people as were killed by heterosexuals, on a proportional basis. Homosexuals committed multiple murders twenty-two times as much as heterosexuals, on a proportional basis. These are tremendously high ratios, and those who cannot recognize the violently dangerous nature of homosexuality that is encouraged and allowed to degenerate in its natural directions must indeed be hiding their heads in the sand. We should consider, too, what Dr. Paul Cameron and the homosexuals Kirk and Madsen said about how continued homosexuality develops into the more violent and destructive acts, and the reasons for this degeneration, as was previously related herein. It quite obviously does terrible things to the mind and emotions of those engaged in it.

There has been a baffling bias of the news media in favor of homosexuality since the beginning of the homosexual movement in this country. Fortunately, as hard as the media have tried to influence the general public in that direction, with its name-calling and misuse of such words as bigotry and homophobia, it has been unable to do so. The *AIM Report*, Accuracy in Media, Inc., May-A 1996, contained the following under the title "Media and Homosexuals:"

> In a panel on homosexual activism, **Dr. Stanley Monteith**, a retired orthopedist and publisher of the newsletter HIV Watch, said that AIDS should never have reached epidemic proportions. "At every stage that this epidemic has progressed, there has been an organized effort from the gay community to block doctors from doing what's been logical to save the very lives of the members of the gay and homosexual community," Monteith said. As examples, he cited resistance by homosexual leaders at the onset of the AIDS crisis to closing down gay bathhouses in San Francisco and gay activist opposition to testing for Hepatitis B in blood transfusions, which has led to the deaths of 3,000 hemophiliacs.
>
> **Peter LaBarbera**, director of Accuracy in Academia and publisher of *Lambda Report on Homosexuality*, said the media are increasingly out of touch with Americans on the homosexual issue. He cited a survey of media by the Times Mirror Center for The People which found that only 4% of the nation's media believe homosexuality should be discouraged in society compared to 53% of the American public. Zero percent of media executives surveyed said homosexuality should be discouraged.

It has also been my experience and belief, reinforced by research and reading, that when the public in an area is sufficiently educated on the actual acts in which homosexuals engage, and by which they gain that classification, members of the public who are in favor of discouraging homosexuality are much higher than 53%.

In ordinary reading of local newspapers for several years, and with the help of my wife and secretaries, I have attempted to gather up articles and news items on multiple murders and assaults by homosexuals. However, this has been made difficult by the way the items are written. The word *homosexual* is seldom used to describe the perpetrators, even when it is abundantly obvious that such was the case; and often the sex of the victims are not even given. The media bias is obvious in this regard. Nevertheless, we have been able to come up with some incidents to add to those listed above, derived from *The Pink Swastika* and *Violence and Homosexuality*. Some of these items have later dates than the dates of the research for those publications. An article in the *Albuquerque Journal*, March 9, 1994, disclosed another homosexual mass murderer, Larry Eyler, who admitted to killing 21 men. This was more than some of those listed, above, from those publications. The article stated:

> A suspected serial killer who died of AIDS on death row confessed to killing 21 young men in a methodical murder spree in which he lured victims with drugs, alcohol and money, his attorney said . ...
>
> ... Authorities had long considered him the prime suspect in the string of murders across Illinois and Indiana in the early 1980's. However he was convicted on only two killings.
>
> ***
>
> Zellner, who handled Eyler's appeals, said he described the killings to her over the last three years, and that she convinced him to let her release his confession after his death.
>
> She released a list of 21 killings to which she said Eyler had confessed, along with the places and dates where the victims were found between 1982 and 1984. Zellner's list gave no name for seven of the victims; 11 were found in Indiana and 9 in Illinois. One body was never found.
>
> ***
>
> Zellner said an accomplice helped Eyler commit four of the killings....
>
> Eyler lured the victims with offers of liquor, drugs and money, Zellner said, then drove them to remote areas where they were handcuffed, gagged and blindfolded and had their feet bound. Not all of Eyler's victims were homosexuals, Zelner said, and Eyler never had sex during the abductions.
>
> ***
>
> Zellner described Eyler as a brilliant, manipulative man whose urge to kill was sparked by fights with his lover and fueled by drugs and alcohol.
>
> ***

Eyler was sentenced to death for the 1984 slaying of a 15-year-old male prostitute whose dismembered body was found in trash bags near Eyler's Chicago home. He also pleaded guilty in 1990 to participating in a 1982 killing in Terre Haute, Ind., and was sentenced to 60 years in prison.

In an article from the *Albuquerque Journal,* 5-10-94, on Joel Rifkin, a 34-year-old landscaper, who admitted killing 17 women. I do not have sufficient information to label him as a homosexual. However, along with whatever other pathology he may have had, he obviously fits the pattern of a violent sex pervert. But certainly not all sex perverts are homosexuals. He was convicted of second-degree murder in the first slaying to come to trial, in Nassau County, New York. He was under indictment for some of the other killings. As to the woman he was convicted of killing, her decomposed body was found in his pickup. The killing was admitted and insanity was pleaded, and rejected by the jury. Rifkin's attorney claimed:

> Rifkin did not know what he was doing and often after strangling women would continue to drive them around in his car, talking to them as if they were alive ....

The article further states:

> The defendant's sole witness, psychologist Barbara Kirwin, testified that Rifkin is a paranoid schizophrenic and suffered hallucinations.
> But Klein (the prosecutor) said Rifkin "knew exactly what he was doing. His behavior was very purposeful."
> The prosecutor said Rifkin even pulled out the teeth and cut off the fingertips of several victims so they couldn't be identified. Several of his victims were prostitutes he picked up.
> He also told jurors for the first time what was found in Rifkin's truck the day police found Bresciani's body: two large kitchen knives, a bolt cutter, rubber gloves and a cooking pot.
> "He intended to dismember her body like he had done to at least three other victims." Klein said. "He was going to cut through her

flesh, use the bolt cutters to break her joints and put her head in the pot." Two jurors became visibly ill.

As illustrated by the two jurors who became ill, the ghastly things that people do, like these sex perverts, in most cases homosexuals, are extremely difficult to fathom by ordinary decent people. This is also true as to the sexual acts in which homosexuals engage.

An article in the *Albuquerque Journal*, 1-5-93, was about the Washington State Supreme Court's refusal to block the execution of Westley Allan Dodd. It stated in part:

> Dodd, a 31-year-old shipping clerk, was sentenced to death in 1990 for the 1989 sex murders of three boys in the Vancouver area in southwestern Washington. The crimes were so grisly that some of the jurors who sentenced him sought psychiatric help afterward.

An article in the *The Albuquerque Tribune*, 6-5-93, was on an Arkansas case where three young men, Michael Wayne Echols, eighteen, Jessie Lloyd Misskelley, seventeen, and Jason Baldwin, sixteen, were each charged with three counts of capital murder in the deaths of three eight-year-old school boys. An *Albuquerque Tribune* article, 6-7-93, on the same case states:

> One of three teenagers accused of killing three 8-year-old boys told police that one victim was sexually mutilated and another was raped as part of a cult ritual, a newspaper reported today.

A case, both comical and tragic, was reported in the *Albuquerque Journal*, 11-6-93, about a child molester imprisoned in New Mexico who was suing the state. "Pain drove an imprisoned child molester to cut off his own testicles, which were too heavy for his prison-issued boxer shorts, his lawsuit alleges." Jerry Walker, 42, was charged with sexual assault on a four-year-old girl, pleaded guilty to lesser charges, and admitted being a habitual offender. The article said that Walker had a prior felony conviction in Texas for indecency with a child by contact, and a misdemeanor conviction in Texas for attempted indecency with a minor child by exposure. The sex of the Texas victims was not given.

The Albuquerque Tribune, 12-2-93, contained a gruesome story about husband-and-wife sex perverts who apparently sexually abused and killed two teen-age girls in 1991, in or near Toronto. Canada. Facts are skimpy because of a judge ordered a news blackout. Paul Teale's trial was pending and his estranged wife, Karla Homolka, had been sentenced to twelve years for manslaughter on a plea bargain in which she agreed to testify against Teale. The article stated in part:

> Reporters and police officers were said to have been in tears at what they heard about the killing of the girls, and how Homolka drugged her own 14-year-old sister for her own and Teal's sexual enjoyment, preserving the scenes on video.
>
> ***
>
> The account, describing how one of the teen-age victims was kept alive for 13 days before being slain, was published in the paper in Buffalo, N.Y.

A California case was reported in the *Albuquerque Journal*, 12-23-93, as follows:

> A woman whose lover's decapitated body was found stuffed in a wicker hamper in a field faces trial in her death.
>
> Roseanne Peterson, 24, was ordered to stand trial for murder after a hearing Tuesday during which a friend testified that Peterson had confessed to killing Laura Venable. Venable, 29, disappeared in March. Her decomposed body was found in May.
>
> ***
>
> Venable and Peterson had lived together in Vallejo for about 18 months when Venable disappeared.

The Albuquerque Tribune, 1-26-94, reports:

> San Francisco Police Inspector P. Thomas Cady, who won a landmark ruling by proving that he contracted the AIDS virus in the line of duty, had died of AIDS complications. He was 47.
>
> ***
>
> In June 1992, he won his three-year battle when an administrative law judge ruled that Cady had been infected with HIV in 1984 when a suspect bit him on the hands.
>
> ***

Julius (the suspect), convicted in 1989 of murder, was admitted to the California Medical Facility in Vacaville and in early 1990 tested positive for the AIDS virus.

An article in *The Albuquerque Tribune*, 2-15-94, on a serial murderer pleading guilty, failed to even identify the sex of the victims, or to give their names. It did state:

Rolling, 30, already is serving three life terms for a string of burglaries and robberies.

He was about to go on trial in the 1990 slayings of five young people, all students at the University of Florida or nearby Santa Fe Community College, in their campus-area apartments. Three of the five victims were mutilated.

The *Albuquerque Journal*, 3-1-94, on a Florida case:

An HIV positive man was found guilty of attempted murder for raping a boy, with the jury concluding that his AIDS was a lethal weapon.

... He also was found guilty of kidnapping, lewd and lascivious assault and sexual battery.

It was the first prosecution of an HIV-positive rapist for first-degree attempted murder in the United States ....

***

Perea still faces charges in the alleged rapes of two other boys in November 1991. None of the boys contracted the AIDS virus.

Perea was given a life sentence. The ages of the boys were eleven to thirteen. (*The Albuquerque Tribune*, 3-26-94)

An article in *The Albuquerque Tribune*, 4-25-94, on a serial murder in England:

Police have charged Rosemary West with murder in one of the 10 cases in which her husband also faces homicide charges.

... Rosemary West was charged Sunday in the murder of Linda Gough. Fredrick West, 52, has been charged with killing Gough and nine other women.

Gough's body and those of eight other women, including the Wests' 16-year-old daughter, Heather, were found buried under the Wests' house in Gloucester.

The bones of West's first wife were found in a corn field in Kempley, 10 miles northeast of Gloucester.

Bennett (detective) said police would begin a third search Tuesday....

Last week police charged Rosemary West with raping an 11-year-old girl between 1974 and 1976 and assaulting a 7-year-old boy between 1972 and 1974. She was also charged Friday with a serious sexual offense. Further details of that charge were to be presented in court, police said.

Fredrick West hung himself in prison before his trial. "One of Britain's worst serial murderers went to jail for life Wednesday, protesting she was innocent of torturing and killing 10 women and girls, including a daughter and a stepdaughter." She blamed all of the murders on her husband. She "admitted being a prostitute, having a string of affairs with both sexes, and having children by other men." (*Albuquerque Journal*, 11-23-95)

John Wayne Gacy (a homosexual, listed above as the top U. S. serial killer) was executed in Illinois on May 10, 1994. (*Albuquerque Journal*, May 10, 1994)

The Albuquerque Tribune, 5-14-94:

AUSTIN, Texas — A man charged with molesting and stalking a boy shot him to death as the 15-year-old's grandmother pleaded for his life, police said.

Dennis Queen, 28, was jailed without bail on a murder charge Friday in the death of Eric Krause. If convicted, he could face the death penalty.

The two met six years ago, when Queen worked at the day care center Krause attended, Sgt. Dusty Hesskew said.

"He kind of took over as a 'big brother' of this kid," Hesskew said.

But their friendship soured recently. Queen began stalking Krause in March, when the high school honors student started dating a girl, Hesskew said.

Krause tried to hide at his grandparents' house, but Queen found him there Thursday and shot him in the head. ...

Albuquerque Journal, 11-7-94:

TEL AVIV, Israel — Yeshayahu Demner was a respected engineering professor described by students as a reserved, kindly man.

Now police suspect the 46-year-old bachelor led a double life, dedicating the last year of his life to spreading the AIDS virus until he was murdered last week.

... Gay activists fear their struggle for acceptance in a conservative society has been set back years. ...

***

Police said that meticulous personal records found in the apartment revealed a dual identity.

David Tuval, the detective in charge of the case, said the documents showed that Demner discovered he had HIV, the sexually transmittable virus that leads to AIDS, in the fall of 1993. After that, he had sex "with many dozens of men" on condition that no protection be used, Tuval said.

Police sources said the murderer might be a sex partner who discovered Demner was HIV-positive. They refuse to say if they have any suspects.

The Albuquerque Tribune, 5-6-93:

A sixth patient of a Florida dentist, David Acer, who died of AIDS in 1990, has tested positive for HIV.

***

The girl is one of six former patients of Acer who have tested positive for HIV, which causes AIDS, One of them, Kimberly Bergalis, died of AIDS in 1991. ...

The *Albuquerque Journal*, April 12, 1994, contained an article by a Boston dentist and public educator, Leonard Horowitz. Horowitz claimed, in a talk at the New Mexico School of Pharmacy, and in a book he wrote, *Deadly Innocence*, that the dentist, Acer, referred to above, was a serial killer and infected his patients purposely by injecting them with his blood. In arriving at his conclusion, Horowitz claimed that he had made a study of thirty-six sexual serial killers, and that his findings were "the closest thing to a smoking gun." He also said that he had done an investigation of the matter, working on it seven days a week for seven months, and that his conclusions were based on circumstantial evidence. However, I found nothing in the article that amounted to the description of any real evidence that supported the conclusion. The article said that the CDC has yet to publicly release an opinion. The article also said that Dr. Stephen Carter, a Georgia dentist crusading to overturn the American Dental Association policy opposing mandatory AIDS testing for dentists, believes small amounts of tainted blood leaked through Acer's gloves. There was no explanation as to how or why the dentist would have blood in his gloves so many times. To me, the case is still a mystery.

An article in *The Albuquerque Tribune*, 11-28-95, is a prime example of the newspaper, either purposely or through inadequate reporting, failing to give sufficient facts about an incident for people to make a proper judgment as to the full nature of the incident. Raymond Corriz, thirty, was given thirty-seven years in prison for tying up and raping three children who were five years old and younger. His ex-wife, Loretta Corriz, twenty-three, was sentenced to three years in prison for allowing the rapes to occur. The article does not give the sex of the victims. It also does not even give the kinship of the children to the defendants, although it would appear that they must have been the children of one or both of the defendants. It did say that the children had been placed in five different foster homes since July because it is difficult to find an appropriate place for them. An *Albuquerque Journal* article, 11-28-95, was less protective, and gave a more complete account of the homosexual nature of the crimes of Raymond Corriz:

> Waggoner (prosecutor) said the eldest child, a girl, recalled being raped several ways by Corriz, beginning when she was 4. When he began to abuse her younger brother, she would offer to perform oral sex on Corriz if he would stop abusing her brother.
>
> But Corriz continued to abuse them and also raped their younger brother, Waggoner said. Corriz would beat them sometimes and threaten them, she said.
>
> According to testimony Monday, the three children have been placed in five different foster homes since July and that the children are confused, scared and have numerous psychological problems as a result of the abuse.
>
> Therapists and social workers said the children, who were not in court, asked that Raymond Corriz be imprisoned for many years, then killed.

The middle child, now 7, is obtaining inpatient psychological treatment, and the boy's therapist told the judge he believes the boy's chances of leading a normal life are slim to none because of the severity of abuse.

Albuquerque Journal, 1-19-96:

LOWELL, Mass. – A couple were arrested on charges they injected their four sons with drugs and repeatedly raped them over a six-month period.

"The people are monsters. They are absolute monsters," Detective Lt. William Taylor said, "I can't imagine what else you could do to these kids that could be worse."

The couple, ages 39 and 33, were arrested Wednesday and held without bail on charges including rape of a child with force and distribution of cocaine and marijuana to a youngster. The boys range in age from 9 to 12.

Police investigating a complaint of a domestic dispute in November found what they said were signs the boys were neglected and abused.

The children were taken to a hospital, where they tested positive for cocaine, Taylor said.

The *Albuquerque Journal*. 5-31-97, contained what appears to be a follow-up on the above:

Couple Convicted of Drugging, Raping Kids

CAMBRIDGE, Mass. — A couple was convicted Friday of raping their four sons and drugging them with cocaine for a year in an ordeal that ended on Thanksgiving Day when one boy called 911.

Corby Adkinson, 40, was convicted of child rape, drug distribution, indecent assault and other offenses, while Nancy Adkinson, 35, was convicted of child rape, indecent assault on a child and drug possession. ***

Middlesex Superior Court Judge Robert Barton could sentence the pair to up to life in prison on the child rape charge on June 19.

"You'll never burn another kid again," Mrs. Adkinson's former husband, Kenneth Bock, shouted as the couple were led from the courtroom.

Mrs. Adkinson, of Lowell, had denied performing oral sex on her sons, now aged 12, 10, and 11-year-old twins, in 1995, and injecting the boys with drugs. Syringes that were in the house were for medication for bee-sting injuries, she said.

But a prosecutor pointed out that Mrs. Adkinson also told police she pretended to have sex with the boys, and said there were traces of cocaine in the children's blood. ***

The *Albuquerque Journal*, 5-30-97:

6 Accused of Molesting Kids

YPSILANTI, Mich. — Six people were accused Thursday of luring children into a filthy, roach-infested house and molesting them.

The four men and two women got some of the youngsters inside by offering free baby-sitting to their parents, investigators said.

State police said that as many as 15 children, ages 5 to 12, were sexually assaulted between July 1996 and January of this year.

Troopers on April 16 arrested a 31-year-old Harvey Santure in the house, which sits in a quiet, tidy neighborhood west of Detroit. Police arrested five other adults Wednesday on criminal sexual conduct charges: three men, ages 30, 31, and 72, and two women, ages 50 and 64.

Police said three dogs seized from the home also may have been sexually abused.

An article in the *Albuquerque Journal*, 12-2-95, entitled "Lover Charged With Slaying of Portales Professor," was on first-degree murder charges being filed against Rhea Gaines, thirty-nine, for slaying her "lover," Kelly McGarrh, a thirty-four-year-old college professor, and states:

Roosevelt County (New Mexico) Sheriff Bob Dodgin said problems in the women's relationship apparently led to a disagreement that ended in gunfire.

"They were a couple. They were partners," Dodgin said. After moving together from Tennessee to Portales after McGarrh got a teaching job at Eastern New Mexico University, the couple was having problems, he said.

"Their relationship," Dodgin said, "had kind of soured."

An Associated Press article in *The Albuquerque Tribune*, March 19, 1994, entitled "Teen killers may get the death penalty," relates the jury conviction at Jonesboro, Arkansas, of Damien Echols, nineteen, and Charles Jason Baldwin, sixteen, on three counts of capital murder of three eight-year-old boys who disappeared May 5 while riding bikes near their homes. The article states in part:

> ... Their nude, hog-tied, battered bodies were pulled from a drainage ditch the next day. ***
>
> Echols and Baldwin were arrested June 3 after a friend, Jessie Lloyd Misskelley Jr., made incriminating statements to police.
>
> Misskelley, 18, was convicted in a separate trial of one count of first-degree murder and two counts of second-degree murder. He is serving a prison sentence of life plus 40 years.
>
> Misskelley said he watched Echols and Baldwin beat the boys, rape two of them and castrate one. At one point, Misskelley said, he chased down Michael Moore (one of the little victims) and prevented him from escaping.
>
> Prosecutors presented evidence suggesting Echols was a devil worshiper and Baldwin his loyal follower. Witnesses said both of them bragged about killing the boys. ***

One who studies these homosexual murders will note the apparent psychopathic obsession with such things as nudity of the victims, cruelty to them, and often mutilation of them, and in some instances, even eating parts of the victims. To me this ties in with the descriptions of Dr. Paul Cameron, and the Harvard-educated homosexuals, Marshall Kirk and Hunter Madsen, in regard to how homosexual activity often seems to regress into acts that are more violent, and often heinous.

Homosexual acts are unnatural acts that by their very nature degrade both – or, in the multiple-party orgies, all parties to the acts. Such things cannot possibly involve real love, and therefore cannot possibly give the participants the satisfaction that results from natural heterosexual relationships that encompass true love and decent sexual relations. For these reasons there is no way that homosexual acts can ever result in the elusive satisfaction and peace of mind homosexuals seem to be pursuing. The resulting frustration and unfulfilled desires seem to lead many of them further and further down the ladder toward a real living hell. It does not often lead to such violence as murder, but often cruelty and violent acts are involved, and, as we see, many murders have resulted.

William George Bonin, the "Freeway Killer," listed above as one of the top homosexual serial killers was executed in the San Quentin, California, prison on February 23, 1996. (*The Albuquerque Tribune*, 2-23-96) The serial killer listing above, from *The Pink Swastika*, numbered his victims fourteen. This news article on his execution says that he "was executed early today for torturing and murdering 14 boys and dumping their nude, mutilated bodies along Southern California highways. The article also states that Bonin says that he had killed 21 people. However, not all of Bonin's victims were murdered. The article includes a large picture of ten men with raised glasses over the caption, "Victims of California 'Freeway Killer' William Bonin offer a champagne toast to Bonin's execution ...." The ages of the victims at the time of the crime were 12 to 19. They "were sexually abused, tortured and, except for one, strangled. The exception was a 17-year-old German tourist, who was stabbed about 70 times." Two of Bonin's accomplices, James Munro and Gregory Miley, testified against him in exchange for lighter sentences. Another hanged himself before trial. An *Albuquerque Journal* article, 2-19-96, says that before the young men and boys were murdered, they were "sodomized."

There was an article in *The Albuquerque Tribune*, 3-14-96, and articles in the *Albuquerque Journal*, 3-14-96 and 3-15-96, about Thomas Hamilton who had just shot and killed eleven girls and five boys in Scotland and then killed himself. It was rumored that he was a pedophile, but this was apparently never determined on any credible evidence. However, there are several facts that point in that direction. First, there is the pathological violence. Secondly, he had been "kicked out" of the Boy Scouts, and barred from activities in a local boys' club, for his peculiar behavior. He seemed to have a peculiar liking for having boys take their clothing off above their waist, and taking pictures of them sticking out their chests. He lived alone and tried to get boys to go to his house with him.

Erik Menendez, twenty-five, and his brother, Lyle, twenty-nine, were found guilty of first-degree murder in March, 1996, for the shotgun slayings of their parents. (*The Albuquerque Tribune*, 3-21-96) An article in the *Albuquerque Journal*, 4-10-96, states:

> LOS ANGELES — A psychiatrist testified Tuesday that Erik Menendez's lead attorney ordered him to delete reference to homosexual relationships, parent-hating and hints of premeditation from notes of interviews with the murder defendant.

The following is from and article in the *Albuquerque Journal*, 5-19-96:

> CHICAGO — Richard Speck horrified the public with his savage killings of eight student nurses in 1966. Now, four years after his death, he's shocking people again as the grotesque star of a drug-and-sex videotape that suggests a prison system run amok.
>
> ***
>
> ... Kurtis' production company obtained the tape from a lawyer who remains anonymous.
>
> The tape was apparently made with prison video equipment in 1988 somewhere in the sprawling Stateville Correctional Center, one of Illinois' four maximum-security prisons.
>
> Speck who died of heart attack in 1991 while serving a life sentence, details his killings, along with a lesson on strangling: "It ain't like you see on TV. ... You have to go at it for about 3- minutes."
>
> Later, the fleshy, middle-aged murderer strips off his prison coveralls to reveal blue women's panties and heavy breasts. He has sex with a fellow inmate, and the two snort what appears to be cocaine and flash what looks like a wad of cash.

An article in the *Albuquerque Journal*, 5-14-96, quotes Speck as saying on the tape: "If they knew how much fun I was having in here they would turn me loose."

In the *Albuquerque Journal*, May 21, 1997, was an article, "Case of Convicted Molester Haunts Ariz. Lawman", by Linda Basheda, from *The Orange County Register,* Santa Ana, Calif. The article concerns James Lee Crummel, and states in part:

Crummel also has been named a suspect in the disappearance of a Big Bear boy. He is being questioned by Costa Mesa police in the 1979 death of James Trotter. And Pomano police want to re-question Crummel about the 1981 slaying of Anaheim Hills 6-year-old Jeffrey Vargo.

Sexual Predator

Crummel was born Jan. 27, 1944, in Kalamazoo, Mich., the second of five children to Loretta Beisehi.

When he was 8 years old, he later told prison psychiatrists, he performed a sex act on a neighborhood boy for a pocketful of pennies. He quit school after being expelled in the ninth grade for punching out a student and knocking down his principal.

When he turned 17, Crummel enlisted in the Army. But one year later, in 1962, he was court-martialed in Missouri for molesting two boys and a girl.

Crummel was sentenced to 10 years in Fort Leavenworth, Kan.

In 1966, he was caught in a lewd act with another inmate.

In 1966, he was set free after serving four of the 10 years.

In 1967, Crummel turned up in Drexel Heights, Ariz., and moved into a mobile home with his partner, Steve Shimer.

One late afternoon in February, fourth-grader Frank Clawson rode up on his banana-seat bike to the back door of his best friend, Gary Bynum — just down the road from Crummel's trailer. (The other boy was not able to go play.) ***

Later that night, the (Clawson) boy's parents found his bike in the middle of the street in front of their home.

By daylight, a police officer found him strangled with his own belt in a ditch under a mesquite tree a couple of hundred yards from his house.

Five days later, Crummel and Shimer left town.

On the way, Shimer later told police, Crummel admitted killing Frank.

Six months later, on Aug. 29, 14-year-old Steve Scallon was hitchhiking home from football practice in a Milwaukee suburb when, court records show, Crummel picked him up in his laundry-delivery truck.

He stopped and got some ice cream. Then he asked Steve Scallon if he wanted to go on a delivery. Scallon said sure. A few miles down the road, Crummel invited the boy to take a walk in a wooded area.

He molested the boy after tying him up. Later Crummel molested him again, records show.

The boy blacked out. Crummel took a tree limb and beat him severely and tossed him into a ravine.

Scallon crawled out the next day and neighbors found him, his head swollen and bloody, his skull fractured.

Crummel was arrested two days later. When police interviewed Shimer, he told them about the alleged confession. (My comment: What kind of a person was Shimer, who apparently lived with Crummel all this time after he admitted to the murder of the Clawson boy?) ***

(Bob Lough) moved to Pima County (Ariz.) in 1974 and applied for a job at the Sheriff's Department. He worked narcotics, patrol, and robberies.

In 1980, his first day in homicide, Lough walked into the sergeant's office.

"I want the Clawson case," he told them. "It's a solvable case. Crummel's dangerous."

Lough found Crummel pretty quickly. He was living with a Newport Beach psychiatrist. Crummel was calling himself Jimmy Savage.

Lough went to work, methodically retracing Crummel's steps.

He found Shimer in Texas. And tracked down dozens of Crummel's former prison inmates, old friends, family members, victims and psychologists.

Crummel's prison sentence for the Steve Scallon beating was unlimited, to be reviewed periodically. After serving five years, the prison recommended he serve at least five more. The courts came to a different conclusion. Crummel walked on Aug. 23, 1972.

Crummel broke into tears when Lough arrested him in Newport Beach on May 19, 1982, and escorted him back to Arizona.

But the next month, at a preliminary hearing, Shimer recanted his statements about Crummel's confessing.

The case was dismissed.

Crummel returned to California. On Halloween, he showed up at a party in Costa Mesa. Later, the host of the party went to check on his son. There was Crummel kneeling at the boy's bedside. The boy's father attacked Crummel. Other party goers ran in and started beating him.

While he was still sitting in jail awaiting trial, there was a change in case law in Arizona that let Shimer's former statements about Crummel's confession into trial — even if he wouldn't cooperate.

Lough got a warrant in February 1983. Crummel was on his way back to Arizona, after being acquitted of charges in the Halloween incident.

On Nov. 15, 1983, he was convicted of killing Frank Clawson. It took the jury one day. He was sentenced to life in prison.

One year later, Crummel's new attorney convinced the judge that their client got a raw deal. His original attorney failed to adequately represent him, failed to cross-examine key witnesses.

The prosecution didn't have enough for a new trial. In 1987, Crummel pleaded to kidnapping.

Crummel walked out of prison later that year. Lough quit homicide. Now he's on patrol.

The following is from an article in *The Observer* (Rio Rancho, N.M.), 5-23-97:

*** Willard Dan, 35, and Darwin Dan, 32, have been charged with criminal sexual penetration of a minor [a 5-year-old boy], criminal sexual contact of a minor, false imprisonment and enticement of a child.

They were arrested after the mother of the boy took him to the University of New Mexico Hospital and doctors there said he showed signs of sexual penetration. ... the boy told a doctor who examined him that the two men had sexually penetrated him and he was in pain.

The youngster also told the doctor that the suspects showed him a magazine with pictures of naked girls and boys. In addition, he said the men hit him with a bat and fists for telling his mother they had previously sexually abused him and the men threatened him not to tell anyone. The boy indicated that Willard Dan wore a condom during the assault.

The suspects had been staying at the home of Willard Dan's mother-in-law, who is the boy's neighbor.

The brothers have extensive criminal records, [Deputy] Rivera said. Both were charged in 1987 with murder. Darwin Dan was convicted and served seven years at the Western New Mexico Corrections facility. Willard Dan has served time at the Santa Fe Penitentiary for auto burglary.

The Dans are each being held on $100,000 cash-only bonds. No trial has yet been scheduled, Rivera said.

An Associated Press article, "Lesbian faces life in taped slayings," *Albuquerque Journal*, 5-23-96:

> MIDDLETOWN, Conn. — A jury recommended life in prison Wednesday for a woman who killed two Wesleyan University employees over a failed lesbian relationship in a grisly murder that was recorded on an answering machine tape.
>
> The seven men and five women determined that Janet Griffin, 49, killed her victims in a cruel and depraved manner but found at least one mitigating factor to spare her from the death penalty. They didn't say what the factor was.
>
> Griffin, of Rutland, Vt., was convicted last month in the fatal shooting, stabbing and beating of Patricia Lynn Stellar, 43, and Stellar's nephew Ronald King, 26, in November, 1993.
>
> The prosecution said Griffin was driven by rage and jealousy after her former lover, Gena Coccia, left her and moved in with Steller.

Family Research Report, Family Research Institute, March-April, 1996:

> *Gay Violence:* From *Philadelphia* comes wealthy John du Pont. Seems he liked men — wrestlers, cops, swimmers. And he liked to touch men's privates. One day in January he shot Dave Schultz, an Olympic Gold medalist, dead.

"In 1992, two Jeffersonville, Indiana, lesbians, aged 17 and 16, abducted a 12-year-old girl whom they accused of trying to 'steal a girlfriend.' The little girl was pushed into the trunk of a car, stabbed repeatedly, and beaten with a heavy metal bar. While still struggling, they poured gasoline on her and set her ablaze." (*Violence and Homosexuality*, supra)

In 1992 in Fort Lauderdale, Florida, a fourteen-year-old boy was convicted of first-degree murder for helping to kill his forty-year-old father. The father "was stabbed 45 times and beaten so badly with an iron skillet that the skillet shattered." The boy confessed that he helped his father's former homosexual lover and roommate kill him so that he and the thirty-one-year-old homosexual "could live together." (*Violence and Homosexuality*, supra)

Homosexuals murdering homosexuals certainly is not uncommon. From my unscientific study of the problem, it appears clear that most murders of and most attacks on homosexuals are by other homosexuals. There is no question that the ratio would be exceedingly high when weighted by population percentages. And heinous murders are committed by lesbians as well as homosexual men. The following are two more examples reported in *Family Research Report*, Family Research Institute, Sept.-Oct. 1997:

Richmond, VA: ... On July 4th, Stacy Hanna, 19, moved in with a group of 4 lesbians aged 18, 18, 19, & 18. Soon there was a romantic interest and involvement. By July 27 Stacy was found "face down in the mud. She had been severely beaten, her skull fractured, and her throat slashed." The accused lesbian killers are all active in the Richmond Organization for Sexual Minority Youth! The murder was a team affair with one lesbian admitting to stabbing Hanna several times in the chest, another throwing a cinderblock at Hanna's head, and another cutting her throat. (*Washington Blade* 9/19/97)

Toms River, NJ: Seems a 43-year-old gay blade from New York, Stephen Simmons, wanted a little "younger action." So he met a 14-yr old boy on the Internet and got together with him a number of times for sex in 1996. A year later, 11-yr old Eddie Werner was selling candy and wrapping paper door-to-door. Eddie happened to knock at the door of the lad who had been molested by Simmons. Before he was killed, Eddie was sodomized by the now-15-yr old lad. ... (*Washington Times* 10/3/97)

The *Albuquerque Journal*, October 10, 1996, in an Associated Press article, "Grisly Indiana Discovery locates Missing Gay Men," reports that at least four missing gay men were found among the bodies of at least seven bodies discovered on the estate of Herbert Baumeister, forty-nine, who lived there until he went to Canada, where he shot himself to death. The dead were found on Baumeister's estate along with spent shotgun shells and handcuffs. "...Baumeister's ties to the Indianapolis gay community are unquestioned. Police have spoken to men who had sexual encounters with Baumeister," said Sgt. Ken Whisman, the lead investigator on the case. "We put him in every gay bar in the city," Whisman said. "Whisman, however, refused to call Baumeister a serial killer, saying that since the causes of death remain undetermined, the cases aren't even classified as homicides."

Probably the greatest mass killer of victims in the U. S., and certainly of homosexuals, was Gaeton Dugas, referred to above in the part of this chapter on spreading the AIDS virus. *The Pink Swastika*, supra, p. 176, states:

> In a spree of "gay-on-gay" violence not seen since Nazi Germany, one homosexual man, Gaetan Dugas, was directly responsible for killing over a thousand homosexual men by deliberately infecting them with the AIDS virus. Indirectly he may be responsible for tens of thousands, eventually perhaps hundreds of thousands of AIDS deaths. One of the first known AIDS carriers, Dugas was known as "Patient Zero" because he caused so many of the earliest infections (Clowes, Brian. <u>Debating the "Gay rights" Issue</u>, Brooks Oregon, Oregon Citizens Alliance, 1993.) Even after his diagnosis Dugas "justified his continued sodomy with the excuse that he was free to do what he wanted with his own body. Even when he was in the final stages of AIDS, he would have anonymous sex with men in homosexual bathhouses, and then show his sexual partners his purple Kaposi's Sarcoma blotches, saying, 'Gay cancer. Maybe you'll get it'" ("The Columbus of AIDS." *National Review*, November 6, 1987:19)

The greatest mass murders of all time by homosexuals were surely the Nazi killers in Germany, during the Hitler regime.

The Homosexual Deception: Making Sin A Civil Right, supra, pp. 36-37, states:

> Homosexual activists often attempt to gain sympathy by recalling the extermination of thousands of homosexuals under the tyranny of Hitler's Third Reich. But Reisman points out the paradox: "The World War II notion of Hitler's persecution of homosexuals is based on his assault of 'fems' not homosexual Nazi supermen. Many of Hitler's 'Inner Circle,' and the key men who recruited for the party, and who led the party, including the most brutal military brigades, the Storm Troopers (SA), and the Infantry School—were homosexual: Ernest Roehm [head of the SA], Rudolph Hess and Gerhard Rossbach, while the infamous Goering was said to be a type of transvestite . . . Walter Langer, writing in *The Mind of Adolf Hitler* (1972), noted that Rudolph

Hess 'was generally known as Fraulein Anna.' There were many other [homosexuals close to Hitler] and it was supposed, for this reason, that Hitler too belonged in this category" ("A Content Analysis of *The Advocate* [a national homosexual magazine] 1972-1991," by Dr. Judith Reisman, President of The Institute for Media Education, not-yet published study, pp. 57-58)

Reisman adds in a footnote: "See Berhold Hinz, *Art in the Third Reich* (Pantheon Books: New York, 1979) about the display of brazenly homosexual Nazi male imagery and concepts, and see especially S. William Halperin, writing in *Germany Tried Democracy: A Political History of the Reich from 1918-1933* (Norton Books: New York 1946). Here, Halperin describes the role of public homosexual activists within Hitler's Nazi party, even in "major posts of import" (Ibid., p. 65)

The report, *Violence and Homosexuality*, supra, was quoted above, as to the statement about the homosexual Nazi executioner, Ludwig Tiene, murdering as many as 100 persons a day.

By far, the most complete work that I have found about homosexuals in the Nazi party, and the atrocities and murders committed by them, is *The Pink Swastika*, supra. The following is taken from this book.

Rudolph Hess, a homosexual, was one of Hitler's closest friends, and became the Deputy *Fuehrer* of the Nazi party. (p. 62)

As to whether Hitler himself was a homosexual, the authors state:

The short answer to this question is 'probably not.' Hitler was certainly not an exclusive homosexual in any case." (p. 82) Langer [Langer, Walter C., "The Mind of Adolph Hitler," The Secret Wartime Report, Basic Books, Inc., New York, 175f.] suggests that Hitler may very well have engaged in homosexual behavior, saying "persons suffering from his perversion sometimes do indulge in homosexual practices in the hope that they might find some sexual gratification. Even this perversion would be more acceptable to them than the one with which they are afflicted. (p. 83)

At this point I interrupt the discussion of *The Pink Swastika* and give my own opinion as to whether or not Hitler was a homosexual. The definition I have used for homosexual in this book is one who voluntarily engages in sex with a person of the same sex. This would include bisexuals. I see no moral or other real difference between the two. Also, as pointed out above, bisexuals seem to be as heinous as homosexuals, and sometimes more so, in the vile acts in which they engage. In this regard I believe that the authors of The Pink Swastika were overly cautious and conservative, and I believe that in the light of further research they have done, that they would agree with my conclusion on this, if bisexuals are included. Also, I think that most anyone would agree that Hitler was a vicious sex pervert with no morality at all. This appears to be true in many homosexuals. It should also be pointed out that Rohm and Roehm are different spellings of the name of the same person. Scott Lively, one of the authors of The Pink Swastika, explains that this spelling confusion is brought about by a German symbol which is not in English. (I would also note that I have found the first name of Hitler to be spelled in two ways, Adolph and Adolf.) Lively has continued to research and write on the subject of the influence of homosexuality in Nazism, and the following is from his recent book, **The Poisoned Stream - *"Gay" Influence in Human History*, by Scott Lively, Vol. 1,** Founders Publishing Corp., 1997, pp. 80-81:

> In 1945, a Jewish historian by the name of Samuel Igra published *Germany's National Vice.* (London: Quality Press Ltd. 1945), in which he called homosexuality a "poisoned stream" that ran through the heart of Nazism. (In the 1920s and 1930s, homosexuality was known as "the German vice" across Europe because of the debaucheries of the Weimar period). Igra, who escaped Germany in 1939, claims that Hitler "had been a male prostitute in Vienna at the time of his sojourn there, from 1907 to 1912, and that he practiced the same calling in Munich from 1912 to 1914" (Igra: 67) Desmond Seward, in *Napoleon and Hitler*, says Hitler is listed as a homosexual in Viennese police records (Seward: 299) Lending credence to this is the fact, noted by Walter Langer, that during several of those years Hitler "chose to live in a Vienna flophouse known to be inhabited by many homosexuals." (Langer: 192) Rector writes that, as a young man, Hitler was often called *"der schoen Adolph"* (the handsome Adolph) and later his looks

"were also to some extent helpful in gaining big-money support from Ernst Rohm's circle of wealthy gay friends" (Rector, Frank, *The Nazi Extermination of Homosexuals*, New York, Stein and Day, 1981).

(Walter C.) Langer, a psychiatrist, was commissioned by the allies in 1943 to prepare a thorough psychological profile of Hitler. His report, kept under wraps for 29 years was published in book form (by Signet) in 1972 as *The Mind of Adolph Hitler*. Langer writes that Hitler was certainly a coprophile (a person who is sexually aroused by human excrement) and may have practiced homosexuality as an adult. He cites the testimony of Hermann Rauschning, a former Hitler confidant who "reports that he has met two boys who claimed that they were Hitler's homosexual partners, but their testimony can hardly be taken at face value. More condemning," adds Langer, "would be the remarks dropped by [Albert] Foerster, the Danzig gauleiter, in conversations with Rauschning. Even here, however, the remarks deal only with Hitler's impotence as far as heterosexuality relationships go without actually implying that he indulges in homosexuality. It is probably true that Hitler calls Foerster "Bubi," which is a common nickname employed by homosexuals in addressing their partners. This alone is not adequate proof that he has actually indulged in homosexual practices with Foerster, who is known to be a homosexual (Langer: 178). However, writes Langer, "Even today, Hitler derives sexual pleasure from looking at men's bodies and associating with homosexuals" (Langer: 179). Too, Hitler's greatest hero was Frederick the Great, a well known homosexual (Garde, Noel I., *Jonathan to Gide: The Homosexual in History*, New York, Vantage Press, 1969, p. 44).

Like Langer, Waite (Waite, Robert G. L., *The Psychopathic God Adolf Hitler*, New York, Signet Books, 1977) hesitates to label Hitler a homosexual but cites substantial circumstantial evidence that he was:

> It is true that Hitler was closely associated with Ernst Rohm and Rudolf Hess, two homosexuals who were among the very few people with whom he used the familiar *du*. But one cannot conclude that he therefore shared his friends' sexual tastes. Still, during the months he was with Hess in Landsberg, their relationship must have become very close. When Hitler left the prison he fretted about his friend who languished there, and spoke of him tenderly using Austrian diminutives: 'Ach mein Rudy, mein Hessert, isn't it appalling to think that he's still there.' One of Hitler's valets, Schneider,

made no explicit statement about the relationship, but he did find it strange that whenever Hitler got a present he liked or drew an architectural sketch that particularly pleased him, he would run to Hess – who was known in homosexual circles as "Fraulein Anna" – as a little boy would run to his mother to show her a prize .... Finally there is the nonconclusive but interesting fact that one of Hitler's prized possessions was a handwritten love letter which King Ludwig II had written to a manservant (Waite, 1977:283f.).

Hitler, if homosexual, was certainly not exclusively so. There are at least four women, including his own niece, with whom Hitler had sexual relationships, although these relationships were not normal. Both Waite and Langer suggest that his sexual encounters with women included expressions of his coprophilic as well as extremely degrading forms of masochism. It is interesting to note that all four women attempted suicide after becoming sexually involved with Hitler. Two succeeded. (Langer: 175f.).

Jewish writer, Howard L. Hurwitz, in **The Truth About Homosexuals and the Holocaust**, *Human Events, 8-29-97 and 9-5-97*, also states: "Hitler himself is listed in Austrian police archives of the early 1920s as a male prostitute."

Hitler certainly had all of the symptoms and indications of a progressed homosexual or bisexual. These are various kinds of perversions, cruelty, and a complete lack of morality. It is also clear that a large part of the mass murderers in history were homosexual.

When a mind becomes so demented that sodomy is considered good and admirable, the progression to more bizarre and violent activities may soon follow as a matter of course, as is explained herein. It therefore appears to me that the great preponderance of the evidence is corroborative of the direct statements that Hitler was a homosexual. I therefore agree with the statements of Samuel Igra, and with the ideas of British Consul-General R. T. Smallbones, infra.

Until I began studying the homosexual movement, and homosexuality, I was never able to comprehend how a group of people in a civilized nation, such as Germany, could commit such depraved acts as the atrocities against the Jewish people, including the Holocaust. I believe that I now understand what was behind it and what the moving impetus was. It was the demented minds of perverts who had lost all sense of what is right and what is wrong; following their leader, Hitler, who was possessed of the same sickness.

We now have the same sickness working in this country, and in much the same way it debilitated Germany. We have attacks against our churches and traditional values. The homosexualists are successfully promoting their propaganda through all forms of our media. They have a firm grip on the Clinton administration. And worst of all, a large part of our schools and universities have already been successfully infiltrated and students are being brainwashed with homosexual propaganda.

We now continue with *The Pink Swastika.*
At page 85:

> ... Hitler not only knew that the Nazi Party was a virtual homo-
> sexual social club, it seems that this was the way he wanted it.
> Finally in our look at Adolph Hitler, the man, we turn to Samuel
> Igra, a Jew who fled Germany in 1939 after twenty years of observing
> Hitler and the Nazis:
>
> > For the purposes of the present investigations Hitler is important
> > for what he represented. . .when he embarked the German people
> > on the policy that brought about the world catastrophe. He was
> > the central figure around which a number of men grouped them-
> > selves, from the 1920's onwards, in a movement to gain supreme
> > control of the German people. As the movement developed they
> > were aided and abetted and supported financially as well as po-
> > litically by the industrial capitalists of the Rhineland; but the ini-
> > tiative did not come from the latter. It came from Hitler as the
> > condottiere [leader] of a band of evil men who were united to-
> > gether by a common vice [homosexuality]. (Igra, Samuel,
> > "Germany's National Vice," London: Quality Press Ltd., 1945)

Hitler learned that public opinion was not with him in the matter of homosexuality, despite Germany's international reputation as a haven for homosexuals. Roehm's homosexual activities were becoming widely known and embarrassing to Hitler, and exacerbated conflicts between Hitler's lieutenants. The greater part of these conflicts were between the homosexuals, themselves. (p. 87) They "quarreled and feuded as only men of unnatural sexual inclinations with their peculiar jealousies can." (Shirer, William, "The Rise and Fall of the Third Reich," New York, Fawcett Crest, 1960, p.172). Hitler set up a party court to try to settle disputes and prevent his comrades from washing their dirty linen in public. It was considered a sham, because Hitler assigned Major Walther Buch, and two assistants, Ulrichs Graf, the former butcher who had been Hitler's bodyguard, and Hans Frank, a young Nazi lawyer. Both Graf and Frank were homosexuals, and Buch may have been, also. The only purpose of all this sham was to hide the perversions of the party hierarchy from the public. (pp. 87-89)

In February, 1933, Hitler banned pornography, homosexual bars and bath-houses, and groups which promoted "gay rights." The masculine homosexuals in the Nazi leadership selectively enforced this policy only against their enemies and not against all homosexuals.

On May 6, 1933, the Nazis attacked and destroyed the Sex Research Institute of Berlin, which served as a center for the "study" of homosexuality, and was the headquarters for the effeminate branch of the German "gay rights" movement.

"However, the attack on the Institute was not motivated solely by the Nazi enmity against effeminate homosexuals. It was an attempt to cover up the truth about rampant homosexuality and other perversions in the Nazi Party. Sklar writes that 'Hitler attempted to bury all his earlier influences and his origins, and he spent a great deal of energy hiding them ... . [In this campaign to erase his past] Hitler ordered the murder of Reihold Hanish, a friend who had shared his down and out days in Vienna [where Hitler is suspected of having been a homosexual prostitute] (Sklar, Dusty, "The Nazis and the Occult," New York, Dorset Press, 1989). (pp. 99-101)

"The event in history most frequently cited as evidence of Nazi persecution of homosexuals is known variously as the Blood Purge, the Night of the Long Knives, and the Roehm Purge." However, the Roehm purge was driven by political, not moral concerns. Roehm, as leader of the SA, had become a serious political threat to Hitler. Hundreds of his political enemies were assassinated in one bloody sweep. (Eight authors and historians are cited for this information.) (pp. 102-106)

It has been claimed that Heinrich Himmler, head of the SS and Gestapo, was a fanatical anti-homosexual member of the Nazi party. This does not seem to square with the following:

> Himmler may have been a homosexual. Filmmaker Walter Frenz, who worked closely with the Nazi elite including a stint as Hitler's private filmmaker, is reported to have traveled to the Eastern front with Himmler "whose pederastic proclivities he captured on film" (*Washington City Paper*, April 4, 1995). Himmler, like Hitler, was closely associated with homosexuals during his entire adult life. His path to Nazi leadership, however, was not like that of so many others, through the German "gay rights" movement. It was, instead, through the occult movement, and his Nazi career was defined by his passion for the occult. We have seen how Himmler was profoundly influenced by Guido von List and Jorg Lanz von Liebenfels, the homosexual gurus of nationalistic and anti-Semitic occultism. ... (p. 112)

Reinhard Heydrich, a homosexual known as "The Blond Beast," was one of the most famous of the persecutors of the Jews. (pp. 115-122) Consider the following:

> Perhaps the single most infamous incident orchestrated by Heydrich was the November 9, 1938 *progrom* known as *Kristallnacht* ("Crystal Night"), in which hundreds of Jews were killed and synagogues and businesses were destroyed across Germany. "In fifteen hours," writes Snyder, "101 synagogues were destroyed by fire, and 76 were demolished. Bands of Nazis systematically destroyed 7,500 Jewish owned stores. The pillage and looting went on through the night. Streets were covered with broken glass, hence the name *Kristallnacht*" (Snyder, Dr. Louis L., *Encyclopedia of the Third Reich*, New York, Paragon House, 1989) Michael Berenbaum, In <u>The World Must Know</u>, adds that ninety-six Jews were killed and thirty thousand were arrested and sent to the camps. Jewish cemeteries, schools and homes were destroyed. As a final insult, the Jews were held responsible for the damage and collectively fined one billion Reichsmarks (Berenbaum:54). (p. 118)

It was of course difficult for the world to understand how such atrocities could happen in this modern world. The following is an account of an explanation offered by British Consul-General R. T. Smallbones (pp. 121-122):

> ... "The outbreak of sadistic cruelty may be that sexual perversion, and, in particular, homosexuality, are very prevalent in Germany. It seems to me that mass sexual perversion may offer an explanation" .... I am convinced that this explanation is the correct one [writes Igra]. For, as a matter of fact, the widespread existence of sexual perversion in Germany ... is notorious. And authorities on criminal sociology are agreed that there is a causal connection between mass sexual perversion and the kind of mass atrocities committed by the Germans [Igra, supra, p. 7].

"We have now arrived at one of the most sensitive topics in our discussion of homosexuality in Nazi Germany. Revisionists have attempted to define homosexuals as a class of people who were 'targeted for extermination' by the Nazi's. One homosexual group went so far as to stage a high-profile 'pilgrimage' to the Yad Vashem Holocaust Memorial in Jerusalem in May of 1994. They were met by a delegation of Jewish Holocaust survivors who were so overcome with outrage that some of them had to be restrained from physically assaulting the contingent of (mostly American) political activists. One man cried "My grandfather was killed for refusing to have sexual relations with the camp commandant. You are desecrating this place..." (*The Jerusalem Post*, May 30, 1994). (p. 123)

The authors reject the idea that homosexuals should be considered victims of genocide, as the Jewish people were. "Homosexuals who died were 'a small fraction of less than 1 percent of homosexuals in Nazi occupied Europe..., compared to more than 85 percent of European Jewry. ...many of the guards and administrators responsible for the infamous concentration camp atrocities were homosexuals themselves, which negates the idea that homosexuals in *general* were being persecuted and interned. (pp. 123-124)

"An additional point that deserves mention here is that the uniform pattern of brutality for which the camps are known was established as a deliberate and calculated policy by the SA under Ernst Roehm in 1933. Heiden writes that '[t]he SA had learned ... that the will of an imprisoned mass must be broken by the most loathsome cruelty' (Heiden, Konrad, 'Der Fuehrer: Hitler's Rise to Power,' Boston, Houghton Mifflin Co. 1944, p. 565). He later adds '[f]rightening reports also trickled through from the concentration camps, and the public began to realize that Fuhrer's picked troops had organized artificial hells in Dachau ... Roehm admitted publicly that these things seemed unbearable to many people, but said he saw no reason for stopping them' (ibid..:732f.). Though Roehm was soon killed, his system of mass torture and degradation endured." (p. 125)

Grisly accounts of homosexual sexual acts, torture, atrocities of all kinds, and murder by homosexuals who were guards and in charge of camps at Auschwitz, Treblinka, and Buchenwald are described. (pp. 126-134)

"This extreme savagery exhibited by the Butch homosexuals of the camps was not rare, but some accounts of brutality are more gruesome than others. At Auschwitz, for example, *Kapo* Ludwig Tiene became the most prolific mass murderer of all time by strangling, crushing and gnawing to death as many as 100 boys and young men a day while he raped them (Rector, Frank, *The Nazi Extermination of Homosexuals*, New York, Stein and Day, 1981, p. 143). It is not clear if Auschwitz's Commandant Hoess was homosexual, though we know that he had at one time been a close friend of Edmund Heines (Snyder, supra, p. 301), the procurer of boys for Roehm's pederastic orgies." (p. 130)

"Perhaps the most grotesque story of all, however, is told by Rector in his chapter on the camps, grotesque not because it is bloodier, but because it reveals how widespread and acceptable this level of perversion had become among the Nazi elite. He writes,

> As for the SS, their behavior was typical among those who engaged in sexual bestiality. An example is a film, in color with a sound track, that was secretly made for the pornographic enjoyment of a select coterie of Nazis showing a wild drunken orgy of beautiful boys and handsome young men being whipped, raped and murdered by the SS (Rector: 144). (Note: Rector adds that this film is still today "very discreetly and very privately shown to only an inner circle of certain homosexuals in Europe"). (p. 130)

"Before we leave the subject of guards and *Kapos*, we can find one of the few mentions of lesbians in Nazi history connected with the prison system. In <u>Paris Under the Occupation</u>, Historians Perrault and Azema describe the activities of the French Gestapo. They identify 'Sonia Boukassi, a drug addict, and Violette Morris, onetime French weight-lifting champion, both lesbians, [as] the chief women's interrogators' in the notorious torture chambers of *La Carlingue* (Perrault and Azema: 38)." (p.131)

How such atrocities of the Nazis could have been allowed to occur by the civilized people of Germany will forever be a puzzle to decent and normal people. The authors of *The Pink Swastika* offer some explanations.

"Guido von List targeted his hatred more specifically against Christians, and developed an elaborate mythology to justify attacks against Christianity. ... the rise of homosexuality in a Judeo-Christian-based culture necessarily represents the diminution of Biblical morality as a restraint on human passions. Consequently, where Judeo-Christian ideals decrease, violence and depravity increase." (p. 135)

The authors comprehensively detail the attacks on religion and Christianity, and the resulting weakening of the church structure. Neo-paganism entered the weakened churches. The Nazis replaced Christian holidays with pagan celebrations. The schools were heavily targeted in the strategy to de-Christianize the young. Mandatory school prayer was stopped in 1935. (pp. 133-142)

"In an obscene twist, the Nazis used former Christian religious facilities, seized by the government, to establish schools in which students were trained in male supremacist ideology, using teachings from the works of homosexual theorists such as Otto Weininger (Rosenthal, A. M., and Gelb, Arthur, *One More Victim: The Life and Death of a Jewish Nazi*, New York, The New American Library, Inc., 1967)." (p. 140)

The strategy worked well in Germany, and we see much of the same strategy being used in this country for the past forty years, and today. It is also having amazing success here, with the help of the liberal media and the liberal politicians. We are being taught that homosexuality is great and acceptable. Religion is continually denigrated. It is even ridiculed and called superstition. People who support the Judaic-Christian principles on which this country was built are called bigots, "Christian Fundamentalists," individuals and churches are physically attacked by the homosexual groups, and property is burned and destroyed. Threats and pressure are successfully used against such groups as the American Psychiatric Association, schools, and private businesses, to accomplish the goals of the homosexual agenda. These things will be discussed in detail in Chapters 6 and 7.

Various threats, including violence, destruction of property, intimidation, deliberate AIDS infections, and contamination of blood supplies, have been previously outlined in this chapter.

Chapter 7, "American Nazis," of *The Pink Swastika*, pp. 143-199, is a complete and very informative chapter on the current Nazi movement, and activities, primarily in this country; but it also touches on the current Nazi "skinhead" movement in Germany and other countries. It details the Nazi connections with and ideas used by the homosexual movement in this country. There are striking similarities to the methods used by the homosexual Nazis in the rise of the Third Reich, including the use of propaganda, threats and intimidation, attacks on citizens with opposing views, attacks on churches, and destruction of property. For the sake of some brevity in trying to reasonably cover a few of the incidents detailed in The Pink Swastika, a large number of the citations and references will be omitted, but the book is well documented for those interested in verification.

The Pink Swastika, supra, pp. 143-144:

The most famous incident in the history of the American Nazi Party resulted from its 1977 demand to stage a march through the largely Jewish neighborhood of Skokie, Illinois, a Chicago suburb and the home of many holocaust survivor. This plan was devised by Frank Collin, who often appeared with his followers "in full Nazi regalia: brown shirts, black boots, and armbands with swastikas" and who "advocated that all African-Americans, Jews and Latinos be forcibly deported." ... Civil authorities effectively blocked the march at first, but the American Civil Liberties Union (ACLU) rose to Collin's aid and forced the City of Chicago to allow it.

Frank Collin was a homosexual. In 1979 he was arrested "for taking indecent liberties with boys between ages 10 and 14" and was sentenced to seven years in prison. (Ibid., pp. 143-144)

Another branch of the American Nazi movement, the National Socialist League (NSL), is openly homosexual. This San Diego based organization of the NSL was founded in 1974 by defecting members of the National Socialist White People's Party, and is unique in restricting its members to homosexual Nazis. (Ibid., p, 144)

A simple perusal of *The Advocate*, the leading "gay" magazine, reveals that Nazi themes are common in the homosexual community. (Ibid., p. 146)

One "popular" film, by a Finnish "gay rights" advocate Iippio Pohjala, entitled "Daddy and the Muscle Academy" (1992), was shown in San Francisco on June 26, 1992, at the Castro Theater as part of the 16th Annual Gay and Lesbian Film Festival. The "hero" in the film is a homosexual fascist and pornographer, and the film combines themes of pederasty and Nazi glorification. (Ibid., p. 146)

A description by Susan Leigh Star, a Jewish sociologist, is given (Ibid., p.147):

> For years I have lived in the Castro section of San Francisco.... When I walk down the street in my neighborhood, I often see people dressed in black leather, wearing chains and sometimes carrying whips. In the magazine stores there are many sadomasochist publications. Often these include pictures of people wearing replicas of Nazi Germany uniforms. Iron crosses, storm trooper outfits, military boots. And swastikas. Once and a while someone on the street is dressed in full Nazi regalia ... .

(Scenes as described, above, by Ms. Star, were some of the dominant factors in all of the "gay and lesbian" parades and celebrations shown on the video tapes described above, and the kinds of garb described were worn by both men and women.)

Nazi and Fascist type actions of the homosexual organizations, ACT-UP, Queer Nation, and Bigot Busters are detailed. As Eric Pollard, founder of the Washington, D. C., ACT-UP later regretfully admitted in a letter to the Washington Blade, January, 1992, they used "subversive tactics,

drawn largely from the voluminous _Mein Kampf_, which some of us studied as a working model." Pollard recommended a termination of these
tactics. (But my observation is that they have continued right up to the
present.) Within a few months after Larry Kramer founded the first
ACT-UP, in March, 1987, its members gained national attention by invading Catholic churches in New York, screaming obscenities and stomp-
ing on Communion wafers. Catholic churches were targeted in a number
of other places. Newspaper boxes were smashed in Sacramento to "punish an editor for his views." Bigot Busters threatened and harassed people
trying to get up a petition for a law to prohibit "gay rights bills." Petitions were ripped from circulators hands or doused with paint, activists
blockaded petition tables, and several circulators were physically assaulted. Hundreds of false signatures were put on petitions in an effort
to invalidate them. (Ibid., 169-174)

It is unbelievable that this country has allowed the things that have
gone on in "our homosexual capital," San Francisco. The riot when
Governor Pete Wilson vetoed the first "gay rights bill" was described
above. I suppose that he was so intimidated that he signed the next one.
Assaults and criminal attacks were made against churches and church
people, and I have yet to hear or read of one person being prosecuted for
the many felonies committed in these incidents, or even for any serious
misdemeanor.

In 1973 Chuck McIlhenny became pastor of the First Orthodox Presbyterian Church in San Francisco. Since then he has lived there with
his wife, Donna, and they raised three children. The pastor greatly offended the homosexual community by preaching the Bible, on which
his religion was based, including the passages against sodomy. They
opposed the homosexual movement. An organist was hired at the church,
and was removed after he admitted being a practicing homosexual.
McIlhenny and the church were sued over this, but won the lawsuit.
These things enraged the homosexual community, and the persecution
of all of the McIlhennys began, and has never terminated. The details of
the mistreatment allowed by the authorities against these people are
related in the book by Chuck & Donna McIlhenny and Frank York,

When the Wicked Seize a City, Huntington House Publishers, Lafayette, La., 1993. The following is taken from this book.

Homosexuals threw rocks, beer bottles, and beer cans through the church windows on many occasions. They carved swastikas in the church doors and drew them on McIlhenny's house next door. A window in their car was smashed. Homosexuals sprayed graffiti all over the church, house, and sidewalk. Anti-Christian, pro-homosexual leaflets were scattered around the neighborhood calling the McIlhennys Nazis, anti-gay, etc. Demonstrators often came in and disrupted Sunday worship services, vocally and by writing protests in the hymn books. They made death threats against the family. They made phone calls to them at all times of the night and day, screaming obscenities. Sometimes callers described their children by name, where they attended school, and when they got out of school. Homosexuals described the sexually deviant behavior they would practice on the children before killing them. At least three times the death threats became so severe that the McIlhennys flew their children down to Los Angeles to stay with relatives. The threats to kill were not idle threats. (pp. 109-110)

Donna McIlhenny describes the fire on May 31, 1983, which could only have been attempted murder (pp. 110-113):

> It had been a long day at the law firm where I work, and when I got home it seemed that I had a hundred different things to do before going to bed. It was nearly 12:30 a.m. by the time I locked up for the night and headed for bed. The children had already been asleep for hours, and Chuck had gone to bed shortly before me.
>
> As I crawled into bed, I heard what I thought were the garbage cans banging together in the fierce May wind. Experience had taught me to check out any strange noises; however, I was so exhausted that I simply listened for a moment and lay down to sleep. The church and the house are right next door to each other, attached by a small alleyway. Our bedroom was right next to the alleyway. As I lay down, I was looking toward the alleyway windows. I saw something flicker, and before I could even wonder what it was, a huge ball of fire rolled up the alleyway wall and burst through the window into the bedroom, breaking the quarter inch pane of glass.
>
> I yelled at Chuck to get the kids. He was out of bed and down the hall to their rooms in a flash! I heard him barking orders to them, and

in just seconds, they were lined up on the sidewalk in front of the house like three little troopers.

As Chuck got the children, I ran for the phone in the kitchen and called 9-1-1. (I was firmly reprimanded for it by the firemen afterwards—always leave the house first and then find a phone to call.) By the time I hung up the phone smoke had begun to fill the house.

***

The fire trucks arrived within minutes of my call. Some manned the hoses and some began chopping at the church doors with axes. Even though the strong winds were whipping the flames around, the firemen were able to extinguish the blaze before the entire house and church had gone up in flames.

***

...The fireman showed me two charred gasoline cans and told me that this was indeed arson, and the real seriousness of our situation struck me. I was filled with terror. I asked whether this had merely been an attempt to scare us—somehow it was too terrifying for me to comprehend that someone had actually tried to kill us, especially little children! The fireman replied: "The intent was to kill. It's as if someone pointed a gun in your face and pulled the trigger . . . only, in this case, the gun misfired!"

***

We packed a few things for ourselves and the kids and went to Scott and Joy's for the night.

It was several weeks before they could go home. After staying with friends they stayed in several motels. Mrs. McIlhenny describes the first one (p. 114):

Although the motel we had chosen was supposed to be in a "good part of town," it was a disaster! ...the worst thing was the view we had. ...Directly across the parking lot was a house with the shades open and the lights on. There were two men in front of the window engaged in exactly that activity for which this city has become so well known. We closed the curtains and told the kids not to look our the window.

The threats, the attacks, and the disruptions in their church continued. This was particularly true after Rev. McIlhenny worked on a petition to put a domestic partners ordinance passed by the city to a vote of the people. He was sued by some lesbians over this. On March 22, 1990, their house and the church was again violently attacked. Graffiti was sprayed on them. Windows were broken out, and vandals beat on the door with hammers or tools of some kind. When the police finally arrived, four or five people were still there and ran from the scene, leaving behind several spray paint cans. (pp. 128-172)

Chapter 5 of the book (pp. 80-93) gives an account of how the homosexuals had gained influence and control in San Francisco.

Mrs. McIlhenny states (p. 112):

> To date, as of the writing of this book, nothing has been turned up by the police and fire department investigations as to who may have set the fire. No leads, no clues, and no person has ever been questioned!

The following is from an article, "Gay Activists Threaten to Torch Church," *Lambda Report*, November 1993:

> Last month's LR reported on the riot/protest by militant gays who took over the grounds of the Hamilton Square Baptist Church in San Francisco September 19. About 75-100 activists protested a speaking appearance at the church by Rev. Lou Sheldon, who heads Traditional Values Coalition, a leading group opposing the homosexual political agenda.
>
> ... homosexuals pounded on the emergency side doors of the church to get in as the evening worship service began. The noise inside the church was so loud that children began crying and an elderly blind woman thought someone was firing a gun.
>
> Thanks in part to the prodding of Hamilton Square pastor David Innis, police are preparing to charge "three or four" of the ringleaders of the church protest the *San Francisco Chronicle* reported October 28.
>
> Police Inspector Robert O'Sullivan called the riotous scene "the worst church protest in [San Francisco] since 1983, when arsonists burned the First Orthodox Presbyterian Church where a conservative minister had preached against homosexuality," the *Chronicle* reported.

That minister was Pastor Charles McIlhenny, who with his wife Donna had to push through the angry crowd to get into the Hamilton Square service September 19. ...Suffice it to say McIlhenny appreciates like no other the severity of the following phone threat received by Hamilton Square October 13:

> ...We understand you're going to try to sue the Sentinel [the gay newspaper that ran an ad urging readers to protest at the church]. Ha, ha, ha, ha, ha, ha! Well, let me tell you something my little devil worshiper. You think that last demonstration was unpleasant? What do you think will happen if you try this? Can you imagine jars filled with gasoline coming through your glass windows? ...

The Lambda article says that video and audio tapes were made of the September 19 protest. In the prior incidents involving the McIlhennys and their church, gasoline cans and spray paint cans were left behind. As brazen as these perpetrators have been it is hard to believe that there were no fingerprints, clues, or witnesses from which a case could have been made with any serious investigation. But I have not yet heard or read about any prosecution.

Why are these things being allowed to happen in this country? Are we now succumbing to these ghastly homosexual and Nazi ideas and values as did Germany?

Homosexual activists try to convince us that their acts are normal. If these vile and destructive acts have now become normal, then the world is in bad shape, indeed. The worst harm that they do by such false arguments is to themselves. They should be receiving treatment for their sickness of mind, but they first have to accept the truth, which is that it is a sickness of mind. Because they have gained greater public tolerance in the past thirty years, their destructive acts and promiscuity has greatly increased, resulting in unprecedented harm to the public through moral breakdown, and through the spread of AIDS and other sexually transmitted diseases.

The vile and destructive acts of homosexuality should never be accepted, and, on the contrary, should be strongly and legally discouraged. This is the direction that is best for the country; and it is the best one for homosexuals, because it is the path that will encourage them to leave their lifestyle and become decent members of society.

CHAPTER 2

CAUSES OF AND CURES
FOR HOMOSEXUALITY

At this point, I clarify one point of contention: the *Ten-Percent Lie*. For purposes of their agenda, the homosexual activists and their supporters continually and falsely state that 10 percent of the population is homosexual. A well-documented article, "Homosexuality: The 10% Lie," *The Family Report*, Family Research Institute, Inc., (FRI), 1992, covers at least six reputable surveys since 1986. As to one of these surveys, the article states: "In the on-going U. S. Govt. survey of 109,364 adults, less than 3% of men admitted to *either* homosexual sex or IV drug use since 1977." "But not even one well-done study, however, supports the 10% figure." FRI concluded: "Our review of the world's scientific literature concludes that at most 3% and, more likely, less than 2% of adults are currently bi- or homosexual."

Many activist homosexuals alternatively argue that they "were born that way" and then take a completely contrary stance that homosexuality is something that is "good and beautiful" and is therefore a natural choice—and that they are just the same as anyone else. They choose whichever of these opposite arguments that seems to suit their particular purpose at the time. The great preponderance of the evidence supports the argument that homosexuality is something that comes about primarily from environmental and social causes, including younger victims being enticed by older men or women who are homosexuals.

There is no way that anyone could be born to engage in the many vile acts in which homosexuals, both men and women, engage. They are too many and too varied. In addition, no one is forced by nature to engage in any sexual acts, except in cases where rape is involved. They may be born with inclinations, but the acts in which they engage are by choice. Also, although it enrages homosexual activists, the evidence is abundant and clear that heterosexuals have become homosexuals, and homosexuals have become heterosexuals. Therefore, there could be no genetic makeup that forces upon us either one or the other. Then there are those who are considered "bi-sexual" and who engage in both heterosexual and homosexual acts. There is no logic to an idea that someone could be born both ways. Some men are born more effeminate than other men but that does not make the more effeminate a homosexual, because many are not. And some women are born with more masculine traits than others, but that does not mark them as homosexual, because many women who appear to have some masculine traits are not homosexual; but, as with the men, there are lesbians who take the masculine part, and there lesbians who take the more feminine part. There are the "butches" and the "femmes" in both male and female homosexuality.

Although some men may have been born with more effeminate characteristics than other men, all boys who may have been considered as "sissy" do not turn out to be homosexuals. We also learn that the most brutal and militant of the homosexual men appear to be the extreme masculine types. As was shown by the information from *The Pink Swastika*, there was rivalry between the two groups, and many of the "butches" despised the "femmes,"

It is my opinion, from reading many studies on the question, that it has not yet been established whether or not a person may be born with more tendencies toward homosexuality than the average. But I also believe that two things are certain. One is that no one is born with anything that forces the person to engage in anything as vile as homosexual acts. The second is that it is clear that regardless of how the tendencies were acquired, a person can overcome those tendencies, even after becoming a homosexual, and live a decent, fruitful, and enjoyable heterosexual life. Also, there are those who abstain from any sexual activity for a variety of reasons.

It should make little difference to society even if it were proved that some people are born with homosexual inclinations. The same arguments could be made, and have been made, for child molesters, those who commit incest, rapists, and many other such deviants. There are certain things that are so evil and destructive that they should not be tolerated by society, and homosexual acts are certainly among them.

There have been a spate of news articles over the last several years, since the homosexual movement took hold of the country, on so-called "studies" that purported to show that homosexuality was a biological or genetic condition with which these perverts are born. Many of these studies were conducted by homosexuals. It cannot be determined, from the material I have read, whether or not all who made the studies were homosexual, as most of the news articles do not say. None have withstood the verification and replication of the scientific community necessary for such studies to be considered proof of the premises propounded. They are hardly worth spending our time on, but since the public is continually exposed to these things, most of which amount to little more than propaganda, a few will be referred to. We should also keep in mind that there is no way that a person could be born to engage in any one of the disgusting acts, on which statistics were given in Chapter 1, let alone all of them. It has been established that some people, at some time in their lives, have had a sexual attraction for those of the same sex. We will see that the evidence greatly preponderates toward this being an acquired condition, and not something with which a person is born. It is also established, beyond any reasonable doubt, that those who are sufficiently motivated, through religion or otherwise, can change this unhealthy and destructive orientation. By destructive, I mean physically as well as mentally. But as we have seen from the material, above, the most terrible destruction is emotional or mental. And accepting such a condition as normal or good only aids in destroying any moral soul that such a person may have left. This is the primary reason why the homosexual movement and the homosexual agenda is so detrimental to homosexuals, themselves, as well as to society.

Another thing that we should keep in mind is that anything that is written by a homosexual should be considered suspect. I consider it clear that, as a class, they have no regard for the truth, and, often, do not seem to have the ability to recognize truth. It seems to be inherent in the sickness of mind that accompanies homosexuality. Perhaps it is how they are able to live with themselves. This factor will be further discussed later in this book.

The Albuquerque Tribune, 3-12-93, "Genes linked to lesbianism in women, study says": This was a study by J. Michael Bailey, who also conducted the study referred to below. The study, appearing in the March issue of the Archives of General Psychiatry, examined seventy-one sets of identical female twins, thirty-seven sets of fraternal twins and thirty-six sets of adoptive sisters. The study found that 48 percent of the identical twins who said they were homosexual or bisexual had twins who also were lesbian, as did 16 percent of the fraternal twins and 6 percent of the adoptive sisters. The first thing statistically wrong with this study, as well as all other such studies listed herein, is that there is no evidence that they were done by random sampling, rather than advertising for subjects. Why would an ordinary decent citizen want to participate in such a study? No information has been given to show the effect or degree of similarity of identical twins and the other twins, nor the nature and length of the environmental influences. Bailey states: "Our research shows that environment clearly matters in at least some cases." Even so, he said: "I would say that this is very strong evidence in favor of the argument that heredity plays a role in determining sexual orientation."

The Albuquerque Tribune, 3-25-93, "Lesbianism runs in family, study finds": A study by J. Michael Bailey, an associate professor of psychology at Northwestern University, and a colleague, Deana S. Bernishay, of ninety-nine sisters of lesbians and eighty-three sisters of heterosexuals showed that 12.1 percent of the former and 2.4 percent of the latter were lesbian or bisexual. The article itself establishes its inapplicability to the issues at hand by the statement: "But its unclear whether it's heredity or environment at work."

The Albuquerque Tribune, 7-16-93, "Study tentatively points to gay gene": Dr. Dean Hamer, a National Cancer Institute molecular biologist headed a study. The study found a "similar stretch of DNA in a region of the chromosome known as Xq28" of thirty-three of forty pair of gay brothers studied. They had turned their attention to the X-chromsome because it is the only one that men inherit from their mothers, and a previous analysis of the family histories of seventy-six gay men revealed a tendency for a significant subset of relatives on their mothers' side to be gay, and moreover, they had fourteen gay brothers. As to these gay brothers of the seventy-six gays, the "scientists suggest" that this is "more than six times higher than appears in the general population." "The failure of the study to find such a similarity in nearly 20 percent of the men studied shows 'that you cannot just look at the DNA and predict who will or will not be gay,' Hamer said." If this is an accurate account of the extent of the studies, there are other inherent statistical errors. As to the family history study, the results could be environmental as well as inherited. As to the DNA studies, these were not controlled studies. Studies should have been made of forty pairs of heterosexual brothers chosen by random process, and comparisons made.

On the *MacNeil-Lehrer Newshour*, Public Television, 1-4-94, a part of the program was by someone from Discover Magazine on the search for genes that cause various kinds of behavior, including violence and homosexuality. The gist of the information was that none had been found or proved, and that people have a lot of control over their behavior.

Concerned Women for America, *The Homosexual Deception: Making Sin a Civil Right, pp. 29-30:*

> Recently a "study" has surfaced correlating the supposedly common homosexual behavior of fraternal twins as "proof" of a possible genetic origin for homosexuality. But significantly, the "study" (by Bailey and Pillard [a homosexual]) fails to compare twins raised in separate environments. Only studies of twins raised separately in a very different environment might even conceivable be true indicators of physiological origins of homosexuality. Anne Fausto Stirling, a developmental biologist at Brown University has said, after analyzing Bailey's and Pillard's study: "In order for such a study to be at all meaningful, you'd have to look at twins raised apart. It's such badly interpreted genetics" (*Newsweek*, Feb. 24, 1992, p. 48).
>
> Simon LeVay's study of the hypothalamus in the brains of 19 homosexual male corpses (all of whom died of AIDS complications) noted a difference in size compared with that of a group comprising 16 presumably heterosexual male and six female corpses. Dr. Paul Cameron has commented:

> If ... all homosexual brains contained smaller INAH3s [a
> neuron group], then we might have an interesting hypothesis
> to work with. But that's not the case. First LeVay couldn't
> verify the sexual orientation of his non-homosexual subjects—
> a fact that seriously limits the meaning of general differences
> in his study.
>
> Second, 3 out of 19 homosexuals had a larger INAH3
> than the mean size for "heterosexuals" (the 2nd largest INAH3
> belonged to a homosexual) and 3 out of 16 "heterosexuals"
> had a smaller INAH3 than the mean size of homosexuals...
>
> According to [LeVay's] theory, 3 of the "heterosexuals"
> "should" have been homosexual, and 3 of the homosexuals
> "should" have been heterosexual. When you completely
> misclassify 6 of 35, you don't have much of a theory.

***

LeVay himself has admitted that, even if his findings were totally
consistent, they would not distinguish whether the observed difference in brain size was a probable cause of homosexual orientation, or
an effect of AIDS infection or the homosexual lifestyle itself.

The Albuquerque Tribune, 2-15-95, "Scientists study 'gay gene' possibility": Sandra Witelson, a researcher at McMaster University, Ontario,
Canada, says that her studies have indicated that the brains of homosexual men have features that resemble female brains. She says that
more homosexuals tend to favor using their left hands than heterosexuals, and that homosexuals tend to score differently on perception tests
than heterosexuals. Roger Gorski, a geneticist with the School of Medicine at the University of California, Los Angeles, says his research indicates that all humans begin development with a "female" brain, but that
most males have changes produced by testes. Improper development,
he claims, can result in either female or male homosexuality. No details
or other information that would have any weight in validating these
studies were given in the article.

An article, "Is there a 'gay gene'?," U.S. News and World Report,
November 13, 1995, p. 94, notes:

> Now, everyone is waiting for Hamer's findings to be replicated by
> others, and studies are being planned. Hamer's work "is well done,"

says... Michael Bailey (referred to above), who has studied gay siblings, "[But] I wouldn't say the finding is definitive." Some scientists accuse Hamer of choosing his study subjects so selectively that he found something that isn't really there. And Hamer is under investigation by the federal Office of Research Integrity for allegedly skewing his 1993 data.

"Nature Plus Nurture," *Newsweek,* November 13, 1995, p, 72:

> None of the studies on gay brains, gay genes or transsexual brains has been replicated by other labs. One of Hamer's ex-collaborators even accused him of selecting only data that support his hypothesis; ... .

As previously stated, even if a person is born with an inclination or an orientation for this perverse conduct, it still should not be condoned by society. It is also proved that homosexuals can become heterosexuals. Nevertheless, the news media have made a big thing (out of nothing) with these various studies designed to convince people that homosexuality is biological. This proposition is refuted by so many articles that it certainly is counter-productive to try to cover all of them.

"Natural-born deviates?", *CFV Report,* Colorado for Family Values, Colorado Springs, Co., August 1995:

> Contrary to what you might have heard, a strong majority of serious scientific opinion continues to hold that homosexuality is abnormal, a product of nurture and not nature. One of the most obvious signs of this ... is the existence of the National Association of Psychoanalytic Research and Therapy of Homosexuality, comprised of "... psychoanalysts and psychoanalytically informed individuals who believe that obligatory homosexuality is a treatable disorder...." Because of increasing attempts to censure and even prevent homosexuals from obtaining treatment (tens of thousands have successfully and voluntarily left the lifestyle, through the help of several therapeutic organizations worldwide), it is forced to "combat efforts to declare homosexuality a 'non-condition' and label those who treat it as 'homophobic' and 'unethical.'"
>
> The landmark text, *Homosexual Behavior Among Males,* espouses the prevailing view that sexual behavior is not genetic in origin. ...

(Wainright Churchill, *Homosexual Behavior Among Males* (New York: Hawthorne Books, 1967, p. 101)

***

Dr. Judd Marmor, past president of the American Psychological Association, has written, "No one has ever found a single, replicable genetic, hormonal or chemical difference between heterosexuals and homosexuals." (Dr. Judd Marmor, *Homosexual Behavior: A Modern Reappraisal* [New York: Basic Books, 1982])

[This article then goes on to analyze various more modern studies, and arrives at the same conclusion, that "homosexuality is not a product of genetics." I also consider this conclusion well supported by the presently available data that I have reviewed.]

In *The Gay Agenda*, supra, Dr. Nicolosi states:

> The gay movement today, is very much threatened by the kind of therapy that I do. Because the therapy that I do can demonstrate that people can change. And it is essential to the gay movement that it convinces American society that homosexuality cannot change, that a person is born gay, that there's nothing they can do about it but to accept it. So when you have individuals who can move on to marriage, have a family, then, that threatens the assumption of the gay movement.

Psychotherapy claims about a 30% cure rate, and religious commitment seems to be the most helpful factor in avoiding homosexual habits. (*What Causes Homosexual Desires and Can It Be Changed*, The Family Research Report, Family Research Institute, Inc., 1992) This publication also states that homosexuals were able to change both their habits and their desires as a result of psychotherapy, and that others were prompted to change by a religious or spiritual conversion. It further states:

> ...Whatever the mechanism, in a 1984 study almost 2% of heterosexuals reported that at one time they considered themselves to be homosexual. ...
> Certainly, as noted above many people have turned away from homosexuality – almost as many people as call themselves "gay."

The following is from *Born What Way?*, The Family Research Report, Family Research Institute, Inc., 1993.

"Gay activists regularly claim that they were 'born that way' and thus cannot change their desires or stop their activities. Yet there are numerous documented cases in which homosexuals have changed."

"The Masters-Johnson Institute reported that:

A 25-year-old man had had his first sexual experience when he was 13 years old. It was arranged by his lesbian mother with an older gay man. After the episode, his imagery and interpersonal sexual experience were exclusively homosexual.... The man was motivated to establish a heterosexual life style because he was sincerely distressed by public disapproval of homosexuality and his personal loneliness. [After treatment, he] has been followed for 3 1/2 years. His sexual interaction has been exclusively heterosexual. He has moved out of the gay community and has changed ... his life style. (Schwartz, M. F., and Masters, W. H. The Masters and Johnson treatment program for dissatisfied homosexual men, *Amer. J. Psychiatry*, 1984:141; 173-81)"

(As to the argument that homosexuality is genetic—people cannot change their genetic makeup. This is exactly why homosexual activists do not want to recognize the fact that homosexuals can become heterosexuals.)

"Two prominent 'homosexual' psychiatrists, examining their own lives as well as those of others came to different conclusions in this long-running debate. The first of these, Sigmund Freud, saw his homosexual urges as pathological. Through self-analysis, he overcame them and eventually rejoiced in the 'greater independence that results from having overcome my homosexuality.' (1910 letter to Sandor Forenczi) The second of these, Richard Isay, confronted his desires, pronounced them 'natural,' divorced his wife and joined the gay subculture. (*Wall Street Journal*, 4/21/93, p. A6)"

"In 1992 Isay admitted that the 'conviction among most, though not all, dynamically oriented psychiatrists in general and psychoanalysts in particular [is] that homosexuality can and should be changed to heterosexuality. (Homosexuality and psychiatry, *Psychiatric News*,

Feb. 7, 1992, p. 3) Yet, while acknowledging this consensus among his colleagues, Isay called attempts to change homosexual desire 'the greatest abuse of psychiatry in America today.' Why? Because the 'attempt to change is very harmful.' (*Wall Street Journal*, 4/21/93, supra) Instead, *society* should change to accommodate homosexuality."

Dr. Isay, who chairs the American Psychiatric Association's committee on *Gay, Lesbian, and Bisexual Issues,* argues that homosexuality is biological, and for support cites two 1991 studies: The 'gay brains' research of Simon LeVay, and the "gay twins" study of Bailey & Pillard.

In 1993, Drs. William Byne and Bruce Parsons, researchers at the New York State Psychiatric Institute, critically reviewed "the evidence favoring a biologic theory" presented by LeVay and Bailey & Pillard. They concluded that there is no evidence at present to substantiate a biologic theory. (Human sexual orientation: the biologic theories reappraised, *Archives General Psychiatry*, 1993:50; 228-239)

"Byne & Parsons remembered that from the 1940s through the 1970s it was widely argued and believed in the scientific community that male homosexuals had a deficiency of male hormones. However, only 3 'studies had indicated lower testosterone levels in male homosexuals, while 20 studies found no differences based on sexual orientation, and two reported elevated levels in male homosexuals.' In spite of these studies, textbooks alluded to the supposed 'fact' of hormonal differences for three decades.

"But this 'scientific' belief was false."

" ... LeVay compared human brains with rat brains *but failed to locate the analogous region.* Instead of the 'bullseye' that Isay and the mass media celebrated, it was an embarrassing *miss*!

"Levay's study also had numerous technical problems. For instance, his samples included 19 brains of gays who died of AIDS and 16 brains from men whose sexual orientation was unknown. He assumed the 16 were heterosexual, even though 5 had died of AIDS." (Further criticism of the LeVay study was included above from the article, *The Homosexual Deception: Making Sin a Civil Right, pp. 29-30)*

"Bailey & Pillard reported that 52% of identical twins of homosexuals were also homosexual. But after the media finished hyping Bailey & Pillard's results, King & McDonald (King, M. and McDonald, E., Homosexuals who are twins: a study of 46 probands, *Brit. J. Psychiatry*, 1992, 160: 407-409) published a new 'sexual orientations of twins' study, which found concordance rates for homosexuality of 25% in identical twins. That's half of the 52% reported by Bailey & Pillard. Drs. Byne & Parsons noted that large proportions of identical twins in both studies 'who were discordant for homosexuality despite sharing not only their genes but also their prenatal and familial environments... [which] underscores our ignorance of the factors that are involved, and the manner in which they interact, in the emergence of sexual orientations.'"

"That sexual desire and behavior are flexible was demonstrated by the Kinsey Institute in 1970. It reported [Bell, A. P. and Weinberg, M. S., *Homosexualities: A Study of Diversity Among Men and Women*, New York, Simon & Schuster, 1978 and Hammersmith, S. K., *Sexual Preference: Statistical Appendix*, Bloomington, Indiana University Press, 1981] that 81% of 684 gays and 93% of 293 lesbians had changed or shifted either their sexual feelings or behaviors after age 12. 58% of the gays and 77% of the lesbians reported a second shift in orientation; 31% of the gays and 49% of the lesbians reported a third shift; and 13% of the gays and 30% of the lesbians reported even a *fourth* shift in sexual orientations before 'settling' into adult homosexuality."

(Certainly, changes like this could not be either biological or genetic.)

A table of an analysis by a Dr. Christopher Hewitt of various different societies shows that societies that accept homosexuality have more of it and those that disapprove of and punish it have considerably less of it.

"When Kinsey asked 1700 homosexuals in the 1940s how they 'got that way,' only 9% claimed that they were 'born gay.' In 1970, a similar percentage was recorded for 979 gays in San Francisco. But in 1983, after the gay rights movement started to politicize the issue of homosexual origins, 35% of a random sample of 147 gays said that they were 'born that way.'"

"Perhaps those who commit adultery, molest children or practice homosexuality are 'born with' unusual biological influences. But there is no hard evidence of this. In fact, it appears that participation in these activities, like drug abuse or any other chosen behavior, is a combination of will and opportunity. No matter how such desires come about, members of society are rightly expected to control their behavior and not endanger others."

John Smid (**The Gay Agenda**, *The Report*, Video, 1992) states:

> The gay community today appears as though they would like to discount the work of many popular psychologists such as Joseph Nicolosi, Dr. Elizabeth Moberly, and Joe Dallas that are working with people who want to change their homosexual behavior. One of the things we hear commonly is, "Well if you change your homosexuality, then you must not have been gay to begin with." And all I can say to that from my personal experience is that I know what I know from my own life. I know that I was gay.
>
> ***
>
> At one time in my life, when I was in my early twenties, I was stuck in that little-boy stage of hungering for a relationship with other little boys, the same thing all grade school boys go through. But I was stuck as an adult, twenty years old in a grade-school mind. And I saw that that immaturity of growth is preventing me from seeing marriage as being valuable, prevented me from seeing women as being valuable, in terms of my relationship to them. I saw women as buddies, as friends, as though I was amongst them, as though I was like them, but I knew my body did not line up with that. And in the process of coming out of this, I began to see the difference between men and women, and I began to see the value in that. And now my wife and I have a relationship that never grows dull, it never grows bland. I will never fully conquer my wife, because the male/female relationship has a dynamic about it that will constantly change and evolve and rotate throughout life.

It certainly would appear that the Olympic diver Greg Louganis presents a case that weighs heavily in favor of acquired rather than inherited homosexuality. The following is information from an article by Peter LaBarbera, **Louganis Said To Typify "Made" Homosexual**, *Lambda Report*, April-June 1995.

> A leading expert in "reparative therapy" for homosexuals says Olympic diver Greg Louganis' new autobiographical book (*Breaking

the Surface) reveals a "classic case" of how a troubled father-son relationship can help cause the son's homosexuality. ***

"The Greg Louganis story is the perfect triatic relationship that psychologists have repeatedly observed in the lives of gay males," said Joseph Nocolosi, a clinical psychologist who has treated over 350 homosexual males. "A distant, detached and critical father, an over involved domineering mother and a sensitive boy."

Louganis' book ... chronicles his distant and at times abusive relationship with his adoptive father, his love hate relationship with a sadomasochist male lover who beat and abused him, and his growing up as a highly sensitive and perfectionist boy. The three-time Olympic gold medalist revealed last year that he has the AIDS virus, after announcing publicly that he was gay.

... Louganis writes repeatedly that he was "starved" for affection, leading him to continue his early homosexual relationships. Describing an affair he had at age 16 with a man 20 years his senior, he writes, "I kept going back for the affection, the holding, the cuddling—more those than the sex. I was starved for affection . . . ."

"The only difference between Greg Louganis and all the other guys I've seen [in therapy] is that they don't dive as well," said Nocolosi, Director of the National Association for Research and Therapy of Homosexuality (NARTH), based in Encino, California. ***

... Nicolosi said the character traits exhibited by Louganis offer an uncanny model for the gay men who've come to him for help. He cited the diver's perfectionism, the same trait he said drives so many homosexual men to rigorous body-building, tanning, and other self-improvement efforts. ***

He said some of his clients have sent Louganis copies of his book on "reparative therapy" because the similarity between his troubled childhood and theirs is so great. ***

Chris Camp, a homosexual counselor, criticized Nicolosi's ideas about Louganis, saying it is a "bad scientific method" to generalize from the troubled life of one man. Camp, a graduate of an evangelical seminary, said that he had spent seven years trying to resist his homosexuality. He said that there are many gay men like himself who did not experience a tortured childhood. The article does not state how Camp thinks that he and others like him became homosexuals. Certainly there may be many ways by which a person may become a homosexual, other than by genetic heredity.

Also, Camp's implication that Nicolosi was generalizing "from the troubled life of one man" is incorrect. He was comparing the Louganis case with many other similar cases in his experience.

Submitted with the article were a number of statements from Louganis' book showing the lingering disturbance in his life, because he felt his father did not love him, show affection to him, and take an interest in him and what he was doing. He states how he envied another man's sons, because "he was the kind of father I wanted."

> I consider significant Louganis' statement that he kept going back to the older man and submitting to sex because "I was starved for affection, and he was happy to give it to me." Also, what may be a further insight into homosexuality generally: "I know that plenty of gay men and lesbians can tell stories about having had similar experiences with older men and women when they were teenagers. Most will tell you that they were willing to participate . . . ."

It is interesting to consider the information about Greg Louganis in connection with the research paper, What Causes Homosexual Desire and Can It Be Changed?, Family Research Institute, 1992. The following is from that pamphlet. (The many footnotes and references are omitted.)

> Most of us fail to understand why anyone would want to engage in homosexual activity. To the average person, the very idea is either puzzling or repugnant. Indeed, a recent survey indicated that only 14% of men and 10% of women imagined that such behavior could hold any "possibility of enjoyment."
>
> ... What does the best research really indicate? Are homosexual proclivities natural or irresistible?
>
> At least three answers seem possible. The first, the answer of tradition, is as follows: homosexual behavior is a bad habit that people fall into because they are sexually permissive and experimental. This view holds that homosexuals choose their lifestyle as the result of

self-indulgence and an unwillingness to play by society's rules. The second position is held by a number of psychoanalysts (e.g., Bieber, Socarides). According to them, homosexual behavior is a mental illness, symptomatic of arrested development. They believe that homosexuals have unnatural or perverse desires as a consequence of poor familial relations in childhood or some other trauma. The third view is "biological" and holds that such desires are genetic or hormonal in origin, and that there is no "choice" involved and no "childhood trauma" necessary.

Which of these views is most consistent with the facts? Which tells us the most about homosexual behavior and its origins? The answer seems to be that homosexual behavior is learned. The following seven lines of evidence support such a conclusion.

1) No researcher has found provable biological or genetic differences between heterosexuals and homosexuals that weren't caused by their behavior.

Occasionally you may read about a scientific study that suggests that homosexuality is an inherited tendency, but such studies have usually been discounted after careful scrutiny or attempts at replication. No one has found a single heredible genetic, hormonal or physical difference between heterosexuals and homosexuals—at least none that is replicable. While the absence of such a discovery doesn't prove that inherited sexual tendencies aren't possible, it suggests that 'none has been found because none exists.'

2) People tend to believe that their sexual desires and behaviors are learned.

Two large studies asked homosexual respondents to explain the origins of their desires and behaviors—how they "got that way." The first of these studies was conducted by Kinsey in the 1940s and involved 1700 homosexuals. The second in 1970 (AP Bell Homosexualities: their range and character, *Nebraska Symposium on Motivation* 1973 JK Cole & R Dientsbier (eds) U Nebraska Press), involved 979 homosexuals. Both were conducted prior to the period when the "gay rights" movement started to politicize the issue of homosexual origins. Both reported essentially the same findings. Homosexuals overwhelmingly believed their feelings and behavior were the result of social and environmental influences. [The accompanying table for the 1940s and 1970 studies showed that only 9 percent of the combined groups believed that they were "born that way."]

In a 1983 study conducted by the Family Research Institute (FRI) involving a random sample of 147 homosexuals, 35% said their sexual desires were hereditary. Interestingly, almost 80% of the 3,400 heterosexuals in the same study said that their preferences and behavior were learned ....

While those results aren't conclusive, they tell us something about the very recent tendency to believe that homosexual behavior is inherited or biological. From the 1930s (when Kinsey started collecting data) to the early 1970s, before a politically correct answer emerged, only about 10% of homosexuals claimed they were "born that way." Heterosexuals apparently continue to believe that their behavior is primarily the result of social conditioning.

3) Older homosexuals often approach the young

There is evidence that homosexuality, like drug use, is "handed down" from older individuals. The first homosexual encounter is usually initiated by an older person. In separate studies 60%, 64%, and 61% of the respondents claimed that their first partner was someone older who initiated the sexual experience.

How this happens is suggested by a nationwide random study from Britain: 35% of boys and 9% of girls said they were approached for sex by adult homosexuals. Whether for attention, curiosity, or by force, 2% of the boys and 1% of the girls succumbed. In the US, 37% of males and 9% of females reported having been approached for homosexual sex (65% of those doing the inviting were older). Likewise, a study of over 400 London teenagers reported that "for the boys, their first homosexual experience was very likely with someone older: half the boys' first partners were 20 or older; for girls it was 43%. A quarter of homosexuals have admitted to sex with children and underaged teens, suggesting that homosexuality is introduced to youngster the same way other behaviors are learned—by experience.

4) Early homosexual experiences influence adult patterns of behavior

In the 1980s, scholars examined the early Kinsey data to determine whether or not childhood sexual experiences predicted adult behavior. The results were significant: Homosexual experience in the early years—particularly if it was one's first sexual experience—was a strong predictor of adult homosexual behavior, both for males and females. A similar pattern appeared in the 1970 Kinsey Institute study: there was a strong relationship between those whose first experience was homosexual and those who practiced homosexuality in later life. In the FRI study two-thirds of the boys whose first experience was homosexual engaged in homosexual behavior as adults; 95% of those whose first experience was heterosexual were likewise heterosexual in their adult behavior. A similar progressive pattern of sexual behavior was reported for females.

It is remarkable that the three largest empirical studies of the question showed essentially the same pattern. A child's first sexual experiences were strongly associated with his or her adult behavior.

5) Sexual conduct is influenced by cultural factors—especially religious convictions

Kinsey reported "less homosexual activity among devout groups whether they be Protestant, Catholic, or Jewish, and more homosexual activity among religiously less active groups. The 1983 FRI study found those raised in irreligious homes to be over 4 times more likely to become homosexual than those from devout homes. These studies suggest that when people believe strongly that homosexual behavior is immoral, they are significantly less apt to be involved in such activity.

Recently, because of the AIDS epidemic, it has been discovered that, relative to white males, twice as many black males are homosexual (Chu S *et al* Aids in Bisexual Men in US *Amer J Public Hlth* 1992, 82: 220-224) and 4 times as many are bisexual. Perhaps it is related to the fact that 62% of black versus 17% of white children are being raised in fatherless homes. But even the worst racist wouldn't suggest that it is due to genetic predisposition.

Were homosexual impulses truly inherited, we should be unable to find differences in homosexual practice due to religious upbringing or racial sub-culture.

6) Many change their sexual preference

In a large random sample, 88% of women currently claiming lesbian attraction and 73% of men claiming to currently enjoy homosexual sex, said that they had been **sexually aroused** by the opposite sex.

- 85% of these "lesbians" and 54% of these "homosexuals" reported sexual relations with someone of the opposite sex in adulthood,
- 67% of lesbians and 54% of homosexuals reported *current* **sexual attractions** to the opposite sex, and
- 82% of lesbians and 66% of homosexuals reported having been **in love with** a member of the opposite sex.

Homosexuals experiment. They feel some normal impulses. Most have been sexually aroused by, had sexual relations with and even *fallen in love with* someone of the opposite sex.

Nationwide random samples of 904 men were asked about their sex lives since age 2, and more specifically in the last year. As the figure reveals, 1.3% reported sex with men in the past year and 5.2% at some time in adulthood. Less than 1% of men had *only* had sex with men during their lives. And 6 of every 7 who had sex with men, also reported sex with women.

It's a much different story with inherited characteristics. Race and gender are not optional lifestyles. They remain immutable. The switching and experimentation demonstrated in these two studies identifies homosexuality as a *preference*, not an inevitability.

7) There are many ex-homosexuals

Many engage in one or two homosexual experiences and never do it again – a pattern reported for a third of the males with homosexual experience in one study. And then there are ex-homosexuals – those who have continued in homosexual liaisons for a number of years and then chose to change not only their habits, but also the objects of their desire. Sometimes this alteration occurs as the result of psychotherapy, and in others it is prompted by a religious or spiritual conversion. Similar to the kinds of "cures" achieved by drug addicts and alcoholics, these treatments do not always remove homosexual desire or temptation. Whatever the mechanism, in a 1984 study almost 2% of heterosexuals reported that at one time they considered themselves to be homosexual. It is clear that a substantial number of people are reconsidering their sexual preferences at any given time.

What causes homosexual desire?

If homosexual impulses are not inherited, what kinds of influences do cause strong homosexual desires? No one answer is acceptable to all researchers in the field. Important factors, however, seem to fall into four categories. As with so many other odd sexual proclivities, males appear especially susceptible:

— Homosexual experience:

• any homosexual experience in childhood, especially if it is a first sexual experience or with an adult

• any homosexual contact with an adult, particularly with a relative or authority figure (in a random survey, 5% of adult homosexuals vs 0.8% of heterosexuals reported childhood sexual involvement with elementary or secondary school teachers).

— **Family abnormality, including the following:**
- a dominant, possessive, or rejecting mother
- an absent, distant, or rejecting father
- a parent with homosexual proclivities, particularly one who molests a child of the same sex
- a sibling with homosexual tendencies, particularly one who molests a brother or sister
- the lack of a religious home environment
- divorce, which often leads to sexual problems for both the children and the adults
- parents who model unconventional sex roles
- condoning homosexuality as a legitimate lifestyle – welcoming homosexuals (e.g., co-workers, friends) into the family circle

— **Unusual sexual experience, particularly in early childhood:**
- precocious or excessive masturbation
- exposure to pornography in childhood
- depersonalized sex (e.g., group sex, sex with animals)
- for girls, sexual interaction with adult males

— **Cultural influences:**
- a visible and socially approved homosexual sub-culture that invites curiosity and encourages exploration
- pro-homosexual sex education
- openly homosexual authority figures, such as teachers (4% of Kinsey's and 4% of FRI's gays reported that their first homosexual experience was with a teacher)
- societal and legal tolerance of homosexual acts
- depictions of homosexuality as normal and/or desirable behavior

Can homosexuality be changed?

Certainly. As noted above, many people have turned away from homosexuality – almost as many people as call themselves "gay."

Clearly the easier problem to eliminate is homosexual behavior. Just as many heterosexuals control their desires to engage in premarital or extramarital sex, so some with homosexual desires discipline themselves to abstain from homosexual contact.

One thing seems to stand out: Associations are all important. Anyone who wants to abstain from homosexual behavior should avoid the company of practicing homosexuals. There are organizations, including "ex-gay ministries," designed to help those who wish to reform their conduct. Psychotherapy claims about a 30% cure rate, and religious commitment seems to be the most helpful factor in avoiding homosexual habits.

An article, "Once Gay Always Gay?", *The Edge*, May 1994, Christian Broadcasting Academy, Albuquerque, N.M., is about an ex-lesbian, Jami Breedlove, and an ex-homosexual, David Davis. Mrs. Breedlove had been a lesbian for twelve years. She left that lifestyle and is now happily married with two children. She attributes her change to religion and love of her husband. Mr. Davis was a homosexual for four and a half years. He is now happily married for thirteen years, with five children. He attributes his change to the spiritual help he received.

Lambda Report, Washington, D. C., Dec.-Jan. 1993-4, has an article about John Paulk, the ex-homosexual referred to in "The Gay Agenda," supra, and his wife, Anne, an ex-lesbian. At the time of the article they were approaching their second wedding anniversary. Both were helped out of their lifestyle by their Christian faith.

"A Way Out," *Christian American,* Christian Coalition, July/August, 1996, Chesapeake, Va., is an article about an ex-homosexual, Jim Johnson, and an ex-lesbian, Jane Boyer, who left their lifestyles with spiritual help.

"No Longer Gay," *The Albuquerque Journal,* April 21, 1994, is an article about an ex-lesbian, Barbara Swallow, and an ex-homosexual, Mark Canavan, who both left their lifestyles with the help of faith and Christian counseling. I have worked with these two against the homosexual movement, and "gay rights" bills in New Mexico, and have been acquainted with them for several years. There is no doubt in my mind that these two have certainly changed.

"A Gift Beyond Measure," SPHA Bulletin, March/April, 1996, Honolulu, Hawaii, is an article about Bob Winter who left his homosexual lifestyle and served as a director of AIDS Services at Love in Action, an ex-gay ministry based in Memphis, Tennessee, before he died of AIDS in December, 1989. He said before his death:

> I have made such a mess of my life by following my own stubborn will. Now I want God's will, even if that means dying. Through all He's done in my life, God has shown me how much He loves me. I know that whatever He has for me, that's the best possible plan. And the assurance I have His love is a gift beyond price He's given me.

There will continually be new studies that purport to establish that homosexuality is genetic or hereditary—particularly as long as the homosexual movement is being pressed on the country. They should be approached with skepticism. It should be determined if the studies were by homosexualists. Any other inherent biases should be determined.

HOMOSEXUALITY—WHETHER OR NOT IT SHOULD BE TREATED

The most serious damage that the homosexual movement has done, both to homosexuals and to our society, is the promotion of the idea that homosexuality should be considered as normal, and therefore should not be professionally treated.

Later in this book we go in detail into the propensity of homosexual activists to make false statements, to teach us the exact opposite of the truth, and the apparent inability to even recognize the truth.

They vigorously attack as false anything that is said against their agenda, they personally attack those who oppose their agenda, and they have a special hate for people like Dr. Paul Cameron, Dr. Joseph Nicolosi, and many others who believe in treating homosexuals for their deviancy. They also have a very special wrath for the many who have overcome their homosexuality, and then work against the homosexual agenda or go public with the fact that they have overcome their homosexuality.

They even call unethical any professional who treats homosexuals trying to overcome their homosexuality, or who advocate such treatment.

They are trying to get the American Psychiatric Association and the American Psychological Association to declare such treatment or advocacy as unethical. And with the direction these associations are going they may indeed declare such treatment and advocacy as unethical.

Continual attacks, many of which have little or no basis in fact, are made on Dr. Cameron and others, in public, in publications, including professional publications, and even in court.

Examples will be given on two specific attacks on Cameron which are typical.

In *The New Republic*, October 3, 1994, in an article, "Queer Science," p.10, Mark E. Pietrzyk, makes a vicious attack on Dr. Cameron. Pietrzyk at the time was a research analyst for Log Cabin Republicans, a homosexual organization. The substance of his attack was:

> *** During the 1980s he [Dr. Paul Cameron] published hysterical pamphlets alleging that gays were disproportionately responsible for serial killing, child molestations and other heinous crimes.
>
> Shortly after Cameron made these claims, several psychologists whose work he had referenced – including Dr. A. Nicholas Groth, director of the Sex Offender Program at the Connecticut Department of Corrections – charged Cameron with distorting their findings in order to promote his anti-gay agenda. When the American Psychological Association (APA) investigated Cameron, it found that he not only misrepresented the work of others but also used unsound methods in his own studies. For this ethical breach, the APA expelled Cameron in December 1983. (Although Cameron claims he resigned, APA bylaws prohibit members from resigning while under investigation.) ***
>
> (Pietrzyk also claimed that Cameron's studies on life expectancy of homosexuals was flawed.)

I consider the above accusations to be unsupported and a typical homosexualist attack on those who fight their agenda.

This book is replete with studies, news articles, and information from many sources other than Cameron, that indeed corroborate "that gays were disproportionately responsible for serial killings, child molestations and other heinous crimes." I think that there is no doubt whatsoever about this statement. And, as usual, it is claimed by the homosexualists that figures are "distorted," but they never say exactly how—and they never refer to reputable studies that might give what they consider the correct figures. This approach is what truly is the unprofessional practice. But it is one that I find used over and over by homosexualists.

Furthermore, I researched publications of the American Psychological Association, and found nothing that would corroborate that it had held any hearing, made any findings, or took any formal action that corroborated the claim that Cameron had been expelled for cause. And I think it is clear that he did not even attend any hearing. He had been at odds with the Association ever since it officially began considering reprehensible homosexual deviancy as "normal."

In a letter published in response to the claims of Pietrzyk, *The New Republic*, 10-31-94, p.8, Dr. Cameron stated:

> ... Mark Pietrzyk accuses me of inaccuracies. As it happens, there are a number of inaccuracies in his article.
>
> (1) I was an associate professor in human development and the family, and not an "instructor of psychology," at the University of Nebraska.
>
> (2) I was not expelled from the American Psychological Association for misrepresenting the work of others and using unsound methods in my studies. In fact, I resigned from the American Psychological Association in November 1982. It was only later, in December 1983, that the organization "dropped" me from membership.
>
> (3) I have never proposed "extermination of homosexuals."
>
> (4) Twelve percent of heterosexual men in our random sample said that they had "attempted to kill, engaged in activities designed to kill or deliberately killed another human being" not as Pietrzyk reported, "have either committed or attempted to commit murder." Since about one-third of American men have served in the Armed Forces, our finding is not unreasonable.
>
> (5) Our study of lifespan of homosexuals includes not only obituaries but a review of the last 140 years of published material.
>
> Though Pietrzyk found professionals who disagree with me he failed to specify and correct a singe inaccuracy. Pietrzyk broadcasts that I am a "professional sham." Yet I have published more than fifty articles in referred scientific journals, my research is cited in

contemporary textbooks and I have been paid for my expertise by federal and state governments.

Scientists besides myself have noted the addiction to falsehood and deception that is characteristic of homosexuals. Why didn't *The New Republic* reveal that your author is a member of a gay rights group? As a licensed psychologist since 1981, I could have been called by the Board of Examiners to account for any of the above, but I haven't on any issue. What may be proof to TNR isn't even worth an investigation to a state board.

I have written letters to the City of Albuquerque opposing ordinances providing for "hate crimes" and benefits for homosexuals, when Martin Chavez was mayor. For years Chavez has supported the homosexual agenda, and when he was a New Mexico senator, he supported the "homosexual rights" bills. He was a typical liberal Democrat. I had submitted with the letter some statistics on homosexual acts from a book of Dr. Cameron. He came back with the familiar homosexualist line that Dr. Cameron had been discredited. He said that a federal judge had "discredited" Cameron in the case of *Baker v. Wade*, 553 F.Supp. 1121 (N.D. Texas 1985). Although Chavez was an attorney, and knew better, he failed to say that the case had been reversed. I consider the only one who was discredited to be the liberal federal judge who was trying to pull off some judicial legislation. The decision was supplemented by a written opinion, in the same case, *Baker v. Wade*, 106 F.R.D. 526 (N.D. Texas July 1985). The judge ruled that a Texas statute making sodomy a crime violated the constitutional right to privacy and due process clauses of the United States Constitution. The opinion contained phrases clearly showing his liberal bias and the following of the homosexual propaganda, such as: "although 'homophobia'—an exaggerated fear of homosexuals—may exist among many heterosexuals, there is no rational basis for it." It is hard to imagine a federal judge in Texas making such an asinine remark. Texas probably had laws against sodomy ever since it was a state, as did most of, if not all of the states. The United States Court of Appeals for the Fifth Circuit promptly reversed the case. in *Baker v. Wade*, 769 F.2d 289 (5th Cir. Oct. 1985). The Fifth Circuit noted that a Virginia sodomy statute, similar to the Texas statute, was upheld by a three judge district court, and summarily affirmed by the

United States Supreme Court in *Doe v. Commonwealth's Attorney*, 425 U.S. 901 (1976). The Dallas judge had to know he was going against established law, and there is no excuse for this attempted usurpation of legislative authority of the states. I consider the act against the judge's oath of office and dishonest. He accused Dr. Cameron of fraud and misrepresentation because he distorted data of Kinsey, of all people, and concluded that homosexuals were forty-three times more likely to commit crimes than the general population. It is clear that all he had to go on was testimony of other experts. My guess is that the judge misconstrued Dr. Cameron's statistics, much of which I have studied. But there is no question that homosexuals are more apt to commit crimes other than sodomy than the general population. And many of them continually commit crimes as sodomy is a crime even now in many states. In reversing Baker v. Wade, and upholding the Texas sodomy statute, the Fifth Circuit noted the "strong objection to homosexual conduct which has prevailed in Western culture of the past seven centuries." It also cited the United States Supreme Court in *Berman v. Parker*, 348 U.S. 26, for the principle that "implementing morality" is "a permissible state goal." As explained in Chapter 3, in 1986, in *Bowers v. Hardwick*, infra, the United States Supreme Court upheld a Georgia sodomy statute which made sodomy a criminal offense, punishable by up to 20 years in prison.

Homosexuals have now made a farce of the two APAs. The American Psychiatric Association first capitulated to the homosexual movement, and then the American Psychological Association followed suit.

The most comprehensive writing I have found on the capitulation of the American Psychiatric Association to the homosexualists is a 216 page book by Ronald Bayer, **HOMOSEXUALITY AND AMERICAN PSYCHIA-TRY – The Politics o***f Diagnosis*, Basic Books, Inc., New York 1981. (The following contains comments on and excerpts from that book. Generally, footnotes and references, of which there are many, are omitted.)

It appears that Dr. Bayer was sympathetic to the homosexual movement, but he nevertheless seems to have presented his factual material accurately, and gave the pros as well as the cons.

As to the reason he wrote the book, Bayer states in the Acknowledgments:

> The idea of doing this book emerged during a postdoctoral year spent at the Hastings Center. Aware of my interest in the relationship between psychiatry and society, Willard Gaylin, the Center's president, suggested that I might find it rewarding to study the 1973 dispute over homosexuality within the American Psychiatric Association. He was right. ***

From the book:

> Under attack from many quarters and torn by internal disputes regarding its appropriate mission, psychiatry was especially vulnerable to the challenge of an increasingly militant Gay Liberation movement. Though symbolically powerful, psychiatry was in fact a target that could be attacked with relative impunity. Thus it was with stunning ease that the Gay Liberation movement was able to force the American Psychiatric Association to reconsider the inclusion of homosexuality in it official nomenclature of disorders, the *Diagnostic and Statistical Manual*. (p. 12) ***
>
> Between 1970 and 1973, in a period of only three years, what had been an article of orthodoxy in psychopathology was reversed. Because the change occurred so rapidly, the factors that are always at play were placed in stark relief, allowing us to observe some features that are often obscure. (p. 13) ***

On pages 49-53, Bayer relates the importance of one study of psychologist Evelyn Hooker to the homosexual agenda. Even though: "Acknowledging that these men were not a random sample, she justified her procedure by arguing that since homosexuality was a largely cover phenomenon, it simply was not possible to study a more representative population." "... she claimed that the 'disturbed' behavioral patterns of homosexuals were 'ego defensive,' traceable to the victimization they had experienced ... ." (p. 52)

(The book then goes on to explain how Hooker became the darling and the heroine of the homosexual movement, even though she had published one very short paper on a small amount of research on a small selected population that was not random or representative, and which she was " 'pressed' ... to put into print despite her own belief that the analysis was still preliminary." They were indeed desperate for something to support them.)

> The appearance of Hooker's work in the mid-1950s was of critical importance for the evolution of the homophile movement. Her findings provided "facts" that could buttress the position of homosexuals who rejected the pathological view of their condition. ... Her collaborative relationship with the Mattachine Society went beyond using it as a source of informants. She spoke to its members, published in its *Review*, attended its meetings, and received its honors. She became not only a source of ideological support, but an active participant in the homosexual struggle. (p. 53)

The book outlines a number of professional criticisms of the study and conclusions of Hooker and several others who seemed to be leaning toward the idea that homosexuality was normal. One was by Irving Beiber et al, *Homosexuality*, (New York: Basic Books, 1962), pp. 304-6.

> ... Finally, with reference to Evelyn Hooker, Bieber argued that the only plausible explanation for the discrepancy between her findings and his was that "the tests themselves or the current methods of interpretation and evaluation are inadequate to the task of discriminating between homosexuals and heterosexuals." *** (P. 66)

Dr. Bayer then goes into the nature of the attack on the APA.

> Far more significant, however, was a shift in the role of demonstrations from a form of expression to a tactic of disruption. In this regard gay activists mirrored the pattern of confrontation politics that had become the cutting edge of radical and antiwar student groups. The purpose of protest was no longer to make public a point of view, but rather to halt unacceptable activities. With ideology seen as an instrument of domination, the traditional willingness to tolerate the views of one's opponents was discarded. ...
>
> ... gay activists held a sit-in at the offices of the American Broadcasting Company to demand that a Marcus Welby show be withdrawn because it characterized homosexuals as "guilt-ridden mental cases."
>
> No longer content with the mere picketing of professional meetings, homosexuals began to engage in disruptions, "zaps," designed to

put a halt to discussions considered inimical to their interests. In October 1970 the Second Annual Behavior Modification Conference in Los Angeles was the target of such an action. During the showing of a film depicting aversive conditioning techniques to eliminate homosexual behavior, members of the Gay Liberation Front interrupted with cries of "barbarism," "medieval torture," and "This is disgusting." ... One demonstrator announced to the startled and furious audience:

> We are going to reconstitute this session into small groups with equal numbers of Gay Liberation Front members and members of your profession and were are going to talk as you have probably never talked with homosexuals before, as equals. We're going talk about such things as homosexuality as an alternative life style.

This disruption was in fact a replay of one that had occurred in San Francisco six months earlier, when homosexuals created a chaotic situation after their first direct attack on the American Psychiatric Association. That action represented the opening salvo in a battle that was to last three years, and was to bring homosexuals into direct conflict with organized psychiatry over the official classification of homosexuality as a disease. (pp. 98-100) ***

In the wake of the American invasion of Cambodia in May 1970, the killings at Kent State, and the subsequent convulsion of protest that swept the nation, gay groups in alliance with feminists engaged in the first systematic effort to disrupt the annual meetings of the American Psychiatric Association "When we heard that Bieber and company were coming," said one activist, "we knew we had to be there." Guerrilla theater tactics and more straightforward shouting matches characterized their presence. At a panel on transexualism and homosexuality, Irving Bieber experienced his first face-to-face denunciation. Having become accustomed to the written attacks of those who had labeled him Public Enemy Number One, he was still unprepared for the kind of rage that greeted him. His efforts to explain his position to his challengers were met with derisive laughter. Since the norms of civility were considered mere conventions designed to mute outrage, it was not difficult for a protester to call him a "motherfucker." "I've read your book, Dr. Bieber, and if that book talked about black people the way it talks about homosexuals, you'd be drawn and quartered and you'd deserve it." This verbal attack with its violent tone caused Bieber considerable distress.

It was not, however the confrontation with Bieber that provided the most dramatic encounter at the convention, but one that occurred at a panel on "issues of sexuality." In a room filled with several hundred psychiatrists, homosexuals and feminists expressed their strongest outrage during the presentation of a paper by Nathaniel McConaghy, a young Australian psychiatrist, who was discussing the use of aversive conditioning techniques in the treatment of sexual deviation. Shouts of "vicious," "torture," and "Where did you take your residency, Auschwitz?" greeted the speaker. As that paper came to an end, and the chair prepared to announce the next presentation, demonstrators exploded with the demand that they be heard. "We've listened to you, now you listen to us." When urged to be patient, they retorted, "We've waited five thousand years." At that, the meeting was adjourned and pandemonium ensued. As one protester attempted to read a list of gay demands, he was denounced as a "maniac." A feminist ally was called "a paranoid fool" and "a bitch." Some psychiatrists, enraged by the intrusion and the seeming inability of the Association to protect their discussions from chaos, demanded that their air fares to San Francisco be refunded. One physician called for the police to shoot the protesters. While most of those who had assembled for the panel left the room, some did not, staying to hear their profession denounced as an instrument of oppression and torture. (pp. 102–103) ***

... When told that homosexuals wanted to present a panel at the next APA convention, to be held in Washington, D.C., [Kent Robinson] agreed to convey that demand to the Association's leadership. (p. 104)

(Now the cowardice of the APA begins to take over.)

It was against this background of this chaotic challenge to the APA that Robinson approached John Ewing, chair of the Program Committee, warning him that unless the request for a panel was met, there was a grave risk that the entire 1971 meeting would be disrupted. "They're not going to break up just one section.". Noting the coercive terms of the request Ewing quickly agreed, stipulating only that, in accordance with APA convention regulations, a psychiatrist chair the proposed session. (p. 104) ***

... Aware of the organizational weakness of his own Mattachine Society, Frank Kameny turned to a Gay Liberation Front collective in Washington to plan the May 1971 demonstrations. Together with the collective, Kameny developed a detailed strategy for disruption, paying attention to the most intricate logistical details, including the floor plan of the hotel in which the convention was to be housed.

... the APA's leaders decided to avoid, at all costs, any reliance upon a show of force by uniformed guards or police. A less provocative posture, one that entailed a willingness to ride out rather than to prevent demonstrations, was agreed upon.

The planned disruption occurred on May 3, when gay and anti-war activists stormed into the prestigious Convocation of Fellows. During the ensuing uproar, Kameny grabbed a microphone and denounced the right of psychiatrists to discuss the question of homosexuality. Borrowing from the language of the antiwar movement, he declared, "Psychiatry is the enemy incarnate. Psychiatry has waged a relentless war of extermination against us. You may take this as a declaration of war against you." Fist-shaking psychiatrists, infuriated by the invaders, compared their tactics to that of Nazi stormtroopers.

The tone and mood of intimidation produced by this encounter pervaded the convention from that point. Using forged credentials, gay activists gained access to the exhibit area and, coming across a display marketing aversive conditioning techniques for the treatment of homosexuals, demanded its removal. Threats were made against the exhibitor, who was told that unless his booth was dismantled, it would be torn down. After frantic behind-the-scene consultations, and in an effort to avoid violence, the convention leadership agreed to have the booth removed. Robinson, who had been acting as an intermediary between the APA and the homosexuals, was himself taken aback by the intensity of the rage and cautioned Kameny to temper the tactics of his co-demonstrators. His call for moderation was dismissed. Robinson continued to perform the self-described function of "bagman" with the Association's quest for order being held at ransom. (pp. 105-106) ***

The panel set up for the homosexuals was then discussed.

Both the tone and the content of the open discussion that followed the panel suggest that those who opposed the homosexual presence at the convention had either avoided the session or been intimidated into silence. ...

Toward the end of the convention Kameny and Littlejohn informed Robinson that they wanted to present their demands for the deletion of homosexuality from the APA's official nosology, *DSM II*, to members of the Association's Committee on Nomenclature. ...

Reliance upon disruptive tactics and rancorous denunciation was largely absent from the homosexual involvement in the 1972 APA convention held in Dallas. ... Since the Psychiatric Association had accommodated itself to the inevitability of homosexual pressure, those who continued to challenge the designation of homosexuality as a disorder displayed a willingness to meet their opponents on terms less threatening to professional decorum. (pp. 108–109) ***

... The tactical reliance upon disruption and force in earlier years had been vindicated. ... (p. 111) ***

... Interested in avoiding conflict, the leadership chose to sidestep the dispute over homosexuality. Despite their sharply divergent evaluations of the motives of those involved, [Dr. Charles Socarides] stressing venality and [Robert Osnos] timidity, both provided unmistakable evidence of the extraordinary degree to which political factors and fractious spirit had begun to affect psychiatric decision-making on the issue of homosexuality. (p. 114) ***

The author explains the continuation of organized disruptions and intimidation against the association and its meetings.

... Toward the end of 1972 Lawrence Harmann, chair of the Branch's Social Issues Committee, decided to have his group take up the issue of homosexuality. Concerned about both the scientific and civil rights aspects of the problem, he thought it an appropriate moment for the Branch to go on record as favoring the deletion of homosexuality from *DSM II* as well as supporting an aggressive campaign to combat discrimination against gay men and women. *** (p. 122)

(That amounted to the capitulation of professional science to homosexual politics.)

The book then details the papers and the routes through the committees of the proposal to change the diagnosis. On December 15, 1973, the Board of Trustees of the American Psychiatric Association, approved the change in the DSM-II manual:

> ... On a final poll, with a vote of thirteen to zero and two abstentions, the board approved the deletion of homosexuality and its replacement with the classification "sexual orientation disturbance." ***
>
> In addition, the trustees, with only one abstention, approved Spitzer's far-reaching civil rights proposal, placing the American Psychiatric Association on record as opposing both the use of criminal sanction against private consensual homosexual activity and the deeply embedded pattern of social discrimination against gay men and women. *** (pp. 132-137)
>
> On a clinical level, concern was greatest over the implications of the Association's decision for the psychotherapeutic effort to assist adolescents experiencing conflict over their sexual identities. The removal of homosexuality from the list of psychiatric disorders would signal to these confused young men and women that it mattered little whether they chose a homosexual or heterosexual orientation. One psychiatrist wrote to the *Psychiatric News*: "The Board of Trustees has made a terrible, almost unforgivable decision which will adversely affect the lives of young homosexuals who are desperately seeking direction and cure. That . . . decision will give young homosexuals an easy way out and make the job of practitioners like myself much more difficult."
>
> In attempting to explain the decisions of the board and the other APA bodies, dissenting psychiatrists frequently asserted that those who had supported the deletion of homosexuality from *DSM-II* acknowledged privately that such sexual behavior represented a pathological condition, but refused to say so publicly. *** (p. 140)
>
> ... Perhaps the gravest prediction of the costs to psychiatry came from Abraham Kardiner, a senior figure who had pioneered in the effort to merge the insights of psychoanalysis and anthropology. Viewing homosexuality as a symptom of social disintegration, he wrote to the editors of *Psychiatric News*:

> Those who reinforce the disintegrative elements in our society will get no thanks from future generations. The family becomes the ultimate victim of homosexuality, a result which any society can tolerate only within certain limits.

If the American Psychiatric Association endorses one of the symptoms of social distress as a normal phenomenon it demonstrates to the public its ignorance of social dynamics, of the relation of personal maladaption to social disharmony, and thereby acquires a responsibility for aggravating the already existing chaos. (p. 141) ***

The APA then held a vote on the decision of the trustees for the change with 10,091, casting ballots 58% approved, 37% opposed, and 3% abstained.

(The capitulation to the militant homosexuals was now completed.)

The continued widespread opposition by America's psychiatrists to the APA's official position on homosexuality was evident in a survey conducted in 1977 by the journal *Medical Aspects of Human Sexuality.* Though APA's 1974 referendum had made clear the presence of a serious split among its membership, these new finding suggested that the leadership no longer represented the majority position. Analysis of the first 2,500 response to a poll of 10,000 psychiatrists found that 69 percent believed that homosexuality usually represented a pathological adaptation. Only 18 percent disagreed with this proposition. Sixty percent of the respondents asserted that homosexual men were less capable of "mature, loving relationships" than their heterosexual counterparts. Finally, 70 percent supported the view that the problems experienced by homosexuals were more often the result of "personal conflicts" than of stigmatization. (p. 167) ***

More recently, Fritz Redlich, a leading academic psychiatric researcher, also underscored the powerful role of cultural influences on definitions of mental health and illness. For him, discussions of normal and abnormal behavior turn out, on closer examination, to be discussions about good and bad behavior. Bluntly acknowledging the extent to which psychiatrists were bound by such considerations, he and Daniel Friedman, Chair of Psychiatry at the University of Chicago, wrote, "The judgments of psychiatrists cannot in reality be far removed from those of the *common man*, of the societies and cultures in which psychiatrists and patients live." The symptom of disorder in one society might thus well be the sign of achievement in another. (p. 181) ***

What can account for the speed with which so many psychiatrists and so many other allied mental health professionals have altered their thinking on homosexuality? What made the arguments of gay activists appear so credible when the work of Hooker, Kinsey, and Ford and Beach had been dismissed so readily for more than two decades? Those who have denounced the deletion of homosexuality from *DSM-II* claim that the American Psychiatric Association was intimidated into taking its action, and that despite the Association's official posture, a vast majority of psychiatrists continue to view homosexuality as a pathological condition. That the American Psychiatric Association responded to the concerted pressure of an angry militant movement that had made full use of coercive and intimidating tactics is undeniable. To assert, however, that the decision of December 1973 represented nothing more than a capitulation to the face of force involves a great distortion. Though it is difficult to determine the precise proportion of psychiatrists who have adopted the nonpathological view, it is clear that the numbers are substantial. (p. 189) ***

... With the theoretical foundations for classifying homosexuality as a psychiatric disorder uncertain, it was possible for "extra professional" values to assume greater salience than otherwise might have been the case. This point is underscored by the fact that psychoanalysts, typically more liberal than other psychiatrists, remained steadfastly committed to the pathological perspective. ... Because of their powerful professional ideology involving a highly developed theoretical orientation, psychoanalysts were protected against the pressures exerted by the homosexuals. They were, in fact, able to argue that the deletion ... was against the "true interests" of those who so urgently and wrathfully pressed for change. ... (p. 191) ***

A CRITICISM OF THE WORK OF EVELYN HOOKER

In the very early days of the homosexual movement, homosexual activists were desperately searching for something scientific upon which they could base a claim of normalcy. Evelyn Hooker came up with some rather feeble work and conclusions, but it was the best they had, and she became the heroine of their cause. They were also learning that facts and truth could be far less effective then persistence, force, and intimidation. After large doses of the latter was applied to the American Psychiatric Association in the early 1970s, they even convinced the APA that Hooker's work was valid and acceptable—even though the only study results she ever published was published in 1957 and little importance had been placed on it, and little acceptance was given it in professional circles. But it gave the APA one of its excuses to use in an explanation of its capitulation to the homosexuals.

From my research, it appears that she did one very limited study, and published one report on it. I searched professional journals and found two publications by Dr. Hooker—the one in 1957 and "Reflections of a 40-year Exploration," by Evelyn Hooker, *American Psychologist*, April 1993, pp. 450-453. This article was not a professional report, but was primarily about her career of supporting the homosexual movement. With the article was a editor's note that the article was originally presented when Dr. Hooker was given an award by the American Psychological Association in August 1992. The author's note of Dr. Hooker:

> I was especially proud to receive this Distinguished Contribution award because it was in the public interest, and I wish to share the award with the gay and lesbian community—whose achievements are equal to, if not greater than, my own. It pleased me enormously that my research and my long advocacy of a scientific view of homosexuality have not only contributed to the well-being of gay men and lesbian women, but have contributed to their extended families and the general public as well.

Evelyn Hooker was completely immersed with the language and thinking of homosexual activism. It was evident in the article referred to above, and it was evident even in her report on her research published in 1957. This alone is sufficient to substantially impeach her credibility. Following are comments on and quotes from her 1993 article. It seems that from the outset she came from far out in left field.

Speaking of 1953 when she applied for a grant for her study:

> ... It was the height of the McCarthy era: Communists and homosexuals were the objects of destructive witch hunts.

Giving further insight to the politics of her husband and herself:

... he fought very hard against the University of California loyalty oath, as did I.

Showing her bias when she commenced her studies:

... I told him I was studying "normal male homosexuals."

When she commenced her studies, that statement was a complete scientific misnomer.

Dr. Hooker's writing indicates that her husband died during her research.

She makes statements that are contrary to her own theories and conclusions, such as:

Working alone in such a high stress- and trauma-laden field inevitably entails high psychological costs. ... I hasten to make clear that, when I characterize conducting research with gay men as stressful, I am only referring to the McCarthy era when the penalties were barbaric.

I lived through the "McCarthy" period, and I never heard of McCarthy having anything to do with sodomy penalties. He was a United States senator who vigorously pursued communists at the height of the cold war—some thought too vigorously—particularly the communists. But regulation of sodomy has always been left to the states. And I have never heard of sodomy being a capital offense in the states, even in colonial days, as it has been in other countries. We also had very high morality in this country then—compared to now. I am sure that Dr. Hooker thought that any penalty for sodomy was "barbaric."

Her statements give us some insight into her general involvement in the "gay community—and keep in mind that homosexual acts were then undoubtedly a felony in California, where she was conducting her "research."

... I accepted invitations to gay parties, gay organizations, gay after-hours clubs, and gay bars. ...

... Camping, for example, is a dramatic form of behavior in both its high and low comic and tragic aspects. Perhaps an illustration will convey something of both. One evening at a dinner party attended by a number of distinguished writers and myself as the only woman, attention turned to how the guests could enhance my knowledge of gay institutions, for example gay baths. My friend, Christopher Isherwood, then began a very dramatic story about how he would take me to the Crystal Baths on the Santa Monica beach, and what we would see, beginning on Level 1—nude men in various sexual activities—complete with hilarious descriptions of the activities on each of the various levels until we reached the top. And then, he said, I would be killed, because no woman is allowed to know the secrets of the gay world and live.

Dr. Hooker never said whether she took the trip to the Crystal Baths—anyway she lived to publish her one report. My recollection is that she died a natural death a few years ago. Without question, the sexual acts being described were the most common ones as noted in the prior chapter—each and every one of which reflect a sick mind. Common sense tells us that there is something amiss with anyone who describes a person who engages in such acts as "normal"—and that includes Dr. Hooker.

She made comments on what she claims the "judges" found from her data. Her comments show what she was hoping to accomplish from the outset even though it was contrary to established science:

> ... You know now that the two groups, homosexuals and heterosexuals did not differ in adjustment psychopathology. When I saw that, I wept with joy. I knew that the psychiatrists would not accept it then. But sometime!

Her article relates her trips abroad promoting the homosexual agenda, which she refers to as speaking and presenting papers. The article notes that a documentary film was made about Dr. Hooker and shown at the Berlin Film Festival in February 1992 entitled: *Changing Our Minds: The Story of Evelyn Hooker.*

She notes that approximately $500,000 has been put up with the American Psychiatric Association and earmarked for certain research, and she hopes to cure the rest of us who do not accept sodomy as a commendable goal for society:

> ... The future research on homophobia seems assured, at least financially. I would hope also that some effort would

be made to present positive but accurate pictures of gay and lesbian life-styles.

The small amount or research, and the publication of the one study report, certainly did not warrant the propelling of Evelyn Hooker into the limelight and fame. Little attention was paid to her work until the big homosexual push against the APA's. With the force of the homosexual assault, and the cowardice of the organizations, Dr. Hooker's previously unacceptable ideas became acceptable. The powerful homosexual community then propelled her onward and upward. And it has helped push our country into the muck of depravity.

The following are comments on and quotes from the published report on her studies: Evelyn Hooker, "The Adjustment of the Male Overt Homosexual," *Journal of Projective Techniques*, 1957, Vol. 21, No. 3, pp. 18-31.

On the first page of the paper, Dr. Hooker adopts a statement issued by a psychiatric group. Statements, such as the following, have long been a line of homosexual activists:

> "It is well known that many people, including physicians, react in an exaggerated way to sexual deviations and particularly to homosexuality with disgust, anger, and hostility. Such feelings often arise from the individual's own conflict centering about his unconscious homosexual impulses. ..."(p. 18)

Let us consider this kind of thinking from a standpoint of common sense. If the vile and depraved acts of homosexuals, as described in Chapter 1, are disgusting to a person, then it may be a sign of his or her own "unconscious homosexual impulses." Homosexuals, using this kind of thinking, have called in when I have appeared on radio talk shows opposing the homosexual agenda—and accused me of being a repressed homosexual. But I was in good company. They say the same thing about the Apostle Paul, and even Jesus was accused of being a drag queen. See Chapter 4 for examples. In other words, if such repulsive acts are repulsive to a person, then he or she is probably a repressed homosexual. They say we are the ones who should be treated and cured of our homophobia.

To compare the psychological adjustment of homosexuals and heterosexuals, it would be necessary to take a random sample of each population. Dr. Hooker's report makes it clear that she set out to try to find homosexuals that would be most likely to have the same adjustment factors as heterosexuals. At the beginning of the report, she explains that, rather than doing a random sample, "... I set out to investigate the adjustment of homosexuals ... who had a chance of being individuals who, on the surface at least, seemed to have an average adjustment, provided that (for the purpose of the investigation) homosexuality is not considered to be a symptom of maladjustment." (p. 18)

This statement tells us something else. Although for centuries Western Civilization has considered homosexual acts to be unnatural and loathsome acts, and a very serious deviancy from the norms of acceptable conduct, Dr. Hooker was assuming that it was "normal" behavior and not a deviancy showing any maladjustment. This was also contrary to the accepted norms of both psychiatry and psychology at the time, as shown by the information from Dr. Bayer's book, referred to above.

Dr. Hooker states: "No one knows what a random sample of the homosexual population would be like ... ." (p, 19)

She had the Mattachine Society (a homosexual organization) help her find homosexuals that might fit the category she was trying to find.

Her efforts to get matched groups of heterosexuals and homosexuals even went to the extent of screening them. (pp. 19–20)

> In both groups subjects were eliminated who were in therapy at the time. If, in the preliminary screening evidence of considerable disturbance appeared, the individual was eliminated ... . (p. 20)

The article does not say whether or not tests were given before hand as a part of this screening.

Another odd thing occurred. It appears that Dr. Hooker eliminated heterosexuals who had strong feelings against homosexuality. This would eliminate heterosexuals who had strong natural feelings of decency and morality. Consider the following:

> ... I then asked whether he had had any homosexual inclinations or experience. This question was put in a matter of fact way and only

after a good relationship of cooperation had been established. If the individual seemed to be severely disturbed by the question, or responded in a bland way, or denied vehemently, I did not include him in the sample of 30. It is possible, though I doubt it, that there are some heterosexuals in my group who have strong latent or concealed overt homosexuality. (p. 20)

So we also see that not only was Dr. Hooker even using screening to find homosexuals that fit the type she was hoping would best fit what she considered reasonably well-adjusted homosexuals, but she was screening and selecting heterosexuals who had no strong aversions to homosexuality. So we see that neither group at all fits any kind of a representative sampling of the population of the two groups. Very odd indeed.

All this "research" amounted to was an attempt to find a group of homosexuals and a group of heterosexuals, with similar intelligence quotients, who would be most likely to show similar results on three psychological tests. Thirty homosexuals and thirty heterosexuals were selected. I certainly do not consider this any scientific way to compare the psychological health of homosexuals and heterosexuals.

The three tests used were the Rorschach, TAT, and MAPS. The report does not disclose who administered the tests.

Two clinicians, who were also considered experts in Rorschach, analyzed the Rorschach test information. They were designated as Judges A and B, and tables were given of the results. Five categories were listed, with the first being superior adjustment, and the fifth being maladjustment or the bottom limit of normal.

The following are interesting comments of Hooker on the agreement of these two judges and the suitability of tests given to a group selected like this to give any meaningful results:

> ... Although a Tschuprow coefficient between the ratings of Judge "A" and Judge "B" is only 0.33, it is important to point out that the situation is not as bad as this low coefficient would seem to indicate.
> ... it is safe to say that in two-thirds of the total distribution there is high agreement.
> ... But caution is needed. As clinicians, we are well aware, in daily practice, of limitations of projected material analyzed "blind." ***

... both judges commented on the fact that the records which they thought to be homosexual were unlike the ones they were familiar with in the clinic. They were not the disturbed records ordinarily seen. ... It may be pertinent to reiterate that I had made an effort to secure records of homosexuals who ordinarily would not be seen in a clinic. ... At a minimum, healthy skepticism about many (but not all) so-called homosexual content signs in the Rorschach is, I think, called for. *** (pp. 22-23)

One professional examined the MAPS and TAT protocols for Dr. Hooker.

... The problem of identifying the homosexual protocol from this material was essentially a much easier one than that encountered with the Rorschach, since few homosexuals failed to give open homosexual stories on at least one picture. ***

... homosexuality was openly revealed in some TAT records and not in the MAPS (for the same man), and vice versa. ...

... Determining the degree of agreement between the ratings on the Rorschach and TAT-MAPS constitutes a difficult problem, since two variables are involved: the judges and the test materials. A Tschuprow coefficient between either Rorschach judge and the TAT-MAPS judge is 0.20. ... When the ratings of all three judges are put together, there is agreement on 14 homosexuals (approximately one-half of the group) as being 3 or better in adjustment, and 14 heterosexuals. (p. 25) ***

One of the specific examples of the subjects tested tells anyone with common sense that there is something wrong with either the method of testing or the results—and certainly something wrong with Dr. Hooker's ideas and conclusions. The following are statements about subject #50:

[Subject #50] was placed in adjustment categories 1 or 2 by both Rorschach judges and misidentified as being heterosexual. ...

... He lives alone in an apartment, though in an apartment house in which other homosexuals reside. His homosexual pattern involves rather a large number of homosexual partners. He is thoroughly immersed in the homosexual way of life, but apart from this I see no particular evidence of disturbance.

The TAT was analyzed first, and on the TAT he talks about homosexuality, thus revealing that he is a homosexual. The judgments to which the clinician comes are essentially that he is a promiscuous, driven person; that there are compulsive elements; that he goes from one relationship to another, not even aware of what he is seeking, a fairly lonely man, although with an adjustment slightly below 3. The first four stories of the MAPS were described by the judge as being definitely heterosexual. On the last story, the Dream, I should like to quote the judge directly: "I am surprised, because what this means is that this is the record of a homosexual; and it means that I had not seen this at all up to this point. It means, also, that he doesn't show it except over the jealousy and rivalry of homosexual partners. ... One of the statements about him is that he is a normal homosexual. ... If you want proof that a homosexual can be normal, this record does it." (pp. 26–27) ***

To say that #50 is a normal person defies the reasoning of anyone with common sense and natural sensibilities.

The article states:

... Another way of looking at the data from the projective tests may be that the homosexual "pathology" occurs only in an erotic situation and that the homosexual can function well in non-erotic situations such as the Rorschach, TAT, and MAPS. Thus, one could defend the hypothesis that homosexuality is symptomatic of pathology, but that the pathology is confined to one sector of behavior, namely, the sexual. (p. 30) ***

What are the psychological implications of the hypotheses that homosexuality is not necessarily a symptom of pathology? I would *very tentatively* suggest the following:

1. Homosexuality as a clinical entity does not exist. Its forms are as varied as are those of heterosexuality.

2. Homosexuality may be a deviation in sexual pattern which is within the normal range, psychologically. This has been suggested, on a biological level, by Ford and Beach (2).

3. The role of particular forms of sexual desire and expression in personality structure and development may be less important than has frequently been assumed. Even if one assumes that homosexuality represents a severe form of maladjustment to society in the sexual sector of behavior, this does not necessarily mean that the homosexual must be severely maladjusted in other sectors of his behavior. Or, if one assumes that homosexuality is a form of severe maladjustment

internally, it may be that the disturbance is limited to the sexual sector. (pp. 30–31)

What the published results by Dr. Hooker boils down to is that if one assumes that homosexuality in itself is not a psychological maladjustment, then the tests will not reflect any maladjustment, in some individuals who are particularly selected so as not have any signs or records of such maladjustment.

The initial and basic premise is false to a sensible person with natural and normal sensibilities. And the methods of screening and testing done by Dr. Hooker were particularly designed to eliminate any random sampling of homosexuals. Also, if one would fully accept her conclusions, it means only that there may be some homosexuals who are so calloused and satisfied with their reprehensible activities that they have no other major psychological disturbances that substantially interfere with their non-sexual activities in society. This was rather a meaningless study. But I am sure that with the cultural war in which the homosexualists are engaged with those trying to protect our traditional values of morality and decency, there will be many more such studies as tools for homosexual propaganda.

Kuchta, John C., Ph.D., "Homosexuality, Psychiatry & Amendment 2: The Whole Story," *Tri-Lakes Times*, March 3, 1993, reprinted in *The Colorado Model*, Colorado for Family Values, Colorado Springs, Co. 1993, states:

The uproar over Amendment 2 created by the gay and lesbian ayatollahs and their supporters from the political Left has generated more heat than light. Boycotts, character assassinations, pejorative terms of abuse such as "homophobe" and "hate monger" and the clever propaganda employed by screechy gay activists represent a hysterical response to what they perceive as a threat to their sociopolitical agenda. As a practicing clinical psychologist of 38 years, which includes therapeutic work with homosexuals, it is my purpose in this essay to cast some light on the homosexual controversy from a psychiatric perspective as well as to discuss some associated politics and sociocultural consequences of the Gay Liberation Movement. For the most apart, the realities of this account are habitually concealed or obscured by the ruling liberal media.

***

Medical and mental health professionals had always considered homosexuality a sexual disorder, until the Gay Liberation Movement emerged from the shadows in the late sixties to take advantage of the climate created by the hedonism, narcissism and nihilism of the counter-culture revolution. It was a time when senseless mischief gradually escalated into stark destructiveness. It was a time when ghetto thugs like the Black Panthers could be anointed as political saviors; when avenging malcontents became social evangelists spreading the gospel of drugs and sexual vagrancy; when our traditional values and assumptions which provided stability and continuity to the American experience for two centuries were assaulted and discredited one after another.

Quick to exploit the situation, [gay activists] took up the liberal call for "victimhood" and self-obsession and denounced all traditional values as "oppressive", impetuously establishing their own liberated zones where they pursued an ideal of liberated sex. Their bathhouses became institutional symbols and political organizing halls, as well as the sexual gymnasiums of their movement. In time, these sites would become disease laden pleasure palaces, culturing a virulent brew of established venereal organisms and introducing a new one, human immunodeficiency virus (HIV).

The gay activists eventually created a political juggernaut so powerful that public health officials in San Francisco, New York and Los Angeles were intimidated from closing down these disease infested bathhouses for fear of trespassing against a "minority lifestyle." Proven public health measures were rejected as an infringement of "gay civil rights." According to Randy Shilts, a gay author of the best seller, *And The Band Played On*, AIDS might never have reached epidemic proportions and become the medical problem it is today had these "joy houses" been closed down. He describes the atmosphere on the eve of its outbreak:

Gay men were being washed by tide after tide of increasingly serious infections. First it was syphilis and gonorrhea. Gay men made up about 80 percent of the 70,000 annual patient visits to San Francisco VD Clinics. Easy treatment had imbued them with such a cavalier attitude toward venereal diseases that many gay men saved their waiting-line numbers like little tokens of desirability, and the clinic was considered an easy place to pick up both a shot and a date.

It was in this climate of cultural liberation and totalitarian passion for a new social order that homosexuals began to demand that their lifestyle be recognized as an acceptable alternative to traditional arrangements. However, in order to achieve this goal the gay community quickly realized that their first task would be to effect the removal of homosexuality as a mental disorder from the *Diagnostic and Statistical Manual of Psychiatric Disorders*. Without this dispensation from the sweep of psychiatric disorders, homosexuality could never be accepted as the equal of heterosexuality and the revolution would languish and die. In a very real way the American Psychiatric Association (APA), which controlled these diagnostic entries, ultimately held the fate of the movement.

From 1969 to 1971 gay activists made a concerted effort to storm the annual meetings of the APA and demand the normalization of homosexual behavior. With each successive meeting the intensity of their effort increased geometrically. In fact, their strategy set the standard for any special interest group who might want to run roughshod over an organized society. A veritable high noon was reached in 1971 when a homosexual horde descended on the annual meeting like an invading army, screaming and kicking, and destroyed whatever hopes the members had concerning a peaceful and orderly discussion of the homosexual issue. Microphones were seized and psychiatry was denounced as "the enemy incarnate". The gay plan to silence opposing medical opinions even extended to the literature being distributed at the convention. Using forged credentials, gay activists gained access to the exhibit area and demanded that a display marketing conditioning techniques for the treatment of homosexuals be removed. The exhibitor was told that unless his booth was dismantled, it would be torn down. Yielding before this threat, the booth was removed in order to avoid violence. In response to this bullying, physical intimidation and dishonesty, the members of the APA Nomenclature Committee led by Robert Spitzer eventually initiated a movement to *normalize* homosexual behavior. This normalization was subsequently endorsed by the Board of Trustees of the APA in December of 1973.

By that time the homosexuals were a fully institutionalized presence at the annual meetings.

Many members of the association strongly objected to this change on the grounds that it was scientifically unsound and ignored the results of decades of research and clinical work. Galvanized by their exasperation over the "Spitzer gambit," these dissident members then initiated a referendum of the entire APA membership in an attempt to reverse the decision of the Board of Trustees and restore the original classification of homosexuality as a mental disorder. This referendum was the first in the history of the APA and was defeated by a margin of 58 to 42 percent. Consequently, homosexuality was regarded thereafter simply as a variant of sexual orientation, a position which was subsequently endorsed by the American Psychological Association. A homosexual was to be considered as suffering from a mental illness only when in conflict with his homosexuality; however, even this so called "Ego-Dystonic Homosexuality" was subsequently removed from the diagnostic manual in 1986. Of interest is the fact that the American Medical Association was also surveyed at about the same time of the "big switch" and only 18 percent considered homosexuality a variation of normal, while 69 percent agreed it was pathological.

This event marked the first time that a disorder was eliminated by a vote, and that a special interest group's own evaluation was a criterion for determining if a specific behavior constituted an illness or not. If all that is needed to remove large numbers of individuals from the ranks of the mentally ill is a vote by the APA, then surely other diagnostic classifications are suspect. Furthermore, why should not other disorders be removed when there is no conflict, like pedophilia, zoophilia, alcoholism, and anti-social personality disorder.

Many mental health practitioners and researchers, including this writer, saw this normalization of homosexual behavior as a misguided response to concentrated and dogged political pressure by a special interest group. Were it not for this mobilized coercion, homosexuality would still be recognized today as a psychiatric disorder. Within a twenty-four month period the APA had completely surrendered its integrity and self-determination to the gay activists. They had demanded and received an unprecedented "preferred status" in the profession. They had gained this advantage only because they had violated all the rules of formal scientific discourse. If you want to know when the ultimate politicizing of American health care occurred, you need look no further. So much for science contaminated by a political blitzkrieg. The tactical reliance upon disruption and force had been vindicated.

Reinforced by their success in the mental health arena, such "brownshirt tactics" became the modus operandi for gay activism from issues of AIDS to public education. A very recent example of such an assault was the response of ACT UP, a gay activist group, to Stephen Joseph's book, *Dragon Within the Gates,* in which he scolds homosexual organizations for exaggerating the incidence of AIDS and enlarging the scope of the epidemic to include all demographic groups when the wellspring of AIDS is gay sexual behavior. The gay response included shouting Joseph down at public meetings, barging into his office with a video-camera, intimidating him with obscene phone calls, threatening his life as well as his wife's, and protesting outside his home. I find it quite incredible that these are the same people who accuse others of bigotry, closed-mindedness, and oppression.

The tragedy of this ill-conceived normalization of homosexual conduct is that it did a great disservice to nonvocal homosexuals. By endorsing their sexual behavior as normal, the APA came out, by implication, against therapy for this disorder. Moreover, therapy has itself been mythologized, in the polemics of the Gay Liberation Movement, into a monstrous plot geared toward a coercive change in sexual orientation. The defensiveness implicit in such mindless charges speaks for itself. This antitherapeutic attitude of the APA has led to unwarranted pain and discomfort for many homosexuals who are intimidated by the power and control exerted by gay activists.

Dr. Kuchta is a Clinical Psychologist for General Adult Psychiatric Services at the Colorado Mental Health Institute of Pueblo, Colorado.

As previously stated, Dr. Joseph Nicolosi is one of the foremost authorities in the country engaged in reparative therapy for homosexuals. An article, "Born or Bred," *Newsweek,* Feb. 24, 1992, states:

> Some psychiatrists still see the removal of homosexuality from the official list of emotional disorders as a mistake. ..."Psychology and psychiatry have essentially abandoned a whole population of people who feel dissatisfied with their feeling of homosexuality," says psychologist Joseph Nicolosi, author of "Reparative Therapy of Male Homosexuality" (*Jason Aronson,* 1991). In graduate school, says Nicolosi, he found the stance was that if a client came in complaining about his

gayness, the therapist's job was to teach him to accept it. "It was like the old joke of the patient who tells the doctor his arm hurts when he bends it and the doctor advises him not to bend it."

Certainly there are genetic, organic, physiological, and psychological disorders that cause or contribute to sickness of the mind, as well as sickness of the body—even complete insanity. But this certainly does not mean that such mental illness should not be treated, and should be considered as normal and good, just because it is caused by or contributed to by factors that are not purely psychological. This would eliminate a large part of the highly beneficial work done by psychiatrists, other medical doctors, and psychologists.

Let us consider an example. In my work, I have studied the medical records of a good many people. One lady was an attractive, well educated, and seemingly bright young married woman. She developed a mental illness that was considered to have physiological and hereditary root causes. She engaged in bizarre conduct such as indiscriminately giving away valuable possessions. When visiting people, she would undress and show her nakedness, quite inappropriately. At her worst, she was huddled in the corner of her room in a psychiatric hospital, defecating on the floor, and eating her excrement. (When I learned of some of the things that some homosexuals do, as described above, I was reminded of this lady.) Later she was put on a new medicine that had been developed, which effectively controlled her condition. She lived fifteen to twenty years after she began taking the medicine, generally appeared to be happy and productive, and to function as a normal person.

There are many people that have serious mental illnesses that have physiological, genetic, and hereditary causes. Prior to proper treatment, they have engaged in conduct that was seriously destructive to society, and to themselves. With proper treatment in the form of medicine, therapy, and often both, they have been able to lead happy and productive lives, and apparently function as normal human beings.

Nevertheless, it appears to me that the available evidence is very heavily weighted toward homosexuality being psychological, and caused by events in one's life, rather than organic or genetic. However, whatever the cause, professionals in the related fields should continue research to better define the causes. There may well be several causes, and there may be causation differences between particular cases. Likewise, for the benefit of homosexuals and our society, research should be continued to determine the most effective treatment of this seriously deviant condition.

It is indeed a shameful thing that the American Psychiatric Association and the American Psychological Association, the two professional organizations that should have primary responsibility for such work, have abandoned homosexuals and society because of politics and intimidation. There is no question whatsoever that homosexuality is a destructive deviation from the norms of society. Even worse, there are a substantial and growing number of the members of both organizations who consider it unethical to even treat homosexuals and help those who wish to overcome their homosexuality. This is particularly disgusting, and points up the extent to which these organizations are controlled by the homosexualists.

It reminds me of the terrible incident described in Chapter 1 where the young man went to two priests for help to overcome his homosexuality and was sodomized by both.

Now the American Psychiatric Association appears to be working toward normalizing "pedophilia" in the same way that it "normalized" homosexuality. It has removed acts of pedophilia from its criteria for disorders. Under the present definitions, such behavior must be accompanied by "distress" or "impairment in ... areas of functioning." Under this definition, a pedophile who continues to function well in other areas, and is not distressed by his or her heinous acts, may have sex with children, and still be considered normal. The APA denies this, but the wording speaks for itself. The article from which this information was derived is "Psychiatric Group Denies It Is Normalizing Pedophilia," by Mark Kelly, Baptist Press, *Lambda Report*, April-June 1995. The article sets out the following wording:

CHANGES IN THE DSM ON PEDOPHILIA

The following are texts for the APA's *Diagnostic and Statistical Manual of Mental Disorders for* "pedophilia." This is Point "B," one of three criteria for the disorder:

1987 (DSM III)

"The person has acted on these urges, or is markedly distressed by them."

1995 (DSM IV)

"The fantasies, sexual urges, or behavior cause clinically significant distress OR impairment in social, occupational, or other important areas of functioning."

The APA can try to fool the public all it wants, but "acted on these urges" of molesting children is "behavior;" and behavior is specifically allowed as normal unless the "clinically significant distress or impairment" is caused by the behavior. This is certainly a significant change in what may be considered normal.

Not only that, according to the article, Michael First, who headed the DSM-IV group on "paraphilias," sexual disorders such as sexual sadism, masochism, exhibitionism, transvestitism, voyeurism, and pedophilia, contradicted himself in trying to argue that the definition did not normalize pedophilia if there was no clinically significant distress or impairment. He said that the APA would probably clarify the entry on pedophilia to eliminate any notion that it was being normalized. But First said that the APA would not change the identical language applying to the other "paraphilias" such as sexual sadism, masochism, exhibitionism, transvestitism, and voyeurism. It is ridiculous and against all common sense to consider such things normal, whether or not they cause clinically significant distress or impairment. And, as of now, I have not heard of the APA even changing the wording on pedophilia. So now we have the outrageous situation that the APA considers homosexuality normal, as well as all of these other things, if they do not cause significant distress or impairment of the pervert in "social, occupational, or other important areas of functioning."

Any normal individual with ordinary common sense knows that all of these thing are abnormal and a perversion. As it did with homosexuality, the APA has again capitulated to the pressure and politics of the homosexual activists, to the detriment of the profession, of the public, and of the homosexuals themselves. We should also bear in mind that all of these disorders under discussion are among the things commonly done by various homosexuals, although not many of them, if any, do all of them.

Whatever the work group's reasoning for the new criteria, the changes reflect "the continuing massive erosion of moral standards" among APA psychiatrists that began in the 1960s, said Jeffrey Satinover, a member of Focus on the Family's Physicians' Research Council.

> "Most mental health professionals are now convinced there exists no objective criteria by which to define homosexuals as ill," Satinover said. The new diagnosis criteria lay the foundation for "full acceptance of all sexual perversions as a normal variants of homosexuality—pedophilia included." ***
>
> Satinover notes that if pedophilia is no longer considered abnormal, only age of consent laws prevent open adult-child sexual relations. "Youth emancipation" is not only the political agenda of pedophile groups but also frontline liberal activists he said.
>
> American Society no longer shares any moral values that allow it to discern right from wrong, said Richard Land, executive director of the Christian Life Commission of the Southern Baptist Convention.
>
> "When you don't have a prevailing ethic that defines moral and immoral behavior, you are left with nothing but opinion polls to determine what's normal and what's abnormal," he said. "Even when it comes to something as grotesque as pedophilia, we evidently cannot force ourselves to say, "This is wrong; and we're going to treat it that way." ***
>
> "The next step will be a strong effort to lower the age of consent," Land asserted. "In Scandinavia and certain parts of Europe we have seen a softening of the laws concerning sex between adults and children and an attempt to autonomize the child, lowering the age of consent and thus decriminalizing sex acts between adults and children." *** (*Lambda Report*, ibid.)

The homosexual organization, the North American Man-Boy Love Association (NAMBLA), has long been working to lower the age that children may consent to sexual acts with adults, and with some success.

Another insight into the insanity and immorality gripping these organizations is the following on the push of homosexuals for three-way or multiple marriages (*Lambda Report*, Jul.–Sept. 95):

... Dr. Jack Drescher, M.D., a homosexual activist within the American Psychiatric Association (APA), gave a rationale of sorts to the concept of homosexual "three-ways."

"Our culture tells us that we're supposed to find satisfaction in *one* person. But not everyone can find everything they need from one man," said Drescher, a psychoanalyst who co-chairs the Committee on Gay and Lesbian Issues for the APA's New York chapter.

Another homosexual referred to in the article (Ibid.) puts things in a more realistic perspective:

Larry Ringer, who lost his male lover and business partner to a homosexual "couple," was bitter about the whole three-way concept.

"Face it. We're sluts, most of us," Ringer told *Genre* (magazine). "So why stop at two husbands? We can't copy straight marriages and make it work, so we go the opposite direction and make a mockery of the whole concept of marriage."***

The following is from an article in *The Wall Street Journal*, 1-9-97, by Charles Socarides, Benjamin Kaufman, Joseph Nicolosi, Jeffrey Satinover and Richard Fitzgibbons. Dr. Socarides is a clinical professor of psychiatry at Albert Einstein College of Medicine. Dr. Kaufman is a clinical professor of psychiatry at the University of California, Davis. Dr. Nicolosi is a director of a clinic in Encino, California. Dr. Satinover is a Westport, Connecticut, psychiatrist. Dr. Fitzgibbons is director of a clinic in West Conshocken, Pennsylvania.

DON'T FORSAKE HOMOSEXUALS WHO WANT HELP

*** Every day young men seek help because they are experiencing an unwanted sexual attraction to other men, and are told that their condition is untreatable. It is not surprising that many of these young men fall into depression or despair when they are informed that a normal life with a wife and children is never to be theirs.

This despair can lead to reckless and life-threatening actions. Many young men with homosexual inclinations, feeling their lives are of little value, are choosing to engage in unprotected sex with strangers. Epidemiologists are well aware that the number of new HIV infections among young men involved in homosexual activity is rising at an alarming rate; within this population the "safer sex" message is falling on deaf ears. One recent study revealed that 38% of homosexual adolescents had engaged in unprotected sex in the previous six months.

Young men and the parents of at risk males have a right to know that prevention and effective treatment are available. They have a right to expect that every professional they consult will inform them of their therapeutic options and allow them to make their own choices based on the best clinical evidence. A variety of studies have shown that between 25% and 50% of those seeking treatment experienced significant improvement. If a therapist feels for whatever reason that he cannot treat someone for this condition, he has an obligation to refer the patient to someone who will.

Also, these young men and their parents have the right to know that, contrary to media propaganda, there is no proven biological basis for homosexuality. A November 1995 article in Scientific American pointed out that the much-publicized brain research by Simon Le Vay has never been replicated and that Dean Hamer's gene study has been contradicted by another study.

The truth is that the clinical experience of many therapists who work with men struggling with same-sex attractions and behaviors indicates that there are many causes for homosexuality. ...

... many find the freedom they are seeking and are able to have normal relationships with women.

Help is available for men struggling with unwanted homosexual desires. The National Association for Research and Treatment of Homosexuality offers information for those interested in understanding the various therapeutic approaches to treatment. In addition, a number of self-help groups have sprung up to offer support to those who suffer from this problem.

As we grieve for all those lives so abruptly ended by AIDS, we would do well to reflect that many of the young men who have died of AIDS have sought treatment for their homosexuality and were denied knowledge and hope. Many of them would be alive today if they had only been told where to find the help they sought.

The following is from an article by Cal Thomas, *Christian American,*
Jan/Feb 1998:

GAY CONVERSION: A REALITY PSYCHOLOGISTS IGNORE

The American Psychological Association (APA) has adopted a resolution it hopes will limit treatment designed to change the behavior of
homosexual men and women. Known as "reparative therapy," the
technique seeks to help homosexuals troubled by their lives.

[Why do the homosexual lobbies oppose such treatment?]
If homosexuals can change their behavior, then their argument for
special protection under civil rights laws ... falls apart. That's why
they have stepped up the media assault, including 30 gay and lesbian
characters showing up on television this coming season, according to
the Gay and Lesbian Alliance Against Defamation. It is also why they
conduct organized letter-writing campaigns to newspapers demanding the censoring of any writer who does not embrace and promote
their view.

The APA backed away from wording that would have deemed reparative therapy "unethical" but it's only a matter of time before such
a resolution is approved, given the political direction of the organization. It has an office dedicated exclusively to gay, lesbian and bisexual
issues that helped craft the approved resolution.

But the facts (as opposed to the politics) are that people who want
to change *can* change, because it is a behavior issue – not race, gender
or physical abilities. ***

One of the most successful at reparative therapy is the National
Association for Research and Therapy of Homosexuality (NARTH).
In May, NARTH released the results of a two-year study conducted
among nearly 860 individuals struggling to overcome homosexuality
and more than 200 psychologists and therapists who treat them.

The survey found that before treatment 68 percent of respondents
perceived themselves as exclusively or almost entirely homosexual,
with another 22 percent stating they were more homosexual than heterosexual.

After treatment, only 13 percent perceived themselves as exclusively or almost entirely homosexual, while 33 percent described themselves as either exclusively or almost entirely heterosexual.

Ninety-nine percent said they believe treatment to change homosexuality can be effective and valuable.

Even their thought-life had been transformed, with 63 percent indicating they had frequent and intense homosexual thoughts before treatment and only 3 percent indicating they had such thoughts after treatment. Among the psychotherapists, 82 percent said they believe therapy can help change unwanted homosexuality. ***

Why would the APA oppose treatment that is not coercive and that is conducted only with those who seek it unless it has a political agenda?

Are these psychiatric and psychological organizations now controlled by the mentally ill or merely by the spineless?

If America ever succumbs to accepting the vile and destructive acts of homosexuality and its related perversions as normal and good behavior, it will have reached the dregs of depravity. Those who oppose the homosexual agenda must continue to speak the truth about the causes and the cures of this sickness.

CHAPTER 3

WHY SODOMY IS WRONG

T he following is the complete definition of sodomy given in Webster's New Twentieth Century Dictionary—Unabridged, Second Ed., 1964, The World Publishing Co., Cleveland and New York:

> [A]ny sexual intercourse regarded as abnormal, as between persons of the same sex, especially males, or between a person and an animal.

As used in this book, the word *sodomy* is used to encompass all of the sexual acts between persons of the same sex, and all of the sexual acts described in Chapter 1, as acts in which homosexuals engage. Sodomy is used interchangeably herein with homosexuality.

The Encyclopedia Britannica (1973), Vol. 20, p. 828, states: "Sodom and Gomorrah, cities of legendary wickedness, were destroyed by a rain of 'brimstone and fire' (Gen. 19:24). Their most likely location is beneath the shallow waters of the southern end of the Dead Sea ... ."

Sodom and Gomorrah, in the Bible, and since biblical times to this day, have been held up as the epitome of evil and depravity in civilized society. The Bible states that this is why they were destroyed. The primary evil described in the Bible was the homosexuality engaged in by their inhabitants, both men and women, and it is from these biblical accounts that the words sodomy and sodomite are derived, as they are used today.

However, as explained in Chapter 1, we have video proof of worse depravity taking place in San Francisco, New York City, and Washington, D. C., than the acts described in the Bible.

Each and every one of the homosexual acts described in Chapter 1 should be shocking and revolting to any sane and decent human being, without resort to or consideration of the Biblical condemnations. They are inherent crimes against nature and mankind. They are destructive to the minds and to the bodies of those who engage in them. But the homosexual activists try to convince us that their acts are good and acceptable, and use every conceivable fallacious argument to try to support their position, including completely misconstruing the Bible. Later, herein, we will show the unqualified condemnation of homosexuality in the Bible, in both the Old Testament, the basis of the Jewish religion, and the New Testament, the primary basis of the Catholic religion. Most Protestant religions are based both on the Old and New Testaments.

In an interview with President Clinton on ABC News in March, 1994, in defense of his support of the homosexual movement, he noted that nothing against homosexuality made its way into the Ten Commandments. I consider this a typical statement from a man who I believe represents the epitome of hypocrisy.

A similar argument is made by many homosexuals and their supporters when trying to falsely argue that homosexuality is not condemned in the New Testament, because Christ said nothing about it. As to the Old Testament they say that Leviticus, which strongly condemns homosexuality, also says that we should not touch pig skins, with the implication that this is so foolish that the parts about sodomy should be ignored.

In other words, these people want to claim that they follow the Christian beliefs, which are based both upon the Old and New Testaments, both of which strongly condemn sodomy. To do this they must violate long-accepted principles of both logical and legal construction of the text involved. These principles state that all parts of a governing text must be construed together and in such a way that all parts are consistent and compatible; and that specific statements on a subject control over general statements which may be applied to other subjects as well.

One part of a writing should not be interpreted so as to make its other parts ineffective and meaningless.

In twisting the scriptures, they manage to ignore the specific and unequivocal statements condemning sodomy so strongly that Sodom and Gomorrah were destroyed because of their sinfulness, and the Apostle Paul's extremely strong condemnation of homosexuality. Instead they dwell on such general statements as "love thy neighbor" and "judge not others." Really? No matter how heinous a person's crimes or acts are, we should love them and never judge them. If no one must be judged and criticized for anything, then certainly no one should be executed or put in jail—even murderers and rapists. How absurd have we become?

As to Clinton's statement that nothing against homosexuality made its way into the Ten Commandments. Neither did prohibitions against rape, incest, bestiality, prostitution, fornication, child abuse, child sexual molestation, wife abuse, cruelty to animals and humans, and many other reprehensible things strongly condemned by both the Old and New Testaments.

A careful study and search of the Bible has convinced me that, next to murder, sodomy is the most strongly condemned of anything else in the Bible. Let us consider some of the things the *King James Version of the Holy Bible* says about this subject.

THE OLD TESTAMENT

Genesis 13:13: "But the men of Sodom were wicked and sinners before the Lord exceedingly."

Genesis chapter 18 relates the Lord considering whether or not to destroy the cities of Sodom and Gomorrah, "because their sin is very grievous." On questioning by Abraham, the Lord said that if ten righteous people could be found, he would not destroy the cities.

Genesis tells of the visit of Lot, the nephew of Abraham, to Sodom, and his learning of their wickedness, and their seeking of the men with him for their evil purposes:

And they called unto Lot, and said unto him, Where *are* the men which came in to thee this night? bring them out unto us, that we may know them.

And Lot went out at the door unto them, and shut the door after him.

And said, I pray you, brethren, do not so wickedly.

Behold now, I have two daughters which have not known man; let me, I pray you, bring them out unto you, and do ye them as is good in your eyes; only unto these men do nothing; for therefore came they under the shadow of my roof.

And they said, Stand back. And they said *again*, This one *fellow* came to sojourn, and he will needs be a judge: now we will deal worse with thee, than with them. And they pressed sore upon the man, *even* Lot, and came near to break the door.

But the men [Angels of the Lord] put forth their hand, and pulled Lot into the house to them, and shut to the door.

And they smote the men that were at the door of the house with blindness, both small and great: so that they wearied themselves to find the door.

And the men (Angels of the Lord) said unto Lot, Hast thou here any besides ? son in law, and thy sons, and thy daughters, and whatsoever thou hast in the city, bring *them* out of this place:

For we will destroy this place, because the cry of them is waxen great before the face of the Lord; and the Lord has sent us to destroy it.

And Lot went out, and spake unto his sons in law, which married his daughters, and said, Up, get you out of this place for the Lord will destroy this city, But he seemed as one that mocked unto his sons in law.

And when the morning arose, then the angels hastened Lot, saying, Arise, take thy wife and thy two daughters, which are here; lest thou be consumed in the iniquity of the city.

And while he lingered, the men laid hold upon his hand, and upon the hand of his wife, and upon the hand of his two daughters; the Lord being merciful unto him: and they brought him forth, and set him without the city.

***

The sun was risen upon the earth when Lot entered into (Zoar).

Then the Lord rained upon Sodom and upon Gomorrah brimstone and fire from the Lord out of Heaven.

And he overthrew those cities, and all of the plain, and all the inhabitants of the cities, and that which grew upon the ground. (Genesis 19:5–16, 23–25)

When the Lord God was stating His laws to the Israelites, He specifically addressed sodomy. Look at Exodus 22:19: "Whosoever lieth with a beast shall surely be put to death."

Leviticus 18:22–25:

Thou shalt not lie with mankind as with womankind: It is an abomination.

Neither shalt thou lie with any beast to defile thyself therewith: it is confusion.

Defile not ye yourselves in any of these things: for in all these the nations are defiled which I cast out before you;

And the land is defiled: therefor I do visit the iniquity thereof upon it, and the land itself vomiteth out her inhabitants.

Leviticus 20:13: "If a man also lie with mankind, as he lieth with a woman, both of them shall surely be put to death; their blood shall be upon them." Deuteronomy 22:5: "The woman shall not wear that which pertaineth unto a man, neither shall a man put on a woman's garment; for all that do so are abomination unto the Lord, thy God." Deuteronomy 23:17 "There shall be no whores of the daughters of Israel, nor a sodomite of the sons of Israel." 1 Kings 14:24: "And there were also sodomites in the land; and they did according to all the abominations of the nations which the Lord cast out before the children of Israel." 1 Kings 15:11–12: "And Asa did that which was right in the eyes of the Lord, as did David his father. And he took away the sodomites out of the land, and removed all of the idols that his fathers had built."

THE NEW TESTAMENT

Mark 6:11 (These are the words of Jesus): "And whosoever shall not receive you, nor hear you, when ye depart thence, shake off the dust under your feet for a testimony against them. Verily I say unto you, it shall be more tolerable for Sodom and Gomorrah in the day of judgment, than for that city."

Mark 7:21–23 (Again, the words of Jesus):

For from within, out of the heart of men, proceed evil thoughts, adulteries, fornications, murders.

Thefts, covetousness, wickedness, deceit, lasciviousness, an evil eye, blasphemy, pride, foolishness:

All these evil things come from within and defile the man.

Romans 1:24–32 (the words of the apostle Paul):

Wherefore God also gave them up to uncleanness through the lusts of their own hearts, to dishonour their own bodies between themselves:

Who changed the truth of God unto a lie, and worshipped and served the creature more than the Creator, who is blessed for ever. Amen.

For this cause God gave them unto vile affections; for even their women did change the natural use unto that which is against nature:

And likewise also the men, leaving the natural use of the woman, burned in their lust one toward another; men with men working that which is unseemly, and receiving in themselves that recompence of their error which is meet.

And even as they did not like to retain God in their knowledge, God gave them over to a reprobate mind, to do those things which are not convenient;

Being filled with all unrighteousness, maliciousness; full of envy, murder, debate, deceit, malignity; whisperers,

Backbiters, haters of God, despiteful, proud, boaster, inventors of evil things, disobedient to parents,

Without understanding, covenantbreakers, without natural affection, implacable, unmerciful:

Who knowing the judgment of God, that they which commit such things are worthy of death, not only do the same, but have pleasure in them that do them.

1 Corinthians 6:9–10:

Know ye not that the unrighteous shall not inherit the kingdom of God? Be not deceived: neither fornicators, nor idolaters, nor adulterers, nor effeminate, nor abusers of themselves with mankind,

Nor thieves, nor covetous, nor drunkards, nor revilers, nor extortioners, shall inherit the kingdom of God.

1 Corinthians 10:8:

Neither let us commit fornication, as some of them committed, and fell in one day three and twenty thousand.

2 Corinthians 12:20–21:

For I fear, lest when I come, I shall not find you such as I would, and that I shall be found unto you such as ye would not lest there be debates, envyings, wraths, strifes, backbitings, whisperings, swellings, tumults:

And lest, when I come again, my God will humble me among you, and that I shall bewail many which have sinned already, and have not repented of the uncleanness and fornication and lasciviousness which they have committed.

1 Thessalonians 4:2–5:

For you know what commandments we gave you by the Lord Jesus.

For this is the will of God, even your sanctification, that ye should abstain from fornication:

That every one of you should know how to possess his vessel in sanctification and honour;

Not in the lust of concupiscence, even as the Gentiles which know not God.

2 Timothy 3:1–4:

This know also, that in the last days, perilous times shall come

For men shall be lovers of their own selves, covetous, boasters, proud, blasphemers, disobedient to parents, unthankful, unholy,

Without natural affection, truce-breakers, false accusers, incontinent, fierce, despisers of those that are good,

Traitors, heady, highminded, lovers of pleasures more than lovers of God;

2 Peter 2:6–10 (the words of Simon Peter, the first of the twelve disciples of Jesus Christ):

And turning the cities of Sodom and Gomorrah into ashes condemned them with an overthrow, making them an ensample unto those that after should live ungodly;
And delivered just Lot, vexed with the filthy conversations of the wicked;
(For the righteous man dwelling among them, in seeing and hearing, vexed his righteous soul from day to day by their unlawful deeds;)
The Lord knoweth how to deliver the godly out of temptations, and to reserve the unjust unto the day of judgment to be punished:
But chiefly them that walk after the flesh in the lust of uncleanness, and despise government. Presumptuous are they, selfwilled, that are not afraid to speak evil of dignities.

Jude 1:7–8:

Even as Sodom and Gomorrah, and the cities about them in like manner, giving themselves over to fornication, and going after strange flesh, are set forth for an example, suffering the vengeance of eternal fire. Likewise also these *filthy* dreamers defile the flesh, despise dominion, and speak evil of dignities.

The scriptures above are far from the only biblical references condemning sodomy. It is condemned throughout the Bible. The following are references, including the above, that I consider relevant to sodomy and sexual perversions, and I am sure that there are others: Genesis 13:13, Genesis 19:4–14, Genesis 19:24–25, Exodus 22:19, Leviticus 18:22–23, Leviticus 20:13–17, Deuteronomy 22:5, Deuteronomy 23:17, Deuteronomy 27:21, Judges 19:22, 1 Kings 14:24, 1 Kings 15:12, 1 Kings 22:46, 2 Kings 23:7, Job 36:14, Isaiah 3:9, Ezekiel 16:49–50, Hosea 4:14, Matthew 11:23–24, Mark 6:11, Romans 1:22–32, 1 Corinthians 6:9, 1 Corinthians 6:18, 1 Corinthians 10:8, Galatians 5:19, 1 Thessalonians 4:3–4, 1 Timothy 1:9–10, 2 Timothy 3:1–9, 2 Timothy 3:13, Jude 1:7–8. These references do not include the condemnations of incest and such things in Chapter 20 of Leviticus, and in other parts of the Bible.

It is decisively and unquestionably clear that homosexuality is exceedingly and strongly condemned in the Bible, in no uncertain terms. It is clear, unconditional, and unambiguous, and there is no logical or reasonable way that it can be construed to the contrary.

The destruction of Sodom and Gomorrah was the only instance in the Bible where people so offended God that he chose to destroy two cities in their entirety. It is equally clear that their primary sins with which God was displeased were "the filthy conversations of the wicked." And that conversations as used in that passage meant sexual intercourse, which has been a common meaning of that word until this day. Without question, from these biblical passages the word "sodomy" was developed, as synonymous with homosexuality. And from Bible times until modern times, Sodom and Gomorrah were considered the ultimate of vileness and depravity. Now we are being taught by the liberal and godless segments of society, including President Clinton, that there is nothing wrong with the vile and destructive acts of sodomy, and that it should be accepted as a wholesome "alternative lifestyle." This is the low ebb of our civilization.

Homosexualists (homosexual activists and their liberal supporters), in addition to presenting such illogical statements as the one referred to by President Clinton, in support of the absurd argument that homosexuality is not condemned by the Bible, also bring up the quotation from Jesus, "Judge not that ye be not judged." It takes quite an illogical stretch of the imagination to use this general statement for the false argument the things that are wrong and condemned in the Bible should not be considered wrong by us, and taught to our children as wrong. This statement by Jesus was merely an indictment of hypocrisy, and in no way meant that the other teachings of the Bible should be discarded or disregarded. The same is true with other general statements in the Bible.

Matthew 7:1–3 states these words of Jesus: "Judge not that ye be not judged. For what judgment ye judge, ye shall be judged: and with what measure ye mete, it shall be measured to you again. And why beholdest thou the mote that is in thy brother's eye, but considerest not the beam that is in thine own eye?"

In other words, Jesus is saying to judge yourself first, because you will be held to the same standard you hold others to.

However, in regard to the extremely strong condemnation of sodomy in the Bible, no one should conclude that homosexuals should be gathered up and executed or indiscriminately punished, because of the statements in the Old and New Testaments that such acts are worthy of death. The Old Testament, and more particularly the New Testament, do not appear to substantially dwell on or prescribe punishments to be meted out by others to those who sin. All of us are or have been sinners. Punishment in the Bible is usually left to God. Also we should consider the fact that death, as used in the statements referred to, is generally meant to be the opposite of eternal life, in both the Old Testament and the New Testament.

> In the Old Testament, we have Daniel 12:2: "And many of them that sleep in the dust of the earth shall awake, some to everlasting life and some to everlasting torment."
>
> In the New Testament, we have the words of the apostle Paul in Romans 6:23: "For the wages of sin is death, but the gift of God is eternal life through Jesus Christ our Lord."

However, neither should we be misled into thinking that we should not pass the necessary laws to protect and promote a moral and decent society, which this country followed for the first two hundred years of it existence. Our laws were clearly based on Judaic-Christian principles. Consider the words of Jesus' disciple, Peter, quoted above. He not only condemned the "filthy conversations" of the sodomites, but he also decried "their unlawful deeds," and that they "despise government," and "speak evil of dignities."

Although a number of our churches have caved in to the pressures of the homosexual movement, abandoned a great part of the Scripture on which their religion is supposed to be based, condoned homosexuality, and even admitted practicing homosexuals as ministers, not all have sunk to that level. As of the end of 1996, on a national basis, the Roman Catholic, Baptist, United Methodist, Presbyterian, and Episcopal churches, plus all Pentecostal churches, were still among the churches which bar practicing homosexuals as ministers, and condemn homosexuality. Pope John Paul II has steadfastly stood by the tenets of the Catholic religion and condemned sodomy and homosexual marriages. They of course do not bar homosexuals from their membership or services. The primary purposes of the churches are to help sinners change their ways. As many have said, "we love the sinner, but hate the sin."

The following is from a thoughtful and comprehensive article about homosexuals who are trapped between a life-style they have rejected, and Christians who reject them:

> Thus, Christians should accept repentant homosexuals into fellowship just as they accept any repentant sinner—thankful that God has extended his mercy and grace to a fellow human being. (Halford, John, and Luker, Dennis, "Understanding the Struggle of Homosexuals," *The Plain Truth, May/June, 1994.*)

In 1986, The United States Supreme Court, in a five to four vote, upheld the Georgia sodomy law which made sodomy a felony and provided a penalty of up to twenty years in prison. *Bowers v. Hardwick*, 478 US 186, 106 S.Ct. 2841, 92 L.Ed.2d 140 (1986). Justice White wrote the majority opinion, joined by Chief Justice Burger and Justices Powell, Rehnquist, and O'Connor. Those dissenting were Blackmun, Brennan, Marshall, and Stevens. The opinion states, in part:

> ...The issue presented is whether the Federal Constitution confers a fundamental right upon homosexuals to engage in sodomy and hence invalidates the laws of the many States that still make such conduct illegal and have done so for a very long time. ...
>
> ***
>
> Precedent aside, however, respondent would have us announce, as the Court of Appeals did, a fundamental right to engage in homosexual sodomy. This we are quite unwilling to do. It is true that despite the language of the Due Process Clauses of the Fifth and Fourteenth Amendments, which appears to focus on the processes by which life, liberty, or property is taken, the cases are legion in which those clauses have been interpreted to have substantive content, subsuming rights that to a great extent are immune from federal or state regulation or proscription. ...
>
> It is obvious to us that neither of these formulations would extend a fundamental right to homosexuals to engage in acts of consensual sodomy. Proscriptions against the conduct have ancient roots. See generally Survey on the Constitutional Right to Privacy in the Context of Homosexual Activity, 40 U of Miami L Rev 521, 525 (1986). Sodomy was a criminal offense at common law and was forbidden by the laws of the original 13 States when they ratified the Bill of Rights.

In 1868, when the Fourteenth Amendment was ratified, all but 5 of the 37 States in the Union had criminal sodomy laws. In fact, until 1961, all 50 States outlawed sodomy, and today, 25 States and the District of Columbia continue to provide criminal penalties for sodomy performed in private and between consenting adults. ...

***

Respondent, however, asserts that the result should be different where the homosexual conduct occurs in the privacy of the home. ...

...The right pressed upon us here has no similar support in the text of the Constitution, and it does not qualify for recognition under the prevailing principles for construing the Fourteenth Amendment. Its limits are also difficult to discern. Plainly enough, otherwise illegal conduct is not always immunized whenever it occurs in the home. Victimless crimes, such as the possession and use of illegal drugs, do not escape the law where they are committed at home. ...And if respondent's submission is limited to the voluntary sexual conduct between consenting adults, it would be difficult, except by fiat, to limit the claimed right to homosexual conduct while leaving exposed to prosecution adultery, incest, and other sexual crimes even though they are committed in the home. We are unwilling to start down that road.

Even if the conduct at issue here is not a fundamental right, respondent asserts that there must be a rational basis for the law and that there is none in this case other than the presumed belief of a majority of the electorate in Georgia that homosexual sodomy is immoral and unacceptable. This is said to be an inadequate rationale to support the law. The law, however, is constantly based on notions of morality, and if all laws representing essentially moral choices are to be invalidated under the Due Process Clause, the courts will be very busy indeed. ...

Chief Justice Burger wrote a concurring opinion in *Bowers v. Hardwick*, ibid..., adding the following historical comments:

I join the Court's opinion, but I write separately to underscore my view that in constitutional terms there is no such thing as a fundamental right to commit homosexual sodomy.

As the Court notes, ante, at 192, 92 L Ed 2d, at 146–147, the proscriptions against sodomy have very "ancient roots." Decisions of individuals relating to homosexual conduct have been subject to state intervention throughout the history of Western Civilization. Condemnation of those practices is firmly rooted in Judeao-Christian moral and ethical standards. Homosexual sodomy was a capital crime under Roman law. See Code Theod 9.7.6; Code Just 9.9.31. See also D. Bailey, Homosexuality and the Western Christian Tradition 70–71 (1975). During the English Reformation when powers of the ecclesiastical courts were transferred to the King's Courts, the first English statute criminalizing sodomy was passed. 25 Hen VIII, ch 6. Blackstone described "the infamous crime against nature" as an offense of "deeper malignity" than rape, a heinous act "the very mention of which is a disgrace to human nature," and "a crime not fit to be named." 4 W. Blackstone, Commentaries *215. The common law of England, including it prohibition of sodomy, became the received law of Georgia and the other Colonies. In 1816 the Georgia Legislature passed the statute at issue here, and the statute has been continuously in force in one form or another since that time. To hold that the act of homosexual sodomy is somehow protected as a fundamental right would be to cast aside millennia of moral teaching.

I became interested in the book *Perfect Enemies,* by Chris Bull and John Gallagher, (New York; Crown Publishers, Inc., 1996), on October 21, 1996, while watching the Jim Lehrer Newshour on public television. David Gergen, editor-at-large of *U.S. News and World Report*, interviewed one of the authors. The interview seemed a rather anemic and innocuous promotion of the book and the view of the authors. We did learn that the book was about the "religious right" and the "gay movement," but it sounded like the book was somewhat neutral, and was arguing that both sides should come to some kind of a cultural compromise, quit fighting and reconcile their differences. Such views sounded somewhat intriguing, although impossible. Neither Mr. Gergen nor the author informed the public of the bias of the authors, and that the book was merely another book trying to insidiously promote the homosexual movement. Neither Mr. Gergen nor the author even saw fit to inform the public as to whether or not the authors were themselves homosexuals. I am firmly convinced, from the content of the book and the information given on the cover of the book about the authors, that both are homosexuals. It was decided that parts of the book would be covered because of the peculiarity of the argument, and because there may be others that might place the importance on it that Mr. Gergen seemed to. The following are my comments.

Chris Bull is a former correspondent for *The Advocate*, a leading national homosexual publication. He received the National Lesbian and Gay Journalists Association's 1994 honors for coverage of gay youth suicide. John Gallagher was a national correspondent for *The Advocate* for the past five years.

The gist and the central thrust of the book seems to be that both sides have been able to raise and spend large sums of money because of their bitter cultural fight. And that they should somehow compromise their cultural differences on some kind of a middle ground that would recognize homosexuality as an acceptable lifestyle, and be tolerant and uncritical of it. All that the religious right would have to do to accomplish this is to turn away from their faith and repudiate the Judaic-Christian principles that have formed the backbone of our country.

Like the writing of all homosexual activists that I have read, the book is replete with unsupported and illogical statements. Its general theme is unsupported attacks on anyone who is opposed to acceptance of homosexuality as righteous and wholesome conduct in our society, and particularly any professional person who opposes it on a scientific basis. "Homophobic" is used throughout the book to describe those opposed to the acceptance of sodomy, and those opposed to the destructive homosexual movement. "Even in Republican circles, evangelical Christians were still widely considered part of the crackpot fringe for their extreme politics and faith in the inerrance of the Bible." (p. 2) Evangelical Christians and the Bible are similarly denigrated in other parts of the book.

The authors have a special hate for Dr. Paul Cameron. They state: "It is hard to imagine a more discredited figure than Cameron." His work is described as "shoddy research" and "crackpot theories." (p. 26) They state :

> Cameron has spent the better part of the AIDS epidemic devising studies to demonstrate that gay men brought AIDS on themselves and the rest of the world. ... (p. 26)

First, I would like to say that it is certainly well established that in this country homosexuals caused the AIDS epidemic among themselves, and caused many innocent people to get AIDS—both through the contamination of blood supplies and by contacts through their promiscuous sexual contacts.

Secondly, I would like to say that this book is one of the most poorly referenced and poorly supported books of this kind that I have ever read. The authors make all kinds of assertions about the work of Dr. Cameron and others, such as the above, yet they give no references to support their emotional assertions. I suppose that they figure that this is the best method to conceal their falsifications. The book attacks the statistical data of Cameron and others, but no where do they point out how they are false, or what the correct figures are. This kind of "factual" writing is completely unacceptable. If an author has first-hand knowledge of a matter, the time, place and circumstances should be explained. If a statement of another author is attacked as wrong, a proper reference should be made to the questioned material, giving the name of the book or writing and the page number, so that a fair comparison may be made. It is hard to believe that a book like *Perfect Enemies* would even be published by a reputable publisher were it not in support of the homosexual movement—something currently favored by the elitist media. This is truly a "shoddy" and "discredited" work.

To contrast the difference between documented references and unsupported assertions, please refer back to the subheading, "Spreading the Aids Virus" in Chapter 1. Look at the actual quotation from the publication of Family Research Institute, *Medical Consequences of What Homosexuals Do,* 1993, on spreading the virus. Dr. Paul Cameron is chairman of the Family Research Institute, and this is undoubtedly the writing referred to by the authors of Perfect Enemies. This is a well-referenced and a professional writing. Then reread the material under this subheading from the other sources on this subject. There is no question about the solid scientific documentation of the statements referred to in the publication of Dr. Cameron's organization. *A Time of AIDS - The Zero Factor,* supra in Chapter 1, explains what were probably the most extensive investigations that have been done in tracing down the cause and spread of AIDS, and it is entirely consistent with Dr.

Cameron's research and publications. It is the homosexualist propaganda by the authors in *Perfect Enemies* that is false and unsupported.

The authors make general attacks on Dr. Cameron's statistics on murder, child molestation, and everything else, but they give no details as to which statistics are actually incorrect or what the correct statistics are. They give no references at all to support the authors' statements. Dr. Cameron and his organization have done many studies on these subjects, later than 1983, but all the authors do is talk about one of his 1983 studies, and give no references, give no figures that they claim are correct, and, in fact, do not even explain in what regard the figures are wrong. The book continually makes such general unsupported attacks on statistics and figures that show the vile acts of homosexuality and the resulting destruction to the ones involved, and to society.

"For all its flaws, the religious right was dependent on Cameron's research to supplement its biblical arguments about the supposed deleterious social consequences of homosexuality." (p. 28) The falsity of this statement is clearly demonstrated in the limited confines of Chapter 1, above, which shows the large number of authorities, other than Dr. Cameron, who all demonstrate the "deleterious social consequences of homosexuality."

"Indeed, an accumulation of cooked statistics and questionable behavior led to Cameron's expulsion from the American Psychological Association in 1983. Cameron would later claim he resigned, or, alternatively, had been drummed out by radical supporters of gay rights upset at his research. The group however does not allow resignations of members under investigation." (p. 28) This unreferenced and unsupported statement is a little ridiculous on its face. No such organization may stop a person from resigning and terminating his relationship. I will certainly give more credence to Dr. Cameron, who had a first-hand knowledge of the facts in question, than to the biased and unsupported statements of these authors. It is also clear that Dr. Cameron was not the only one at odds with the American Psychological Association and the American Psychiatric Association, for their caving in to the homosexual activists, and changing their prior views on homosexuality, which had been long accepted and recognized. The prior views were arrived at by objective research and study, and not by the false views that took their place, which were arrived at by bowing to politics and intimidation. The fiasco of these professional organizations was covered at length in Chapter 2, as was Dr. Cameron's fight with the APA.

In their criticism of the Oregon Citizens Alliance for its opposition to "gay rights" laws, the authors state (p. 51):

> Yet, the Alliance was not content with civil rights arguments alone. The group went much further, characterizing gay life and practices as repulsive and dangerous. In voters' pamphlet distributed before the election, Phillip Ramsdell, the group's political director, outlined his version of gay sexual habits in graphic detail: "Studies by leading researchers show that the following practices are regularly engaged in by homosexuals: fellatio 100%, fisting 41% (inserting fist and forearm into rectum), rimming 92% (licking rectum), water sports 29% (urinating on partners, drinking urine), mud wallowing 17% (defecating on partner), sado-masochism 37% (beating, piercing another person for sexual pleasure), public sex 66% (public restrooms, bathhouses, parks), pedophilia 46% (sex with minors)."

The writing is so general and vague, it's hard to figure out whether the authors are trying to convince us that such acts are not repulsive and dangerous, or whether they are trying to convince us that the statistics are wrong. To any decent person, it is quite obvious that such practices are repulsive and dangerous. As to accuracy, a comparison to the figures set out for such acts in Chapter 1 show no material differences. Why do they not give us what they consider correct statistics for the sexual acts in which homosexuals engage? Why do they not tell us what acts they think are not repulsive, and what acts, if any, they think are repulsive to decent people? Why do they just give general, unsupported, and unreferenced criticism for all of those who do give statistics? This whole book is a classic example of trying to convince society of the very opposite of the truth on the issues discussed. Such fallacies are consistent with activist writings of homosexualists.

On pages 131–139, General Colin Powell and Lt. Col. Robert Lee Maginnis, Inspector General of the Army, are criticized for their opposition to allowing homosexuals to serve in the military. On pages 138–139, they state:

> In January of 1993, Maginnis was tapped by the Army to serve on a five-member panel known as the Homosexual Working Group to

assess the impact on the military lifting the ban. Like the Family Research Council's, Maginnis's work relied heavily upon discredited antigay research. His carefully footnoted articles were filled with references to Paul Cameron, president of Family Research Institute, and Joseph Nicolosi, a therapist who was dedicated to "converting" gay patients to heterosexuality, a practice the American Psychological Association considers a form of patient abuse.

It should be noted that the Family Research Council and the Family Research Institute are two different organizations. To these authors, anyone who opposes the homosexual movement is thereby discredited, and they seem to have a particular dislike for those who still dare to treat homosexuals for their deviant lifestyle.

On page 256 is a diatribe about the Reverend Lou Sheldon, president of the Traditional Values Coalition, who also opposes the promotion of sodomy. Rev. Sheldon had quoted psychiatrist Charles Socarides, who wrote the book, *A Freedom Too Far,* and referred to him as the foremost authority on homosexuality. The authors "discredit" Dr. Socarides by their general terms of saying that he "continues to engage in unethical 'reparative therapy,' which seeks to 'convert' gays to heterosexuality." These authors seem to think that it should be a hanging offense for a professional person to try to help a homosexual who wishes help in leaving the depraved deviancy into which he has fallen.

The book relates a controversy over pornographic and homosexual "art" of Robert Maplethorpe, including the piece that showed the bullwhip protruding from his rectum, and the *Piss Christ* scene of Andres Serrano, both of which were discussed in Chapter 1. It states: "The Maplethorpe controversy was the most visible eruption of a long-standing crusade by conservative Christians against forms of expression that they considered immoral or blasphemous." (p.164) Apparently such things are not considered immoral or blasphemous by the authors.

Chapter 7, "Family Values," of *Perfect Enemies,* amounts to an insidious argument for accepting homosexual families on the same basis as our traditional families, including marriage, adoption, and all of the other aspects. "Yet the religious right, hell-bent on depicting gays as threats to the heterosexual family, refused to recognize that many gays and lesbians maintained stable, loving relationships that are virtually identical to those of heterosexuals in substance, if not in form." (p.202)

If the "religious right" ever accepts the above premise, then religious would be changed to heretical and right to left. In addition, I have yet to hear of a blood relationship of family ties resulting from a homosexual relationship. Also, this is a terrible misuse of the word "love." Love, to me, is something that is not even connected with most acts of sex, although it is often sadly misused in that connotation. A person may or may not truly love a person with whom he or she is engaged in passionate sex. Real love is a natural feeling one has for a husband or wife, parents, brothers and sisters, close members of the family, friends, or even pets. It is a deeply kind and loving affection, and has no sexual overtones, desires, or involvement. It is something a soldier has for a friend for whom he will willingly risk his life on the battlefield. It is not something that causes a person to defile and degrade both himself and his partner by engaging in the vile acts of sodomy. This is indeed a sick use of the word.

On page 277 the authors try to disconnect homosexuals from the Hitler and Nazi movement, and from the Holocaust. Finally they state: "The religious right's use of the Holocaust is an attempt to wrest control of the ultimate symbol of political repression away from gay activists, not legitimate historical inquiry." It is hard to believe that the authors make such a statement about such a complicated subject, on which so much has been written, without one reference whatsoever. These authors have to be educated enough to know how completely unacceptable this type of writing is on factual subjects. It is surely being done for the purpose of intentionally deceiving the gullible reader. It is hard to believe that they are too ignorant to not know better. Not one mention was made of *The Pink Swastika*, supra, the most comprehensive book that I have found on this particular subject.

The last chapter of the book, "From Arms to Armistice," seems to be the summation for the argument that the religious right and the homosexualists should resolve their differences and quit opposing one another. To do this all the religious right has to do is to agree that their is nothing wrong with sodomy, and defer to the homosexual movement. Throughout the book they realize the problem of reconciling such a stance with the Scripture. To overcome this problem they simply teach us that the Bible should not be read or interpreted literally. "For Falwell and the religious right, the tension between adhering to a literal inter-pretation of the Bible and allowing the compromise inherent in main-stream politics never fully eased." (p. 24) Not once in the book is reference made to any particular passage of the Scripture, which it in-sists should not be read "literally."

In the last chapter, they seem to adopt the following: "As the con-servative evangelical leader Tony Campolo has demonstrated, it is in-deed possible to adhere to a strict interpretation of biblical dictates against sex outside of traditional, heterosexual marriage while granting that, as hardworking, tax-paying, God-fearing American citizens, gays and les-bians deserve an equal place in the military and in all aspects of Ameri-can life." (p. 280) There seems to be an irreconcilable conflict in this last statement, if that is what Campolo said. (No reference is given, as usual.) It is somewhat difficult for me to see how a person can be clas-sified as "God-fearing" and at the same time be engaged in homosexual acts, and even worse trying to convince us that homosexuality is an acceptable and righteous "lifestyle."

The whole theme and basic premise of the book *Perfect Enemies* is a contradiction. It tries to reconcile that which is irreconcilable. The religious right could not retain its definition and accept homosexuality as not being a detriment to society, and a sin against God, nature, and humanity.

In contrast to the nebulous, incomprehensible, and fallacious theo-ries and ideas of *Perfect Enemies*, contrast the clear statements of the great Christian author, David Jeremiah:

> We must reject totally the idea that one can be a Spirit filled Chris-tian and a practicing homosexual at the same time. The biblical evi-dence will not allow that position. It is impossible to enter the Kingdom while rejecting and violating the standards of the King. We cannot maintain our Christian integrity if we condone what God condemns. To recognize a gay church as a church in the biblical sense of the word is to degrade the term "Church." You might as well have churches for

fornicators, adulterers, and robbers. The church is called to bring back the straying sheep. We are not called to say to the straying sheep that they are okay in their wanderings and that we ordain their devious paths as alternative lifestyles. [*The Rebirth of America*, Nancy Leigh DeMoss, Editor, (Arthur S. DeMoss Foundation, 1986), p. 108]

The argument that the passages of the Bible directly, unequivocally, and emphatically condemning homosexuality should not be read literally is erroneous on its face. The intent of those particular passages are literal, and that is the only reasonable way that they can be read. These statements in question were not parables. There is nothing about them that is symbolic, figurative, metaphorical, or allegorical.

The Scripture may be accepted or rejected, but it remains forever as it is. And it is a meaningless farce to try to make it out the opposite of what it is.

Homosexuals are not alone in falling into the trap of making themselves believe that there is nothing wrong with particular things in which they engage that are against traditional and long established ideas of what is right and wrong. Many heterosexuals do the same thing. When one fails to recognize that something he or she is doing is wrong and sinful, because it is something that such person is doing and wants to do, and is being done by others, then one is becoming psychologically sick. When others begin to think the same way, then it becomes destructive to the mores of the community. Examples in our society are couples having sex and living together out of wedlock, having illegitimate children, using drugs, and excessively using alcohol. First they are tolerated, then they are accepted. And then they become a cancerous pathological sickness of our society.

God and nature made women with female sexual organs and men with male sexual organs. The primary reason and intent was quite obviously for procreation and continuation of the species. The fact that there is satisfaction or enjoyment in sexual acts is a natural part of the overall plan and purpose. Men are not made with organs meant to receive the sexual organ of another man; and women are not made with any organ meant to be inserted in the sexual organ of another woman. Throughout time people have recognized this, and this is why sodomy is called a crime against nature.

Any person with natural sensibilities has a natural aversion to all acts of sodomy and is repulsed by those who engage in such acts. Throughout history such acts were considered to be highly depraved conduct to the extent that advanced societies have throughout history made sodomy a criminal act. In some societies such acts were considered so heinous that the sentence for the crime was death.

Now the liberal homosexualists would teach us that nature is wrong, that the Bible is wrong, and that their despicable acts of sodomy are normal and acceptable. And that we who retain natural feelings and sensibilities, and certainly those who still hold to Christian-Judaic principles, are the ones who are deviant, being beset by the made-up illness of "homophobia." They insist that all of us, including small children, must be brainwashed until we fully accept their corruption as perfectly right. What is utterly amazing is the success that they have had!

It truly appears that our blind acceptance of modern liberalism is making us a nation of fools.

CHAPTER 4

OUR RAPID DECLINE IN MORALITY

The destruction reaped from the moral decline in this country, for just the past thirty years, is indeed tremendous. Thirty years ago I could not have imagined the depth of the depravity into which this country would slip, slide, and fall.

By having the idea that no one should be discriminated against, regardless of their moral character and conduct, pounded into us for thirty years by the various leftist movements and their media supporters, we are fast becoming a mindlessly permissive society with the inability to distinguish between right and wrong.

We have, because of this moral decline, been forced into a fight for our personal survival. We are not even safe in our homes, and certainly not on our streets. Children are murdering other children in our schools and on our streets. Drug use and teen-age pregnancy, and immorality generally, are prevalent in our public schools. Children murder older people and helpless people in their homes. The mayor of Washington, D. C., the capital of our nation, has recently asked that the National Guard be called out to protect the residents of the seat of our government from their fellow citizens who are on a rampage of crime and murder. But the worst and most dangerous thing is the apparent inability of our people to even recognize what has caused and is causing these things to occur.

Our moral degradation and its resulting violence and degenerate behavior of our children is blamed by the liberal media and the liberal politicians on such things as poverty and the availability of guns. When people even suggest the real cause, which is the decline of religious and moral values, they are called fundamentalist religious bigots by the liberal media and politicians. These leftists even support and promote sodomy, which is the epitome of vile and depraved conduct.

When this country was in its infancy, when we were fighting for our independence, there existed a level of poverty and hardship which was unbelievably greater than anything that existed in this country during the last thirty years. And almost all people had guns. Those guns were what our forefathers used to fight the British for their independence. But the people were highly religious, and moral values were of the greatest importance to them. Our society then was not the permissive society we have now. Sodomy, the cohabiting of unmarried couples, having children out of wedlock, sex between unmarried couples, sex and even sodomy between children, and the idea that those who work and are productive should be taxed to support those who choose not to work and those who choose to have illegitimate children they cannot support, were things that were not accepted or condoned. Such ideas just did not exist in that society. This is the basic reason that the United States of America exists today.

During the period of the Great Depression, in the 1930s, I lived in the panhandle of Texas, an area plagued by extreme drought. There in the dust bowl, and in many other parts of the country, there were substantial periods of unemployment as high as forty and fifty percent. Compared to today, the hardship and poverty that existed was tremendous. But people survived, primarily because of their morality, basic religious beliefs, hard working ethics, and helping one another. All of these principles and basic beliefs are complementary and harmonious.

Back then, in the town in which I lived, people did not have bars on their windows, and many never even locked their doors when they were absent. The same was true in the country. If someone dropped by for a visit, and you weren't there, they would often go into the house and make themselves at home while they waited for you to get home. Can you even imagine such things as that in this day and time? People did not live in continual fear for their lives, and of having everything they owned carted off by thieves if they were not guarding their property for a few moments. People had and knew how to use guns, but our streets were safe to travel, even on foot, and at night. It was generally unheard of for school children to become pregnant, or for them to use drugs or murder each other. Sodomy was considered to be as vile and as depraved an activity as one could engage in, and was a felony. I went through public grade school and high school, served in combat in World War II for over three years. I never personally knew any school girl who became pregnant, I knew of no murders by schoolchildren, or even assaults, other than fist fights between boys. I never personally knew a person who used drugs, until the last thirty years, although I knew a lot of cowboys and soldiers who drank plenty. I never personally knew a student, a soldier or a sailor who was a homosexual, or any other kind of a sex pervert. I certainly am not saying that everything we did was right and moral, because it wasn't. But we had not yet entered into the moral decay that has resulted in the degeneration and degradation that exists today.

People now have their community meetings and wring their hands about what is going on in our public schools. Yet they seem unable to even comprehend what is causing the problems, or what to do about it. There are comparatively few of them that even mention the need to return to the basic moral and religious principles on which this country was founded, and those who suggest such things are referred to as dinosaurs or unenlightened bigots. "This is the new millennium," they say. With this outlook, things can only get worse. Banning guns, passing out condoms to school children, and teaching them that engaging in sodomy is an acceptable alternative lifestyle will not cure the problems in our society. Such ideas are part and parcel of the problem, and only sink us further into the quagmire of our immorality. Until a sufficient number or our citizens return to the moral and family values which were the basic foundation of our country, and which made it a great country for so many years, the disintegration of our society will continue.

How did we drift into this quagmire? Certainly things that were good for this country, and needed changes, grew out of the civil rights movement for blacks. But that movement was not the only one going on in this country. Along with it there was a hotbed of liberalism, ideas of "tolerance," and the "anything goes" attitudes that have reduced the morals of this country to the depths of depravity. There were demonstrations, civil disobedience, riots, lawlessness, and legal litigation against those who disagreed with certain views, against owners lawfully using their property, and against those properly carrying out their legal duties in government offices. Flower children, hippies, and draft-dodgers became common in the 1960s. A generation grew up with little morality, and now have raised children with no sense at all of what is right and what is wrong. The cultural decline produced poor work ethics, unwed mothers, crime, drug use, homelessness caused by dereliction, and open homosexuality.

Jenkin Lloyd Jones wrote an article, "An Editor's Outlook," for the Los Angeles Times, published under the title, "Report About Class of '65 Tragedy Not Overdrawn," in the *Albuquerque Journal*, 10-18-76. The article started out by referring to the book, *What Really Happened to the Class of '65*, by David Wallenchinsky and Michel Medved, about the 1965 graduating class of the Los Angeles Palisades High School, just down Topanga Canyon from UCLA and Beverly Hills. These graduates were a group of young people from prosperous families who had all of the advantages and a good prospect for making something good and useful of their lives. The authors wondered "if there were any normal young-life histories among those particular graduates." Their book was built on sixty-five interviews of these students. Of those, "fifty lives turned sour," and the writers claimed to have skipped over some of the gloomiest cases. *Time* magazine had selected that very class eleven years before for a special article, saying that this class was "on the fringe of a golden era." What happened?

Mr. Jones said:

> From the classmate voted "most popular," who killed himself six years later, to the woman who fell into a heroin-induced stupor even as she was being interviewed, there emerges the picture of a rudderless, confused unhappy and even self-destructive generation.

But why? I agree with Jones's assessment:

> Growing up has always been a problem in America or any other land. But here was one that grew up blind. Their parents, who had

remembered the Great Depression as children and the privations of World War II, were determined to give them everything but values.

It was a society in which religion, where it existed at all, was usually shallow and perfunctory, where horsepower, clothing labels, price tags and swimming pools were gods, and where the Beatles were the prophets.

And so it was the generation of the up-chucking, of fierce revolt, of a wistful effort to find something—anything —to believe in.

As such, it was a sucker for hedonism, for if there are no other values what is more natural than to do what comes naturally, to "let it all hang out" as the commandment went? Pot is a positive good, pills a way around perplexities, LSD a road to revelation, and casual sex a healthy recreation. ***

Home had not laid down any law. Home had bowed to demand and whim. Schools had long since ceased to impart moral homilies. Doing your own thing, however useless, trivial or self-damaging, was in. ***

It was deprived of the knowledge that liberties will never last for those who will risk nothing for them, and that tyranny is unafraid of magic symbolism, such as flowers painted on Volkswagens. It was even robbed of love, being untaught that casual orgasms are not the stuff of which love is made. ***

Certainly, in the 1960s and 1970s, we had tremendous damage done to our country by the prevalence of drug users, flower children, sex revolutionists, draft dodgers and war protesters. With the help of the liberal media and the liberal politicians, we lost the Vietnam war—a shameful first for our country. We cowardly forsook our ally and let South Vietnam be taken over by the Communists. This will forever be a blot on American history. The United States had the full capability to end this war in a matter of weeks—and without even using our atomic power. The North Vietnam forces were so strung out and stretched that by the use of strategic bombing, as was done in World War II, against the power plants, factories, and transportation centers in North Vietnam, we could easily, and in a very short period of time, have destroyed the ability of North Vietnam to conduct war. But instead our government was sending our young people to be exposed to the dangers of war for long periods of time—with no will or purpose to even win the war.

Never should a soldier be forced continually, day after day, to put his life on the line in battle, without an all out effort by his country to win the war. This degrades the life of the soldier to an unbearable and unforgivable degree. But as demeaning and destructive as these radical ideas were in this period—the worst was yet to come. The more permanent damage was just beginning.

The real damage occurred when many of these gutless radicals— still devoid of traditional morals—took over as teachers, professors, and administrators of our schools and universities. Later, they became officials running our national and local governments. And, to our shame, one of them even became our president.

Consider an article by columnist James J. Kilpatrick, about the corruptness in our universities and the harm being done the students:

Radicals Are Ruining American Universities

Are their minds being enriched? Two authors in recent months have come up with the same answer: No, their minds are not being enriched. Their brains are being washed. In many of the nation's top colleges and universities, radical professors and militant students have succeeded in ravaging the traditional groves of academe.

These conclusions are advanced by Roger Kimball in "Tenured Radicals" and by Charles J. Sykes in "The Hollow Men." The works ought to be on best-seller lists, but neither one has received the audience it deserves. Kimball captures the corruption of the humanities (the political infection of art, architecture, philosophy, and social studies). Sykes focuses more narrowly on the corruption of one institution that he once admired: Dartmouth. He methodically chronicles the cowardice of Dartmouth's administrators and the bullying tactics of the radicals. It is an ugly, ugly story.

... A new breed of professors create a pretty smorgasbord of courses that offered easy alternatives to disciplined learning.

(There was an outright revolution in 1964 replacing meaningful and traditional curriculum with radical ideas and material.) Dartmouth was not alone.

This was the period that saw the rise of Black studies. [Here the terrorizing of Cornell and its president James Perkins is described, which is covered below in reference to Judge Bork's book.] Thus terrorized, [Perkins] turned to jelly [and praised the incident as a great thing for Cornell]. *** (*Albuquerque Journal*, 11-14-90)

The article goes on to explain further incidents, primarily in the 1960s, at other universities, as well as more incidents at Dartmouth. The liberal and cowardly faculty at Harvard voted 248 to 149 "not to criticize the violent seizure of the administration building." "At Stanford, militants pelted Vice President Hubert Humphrey with urine and excrement. The disrupting students were quickly forgiven." At Dartmouth, students drove Alabama Governor George Wallace off the campus, "rocking and pounding on his car," and no punishment was imposed. There, in 1968, they invaded the office of President John Sloan Dickey, pushed him down a flight of stairs, and he then caved in to their demands to phase out the ROTC program. "After the violence finally subsided, 22 Dartmouth professors issued a joint letter defending the students as "sincere, dedicated and thoughtful young people."

These things described herein are only a small part of the incidents relating the capitulation of our educational institutions, and a large segment of our society, to the radicalism that gained a strong foothold in the 1960s, and continues until now—ever increasing.

The climate was a natural one, back in the sixties, for the beginning of the homosexual movement—and begin it did.

Homosexuality is considered as playing an important part in, and at the same time being a terrible result of, our cultural decline. The two factors feed on and increase the other. If a society can be desensitized and conditioned into accepting something that is as vile and unnatural as homosexuality, and as strongly condemned by the Bible; then there is little left that may be too sinful and destructive to become acceptable.

With all of this there has developed a liberal news media that is an extreme detriment to our society. They continually and systematically intone their anti-religious ideas, and their modern liberal views that are contrary to traditional values of this country, into what is supposed to be the reporting of facts that constitute the news. It has become very difficult to get unbiased and factual news.

Let us consider some of the ideas, depravity, and tragedy resulting from our moral decline. The fact that a steep moral decline has occurred in the last half of this century should be obvious to any thinking person. The causes are more complex. They are a complete mystery to the atheistic element of this country because it is blinded to the benefits this country derived form its religious beliefs. Many seem not to understand that the driving force of the founders of this country in forming our constitution was their religious beliefs. Morals based on religious beliefs were the basis of our laws for the first two hundred years. Laws were for the purpose of doing justice among people—and justice was considered to be what was right and fair—and was based on Christian and Judaic ethics and principles.

Morals necessarily have a religious basis—a basis that does not change with the new ideas of individuals. Otherwise we have a moral anarchy, in which each individual has as much right as the other to determine what is right and what is wrong. There would be as many sets of morals as there are individuals. Each person's idea on morality would be as valid as the next one's, and none would really have any validity at all. We are adrift with no anchor and with no compass. This lack of absolutes is the basis of secularism and "humanism" that are at the root of the great moral decline and moral decay in our country. In this chapter we consider the causes of our moral decline, and the destructive results of it. We consider the part that homosexuality has played in it. In Chapter 8, we will explore what can now be done, if anything, to bring this country back toward the morality and greatness it once enjoyed.

A number of prominent individuals and writers have wrestled with the problems of our cultural decline. Three excellent books that I would recommend on the subject are:

Bennett, William J.; *The Index of Leading Cultural Indicators* (Simon & Schuster, New York [and other major cities], 1994)
The Rebirth of America, Nancy Leigh DeMoss, Editor (Arthur S. DeMoss Foundation, 1986)
Bork, Robert H.; *Slouching Towards Gomorrah* (HarperCollins Publishers, Inc., New York, 1996)

These books are a rich source of ideas, and each is a warehouse of factual information on the causes and effects of our moral decline, the devastating results; and possible ways to reverse the decline. They deal with the decline in a much more general sense. For my purposes, the general decline is of great importance, but this book concentrates on the part played by the homosexual movement.

Each of these three books will be reviewed in the order listed above. The facts and ideas reported and brought out from them should be compared. They are entirely consistent. Together, they show the decay and degradation of our society, but they also point the way back to a decent and worthwhile life for our country, by recapturing our traditional religious and moral values. These values must again be instilled in our children. Any idea that a civilization is going to have good morals, without a religious base and mooring is indeed a fallacy that is well demonstrated.

The following is information derived from *The Index of Leading Cultural Indicators*, By William J. Bennett, supra. Mr. Bennett is co-director of Empower America, a distinguished fellow in Cultural Policy Studies at the Heritage Foundation, and a senior editor of *National Review* magazine. He has served as director of the Office of National Drug Control Policy, Secretary of Education, and chairman of the National Endowment for the Humanities.

The book has a very large and comprehensive compilation of statistics, and comments on their interpretation and meaning. The sources were primarily agencies of the federal government which compile such information, although a few other reputable sources are used. The following is stated in the Introduction, page 8:

> Over the past three decades we have experienced substantial social regression. Today the forces of social decomposition are challenging— and in some instances, overtaking—the forces of social composition. And when decomposition takes hold, it exacts an enormous human cost. *Unless these exploding social pathologies are reversed, they will lead to the decline and perhaps even the fall of the American Republic.*
>
> Since 1960, population has increased 41 percent; the Gross Domestic Product has nearly tripled; and total levels of spending by all levels of government (measured in constant 1990 dollars) have risen from $143.73 billion to $787.0 billion—more than a five-fold increase. Inflation-adjusted spending on welfare has increased 630 percent and inflation-adjusted spending on education has increased more than 200 percent. The United States has the strongest economy in the world, a still-healthy work ethic, and a generous attitude—good signs all.

But during the same 30-year period there has been more than a 500 percent increase in violent crime; more than a 400 percent increase in illegitimate births; a tripling of the percentage of children living in single-parent homes; and a drop of almost 75 points in SAT scores. Modern-day social pathologies have gotten worse. They seem impervious to government spending on their alleviation, even very large amounts of spending.

Pages 9–10:

This palpable cultural decline is the manifestation of a marked shift in the public's beliefs, attitudes, and priorities. Social scientist James Q. Wilson writes that "the powers exercised by the institutions of social control have been constrained and people, especially young people, have embraced an ethos that values self-expression over self-control." According to pollster Daniel Yankelovich, our society now places less value than before on what we owe others as a matter of moral obligation; less value on sacrifice as a moral good; less value on social conformity, respectability, and observing the rules; and less value on correctness and restraint in matters of physical pleasure and sexuality. Higher value is now placed on things like self-expression, individualism, self-realization, and personal choice.

...Nobel Prize-winning author Aleksandr Solzhenitsyn, in a recent speech, said, "The West ... has been undergoing an erosion and obscuring of high moral and ethical ideas. The spiritual axis of life has grown dim." And novelist John Updike has put it this way: "The fact that, compared to the inhabitants of Africa and Russia, we still live well, cannot ease the pain of feeling we no longer live nobly."

In 1960, the percentages of illegitimate births of all births in this country, were 5.3 for all races, 2.3 for whites, and 23.0 for blacks; in 1991, the respective percentages were 29.5, 21.8, and 67.9.(p. 46) Certainly, all of the increases are troubling and deplorable, but the almost ten-fold increase for whites is consistent with their particularly alarming decrease in moral values.

"By 2000, according to some projections, 40 percent of all American births and 80 percent of minority births will occur out of wedlock." (p. 47)

Some consider illegitimate births—and the fatherless children that result— the most important problem we have today. They are not only a sign of the moral destruction of our society, but they are the cause of even further destruction. They increase poverty, crime, and immorality, generally.

From 1960 to 1991, the marriage rate decreased from 74 to 54 marriages for every 1,000 unmarried women; a decrease of 27 percent. For the same period, divorces increased form 9 to 21 per 1,000 married women; an increase of 133 percent. (p. 58)

Children in poverty went from 26.9 percent in 1960 down to 15.1 percent in 1970, and then back up to 21.8 percent of our children in 1991. (p. 61)

Children on government welfare went from 3.5 percent in 1960 to 12.9 percent in 1991. (p. 64) This burden on the productive segment of our society, the taxpayers, more than tripled.

"In the 1950s, before the 'War on Poverty' was launched as part of [President] Lyndon Johnson's Great Society, nearly one-third of all poor families were headed by adults who worked full-time during the year. In 1990, only 15 percent of all poor families had working heads of households. Half of poor, non-elderly adults do not work at all." (p. 65)

It appears that our welfare programs actually increase poverty and idleness, instead of decreasing them as was intended. Not only have they failed their intended purpose, but they have encouraged the breakdown of the traditional family, where a working man was the head of the household.

The rate for unmarried teenage births per 1,000 teenage girls, went up from 15.3 in 1960, to 44.8 in 1991. (p. 72) The rate of unmarried teenage pregnancy rates, per 1,000 unmarried teens, went up from 49.4 in 1972, to 99.2 in 1990; and the rate of teenage abortions, per 1,000 teenage girls, went from 19.9 to 43.8 for the same period. (pp. 74–75)

Teenage suicide rates more than tripled in 30 years, going up from 3.6 in 1960, to 11.3, in 1990, per 100,000 children 15 to 19 years old. (p. 78) It is also noted that for every successful suicide there are at least fifty to one hundred adolescent suicide attempts. (p. 79)

From 1960 to 1990, total expenditures on elementary and secondary schools, adjusted to constant 1989 dollars, increased from approximately $90 billion to $250 billion. Yet during the same period SAT scores went from 975 to 902. (pp. 83–84)

A comparison was made of the 1989 expenditures per student by seven of the more modern and industrialized countries, and the United

States made the greatest expenditures, adjusting all to 1989 dollars. The order of ranking from the highest of just under $4,000 per student, to the lowest of just over $2,000 per student, were the United States, Canada, Italy, West Germany, France, United Kingdom, and Japan. (p.91) In 1988, International Assessment of Educational Progress exams in science were given to students of five countries. The United states ranked the lowest. Their rankings were (mean scores, 0 - 1,000): Korea 568, Spain 512, United Kingdom 510, Ireland 504, United States 474. (p. 85) This is indeed a sad commentary.

It also appears that education is another area where merely spending more money seems to have the opposite of the intended effect; and that the entry of the government into the education field has had a detrimental effect.

However, to me the saddest thing of all was the results of a survey of the American public schools on the top disciplinary problems of public school teachers for the years 1940 and 1990, published in the *Congressional Quarterly*, and shown on page 83 of Mr. Bennett's book. They were, ranked in order of importance:

1940	1990
Talking out of turn.	Drug Abuse.
Chewing gum.	Alcohol Abuse.
Making noise.	Pregnancy.
Running in the halls.	Suicide.
Cutting in line.	Rape.
Dress-code violations.	Robbery.
Littering.	Assault.

Please note that not one of the minor things listed in 1940 were even listed for 1990, and vice-versa. These things show, above all, our serious moral degeneration. When children have no morality when they enter school, or turn bad before they even leave school, our country is in serious trouble.

Although total church membership has slightly increased during the past thirty years, from 1960 to 1990; as a percentage of the population, it has slightly decreased, from 63.3 percent to 59.3 percent. (p. 115)

Page 117:

Commentary on Religion
"Of all the dispositions and habits which lead to political prosperity, Religion and Morality are indispensable supports. In vain would that man claim the tribute of patriotism who should labor to subvert these great pillars of human happiness, these firmest props of the duties of men and citizens.... And let us with caution indulge the supposition that morality can be maintained without religion. Whatever may be conceded to the influence of refined education on minds of peculiar structure, reason and experience both forbid us to expect that national morality can prevail in exclusion of religious principle."

—George Washington, 1796

"While the church may seem to be experiencing a season of growth and prosperity, it is failing to move people to commitment and sacrifice. The hard truth is that we have substituted an institutionalized religion for the life-changing dynamic of a living faith.... When compared with previous generations of believers, we seem among the most thoroughly at peace with our culture, the least adept at transforming society, and the most desperate for a meaningful faith. Our *raison d'être* is confused, our mission obscured, and our existence as a people in jeopardy."

—Charles Colson
Prison Fellowship

"There is little hope for democracy if the hearts of men and women in democratic societies cannot be touched by a call to something greater than themselves. Political structures, state institutions, collective ideals are not enough. We Parliamentarians can legislate for the rule of law. You the Church can teach the life of faith. When all is said and done, a politician's role is a humble one.

—Margaret Thatcher
Prime Minister of Great Britain,
1979-1990

The Rebirth of America is a collection of fine writings and expressed thoughts that go back in history to the beginning of our country, and come up to our modern times and problems, with thoughtful editorial comments. It includes statements and thoughts from such people as George Washington, at the beginning of our country, to Ronald Reagan in modern times.

Throughout the history of our country, the greatest minds and thinkers — our leaders, have stressed the importance of our traditional religious values in keeping this country on its course, and in making democracy work. We had the admonition of George Washington, in 1796, set forth above, out of *The Index of Leading Cultural Indicators*.

From *The Rebirth of America*, page 21, we have the admonition in 1851 of Daniel Webster, one of the great senators and statesmen of this country:

> Let the religious element in man's nature be neglected, let him be influenced by no higher motives than low self interest, and subjected to no stronger restraint than the limits of civil authority, and he becomes the creature of selfish passion or blind fanaticism.
>
> On the other hand, the cultivation of the religious sentiment represses licentiousness ... inspires respect for law and order, and gives strength to whole social fabric, at the same time that it conducts the human soul upward to the Author of its being.

(In this section, further references to *The Rebirth of America* will be made only by giving page numbers in the book.)

At pages 78–79, we have the clear assessment of Senator Jesse Helms, in 1976, as to what we had already fallen into in our time:

> In the brief history of our country since we gained our independence, we can look back upon a tremendous heritage of political freedom founded upon a biblical faith and a biblical understanding of the nature of man. Moreover, we can look back upon the material signs of God's blessing in a fruitful and bounteous country, with success in almost every enterprise in war and peace.
>
> But within my own lifetime, I have seen the most ferocious assaults on Christian faith and morals; first on the part of the intellectual community, and then on the part of the government. Especially

in the last 25 years, the federal government has not even tried to conceal its hostility to religion; now, with many of our churches in disarray, the attack is being prepared against the family as the last bastion opposing the totalitarian state. Militant atheists and socialists have gone very far in imposing their view of life and man on almost every American institution.

And what have we reaped as a nation from our many personal and collective delinquencies? Atheist schools, rampaging crimes, God forsaken homes, drugs, abortion, pornography, permissiveness, a sense of cynicism, and spiritual desolation absolutely unprecedented in our country's history.

(Senator Jesse Helms continues to this day fighting the cultural decline in this country, which he long ago recognized. In 1996, he played a major part in the defeat of the homosexual employment rights bill; and in passing the Defense of Marriage Act, so that states would not have to recognize homosexual marriages that might be legalized in other states.)

Even by 1982, David Jeremiah recognized the evil onslaught on our culture by the homosexual movement, and its destructive successes. He stated (p. 106):

> ...Certainly there have been homosexuals in America since the early days of our country, but the militant and open flaunting of homosexual perversion is a relatively recent development.
>
> The following are just a few of the many advances of the Gay Rights Movement in our country today:
>
> • The "Blueboy," a magazine something like a homosexual "Playboy," is published by Donald Embinder, a 44-year-old gay publisher. At the last check, the magazine had a circulation of over 135,000.
> • 39 cities, towns and counties, including Detroit, Washington, D.C., and Minneapolis, have enacted ordinances forbidding discrimination against homosexuals in jobs and housing.
> • 120 major corporations, including AT&T and IBM, have announced that they do not discriminate in hiring or promoting people because they are homosexuals.

- TV and movies are treating gay themes more openly and sympathetically. ABC's hit series "Soap," for example, had two homosexual characters, one a macho football player.
- The Metropolitan Community Church, largely made up of homosexuals, is headquartered in Los Angeles, and has 110 congregations and mission stations. It even sends "missionaries" to organize new churches throughout the U.S., Canada, and Europe.
- Gay rights legislation is being sought that would elevate homosexuality to normalcy along with heterosexuality, give gays increased leverage to secure jobs on a quota basis, force the military and public schools to hire avowed homosexuals, and make it impossible for even church organizations to fire a homosexual if he or she were discovered after hiring.

The observations by Mr. Jeremiah, in 1982, of the extent to which the homosexualists had degenerated this country by then were only a harbinger of things to come.

Dr. D. James Kennedy relates:

One woman went to her son's school to speak to the teacher. She had heard something about the new social studies textbooks, or a series of them called "The Promise of America." The teacher was a bit embarrassed and finally said, "We don't show some textbooks to parents." The woman said that she felt a little bit bad about it, but when all the students were out at recess, she went in and borrowed her son's textbook. She read it and was astounded! No wonder they do not show those textbooks to parents! It was filled with all sorts of profanity and blasphemy and obscenities — gutter language. It endorsed illicit sex, sex out of marriage, homosexuality and abortion. It dragged the church and God in the mud, it was unpatriotic, it recommended draft dodging, and a number of other "wholesome values" that were being taught our children. Yet, most of the parents are completely oblivious to the whole thing. (pp. 124–125)

Now let us move on a decade, and consider the further decay that has become so evident in our society.

Robert H. Bork, author of *Slouching Towards Gomorrah*, supra, was nominated by President George Bush, during his presidency, to be a justice of the United States Supreme Court. In my opinion, there could not have been a better man for that position. Judge Bork was successful in the private practice of law with a major law firm, taught constitutional law as the Alexander M. Bickel Professor of Public Law at the Yale law school, served as Solicitor General, and served as a highly respected United States Court of Appeals Judge. There was a democratic majority in the senate, full of liberals, and Judge Bork could not gain approval. The sole reason was that Judge Bork was a conservative, and believed in interpreting the law and the Constitution according to its plain wording, and the intent of the framers of the Constitution, the bodies which promulgated amendments, and the bodies that pass the laws in question. This is contrary to liberal ideology, as liberal judges are prone to make decisions according to their own liberal political ideas. This is called judicial legislation, and is one of the most destructive aspects of modern liberalism. Judge Bork focuses on such judicial legislation, particularly as to the United States Supreme Court, in Part I. Chapter 6, of his book. I take it up at some length in Chapter 8 of this book.

I consider *Slouching Towards Gomorrah* to be one of the finest and most meaningful of any factual and philosophical books I have ever read. Judge Bork describes the unrelenting assault on and destruction of our society. The following relates to facts and thoughts derived from that book.

> "With each new evidence of deterioration, we lament for a moment, and then become accustomed to it. We hear one day of the latest rap song calling for killing policemen or the sexual mutilation of women; the next, of coercive left-wing political indoctrination at a prestigious university; then of the latest homicide figures for New York City, Los Angeles, or the District of Columbia; of the collapse of the criminal justice system, which displays an inability to punish adequately and, often enough, an inability even to convict the clearly guilty; of the rising rate of illegitimate births; the uninhibited display of sexuality and the popularization of violence in our entertainment; homosexuality, environmentalism, animal rights—the list could be extended indefinitely." (pp. 2–3)

(Environmentalism and animal rights groups are destructive to society when their ideas are carried to the extreme that some are today. Some advocate usurping both individual and property rights, and some such radicals are advocating the elimination of all hunting and fishing. And some would even prevent us from eating animals and fish. These are the kind of things Judge Bork includes in "modern liberalism." No reasonable person objects to a balanced approach to the protection of our environment, nor does he believe in the mistreatment of animals. We have long had laws against such things.)

The following relates to how we are being desensitized to the point of a complete callousness to the moral degradation taking place around us:

> So unrelenting is the assault on our sensibilities that many of us grow numb, finding resignation to be the rational, adaptive response to an environment that is increasingly polluted and apparently beyond our control. That is what Senator Daniel Patrick Moynihan calls "defining deviancy down." Moynihan cites the "Durkheim constant." Emile Durkheim, a founder of sociology, posited that there is a limit to the amount of deviant behavior any community can "afford to recognize. As behavior worsens, the community adjusts its standards so that conduct once thought reprehensible is no longer deemed so." ... (p. 3)

(At this point I would like to inject some thoughts from two other great thinkers on this subject. One is William J. Bennett, of our current times, and one is from the time of the founding of this country—by Abigail Adams, wife of John Adams, our second president. These ideas are from *Our Sacred Honor*, by William J. Bennett, Broadman and Holman, Nashville, Tenn. 1997, pp. 241–242. Mr. Bennett calls this phenomenon "getting used to decadence." Mrs. Adams' ideas were set forth in a letter to her sister, Mary Crouch, February 20, 1785. She was primarily complaining about things she had seen in Paris and Europe, and about the scantily clad dancing girls in Paris. She said, "I have been more than ever convinced that there is no summit of virtue, and no depth of vice of which human nature is not capable of rising to, on the one hand, or sinking into on the other. I have felt the force of an observation I have read, that 'daily example is the most subtle of prisons.' I have found my taste reconciling itself to habits customs and fashions, which at first disgusted me." But at the end of the letter, she concludes, "my abhorrence is not lessened, and neither my reason or judgment have accompanied my sensibility in acquiring any degree of callousness." What we all need today is the ability of Abigail Adams to retain the principles handed down to us by the great people who paved the way for us in this country. They made it a great country, but today its people are sinking it to depths of degradation that Abigail and John Adams could not have imagined.)

The following is related by Judge Bork from writing of the well-known and respected columnist Charles Krauthammer: "As a part of the vast social project of moral leveling, it is not enough for the deviant to be normalized. The normal must be found to be deviant." (pp. 3–4) A more fitting description could not be made of the project of the homosexualists to teach us that homosexuality is normal and acceptable, and that those who think otherwise are now to be considered abnormal—they are "bigoted" and "homophobic." Although the homosexual assault on us is the most vicious and base that has ever been made on American civilization, we have already become largely numb and acceptable to fornication, adultery, drug use, clean needles for drug addicts, sex and AIDS education, illegitimate pregnancies and births, abortions for birth control, and many other evils. The acceptance of these immoralities in our society has substantially desensitized us and paved the way for the acceptance of the most vile thing yet—homosexuality. And the homosexuals are rapidly and very effectively carrying out their well laid plan of "First let the camel get his nose inside the tent—and only later his unsightly derriere!", as explained in Chapter 6.

Judge Bork chooses to use the term, "modern liberalism," for the current form of liberalism that is wreaking havoc to our social structure. (pp. 4–5)

Perhaps one of the most important contributions the book makes to our historical and philosophical literature, is the explanation of the destructive effect of modern liberalism in our universities. Judge Bork not only had a first hand knowledge of much of this, but has also made a careful study of the matter. He explains that those with the radical and destructive ideas of the sixties were not defeated; many of them occupied our places of higher learning and influenced the curriculum. (p. 13). They became instructors and professors in our universities. This is undoubtedly how they have wreaked the greatest havoc to this country—they have injected their poisonous influence and ideas into the minds of students when they are in the most receptive stages of their lives. The revolt was not just against the Vietnam War, but against our entire culture. This radical element considered the United States "deeply immoral, being racist, sexist, authoritarian, and imperialistic." (p. 32) The radicals now control the institutions they formerly attacked (p. 34).

At the beginning of the introduction (p. 1), Judge Bork describes one morning on his way to teach a class, when he came upon smoldering books that had been burned in the law library. In Chapter 2, there is a section, THE SACKING OF THE UNIVERSITIES. Further turmoil at Yale is described, such as "student strikes, arson in the university buildings, (three episodes in the law school alone), angry demonstrations, classroom disruptions, rejection of rationality as reactionary, obscenities shouted at faculty members, the usual assortment of barbarities. (p. 37)

Faculty members took their work and research home with them to avoid destruction. Professors at other universities had suffered losses of years of work. A minority of radicals, because of their aggressiveness and militancy were able to set the tone and effectively control the institutions. (p. 38)

Bobby Seale, a national Black Panther leader, and other Panther members were indicted and to be tried for murder. None of his crimes had anything to do with Ivy League universities, but in 1970, when the time for trial neared, black students and radical whites set out to sack these universities. That the victim had been murdered and tortured seemed to matter little to the radical students, or even to some of the radical members of the faculty. Little was done to Yale, because it had advance warning and there was a massing of federal troops and police to protect it. Cornell collapsed. Rifle-carrying black students trashed a library and occupied a building. The president, James A. Perkins, publicly acquiesced to the leaders of the riots and demonstrations. They had him sitting cross-legged on the stage, while they mocked and berated him, and while they made their speeches. President Perkins then exhibited the extreme lack of courage of then submissively telling the crowd that their disobedience and destruction was "probably one of the most constructive, positive forces that have been set in motion in the history of Cornell." (p. 43)

The cowardice described above was not limited to Cornell. It was also exhibited by most of the colleges and universities in the country, and sadly enough, it continued to be exhibited, and still exists in them today. Today, they are capitulating to the homosexual movement the same way that they did to the radicalism of the sixties and seventies. As an example, you will recall the homosexual activities described at Harvard in Chapter 1. I believe that most of the places of higher learning in the country have embraced the anti-discrimination part of the homosexual movement. Homosexuals are at will to conduct their activities and have their organizations on campuses, but religious organizations have been sorely limited, and lawsuits have had to be brought to obtain even the allowance of religious organizations on campuses. The march of our universities to the tune of the radical liberals has resulted in some of the greatest harm that has ever befallen this country. Instead of getting the quality of education they should, our young people, when they are the most impressionable, are indoctrinated with an attack on our traditional morals and culture, in the form of radical liberalism. I once talked to a bright young law graduate from the University of New Mexico about coming into my office. He had written and had published a law review article about an appealed case that I had handled, and his excellent legal writing and understanding got my attention. But he had just accepted a scholarship for a graduate degree at George Washington University and wanted to finish that project. He was there during the period of the riots and disturbances related by Judge Bork. He later informed me that his views had changed, and he was no longer interested in practicing the type of law in which my office was primarily engaged — civil trial work. He was more interested in defending criminal defendants, who he seemed to think were being generally mistreated by our society. He came back a liberal and an ACLU type that I would not have had in my office.

Now back to *Slouching Towards Gomorrah*.

In the spring of 1970, the U.S. made an invasion of Cambodia to try to eliminate a sanctuary from which our troops in South Vietnam were being attacked. This enraged the Communist sympathizers of the radical left throughout the country. "About a thousand demonstrations erupted on more than two hundred campuses. Arson bombing and window-smashing wreaked damage in the millions of dollars. (p. 44) (There were also riots and destruction by students in cities throughout the country, including some I personally witnessed in Albuquerque, New Mexico.)

Some of the worst riots and destruction occurred at Kent State University and the town at which it was located. Ohio National Guardsmen were attacked with chunks of concrete, cinderblocks, and canisters, and fifty-eight of them were injured. Finally, the guardsmen fired on the students, killing four and wounding ten. The Guardsmen were exonerated by a grand jury that found that they fired in legitimate fear of their lives. (pp. 45–46)

Judge Bork quotes from Edmund Burke (p. 51):

By the early Seventies, a subtle panic had overtaken the Movement. The revolution that we had awaited so breathlessly was nearing the end of what we now realized would be a dry labor. The monstrous offspring of our fantasies would never be born. People who had gathered for the apocalypse were dropping off into environmentalism and consumerism and fatalism. . . . I watched many of my old comrades apply to graduate school in the universities they had failed to burn down so that they could get advanced degrees and spread the ideas that had been discredited in the streets under an academic cover.

Judge Bork explains that a large number of this radical type were not the kind to go into the business or conventional professional field.

(I would except the legal profession from this—many radicals seem to have made a natural migration into the field law, and unfortunately, many have become judges and have wreaked more damage to their country than they did to their schools. Also, in Chapter 8 the case of *Romer v. Evans* is discussed, and it is noted that Justice Scalia's dissent points out that the Association of American Law Schools requires its members to agree to the willingness to hire homosexuals. Such law schools can now claim full membership in the paganistic and vile culture of the homosexuals.)

"They didn't go just into the universities. ...They were part of the chattering class, talkers interested in policy, politics, and culture. They went into politics, print, and electronic journalism, church bureaucracies, foundation staffs, Hollywood careers, public interest organizations, anywhere attitudes and opinions could be influenced." (p. 51)

Judge Bork explains that the radicalism of the sixties has now permeated our language, cultural, and sexuality mores. Ideas of "political correctness" are a disease and a sickness that permeate not only our universities, but our general culture. Oppressive levels of "political correctness" now prevent truthful examination of facts and events, and project false ideas about the oppression of women, Western imperialism, colonialism, racism. This PC madness is not confined to the enclaves of the academy. It is now to be found in museums, art galleries, seminaries, foundations—all the institutions relating to opinion and attitude formation. (pp. 53–55)

(I would add that next to the universities, probably the worst harm has been done by the infiltration and pervasion of our news and entertainment media with these radical and false political ideas. The latest thing they have done is to promote homosexuality as acceptable and good, and they are now doing the same with homosexual marriage. If there is any morality at all left in the liberal news and entertainment media, it has been very difficult for me to discern. They pervert the use of words like "love, fairness, equality, and discrimination" to deceive the gullible into accepting the most vile and degrading acts that exist as good and commendable. In all instances, we are taught the exact opposite of the truth. But the saddest part of all of this is the success it has had.)

In Chapter 6, Judge Bork explains the effect of modern liberalism on the United States Supreme Court, and the influence exerted by the American Civil Liberties Union which argues, litigates, and lobbies for rights to abortion, to practice prostitution, for the acceptance of homosexuality, homosexual marriage (p. 97). (The same is true of atheism and flag burning. But when it comes to individual rights that are not a part of the radical left and atheistic ideas, the ACLU takes the opposite view.) It supports affirmative action, government limitations on the freedom of businesses to discharge unsatisfactory employees. (p. 98) (It also believes in forcing people to hire homosexuals, to rent to them, and to have them on their premises. They wish to prevent people from taking moral character into consideration in determining with whom they deal, or else to accept the views of the ALCU and other homosexualists as to what constitutes good moral character.)

Chapter 7 is entitled, The Collapse of Popular Culture.

The trash that is called "rap music" is referred to, and the following is quoted from Snoop Doggy Dogg's song "Horny":

> I called you up for some sexual healing. I'm callin' again so let me come get it. Bring the lotion so I can rub you. Assume the position so I can f. . . you. (p. 123)

Nine Inch Nails' song, "Big Man with a Gun":

> I am a big man (yes I am). And I have a big gun. Got me a big old [expletive] and I, I like to have fun. Held against your forehead, I'll make you suck it. Maybe I'll put a hole in your head. . . . I can reduce it if I want. I can devour. I'm hard as [expletive] steel and I've got the power. . . . Shoot, shoot, shoot, shoot, shoot. I'm going to come all over you. . . . me and my [expletive] gun, me and my [expletive] gun. (p. 124)

(Actually the term "trash" for the above degrades the word trash. Sick filth is much more appropriate.)

Records like Ice-T's "Cop Killers," and other popular music is discussed.

Pages 127–129 state:

> Perhaps popular culture is inevitably vulgar but today's is more vulgar than at any time in the past. Sex in sitcoms, previously pervasive, has recently exploded. A Super Bowl half-time show stages an elaborate sequence in which the central feature was Michael Jackson writhing and clutching his private parts for the edification of family audiences. But the television talk shows are perhaps the most astonishing. There are about twenty-five hosts competing for audiences and they generate about a hundred hours of programs weekly. I learned from a Montel Williams show about the institution of shore parties: people take vacations, engage in as much random sex as possible, and

keep the score on a paper fastened to the refrigerator door. There was a show on women who marry their rapists and another about mothers and daughters having affairs with the same man. "In one Richard Bey outing last week," wrote Walter Goodman, "I met Karen, who admitted that she had offered her husband to Donna as a sleeping companion; Carolyn, who said her brother had slept with her boyfriend, and Geena, who said she had slept with an old friend's fiancé. . . . Geena presented her old friend with a birthday cake on stage before confessing to her, and got the cake back in her face. The audience whooped." ***

One evening at a hotel in New York I flipped around the television channels. Suddenly there on the public access channel was a voluptuous young woman, naked, her body oiled, writhing on the floor while fondling herself intimately. Meanwhile, a man's voice and a print on the screen informed the viewer of the telephone number and limousine service that would acquaint him with young women of similar charms and proclivities. I watched for some time—riveted by the sociological significance of it all. Shortly after that, men only slightly less nude advertised homosexual prostitutes.

(The vileness described permeates modern movies and televisions shows. Such trash has been promoted and advocated as a civil right by the ACLU. And by United States Supreme Court decisions that have encouraged this filth, as a right of free speech, contrary to earlier decisions when the majority of our courts were able to recognize the difference between worthless pornographic filth, and acceptable speech.)

In Chapter 8, "The Case for Censorship," a case is made for going back to reasonable censorship. We did not use to have the utterly filthy displays that are commonplace today. They were not allowed. It is also true that: "The period of Hayes office censorship was also, perhaps not coincidentally, the golden age of movies." (p. 141) (We no longer have many great and classical movies that were common in that time. Trash, filth, and violence now prevail. Even many cartoons for children reflect the lack of morality and violence into which we have fallen.)

Chapter 11, "The Politics of Sex," describes the harm done to our culture, to our schools, and even to our military by radical feminism.

Instead of useful education, many schools are furnishing an indoctrination of false and radical ideologies.

Judge Bork considers modern feminism to be the most fanatical and destructive of the radical movements coming down to us from the Sixties (p. 193). Perhaps this is so, particularly in light of its melding with the homosexual movement. Now they continually work together and are intertwined. This is undoubtedly one of the reasons for the successful indoctrination of the teachers' union, the National Education Association, with the activist homosexual views.

In addition to the "minority" studies that have been foisted upon the schools, there are now a large number of "Women's Studies," and such courses as "Gay and Lesbian Studies." There are more than six hundred undergraduate and several dozen graduate programs in Women's Studies alone in our colleges and universities. These are not courses of factual integrity, but of feminist propaganda, and "political correctness." The same kinds of misinformation is making considerable headway in high schools and elementary schools. Students who show signs of retaining some semblance of factual integrity are forcefully brainwashed with "sensitivity courses." (pp. 208–209) These courses consist of irrational dogma and hatred. They do not include mathematics, science, or logic, and they are not factually supported. (pp. 210–211) (There is no way that such tripe could be considered educational.) The following is quoted from the respected columnist and television personality, George Will, about the feminists' reinterpreting of literature (p. 212):

> Shakespeare's "Tempest" reflects the imperialistic rape of the Third World. Emily Dickinson's poetic references to peas and flower buds are encoded messages of feminist rage, exulting clitoral masturbation to protest the prison of patriarchal sex roles. Jane Austen's supposed serenity masks boiling fury about male domination, expressed in the nastiness of minor characters who are "really" not minor. In "Wuthering Heights," Emily Bronte, a subtle subversive, has Catherine bitten by a *male* bulldog. Melville's white whale? Probably a penis. Grab a harpoon.

As a part of the radical feminist movement, lesbianism is not only an accepted lifestyle, but a promoted one. (p. 213) (It removes women from their "hated" and "oppressive" dependence on men for their sexual needs.) They want lawful lesbian marriages, "reproductive rights" and adoption rights. (p. 213) Such ideas are pervasive in the women's studies courses. (p. 214) At the University of Washington, a women's studies instructor showed the class how to masturbate, stating that "the preferable tool is a tongue, a woman's tongue." (p. 214)

In Chapter 8, U. S. Supreme Court Justice Scalia's dissent in *Romer v. Evans* is discussed. The opinion noted that the Association of American Law Schools required a pledge from its members to hire homosexuals. This is undoubtedly the same organization referred to by Judge Bork as the "American Association of Law Schools." He relates that a young man he knew went to a convention of that organization, which was a traditional market opportunity for those desiring teaching jobs. He found that the convention had a "Women's Hospitality Room" and a "Minorities Hospitality Room," but there was no hospitality room with any category including white males. (p. 214)

The young man was well qualified, having a splendid record at Harvard, in both the college and the law school, and had been a law clerk for U.S. Supreme Court Justice Anthony Kennedy—"the sort of credentials law schools used to hunger for in their teaching applicants." He applied for a position at the University of Texas law school. A Mexican-American lesbian with much lower grades and credentials was selected for the job, instead of him. "A memorandum from a member of the appointment committee explained to the faculty that she should be hired because 'she does appeal to three constituent groups'" (p. 214)

These things related by Judge Bork are concrete examples of not only the complete lack of morals into which we have fallen, but the utter stupidity that necessarily accompanies these liberal ideas. This is the kind of discrimination that we need to worry about, not discrimination against vile and destructive behavior, which would not be allowed at the same schools. Instead of a sensible and valuable education, students are being taught that right is wrong and wrong is right, and are receiving an indoctrination of the most evil of values, instead of receiving an education. They tend to leave school with a state of mind that will result in further destruction to our society, instead of the critically needed moral attitude that will be necessary to change the destructive direction of our society. The State of Texas and the University of Texas, were once moral and conservative bastions that contributed to the improvement of our society. It is indeed disheartening to see the sickening reverse in direction, but it is even more prevalent in the more liberal parts of our country, particularly in our large coastal cities.

Schools, state and local governments, and even large corporations have surrendered to the homosexual intimidation and onslaught. The very worst thing that they have done is to even require "sensitivity" training for those who retain or express any semblance of traditional morality. Under President Clinton, the federal government has even invoked sensitivity training to promote homosexuality. "Sensitivity training" is merely enforced brainwashing which teaches that homosexuality and other such deviant behavior is good and wholesome, and that ideas to the contrary are ignorant and "bigoted." It is subversive thought control. How could a once religious and moral country have slipped down into such slime and depravity? Apathy and cowardice have played a great part.

Our colleges are using this indoctrination and thought control to try to shape the attitudes of students who have not even displayed any adversity to the radical liberal ideas. An example is given of a training session at Cornell where resident advisers are shown an X-rated homosexual movie, and pictures were taken of the viewers to try to detect reactions that would indicate "homophobic squeamishness." Students are indoctrinated with the politically correct attitudes, not only toward minorities, but toward the radical feminist ideas, and toward homosexuality. (p. 216)

The following is a warning that a Professor Sommers thought should be placed on the first page of bulletins to parents who might be planning to enroll their daughters in some of the institutions known for their radical views, such as Wellesley College, Mount Holyoke, Smith, Mills and the University of Minnesota:

> We will help your daughter discover the extent to which she has been in complicity with the patriarchy. We will encourage her to reconstruct herself through dialogue with us. She may become enraged and chronically offended. She will very likely reject the religious and moral codes you raised her with. She may well distance herself from family and friends. She may change her appearance, and even her sexual orientation. She may end up hating you (her father) and pitying you (her mother). After she has completed her reeducation with

us, you will certainly be out tens of thousands of dollars and very possibly be out of one daughter as well. (p. 217)

When President Clinton first came into office in 1993, one of his first acts was to try to force the military to accept homosexuals. He was substantially impeded by Congress, and what we ended up with was called the "Don't Ask Don't Tell" policy. The substance seems to be that homosexuals could be allowed into the military, if their homosexuality is not stated or known, and if they do not flaunt it or engage in sodomy while in the military. Sodomy is still a criminal violation of military code. Clinton then, more successfully, commenced the imposition of the radical feminist views on the military. The military is even forced, against the recommendations of top officers and prominent retired officers, to put women in certain combat roles. It seems that our president is intent on destroying to a large extent the effectiveness of our armed forces. There has been recent large turmoil, allegations of sexual harassment, and prosecutions for sexual harassment and sexual relations between members of the armed forces that certainly was predictable from the way men and women were being mixed up and put in close contact with one another. Although *Slouching Towards Gomorrah* was written before these latest episodes in the services, it does detail a large number of destructive and absurd things that have happened in such a short time. Of course, some of these things were going on prior to Clinton's administration, as the effect of many years of a liberal congress and its pressures along with the feminist movement. But, with Clinton, things became utterly ridiculous. There are considerable differences between men and women, and there needs to be certain privacy divisions between them. But such common sense seems never to have entered the minds of the liberals and the feminists.

Judge Bork explains that the havoc wreaked by feminists to the military services is similar to that to our educational systems. (p. 218)

Instead of using the military to defend our country, it is being used to reform our society. Contrary to the propaganda fed to the public, both our training and capability standards have been lowered to accommodate women and to give the false appearance that they are on a par with men in military combat roles. (p. 218–219) (This program is not only ridiculous and false, but is highly dangerous to the women involved, and even more importantly, to our military capability. This is only one of the ways in which Clinton is doing great harm to our military forces and to their ability to defend this country.) One example resulted in the death of Navy Lieutenant Kara Hultgreen and the destruction of the fighter plane she was trying to fly in October 1994. (It was fortunate that when she crashed her plane, it went into the ocean instead of the aircraft carrier on which she was trying to land.) She had failed the landing phase of her training in April, but the Navy let her take it again, and she finally passed it once. (She was given the same help in passing that "minorities" are often given in colleges and universities. What results is a detriment [and in this case highly dangerous] to the individuals involved, and to society.) Lieutenant Hultgreen was allowed to continue although (in training sessions of simulated flight) she recorded seven crashes in combat conditions. A male pilot with her record would have been grounded. Although a public cover-up was made of the true results of the Navy investigation , the private Navy conclusion was that her death and the loss of the plane was due to pilot error. Feminist Colorado Congresswoman Pat Schroeder tried to make the accident look like it was caused by engine failure. This was of course false. The real story was how little interest the liberal media (and our liberal representatives) had in trying to determine and let the public know the true cause. (pp. 219–220) It was not a "politically correct" result.

Our career military officers are intimidated and are in justified fear of losing their careers if they express disagreement with the feminist approach of the Clinton administration as to the proper role of women in the military. An example is Lieutenant Commander Kenneth Carkhuff. "On July 26, 1994, Carkhuff's superior officer recommended him for early promotion ahead of his peers because he was an 'extraordinary department head,' a 'superior officer in charge' with 'unlimited potential destined for command and beyond.'" Six weeks later he stated, in a private conversation with his commanding officer, that his religious views made him doubtful about putting women in combat, although his views also required him to lead them into combat if ordered by his superiors. His overall performance was then downgraded to unsatisfactory and he was discharged from the Navy. The matter (which amounted to a performance in stupidity by the Navy) was summed up by his superior: "A bright future has been lost and otherwise superb performance completely overshadowed by this glaring irreconcilable conflict with Navy policy." (p. 220) (Now our "Commander in Chief" is not only requiring absurdity in our military services, but he is requiring brainwashing of our officers who have some common sense, and the elimination from the armed forces of those who have the temerity to display any, even in private conversations. Our country is most fortunate that such "enlightened" leadership did not exist during the Second World War. Otherwise, we would probably now be under the rule of some foreign power—either Germany or Japan or both.)

Performance in our military academies has been downgraded to accommodate the women cadets. For example, men are no longer required to run carrying heavy weapons, because the women are not able to do that. Women cannot perform nearly as well as men in the training programs. (p. 221)

"Pregnancies due to sex during the preceding phase, Desert Shield, was the primary reason the non-deployability rate of women was many times higher than that of men when the troops were called to battle in Desert Storm." "Three 'Top Gun' flight commanders had their careers destroyed because they were present at or performed in the Tom Cat Follies, which included a rhyme denigrating Pat Schroeder. President Bush and Vice President Dan Quayle were also lampooned, but only parodying a fierce feminist congresswoman was considered a grave offense." (p. 221)

In Air Force Academy physical fitness tests, very few women could even do one pull-up on a horizontal bar, so the women were given credit for the time that they could merely hang up on the bar. Female cadets averaged about four times as many visits to the medical clinic as males. At West Point, the injury rate of women in field training was fourteen times that of men, and 61 percent of the women failed the complete physical tests, as compared with 4.8 percent of the men. "During the Army basic training, women broke down in tears, particularly on the rifle range." (p. 221)

It has been reported that ships have been recalled from missions because of pregnancy of female sailors. (p. 221) (This appears to be one immutable difference between women and men that not even Pat

Schroeder and United States Supreme Court Justice Ruth Bader Ginsburg, together, could change.)

"A male and a female sailor on the aircraft carrier USS *Dwight D. Eisenhower*, both married to others, videotaped themselves having sex in a remote part of the ship. There had been thirty-eight pregnancies since the crew went aboard the *Eisenhower*, fourteen of them after the ship was deployed. The Navy said that there was no indication that any of the pregnancies resulted from sex on board the ship. Those who wish to may believe that." (p. 222)

In the Gulf War, a female American pilot was captured, raped, and sodomized by Iraqi troops. She declared that this was just part of combat risk. (Certainly this is true, and just one of the many cogent reasons that women should not even be in zones of direct combat.) "The Israelis, Soviets, and Germans, when in desperate need of front-line troops, placed women in combat, but later barred them. Male troops forgot their tactical objectives in order to protect the women from harm or capture, knowing what the enemy would do to female prisoners of war. This made combat units less effective and exposed the men, also, to greater risk. (p. 222)

A little common sense would tell us what the Israelis, Soviets, and Germans learned, besides the fact that knowledge of their experiences are available to us. This country seems to have lost all sense of reason in cowering before the radical movements that have beset it.

The Clinton administration has been able to do more harm to the military forces by its feminist views than by it homosexual agenda, because congress fortunately curtailed the homosexual agenda to a substantial degree. However, as noted above from disclosures in Judge Bork's book, the feminist movement has wreaked great havoc to our armed services. Of late, serious charges of everything from rape to sexual harassment have been rocking the military forces. As previously noted, this was certainly predictable and is only a small part of the damage to the military capability of the armed forces that has been caused by the mixing of young men and women together in situations that are contrary to the common sense of any experienced military personnel.

Columnist Suzanne Fields wrote an excellent article on this subject, "Pressures of Unisex Military Weakening Armed Forces," which was published in the *Albuquerque Journal* on January 20, 1997. It states in part:

> ... maybe it takes James Webb—a twice-wounded veteran of the Vietnam war and secretary of the Navy and an assistant secretary of defense under Ronald Reagan—to sound the most eloquent warning yet that the most dangerous military experiment in the history of our country threatens to destroy the nation's defense. ***
>
> In our rush to assimilate women throughout the military, we're destroying leadership, encouraging officers to lie about the most crucial elements of command, and lowering morale of both men and women in the ranks. Cynicism blossoms.
>
> ... talented women as well as men lose in a Faustian bargain. Writes Webb in The Weekly Standard: "This cynicism feeds a backlash, which increases tensions, even in areas where women perform well and where their presence is not counterproductive to the military's mission."
>
> Soldiers traditionally have little privacy, but, says the soldiers' newspaper Stars and Stripes, they're skilled at finding places for furtive sexual encounters. This may require a study of positions from the Kamasutra, to adjust to the back seat of a Humvee, a latrine, a corner of a group tent or even an underground bunker with three inches of water on the floor
>
> ... on average, an American servicewoman turns up pregnant every third day.
>
> The jokes about "love boats" and pregnant soldiers provoke laughter in the mess hall, but elsewhere they're no laughing matter. By placing young men and women in close sleeping quarters on ships at sea in the Middle East and under tents in Bosnia, away from a conventional social life and the easy, everyday affections of friends and family, the Army is begging for trouble. Trouble, like a good soldier, obliges on cue. ***

During the Second World War, and since then, until the feminist movement destructively gained a foothold in the military, women served honorably and effectively in all services. They were separated from the men, and they were assigned to duties that were reasonable under the circumstances, and that they were capable of performing. But there are rather obvious emotional and physical differences between men and women, and there are combat and other roles to which women should not be assigned. Never should women and men be mixed together in the field in military activities, and never should they be mixed in living quarters on a base. They should not undergo physical training together. Such things are worse than absurd. Women should be trained with women in physical training which they are reasonably capable of performing. They should never be mixed with men in physical training, and thereby drag down the standards that would otherwise be required of the men.

Chapter 14 of Junde Bork's *Slouching Towards Gomorrah* is entitled "The Trouble in Religion." It deals with the decline in our morality as religious influence declined, and secular influences increased.

> Whether the link between religion and morality can be demonstrated conclusively, as I have come to believe it can, it is true that the coming of trouble in our culture coincided with a decline in the influence of religion. "In the mid-nineteenth century England and America reacted to the consequences of industrialization, urbanization, immigration and affluence by asserting the ethos of self-control," James Q. Wilson writes, "whereas in the late twentieth century they reacted to many of the same forces by asserting an ethos of self-expression." Religion and the voluntary associations inspired by religious life were the source of the ethos of self-control working through the processes of habituation in the family, the schools, the neighborhood, and the workplace. The secular ethos of self-expression led to excesses, according to Wilson, because of the unwillingness of certain elites to support those processes of habituation. He does not draw a conclusion about the importance of religion, but his observations do more than merely suggest that importance. (pp. 273–74)

On religion, I agree with Judge Bork that our only chance to bring this country out of the degradation into which it has fallen is by regaining the religious moral principles which once guided us. But our churches, generally, have so far failed us.

Reverend Billy Graham is considered by many to be the greatest evangelical preacher of our time. But I have long waited in vain for him to enter into combat with the one greatest threat to our traditional religion that there has ever been—the homosexual movement. I have listened to many of Graham's benign sermons, and I have read much of his literature, but, until the fall of 1997, I did not hear or read anything from him on this subject. Could it be that he lacks true biblical convictions? I doubt that this is it. And he could not be ignorant of the clear and unqualified condemnations of sodomy in both the Old and New Testaments, which he professes to believe. Could it be that he just lacks the courage? Was Graham afraid of losing the huge crowds that flock to his sermons? Was he afraid of losing the large income to his organization? Will his son who now follows him be the same? I wish I knew the answers to these questions. But one thing I do know, and that is that the great praising of the Lord and the benign preaching of motherhood and apple pie has failed mankind. During his heyday the country has regressed at a fast rate into the deepest depths of degradation that it has ever been.

Finally, in 1997, I read a news report on Graham's answer when directly asked in a news conference about whether or not he considered homosexuality a sin. "Graham said that according to the Bible, 'their lifestyle ... is wrong. It is a sin. But there are other sins. Why do we jump on that sin as though it's the greatest sin?' " (*The Albuquerque Tribune*, 9-25-97) This timid and impotent statement was clearly contrary to the teachings of the Bible on the gravity of the sin. It plays down how vile, depraved, and destructive homosexual acts are. Rev. Billy Graham has let down our society in failing to lend his voice to combat this war against the good and decent values of our society.

It appears that Billy Graham has now become an apologist for sodomy. He has also become an apologist for the one who has done the most to promote sodomy in America, our President Clinton.

During the period of March 5, 1998 to March 8, 1998, it was reported several times on CBS News, and CBS Meet the Press, the Rev. Billy Graham's answers as to what he thought about the allegations against President Bill Clinton. There were at that time a number of allegations against Clinton, including adultery with various women, allegedly trying to get two women to perform oral sex on him, perjury, subornation of perjury, obstruction of justice, in connection with his activities with various women, and in connection with the Whitewater savings and loan scandals. In response to these allegations, Graham's statement was:

I—I forgive him—I don't know what the average person—but I mean—certainly I forgive him. Because I know the frailty of human nature. And I know how hard it is for a strong vigorous young man like he is and he has such a tremendous personality—that I think the ladies just go wild over him.

Can you imagine such a statement from the best known and most respected Christian evangelist of our time? Graham must have assumed that there was substantial truth to the allegations, as most people do. He certainly assumed that the president had done something that he was "forgiving" him for. However, the Christian idea of forgiveness is that first there should be truthful confessions and real repentance. Clinton was still denying to the people and swearing under oath that he did not do most of the things of which he is accused.

The sad and frightening thing is that the public opinion polls show that most of the people, as it seems does Billy Graham, want Clinton to remain president, even if he has done all of the things of which he is accused. It would therefore appear that a majority of Americans are willing to tolerate, overlook, and accept sodomy, adultery, perjury, subornation of perjury, fraud, and misbehavior of all kinds—even if committed by the President of the United States. People used to believe that the president should be one who the children of the country could look up to as an exemplary person. How things have changed in a short period of time! And when even the top Christian evangelist in the country thinks that we should overlook and "forgive" such things, we are in real trouble.

My heart is sick for my country. And I am reminded of Judge Robert Bork's doubts about whether our moral decline has already been so great that we no longer have the ability to recover.

We are farther from living the true teachings of the Bible than we have ever been in our history. Those who dare express true biblical beliefs outside of the church building or a religious congregation are scorned by the "educated" elite, by the media, and by their government. Little that is so deeply wrong with this country actually takes place within the church building or at a religious congregation. The sinfulness wreaking havoc to us is taking place in our homes, in our schools, and in our streets. Our ministers seem to be ministering in the wrong places. Most of the preaching seems to reach only the choir. Our preachers, above all people, should be joining in the cultural war in which we are up to our necks. They will not find the enemy in their churches—there will be little engagement there. The enemy has taken over our schools, our political organizations, and our young people. These are the areas where any effective engagement must take place. Organized churches and religions can only be the headquarters—the war can only be won in the trenches—the places where the enemy operates. Enlarging congregations and great building projects have not and will not get the job done.

Let us consider where Christ did His work. Always among the people—ministering where He was needed—facing all condemnation and danger—even ministering to His crucifiers and to a thief hanging beside Him while He was nailed upon the cross. (See Luke 23:34–43.) I have to believe that this man of courage and convictions was truly the Son of God.

Things discussed in other chapters of this book certainly show the depravity going on in this country. We will now consider some more of the specific results we have reaped from our decline in morality in the past thirty years. The things that have happened may seem different and unrelated, but a little thought will show that they are directly related in that they would not have happened had those involved followed traditional religious moral values.

GENERAL MORAL DECLINE

Probably the greatest and fastest moral decline ever witnessed in this country, in such a short period of time, was during the four years of President William Clinton's first term, and he was a major contributor to it. He led the way. It began immediately.

The following information was derived from Dr. James C. Dobson's newsletter, "1993 in Review," *Focus on the Family*. Colorado Springs, Co., Jan., 1994:

January. After being elected, but prior to his taking office, Bill Clinton received a letter signed by 51 members of Congress, including Patricia Schroeder, D-Colo., and self-identified homosexuals Barney Frank, D-Mass. and Gerry Studds, D-Mass. The substance of their message was:

We are writing to express our support for an executive order ending the ban on lesbians and gay men serving in the Armed Forces as soon as possible upon taking office in January. We will stand with you as you execute this historic executive order and will work with you to oppose any attempts to legislate this type of discrimination in the future.

(Clinton lost no time in trying to implement his pro-homosexual and other liberal ideas.)

On Jan. 23, the third day of his administration, Clinton issued five controversial executive orders, designed to:

1. Lift the ban on homosexuals in the military.
2. Lift the ban on fetal tissue research.
3. Lift the ban on abortion counseling in federally funded clinics.
4. Begin the process of approving the importation of the abortion-inducing medication RU 486.
5. Provide for the first time for abortions in military hospitals overseas.

February. The *Washington Post*, 2-1-93, in a front page story by Michael Weisskoph, referred to members of the so-called religious right as "largely poor, uneducated, and easy to command." "Only Christians could be characterized today in such disrespectful terms."

Clinton nominated Roberta Achtenberg, an avowed lesbian activist, to become assistant secretary for fair housing and equal opportunity at the Department of Housing and Urban Development. Achtenberg has a long history of radical activities and spearheaded an attack on the Boy Scouts in San Francisco because the organization barred homosexuals as scoutmasters. She said: "Do we want children learning the values of an organization that ... provides character building exclusively for straight, God-fearing male children?"

Clinton attempted (by executive order), to lift the restriction on immigrants who were HIV positive. This effort was quickly overturned by Congress.

March. The *New York Times*, 3-29-93, ran a story on the "Spur Posse," a high school gang in Lakewood, Calif., whose members were accused of raping and exploiting hundreds of girls as young as ten. One of the members, Eric Richardson, said: "They pass out condoms, teach sex education, and pregnancy-this and pregnancy-that. But they don't teach us any rules."

April. Gannett News Service reported, 4-2-93, Clinton's attempt to repeal the Hyde Amendment, which prohibits federal funding of abortions. Congress blocked this effort later in the year.

Surgeon General nominee Joycelyn Elders was quoted in the *National Review*, 4-26-93: "I tell every girl that when she goes out on a date — put a condom in her purse."

"Defense Secretary Les Aspin ordered the Pentagon to lift the ban on women in combat, summarily discarding 217 years of military tradition."

June. Clinton signed into law a bill lifting the restriction on fetal tissue research, following through on what he began on January 23.

Clinton appointed feminist and ACLU activist Ruth Bader Ginsburg to be an associate justice on the Supreme Court. Ginsburg believes that:

1. The traditional family concept of the husband as a breadwinner and wife as a homemaker must be eliminated.
2. The federal government must provide comprehensive child care.
3. The Homestead Law must give twice as much benefit to couples who live apart from each other as to a husband and wife who live together.
4. In the military, women must be drafted when men are drafted, and women must be assigned to combat duty.
5. Affirmative action must be applied to equalize the number of men and women in the armed forces.
6. The age of consent for sexual acts must be lowered to 12 years of age.
7. Prostitution must be legalized. She wrote: "Prostitution as a consensual act between adults is arguably within the zone of privacy protected by recent constitutional decisions."
8. All-boy and all-girl organizations must be sexually integrated, as must all fraternities and sororities. The Boy Scouts and the Girl Scouts must change their names and their purposes to become sex-integrated.

Ms. Ginsburg was confirmed in the Senate by a vote of 96–3, with one abstention.

One June 19, Clinton sent a letter to Jon Larimore of the Gay and Lesbian Information Bureau, stating in part:

> I want to extend my appreciation to the many members of the Gay and Lesbian Information Bureau who are selflessly giving their time to support my administration. ...
>
> The response we received to our request for help has been remarkable. All of you who joined our ranks are making a real contribution to the future of this nation.

(The homosexual lobby was a prime contributor to Clinton's campaign.)

Clinton named Kristine Gebbie, a lesbian, as the new AIDS czar. She expressed her views on morality as:

> [The United States] needs to view human sexuality as an essentially important and pleasurable thing. [Until it does so], we will continue to be a repressed, Victorian society that misrepresents information, denies sexuality early, denies homosexual sexuality particularly in teens, and leaves people abandoned with no place to go. I can help just a little bit in my job, standing on the White House lawn talking about sex with no lightning bolts falling on my head.

July. U. S. Surgeon General nominee Joycelyn Elders was quoted by Suzanne Fields in *The Washington Times*, 7-15-93, as follows: "We taught them [teens] what to do in the front seat [of a car]. Now it's time to teach them what to do in the back seat."

August. The National Endowment for the Arts agreed to fund three "gay" and lesbian film festivals. The NEA gave $17,500 to festivals in Pittsburgh, New York and Los Angeles. "We're delighted that the NEA has reinstated the funding. It's a sign of validation from the highest office for arts funding in this country," said Larry Horne, executive director of the Gay and Lesbian Media Coalition. (8-27-93)

September. Clinton took action against the federal Title XX initiative, a holdover from the Bush Administration which earmarked a tiny amount of money for the teaching of abstinence to teenagers. "The funds were diverted into 'safe sex' programs promoting condom usage."

"The U. S. Senate confirmed Dr. Joycelyn Elders as the new surgeon general by a vote of 65–34. She holds the most radical views of any person ever appointed to that position. This was a sad day for the nation's youth, and indeed, for all of us!"

Senator Paul Wellstone, D-Minn., said of Elders: "I think we're talking about a woman who'll be a healing force for our country. She'll be the kind of surgeon general who will unite us and bring us together."

September. On September 19:

> Members of Hamilton Square Baptist Church in San Francisco were attending their Sunday evening service when they were attacked viciously by the gay-activist groups, Act-Up and Queer Nation. The church was surrounded by more than 100 rioters who screamed obscenities and roughed-up parishioners who were attempting to attend the service. When the protesters saw boys and girls inside the church, they shouted, "We want your children, give us your children!" a nine-year old boy was crying hysterically, "They are after me. It's me they want."
>
> The pastor, Dr. David Innes, begged for additional police support but his request was denied. He was told, "You must understand, this is San Francisco." No arrests were made.

October. CBS, on October 12, presented nationwide its program, "Other Mothers," a broadcast special for young people described as "an honest and straightforward depiction of prejudices faced by lesbian parents and their children."

Girl Scouts decided not to require allegiance to God in their oath. Angie Grieling, a Girl Scout delegate, was quoted by the Associated Press, "I believe that the Girl Scouts are an inclusive organization, and the ideas is that we are across all lines, not focusing on one group or religion or race." (10-30-93.)

November. Two articles of November 1, in *Time* magazine reflect the bias of that magazine. An article by reporter Jill Smolowe, editorialized sarcastically that "when conservative Christians try to be involved in their children's education, they only 'impede [teachers'] work' and 'tie up meetings with arguments.'"

An article of the same date, in *Time,* was about Peter Melzer, a physics teacher at New York City's prestigious Bronx High School of Science. Melzer is stated to be a leader and promoter of NAMBLA, the North American Man/Boy Love Association. "This organization's goal is to achieve the legalization of sex between minors (including little boys) and men. A controversy developed over Mr. Melzer's individual rights and whether his affiliation with NAMBLA disqualified him to teach high-school students." The *Time* article states: "Given the free-speech issues it raises, Melzer's seems like exactly the kind of case the American Civil Liberties Union was created to defend."

On November 2, homosexual and lesbian appointees of the Clinton Administration held a "coming-out breakfast" for the press. The original goal, they said, was to secure five gay appointments by the White House. Already they have obtained twenty-two, and more are expected. Bruce Lehman of the Gay and Lesbian Victory Fund said, "For the first time in the history of mankind, a president has sought to break this barrier, this taboo. For that Bill Clinton is going down in history."

U. S. News and World Report, 11-8-93, reported that more than 3 million crimes a year are committed in or near the 85,000 U.S. public schools. A University of Michigan study reports that 9 percent of eighth-graders carry a gun, knife or club to school at least once a month. In all, an estimated 270,000 guns go to school every day. Twenty percent of suburban high schoolers surveyed by Tulane University researchers thought it was appropriate to shoot someone "who has stolen something from you." Eight percent believed it is all right to shoot a person who had "done something to offend or insult you." One authority said a "juvenile Armageddon" may be approaching.

(A November 8, 1993 *Newsweek* article on teens experimenting in homosexuality and bisexuality, is discussed. Detailed information is presented on this article, in Chapter 6.)

On November 28, the San Francisco Board of Supervisors created a 20-member group that included three former prostitutes to consider legalizing prostitution and other steps that might help neighborhoods where men and women sell sex on street corners.

On November 30:

Rap artist Snoop Doggy Dog was due in court to face first-degree murder charges. He had been free on $1 million bail, permitting him to tour the country promoting his new album, which sold 800,000 copies in its first few weeks. Contained in this recording are lyrics describing the murder of a policemen, the killing of a rival, hatred for women, and explicit sexual language. It is, literally, too foul to be aired on radio or television. The artist, whose sneering picture was on the cover of *Newsweek* (Nov.29), had already served time for dealing drugs and carrying a concealed weapon, Yet his new album was at the top of the best-selling charts, and he had become a role model for millions of teens. Referring to the album, the *L. A. Times* stated, "its ideas could inspire rap for years to come."

December. On December 1, designated World AIDS Day, French AIDS activists placed a 72-foot pink condom over the Obelisk in the Place de la Concorde in Paris.
On December 3:

The *Rocky Mountain News* reported on Planned Parenthood's "Dollar a Day" program. It offers $1 to participating teenagers for each day they don't get pregnant. Of course, the girls can be sexually active and still get the money, as long as they use birth control devices. The program cost $657 per girl in 1993. One of the teenagers in the program said, "Some of the girls have been in the group since they were 12." An adult coordinator added, "No one was sexually active then. And now, everyone, of course, is."

News items of December 7 and 8 are reviewed. AIDS czar Kristine Gebbie announces an ad campaign to provide explicit information on the use of condoms. Surgeon General Joycelyn Elders Says: "We could markedly reduce our crime rate if drugs were legalized." The White House and other governmental departments add "sexual orientation" as a part of the nondiscrimination policies.
On December 11:

A song written by convicted mass murderer Charles Manson was included in a new hard rock album by Guns 'N Roses, reported *Billboard*. When lead singer Axl Rose was asked in a television interview why he included Manson's song in the album, he said, "Manson is cool."

Dr. Dobson remarked about the year:

Well, those are just a few of the developments that served to undermine traditional moral values and weaken the family in the past 12 months. Can there be any doubt, hearing these echoes from the culture, that a great Civil War of Values is being waged in Western nations, or that radical anti-family forces are making dramatic alterations in the way we think and act? I've seen that upheaval coming for almost a decade, but it is now evident to anyone who watches the evening news on television. The family is not simply disintegrating from natural forces and pressures. Its demise is being orchestrated at the highest levels of government, and by radical special-interest groups.

I consider 1993 as one of the worst years in our nations history. We are beset by a vile sickness that is actually promoted by the Clinton administration, while our President and "First Lady" piously and hypocritically go to church on Sunday, and have news reporters on hand when they come out, to have their pictures taken carrying the Holy Bible. The administration is greatly assisted and supported by the liberal news media, which has also reached a decadence and immorality never before witnessed in this country.

Dr. Dobson also stated, in the Jan. 1994 newsletter: "Am I concerned by these recent trends? Yes, the pattern of events reveals a society in dramatic decline. Indeed, the value system that has served us so well for 217 years may not survive the next decade." The concerns of Dr. Dobson are not materially different than those of Judge Bork, previously referred to in *Slouching Towards Gomorrah*. I have the same concerns and doubts. Dr. Dobson goes on to explain that there is hope in that there seems to be a revival beginning in some of our churches and evangelical movements.

However, since the news letter, this country has again elected Bill Clinton as president. Even worse, polls showed that a majority of the

American people were reasonably aware of his immorality, and had doubts about his veracity.

Polls Suggest Voters Don't Care If Clinton Is Dishonest

WASHINGTON — When the Gallup Poll (June 18–19, 1996) asked whether the words "honest and trustworthy" apply to Bill Clinton, Clinton lost 49 percent to 46 percent. (Two weeks later, in another poll, same question, Clinton was losing 54–40) And when Gallup asked whether Clinton has the honesty and integrity to serve as president, Clinton won 62–36, a landslide bigger than Lyndon Johnson's.

... A large number of Americans think their president crooked *and* ethically fit for office. *** (Charles Krauthammer, Columnist, *Albuquerque Journal,* 7-7-96)

It is indeed a sad point in our history that the morality of the people has declined to such an extent that they elect a man for president that they do not believe is honest or has good moral character. It seemed that a large number of the voters, including many older people, were primarily interested in what the government was going to do for them. They were interested in the money they could get out of the government. There appeared to be little concern for what was right and good for the country. The many years that the Democrats had been buying votes by passing out tax money and passing laws to benefit special interest groups paid off in a big way. People seemed little concerned that the interest alone on the national debt that had been built up buying their votes, was becoming close to impossible to support, let alone actually reducing the debt that is now running in the trillions of dollars. It has become so large that it seems incomprehensible to many taxpaying citizens.

Not only have these things broken our government and our country financially, but they have now broken our government and our country morally. It is certainly literally true that our country, and particularly our government, is now morally bankrupt.

Singer is cited for lewd stage act

AUGUSTA, Ga. — Police have issued a citation to singer Bobby Brown for simulating a sex act in front of an underage audience during a concert in Augusta, Ga. *** Police spokesman Mark Cowan said

Brown and Queline Young, a female member of his group, simulated intercourse in a bed on stage during a filthy song of Wednesday night's concert at the Civic Center. *** (Pepper Williams, Brown's publicist) said Brown—who married singer Whitney Houston in July of last year—was on the road and could not be reached for ... comment. ... (*The Albuquerque Tribune*, 1-15-93)

Writer V. B. Price, in an article in *The Albuquerque Tribune*, 10-8-93:

Why are kids bad? Because we're a nation of hypocrites *

While campaigning politicians have been threatening to get tough on Albuquerque's teen-age gangs, the rest of the city has been riveted by reports of violence and vandalism by affluent kids in Far Northeast Heights.

Apparently well-to-do kids with cars and weapons are hanging out in parking lots near shopping malls and fast-food eateries drinking, fighting, harassing passers-by, doing drugs and generally making a public menace of themselves. How can kids from good families do such a thing? people ask, shaking their heads.

Maybe those kids really don't come from good families after all. Maybe American culture is on the verge of making it an act of moral heroism for some folks to be serious parents. Maybe what used to be a cultural imperative — raising kids with a social conscience — is about to be seen as a noble luxury.

How could that be? Have American cultural values become unbelievable and meaningless for kids? Do they just think it's all a bunch of bunk? I think many do. And the reason they do is tragic. I think it's because we've become a nation of hypocrites. ***

Consider the following article, where the parents—although well educated and well off financially—were the ringleaders, and participated with their grown children in what amounted to grand larceny, as reported by the authorities.

Rich Family Hired Shoplifter, Cops Say

ROSEVILLE, Minn. — A wealthy family allegedly used a personal shoplifter to acquire some of life's finer things—until their five-finger discounter turned informant and they got stung.

The family simply made a list of things they wanted from a nearby Dayton's department store and had a convicted thief lift the items for them, paying him a fraction of the retail cost, authorities said.

Gerald Dick, a 58-year-old dentist, his 56-year-old wife, Judy, and two of their children—James Dick, 32, who played for the Minnesota Vikings briefly in 1987, and Stacy Zehren, 33, an attorney—were charged Thursday with two counts each of receiving stolen property.

Their undoing, police said, began a week before with the arrest of Gregory E. Thomas, who told police he had sold about $250,000 worth of goods to the family over the years—although police said that claim was not substantiated.

[The article goes on to say that an investigator went along with the informing thief, posing as a store employee, and sold various items to the family. When police went back to recover the property, they said that Mrs. Dick said, "OK, you caught us red-handed, now what?"] *** (*Albuquerque Journal*, 12-7-96)

Not only are parents failing their children, but so are their schools, their churches, and their government.

Principal paid 12-year-old lover's mother $15,000 to keep affair quiet
CLEVELAND — For nearly a year, 52-year-old Nancy Marks carried on an affair. Among the gifts she gave her lover; toys. *** She was an elementary school principal. The object of her affections was a sixth grade boy. *** "Part of his psyche was missing and I wanted to make him whole. ..." Marks said .... *** She began to shower the boy with spending money, toys and other gifts. *** Police said she gave even more money to the boy's mother, Robbie Robinson, who extorted $15,000 in exchange for silence about the affair. *** Both women were charged, convicted and sent to prison. The boy's brother, 17 at the time, also was convicted of extortion. *** "My dog has better maternal instincts than you do," Common Pleas Judge Kathleen Ann Sutula told Robinson. *** (*The Albuquerque Tribune*, 12-14-96)

The following is from an article of Dr. John Rosemond, a family psychologist practicing in Charlotte, N.C.:

Liberal Scheming Could Undermine Family
Impossible to Separate Politics From Parenting ***

- A growing number of "helping" professionals are lending influential support to organizations such as End Physical Punishment of Children and the National Committee to Prevent Child Abuse to bring about legislation that would make spanking by parents a crime. Most anti-spanking proposals would require that offending parents receive "help" from none other than a "helping" professional. That's tidy, eh?

- Groups including the National Task Force for Children's Constitutional Rights and the National Committee for the Rights of the Child are lobbying vigorously for a Children's Rights Amendment. Their strategy is to first succeed on a state-by-state basis, thereby gathering a broad base of support for an amendment to the U.S. Constitution that would affirm the right of every child to "a home that is safe and healthy" and "the care of a loving family." That safe healthy homes and loving families are in the best interests of children is self-evident. The problem is in the eyes of judicial beholders when it comes to interpreting such ambiguities as "safe," "healthy" and "loving." ***

... Should any of this mischief become reality, state social workers will be considerably freer to force access to and influence upon a family whenever they suspect that a parental action of one sort or another has violated a child's nebulously defined rights. ***

English historian Paul Johnson reminds us that the intact, autonomous family unit is our best defense against the overweening, and ultimately totalitarian state. ...

... President Clinton recently signed the United Nations Convention [resolution] on the Rights of the Child, to which the first lady, during her tenure on the board of the Children's Defense Fund, lent her strong support ... Stay tuned next week for an in depth look at the Pandora's Box the president has opened with a mere stroke of his righteous pen. *** (*Albuquerque Journal*, 5-11-95)

AIDS Czarina: Enjoy Promiscuity.

"Clinton's AIDS czarina, Kristine Gebbie, advocated free love at a conference on teenage pregnancy. Her position is charged with finding policies to fight the spread of AIDS infection. Her mandate, by any reasonable analysis, is completely counter to fostering promiscuity. *** Gebbie said Americans must start viewing sex as an 'essentially important and pleasurable thing ... and that until they do so, we will continue to be a repressed Victorian society that misrepresents information, denies sexuality early, denies homosexuality — particularly in teens — and leaves people abandoned with no place to go.'" (*Washington Inquirer*, 10-29-93)

Social Security Pays for Druggies and Drunks.

"Under a law passed in 1974, on disability, the government is now paying social security benefits to drug addicts and alcoholics. In 1992, 31,000 such derelicts were drawing SSI benefits. "This money isn't intended to buy drugs or booze." "Ruddy (a New York Post reporter) wrote that getting money for drugs or booze is as easy as calling the toll-free hotline for Social Security claims. One vagrant told Ruddy, 'you don't even need a Social Security number. You just make up a name. They give it to you. They have to.'" (Accuracy in Media, *Washington Inquirer*, 10-29-93)

Porn's Human Toll Presented.

"Is pornography harmless? Consider Ted Bundy. His escalating appetite for pornography propelled him from a Christian upbringing to the sexualized murder of more than 30 women. *** Just before his Florida execution for the murder of a 12-year-old girl, Bundy cited pornography as the catalyst of the trail of death and anguish he left from Washington to Florida. *** 'American Tragedy' (shown on Coral Ridge Hour, 11-7-93) offers further proof that pornography is anything but harmless in the statements of men who, seeking to overcome their sexual addictions, have left families and jobs to spend six months at a Christian retreat farm in northern Kentucky. One young former minister, married with two children, said, 'It has its hooks into me so deep that I act like a fool and I'm willing to throw away the most precious things.' *** Children are pornography's most innocent victims. Each year some 300,000 children are used to produce child pornography in America and another 900,000 are involved in prostitution." (*Impact*, Coral Ridge Ministries, Nov. 1993)

The Clinton administration goes on in high gear — promoting homosexuality and promoting general moral decay.

Official Advocates

"In the March 22 edition of the glossy homosexual magazine, *The Advocate*, Surgeon General Joycelyn Elders says, 'Society wants to keep all sexuality in the closet. We need to be more open about sex . . . a normal part of any healthy part of our being, whether it is homosexual or heterosexual.' In Feb. 22 edition, National Endowment for the Arts Chairwoman Jane Alexander unveils her mission 'to introduce people gently to gay themes all across the country. And I mean gently, because if you start with kind of an overt thing, people get scared.'" (*Washington Watch*, Family Research Council, March 18, 1994)

The above quote from Jane Alexander should be entitled "**The Delicate Brainwashing of the Stupid American People into Sodomy.**" Fortunately, a large part of the American people are not as stupid as the Clinton Administration considers them to be. However, in spite of all these things the people did elect him to another term. And the success of the homosexual movement has been utterly amazing.

Unsafe at Any Age.

"White House Aids czarina Kristine Gebbie was the keynote speaker at a Feb. 12 'peer educator conference' in New York that was limited to people aged 12 to 24 (thereby excluding parents). Available were explicit materials from Gay Men's Health Crisis that advised black boys that if they 'do men,' they can 'safely' engage in anal sex and other (unprintable) practices. A pamphlet aimed at girls graphically touted a variety of lesbian sex acts, including a practice that can cause infertility and require corrective surgery." (*Washington Watch*, Family Research Council, March 18, 1994)

Explained above was Clinton's attempt to allow people infected with the AIDS virus to immigrate to this country. For many years, and perhaps since this country had an immigration policy, moral character was a factor in determining qualifications of immigrants, and homosexuals were not allowed as immigrants. Also, people with venereal diseases were not allowed as immigrants. Clinton tried to do away with this in one fell swoop by administrative orders. To some extent, in spite of Congress's authority in the subject, he has been successful. He tried to eliminate sexually transmitted diseases as a disqualification for the purpose of qualifying the most deadly of all, AIDS. Not only would this be highly detrimental to the health of this country, it would put untold expenses on us.

Above we noted that Social Security was paid to alcoholics and drug addicts. It is also paid to people disabled with AIDS. This is true, even though the disabilities came about by their own wrongful acts and derelictions. Now the government has found an additional way to inflict harm on innocent people, and expense on taxpaying citizens, in response to the homosexual movement. This is by use and interpretation of the Americans With Disabilities Act (ADA).

An article, **"Disabilities Law, Health Hazard,"** by James Bovard, in *The Wall Street Journal*, March 23, 1994, states in part:

> Employers are now required to hire people with contagious diseases unless they can prove that the person poses a large risk to other workers or their customers. The Equal Employment Opportunity Commission, in its implementing regulations for the ADA, announced: "Determining whether an individual poses a significant risk of substantial harm to others must be made on a case by case basis." "Significant risk" was defined in congressional reports authorizing the law as a high probability of substantial harm.
>
> Restaurants are now obliged to give the benefit of the doubt to potentially contagious job applicants. James Coleman, an attorney for the National Council of Chain Restaurants, observed in 1992, "What we were told in no uncertain terms was 'We [Congress] are going to use the restaurant industry as a vehicle for forcing a change in public attitude with respect to AIDS. If it costs you money, too bad.'"
>
> ***
>
> Federal regulations are resulting in a cloak of secrecy being imposed on what may be life-or-death information to patients. The ADA gave health care workers the right to continue performing invasive surgery without disclosing to patients that there is a risk that they could contract AIDS from the health care provider.
>
> ***
>
> The ADA is also restricting how health care workers may protect themselves from contagious patients. (The CDC has identified 120 cases of documented or possible occupational transmission of AIDS/HIV to health care workers, and hepatitis B kills over 200 health care workers a year.) The official news magazine of the American Dental

Association warned dentists last November that "dentists should be . . . aware that they could be charged with discrimination for using 'extra precaution'" while treating HIV patients.

* * *

...The Americans With Disabilities Act is creating a "civil right" that is the antithesis of individual rights—of freedom of contract— and of the right to informed consent. Maybe someday someone will make a movie about it.

Things going on in this country today defy any conventional reason. It often seems that there is a conspiracy on foot to not only completely destroy all conventional morality, but to also give as many people as possible AIDS and other infectious diseases. Could all of these dangerous and unfathomable things be going on just out of pure ignorance on the part of our president, Congress, and the administrative bureaucracies?

One thing seems certain: the people have become so used to being regulated and told what to do—from birth to grave—that they have become numb and resigned. They seem to no longer have the will to stand up for what is right and reasonable. The same is true of our large business corporations. They seem to think that it has become easier and less expensive to comply, than to try to continually fight big government. The same numbness and weariness probably explains why so many big corporations have so easily caved in to the demands of the homosexual activists. Decent and caring people are so beset upon by big government, small-time politicians, special interest groups, and the liberal media supporting them, that they are fast losing any will to fight. They feel helpless and hopeless. They just try to comply with literally thousands and thousands of ridiculous laws and regulations that are imposed upon them at every level of government—from our national government clear down to our counties and municipalities.

The State of Vermont agreed to provide health care benefits to the unmarried partners of state workers—both heterosexual and homosexual partners. (*Albuquerque Journal*, 6-13-94)

Girl Scouts Don't Bar Lesbians, Leader Says. The Girl Scouts, smarting at some advice from Surgeon General Joycelyn Elders, said Thursday their organization does not bar girls or leaders who are lesbians. "The Girl Scouts never have discriminated in any way," said Bonnie

McEwan, national director of communications for the Girl Scouts of the U.S.A. (*Albuquerque Journal*, 6-3-94)

"No-Strings Sex Is Fuel for Societal Decay," by Suzanne Fields, *Albuquerque Journal*, 12-30-93:

***

We talk of the technology of condoms rather that the romance of commitment, protection against disease rather than affection for another, titillation rather than tenderness, exploitation rather than expressiveness.

College women, deprived of protections forged from the accumulated wisdom of the ages, with its strictures against sex without love, now strive to develop codes of behavior for men rather than take responsibility for themselves in a morality drawn by every major faith from the Bible.

***

Hence the astronomical rise of illegitimacy in the underclass. Teenage girls compete for maternity chic and pregnant teen-agers become "role models" for younger girls.

***

When pregnant cheerleaders were barred from the cheerleading squad in a high school in Hempstead, Texas, the National Organization for Women threatened to sue the school district for imposing sanctions.

Sen. Daniel Patrick Moynihan, D-N.Y., wrote an essay 25 years ago noting the signs of danger in the single-parent Black family in the Black community. He was told to mind his own business.

Today more than two-thirds of the children born to Black parents are illegitimate, one-fifth of all White babies are.

***

It's commonplace to observe that generations of fatherless families create cycles of welfare families and endless cycles of criminals. This costs us all big sums of money, reducing the quality of life for everybody.

Large numbers of fatherless sons join violent gangs for male support; fatherless daughters bear babies without fathers.

***

District of Columbia — Washington police get federal help

"Federal cops, including the FBI and Secret Service, will help local police bring order to the violent streets of the nation's capital. *** U. S. Attorney Eric Holder today unveiled plans for assistance to the city's beleaguered 4,200-member police by the FBI, U.S. Capitol and Park police, the uniformed division of the Secret Service and the Drug Enforcement Administration." (*The Albuquerque Tribune*, 3-18-94)

Thomas W. Sowell is a Black man, and a highly respected conservative writer. He is a senior fellow with the Hoover Institute at Stanford University. He writes in an editorial, "Americans are sick of liberals and criminals," *The Albuquerque Tribune*, 12-17-93:

Can the U.S. survive liberalism's legacy of tolerance for crime?

...zealots on the political left, who never seem to want to do anything against criminals, are full of fire when it comes to stopping law-abiding citizens from arming themselves in self-defense.

This is not accidental. It is part of the left-wing vision of the world. As the anointed see it, "society" is to blame for not having treated hoodlums right, and the anointed want to rehabilitate the criminal and society. Merely to protect society by locking up criminals would not allow the anointed to play the morally superior role.

***

The trump card of the liberals is the charge that those who want law and order are closet racists. For a long time that was enough to intimidate those who wanted stronger law enforcement. But today increasing numbers from within the African-American community are not buying that.

African-Americans are the principal victims of African-American criminals, so it is no favor to the people in the ghetto to let hoodlums and murderers walk the streets.

***

The excuse-mongers also ignore that African-American communities did not have anywhere near today's levels of crime, family breakdown and other social problems half a century ago when they were closer to the era of slavery. What the ghettos are suffering from today is much more a legacy of 1960s liberalism.

...A hundred years ago the marriage rate among African-Americans was higher than among Whites—and remained so in every census from 1890 to 1940. Slavery had separated people, but it could not destroy the family feelings they had for each other. Liberal social programs have done that, often by preventing a family from being formed in the first place.

The painful question now is whether we can escape the legacy of liberalism.

"**Pope Blasts Permissive Society.** ROME — He chatted with moms and dads, encouraged children preparing for their first communions and blessed a baby held up in the crowd of parishioners. Then the pope turned stern. *** 'I'm not strict, I'm gentle by nature,' said Pope John Paul III. 'But, when it comes to defending principles, I don't bend.' *** He went on to condemn homosexual marriage. *** The recent parish visit was part of a new crusade against homosexuality, contraception, abortion, euthanasia and other elements of modern society the pope believes have no place in Roman Catholicism." (*Albuquerque Journal*, 3-27-94)

George Will writes:

***

In the process of endorsing adoption of children by homosexuals and embracing the fiction that 10 percent of young people are homosexuals, she says, "sex is good; sex is wonderful." Verily it can be, but Elders' effusions are not exactly all that the nation just now needs to hear from its principal public health official.

Is it good and wonderful sex that is making so many 14-year-old mothers? From boom boxes carried by young males down city streets comes 2 Live Crew's song "Me So Horny" and lyrics about how fun it is to "bust the walls" of vaginas. Not good.

The New York Times reports a resurgence of what it delicately describes as "commercial establishments where people meet for sex." The city is estimated to have about 50 such establishments where people go, often for anonymous sex with multiple partners. The city government also knows that it will have to care for many of the more than 80,000 "AIDS orphans"—children whose mothers died of AIDS—that the nation will have by the end of this decade. (*The Albuquerque Tribune*, 3-31-94)

College Students cheer speaker denouncing Jews.

"WASHINGTON — Almost 2,000 people repeatedly cheered Khalid Muhammad as the controversial Nation of Islam member denounced Jews as 'honkies' and said God had spoken to Colin Ferguson, the Jamaican charged with killing six people on a New York commuter train. *** Muhammad, once a spokesman for the Muslim organization, spoke at Howard University. ***" (*The Albuquerque Tribune*, 4-20-94)

In Germany, four youths were sentenced to jail terms for torching a synagogue. "Five people were sleeping in apartments above the Luebeck synagogue when the youths hurled gasoline-filled beer bottles into the building on March 25, 1994. All five escaped." (*The Albuquerque Tribune*, 4-13-95)

PROFANITY

There have been several articles about the growing use of profanity in this country. It is commonly used by men, women, boys, and girls. Crude foul language is commonly used—openly, in public and in mixed company. It is becoming common in the movies and on television. It is just one more sign of a sick society. An editorial in *The Albuquerque Tribune*, 5-11-94, correctly states: "The nation is coming to accept gutter language as a matter of course." This has all come about within the last thirty years.

"Language and cultural historians trace the nation's growing use of profanity to the societal upheaval of the 1960s.... *** Comedian Lenny Bruce and poet Allen Ginsberg pushed the language frontier, while the sexual revolution and war protests created a 'let-it-all-hang-out' attitude that relaxed conversational norms. *** Profanity was a black-or-white issue in pre-1960 movies like 'Casablanca,' starring Humphrey Bogart and Ingrid Bergman. Movies contained zero profanity because the Hays Production Code strictly forbade it. The code was abandoned in 1966." (*Albuquerque Journal*, 1-6-93)

John Leo, Syndicated Columnist, *Albuquerque Journal*, 4-15-96:

Television Still Pushing Envelope of Public Coarseness
*** General Motors is celebrating the joys of giving other drivers the finger.

Other TV ads are worse. Among the recent themes are defecation (an ad for a Maryland mall) and oral sex (an excruciatingly gross ad for a little-known hamburger chain.)

Nothing makes the declining level of civility more obvious than the fact that large corporations now feel free to cash in on it. Would GM have sponsored a bird-flipping commercial as recently as five years ago? Partly because of the highly publicized furor over Calvin Klein's kiddie-porn ads, partly because the anything-goes ethic is now so strong, corporations are more willing to get attention through aggressive, assaultive advertising. They understand that in-your-face messages that shred social norms can move the merchandise by playing the current sour, ant-social mood. Thus the rapid spread of ads urging us to break all the rules or just make up our own.

***

And all attempts at reform must come to terms with the '60s generation and its belief that social forms and norms are hypocritical masks for the status quo. Sometimes they are. But our levels of political, social and commercial discourse are now so low that it is surely time to try restoring civility from the bottom up. The alternative would seem to be an increasingly stupid and brutal culture.

A start would be zero tolerance for messages and tactics aimed primarily at degrading and enraging opponents, or cashing in on the fashionable nihilism of the day. This new intolerance should apply equally to angry anti-abortion demonstrators harassing doctors at their homes and angry gay demonstrators attempting to degrade the various symbols and trapping of Christianity. Isn't this a modest proposal?

Where have good manners, politeness, civility, pride, and dignity gone? How did they leave us so fast?

School boys go down the street with oversize shirts, baggy pants sagged to expose underwear, with belts twice too large for them with the ends hanging down between their legs. They seem to be in some kind of a contest to see who can appear to be the most sloppy and stupid. And certainly such things are an indication of stupidity—both on the part of the child and on the part of their parents. School girls go around puffing on cigarettes and looking like little hookers. And perhaps some are. Top athletes jump around like monkeys, trying to draw attention to themselves when they make a good play on the football field—exhibiting a complete lack of any quiet pride or dignity—with

no manners whatsoever. There was a time when that kind of exhibitionism would have raised a question of their sanity. And it still makes
intelligent people wonder if some of these athletes are capable of any
abstract thinking. It seems that every influence on young people today
teaches them the opposite of what they should be taught, with the possible exception of some churches, and some of the churches appear to
be doing such things as adopting rock music in an attempt to attract
young people with things in which they seem to be interested, instead
of teaching traditional values and religion.

"Surgeon General Joycelyn Elders, a target of conservatives for her
views on abortion, drug legalization and sex education, was abruptly
ousted by President Clinton on Friday after saying that schoolchildren
should be taught about masturbation. *** Elders was removed a month
after a Republican election landslide seen as a shift toward the right
among voters. Since then Clinton has been struggling to tailor himself
to more centrist positions." (*Albuquerque Journal*, 12-10-94)

Sheriff Sentenced in Sex Case.
PANAMA CITY, Fla. — A Florida Panhandle sheriff was sentenced
to 4 1/4 years in prison for extorting oral sex from women.

It is certainly clear that not all sex perverts are homosexuals.

AMERICANS SHRUG OFF RISK OF SEX DISEASES.
WASHINGTON — Americans don't know their risk for sexually transmitted diseases—and aren't worried about it. *** The survey concluded
that 62 percent of the men and half of the women polled are at moderate
or high risk of catching a sexually transmitted disease. *** But 75 percent
said they weren't worried about it, 62 percent said they know very little
about such diseases—and 46 percent of those at highest risk said they
never use a condom. *** (*The Albuquerque Tribune*, 2-14-95)

Phenomena such as the above I cannot fathom, yet I do not doubt
that it is true. Have people become generally stupid? Are they in an
extreme state of despair? Apparently, when one's life becomes sufficiently
devoid of morals, then life must also become of little value to the person.

THOUSANDS ABANDONED AT BIRTH
22,000 Babies Left In Hospitals: Survey

WASHINGTON — Thousands of babies across the country have been abandoned in their hospital cribs by parents unwilling or unable to take them home. *** They are the tiniest victims of crack-cocaine, poverty, homelessness and AIDS, and one of the reasons the number of children in foster care is inching toward half a million. *** Researchers counted 22,000 abandoned infants and boarder babies in the nations hospitals in 1991, according to a draft report from the Department of Health and Human Services. *** (*Albuquerque journal*, 11-9-93)

George Will, *The Albuquerque Tribune,* 11-1-93:

UNWED WOMEN'S RISING BIRTH RATE BURDENS SYSTEM
The real "health-care crisis" is a crisis in moral behavior.

WASHINGTON — The Senator glanced at the numbers and saw in his mind's eye something frightening: A straight line, ascending.

Pat Moynihan had in hand the 1991 birth statistics which together with those for 1970-1990, produce a graph line pointing straight to calamity.

***

What makes the statistics alarming is the ascending straight line for the whole society. What makes the statistics terrifying is that the graph line of births to unmarried African-American women remains straight. That is the rate of increase is not lowering even at extraordinarily high levels.

Minority births are primarily responsible for the fact that the percentage of births to unmarried women is over 70 percent in Detroit, over 60 percent in Atlanta, Baltimore, Cleveland, Newark, St. Louis and Washington, over 50 percent in Chicago, Miami, Philadelphia and Pittsburgh. But Moynihan surmises that San Francisco's lower ratio—31.5—is the result of a minority: Asian-Americans.

***

What can be done?

One clue may be in William Buckley's words that Moynihan cites: "The most readily identifiable tragedy of modern life is the illegitimate child."

To many people today there is something anachronistic about the word "illegitimate." They find it jarring because it is "judgmental." But reviving the value judgments behind that locution may be the only way to bend down the line on Moynihan's graph.

WELFARE PROMOTES UNMARRIED BIRTHS: STUDY

WASHINGTON — *** The study this week by the Heritage Foundation ***. written by Robert Rector ***.

Rector argues that the welfare system began expanding rapidly in the mid-1960s, when President Johnson launched the War on Poverty. But these "investments" in the poor he said have only led to higher spending and escalating social problems.

Today, one child in seven is being raised on AFDC (Aid to Families with Dependent Children). When the war on poverty began, roughly one Black child in four was born out of wedlock; overall, one child in 14 was born to a single mother.

Now ... two out of three Black children are born out of wedlock and overall, nearly a third of children are born to single mothers.

"The principle is simple: in welfare as in most other things, you get what you pay for. For 30 years the welfare system has paid for non-work and non-marriage and has achieved massive increases in both," Rector wrote.

Rector also argues that by undermining work and rewarding out-of-wedlock births, the welfare system generates its own clientele.

"The more that is spent, the more people in apparent need of aid who appear," he said. (*Albuquerque Journal, 6-8-95*)

People, particularly in the larger cities, will note that the same principles apply to other forms of government handouts. The easier it becomes for people to exist by living off of others and not working, the more people we will have doing it. One example is the "homeless" and "street people." The more they are cared for, the more there are to care for.

This system has even more insidious and harmful aspects.

Forty years ago, it was widely believed that unmarried people should not live together; that single women should not become pregnant; that even married couples should not have children until they, themselves, were ready to properly care for them; and that one should strive to make one's own living, rather than sponging off of the work of others. There was a tremendous stigma on those who violated these beneficial rules of society.

The practice of rewarding the violating of those rules has been one of the factors in the general decline and breakdown of our morality. Many people have begun to believe that not only is there nothing morally wrong with violating what had been these beneficial rules of society, which had developed from the ideas of a religious people, but that they are entitled to support from the government so that they may continue to do so—and in better style. We of older generations are shocked to see such things as unions and societies for the homeless and street people, for welfare people—and for about everyone parasitically living off of the productive taxpayer. And, sadly enough, this is not just limited to those of the "lower class"—it now includes probably a majority of our society that are now benefiting in one way or another from government handouts (buying their vote)—from farmers to old people. Not only do they resist cuts in our destructive deficit spending, but most want even more.

John Leo, the syndicated columnist, wrote in the *Albuquerque Journal*, 11-2-93:

Recent Research Exposes Myth of Victimized Homelessness

"While the 1980s were marked by compassion for the homeless, the 1990s seem to have become the decade of anti-homelessness." (New book by Alice Baum and Donald Bernes, "A Nation in Denial: The Truth About Homelessness)

This is a remarkable shift in public opinion, and it has happened coast to coast, reaching into the most open-minded, tolerant communities. Suddenly, there's a guilt-free consensus that minimum levels of civility and public order are necessary to keep communities functioning.

The New York Times reported recently that even timorous residents now howl about "the broken bottle on the sidewalk, the use of convenient nooks and crannies as public urinals. Middle-class New York is suffering death by a thousand life-style cuts." Beggars seem more numerous, more menacing and more irrational than they did a few years ago. George Kelling, the criminologist, said last week that if people can't exercise the rights to be left alone by aggressive panhandlers and other street folk, "then the only alternative citizens have is to retreat from the public spaces." Actually, middle-class people have another alternative — they can leave the cities, taking much of the tax base with them. ***

With our decline in morality, we have lost our pride in accomplishment, our self respect, and our independence. This is the price we have paid for our government largesse. And at some point our descendants will have to pay for our sinful selfishness.

Time Warner Corners Popular Market on Cultural Degradation

*** The Schlocky Jenny Jones show, the first show on which a guest who was set up to be humiliated later was charged with murdering his (homosexual) humiliator, is a Time Warner product. The most degrading commercial picture book about human sexuality may be Madonna's $49 porn book, which, I am told, pictorially indicates that she is game to have sex with everything but babies and folding chairs. It was published by Time Warner, and (surprise!) chosen as an alternate selection by Time Warner's once respectable Book of the Month Club.

In the movies the all-time low for cynicism and historical lies (Oliver Stone's "JFK") and for graphic, wholesale serial killing presented as fun (Oliver Stone's "Natural Born Killers") were both produced by Warner. In the category of movie nihilism for children, my vote goes to Warner's "Batman Returns," a dark and sadomasochistic film pushed hard to kids through a tie-in with McDonalds.

But it's in the music field that Time Warner does most of its damage. Dr. C. Delores Tucker, chair of the National Congress of Black Women, says Time Warner is "one of the greatest perpetrators of this cultural garbage." She may be understating the case. From the rise of 2 Live Crew and Metallica through the national uproar over Ice-T's cop killing lyrics, down to Snoop Doggy Dog, Nine Inch Nails and Tupac Shakur, the sprawling Time Warner musical empire has been associated with most of the high-profile, high-profit acts, Black and White, that are pumping nihilism into the culture.

Like a junkie quivering toward a fix, Time Warner simply can't resist cashing in on the relentlessly amoral singers who work tirelessly to tear the culture apart, glorifying brutality, violence, and the most hateful attitudes toward women the public culture has ever seen, ranging from rape to torture and murder. *** (John Leo, Syndicated Columnist, *Albuquerque Journal*, 3-21-95)

It is a shame and a disgrace that our country, on the false premise of "freedom of speech," allows the production and distribution of much of this filth. It is even more of a shame that a sufficient number of people buy such garbage that it is profitable. But it is like our plague of dope use. We even use our armed forces to try to interdict the entry of drugs into the country, when our real problem is here—the very fact that we have such a demand for illegal drugs.

Mom: Boys easily plucked porn from computer

WASHINGTON — Dr. Susan Tillman Elliott couldn't figure out why the memory on the family's computer was filling so fast. So she did a directory of the "trash" file — and that's exactly what she found.

Obscene trash, retrieved from a computer on-line service by her 12- and 14-year-old sons. They had gained easy access to a pornographic "chat room" where they copied pictures of humans and animals engaged in sex.

"This is freedom which no 12-year-old needs," Elliott, of McLean, Va., said. "it's far too easy for it to get into our homes."

Elliott was among those testifying Monday before the Senate Judiciary Committee, which held the first congressional hearing on computer pornography.

The panel is considering a bill, which Elliott favors, to make it illegal for on-line computer services to "knowingly" transmit pornography to children or let the system be used as a conduit for pornographic material.

A similar anti-smut provision was included in an omnibus telecommunications bill the Senate passed last month. The measure was approved over the objections of civil libertarians, who complained it violated the First Amendment.

The Clinton administration and House leaders also have objected to the bill, saying it would be difficult to enforce a ban on indecent and obscene materials on computer services and the Internet global computer network.

***

Barry Crimmins, an investigative journalist, told the committee that pornography is pervasive on the Internet and on-line services. He said he found a chat room for sexual abuse survivors, for example, located between a listing for father-daughter incest and one offering pictures of young boys.

"When you go in as a child the pedophiles come after you like they're flies and you're rancid meat," said Crimmins, who pretended to be a 12-year-old boy to lure pedophiles.

"The proliferation of child pornography trafficking has created an anonymous pedophile superstore," he added. *** (*The Albuquerque Tribune*, 7-25-95)

Duke City targeted in child-porn investigation

WASHINGTON — The FBI conducted searches in 20 cities, including Albuquerque ["Duke City"], as part of a nationwide investigation into the use of computer online services and the Internet to lure children into illicit sex and to distribute child pornography.

***

Before Wednesday, the 3-year-old investigation had resulted in 80 arrests, 103 indictments and charges filed by criminal information, 66 felony convictions and 207 searches.

***

"These cases have already revealed the ease and frequency with which criminals have used modern technology to cause grave harm to children," [FBI Director Louis Freeh] said. "These crimes, preying on innocent children, represent every parent's worst nightmare."

***

The nationwide investigation began as a result of widespread electronic distribution of child pornography that was discovered by agents looking into the disappearance of George S. Burdynski, a 10-year-old abducted from his Brentwood, Md. neighborhood in May, 1993. The boy has never been found.

But investigators uncovered adults across the nation using computers to lure minors into illicit sex with pedophiles and to transmit pictures of minors that show full frontal nudity and sexually explicit activities.

Pornographic images of children as young as 2 years old have been displayed online, the FBI said. *** (*The Albuquerque Tribune*, 12-12-96)

Uruguay Prostitutes Entitled to Benefits

MONTEVIDEO, Uruguay — Female prostitutes have obtained the right to a retirement pension, the head of Uruguay's social security system said Friday. [The women are known as "sexual workers."] (*Albuquerque Journal*, 12-16-95)

HIV-Positive Bank Robbers

To be compassionate, Italy passed a law in 1993, forbidding the imprisonment of those infected with HIV. This has turned out to be a boon for a few thousand career criminals. One gang of HIV-infected bank robbers has been arrested numerous times only to be freed within hours of each capture. They are suspected of taking at least $155,000 in their thefts. (*Reason Magazine*, Nov. 1995; *Issues at a Glance*, Concerned Women for America, Feb. 1996)

Incestuous couple sentenced for plot to have husband shot

OXFORD, Miss. — A woman and her grandfather involved in an incestuous relationship for almost 20 years have been sentenced to maximum prison terms for plotting to kill the woman's husband.

Teresa Jean Hutcheson, 30, and William Douglas Hinson, 71, were sentenced Tuesday to five years in prison without parole. The couple, who have two children, pleaded guilty in September to one count of conspiracy to commit murder for hire.

"In my 20 years on the bench, I thought I'd seen everything, but this is the most sordid case I've seen, where the great-grandfather is also the father of his great-grandchildren," U.S. District Judge Neal Biggers Jr. told Hinson. "If I could give you 20 years, I would."

Hinson and Hutcheson had offered $25,000, to be paid out of insurance proceeds on the husband, for a hit man, Assistant U.S. Attorney Charles Spillers said.

Hutcheson and Hinson plotted the slaying of Jimmy Dean Hutcheson, according to court records, as early as November 1993 to obtain more than $200,000 in insurance money. Hinson approached someone at that time about finding a hit man to gun down Hutcheson in an apparent hunting accident.

When that fell through, Hutcheson and Hinson reportedly switched on the electric power in the Hutchesons' New Albany home while her husband was under the house fixing wiring in May, 1994. He suffered burned hands.

Teresa Hutcheson's defense argued for leniency, contending she was under the control of her grandfather through an incestuous relationship that began when she was 11.

But prosecutors claimed taped conversations and other evidence showed she was the key force in the plot. (*The Albuquerque Tribune*, 11-29-95)

Indeed, the truth is stranger than fiction, and, unfortunately, it gets stranger all of the time.

In one day, in the *Albuquerque Journal,* on Valentine's Day, 2-14-96, there were the following two separate and unrelated stories of hideous incest charges:

Location critical in Incest

DADE CITY, Fla. — A judge threw out incest charges Tuesday against a brother and sister suspected of having nine children together, ruling there was no evidence the couple had sex in his county. *** The couple, whose children range in age from 18 months to 22 years, had been charged with incest in the case of their youngest child. The statute of limitations had run out on the other children. *** The couple—he is 66, his sister 44—were arrested March 22 after DNA tests showed that the girl was theirs.

Texas Man May have Fathered Grandchild, Got Her Pregnant

HOUSTON — A man believed to have fathered his granddaughter is suspected of impregnating the 12-year-old girl.

The man, whose name was not released, was arrested Monday on aggravated sexual assault charges and jailed on $300,000 bond. He is charged with molesting the 12-year-old and her 10-year-old sister, whom he did not father, police said.

"We have reason to believe that he's also the father of this unborn baby," Officer Kendal Clark said. "This is the first time I've had a [second generation] and possibly a third generation of incest in one case."

Relatives first alerted authorities to possible abuse in October 1993. The man and the 12-year-old, then 9, were living together at the time, while the mother and other children were living elsewhere.

Clark said the man, a 46-year-old mechanic, denies sexually assaulting the girls and said he is not the 12-year-old's father. He also said he isn't sure he's the father of the girls' 25-year-old mother. ***

Incest Leads to Prison Terms

MILWAUKEE — A brother and sister who had at least three children together were sent to prison Tuesday for incest.

The 45-year-old man received eight years. His 30-year-old sister, who gave birth again just days ago, got five years.

Circuit Judge David Hamsher told them that severe punishment was necessary to keep them apart and stop them from having sex. (*Albuquerque Journal*, 11-12-97)

United Nations Fourth World Conference on Women in Beijing

The following is information obtained from a Newsletter of James C. Dobson, Ph.D., *Focus on the Family,* Colorado Springs, Co., October 1995:

There were 50,000 delegates and observers at the 185 nation conference this fall. Focus on the Family sent a delegation of four to monitor the event.

The liberal and immoral proceedings were entirely predictable. In fact Dr. Dobson had predicted:

"Most of what Christianity stands for will be challenged during this atheistic conference. Every good and perfect gift from the hand of the Creator will be mocked and vilified by many of its delegates."

(He was right.)

When appointing delegates, President Clinton falsely promised and stated: "They come from all walks of life, from different political parties and religions. ... However anyone might try to paint this conference, the truth is, it is true blue to families — to supporting them, to conserving them, to valuing them."

Of the forty-six U.S. delegates, only two Republicans were appointed—both of whom were well-known liberals, and the other forty-four delegates were Clinton allies. None were members of any real pro-family movement. A group of feminist activists, including the radical Bella Abzug, prepared the draft document for the conference at the United Nations.

In a letter to Ambassador Madeleine Allbright, who chaired the U.S. delegation, Congressman Chris Smith (R-N.J.) stated:

"Sections of the document as currently drafted would declare new international rights to abortion, to abortion financing by governments, to non-discrimination on account of sexual orientation, and to rights of 'privacy' or 'sexual rights' that would apply even to young adolescents and could easily be construed as giving them the right to contraceptives and abortions without the consent of their parents. There is little support for any of these new rights within the United States Congress or among the American people."

Mrs. Clinton's group, alone, required five Air Force jets, and cost over one million dollars (of taxpayers' money).

The delegates from the United States, Canada, and European Union countries focused on restructuring the traditional family, reordering male and female roles, distributing condoms and "safe-sex" propaganda to children, weakening parental authority and religious teaching, and promoting "homosexual and lesbian rights."

Even delegates and leaders from Third World countries, including Prime Minister Benazir Bhutto of Pakistan and Dr. Margaret Oogala from Kenya were critical of the conference's agenda, and the claim that it was "mainstream" and "traditional family" oriented. Dr. Oogala said: "Apparently in the United States, the most powerful country in the world, the family is considered as nothing anymore." (What does this tell us about the views of our American feminists such as Hillary Rodham Clinton?)

Most revealing were the actual workshops. The following is a list of some of the topical subjects of the workshops:

- The Role of Inflatable Life-size Plastic Dolls and Dildos in Improving Health (*Description reads: "The inflatable life-size plastic doll will take the brunt off women and help to solve many global problems."*)
- Lesbianism for the Curious
- Spirit and Action: Lesbian Activism From an Interfaith Perspective
- Women in Livestock Development (*Described as "techniques of participatory gender analysis" for livestock officials.*)

- Women in Black: A Gathering of Spirits (*This one tells women attending to wear black and bring a lamp.*)
- Lesbian and Mother: Talking About Being Sperm Donors (*It described as "parenting and donorship within the framework of a lesbian life-choice."*)
- Amphibian Frolic (*Described as a "woman artist's journey into the creature world with costume and dance."*)
- Lesbian Flirtation Techniques Workshop
- How Religious Fundamentalism Helps the Spread of AIDS (*This workshop indicts conservative Christians in the United States for facilitating the spread of AIDS.*)
- Beyond the Trinity Creator, The Mystery of the Virgin Soul
- Hips Hooray! The Healing of Womanhood Through Body Joy
- Lesbians in the Baltics: New Phenomenon of the '90s

Senator Jesse Helms, (R-N.C.) continuing his everlasting fight for family values, sent a letter about the workshops to Brian Atwood, administrator for the U.S. Agency for International Development. He stated:

> I will never understand why this kind of insanity occurs, especially at a conference purporting to be on "women's rights." What, pray tell, does a "workshop" on "flirting techniques for lesbians" have to do with women's rights? I beg you! Please assure me that no U.S. money in the United Nations special trust fund helped pay for this outrageous program!

The Washington Times described one of the radical workshops of Bella Abzug:

> Mrs. Abzug, in one of more than 350 workshops on the second day of the forum, joined hands with other women in a prayerful tribute to "Mother Earth" that mocked orthodox Christian belief. "Give thanks for the fruits of life," said a Brazilian delegate who led the group to prayer. "Thanks to Mother Earth, for you give us life. Thanks for water. People from my community decided no more Crucifixion. We believe in life. We celebrate life, not the Crucifixion. We are power." Mrs. Abzug and several dozen women holding hands then thrust their hands into the air, chanting, "I am power, I am power, I am power."...

With the help of the Clintons and the liberal Democrats, our tax money is now being forcefully taken from us and used to tear down the moral base upon which this country was built, and under which it flourished for two hundred years.

"**GEORGIA ERRED** when it withdrew a job offer in its state attorney general's office to clerk Rubin Joy Shahar, a court says. The state pulled the offer after learning Ms. Shahar was about to marry her lesbian partner in a religious ceremony. In a decision that boosts efforts to win anti-discrimination protection for homosexuals, the U.S. Court of Appeals for the Eleventh Circuit in Atlanta ruled the state violated Ms. Shahar's First Amendment rights to freedom of association, religion and expression." (*The Wall Street Journal*, 1-23-96)

The above news item is one more concrete example of leftist activist courts promoting the homosexual agenda by stating fallacious principles of law that have no valid constitutional basis. For over two hundred years all private persons and government agencies had the right to require good moral character as a qualification for a job. Now, that right has either been removed by such courts, or those who engage in acts of sodomy must be considered to have good moral character. The full acceptance of sodomy is being forced upon us—I consider this to be the one most destructive things going on in our society. How, you may ask, could this be considered more destructive than little girls getting pregnant, children using dope and killing each other, and incest? My answer to this is—that the acceptance of sodomy, is the acceptance of what has historically and Biblically been considered as the ultimate depravity of mankind. It is extremely vile and a crime against nature. When sodomy is accepted, our morality will have been eliminated, and the acceptance and increase of all of these other things will come as a matter of course. These things are literally being forced upon us.

The importance of getting our society back on a wholesome and moral course, and ways to stop the judicial destruction of our right to abide by our own moral beliefs, is discussed in detail in Chapter 8, with recommended changes in our state and federal constitutions.

MORAL DECLINE—YOUNG PEOPLE

How did our standards for young people fall so far in just 30 years?

We old timers over the years have seen many changes in social mores. Moral values have changed dramatically, family units and values have decomposed considerably, and people's changing beliefs and corruption have increased.

What we considered as right and wrong has changed somehow over the last 30 years. We old-timers cannot understand the changes, such as:

- Boys accosting young ladies in elementary and high schools and the young ladies accepting their actions.
- Girls attending classes wearing seductive attire, some with their navels exposed and many with their breast cleavage displayed, leaving no doubt whatsoever as to why its being shown so openly.
- (We old-timers remember the sanctity of womanhood and remember that it was considered totally out of bounds to touch a young lady openly. We also remember that young ladies who displayed, even slightly, their thighs or breasts were thought to be sirens, sluts or tramps. Such displays were simply not accepted.)
- Young students who in their belief that "Joe Camel" helps them to be part of the in-crowd, puffing vigorously to show that they belong, apparently not thinking of how it will affect them or their offspring.
- School authorities encouraging "safe sex" by distributing latex condoms that in some cases are not 100 percent safe. Abstinence should be the message, as it was in the past.
- Young people, some as young as nine or 10, hanging out in parking lots and dark, secluded areas smoking pot and sniffing glue or inhaling the fumes from paint cans. Older youngsters taking them under their wings, leading them to more powerful and dangerous drugs. To obtain such drugs, a great deal of money is needed. Shortly, robberies from their homes as well as others' become an everyday occurrence. Shoplifting, purse snatching, auto heist and armed robbery are the next steps.

***

(Robida, Paul, *The Albuquerque Tribune*, 2-4-95)

Children's Stories Reflect Violent Culture

WASHINGTON— *** As a third-grade teacher for 11 years, Lori Wright of East Silver Spring (Md.) Elementary School has read hundreds of children's stories. In this year's batch:

- *"The Headless Horseman," by a friendly, intelligent boy, which concerned a man who "got shot in the head with a cannonball (by) ... some drunk men." After surviving in the woods by eating the brains of wolves, the man cuts off three people's heads."*

- *A tale by a quiet, imaginative girl concerning two girls being followed by a stranger who later buries them alive.*

- *An articulate boy's story about two youths, Jimmy and his friend Danny, "a lunatic ... who stole some drugs." When Danny strangles Jimmy, Jimmy kicks him in the (testicles)." Danny then pushes Jimmy out a window."*

- *Another boy's story, "I'm King," which reads in its entirety: One day I became king. I killed John and then Joe. Everybody was happy."*

The authors were 8 years old. *** (*Albuquerque Journal*, 11-27-93)

One does not have to be a psychologist to understand that stories such as these are a definite reflection of the detrimental, dangerous, and immoral shift in our children's thinking. At least anyone over fifty years old with a bit of common sense should clearly understand this. Certainly, not all children are like those depicted, but a large and increasing number are.

Pregnant cheerleader ban is reversed

HEMPSTEAD, Texas — Fearing a lawsuit or loss of funds, school officials reversed a ban on having pregnant girls on the cheerleading squad.

The school district cited health concerns when it kicked four pregnant girls off the 16-member Hempstead High School cheerleading squad in September. One girl who had an abortion was allowed to return.

The ACLU and women's rights groups had contended the Hempstead school board's policy is illegal and could threaten federal money received by the district. (*The Albuquerque Tribune*, 11-2-93)

8th Graders Give Classmate a Baby Shower

Officials at Taft Middle School [Albuquerque] say they weren't aware that a group of eighth-graders threw a lunchtime baby shower for a pregnant classmate on school grounds several weeks ago. *** Jaramillo said the girls who threw the shower got permission to do so from the school's counselors. *** (*Albuquerque Journal*, 10-21-93)

Child Prostitution In City Stirs Alarm

On any given day in any major American city, pedestrians and motorists pass prostitutes on the street without a second glance. But if they bothered to look, they might be shocked to see 10-year-old girls and boys selling their bodies for money.

Albuquerque is no exception.

***

..."In these national exploitative networks, Albuquerque is as important a player as New York, Los Angeles and Dallas."

***

...[Police Sgt. Darren White] described how the system — and Albuquerque's role in it — works.

Pimps in cities nationwide are on the lookout for runaways. They befriend the girls and boys, then they travel with them to cities elsewhere.

For example, White said Albuquerque children have been found working the streets in New York, Oklahoma City, Denver and Dallas.

***

On Monday, the U.S. Department of Justice held a training conference at the Law Enforcement Academy in Albuquerque for local officers on how to deal with the problem.

***

In Albuquerque, most teen prostitutes are runaways, White said. Nationally, about half are girls and half are boys. But in Albuquerque, he's seen mostly girls. *** (*Albuquerque Journal*, 11-9-93)

Laughing Teens Anger Audience At Holocaust Film

SAN JOSE, Calif. — When Steven Spielberg released his gritty "Schindler's List," he hoped the film about the Holocaust would provoke a range of responses, from horror to despair to anger. Laughter was not one of them.

... In what appears to be a clash of cultures and generations, theater managers ousted [a group of] Castlemont High School students after other movie-goers complained that they were laughing loudly and contemptuously after one of the movie's most affecting scenes.

"They were laughing at people being murdered by Nazis, laughing out loud," said Allen Michaan, owner of the Grand Lake Theater. "People were shaking with anger. The issue was they weren't permitting other patrons to enjoy the movie." *** (*Albuquerque Journal*, 1-22-94)

Woman on Trial in Out-of-State Abortion

LAPORTE, Pa. — The 13-year-old was pregnant and afraid to tell her mother. So Rosa Hartford, stepmother of the boy involved, drove the teen-ager 60 miles, to an abortion doctor in nearby New York. *** It is the first prosecution in the United States of an adult who drove a girl to another state for an abortion. And the punishment could be severe: up to six years in jail. *** (*Albuquerque Journal*, 10-29-96)

Utah Football Players Confess to 20 Holdups

SALT LAKE CITY — The talk in the locker room was about cars, girls, clothes — and, according to police, the holdups some high school football players committed to pay for it all.

Six members of the Granger High football team were being held Thursday in juvenile detention after police say they confessed to robbing 20 fast food restaurants and other stores. *** (*Albuquerque Journal*, 10-18-96)

It is very saddening and alarming that the above incidents happened in Mormon country. Utah has always been ahead of the rest of the country in having a minimum of crime, violence, drug use, and other indicators of our cultural decline.

In Albuquerque, we recently had an incident that made the papers around the country. A high-school football player, Michael Cito, wore a helmet with a buckle on it honed to a "razor edge" by his father, according to the father's admission, and cut several opposing players in a football game. One of the most discouraging things connected with the incident was that other students demonstrated in favor of the offender. The following article, from which parts are quoted, resulted:

No reason to be surprised at Pius buckle incident

The surprise, given our society's confusion, is that it doesn't happen more often.

***

I was neither shocked nor surprised. Really what do you expect? ...

***

Look what makes headlines in professional sports. Baltimore Oriole Roberto Alomar spits in the face of an umpire and demeans him in public, actually blaming the umpire's cranky disposition on the death of his child. Dennis Rodman head-butts a referee. Albert Belle throws tantrums, and baseballs, at reporters. Michael Irvin has his little dance with hookers and drugs. The list is endless.

Like it or not, these are the people we've told our children to admire and respect. So don't shake your head in bewilderment, wondering where Michael Cito went wrong. ...

And believe me, this isn't just a sports problem. Sports is a mirror that reflects what is truly off course in society in general.

Soon-to-be-former District Attorney Bob Schwartz stopped by the 94 Rock morning show last week, and we asked him after all those years serving as the district attorney what frightened him the most.

He replied that it was the lack of conscience in our youths. Kids are killing kids because they truly don't know the difference between right and wrong. After a shooting, they will show absolutely no remorse for what they have done.

Do you realize how chilling this is? If we are raising a generation that is incapable of knowing the right thing to do, what does this bode for the future? How can you punish someone for a crime when they have no idea they've done something wrong? How can you rehabilitate someone if they feel no guilt or remorse? *** (Trout, T. J., rock radio show host and writer, *The Albuquerque Tribune*, 10-25-96)

On one Sunday morning, almost the entire page of the Albuquerque paper, *The Sunday Journal*, 11-10-96, was taken up with crimes and degradation involving young people. It included the following:

Sex Scandal Grows

The Army suspended an additional 15 training instructors at Maryland's Aberdeen Proving Ground while it examines complaints ranging from verbal abuse to sexual assault.

SPORTSMANSHIP

Is The Foundation Crumbling?

Terry Linton had officiated countless basketball games in the poorly lighted gyms that dot New Mexico, so he was no stranger to the darker side of high school sports.

Boorish coaches, foul-mouthed fans. Athletes—and their parents—wearing chips on their shoulders.

He thought he had seen it all.

He was wrong.

As Linton ran to the officials' dressing room after an emotional Santa Fe Capital-Bernalillo boys' basketball showdown last winter, the veteran referee was showered by a new form of abuse.

Somebody spit on Terry Linton. And it wasn't Baltimore Oriole Roberto Alomar.

***

There is upheaval in the house of New Mexico high school athletics, where increasing examples of poor behavior, misguided principles and frustration are beginning to erode the foundation on which prep sports were built.

As recently as Friday night, football official Allen Bainter was hospitalized after a Wingate High School player allegedly hit him from behind during the Bear's game with Crownpoint. The player was upset because Bainter had just ejected him for unsportsmanlike conduct. [Bainiter was knocked unconscious and was still unaware of what happened as of Saturday night.]

***

Wreck Sobers Socorro

A deadly crash leaves local residents and family members in anguish over toll of drunken driving

[This article related to an accident in late September, 1996. Both drivers, according to blood tests and the district attorney, were drunk. Three men in a pickup were driving into Soccoro, N.M., at about 80 mph in a residential area, when a car driven by Nathan Santillanes, 28, turned slowly into the street in front of the pickup. In the car with Santillanes were his "common-law wife," Liz Meyers, her three children, ages 5, 8, and 9, and her niece, 14. All but the driver were killed. The three men in the pickup survived. The driver of the pickup was Jimmie Guerro, 19. Guerro had no prior record, but Santillanes had a long string of arrests, including three convictions for driving while intoxicated (DWI). His driver's license had been revoked more than once, and there is a long-standing warrant for his arrest for failure to attend DWI classes.]

CRIME AND VIOLENCE—GENERALLY

We now have so many convicted criminals in this country that governmental institutions cannot incarcerate all of them. Felons are turned loose earlier than they should be to alleviate overcrowding. Prosecutors decline to prosecute some cases that were routinely prosecuted before.

Great private prisons are being built to house prisoners.

Governor Gary Johnson of New Mexico announces that the state has contracted to build the largest private run penitentiary in the nation near Hobbs, N. M., and another large one near Santa Rosa, N.M. (*Albuquerque Journal*, 4-27-96) New Mexico, like a number of other states, has had trouble from federal court decrees for a number of years because of jail conditions and overcrowding.

Yet there are still so many criminals running loose and preying on us that we are not safe in our homes, on our streets, and young people are not safe in their schools.

"**America—a mugger's paradise**". "Nine years ago in a New York City subway, Bernard McCummings, 24, hit, pinned and choked half to death Jerome Sandusky, 70, before relieving him of sundry coins, bills and valuables in a contemporary custom commonly known as mugging. *** As McCummings fled the crime scene, a transit policeman alerted by Sandusky's cries fired a bullet into the mugger's back, paralyzing him and eventually landing him in a two-year prison hitch. *** However, a New York jury ruled the officer used excessive force in stopping McCummings, whom it awarded $4.3 million in damages." *** (*The Albuquerque Tribune*, 12-3-93)

Child Molester Back in Jail.

OMAHA, Neb. — A man accused of fondling his 11-year-old stepdaughter in a prison visiting room while serving time for child molestation was sentenced Friday to 20 to 25 years in prison. *** James E. Johnson had been sent to prison in 1989 for sexually assaulting another

11-year-old girl. Instead of being released as scheduled Friday, Johnson received the new sentence. He had pleaded no contest to sexual assault. *** Johnson's wife, Nancy Jo, is charged with child abuse for allegedly bringing his stepdaughter to the prison so he could fondle her. Authorities said the girl was repeatedly assaulted between June 1994 and January. (*Albuquerque Journal*, 4-15- 95)

In the above article we should note that, according to the article, the little girl "was repeatedly assaulted" while Johnson was in prison. What kind of prisons are they running in Nebraska? This seems as ridiculous as what we have in New Mexico, and a number of other places. They are not like the prisons they had in the old South, with hard labor and chain gangs. Those were prisons which convicts made a real effort not to return to when once they got out.

Dad, Son Jailed In Rape Cases

Two Albuquerque suspects are held in adjoining cells while awaiting trials in separate incidents.

An alleged three-time rapist remained behind bars in Albuquerque on Friday evening, awaiting trial.

His father was locked in the cell next door – indicted earlier in the week on different rape charges, officials said. ***

The son, 27-year-old Stacy Simms, and his dad, 52-year-old John Simms, have previous convictions for sexual assault, according to officials and court records.

The older Simms was arrested Feb. 27 on suspicion of raping an Albuquerque woman and punching her "repeatedly" in the face.

According to the criminal complaint filed against John Simms, he told his victim at one point, "you better shut up and let me do what I want or I'll start hitting you again."

Stacy Simms is set to stand trial April 2 on charges that he raped a woman in 1996 after breaking into her Albuquerque home and wrapping a shirt around her neck and face.

The younger Simms also is accused of raping another woman – and kidnapping a third woman – in another criminal case that is still pending. ...

Court records show that Stacy Simms entered an "Alford" plea in 1995 to a charge of raping a woman and was sentenced to five years' probation. In an Alford plea a defendant does not admit guilt but concedes he could be convicted at trial. *** (*Albuquerque Journal*, 3-14-98)

Youth Advocates Oppose Stricter Laws

Adult Punishment 'Doesn't Make Sense'

Spare the rod—save the child.

Youth advocates say the state is taking a system that has "proven" ineffective—adult corrections and punishment—and applying it to juveniles.

***

The category of serious youthful offenders applies to anyone 15 to 18 years old who is indicted for first degree murder. A serious youthful offender can get up to a life sentence—which is 30 years for adults—but juveniles can't get the death penalty.

***

David Schmidt, director of the New Mexico Council on Crime and Delinquency, said the state is heading in the wrong direction by joining a trend that isn't logical.

[Schmidt says]: "The adult system has between a 60 and 70 percent recidivism, while the juvenile (system) has about a 30 percent recidivism."

***

... the average cost of housing juveniles is $30,000 per juvenile per year.

***

[Jerry Ortiz y Pino, director of the New Mexico Advocate for families and children] points to a study done by the Institute for Social Research at the University of New Mexico.

The research found that more than a quarter—28 percent—of the kids in custody in New Mexico juvenile prisons are low risk and can be released to community supervisors.

The state youth department's risk-assessment calculations put the number at roughly 5 percent.

***

[Heather Wilson, Secretary of the Children, Youth and Families Department] defended her department's study.

"I've invited any legislator who believes that there are low-risk kids ready to come back to their community to identify them, come to the parole hearings and they can give them a ride home because I don't think they're there," Wilson said. "Our studies ... show that they're not there, or that they're there but in very low numbers and for a short period of time." (*Albuquerque Journal*, 12-30-96)

New Mexico, like many other states, finally realized that we could not continue to allow a large number of our children to continue to commit murder and other violent crimes, doing nothing but put them in "reform schools" for two years or less and then turn them back loose on the public. We were only then driven to doing something more strict—now the liberals commence their screaming for more of the same thing that brought us to this point.

It is certainly no wonder to anyone with a little common sense that in New Mexico we have a high rate of recidivism in our penal system. Inmates have television, recreational and educational facilities, schooling facilities, and, unbelievably, even conjugal visits from spouses or girlfriends. And even furloughs to go home, and visits to ball games—from which many did not return. Although they are given vocational training if they want, they don't have to work. They are not in the danger they are when they are on the outside and have to rob and steal for a living. Many even get their dope in prison. Many are actually better off in prison than they were on the outside. During the time that our ideas of correction have regressed to this point, crime and recidivism has inversely increased. These are not the old prison systems of hard time, hard labor, and austerity, to which no sane person wanted to return. We are paying the price for our "liberal," "tolerant," and "kind" ideas.

Consider the statement made in the article above: "Spare the rod—save the child." This is the exact opposite of the Biblical teaching that served this country so well for over two hundred years: "He that spareth his rod hateth his son: But he that loveth him chasteneth him betimes [disciplines him diligently]." (*Proverbs* 13:24)

These liberal ideas of disciplining children have been going on for decades, since the advent of Dr. Spock. Because of that liberal teaching, many parents thought that discipline would restrict the personality of their little darlings, so they chose never to resort to spanking. These children, whose parents allowed them to "express" themselves, grew into little monsters, and even murderers.

Such things are common place now that were never heard of when I grew up. Corporal punishment was even used at school then, although it wasn't often needed. The fact that it was available was why it was not often needed. And my father told me that when I got a "whipping" at school, then I would get another at home. Principals and teachers had full authority to enforce proper discipline, and they did so. Let us carefully consider what we have reaped now from our change to tolerance and leniency.

Let us consider this:

At the same time that the old time application of the "rod" has declined, real child abuse has actually and seriously increased. This is another of our legacies of modern liberalism.

Studies show children are beaten, abused often

N. Y. Times News ***

The poll on child discipline, conducted by the Gallup Organization in August and September, asked a representative sample of 1,000 parents nationwide how they handle a child who misbehaves.

If the poll results were projected to the entire population, it would mean that almost 5 percent of parents punish their children by punching, kicking or throwing the child down, or hitting the child with a hard object on some part of the body other than the bottom.

Those acts were classified as abusive in the study, while punishments like spanking, slapping, shouting, cursing or threatening to send a child away were not.

The Gallup poll also found that 1.3 million children a year were sexually abused. ...

***

...the use of milder physical punishments, such as spanking, has been declining in the United States. But severe abuse has not: Indeed, the number of children killed by abuse has increased 50 percent in the last decade. ...

***

Experts on child abuse said the Gallup numbers were not out of line with their research.

***

Physical and sexual abuse were reported three times more often in single-parent families than in two-parent families. *** (*The Albuquerque Tribune*, 12-7-95)

Child abuse doubles, puts strain on system

WASHINGTON — Abuse and neglect of America's children nearly doubled between 1986 and 1993, suggesting that the nation's child-protective services system has reached its capacity, a federal study says.

***

- Children of single parents had a 77 percent greater risk of being harmed by physical abuse, an 87 percent of being harmed by physical neglect and an 80 percent greater risk of suffering serious injury or harm from abuse or neglect than children living with both parents.
- Children from families earning less that $15,000 were 22 times more likely to suffer maltreatment than children from families with incomes above $30,000. They also were 18 times more likely to be sexually abused and 22 times more likely to be seriously injured. *** (*The Albuquerque Tribune*, 9-19-96)

Youth crime by the numbers

Of the 597 juveniles in custody in juvenile prisons on Dec. 1, 1995 (in New Mexico):

- 39 percent had 10 or more referrals in their offense histories.
- 58 percent were 13 years old or younger at the time of their first referral.
- Nearly 67 percent were not attending school before their commitment. (Many of these were probably expelled from school for misbehavior.)
- 48 percent had a known family criminal history.
- 61 percent had immediate family members with histories of substance abuse.
- 63 percent had histories of substance abuse.
- 64 percent had little or no contact with their fathers.
- 34 percent were known to have been victims of abuse or neglect.
- 76 percent were identified as having a gang affiliation.
- More than 62 percent lived in households where the yearly income was less than $15,000. (Most, if not all, of these would have undoubtedly been welfare homes.)
- Only 5 percent posed a moderate or low risk to public safety and could be released to community supervision.
- Roughly 24 percent came from homes where parents were married.

(Source: Children Youth and Families Department's Dec. 1, 1995, snapshot study of youths in custody.) (*Albuquerque Journal*, 12-30-96)

My reading and research indicate that there is not a whole lot of difference between New Mexico and other states, and that, if anything, there are more problems in the more populated states. Our moral decline, and with it the natural harvest from our delinquency, has been general in our country and in many other western civilized countries.

CRIME AND VIOLENCE—SCHOOLS

"Specially trained dogs rummage through secondary schools in New Orleans daily searching for drugs and weapons. Teen-agers in Oklahoma City are scanned with metal detectors before entering school each morning. Close-circuit cameras monitor school buses in St. Johns, Fla. *** Across the country, school districts are trying a variety of disciplinary and security measures to combat a growing 'epidemic of violence,' according to a survey by National School Boards Association released Wednesday. *** Fully 82 percent of the 729 school districts responding to the survey said violence had increased in their schools over the past five years. *** Sixty-one percent of the districts reported weapons incidents, 39 percent said there had been a shooting or knifing at school, 23 percent reported a drive-by shooting in their district and 15 percent reported at least one rape. *** Seventy-eight percent reported student assaults on students; 60 percent reported student assaults on teachers. *** (Article of The Associated Press, *The Albuquerque Tribune*, [I failed to date the clipping, but it was in the last several years.])

Another national survey "found violence to be widespread, it said it occurred predominantly in urban schools and in those with poor academic standards." *** "Teachers and police officials attributed the problem to a lack of supervision at home, lack of family involvement in schools and exposure to violence in the media." (*Albuquerque Journal*, 12-17-93)

McKinley Middle School in Albuquerque enacted a dress code to try to cut down on gang-related violence, and to try to help restore some order to the school. A large number of the students staged a walkout, and protests were made by a number of the parents. (*The Albuquerque Tribune*, 12-14-93)

L. Brent Bozell III, "Prime time turning to family values?", *The Washington Times*, National Weekly Edition, June 6-12, 1994:

***

Given Hollywood's penchant for liberal relativism, it comes as no surprise that homosexual unions are sharing the limelight as well. On a September episode of "Grace Under Fire" a 6-year-old referred matter-of-factly to a classmate who had two "mothers," while a "Herman's Head" protagonist contemplated obliging a lesbian friend's request to father her child.

On NBC's "L.A. Law," a bisexual character fought a child-custody case for a former lover; an episode of ABC's "Civil Wars" dealt with a lesbian "divorce" case, supporting the right of the nonbiological "parent" to sue for custody of a child she helped raise.

Yes, your children continue to be on the receiving end of Hollywood's anything-goes values system. The two-parent household as an ideal continues to be ridiculed by several series. ("The Simpsons," "Roseanne's," "Married ... With Children," "Beverly Hills, 90210," "Other Mothers") ***

School Clinics May Supply Pill

SANTA FE. — Prescriptions for birth control pills were given to 157 teenage girls at two Santa Fe high school clinics in the past several months ... *** [A proposal is sponsored that will also allow the clinics to fill the prescriptions and pass out the pills.] *** Condoms are dispensed along with packages of information about proper use, contraception and preventing sexually transmitted diseases. (*Albuquerque Journal*, 1-6-96)

S. Valley Schools (Albuquerque) Lock Bathrooms During Class

Broken urinals, graffiti and smoking are reasons students have been locked out of bathrooms used during class time at three South Valley schools this semester. *** Recent vandalism has been particularly heavy. *** Urinals and mirrors were broken, paper towel dispensers were ripped from walls and evidence was found that some students were cutting classes and smoking tobacco and marijuana in the bathrooms . ...

Decisions to close the bathrooms were made ... so the schools could better monitor [them]. *** (*Albuquerque Journal,* 3-19-96)

Children have become dangerous and destructive around the country. They indiscriminately shoot into automobiles; break out windows; set business places, schools, and homes on fire; push over and tear up mail boxes; and murder one another, their parents, and strangers. With such young people religious morality is completely lacking. They have been failed by their parents and by public schools.

In many instances the children are merely following the examples of their parents who also exhibit no morality. Their parents live with people to whom they are not married, they have illegitimate children, and many use drugs. They take their trash, discarded furniture and such items, and dump them out in open places, spoiling for everyone nice scenery and country. They would rather spend money for drugs and alcohol than to pay a small amount to properly discard their waste. They are "trash" dumping trash, and generally causing destruction to their community. How could their children be expected to do better?

When I was young, children were taught to try to leave the places they pass through a little better and nicer than when they arrived. People picked up the trash that others may have left in the country, and in the forest, and tried to keep our country beautiful for those who come after us. Have we now turned completely around—to raising destructive little monsters, who have no sense of right and wrong, and no appreciation at all for anything nice and beautiful, and who are an actual danger to society. Certainly, in many cases this is exactly what is happening. As one person said, though more profanely—everything they can't tear up they urinate on!

DRUG USE

Six fourth-graders were caught in Tampa, Florida with bags of cocaine and face charges. (*Albuquerque Journal,* 12-9-93)

"TULSA, OKLA. — A year after getting shot by the father of her twins, two days after seeing her nephews charged in a gang-related murder and the day after police arrested her husband for cocaine possession, Vickie Lynn Alexander smoked $100 worth of crack, went into labor and gave birth to her sixth cocaine baby. *** She named him Ruben Jr. *** Ruben had cocaine in his blood the day he was born, as had five of his brothers and sisters before him. *** One of the sisters was born prematurely and died after a few weeks, her lungs and liver still undeveloped. Another child tested positive for cocaine and died too prematurely to be named. ***" (*Albuquerque Journal*, 12-19-93) Wouldn't it be nice for this kind of thing to be made legal, and sanctioned by our society? Many today think so. But this would merely be giving up on a terrible problem—instead of solving it and eliminating it. Drug problems and any other such problems can be eliminated by simply making penalties sufficiently high, with prompt and sure enforcement. Other countries have demonstrated this.

On the question of whether or not drugs should be legalized, we should consider the following. Many heinous crimes have been committed by people under the influence of drugs, and there is no question that drugs were a direct or contributing factor in the crimes committed. One of the most sad was a widely reported incident that I read about in the late sixties or early seventies—a young mother on LSD butchered her baby in the bathtub. Below, under the section "Murder And Violence—Parents Against Children," we have an incident reported where a cocaine-smoking mother had a child born to her, out of wedlock, and addicted to cocaine. The mother continued with her habit. When her little daughter was six years old, her mother killed her by smashing her against a concrete wall. The little child died from a brain hemorrhage.

I firmly believe that not only should such drugs be illegal, but that penalties for their use should be sufficiently increased to whatever is needed to eliminate the problem. In, addition, I firmly believe that it should be a serious crime for a mother to cause a child she is carrying to become drug addicted.

Our primary drug problem is the use and demand for drugs here at home — not foreign suppliers and the use of our military to interdict them. Our liberalism has given us the inability to understand and eliminate such problems. The average liberal seems to have the inability to comprehend that these things would not be going on were it not for our general decline in religious morality. People who follow Judaic-Christian teachings and principles do not commit such acts.

"**Son faces drug charge**. LITTLE ROCK — The son of Surgeon General Joycelyn Elders, who has suggested the government study

legalizing drugs to reduce crime, is wanted on a felony drug charge. ***
Police issued a warrant for Kevin M. Elders, 26, a week after his mother
advocated research on what effect legalizing illicit drugs would have on
the crime rate." (*The Albuquerque Tribune,* 12-18-93) Prosecutors want
a minimum 10-year sentence for Kevin Elders for selling cocaine. (*The
Albuquerque Tribune,* 7-19-94)

Testifying for her son after he was convicted of selling cocaine, Elders
said, "I don't feel that was a crime." (*The Albuquerque Tribune,* 8-31-94)

Government Doing Little For Drug-Plagued Scotland

GLASGOW, Scotland — The junkies call it "the Gorbals Parade,"
a trash-strewn sidewalk filled with walking dead.

Junkies come to the Gorbals neighborhood, or what's left of it, to
score heroin at $30 a shot. They know it's nuts to mix the junk with
liquid sedatives and shoot it all up, but so what? They know that two
junkies a week are dying in Glasgow, but who cares? They all think
they're already dead.

So here was Pat Kane out on the Gorbals Parade—the worst junkie
street in the worst junkie city in the worst junkie country in Europe—
and she was ready for the next fix.

"I inject it in my neck now," she said. "The groin and everywhere
else is done. I've stopped for a wee while every year for 10, but that's
all. My [unemployment] check isn't big enough for me to buy every
day. The way it's all goin' now, I might have to go back to prostitution,
and I'm terrified in case I do." She burst into tears. She said, "Sorry
for that."

***

The British government—and its local incarnation, the Scottish
Office—has finally confirmed what street level Scots, particularly in
Glasgow, have been saying for more than a decade: The needle is
destroying lives by the thousands here, at a faster rate than anywhere
else in Europe.

***

(Dick Polman, Knight-Ridder Newspapers, *Albuquerque Journal,* 6-12-
94)

We should keep in mind that these drug users in Scotland are not
Blacks in the ghettos of the U.S. We can be sure that they are primarily
Anglos, as are a great many of our own drug users.

U.S. Threatened By Prospect of Heroin Epidemic

WASHINGTON — Soaring heroin production around the world, distributed through some of the struggling democracies of Eastern Europe, has made a cheaper, purer, smokable form of the drug increasingly available on American streets.

Federal and local officials closest to the problem warn that the United States is on the brink of a third heroin epidemic and front-line workers say little is being done to prepare for it.

Hospitals nationwide saw a 44-percent increase in heroin over-doses in the first half of 1993, compared to the year before. Several cities, including Newark, San Francisco and Seattle, report more emergency room admissions related to heroin than cocaine. And what was once considered a back-alley drug is now being sniffed and smoked in the trendy nightclubs of New York and Hollywood.

***

(Vanessa Gallman, Knight-Ridder Newspapers, *Albuquerque Journal*, 6-22-94)

Survey of teens finds 'new wave' of use of dangerous drugs

WASHINGTON — America is seeing a "new wave of adolescent involvement in dangerous drugs," according to a nationwide student survey.

The private drug-prevention group PRIDE, which released the survey, warned that the new rise in illicit drug use could be connected with violent behavior such as carrying guns and joining gangs.

Drug use by students declined steadily for about 15 years, but in the past few years has turned up again, said Thomas Leaton, president of Atlanta-based PRIDE.

Marijuana use is leading the resurgence, especially among African-Americans, the study found

Among African-American males in high school, marijuana use jumped from 19 percent to 29 percent in 1993-94 from the previous year.

Marijuana use among all high school students rose by 5.6 percentage points to 24.6 percent, the biggest increase of all the drugs in the survey.

***

Students use of cocaine, hallucinogens, uppers, downers and inhalants also increased significantly last year, according to PRIDE.

Alcohol use dropped slightly or remained level, the report said.

The group's report was based on 200,000 questionnaires completed anonymously by junior high and senior high students in 34 states.

The survey found a relationship between drug use and violent behavior. Students who reported carrying a gun to school, taking part in a gang or threatening to hurt someone were far more likely to have abused liquor or drugs, it found.

"The PRIDE data confirms what we all know intuitively: that guns and drugs go hand in hand," said Lee Brown, director of the White House Office of National Drug Control Policy. (*The Albuquerque Tribune*, 10-21-94)

Drug-Addicted Baby Left in Hospital

The baby was born addicted to cocaine, and soon after the child's Dec. 1 birth, her mother [25 years old] walked out of University Hospital and didn't return, the report said. (*Albuquerque Journal*, 1-20-95)

Addictions take $77.6 billion from Feds

WASHINGTON — The cost to federal treasury of substance abuse and addiction, including smoking, will be $77.6 billion in federal entitlement payments this year, a study released today estimates. *** The addiction cost estimate comprises $66.4 billion in health care and disability costs resulting from substance abuse, and $11.2 billion in welfare payments to people who are regular alcohol or drug users. *** (*The Albuquerque Tribune*, 2-13 95)

Parents' Drug Use May Be Tied to Rising Rate Among Teens

WASHINGTON — After declining for almost a decade, teen-age drug use is on the rise in the 1990's. Among the possible reasons: Many of today's parents tried illegal drugs themselves and may feel awkward warning their children away from them. *** An annual survey released Friday found that teen-age drug use has risen steadily since 1992, raising fears that the dramatic drop in drug use in the 1980's will eventually be wiped out. *** (*Albuquerque Journal*, 12-16-95)

Academy Drug Probe Spreads

ANNAPOLIS, Md. — An investigation of possible drug use at the Naval Academy has expanded to include 24 midshipmen, five of whom face possible court-martial, the academy announced Monday. *** The probe began last month when two midshipmen were caught with LSD off academy grounds. They and three others are suspected of selling drugs, and Navy lawyers will recommend whether a court-martial should be convened. *** An academy spokesman said the remaining 19 are suspected of using marijuana and LSD and could face other disciplinary action. (*Albuquerque Journal,* 11-7-95)

Teens Use More Drugs, Worry Less

The number of American teenagers using illicit drugs increased again last year for the fourth consecutive year, with fewer young people even worried about the dangers, according to an annual survey.... *** More secondary school students are using marijuana, LSD, hallucinogens, amphetamines, stimulants and inhalants every year, with the levels doubling in several categories since the start of the decade.... [The survey was by the University of Michigan's Institute for Social Research, and considered a reliable benchmark of adolescent behavior because of its consistency and long experience.] (*The Washington Post,* 12-16-95) (*Issues at a Glance,* Concerned Women for America, Feb. 1996)

Fear of Drug Dealers Turns City Neighborhood Into Prison ***

Ten years ago, Louis bought a house that a real estate agent might call a handyman special, but in fact was falling down and in need of more than just fixing up. Louis and his wife rebuilt it and made a home in the old neighborhood.

For seven years, there were no problems. Then one day the prostitutes showed up.

"All of a sudden they were everywhere, "Teresa [Louis' wife] said. "Everything shifted to our street."

Then the drug dealers came.

Death and dealing

First only a few dealers came very late at night. Then the numbers grew and they started to come earlier in the night. Then they came in the afternoon. Then they came in the morning, even at five o'clock, when Luis left for his job.

Then people started dying on the street corner
***

...They shout, drink, fight, throw bottles, squeal the tires of expensive cars and fire guns. [Luis has seen an AK-47 on his street.]

On a good night, Luis gets four hours of sleep.

"Two nights ago, he said, "We call the police. They come in six minutes, but before they come, the people in the street pull this guy up. He was hurt bad. He was knifed. He was completely out. These guys pick him up and throw him in the truck like a dog or something and they leave. The police come and it looks like nothing happened. Everybody's gone."

When the police leave, they come back.

Stand and fight

Luis has talked to his neighbors to see if anyone would join him in standing up to the dealers. He found no one. Every man and woman he talked to said it is better to lock themselves in at night and hope for the best.
***

The word on the street is that two California gangs are fighting a turf war for the drug trade in Luis' neighborhood. In the first eight months of 1995, neighborhood activists logged 75 gunshots in the area. In September alone, they logged 80. *** (Jim Belshaw, *Albuquerque Journal*, 12-3-95)

Drug-Free Zone law faces ACLU challenge

A law that gives Albuquerque police the power to ban people arrested on drug charges from two areas of the city faces a constitutional challenge. *** The American Civil Liberties Union says it will go to court to challenge the city's new Drug Free Zone law, which the City Council passed by a 9-0 vote on Wednesday night. *** (*The Albuquerque Tribune*, 1-4-96)

Heroin on rise as cocaine use stabilizes, study shows

WASHINGTON — Use of powdered and crack cocaine appears to be stabilizing in this country, but more young people are turning to heroin as a strain pure enough to inhale is becoming readily available, a White House study suggests. *** (*The Albuquerque Tribune*, 3-16-96)

DEA trying to stop importation of 'date-rape' drug

Authorities in Texas have made about 500 busts involving Rohypnol, or 'roofies,' in recent months. The sleeping pills were found as authorities were searching for other drugs.

They call it the date-rape drug—a Mickey Finn-type pill known for sending users into a stupor, causing them to black out for 12 to 24 hours. *** A handful of women in Florida have reported being raped after someone doctored their drinks. In Texas, young people like it for the drunken, relaxed state it produces. *** California gang members were using roofies as part of an initiation rite for young girls as long ago as 1989. *** (*The Albuquerque Tribune*, 3-10-96)

Retired All-Pro to keep golf date despite drug bust

MYRTLE BEACH, S.C. — Retired All-Pro linebacker Lawrence Taylor was still planning to play golf in a celebrity tournament today, less than 24 hours after he was charged in a drug sting. *** Taylor, 37, was arrested Friday night when he tried to buy $100 worth of crack cocaine from undercover agents, authorities said. *** Taylor later autographed footballs and pictures at Yesterday's NightLife during a celebrity auction .... (*The Albuquerque Tribune*, 5-4-96)

TV station reports drug buys by Dallas receiver

DALLAS — Michael Irvin, the Dallas Cowboys star under felony indictment, bought cocaine before and after the charges stemming from a motel raid where drugs were seized, according to a broadcast report.

Fort Worth television station KXAS reported Sunday night that Irvin paid $100 for drugs two days before his April 1 felony indictment in connection with a seizure of cocaine and marijuana at the Irving, Texas, motel room.

Anther drug buy two weeks later was also detailed in the report, accompanied by a videotape covertly placed in the back seat of a vehicle in which Irvin was riding. *** (*The Albuquerque Tribune*, 5-6-96)

Michael Irvin did not go to jail, continued to play football, and played until the Dallas Cowboys lost in the playoffs in the first part of 1997. What message does this send to our young people? See the next paragraph.

"On Aug. 20 [1996], the federal government released the National Household Survey (NHS) on Drug Abuse, indicating that an estimated

12.8 million Americans use illicit drugs. Adolescent abuse is especially high. The percentage of teenagers using illicit drugs increased between 1994 and 1995. Since 1992, teenage drug abuse has risen 105 percent." (*Washington Watch*, Family Research Council, Sept. 25, 1996)

Pot Rally Dwarfs Anti-Drug Event
*Boston pro-marijuana gathering draws 50,000, while Just Say No Day tallies less than 500.
*** Police said that about 50,000 people attended the Freedom Rally on the Common, where people openly smoked marijuana. About 60 extra officers were on patrol, but only one arrest was reported, of someone who sold the drug. *** Across town along the Charles River, less that 500 people were at the anti-drug rally. Organizers schedule a race, face painting for children and a softball game. *** (*Albuquerque Journal*, 9-22-96)

The above certainly tells you something about the values of our society in this day and time—particularly in liberal Massachusetts—the home of liberal Senator Edward Kennedy and openly homosexual Congressmen Barney Frank and Gerry Studds.

Regular drug use surging among youths, group says
WASHINGTON — A private study suggests the government may be greatly underestimating the number of teenagers who are regular drug users. And increasing numbers of those teens tend to get "very high, bombed or stoned." *** About 18 percent of students in junior and senior high school say they use illegal drugs every month, according to a study released by the National Parents' Resource Institute for Drug Education *** That's much higher than the findings from a Department of Health and Human Service study released last month that said 10.4 percent of 12- to 17-year-olds used illegal drugs monthly in 1995. The National Household Survey on Drug Abuse said teen-age drug use had nearly doubled from 5.3 percent in 1992. *** Officials don't know why the two surveys differ. Numbers in the annual study by PRIDE, which surveyed nearly 130,000 teen-agers, are historically higher than the HHS survey, which included about

4,500 teen-agers, said Pride executive director Doug Hall. (*The Albuquerque Tribune*, 9-26-96)

Drug Gangs Grip Border With Terror
Ranchers, Patrols Losing Ground to Violence, Fear

EAGLE PASS, Texas — For the second time in a week, an unlikely group huddled in a conference room at the U.S. Drug Enforcement Administration headquarters here—not far from what has become one of the most porous spots on America's border.

They were Americans and Mexicans. Some were former policemen, others life-long cattle ranchers. But most were now cowboys with a deep mistrust of government. And they came to see Uncle Sam, they said, as a last resort before they're simply driven out.

Each owned a slice of land on the Rio Grande. Each was a recent victim of Mexican smugglers who are flooding America with cocaine, heroin, marijuana and illegal migrants.

Even the DEA officials in the room said that morning last May that they were surprised by the number of ranchers who showed up—and alarmed by their message.

'We're losing America'

The ranchers said their problems began a few years ago when migrant-smugglers started cutting through their fences at night. But now, they said, heavily armed Mexican drug gangs were taking their place—terrorizing them in broad daylight as they smuggle record quantities of drugs and migrants through their property and into the United States.

Some of the ranchers had already sold out to smuggling gangs or their front men—a decision almost everyone in the room agreed was on their minds. But neither the U.S. Border Patrol nor any other law enforcement agency said it has the manpower to protect them—or this desolate frontier. *** (*Albuquerque Journal*, 7-7-96; from an article in the *Los Angeles Times*, by Mark Fineman and Craig Pyes.)

Leader of Drug Ring Admits to Murdering 3
Haworth Plea Deal Yields Life Sentence

Richard Michael Haworth admitted Tuesday that he killed three men to further the Las Cruces-Albuquerque marijuana ring he headed—one of them while Haworth supposedly was cooperating with federal authorities.

His admissions brought the 29-year-old life in federal prison with no chance of release, but they also spared him the possibility of death. *** (*Albuquerque Journal*, 1-15-97)

We should continually keep in mind that all of the crimes, murders, and terrorism from drug dealers is directly brought about by one simple factor—the demand for drugs by the people of this country. All we have to do is to have the courage and strength to eliminate that demand—as many other countries have done—and the dealer problems will quickly disappear. Perhaps, as a whole, the people of a country deserve what they collectively put up with, but it is a shame that those who are willing to correct degradation must still suffer because of the liberal element that is not so inclined.

Instead of embracing programs that would help the country, the present administration supports programs that tear down the moral fiber of our country.

Our moral decline was reflected in and contributed to by the people of this country electing Bill Clinton as president, when the people as a whole knew of this man's lack of good moral character. They did not care.

CLINTON REVOKES REAGAN'S ORDER TO PROTECT FAMILIES

The following information is from *Family News From Dr. James Dobson*, Focus on the Family, July, 1997:

In January 1984, President Ronald Reagan met with Dr. Dobson and other religious leaders for the purpose of determining what the administration could do toward the preservation of traditional family values. In 1985, President Reagan appointed Gary Bauer, who was then undersecretary of the Department of Education, to conduct a year-long analysis of government and its role in helping or hurting families.

On September 2, 1987, the president signed Executive Order #12606 that had been carefully designed to protect families from bureaucrats and politicians. The order prohibited government from taking any action until it had answered seven specific questions, as follows:

1. *Does this action by government strengthen or erode the stability of the family and, particularly, the marital commitment?*
2. *Does the Action strengthen or erode the authority and rights of parents in the education, nurture and supervision of their children?*
3. *Does this action help the family perform its functions, or does it substitute governmental activity for the function?*
4. *Does this action by the government increase or decrease family earnings? Do the proposed benefits of the action justify the impact on the family budget?*
5. *Can this activity be carried out by a lower level of the government or by the family itself?*
6. *What message, intended or otherwise, does this program send to the public concerning the status of the family?*
7. *What message does it send to young people concerning the relationship between their behavior, their personal responsibility and the norms of our society?*

(On April 27, 1997, without fanfare, explanation to the public or Congress, Clinton signed a presidential order revoking President Reagan's order on protecting families.)

(This action of the revocation was not publicized by the administration, and escaped public notice until *The Washington Times* broke the story on May 30, 1997. It amounted to a sneak attack, by our President, on traditional family values.)

(The above executive order was never complied with by President Clinton or his administration, even prior to the revocation. Their actions have usually been the opposite.)

> Gary Bauer, now president of the Family Research Council, said this about Clinton's revocation: "We spent over two years in the mid-'80s to establish the groundwork for that executive order, including public hearings and a fairly heated debate within the federal bureaucracy. To see this president destroy all that effort that puts families at the center of public policy broke my heart, and just as importantly has made me more angry than I've been in a long time. We must reverse what he's done."

Dr. Dobson's newsletter further states:

> This president, who has done more to weaken the family and undermine the nation's moral values than any chief executive in history, has now made it more probable that bureaucrats and politicians will run rough-shod over the rights and needs of families. We have to wonder what was behind his decision. Why did he take this action without public disclosure? What is the administration planning to do that Executive Order #12606 would prohibit? ...

The newsletter then details eighteen documented actions taken by the Clinton administration that are vitally contrary to traditional family values, many of which have been detailed elsewhere in this book. The list included the promotion of abortions, including abortions in the military, promotion of homosexuality and homosexuals, and the weakening of child pornography laws. The newsletter also states:

> [President Clinton] became the first president in history to promote the inclusion of "sexual orientation" in federal civil rights law, granting protected class status to homosexuals on the basis of their behavior. ...
>
> He vetoed the ban on the horrible procedure known as "partial-birth abortion," and fiercely defended the continuation of this form of infanticide. ...
>
> If space permitted, this list would include hundreds of related policies, appointments and decisions made by this administration that assault traditional moral values.

This newsletter goes on to show Dr. Dobson's lack of political bias—his views, in my opinion, are without question based on his traditional moral and religious values. The country has been fortunate to have a person of his stature and standing working for our moral values. The Republican leadership is strongly criticized for such things as the failure to cut off funding for the National Endowment for the Arts which "has received $99 million this year despite its consistent support for obscene and profane art," increased funding for the "ultra-liberal Department of Education," giving over $400 million to the International Planned Parenthood Foundation, allocation of "tens of millions of dollars for contraceptive-based sex education services to teenagers; and failure to vote on a religious liberty amendment, and failure to pass a provision to "assure parental consent before minors could receive contraceptives or treatment for sexually transmitted diseases."

Dr. Dobson states that: "If space permitted, this list would include hundreds of related policies, appointments and decisions made by this administration that assault traditional moral values."

DECLINE IN EDUCATION

The United States spends more and more money on education, yet students' level of knowledge continues to fall. Children do not get as good an education now as they did before the federal government began contributing to and to some extent controlling education. It certainly is a large part of our general cultural decline. We have children who get out of high school without the ability to write meaningfully, and without any ability to even do any comprehensive reading. We gave some of the details on these things, above, in reviewing *The Index of Leading Cultural Indicators*, by William J. Bennett.

On November 21, 1996, on ABC Evening News, and on the Newshour with Jim Lehrer on public television, reports covered what Lehrer described as the most comprehensive study yet made comparing the educational abilities of students of different countries. The top ranking three on math ability were: 1. Singapore, 2. Korea, 3. Japan. The United States ranked 21st out of forty-one nations. Mr. Lehrer called this slightly below average. He said we were slightly above average in science, so I assume we would have ranked about 20th in science. Keep in mind that this country spends the most money, and has the most elaborate facilities and equipment.

Abraham Lincoln did much of his studying by firelight, considered himself fortunate to have a few books available, and was largely self-educated. But he had some great assets: A thirst for knowledge, great ability, and a moral background that led him all of his life — and through his fight that ended slavery in this country. How things have changed!

As previously explained, our educational system, generally, is in shambles. The following relates to just a few representative examples. All of us know many others that could be added to this. Not only are students failing to get a meaningful and useful education, but they are exposed to a disturbing and harmful lack of morality.

"Hookers, Pushers, Pimps in 6th-Graders' Math Test. — CHICAGO — *** A test Routen [a teacher] allegedly administered to his sixth-grade class Friday included such word problems as: 'Martin wants to cut his half-pound of heroin to make 20 percent more profit. How many ounces of cut will he need?' Another question on the test said: 'Willis gets $200 for stealing a BMW, $50 for stealing a Chevy and $100 for a 4x4. If he has stolen two BMWs and three 4x4s, how many Chevys will he have to steal to make $800? *** The problems at May Elementary began Friday when parents called school officials complaining about the math exam, which also included word problems dealing with a man's crack habit and how many tricks his prostitutes would have to turn to support his habit." (*Albuquerque Journal,* 3-25-94) This may sound ridiculous, and even humorous, until we consider the influence of such things on impressionable children. Also, a board member stated, "We have dealt with these problems in the past."

Look Who's Teaching Our Children!

At the annual NEA [National Education Association] convention, held this year in New Orleans over the Fourth of July weekend, the headline speaker was Hillary Rodham Clinton....

***

NEA President Keith Gieger's address to the convention lashed out against the "far right," private schools and homeschoolers, "bigotry and oppression," "school funding inequities," and oppression of gays and lesbians. He praised Nelson Mandela, Jesse Jackson, Cesar Chavez, Outcome-Based Education, and the Brady bill.

***

The NEA's Gay & Lesbian Caucus (GLC) was very prominent.

***

"The worst thing that ever happened in education is the radio talk show," declared David Berliner . ... delegates voted to boycott Florida orange juice unless the Florida Department of Citrus canceled its $1 million advertising contract with Rush Limbaugh.

***

The NEA passed its usual list of radical leftist resolutions, including support of nationalized health care, statehood for the District of Columbia, and animosity against parents, private schools, and homeschoolers. A new resolution called "Sexual Orientation Education" put the NEA on record as supporting "the acceptance of diverse sexual orientation and the awareness of sexual stereotyping whenever sexuality and/or tolerance of diversity is taught."

Translated, this means that, whenever a school gives instruction in sexuality, health, family living, multiculturalism, diversity, or tolerance, the curriculum must include teaching the "acceptance" of homosexuality. Another NEA resolution demands affirmative action recruitment and hiring of homosexual teachers. *** (*The Phyllis Schafly Report*, September 1994)

Students' study sessions turned into sex parties

ABINGTON, Pa. — It started out as afternoon homework sessions at the fifth-grade teacher's house, where one pupil says if he got a question right, he got to kiss the teacher's wife.

It degenerated into overnight parties filled with beer, marijuana and sex with the teacher's wife as he watched or joined in, prosecutors say.

Seven students, aged 13 to 17, have come forward to say they drank beer and smoked marijuana that David Miller and his wife, Maryanne, gave them at their house. Two boys say they had sex with Maryanne Miller, one once and the other more than 60 times in the past year.

The Millers have been ordered to stand trial on a list of criminal charges, including involuntary deviate sexual intercourse, statutory sexual assault, criminal conspiracy and intimidation of witnesses.

They have denied the charges, although police say Maryanne Miller confessed to giving the youths beer and marijuana and having sex with one boy with her husband sometimes joining them.

***

Maryanne Miller ... in a brief interview at the couple's home ... acknowledged that a few of the charges were true.

***

David Miller had worked with kids for years, coordinating the before- and after-school programs at YMCA .... He led a Boy Scout troop.

* * *

Two boys and three girls testified during Tuesday's hearing. (*The Albuquerque Tribune,* 11-6-95)

Child predators at schools are being protected

NEW YORK — * * *

Two Professors from Hofstra University, Charol Shakeshaft and Audrey Cohan, conducted a four-year, nationwide study of sexual abuse of students by school personnel.

Their findings showed that the system is essentially rigged against the kids. * * *

They cited one case in which a school superintendent acknowledged that a male elementary school teacher was "patting kids" in various places. ..."The superintendent characterized this behavior as 'not serious,' even though some of the places were the students' breasts, genitals, and buttocks."

The study said, "Another superintendent described a case in which a 'male teacher was involved in fellatio' in the middle of a local shopping center parking lot at 3:10 p.m. The victim was 'an emotionally disturbed female student from his special education class.' The student was told by the district to 'stay away from the teacher.' " * * *

Usually the most vulnerable students are targeted for abuse, especially those with emotional difficulties. * * *

The unwillingness of supposedly responsible adults to recognize that sexual abuse is occurring can be astonishing.

The New York City report said, "In one case substantiated by the [Special Commissioner of Investigation for the New York City School District], colleagues of the offender continued to deny the allegations could be true, despite a full, taped confession by the offender of the conduct alleged."

The simple fact of the matter is that teachers and administrators tend to care much more about their careers than about the welfare of the children in their charge. * * *

Even in those cases where some kind of response is inevitable, the tendency is to take the most minimal action possible. Shakeshaft and Cohan found that school authorities tried to revoke the teaching license of a teacher who sexually abused a student in only 1 percent of the more than 200 cases they surveyed.

They found that far more common was a practice dubbed by teachers and administration as "passing the trash"—transferring a teacher accused of sexual abuse to another district without informing the new district of the allegations. ***(Bob Herbert, New York Times Columnist, *The Albuquerque Tribune*, 5-24-96)

Nation's schools bastions of fear

WASHINGTON — Junior high students are more likely than high schoolers to be involved in weapons offenses at big city schools, but drug and alcohol abuse is more common among the older teens, urban educators reported today.

Two percent of teachers in cities' public schools feel unsafe during the day, twice as many as in the suburbs, the Council of Great City Schools said. After school hours, the figure jumps to 15 percent in cities and 5 percent in suburbs.

In a 1992-93 report card on the state of urban education, the council said more than half the schools systems it represents have gang and crime prevention programs; all the districts have programs to address drug and alcohol abuse. *** (*The Albuquerque Tribune*, 9-27-94)

Nudity In Daily Lobo Starts Fuss

Two photo essays in the arts section of the New Mexico Daily Lobo have the University of New Mexico's student body president seeking to cut off some of the newspaper's funds

David Standridge said Friday the reaction on campus to Thursday's "détoor" section, which featured a photo essay of a gay couple and a separate full frontal photo of a nude man, has been "very negative."

The nude photo was an illustration to go with a story on piercing body parts and showed a man with a stud earring in his penis.

"I've heard from Christian student groups, the Black Student Union and others ... I got 10 phone calls about it at home last night.

"These people are totally appalled," he said. ***

Bob Johnson, a member of the Publications Board and a retired bureau chief of the Associated Press, said the student publication shouldn't be restrained from publishing stories and photos pertaining to student life.

"Student newspapers are designed for experimenting and learning ... so they have a little more leeway than a regular newspaper." (*Albuquerque Journal*, 2-6-93)

It is a tragedy for a decent student trying to get an education in our largest state university to have to be exposed to such trash in the student newspaper. Those who support such filth have no inkling of morality. But then we see from Judge Bork's disclosures, and from the article below, that—even worse—many of our universities teach and even require the reading and viewing of such muck and sewage.

America's Finest Universities Institutionalize Mediocrity

Many students at Swarthmore—and other colleges—are afraid to go public with their objections for fear of being labeled "homophobe," "racist," or "sexist."

"Where's the outrage?" asks Bob Dole.

"Where's the shame?" echoed Ross Perot. Both men are talking about the ethics violations, the law-breaking scandals and "character issues" that plague Bill Clinton.

I offer a simple explanation of what's going on: It's the coarsening of the culture, stupid. Ethical discrimination requires an ability to make distinctions between absolutes of right and wrong, good and bad, moral and immoral and to appreciate the infinite shades of gray that cross the spectrum.

This used to be the ultimate purpose of education . ...

***

Nothing quite prepared me for the contents of the particular envelope (from the Young Americas Foundation). It contained a survey of bizarre college courses at our finest—or at least most expensive—universities, as well as a book entitled "Memories That Smell Like Gasoline," which is required reading for English majors at Swarthmore College. The book was less literary than graphic, filled with explicit drawings of homosexual acts among groups of men, male couples or men and young boys, always focusing on enlarged male genitals.

This is the assigned text at a college which U.S. News and World Report magazine designates as the No. 1 liberal-arts college in the United States. Many students at Swarthmore—and other colleges—are afraid to go public with their objections for fear of being labeled "homophobic," "racist," or "sexist." Other Swarthmore courses include "Lesbian Novels Since World War II," "Epistemology of the

Closet: Literary and theoretical constructions of Male Homosexuality," "Queer Texts and Contexts."

... Women's studies courses outnumber economics classes at most Ivy League schools.

In a choice of 50 colleges, large and small, public and private, the following nonsensical course titles are typical: "Queering the Renaissance," (University of California, Santa Cruz); "Amazons, Valkyries, Nolads, Dykes: Woman-Identified and Lesbian Artists in Europe (Carleton); "Gender and Sexual Desire in Medieval Islam" (Princeton).

My award goes to Harvard for "Fetishism"—"Our capacity to endow objects, people, and institutions—'high heels,' 'Elvis,' 'Harvard,' with an excess of meaning." *** (Fields, Suzanne [a highly respected syndicated columnist], *Albuquerque Journal*, 11-1-96)

Yale Won't Make Concessions to Religious Students
By Herbert London

For anyone who has examined parietals on American campuses over the last few decades, the evidence is stark. Rules and regulations for students exist in form only, with nonenforcement the prevailing sentiment among university administrators.

Consumption of alcoholic beverages at some colleges is an epidemic, with drinking orgies starting on Thursday and ending on Sunday. Coeducational dormitories are the norm, and sexual promiscuity is readily evident on many campuses.

For students with a traditional world-view, the introduction to college life can be jarring. In fact, in a much discussed drama at Yale this fall, five Orthodox Jewish students claim that dorm life is comparable to Sodom and Gomorrah.

The Orthodox students have asked to be excused from the university's requirement that all freshmen and sophomores live on campus. They claim that their religion's rules of modesty and sexual abstinence until marriage are continually challenged in dormitories where condoms are freely dispensed, alcohol is routinely consumed and shared bathrooms and showers are the norm.

Yale's Administration has resisted the request, arguing, in effect, that the college's rules apply to all students. Presumably the administration is saying that despite concessions to ethnic and minority groups over the last few decades, concessions to a conservative religious group will not be made. ***

While Yale bends over backwards to accommodate feminists, homosexuals, and a variety of activists, it seems to be saying to Orthodox Jews, take it or leave it. ***

A nontraditional orthodoxy permeates Yale and many other campuses, in which tolerance exists for what is politically correct and intolerance prevails for traditional religious adherence. (*Human Events*, 10-10-97)

If a student is not extremely well-based in religious moral teaching, and does not have a lot of common sense along with it, then he or she will have been better off not to have even gotten a higher education in such institutions as the above. They not only brainwash students in immoral and false dogma, but they teach false facts, false science, and false history. Suzanne Fields' terminology that they "institutionalize mediocrity" is indeed a most charitable understatement. This is one of the most detrimental things going on in our society. How can a student be expected to withstand such an onslaught of filth and teaching of things that are the opposite of educational—and often intentionally and unequivocally false? They are now bombarded with this tripe from grade school though the universities and colleges, and if the homosexualists and the feminists have their way, it will begin in the kindergarten. It is probably in some kindergartens now.

Our turning away from traditional religious principles, and the resulting decline in morality, has had a devastating effect on family relationships. Fifty years ago, it would have been hard to even imagine the violence and degradation among family members—and the heinous things being engaged in by mere children. We are reaping a bitter fruit from the destructive seeds we have sown. Consider some of the following additional examples.

MURDER AND VIOLENCE—PARENTS AGAINST CHILDREN

The Albuquerque Tribune, 12-16-93, contained an article about a trial in Lubbock Texas, of Steven Carman, 37, and his wife, in which they are charged with killing seven-year-old Stephanie Carman by starving her to death. The child was the daughter of Mr. Carman, and Mrs. Carman was the stepmother of the child. They pleaded not guilty. The article stated in part:

> Pathologist David Hoblit determined the 43-pound girl died of chronic malnutrition. Her death was ruled a homicide.
>
> Prosecutor Rebecca Atchley told the jury in opening statements on Wednesday that the Carmans took Stephanie out of school and ballet class, locked her in her room and fed her so little that her hair fell out in clumps.
>
> "She was caged in her room like an animal. She was given scraps to eat, and as a result, she died," Atchley said. ***
>
> Texas child welfare officials have declined to comment on their contact with the Carmans since the family moved to Lubbock in 1990.
>
> A spokesman for New Mexico's Children, Youth and Families Department said authorities there briefly took custody of the two Carman sisters after Stephanie began showing signs of starvation in 1989. ***

In Quebec, a couple who had previous abuse allegations against them admitted to police that they wrapped their 10-week-old daughter in three plastic bags, stuffed her into a knapsack, and disposed of her body. They claimed that they found her dead in her crib. An autopsy was planned to determine the cause of death. (*The Albuquerque Tribune*, 4-18-94)

Mom Accused of Burning Up Kids

FREEHOLD, N.J. — A mother was charged with incinerating her two youngest children Tuesday in the back seat of her car as it was parked outside of her in-law's house.

Maria Montalvo, 29, was charged with two counts of murder and one count of aggravated arson for the deaths of her 28-month-old son, Rafael Aponte, and 18-month-old daughter, Zonaida Aponte.

Montalvo's mother-in-law, Tomassa Aponte, said she saw flames flare up inside the car after Montalvo threw something on the front passenger seat. (*Albuquerque Journal*, 2-23-94)

Baby thrown in trash — Mother gets 8 months

SANTA FE — A woman who pleaded guilty to child abuse after placing her newborn in a trash bin at her Santa Fe apartment was sentenced to eight months in jail. *** Rosalie Prada apologized Monday to Santa Fe District Judge Petra Maes for wrapping her infant in towels and placing her inside a garbage bag in an outdoors trash bin last March. *** Within 45 minutes of being placed in the bin, the baby was found by a neighbor who heard muffled cries. Hospital workers cared for the child, who has since been adopted. *** (*The Albuquerque Tribune*, 10-18-94)

Mother Denies Killing Son

BATAVIA, Ohio — A woman who said she last saw her 8-year-old son as he headed to school pleaded innocent Tuesday to fatally beating him and dumping him in a ditch. *** Jerry Howell may have been alive when he was thrown from a car Friday at the end of a road about three miles from his home, county Prosecutor Donald White said after a court hearing. *** An autopsy showed he suffered a fractured skull, lacerated liver and punctured lung. ** Rhonda Brown, 41, made no statement as her lawyer entered the plea in Clermont County Municipal Court. She was held on $200,000 bond. ... (*Albuquerque Journal*, 3-8-95)

Mother vents anger by stabbing infant son to death

TULSA, Okla. — Enraged over an argument with her neighbor, Michelle Dawn Murphy (17) returned to her apartment and vented her anger by stabbing her 2-month-old son to death, police said. [She confessed.] *** (*The Albuquerque Tribune*, 9-14-94)

Mom Tells Cops She Killed Boys

UNION, S.C. — The mother who said a carjacker dumped her on a lonely road and drove off with her two young sons in the back seat was charged Thursday with their murders after allegedly confessing.

Susan V. Smith, 23, who made tearful pleas on national television for the boys' return, was in custody and will be arraigned today, Union County Sheriff Howard Wells said Thursday.

The nine-day search for 3-year-old Michael and 14-month-old Alex, which stretched from Georgia to Seattle, ended where it began, in Lake John D. Long ... .

Smith apparently provided information that led investigators to her car Thursday afternoon, Solicitor Thomas Pope said.

Knight-Ridder Newspapers reported that investigators discovered a letter several days ago from a man Smith was dating. The letter said he wanted to be with her but didn't want the children. Investigators said that's what broke the case. ...

Police divers discovered Smith's 1990 burgundy Mazda in the lake with the bodies of [the] two children in the back seat . ...

The car had been driven off a boat ramp [an officer] said ... . ***
(*Albuquerque Journal*, 11-4-94)

Mrs. Smith was later convicted of the murders of her two little boys, and given a life sentence. This was indeed a terrible and incomprehensible crime. The pictures of these children showed two beautiful little boys that many people would have loved and cherished, and would have been happy to adopt.

Dead Baby Thrown to the Dogs

POMONA, Calif. — A teen-ager was charged Thursday with killing her baby and throwing the body into a neighbor's yard where it as mauled by a dog, police said.

The mutilated body of Araceil Garcia's 9-pound newborn boy was found Nov. 4 in a yard where an adult pit bull was penned and a puppy was running free. The puppy attacked the body, but the adult dog couldn't reach him.

Garcia, 19, was charged with murder and endangering a child. The child was Garcia's third and she may have been trying to hide his birth from her parents, with whom she lived, police said.

Garcia's two children, ages 2 and 3, were placed in the custody of her parents, police said. (*Albuquerque Journal*, 11-11-94)

Neighborhood Suspected Mom In Fatal Fire

BALTIMORE — Renee Aulton was gruff with her little girls, often neglected them and didn't even bother to hang curtains in her home, neighbors said.

So when Aulton was charged with killing her two children in a house fire—and confessed—neighbors were appalled but not surprised. ***

As flames engulfed the house with Aulton's children inside, five neighborhood women yelled at her to do something. But Aulton and her boyfriend, Frank Wooters, stood outside the home and watched it burn, neighbors said. ***

Wooters said Friday he did try to save the girls. When he showed up at the house and noticed it was burning, he jumped out of his taxi cab and ran in the front door. "I ran upstairs to get the kids and there was too much smoke. I couldn't get up there," he said.

Aulton, 26, was charged Wednesday with two counts of first degree murder in the deaths of Christina Lambert, 4, and Natalie Aulton, 2. *** (*Albuquerque Journal*, 11-26-94)

The following incident is a good example of what may be expected from an atmosphere of immorality and a resulting exposure of children to the scum and trash of humanity. Without question, many of the incidents in this part of the book were a direct result of exposing children and young people to such detrimental and immoral environments. Not only is much of the damage to them immediate physical harm, but the emotional harm can be permanent. And, in addition, the indirect harm is immense — children tend to follow the teachings and examples of their parents.

Woman faces jail for letting new husband rape her daughter

RIVERSIDE, Calif. — [A 10-year-old boy calls 911, trying to report the assault of his 7-year-old sister.] ***

In the background a woman screams, "Don't! Don't! Don't!" The line goes dead.

It was Jan. 15, 1994, and a child had just been raped by her new stepfather, a crack addict with full-blown AIDS.

No one knew it then, but the assault that stained the girl's polka-dot dress, her cotton underwear and her dress-up white tights with her blood also had infected her with HIV, the virus that causes AIDS.

The attacker was Frank Cisco Bridges, 44, who'd married her mother barely three hours before. Bridges was so stoned during the ceremony that he picked his teeth with the minister's sermon cards and later urinated in a potted plant at the reception.

The woman who screamed and hung up the phone was the girl's mother. Just that morning, she'd bailed Bridges out of jail on a petty theft charge so they could be married at her home in upper-middle class, suburban neighborhood. ***

... Now 8, the girl is displaying diminished motor skills, and early sign of fatal illness, but has not developed AIDS. ***

[The mother, an educated woman with a master's degree in special education, was convicted of child endangerment and being an accessory after the fact to her daughter's rape. She was not yet sentenced, but faced a maximum sentence of only 6 years and 8 months in prison. The man was sentenced to only 38 years imprisonment.] (*The Albuquerque Tribune*, 1-9-95)

Teen Dropped Newborn Out Window, Police Say

CHICAGO — An unwed teen-ager who had concealed her pregnancy from her mother gave birth in her bathroom, then tossed the baby naked out a second-floor window into the bitter cold and went off to school, police said.

Marisol Melendez, 18, was charged Thursday with aggravated battery to a child as the infant—named Zoe, the Greek word for life, by hospital employees—lay in critical condition. ***

The baby had several skull fractures, probably from being dropped and also suffered hypothermia and dehydration, said Mike Maggio, a spokesman at Loyola University Medical Center in suburban Maywood. *** (*Albuquerque Journal*, 1-6-95)

Another young woman who reportedly tosses her newborn baby out a window:

Mom Tosses Newborn, Cops Say

NEW YORK — A young woman who wore baggy clothes to hide her pregnancy from her family was charged with attempted murder Tuesday for allegedly tossing her newborn son from a fourth-floor apartment in Brooklyn.

The baby was in serious condition with a fractured skull.

Kara Bradley, 20, was arrested after she and her mother went to the hospital to claim the baby.

Bradley ... has a year-old daughter ... . ***

The baby landed on a second-floor canopy, where a neighbor found him crying and called 911. *** (*Albuquerque Journal*, 4-5-95)

Woman accused of throwing baby out the window

CHICAGO — A woman trying to stop her baby from crying threw him to his death from an eighth-floor window, police said today.

Deborah Turner said she kicked 16-month-old Tyler Marshall and then threw him out the window after he began crying, police Sgt. Daniel Fitzgerald said.

Turner, 35, was charged with first-degree murder in the Wednesday incident.

The baby, wearing diapers, was found lying on a patch of dirt outside the housing project, where Turner reportedly was visiting friends.

Police were investigating reports the woman was smoking crack cocaine and drinking. (*The Albuquerque Tribune*, 4-13-95)

Stepdad Charged in Tot's Death

A Gallup [New Mexico] man [Alvin Lee, 21] has been charged with the murder of his stepson (who was just under 2 years old), whom he was babysitting while the child's mother was at work. *** An autopsy of the boy showed a ruptured gastrointestinal tract and indications of brain and head trauma, according to a criminal complaint filed in the case. His brain was also swollen. *** [Virginia Begay, the child's mother] told the FBI that the child had received other serious injuries, always while Lee was caring for him. *** (*Albuquerque Journal*, 4-14-95)

Trial begins for mom accused of killing her 'evil' daughter

BANGOR, Maine — Tonia Kigas [30] told police she simply turned up the radio, once for two whole days, to mask her 5-year-old daughter's piercing screams. When the cries stopped Kigas called 911 to say her daughter was dead.

She told police she had withheld food and water for a month from her daughter, Tavielle, because the girl was "evil." She said she didn't kill her daughter, but just "let it happen." ***

If convicted of murder, Kigas would face 25 years to life in prison. *** (*The Albuquerque Tribune*, 6-12-95)

Man accused of killing 2 babies he had with daughter

SCOTTSDALE, Pa. — A man accused of burying alive a baby he had with his daughter 27 years ago has confessed to killing a second child he fathered with her, police said. *** Paul Corvin, 61, was arrested this morning at his home near Scottsdale on a charge of homicide in the second child's death. *** Police in Boynton Beach, Fla., found the skeletal remains of the first child, a boy, Saturday after Corvin's daughter [39 years old] told investigators he buried the baby alive in the family's back yard. She said she gave birth in a bathroom at home, and her father first tried to drown the boy [in the bathtub]. *** (*The Albuquerque Tribune*, 4-18-95)

Mom's Boyfriend Indicted in Tot's Beating

An Albuquerque mother [Gina Gutierrez, 19] and her live-in boyfriend [William Friedrich, 21] have been indicted on child-abuse charges for sever injuries to her 3-year-old daughter, who was punched in the stomach and had her head hit against a wall. *** ... the child remains unconscious. *** [A police affidavit said that Friedrich said he became upset with the little girl because she was playing rough with her sister.] (*Albuquerque Journal*, 4-29-95)

'Baby Killers' Give Each Other Solace

WEST PALM BEACH, Fla. — [This article was about four women, all in the same jail, at the same time, and all awaiting trial for killing their own children. They were Pauline Zile, 24, Clover Boykin, 20, Joanne Mejia, 18, and Paulette Cone, 45. Boykin had confessed to killing two children, her 5-month-old son, and later a 9-month-old girl with whom she was baby sitting. This is without question a record for parental depravity in this country — and probably for all countries — in recorded history. The article below is about the conviction of one of them] (*Albuquerque Journal*, 3-8-95)

Woman Spared in Daughter's Slaying

WEST PALM BEACH, Fla. — A woman who concocted a tale of abduction to cover up the beating death of her 7-year-old daughter was spared the electric chair Wednesday, receiving a sentence of life in prison without parole.

Pauline Zile, 24, did not directly take part in the slaying of Christina Holt but failed to stop the girl's stepfather, John Zile, from beating her Sept. 16, Circuit Judge Stephen A. Rapp said. ***

... Her husband goes on trial Aug. 4. (*Albuquerque Journal*, 6-8-95)

Sex Charges - Neighbors watched home

[ALBUQUERQUE] — Neighbors say all types of people, "even businessmen," frequented the Northeast Heights home of a woman accused of trading the sexual services of her 14- and 15-year-old daughters for drugs.

Traffic in and out of the neatly kept home on the 700 block of Marcell Street Northeast was around the clock over the last year, said a neighbor. ***

Roberta Brusellas, 34, is charged with sexual exploitation of children and other charges. (*The Albuquerque Tribune*, 8-5-95)

Mother pleads not guilty

DAYTON, Ohio — A woman pleaded not guilty Tuesday to a charge of murder in the beating death of her 4-year-old daughter, whose body was found in a water-filled pit. ***

Therressa Jolynn Ritchie, 24, said nothing and showed no emotion as her lawyers entered the plea. Her bail was continued at $1 million.

Ritchie was indicted last week on charges of murder, gross abuse of a corpse, tampering with evidence, inducing panic and making a false alarm in the disappearance and death of Samantha Ritchie.

Ritchie claimed on July 18 that Samantha was missing from her bed when she went to wake her.

Neighbors and volunteers joined the search. Police found the girl's body July 22 at an abandoned iron foundry about a block from her home. (*The Albuquerque Tribune*, 9-6-95)

[A previous article stated: After nearly two weeks of investigation, police arrested Samantha's mother and a neighbor, Ernest Vernell Brooks, late Thursday night. Police said the two confessed but would not give a motive.] (*The Albuquerque Tribune*, 8-5-95)

Mom Admits She Drowned, Smothered 3 Kids

HOUSTON — A woman suspected of trying to strangle her 2-year-old son has confessed to her mother that she drowned two of her infants and smothered a third, the first when she was 14.

Claudette Kibble, 23, was charged with murder Friday in the 1990 suffocation of 9-month-old Quinten Kibble. She was not charged in the other deaths because she was a minor at the time, authorities said. *** (*Albuquerque Journal*, 9-24-95)

Mom charged with soliciting murder of teen-age son

Los Lunas, N. M. — A 46-year-old mother [Mollie Stacey] has been charged with soliciting the murder of her teen-age son [William Edward Stacey, 19] on Halloween, according to State Police who placed her under surveillance. The son was not harmed. *** (*Albuquerque Journal*, 11-9-95) [Ms. Stacey] was arrested ... after she offered to pay $10,000 to someone to kill her ... son in order to collect insurance money. *** (*Albuquerque Journal*, 11-8-95)

Kin Fight Over Girl's Remains - Grandma Jailed in 5-Year-Old's Death

BOISE, Idaho — Five-year-old Ashley Ann McQuillan died on Thanksgiving Day, sending her grandmother to jail on a murder charge and setting off a family fight that threatens to separate her siblings.

Relatives can't even agree on where to bury Ashley.

Ashley's grandmother, Susan Kathleen "Kate" Stovern is accused of drugging and suffocating the 5-year-old and attempting to kill her 3-year-old sister, Alexandria. ***

The children had lived with Stovern [42] while their father lived in Florida and their mother, Stovern's daughter, lived separately in Boise. *** (*Albuquerque Journal*, 11-29-95)

Mom Gave Up 15-Year-Old to Pay Drug Debt, Police Say

DETROIT — A boy who was missing for at least six months had been handed by his mother over to a drug dealer to settle her $1,000 crack cocaine debt, police said after finding the boy Tuesday.

Investigators sorted through conflicting accounts of whether he went voluntarily, sold drugs, was used as a sex slave or was forced to smoke crack himself when he was hungry so his captors could save on food.

Acting on an anonymous tip, police found the boy in a small, rundown house in a neighborhood thick with drug dealers and prostitutes.

His grandmother said he appeared to be addicted to crack. He had lost a lot of weight but seemed otherwise OK, she said

"He's crying a lot. I think he's all right — he said he's all right," she said. "He's as sweet as he can be. He's got one hangup: It's his mother. He loves her." ***

The 33-year-old mother was already in jail on an unrelated burglary charge and could face charges over her son. *** (*Albuquerque Journal*, 11-29-95)

Doctor Waives Extradition in Fatal Blaze

KANSAS CITY, Mo. — A woman accused of setting a house fire that killed two of her three children waived extradition Friday to face arson and murder charges. She remained in jail on $3 million bond.

Dr. Debora Green is charged with aggravated arson and two counts of first-degree murder in the deaths of Tim Farrar, 13, and Kelly Farrar, 6. Green is also charged with two counts of attempted first-degree murder. ***

The investigation included a closer look at a fire about 16 months earlier that damaged the family's previous home and the mysterious illness of the children's father, Dr. Michael Farrar, weeks before the October fire.

Farrar, who filed for divorce the day after the fire, was not at the Prairie Village house when the fire broke out. ***

Johnson County, Kan., District Attorney Paul Morrison said that one of the attempted murder charges stemmed from the fire, the second was related to a poisoning attempt. He would not elaborate. (*Albuquerque Journal*, 11-25-95)

Girl Allegedly Killed By Crack-Addict Mom Buried

NEW YORK — *** Her loving father protected her and, as he was dying, devised a plan to keep her from her crack-smoking, abusive mother. ***

The father died the day he was to have sent her to safety. The judge overruled the objections of teachers and relatives and gave Elisa to her mother.

The mother pulled her out of school, tortured her in attempted exorcisms, and finally, police say killed her by smashing her head against a concrete wall. On Wednesday, they buried 6-year-old Elisa Izquierdo, one more fatally abused child. Year after year, they die at a rate of more than one a week in New York City. This year, Elisa was No. 58. ***

Elisa was born poor, with her mother's cocaine in her veins. Her parents were Awilda Lopez, whom crack addiction had rendered homeless, and Gustavo Izquierdo, a worker at a homeless shelter. They met at Izquierdo's shelter. *** (*Albuquerque Journal*, 11-30-95)

Another article on the above incident:

*** Police found Elisa's body in her apartment a week ago. An autopsy found she died from a brain hemorrhage caused by a blow to the head. Some of her fingers were broken and her skin was scarred by cigarette burns.

Since her death, the details of Elisa's tortured life have emerged. Lopez once allegedly had used Elisa's head to mop the floor and had slammed her head into a concrete wall two days before she died, police said.

Child welfare workers had been warned repeatedly about the abuse but apparently did little to intervene. (*The Albuquerque Tribune*, 11-29-95)

The lack of interest of welfare workers appears to be the result of the liberal attitudes of many of our officials on the state level. Later in this chapter we have an article about the homosexual rape of a young boy by a man who the New Mexico state agency responsible had allowed to become a foster parent of the boy. The article specifically stated that homosexuals and bisexuals were eligible to be foster parents under our regulations. The abuse that any sensible person could have predicted naturally resulted.

Woman sentenced for leaving newborn in outhouse to die
SANTA FE — A 43-year-old Fruitland woman has been sentenced to 12 months and a day in prison for the involuntary manslaughter of her baby, a federal prosecutor said.

Alice Burton pleaded guilty last October.

On Oct. 27, 1994, Burton delivered a full-term baby into an out-house pit near Fruitland, U.S. Attorney John Kelly said in Albuquerque. (*The Albuquerque Tribune*, 1-25-96)

Police fear mother threw twins off bridge

OGLETHORPE, Ga. — Investigators searched a river, the banks and nearby woods for a 3-year-old boy whose twin sister's body was pulled from the water after their mother allegedly threw them off a bridge.

LaSonya Olivia Gipson, 26, has been charged in the death of her daughter, Latoshia, who disappeared along with her son two weeks ago. Authorities believe Gipson's son, Joshua, is also dead. The girl's body was found Wednesday. The search for the boy was interrupted Friday by darkness. It was to resume this morning.

At first Gipson told relatives the children were with their father. Then she said she had left them on a 25-foot bridge over the Flint River. But Sheriff Charles Cannon said he believes Gipson threw them off the bridge on Jan. 14. He said Gipson had a history of mental problems. (*The Albuquerque Tribune*, 1-27-96)

Man found guilty of murdering toddler

[ALBUQUERQUE] — A jury today convicted an Albuquerque man of murder and criminal-sexual contact of a minor for what prosecutors said was the rape and fatal beating of a 23-month-old girl on Thanksgiving Day 1994.

Christopher Mora, 19, was ordered held until his March 21st sentencing. He faces life imprisonment plus three years, prosecutors said.
***

Prosecutors alleged that Mora beat and raped Christina Sierra, his girlfriend's daughter.... *** (*The Albuquerque Tribune*, 2-5-96)

Kids allegedly raped, drugged

CHICAGO — Four children, the youngest now 5 years old, were allegedly raped, drugged and fed fried rats and boiled cockroaches at the hands of their own parents—not once, but again and again over at least four years.

A 1,200-count indictment against Gerald Hill, 52, gives a hellish description of the lives of the youngsters, now 5, 10, 11 and 12. Hill, father of two of the children, was charged with criminal sexual assault, criminal sexual abuse, aggravated battery to a child and aggravated battery. (*Albuquerque Journal*, 2-7-96)

Beheading case to move, judge says

ESTANCIA [N.M.] — [Judge Edmund H. Kase, III, granted a motion for change of venue for the trial of Eric Starr Smith, Sr., who is accused of murdering and beheading his 14-year-old son.] ***

Police have said the Parker, Ariz., man stabbed his son as many as 60 times on the side of the highway ... before decapitating him, as the boy's 13-year-old brother watched. Smith has told authorities that he killed his son because he believed his son was the devil.

Drug tests showed Smith had take methamphetamine before the incident. The drug, known as speed, can make users anxious, paranoid, violent and can cause hallucinations. (*The Albuquerque Tribune*, 4-19-96)

Father says he killed son over toilet training

NEW YORK — The father [Anthony Mikell, 43] of a 2-year-old boy was arrested [and charged with murder] after telling investigators he beat his son to death while trying to toilet train him, police. said. ***

The child had been under the care of the city's child-protection agency but was returned to his parents within the last year. (*The Albuquerque Tribune*, 2-27-96)

Father charged in killing of missing baby girl

LAS VEGAS, Nev. — A father has been charged with killing his baby daughter, who disappeared five years ago after he tried to trade her for a new car, cash and a down payment on a new house.

James Francis Meegan, 39, was jailed without bond on a murder charge Friday, even though the body of little Francine Meegan has never been found.

"We really don't believe that she is alive, but we're not any closer to locating her than we were before," said police Lt. Larry Spinosa. "We are hoping to get some leads which will eventually lead us to her body."

Police, who would not discuss what evidence they have in the case, began questioning Meegan last month.

Initially, Meegan and his wife, Lillian, had no explanation of what happened to the girl, but later said she had been taken from a casino parking lot. They never filed a report on the alleged kidnapping. (*The Albuquerque Tribune*, 3-2-96)

Mom who used daughters as prostitutes gets 10 years

An Albuquerque woman who police say had her teen-age daughters work as prostitutes to finance her heroin addiction is going to prison for 10 years.

Roberta Brusellas of Albuquerque pleaded no contest Friday to three counts of criminal exploitation of a child by prostitution.

She sold sexual favors by her daughters, ages 14 and 15, and a friend of theirs to feed her heroin habit, Bernalillo County prosecutor Stan Whitaker said.

Defense Attorney Edward Benavidez argued for probation, saying Brusellas needed drug treatment and counseling because she was sexually abused as a child.

Both of Brusellas' daughters have been placed in foster care. (*The Albuquerque Tribune*, 3-30-96)

Mom engineered daughter's illnesses, doctors suspect

MIAMI — *** a judge says Jennifer [Bush], now almost 9, should remain in protective custody because there's reason to believe her mother intentionally made her ill, even injecting her with fecal bacteria and duping doctors into ordering 200 hospitalizations.

Authorities say Kathy Bush [the mother] of Coral Springs suffers from Munchausen syndrome (a rare disorder) in which an adult purposely makes a child ill to get attention and sympathy.

Kathy Bush was arrested Monday on charges of aggravated child abuse and fraud, for allegedly obtaining unnecessary medical goods and service for the girl.

She has claimed in the past while appealing for donations that medical bills — the vast majority of which were paid by Medicaid and the state — reached $3 million. *** (*The Albuquerque Tribune*, 4-17-96)

Two-thirds of sex crimes are against kids

WASHINGTON — Children were the victims of two-thirds of the sex offenders in state prisons, a new Justice Department report says.

The report, based on the largest survey ever of state prison inmates, said that children under age 18 bear the brunt of sex offenses and that child molesting remains a crime most often perpetrated by relatives and acquaintances rather than strangers.

The Justice study found that a third of these child victims were the offspring or stepchildren of their attackers. (*The Albuquerque Tribune*, 3-4-96)

Mom, Not Intruder, Charged With Killing Two Sons

BOWLETT, Texas — At a graveside birthday party for one of her two murdered sons, Darlie Routier sprayed Silly String and clutched her sons' photograph while family members sang "Happy Birthday." ***

On Wednesday, she was in jail, accused of stabbing the boys to death then wounding herself to cover the June 6 crime.

Mrs. Routier had told police that an intruder came through a window and stabbed 6-year-old Devon and 5-year-old Damon while they slept in the living room then stabbed her before fleeing.

She said the attacker was a White man, who wore dark clothes and a baseball cap. Police say he never existed.

"On the one hand we had a community thinking that there was a psychopathic killer walking the alleyways at night," Said Sgt. Dean Poos, a spokesman for the police department in this suburb about 20 miles east of Dallas. "On the other hand, we had a crime scene telling us that what Mrs. Routier was telling us didn't happen."

News reports quoting unidentified sources have said blood evidence showed Mrs. Routier was stabbed in the kitchen, not the living room as she told police, and the only set of bloody footprints found in the house belonged to Mrs. Routier.

Reports also said investigators found a knife in a kitchen drawer with metal fragments on it that matched a cut window screen Mrs. Routier said the attacker came through. *** (*Albuquerque Journal*, 6-20-96)

A subsequent article states that Mrs. Routier, referred to above, was given the death penalty by a Texas jury, after conviction for her heinous crimes against her own children. (*Albuquerque Journal*, 2-5-97)

Nebraska Teen Held in Death of Newborn

[ALBUQUERQUE] — A 15-year-old Nebraska girl who came to Albuquerque to spend the summer with her father has been arrested in the death of a new born infant whose body was found Tuesday in a North Valley irrigation ditch.

Melissa Vuchetich, arrested at her father's house Friday night, was being held Saturday — after a physical examination — in the Bernalillo County Juvenile Detention Center.

She was charged with "child abuse resulting in great bodily harm or death," said Ronni Sparks, spokeswoman for the Bernalillo County Sheriff's Department. *** [Information from area residents, and a tip by phone from Nebraska, led to the investigation and arrest, according to the article.] (*Albuquerque Journal*, 6-23-96)

Murder charge filed in death of 2-year-old

An Albuquerque man has been charged with murder in the death of the 2-year-old son of his girlfriend.

The mother [Carmelita Joseph, 26] also was charged Tuesday with negligently permitting her son to be abused by the man, who was her fiance.

The boy, Christian Asante, arrived at a University hospital trauma unit July 16 with a skull fracture, bleeding of the brain, and various fresh and old bruises, according a court document.

The skull fracture was so severe that a doctor likened it to "something sustained from a 30-foot fall."

The doctor told police that the boy was brain dead and was being kept alive by life-support equipment and was not expected to survive.

Asante died at the hospital the next day. *** (*The Albuquerque Tribune*, 7-31-96)

Man Convicted of Trying to Kill Daughter

WILLIAMSPORT, Pa. — A man was convicted Thursday of trying to push his 9-year-old deaf daughter into the path of a pickup truck [driven by a woman accomplice] to collect more than $200,000 in life insurance money.

David Crist's attempted murder conviction in the 1993 plot clears the way for him to be tried in the attempted electrocution of his 4-year-old daughter and the contract slaying of his only brother. In each case, prosecutors said, the motive was greed. *** (*Albuquerque Journal*, 11-22-96)

Dad Gets Life For Raping Daughter, Killing Kids

PALM BEACH, Fla. — Decades ago, Mendum Paul Corvin sexually abused his daughter, then tried to hide the evidence—a child she bore him—by drowning the baby boy and burying him in the back yard of his Boynton Beach home.

Years later, police say Corvin's sexual abuse continued in Pennsylvania. It was there that his daughter bore him a girl, who was killed and buried in a coal bin to hide once again the family's well-kept, sordid secret.

On Wednesday, Covin, 63, stood shackled in a Palm Beach County courtroom and entered guilty pleas to charges of first degree murder and capital rape for the crimes committed in Boynton Beach in 1968. *** (*Albuquerque Journal,* 11-22-96)

Teen Accused of Infant's Death Surrenders
Girlfriend's Son Found in Garbage

WILMINGTON, Del. — [This story was about Brian Peterson, Jr., 18 and his high-school girlfriend, Amy Grossberg, also 18.]

...How did these "good kids" from affluent northern New Jersey neighborhoods end up with their names spread across New York tabloids with headlines calling them "baby slay" teens.

They went off to college this fall—he to Gettysburg College in Pennsylvania, she to the University of Delaware to study art.

They reunited on Nov. 12—Peterson drove three hours to be with her and help her secretly deliver the baby boy in a Newark, Del., motel.

What happened then has not been explained.

He told police he wrapped the tiny body in a plastic garbage bag and dumped the baby in a trash bin before both returned to their dorm rooms.

But they couldn't keep their secret after Grossberg ... was hospitalized with complications from the birth.

A search dog found the body of the 20-inch, 6-pound 2-ounce boy along with bloody linen in the trash bin. An autopsy found the boy died of a skull fracture, but investigators don't know if the injury happened before or after the baby was put in the trash. *** (*Albuquerque Journal,* 11- 22, 1996)

Mom Convicted In Drug Fire Deaths

RIVERSIDE, Calif. — A woman whose stove-top methamphetamine lab exploded in a fire that killed three of her children was convicted Wednesday of murder and faces up to life in prison.

Kathy Lynn James was cooking a batch of "speed" in her illegal drug lab last Dec. 26 when it exploded, trapping children ages 1, 2, and 3 in their burning mobile home. An older son survived and testified against her.

James testified she produced a big batch of methamphetamine each week for about 10 years, sometimes earning thousands of dollars a week. Her lawyer tried to show the fire could have been caused by a propane leak. (*Albuquerque Journal*, 11-28-96)

Attempt To Shoot Fetus Center Of Life Debate

TORONTO — There are no legal precedents in Canada for what Brenda Drummond did: fire a rifle into her womb in an attempt to kill her soon-to-be-born child.

In a country where abortion is legal and a fetus has no rights, prosecutors struggled Thursday to convince a court that she committed a crime. Anti-abortion groups are closely monitoring the case.

Drummond, 28, was charged with attempted murder June 7, eight days after giving birth to a boy in the bathroom of her home near Ottawa.

A brain scan revealed that the ailing infant had a pellet in his brain, and the baby survived surgery to remove it. He suffered no serious permanent damage.

Drummond's lawyer went before an Ontario judge Wednesday to argue that the criminal charge should be dropped.

"If you take the crown's case at its highest level—yes, she was attempting to kill the fetus—well, that is not an offense under Canadian law," said the lawyer, Lawrence Greenspan.

Greenspan said Drummond was attempting to cause a miscarriage on May 28 when she used a rifle to fire a pellet into her vagina while her daughters, 3 and 7, played elsewhere in their home. The baby was born two days later.

"If she had been successful this would not have been a crime—period," Greenspan said. *** (*Albuquerque Journal*, 11-29-96)

Mom Held in Baby's Death

PATERSON, N.J. — A 22-year-old woman who concealed her pregnancy was charged with murdering her newborn daughter by throwing the infant out a third-story window, and a cousin was charged with helping her.

Bacilia Lucero, an illegal immigrant from Mexico, was held in lieu of $500,000 bail pending arraignment on Wednesday, said William Purday, chief assistant Passaic County prosecutor.

The newborn was found Saturday outside a house where Lucero lived with an aunt and uncle.

Relatives all denied knowing anything about the baby, Detective George Jadlos said. But Ms. Lucero's cousin, Juan Diego Lucero, 20, told police ... he helped with the birth and admitted "the baby was thrown out the window," Jadlos said. (*Albuquerque Journal*, 1-7-97)

Mom, Man Accused of Starving Girl

ALUM CREEK, W.Va. — A woman and her boyfriend were charged with starving her mentally disabled 9-year-old daughter, who lay in critical condition Monday at just 12 pounds.

The girl, who had cerebral palsy, suffered from bedsores, suggesting she had been bedridden or restrained, said state police Sgt. G. K. Barnett.

Wendy Smith, 25, and her boyfriend, Josh Phelix, 20, were charged with child neglect Saturday. The could get up to 10 years in prison. (*Albuquerque Journal*, 1-21-97)

10 Kids Found Alone in Crack House

ATLANTIC CITY, N.J. — Police were searching Friday for the parents of 10 children who were left to fend for themselves in a crack house for three weeks with no running water, heat or electricity.

The children, ages 2 to 16, apparently lived on canned vegetables and brought in buckets of water to use in a toilet. Authorities also found a hole in the roof, bedspreads covering a back door, dog feces in a hallway and soggy floorboards ready to collapse.

The situation was discovered Thursday when a neighbor complained that the smell of kerosene was emanating from the two-story rowhouse four blocks from the city's casino strip.

"As soon as you hit the top of the steps, all you could smell was crack," said Garry Alston, the city's chief code enforcement officer. There was evidence of drug use in the house, he said.

When authorities tried to question the children, an 11-year-old boy who appeared to be in charge told them not to talk, according to Hugh Gallagher, a city inspector.

The children were two sets of siblings. Seven of the children were taken to Atlantic City Medical Center to be evaluated. All the children were placed in foster care.

Some of the children told authorities they were from Camden and Philadelphia and that one of the mothers dropped them off at the house three weeks ago.

"The younger ones weren't ready to talk to us. The ones that were talking were getting smacked by their 11-year-old brother for talking to us, telling them to shut up," Gallagher said.

An aunt of at least one of the children lived down the street and was checking on them from time to time, but no adults were staying in the house, Gallagher said. (*Albuquerque Journal*, 1-25-97)

Mother Charged In Baby Death

HOUSTON — A 20-year-old woman who confessed to beating her infant son to death and throwing his body into a bayou is facing capital murder charges.

Evonne Michelle Rodriguez beat 3-month-old Ramiro Valdez Jr. with her hand and choked him with a rosary, according to the formal charge filed late Wednesday night.

The child is the grandson of an Albuquerque couple, Robert and Victoria Rodriguez.

The defendant, previously identified as Evonne Valdez, admitted Tuesday night to killing the baby after insisting all afternoon that he vanished from a restroom in a downtown Houston shopping mall, a police spokesman said.

Police continued to search for the baby's body. (*Albuquerque Journal*, 1-31-97)

Five-Year-Old Poisoned, Put Out With Trash

NEW YORK — The grandmother and mother of a 5-year-old were charged with fatally poisoning the girl, whose body was put out with the trash in front of their Bronx apartment building.

Rosa Wilkerson, 46, and Angelie Burney, 25, were charged with second-degree murder for allegedly forcing Amy Burney to swallow a mixture of ammonia, vinegar, cayenne pepper and olive oil sometime around April 27, Deputy Police Commissioner Patrick Kelleher said Sunday at a news conference.

Child protection officials had been monitoring the family since Feb. 27, when one of Amy's teachers reported she had showed up for school with bruises and scratches on her face.

Police closed that investigation after Wilkerson and Burney told them Amy had fallen off a bed, Kelleher said, but child welfare workers continued to visit the family. They grew suspicious when they were told Amy wasn't home during visits May 9 and May 13.

Wilkerson told reporter Saturday that Amy died of natural causes and her body lay on a mattress for several days before the women realized she was dead. Wilkerson said she and Burney finally threw the body out with the trash. (*Albuquerque Journal*, 5-19-97)

The following is an excerpt from an article on a widely publicized, strange, and shocking crime in 1997. A teen-ager apparently delivered and murdered her baby at a high school prom:

Teen Charged With Murder

NEW YORK — A New Jersey teen-ager who gave birth in a bathroom at her prom, then returned to the dance floor and ate a salad was charged Tuesday with murder after an autopsy found the baby she discarded in a trash can was either strangled or suffocated in a plastic bag.

"The child was alive when he was born," Monmouth County Prosecutor John Kaye said. "It fits the definition of a 'knowing murder.'"

The prosecutor told a news conference Tuesday in Freehold, N.J., that Melissa Drexler, 18, may have used the sharp edge of a sanitary napkin dispenser to cut the umbilical cord on her June 6 prom night before dumping her newborn boy in a bag she found in a bathroom stall.

"Go tell the boys we'll be right out," Kay quoted Drexler as telling a girlfriend who had come into the bathroom to fetch her. *** (*Albuquerque Journal*, 6-25-97)

Cameras Catch Child Abuse

CHICAGO — Hidden video cameras caught parents kicking, punching, slapping and trying to suffocate children who were already in the hospital for injuries from suspected child abuse, researchers said Monday.

The tapes, made by doctors at two British hospitals, show one mother deliberately breaking an infant's arm. Another mother tried to ram a toothbrush down her 3-year-old daughter's throat and then to poison the child with disinfectant.

Abusive parents often switched to loving behavior the moment nurses walked into the room. (*Albuquerque Journal*, 10-28-97)

Baby Found in Coffee Can

TUCSON — A 19-year-old woman was accused Tuesday of drowning her newborn baby in a toilet and hiding the body in a coffee can under a bathroom sink.

Marianne Biancuzzo was charged with murder and child abuse.

Biancuzzo's 15-year-old brother found the body when he went to take a shower the next morning. (*Albuquerque Journal*, 11-12-97)

Woman Who Found Baby Would Adopt

ORLANDO, Fla. — A woman who rescued an abandoned newborn from a toilet at Walt Disney World said Tuesday she is interested in adopting the girl. ***

Investigators have been unable to find the mother of the 7-pound, 21-inch infant, who was nicknamed by hospital nurses "Princess Jasmine" from the movie "Aladdin." *** (*Albuquerque Journal*, 11-12-97)

Teen charged with killing baby

CAMDEN, N.J. — A teen-age mother suffocated her newborn son at home then drove around for hours before taking the dead infant to a hospital, a prosecutor said, accusing the girl of "extreme indifference to the value of life."

The 16-year-old Voorhees girl was charged as a juvenile Friday with aggravated manslaughter. Superior Court Family Judge Robert Page then ordered the teen to stay at Camden County youth shelter and to undergo a psychiatric evaluation.

Autopsy results show the 7-pound infant was born alive Thursday morning at the teen's home and died as a result of unattended delivery and asphyxiation, county prosecutor Lee A. Solomon said. The case follows at lest five other highly publicized New Jersey related infanticides in the past year. (*Albuquerque Journal*, 11-16-97)

Teen Leaves Newborn In Trash Can At School

ST. PETERSBURG, Fla. — Surveillance cameras caught a 10th grader clutching her stomach as she entered a high school bathroom, where she gave birth to a baby and left him in a trash can.

A janitor discovered the boy about 90 minutes later Monday. The boy, called Nicholas by school officials because of Christmas, was ice cold, barely breathing and buried under hand towels.

By Tuesday, his condition was upgraded from very critical to serious. The 6-pound, 10-ounce full-term infant was breathing on his own and may be released by Christmas, Dr. Danilo Escoto said, although his long-term prognosis is not yet known. ***

The teen-ager was back at school Tuesday and summoned for questioning. Pierce said she denied giving birth during a 40-minute interview with police, then admitted the baby was hers after her mother arrived. *** (*Albuquerque Journal*, 12-3-97)

Infant Dies as Mom Sits Silent In Jail

NEW YORK — A jailed prostitute who told no one she had a baby back at her apartment because she was afraid of being arrested for neglect now faces a murder charge for leaving the infant to die, police say.

Neighbors heard the 2-month-old boy crying for days while Lora Pitoscia, 34, spent eight days at the Rikers Island jail. She had been convicted in September of prostitution and drug charges.

When she returned home, she dumped the child's body down a garbage chute, police said.

The baby died a horrible death, said Dr. Winston Price, a pediatrician and trustee for the state chapter of the National Committee to Prevent Child Abuse and Neglect. "He would have screamed incessantly for eight to 12 hours at a time," Price said. (*Albuquerque Journal*, 12-12-97)

It is indeed difficult for a decent person of natural senses to understand this kind of cruelty and disregard for the life of a child. But what does this article also tell us about the neighbors who heard this little baby crying and did nothing. It reminds me of the many reports we have had in this country in the past several years of people observing others being robbed, beaten, and murdered on our streets and doing nothing.

Woman kills boy who was trying to eat

ROCHESTER, N.Y. – A woman has been convicted of killing her malnourished 3-year-old grandson by hitting him with a board after he twice took food without her permission.

Displaying no emotion after a seven-day trial, Barbara Briggs, 42, was convicted Thursday of second-degree murder. She could get 25 years to life in prison at her sentencing May 1.

A defense psychologist testified that Briggs was overwhelmed by schizophrenia and high stress and was borderline mentally disabled.

Keith Sims had moved in with Briggs and her three children because his mother was ill.

Sims weighed 28 pounds when he died in September, and his body was scarred with cigarette burns and whacks from an electrical cord. *** (*The Albuquerque Tribune*, 3-14-98)

The following appears to be heinous incest and murder:

Rubbing Alcohol in Body of Baby

CLEBURNE, Texas – Rubbing alcohol was found in the body of an infant who choked to death last month, raising the possibility that it was poured down his throat, authorities said. ***

Sheriff's investigators arrested 26-year-old Nancy Koerner and her father, 46-year-old Ray Koerner, last month after emergency workers found 11-month-old Gregory Koerner dead in their Johnson County trailer home.

Investigators said the Koerners admitted that they had a three-year sexual relationship and that the child was theirs.

The medical examiner received a toxicology report Monday from a Dallas laboratory that found isopropanol, or rubbing alcohol, in the baby's blood. ***

An autopsy last month found food in the child's lungs, leading authorities to suspect that the baby was force-fed and died or that he choked on vomit. ***

The Koerners were arrested hours after Nancy Koerner called 911 on the afternoon of Feb. 18 and reported that the baby had stopped breathing.

Physical evident and statements that the Koerners made that night led investigators to conclude that the infant was killed hours or days before the call, authorities said.

Hanna [prosecutor] has said that he plans to seek murder or manslaughter charges against the Koerners when a grand jury convenes this month. (*Albuquerque Journal*, 3-12-98)

When it seems that we have seen the worst that humanity can offer, something even more shocking turns up. Surely things can get no more cruel and hideous than the following:

Girl Accused in Infant Death

EAU CLAIRE, Wis. — A 13-year-old girl was accused Monday of killing her newborn son in a YMCA bathroom by squeezing his head and stuffing toilet paper in his mouth.

Lee Vang was charged with first-degree murder and hiding a corpse. First-degree murder carries a mandatory sentence of life in prison.

A YMCA janitor found the infant's body in two plastic bags, one inside the other, in a garbage can in the women's bathroom.

Vang was arrested Saturday during a house-to-house search.

MURDER AND VIOLENCE—CHILDREN AGAINST PARENTS

Mutilation slayer ruled incompetent for trial

SANTA FE —A 20-year-old man charged in the mutilation slaying of his father is incompetent to stand trial and must undergo treatment at the state mental hospital in Las Vegas, N.M., a judge has ruled.

Samuel Vialpando Jr. had told State Police he slit his father's throat with a kitchen knife Sept. 29, then severed the head, legs, arms and penis, court documents say. He told police he had to kill his father because of past abuse, the documents say. *** (*The Albuquerque Tribune*, 12-7-93)

Grandparents Slain After Fight Over Beer: Police

RIO RANCHO — Michael Brown and two friends were ordered out of his grandparent's home because the couple didn't want the teens drinking beer in their house.

But Brown, Jeremy Rose and Bernadette Setser sneaked through a bedroom window and began listening to a rap music tape before stabbing Ed and Marie Brown to death, police said Saturday.

Brown, 16, Rose, 17, and Setser, 16, admitted killing Ed and Marie Brown in a bloody, alcohol-fueled confrontation early Friday morning.

[Brown had left his parents and moved in with his grandparents.] *** (*Albuquerque Journal*, 2-6-94)

[In early 1995, Brown and Setser were sentence to life in prison plus 42 years. Rose pleaded guilty and was awaiting sentencing.] (*The Albuquerque Tribune*, 4-7-95)

Family Admits Doing In Dad

MISSOULA, Mont. — A 15-year-old cheerleader and honor student admitted shooting her sleeping father to death in January, and her younger brother and mother admitted destroying his body. *** [They told the sheriff that the reason was that the father "just treated them all like dirt."] (*Albuquerque Journal*, 2-23-94)

Texas teen found guilty in stabbing deaths of parents

BEAUMONT, Texas — A jury took only 35 minutes to find a 16-year-old ... boy guilty of stabbing his parents to death as part of a plan to run away with a friend to Minnesota and visit the nation's largest shopping mall. ***

[David Travis] sobbed during the trial when he was shown photos of the nude body of his mother, who suffered 13 stab wounds. He also wept while testifying that he began stabbing his mother when she came out of a bathroom and started screaming after she saw the bloody body of his father who was stabbed 11 times.

Travis' friend, Todd Thompson, 16, was killed by a deflected knife blow as Travis' father was trying to fend off the attack. ***

One of Thompsons's notebooks said in a passage dated in November that it was "16 weeks to death." The murders came 16 weeks later. (*The Albuquerque Tribune*, 9-1-94)

Family slaying — Teen sentenced to life

BURLINGTON, Ky. — A teen-ager who killed his parents and two sisters, then went to high school and held his classmates hostage, was sentenced to life in prison. *** [After killing his family, Clay Shrout, 17] then went to school and held his class hostage for about 30 minutes before surrendering to police. He told authorities: "I've had a bad day." (*The Albuquerque Tribune*, 10-15-94)

Phone rules upset teen; she asks friend to kill her mother

DENVER — A 13-year-old girl asked a friend to kill her mother because the girl wasn't allowed to talk endlessly on the phone, police say.

Samantha Burtis was arrested Wednesday in Jefferson County Juvenile Court while appearing on unrelated burglary and theft charges. She was held for investigation of solicitation for first-degree murder. ***

... The girl had attacked her mother several times ... [a detective said]. *** (*The Albuquerque Tribune*, 2-17-95)

2 held in parents' death

MIDLAND, Mich. — Two hulking tattooed brothers were taken to court in shackles today to face charges of beating and stabbing their parents and younger brother to death in Pennsylvania.

Bryan Freeman, 17, and David Freeman, 15, were arrested Wednesday at a rural home near Hope, Mich., along with a cousin and another young man.

Judge James E. Wilson said the brothers are charged with three counts each of homicide and conspiracy to commit homicide in the slayings of Dennis Freeman, 54, Brenda Freeman, 48, and Eric Freeman, 11, whose bodies were found Sunday. (*The Albuquerque Tribune*, 3-2-95)

Another concurrent article on the same incident of the arrest of the Freeman brothers and their cousin, Nelson Birdwell III, 18, referred to them as skinheads, and stated:

*** Police say the brothers had threatened for years to kill their parents as revenge for trying to impose their strict way of life as Jehovah's Witnesses.

The three, all of whom had shaven heads, came into court in blue slippers and green jail uniforms. David has "Sieg Heil!" etched above his eyebrows, while Bryan and Nelson have "Berzerker" tattooed on their foreheads, an apparent reference to Norse folk stories about warriors so fierce they needed no armor. *** (*Albuquerque Journal*, 3-3-95)

These articles are classic examples of the secular, humanist, and immoral influences of modern society substantially outweighing the religious influence that good parents try to exert on their children. Parents today certainly have tremendous obstacles in overcoming the destructive and corrupt influences on children by our current society, including a large number of the schools which they attend. Young bullies like those three boys who have no inhibitions of religious morality and no conscience are extremely dangerous to society, both as a physical danger to their parents and other people, and in their contribution to our general moral decay. Such things have a snow-balling effect. Young people learn from and follow one another.

Teen who shot, killed parents goes on trial

ALLENTOWN, Pa. — Was a Boy Scout a coldblooded killer inspired by TV reports of another slaying when he shot his parents to death? Or did "insanity pull the trigger"?

The two depictions of 17-year-old Jeffrey Howorth emerged in opening statements Monday, with both sides acknowledging he pumped 4 rifle shots into his parents in March and fled in his mother's car.

"This was not madness, it was murder," prosecutor Doug Reichley told jurors.

Prosecutors contended Howorth got the idea from watching news reports of a killing three days earlier and 10 miles away, in which two teen-age brothers killed their parents and a brother using knives and weight-lifting bars.

Seeing reports about those slayings "was a liberating act for Jeffrey Howorth," said Reichley, who later read jurors a rambling note the boy left behind referring to the killings.

"Those kids ... were cool," the note read. "They killed their parents. I would be rough if I did that."

Defense attorney Dennis Charles said his client was nothing like the brothers in the TV reports: avowed neo-Nazis who tattooed "Berzerker" and "Sieg Heil" on their foreheads and went to White power meetings.

Howorth, he said was "a quiet and obedient boy," a churchgoing, varsity swimmer. (*The Albuquerque Tribune*, 10-10-95)

Son Pleads Innocent in Mom's Killing

LAS VEGAS, N.M. — Teen-ager Victor Maestas showed no emotion Friday when he pleaded innocent to charges of stabbing to death his mother, Angela Bergman, 35, and dumping her body in a lake near here.

State Police arrested Maestas, 15, and his mother's lesbian mate, Cynthia Lesly, 36, at about midnight Wednesday. A fisherman found Bergman's body, with a stab wound near the left breast, floating face down in Storrie Lake on the morning of April 9. ***

Lesly was charged Thursday with two counts of contributing to the delinquency of a minor and four counts of evidence tampering ... . ***

... Lesly [had told] police that Bergman had walked away from their residence the night before [the time her body was found] and not returned.

Lesly told police investigators that she and Bergman were married on Feb. 27, 1987 . ...

Affidavits for arrest and search warrants allege that the night before Bergman's body was found, Victor Maestas called and unidentified teen-age friend and told the friend he had just killed his mother and asked for help in getting rid of the body. (*Albuquerque Journal*, 4-22-95)

Rio Rancho teen pleads guilty to shootings, faces 13 years

[NEW MEXICO] — [Peter Rosa, 17] accused of wounding his parents with shotgun blasts in their Rio Rancho home has pleaded guilty to two counts of aggravated battery with a deadly weapon. *** The shooting stemmed from an argument between the parents and their son, police said. (*The Albuquerque Tribune*, 1-5-96)

Peter Rosa) ... who admitted shooting his parents with a shotgun had a fascination with violence and with the main character in the Oliver Stone film "Natural Born Killers," a psychologist testified.

... he wanted to die at an early age, meaning by the time he's 30, was a heavy user of the hallucinogen LSD; once described himself as an anarchist; and once plotted to escape from a treatment center by using a female staffer as a hostage, according to testimony Monday by psychologists. ***

... the shooting stemmed from an argument between Peter Rosa and his parents after his parents became upset when they discovered Rosa's girlfriend had spent the night with him in the family's home. *** (*The Albuquerque Tribune*, 2-27-96)

Peter Rosa, showing no remorse, was sentenced to 12 years in prison. (*Albuquerque Journal*, 5-4-96)

Girl pleads not guilty in mother's strangulation

SALT LAKE CITY — A former Albuquerque teenager has pleaded not guilty to three felony charges in the strangulation of her mother.

Jessica Kaddourah faces charges of murder, fleeing from a police officer and tampering with evidence. The murder charge would be a first-degree felony in the adult system. The other two would be second-degree felonies.

Kaddourah was 13 on Feb. 20 when her mother, Donna Kaddourah Shelton, was strangled and her body left in a Murray pond. The girl turned 14 on Friday, the day she was charged in 3rd District Juvenile Court.

She can't be tried as an adult because Utah law requires children to be at least 14 at the time of the crime to be tried in the adult system. (*The Albuquerque Tribune*, 2-28-96)

Further information about the above crime:

*** Before her death, Donna Shelton apparently fought with her daughter because the girl had returned home later than she was supposed to, [Lt. Pete] Fondaco said.

When questioned about the slaying, Jessica told investigators: "It just happened all of a sudden. It wasn't planned."

She apparently called two 14-year-old friends [girls], who came to the house and helped her load the body into the trunk of the family's leased car, Fondaco said.

Police believe all three teens drove to the pond and threw the body in. *** (*The Albuquerque Tribune*, 2-23-95)

'Vampire Clan' Teens Arrested In Murders

BATON ROUGE, La. — Heather Wendorf wore purple hair and a dog chain around her neck and told friends she was a former demon who had talked with spirits during human blood-drinking rituals.

With her parents found slain and Wendorf missing, authorities feared she had been kidnapped by the killers. Then, they began to suspect her.

Wendorf, an ex-boyfriend and three other teen-agers believed to be in a "vampire cult" in Kentucky were in jail Friday, tracked to Louisiana with the help of one teen's mother.

Roderick Ferrell, 16, Wendorf's ex-boyfriend, and Dana Cooper, 19, both of Murray, Ky. and Scott Anderson, 16, of Mayfield, Ky., were arrested on murder warrants Thursday night, along with Wendorf, 15.

Charity Keesee, 16, of Murray was charged with being an accessory to murder after the fact.

All are wanted in the murders of Richard Wendorf, 49, and his wife Naoma Ruth Wendorf. 53, who were bludgeoned to death Monday night in their Eustis, Fla. home about 20 miles northwest of Orlando.

The Kentucky youths are believed to be in the "The Vampire Clan," a group of about 30 that surfaced about two months ago during an investigation into a break-in at an animal shelter. Two puppies were mutilated and their body parts taken.

"They had stomped one of them to death, and one of them they pulled the legs off," said Sheriff Stan Scott of Calloway County, Ky., about 180 miles southwest of Louisville.

Two youths were charged, including one of the teens suspected in the Wendorf slayings, but other information was withheld because the case involved juveniles.

Baton Rouge Police Capt. Don Kelly said the teens were being questioned by Florida authorities. Extradition proceedings are expected to begin next week.

Kelly said all five have what appear to be self-inflicted cuts on their arms.

"Other than that, they have not exhibited any vampirish behaviors," he said. Some of them wore black but "they're not in black capes and fangs."

"They just look like screwed-up kids," he said. "There's no shortage of those."

David Keesee said his daughter had never been in trouble before.

"She basically ran away from home, but I don't think she knew what she was getting into," he said.

It was Keesee's mother who helped lead authorities to the teens, Scott said. (*Albuquerque Journal*, 11-30-96)

Teen Cult Leader Gets Death

TAVARES, Fla. – The teen-aged leader of a vampire cult was sentenced to death Friday for killing a couple with a crow-bar after traveling to Florida with cult members to help the couple's daughter run away.

Rod Ferrell, 17, pleaded guilty to killing Richard C. Wendorf and Naoma Ruth Queen of Eustis, about 30 miles northwest of Orlando on Nov. 25, 1996.

Ferrell and three members of his blood-sucking cult left Kentucky for Florida to help their [sic] daughter, Heather Wendorf, leave home. She was then inducted into the cult, whose members took drugs, engaged in group sex and drank one another's blood, investigators said. Ferrell told a friend that he needed to kill people to open the "gates to hell." (*Albuquerque Journal*, 2-28-98).

Girl Who Lost Innocence Helps Murder Grandmother

KINGSTON, N.Y. — When her grandmother died, 13-year-old Wendy Gardner was supposed to have the last word.

Wendy had planned to say, "You beat me ... now its your turn to get beaten." But she confessed that even before her boyfriend pulled the kite string around Betty Gardner's neck, plans had gone awry.

"Just do it," she said. Then she fled upstairs and lay down; she sang "Jingle Bells" to blot out the carnage below. ***

Wendy Gardner is polite and pretty with a round face and long brown hair. In school, she earned A's and B's. She plays the flute— pretty sweet melodies—and keeps a diary.

In it she fantasized about ripping an old boyfriend's flesh to pieces.

The contrasts—darkness and innocence—are typical of this child of drug users: a prostitute mother who died after contracting the AIDS virus. A father who boasted of how his own father dropped dead during an argument between them, according to trial testimony.

Betty Gardner [67] took both Wendy and her sister, Kathy into her home in the Hudson Valley town of Saugerties. Wendy was 5, Kathy was 3; their grandmother was a widow who fervently believed in God and discipline, and sometimes the girls were slapped or paddled. ***

Then in October 1994, Wendy met James Evans. James was older—15—and he stole bikes and tortured cats, prosecutors said. Trial psychiatrists diagnosed him as a sociopath.

Before long, Wendy began skipping school. Her grades dropped. Wendy, according to Older [her defense attorney], was becoming like James.

By Christmas 1994, Wendy had essentially lived with James and his mother for two weeks. Betty Gardener ordered her granddaughter home. ***

[James and Wendy then planned the murder.]

[After the murder], James and Wendy had sex in the same room where Betty was killed. She helped James stuff the body into the trunk of Betty's 1984 Mercury. ***

[Both were found guilty of second-degree murder. James was given a sentence of nine years to life, and Wendy had not been sentenced at the time of he article.] (*Albuquerque Journal*, 4-7-97)

Teen Held in Rampage Blames Satanism

JACKSON, Miss. — The teen-ager [16-year-old Luke Woodham] charged with stabbing his mother to death and then fatally shooting two classmates claims it was friends dabbling in satanic worship that persuaded him to turn his loneliness into violence. ***

Prosecutors allege that a group known as the "Kroth" held secretive meetings at Woodham's house.

Woodham is accused of stabbing his mother to death in her bed and then going to school, where witnesses said he pulled a rifle from a long coat and started shooting at students as they waited for classes to begin.

Days later, authorities arrested six alleged members of the Kroth and charged them with murder conspiracy. The trials of five of those are scheduled for February. The sixth case has been transferred to Youth Court.

Grant Boyette, 18, was described by prosecutors as the mastermind of the group. (*Albuquerque Journal*, 11-12-97)

OTHER MURDER AND VIOLENCE BY CHILDREN

Boys brutalized child, prosecutor says

PRESTON, England — Two 10-year-old boys battered a toddler with bricks after luring him from a shopping mall, and dumped his body on a railroad track where it was cut in two by a train, a prosecutor said today.

The boys, now 11, sat in the middle of the courtroom on a specially raised platform so they could see over a railing in front of them. They listened as the prosecutor started their trial by describing the toddler's ordeal.

The boys, the youngest ever charged with murder in Britain, are accused of abducting and murdering James Bulger, 2, who strayed briefly from his mother in the crowded mall in Liverpool, on Feb. 12. ***

Prosecutor Richard Henriques said the two boys took James on a 2 1/2 mile walk across Liverpool, in northwest England, before battering him to death on the railroad track.

"Bricks, stones and a piece of metal appear to have been thrown at James on that railway line," Henriques said. "He sustained many fractures to his skull. "Pathologists concluded that James was already dead when his body was hit by the train, the prosecutor told the jury .... *** (*The Albuquerque Tribune*, 11-1-93)

The Albuquerque Tribune, 12-8-93: "A few weeks ago a court in Liverpool, England, sentenced two juveniles who were found guilty of murdering a 2-year-old to jail for 'as long as Her Majesty may desire.'"

In Chicago, a 10-year-old boy, babysitting for a 1-year-old girl, kicked the baby girl to death to stop her crying, police said. (*The Albuquerque Tribune*, 12-28-93)

In Tampa, Florida, a 14-year-old boy in the ninth grade was charged with attempted first-degree murder. He was accused of dropping rat poison into his teacher's coffee mug. (*The Albuquerque Tribune*, 2-16-94)

Swarm of boys involved in deadly carjacking

A woman whose companion was killed in an early morning carjacking told police that her car was swarmed by a group of boys as she attempted to turn around in a Northeast Heights [Albuquerque] parking lot.

The woman, whose name The Tribune is withholding, said the boys reached into the car and grabbed her and her male companion and demanded keys to the car or "they would blow her head off."

At one point during the Wednesday morning encounter, one of the attackers put a gun to her head and demanded keys, according to Metro Court records.

Marcos Chavez, 17, one of those accused of swarming the car, was to be arraigned today on an open count of murder in connection with a fatal carjacking. ***

Chavez is accused of shooting Earl Wayne West, 30, of Albuquerque, who died of a gunshot wound to the chest during the 3 a.m. carjacking. ***

[A woman who was a nearby resident gave information leading to the arrest of Chavez, and said that she was then threatened by others for giving the information.] (*The Albuquerque Tribune*, 6-2-94)

Boy, 12, Accused of Rape, Sodomy

WILLIAMSBURG, Va. — A 12-year-old boy accused along with a 10-year-old girl of raping and sodomizing a 7-year-old girl may have learned some of the behavior by watching pornographic videos, police said.

Police Capt. Ken Middlebrook of James City County near Williamsburg said the boy told investigators he had watched X-rated tapes and "basically, that's where he learned about this." ***
(*Albuquerque Journal*, 12-5-93)

Boy Hanged in burglary

EAST ORANGE, N.J. — Two teen-agers have been arrested in the death of a 4-year-old boy who has hanged with a belt from a doorknob while his family's apartment was burglarized.

A 17-year-old boy was arrested March 17 and charged with murder, and a 16-year-old boy was arrested Saturday on charges of burglary, robbery and criminal restraint . ...

The toddler, Terrell Edmondson, was found on March 12. His mother, Nicole Edmondson, was charged with endangering the welfare of child because the boy had been left alone.

Teens sentenced in guard beating

Two teen-agers accused of beating and choking a 60-year-old New Mexico Boys School custodian, then stealing his truck to escape from the school, have been sentenced to adult prison. [Robert Gallegos, 18, was sentenced to 9 years, with all but 6 years suspended; and Ricky Romero, 16, was sentenced to 9 years, and all but four years were suspended.] (*The Albuquerque Tribune*, 1-11-94)

With our decline in morality, we have gained another phenomenon. There has been an unprecedented and unthought of rise in violence and crime committed by girls and women. A general viciousness and cruelty has developed among many females that appears to have no historical precedent. I can attribute it only to a combination of the feminist movement and general moral decay—they have gone hand in hand.

Jealous Kids Beat Me, APS Student Claims
Girl: Attack Came After Talk of Becoming Model

Melissa Gomez, 14, said Tuesday that she was attacked and beaten by as many as 15 [both boys and girls] other Hayes Middle School [Albuquerque] students last week. The reason: She's pretty.

Gomez, an eighth-grader [and an honor student] at the Northeast Heights school, said she had been talking about signing with a California modeling agency earlier that day when one of her alleged attackers was overheard saying, "We'll see if she's going to be a model or not."

The beating left Gomez with a concussion, a sprained neck and back, a bruised kidney, a chipped nose bone, two black eyes and a fat lip, according to her mother, Karen Leonard. Since the attack, Gomez said she has had trouble walking and holding up her head. She's been going through tests to determine the extent of her injuries. * * *

Gomez was treated at St. Joseph Medical Center and released later that night. She's been back several times for tests and doesn't expect to return to school any time soon.

And when she does go back, her parents say it won't be Hayes Middle School. * * * (*Albuquerque Journal*, 3-16-94)

Female Gang Planned Valentine's Stabbing

SANTA FE — The gang-style plot was for one girl to distract the boy with a kiss at a Valentine's Day dance at Santa Fe's Alameda Junior High School Gym — and for another student to stab him.

But members of Eastside, a predominantly female youth gang, went to Plan B when the intended kisser backed out, according to a police affidavit that detailed the alleged plot to stab a rival gang member. * * *

It all started when Eastside leader Lupita Velarde, 14, decided to "take down" the 15-year-old seventh-grader, who belonged to a rival gang [the Latin Kings, according to Capt. Andrew Leyba]. * * *

[Erica] Roybal sprayed the victim on the side of the head with a small amount of Mace, then a boy grabbed it and sprayed it directly in the victim's face.

The victim covered his eyes and bent over, and]Alex Flores, 13] stabbed him in the back twice. [The stabbing was not fatal.] *** (*Albuquerque Journal*, 2-24-94)

On August 2, 1993, in Savona, N. Y., a fine endearing little lad of 4 years, Derrick Robbie, was lured into a stand of pine trees a short distance from his home and battered to death. Eric Smith, 13, confessed to the murder. In 1989, the Smith boy had strangled a neighbor's cat with a garden hose. Two years later, when a schoolmate died in a car crash, he called the teenager's family on a few occasions, asking to speak with him. (*The Albuquerque Tribune*, 3-23-94)

Blabbermouth teens arrested in Coney Island rape, beating
NEW YORK — Five teen-agers, who the police said could not resist talking about their crime, have been arrested in the rape and beating of a woman who was attacked as she jogged on a desolate stretch of the Coney Island boardwalk a week ago.
The youths, 14 to 17, years old, were arrested Wednesday after female friends told detectives what the boys were saying. ***
(*The Albuquerque Tribune*, 4-14-94)

What kind of little monsters are being raised, and what kind of a society are we living in, when young people old enough to have some judgment not only do such heinous acts, but think that it is something admirable to brag about to their peers?

FBI says homicides up, especially by kids
The rate of homicides by youths under 18 has doubled since 1985, the article says.
"Over the last seven years, we have seen a major growth in the presence of guns, largely stimulated by a number of young people in the drug business who have guns," said Alfred Blumstein, a professor at Carnegie Mellon University's Heinz School of Public Policy in Pittsburgh. "Playing to a crime-weary public, the Clinton administration is stepping up pressure on Congress to ban 'assault weapons.'"
(*The Albuquerque Tribune*, 5-2-94)
That is a typical liberal response—to ignore personal responsibility. Guns do not cause children to be involved in drugs. Neither do they

cause the moral decline that is the root of every problem mentioned in this book, including those with children. The liberal approach is to limit the traditional and constitutional rights of all people, while contributing to the immorality tearing down all of our traditional values, and resulting in the very problems they are trying to deal with.

Burning Case Shows Holes in Youth Code

[Albuquerque] — It all began with a stolen coin purse.

Larry Montano, one of two teens charged with setting a 14-year-old girl on fire last week, had his first brush with the law five years ago when he was caught with the stolen purse just before his 13th birthday.

He was referred to the juvenile justice system 15 more times before turning himself in April 20 on an attempted murder charge.

Over the years, Montano has been found guilty of charges ranging from selling marijuana to a classmate to stabbing a restaurant manager in the arm. He recently was indicted by a grand jury for allegedly stabbing a man during a West Side beer bash.

The most severe penalty Montano ever received was two years probation. When he violated the probation on at least three occasions, it was extended, according to court records.

But that could change if Montano is convicted of setting Nicole Aragon on fire last week when she allegedly refused to have sex and sniff gasoline with him and co-defendant Pablo Lopez. ***
(*Albuquerque Journal*, 4-29-94)

Cult Slayers Sentenced in Mexico

MATAMOROS, Mexico — The reputed "god mother" [Maria Aldrete] and four other cult members have been sentenced to more than 60 years in prison for the ritual slayings of 13 people, including a Texas college student. ***

Mark Kilroy, a University of Texas pre-med student on spring break, disappeared during a night of bar-hopping in Matamoros, on March 14, 1989. After a month long search, his mutilated body was found at a ranch west of Matamoros.

Fourteen other victims also were unearthed there and at a nearby farm. Authorities said a drug-smuggling cult performed the ritual slayings seeking magical protection from the law and rival drug smugglers.

The murder charges involved only 13 of the 15 victims. ***

[Maria] Aldrete, a student at Texas Southeast College in Brownsville, was accused of being the cult's "high priestess" who lured some of the victims to the ranch. ... *** (*Albuquerque Journal*, 5-4-94)

Teen pleads guilty to role in slaying of 12-year-old girl

[New Mexico] — John Paul Aguilar, one of three teens accused in the August rape and slaying of 12-year-old Crystal LaPierre, today pleaded guilty to three felony counts in the brutal crime and confirmed a chilling statement of facts read by the prosecution.

Aguilar's guilty plea, said District Attorney Mike Runnels, will make it possible for the prosecution to seek the death penalty against 19-year-old Frank Martinez. ***

[After picking up the girl, they drove] up Lobo Canyon road to a clearing called The Oaks, where Aguilar said the boys demanded LaPierre have sex with each of them. When she refused and tried to run away, she was caught, brought back to the car and thrown to the ground by Aguilar, the statement said.

Jaramillo and Aguilar kicked her, Runnels said. Martinez threw LaPierre onto the hood of the Camaro and forced her to have sex; Aguilar and Jaramillo did the same, the statement said. ***

[Aguilar] said they then agreed to kill her and began beating her with their fists and feet. An attempt was made to choke her, stab her, choke her again, before Martinez held her head in a rut filled with water and mud .... The autopsy indicates drowning as the cause of death. *** (*The Albuquerque Tribune*, 5-16-94)

Florida—Youth crime bill signed

TAMPA, Fla. — Spurred by a rash of tourist slayings by teen-agers, Florida has enacted a law cracking down on young criminals.

The $237 million measure creates a department to focus on teen-age criminals; makes it a crime for juveniles to threaten judges or ignore orders to report to detention centers; and requires juveniles of any age to be treated as adults if their rap sheets include three felonies and three stays in a detention center. It also allows prosecutors to try defendants as young as 14 as adults.

(*The Albuquerque Tribune*, 5-19-94)

Teen-agers run over officer with his patrol car

TUCUMCARI, N.M. — A state police officer from Tucumcari was run over this morning when he stopped four teen-agers to check the license plate on the pickup truck they were riding in, a state police spokesman said.

Maj. Frank Taylor of Santa Fe said officer Thomas Dobson, 26, suffered fractures to the lower legs. ***

Taylor said the check found both the license plate and the vehicle had been stolen, and Dobson took the two females and two males into custody.

Taylor said that somehow one of the teens got control of Dobson's patrol car, and ran him down as he stood between the two vehicles.

"It was intentionally done," Taylor said.

The teens then took the patrol car, but were captured a short time later after crashing it into a ditch and taking off on foot, Taylor said. (*The Albuquerque Tribune*, 5-19-94)

The following two news items were in *The Albuquerque Tribune,* of 5-19-94:

Teen accused of murder

A 16-year-old Albuquerque boy faces an open murder charge in connection with the drive-by shooting death of another boy two months ago. ***

Man guilty in shooting

One of two adults charged in the fatal shooting of a 15-year-old boy outside his Southwest Albuquerque home has pleaded guilty to aggravated assault charges

Jeff Graves, 20, was accused of throwing bottles and rocks at the teen and another person before his accomplice opened fire with a handgun. ***

Police say [Carlos Martinez] was shot after gang members got angry because he was wearing a red Chicago Bulls shirt.

Tommy McManaway, 30, has been indicted on murder charges alleging he was the shooter.

Teen pleads no contest in rape

A 16-year-old boy [Ralph Chavez] who pleaded no contest to the attempted rape of a 3-year-old girl has been placed on two years probation and must be tested regularly for AIDS, authorities said. *** Prosecutors said Chavez sexually assaulted the child Feb. 6 while the girl was being cared for by his mother. (*The Albuquerque Tribune*, 6-5-93)

The following is an example of the degradation that has become prevalent in this country — not just in New York and San Francisco — and not just by blacks or other minorities. It is a direct result of our general moral breakdown, accompanied by the disappearance of traditional religious moral values.

In nation's heartland, gang murdered girl for car keys

DAVENPORT, Iowa — In the middle of a silent country night last August 17, 17-year-old Michelle Jensen was shot to death. Her body was left along a dusty rural road, near a cornfield not far from the center of the city.

Three teen-age gang members killed her, a jury ruled last week, for the keys to her Ford Escort. The slaying by the youths from Davenport's blue-collar West End rocked the eastern edge of the state because of the cold-blooded brutality and because the Iowa boys are supposed to join the Boy Scouts, not gangs; they are supposed to commit pranks, not executions.

Three other young men arrested in the case pleaded guilty to lesser charges and testified against the gang members they had vowed to die for. But what seemed to shock people even more than the big-city-style gang violence was the suspects themselves: six white sons of the heartland. *** *The Albuquerque Tribune*, 5-19-94)

Teen-agers laugh while they watch Mister Softee die

PHILADELPHIA — First came the familiar music of the ice cream truck, then an argument, then the sharp sound of gunfire.

As the tinny, tinkling music played on, word spread through the neighborhood that Mister Softee had been shot.

The driver, Mohammad Jaberipour, died 45 minutes after his truck was robbed Wednesday. Neil Lyew, a 16-year-old from the neighborhood, surrendered to police this morning and was charged with murder.

Some witnesses said a group of teen-agers laughed and mocked the driver as he lay dying while music from his truck played.

Jaberipour was 49, an Iranian immigrant, a father of three. He had been on the job only a week and a half, said his boss . ... ***

Witnesses told the Philadelphia Daily News that teen-agers standing nearby laughed and made up songs about the dying driver.

"Mister Softee is dead. He didn't give out enough sprinkles," they chanted. They also laughed. As Jaberipour was loaded into an ambulance, they broke into a rap song: "They killed Mister Softee."

Ehab Elgagry, another Mister Softee driver and a friend of Jaberipour, arrived on the scene shortly after the shooting.

"It wasn't human," he said. "When I got there people were laughing and asking me for ice cream. I was crying. My best friend was killed. They were acting as though a cat had died, not a human being." *** (*The Albuquerque Tribune*, 6-17-94)

Drug present in many NYC slaying victims

NEW YORK — More than three of 10 slaying victims in New York City had cocaine in their systems when they died, according to the Journal of the American Medical Association.

Young women victims had an even higher incidence of cocaine in the their systems than young men.

The journal reported today on a study of 4,298 homicide deaths in the city in 1990 and 1991. *** (*The Albuquerque Tribune*, 7-6-94)

Teen suspect in Florida tourist killing to testify against friends

MONTICELLO, Fla. — A 14-year-old boy who police say crouched in the back seat of a car while his friends fatally shot a British tourist has agreed to testify against them.

Cedrick Green, who faced a first-degree murder charge, pleaded no contest this week to one count of accessory after the fact, a third-degree felony.

Green was 13 last September when Gary Colley was shot and killed during a botched robbery attempt at an Interstate 10 rest stop in this small town east of Tallahassee. Colley's companion, Margaret Jagger, was wounded.

As part of the plea, Green will be treated as a juvenile and could be sentenced to community control, a form of house arrest. (*The Albuquerque Tribune*, 8-13-94)

Jury finds teen guilty in death of 4-year-old

BATH, N.Y. — A jury ignored a defense built around an insanity plea and found Eric Smith, 14, guilty of murdering a 4-year-old boy last summer. *** Tried as an adult, the teen now faces a sentence of nine years to life imprisonment. *** (*The Albuquerque Tribune*, 8-17-94)

Police: Kids Killed Drifter

WENATCHEE, Wash. — Two 12-year-olds killed a drifter who threw rocks at them because they were making too much noise, police say. *** At that point they planned between themselves to hunt him down and kill him, [Det. John Matney] said. *** Both boys shot the man and reloaded. Then one boy "emptied both guns into him from approximately 10 feet. It was cold-blooded murder," Matney said. *** Police found two handguns hidden in bushes. (*The Albuquerque Tribune*, 8-23-94) [A later article said that both boys were convicted of murder and could be sentenced to a detention center until they were 21. It also stated that the boys had gone to the Columbia River area where the killing took place to fire three guns they had stolen.] (*The Albuquerque Tribune*, 1-14-95)

Boys hammered nails into the heels of 8-year-old
who wouldn't shoplift

SOMERSET, Pa. — Eight-year-old Terry Snyder won't talk about the day three boys [ages 14, 10, and 9] dragged him into the bushes and hammered a small nail into each heel because he wouldn't shoplift for them. *** For weeks he hid his wounds out of fear the boys would come after him again, and he has nightmares of being attacked with knives. *** (*The Albuquerque Tribune*, 9-8-94)

Community trying to cope with brutal burning of small boy

HOPEWELL, Va. — The burns ... seared 85 percent of the 3-year-old's body .... *** Two brothers ages 10 and 11, are accused of splashing gasoline on and around Tony Dillhoff and setting him on fire Sept. 19. *** According to neighbors, the accused boys have a history of bullying smaller children. *** (*The Albuquerque Tribune*, 10-6-94)

Boys 10, 11, Drop Child, 5, To His Death

CHICAGO — Despite his brother's frantic effort to save him, a 5-year-old boy [Eric Morris] was dropped to his death from the 14th-floor window of a housing project because he wouldn't steal candy for two older boys, police said.

The suspects, ages 10 and 11, could get up to five years' probation if convicted. Police said they admitted the killing.

"It's truly mind-boggling," said Kay Hanlon. "Every day you think you've seen as bad as it's ever going to get here and something like this happens."

Police said Eric Morris plunged to his death after a desperate struggle Thursday night at the window of a vacant apartment on the South Side.

His 8-year-old brother, Derrick, fought with the two older boys trying to push Eric out the window and pulled him back from the brink once, but then lost his grip when one of the older boys bit Derrick's arm.

The killing was the second horrific episode of child-against-child violence in Chicago in little more than a month.

On Sept. 1, 11-year-old Robert "Yummy" Sandifer was found shot to death after he became the subject of a police search in the shooting death of a 14-year-old girl. Police said Sandifer was killed by fellow gang members worried about an intense police investigation to solve the girl's death. Two boys, ages 14 and 16, are charged in Sandifer's killing.

"Our victims are getting younger and our offenders are getting younger," said police Cmdr. Charles Smith. ***

Both of the boys arrested [in Eric's death] had criminal records. Both said their fathers are in prison. *** (*Albuquerque Journal*, 10-15-94) [A later article reports the conviction of the two boys in juvenile court, and their sentencing to a youth home where they could be held until they are 21.] (*Albuquerque Journal*, 11-29-95)

A follow up article on dropping the little boy:

2 found guilty of dangling, dropping boy to his death

CHICAGO — Eric Morse died when he was 5, dropped from a 14th-floor window because he would not steal candy for two older boys.

His 9-year-old brother lives with the memory of his failed battle to stop them.

Now, the two boys accused in the death face years behind locked doors. The two, who confessed to dropping Eric from the high-rise, on Wednesday were found delinquent in a first-degree murder.

The crime, which took place in September 1994 in a vacant Chicago Housing Authority apartment, drew national attention and outraged the city, where an 11-year-old had been slain by members of his own gang two weeks earlier.

During the two-day hearing, Derrick Lemons testified that he fought the two boys, 10 and 11 at the time, in an attempt to save his little brother. *** (*The Albuquerque Tribune*, 10-19-95)

Chama (New Mexico) boy makes a deal

A 13-year-old Chama boy has admitted to participating in a Sept. 16-17 shooting spree that left one man dead and another seriously injured. *** Jose Ulibarri said he did not fire the gun but was with 16-year-old Javier Manzanares during the shooting in Chama. Manzaneres has been charged with murder and attempted murder. ***
(*The Albuquerque Tribune*, 10-15-94)

4 charged in rape of boy

CHICAGO — Four boys under the age of 14 have been charged with raping a 10-year-old boy twice at a juvenile detention center. *** The victim told police he was attacked by one of the boys while two others pinned his arms as a crowd of youngsters watched television nearby. *** The second assault occurred in a shower room in Cook County Juvenile Detention Center, said State's Attorney Jack O'Malley. *** (*The Albuquerque Tribune*, 10-23-94)

N.Y. Gang Kills Man, Clubs Him With Tricycle

NEW YORK — Angel Lopez Almodover had just brought a new red-and-black tricycle for the 4-year-old son, Jonathan, a gift he was carrying to his Brooklyn home on Halloween night. *** Moments later, the auto mechanic on his way home from work lay dying on the street. *** A gang of nearly 20 young men in masks and painted faces pelted him with eggs and then held him as he tried to fight back by throwing a bottle. *** "Hold this guy," the ringleader told his friends, according to Officer Merri Pearsall, a police spokeswoman. *** Several of the youths surrounded and held Almodovar. The gang leader left as his cohorts restrained the terrified young father. *** The gang leader came back and shot Almodovar in the stomach, sending him sprawling on the pavement, where another bludgeoned him three times with the bike, Pearsall said. Almodovar died in the hospital that night. The suspects were at large Tuesday night. (*Albuquerque Journal*, 11-2-94)

Boy shot his cousin, then caught school bus, police say

KANSAS CITY, Kan. — Shoved during a dispute about a video game, a 14-year-old Kansas City boy pointed two pistols at a younger cousin, shot him in the face and then caught a bus to school, police said. *** The victim, 13, was in critical condition Thursday night at the University of Kansas Medical Center. A slug entered his jaw and lodged in his neck, near the spinal column. ***
(*The Albuquerque Tribune*, 12-3-94)

18-year-old arrested in rape, death of toddler

Police today arrested [Christopher Mora] an 18-year-old Albuquerque man in connection with the rape and death of his girlfriend's 23-month-old daughter. *** An autopsy ... revealed that [the child] died from a skull fracture. *** Injury's to the child's lower body confirmed that criminal sexual penetration had occurred, according to police. *** (*The Albuquerque Tribune*, 12-2-94)

Residents furious over probation for boy who killed elderly woman

CHICAGO —Residents of a neighborhood where an elderly [84-year-old] woman's throat was slit by her 11-year-old next-door neighbor are incensed that the boy was sentenced to home probation [for 5 years] instead of prison. *** Police said that the boy confessed to the killing nearly a year later, and that the only motive he gave was that he hated the woman. *** (*The Albuquerque Tribune*, 12-9-94)

13-Year-Old Carjacker Convicted of Murder

EL PASO — A 13-year-old boy who killed a man, then stole his pickup truck, has been convicted of murder and sentence to 20 years behind bars.

A juvenile court jury ruled Thursday that Miguel Angel Flores engaged in delinquent conduct when he fatally wounded Lionel "Bruno" Jordan during a Jan. 20 carjacking in a Kmart parking lot. ***

His attorney, Sam Medrano, said he will appeal the sentence because jurors might have been swayed by a marijuana cigarette they found while examining the boy's jacket during their deliberations on Wednesday. *** (*Albuquerque Journal*, 6-3-95)

Mother thinks teen was killed for gold teeth

NEW YORK — A teen-ager was shot to death [by "two men"] on a subway platform for his flashy jewelry, although his mother believes the reason was his even flashier Christmas gift—the gold-and-diamond bridgework in his mouth. *** (*The Albuquerque Tribune*, 12-29-94)

Teen arrested in death of student

Albuquerque police have arrested a teen-ager (whose name is not being released) in the shooting death of a 16-year-old Del Norte High School student. *** Police believe the shooting was gang related. *** Manuel Archuleta was shot Monday night after he confronted another teen who had fired a gun at Archleta's car .... ***
(*The Albuquerque Tribune*, 4-11-95)

Two boys, 11 and 13, arrested — 2-year-old raped, beaten

MIAMI — A 2-year-old girl was raped, beaten and nearly drowned because she urinated in her pants, and two young boys left to baby-sit her are charged with attempted murder.

The girl was listed in critical condition today, nearly a week after the attack.

The brothers, ages 11 and 13, are charged with second-degree attempted murder, the 11-year-old also faces sexual assault charges. Both are being held in a juvenile facility.

The girl was left with her godmother while her mother was away on vacation. The woman asked her sons to watch the child while she was at work on July 15.

The boys said they tried to discipline the girl by beating her and holding her head under water after she wet her pants, then the younger boy raped her, police said. (*The Albuquerque Tribune*, 7-22-95)

Two teens arrested

Albuquerque Police Department officers have arrested two teen-agers in connection with a drive-by shooting that occurred Sunday night.

The juveniles shouted out the names of an Albuquerque gang before they shot Michael Carrillo, 15, in the 1600 block of Delgado Drive in Westgate, said Tony Herrera, Police Department spokesman. Carrillo was walking to his home when the suspects fired four shots at him about 8:30 p.m., Herrera said. The suspects fired at Carrillo from a red car, Herrera said.

At least one shot hit Carrillo in the face. He is listed in serious condition at University Hospital, Herrera said.

(*The Albuquerque Tribune*, 7- 31-95)

Dead man's body shown off at party

WHITE CLOUD, Mich. — In a white mobile home in the woods, two teen-age girls had their friends over for a party that police say featured a bizarre attraction — the body of an elderly man they shot together.

"They were laughing about it," said Mike Mercer, undersheriff in rural Newaygo County. "This man was very nice to them, treated them very well, and they killed him for no good reason."

None of the partygoers contacted police until after the body was found by relatives two days later.

Devon Watts, 17, and Kelly Heemstra, 18, were charged Monday with murder in the slaying of 73-year-old Leonard Claude Hughey. They were jailed on $100,000 bond and could get life in prison if convicted.

The pair had lived with Hughey off-and-on for several months, Mercer said, and "bank books and other things around the house" indicated they may have been stealing from the retired widower.

Last Friday an argument erupted about what is not exactly clear — and investigators believe the girls killed Hughey by pulling the trigger of a .22-caliber rifle together.

On Saturday night, the girls invited more than a dozen friends over for a party, Mercer said. The pair apparently bragged about the shooting and led at least two partygoers to the backyard shed where they stowed the body.

One partygoer, 19-year-old Anthony Gilmore, told investigators he saw the corpse. (*The Albuquerque Tribune*, 8-3-95)

Police: 5 bored teens beat, burned homeless man for fun

NEW YORK — Five friends who got bored cruising a park one night stand accused of setting a homeless man on fire to amuse them-selves. They're charged with murder.

The boys and young men, who range in age form 12 to 19, beat Albert Jackson, who was sleeping on a park bench, doused him with gasoline; and lit him with a cigarette lighter, police said. Jackson's body was discovered May 9. ***

Four of the five also were charged in the near-fatal assault of another homeless man six days later. The 30-year-old man was hit over the head with cobblestones and remains hospitalized.

Early Wednesday, police arrested Lawrence Gates, 15, and Frederick Saterfield, 19, on allegations of robbing a park-goer of $4.

One of the two told detectives he intentionally set Jackson on fire and that others were involved, police said. The confession led police to Gerald Roberts, 14, Keith Haytch, 13, and Haytch's 12-year-old brother whose name was not released. *** (*The Albuquerque Tribune,* 8-4-95)

Baby dies after brother, 2, feeds her cocaine

[ALBUQUERQUE] — An 11-month-old Albuquerque girl died after her 2-year-old brother fed her crack cocaine, police say.

The infant, Caylene Gurule, was pronounced dead Tuesday afternoon at St. Joseph Hospital after suffering a heart attack in an ambulance en route to the hospital, Albuquerque police spokesman Tony Herrera said.

Police arrested the baby's mother and the mother's boyfriend, who were at home at the time.

Lynette Berry-Gurule, 20, and Robert Jaukeez Campbell, 18, have been charged with child abuse resulting in death, tampering with evidence and possession and trafficking of crack cocaine, according to City-County Jail records.

"We've had deaths where kids ingest narcotics, but nothing as bizarre as this," Albuquerque police homicide Sgt. Desi Garcia said. ***

Police searched the home and found a "very large" quantity of crack cocaine on a table in the adults' bedroom, Gurule said. *** (*The Albuquerque Tribune,* 10-4-95)

Teens Caught With Head

OGDENSBURG, N.Y. — Three teen-agers are accused of digging up a body in a graveyard, cutting off the head and carrying it around in a plastic bag.

According to statements, the three went to Potter's Field, the gravesite for the poor, to shoot and bury a dog belonging to a brother of one of the youths. After killing the dog early last Tuesday, they began to dig a hole to bury it — but decided to dig up a casket instead.

State police arrested the boys after answering an anonymous complaint of gunfire.

The three, ages 18, 17 and 15, were charged as adults with body stealing, a felony, and opening a grave, a misdemeanor. Both are public health violations, which carry no set penalties.
(*Albuquerque journal*, 10-31-95)

Old Town shootout victim, 15, dies

[ALBUQUERQUE] — A 15-year-old girl who was shot when two feuding teen-agers exchanged gunfire died this morning, authorities said.

Maria Lynnae Lucero, 15, was pronounced dead at University Hospital, where she had been taken Thursday after being shot in the head.

An 18-year-old man [Marcos Lucero] was arrested in connection with the shooting in a neighborhood across Rio Grande Boulevard near Old Town. ***

The other boy with Maria Lucero was shot in the left arm. Clifton Montoya, 14, was treated and released at Presbyterian Hospital, police said. *** (*The Albuquerque Tribune*, 11-3-95)

N.Y. Muggers Steal Man's Artificial Leg

NEW YORK — a Bronx man was in serious condition Tuesday after a group of hoodlums slashed him and stole his artificial leg.

Police said John Hammond, 45, was set upon by three teen-agers and a 20-year-old early Tuesday.

"He was slashed pretty badly on the face and body," said Officer Debra Kearns, a police spokes-woman. She said the gang had also robbed and slashed another man before they attacked Hammond.

A 911 call brought police, who arrested the four young men a short time later. They were charged with first-degree robbery and first-and second-degree assault.

Hammond was taken to the hospital, where he was listed in serious condition. His leg was not recovered. (*Albuquerque Journal*, 11-8-95)

Killer Teen May Serve 14 Years

SAN ANTONIO — A 13-year-old fascinated by the macabre was sentenced to up to 14 years in prison Friday for smothering two children in her care.

Victoria Dalton was convicted last week of killing 2-year-old Renee Gutierrez and her 5-month-old brother, Timothy, in January. The jury could have sentenced her to 40 years.

Victoria's family and that of the murdered children lived together in a two-bedroom apartment with as many as 14 other people at times. (*Albuquerque Journal*, 11-11-95)

I suppose that the lesson that could be gathered from the above is that squalor in living breeds squalor in the thinking, and in the minds of the children exposed to such conditions.

The following two news items were on the same page of the paper on the same day, and cover terrible senseless crimes, from one side of our country to the other, indicating the growing lack of conscience, and a vacuum of any traditional sense of right and wrong, in a great number of young people growing up in our country today.

Baby Sitter Admits Killing Girl

INTERCESSION CITY, Fla. — A baby sitter confessed to drowning his 4-year-old neighbor after she walked in on him as he showered.

Jeremy Lipscomb Skocz, 18, said he wanted to stop Shelby Cox's crying after she refused to leave the bathroom last Monday, and he picked her up to carry her out. He told police he had wrapped a towel around his waist before picking her up and it fell off. Fearing what other children he was also babysitting for at the time might think, he taped her mouth shut and placed her face-down in a full bathtub until she stopped moving, police said.

He was charged with murder on Saturday after he led police to a shed behind his home, where her decomposing body was found. (*Albuquerque Journal*, 11-20-95)

Boy, 8, Shot in Drive-by

COMPTON, Calif. — An 8-year-old boy was killed in a drive-by shooting as he played in a front yard during a family party, police said.

The two gunmen were aiming for three men standing on a sidewalk, but one bullet struck Victor Neal in the head as he played with some other children Saturday night, said Sheriff's Deputy Carrie Stewart.

Victor died early Sunday at a hospital.

No one else was injured in the attack in an unincorporated area near Compton. No arrests had been made Sunday. (*Albuquerque Journal*, 11-20-95)

Two teen-agers arrested in shooting of bystander

Two teen-agers were arrested on an open count of murder in the death of a 30-year-old Albuquerque woman, police officials said.

Gary Atencio, 19, and Bobby Benavidez, 17, were arrested late Sunday afternoon in the shooting death of Susie Baca, said Roni Sparks spokeswoman for the Bernalillo County Sheriff's Office. ***

Baca was shot at 2:46 a.m. Sunday during a confrontation between two rival gang members on the 1600 block of Severo Road in the South Valley, Sparks said. *** (*The Albuquerque Tribune*, 11-27-95)

Boy pleads guilty to manslaughter

OREGON CITY, Ore. — A 10-year-old boy about to go on trial on charges that he shot his little sister to death pleaded guilty Tuesday to a reduced charge of manslaughter.

Brandon Roses had been scheduled to be tried before a judge on a willful-murder charge in the death of his 5-year-old sister, Charolette.

Under the settlement, the boy will be sentenced later. Manslaughter carries a term of up to 10 years.

The shooting occurred June 23 when Brandon was baby-sitting for Charolette and his 6-year-old brother in their home in Mulino, 20 miles south of Portland.

Brandon became upset when his younger sister refused to go to her room, according to a state caseworker. ***
(*The Albuquerque Tribune*, 11-22-95)

Murder Suspect, 14, Known As Partier

[ALBUQUERQUE] — Even Jamie Sedillo's 57-year-old grandmother describes Jamie as a party girl.

"She started getting in trouble when she was 11," said Adlina S. Padilla, who's had custody of her granddaughter since the child was 4. "She'd be at the park drinking with her friends."

That was sixth grade. Jamie was in eighth grade last year. This year she's been charged with murder.

Albuquerque police arrested Jamie on Monday night at a friend's North Valley apartment. She's charged with Friday's slaying of Kenneth "Dirk" Henson, 31, who was shot in the head at Duffy's Bar and Grill on Juan Tabo NE.

Henson's friends at Duffy's say he was protective of his favorite hangout and trying to stop a robbery.

Police say Jamie ran with a rough crowd that's been connected to a yearlong string of violent robberies at stores and restaurants.

Jamie was one of four girls questioned and released in September when police busted a group of young robbers who'd rented two West Side motel rooms for a celebratory bash. The rooms were strewn with cash and guns. Ten young men were charged in about 30 robberies.

"There was gang affiliation. There was dope. There were guns, new clothes. It was party time," said Albuquerque Police Department Sgt. Ted Clingenpeel. *** (*Albuquerque Journal*, 12-13-95)

Upon conviction of first-degree murder, Jamie Sedillo was given a two year sentence to the New Mexico girl's school.
(*The Albuquerque Tribune*, 3-8-96)

Teen charged with long list of crimes in boy's death

[ALBUQUERQUE] — The family of a slain 13-year-old boy cried as the youth accused of killing him stood before juvenile court authorities today. *** Juvenile Court ... ordered Bradley Jay Sosa, 14, held at the juvenile Detention Center after being charged in the shooting death of Mario Hernandez. *** Authorities filed a petition Tuesday charging Sosa with first-degree murder; second-degree aggravated assault with a deadly weapon; unlawful possession of a handgun by a minor; shooting at or from a motor vehicle; auto theft; and eluding police, according to Juvenile Court records. ***
(*The Albuquerque Tribune,* 1-3-96)

Two charged in drive-by shooting

Two teen-agers have been charged with murder in connection with the drive-by shooting of another teen, Jose Andrade, 18, and Efrain Vasquez, 15, both of Albuquerque, were each charged Tuesday afternoon with an open count of murder in the death of John Paul Armijo, 17, of Albuquerque, according to court records

Armijo was gunned down about 3:30 p.m. Monday after being chased by youths near the Rio Grande Zoo.
(*The Albuquerque Tribune,* 1-31-96)

Teens held in killing, torching of girl

[ALBUQUERQUE] — Two teens have been arrested in connection with the death of a 17-year-old girl who was shot in her bedroom and then burned in a nearby field, police say.

Richard Joseph Muniz, 17, and Andre Lamont Williams, 16, were arrested Tuesday on open counts of murder and tampering with evidence, said Tony Herrera, Albuquerque Police Department spokesman.

Police said they were searching for Terry Lee Brown, 19, for questioning about the incident, Herrera said. Brown is an African-American male, about 5 feet 10 inches tall and 170 pounds. He has a tattoo of a black panther on one of his arms, Herrera said. ...

The body of Cassandra DeChiarra, 17, was found about 10:30 p.m. Monday in a field [behind her house]. ***

Nogales said the suspects are gang members, but "there's no indication that the killing was spurred by gang activity. ***
(*The Albuquerque Tribune*, 2-28-96)

School hires guards for unlocked restrooms

[ALBUQUERQUE] — Polk Middle School planned to unlock its student restrooms today and begin paying an adult $5 an hour to supervise them.

The South Valley school wants to prevent vandalism and keep restrooms safe for students, said Principal Rommie Compher.

"We needed tighter security," she said. ***

Restrooms that are outdoors, next to the school's main classroom wing, will now be monitored six hours a day, Compher said. They've been locked up since January, after school officials spent $8,000 repairing broken fixtures and tile and removing graffiti. ***

Polk isn't the only school trying to cope with problems in the restrooms. Harrison Middle School and Rio Grange High, also in the South Valley, will keep certain restrooms locked when students are in classes, said Rick Murray, spokesman for Albuquerque Public Schools.

All of the restrooms are unlocked during the passing periods between classes. Students who need to use a restroom at other times can get a pass from a teacher.

"The schools decided individually to do this because of the vandalism, graffiti and the smoking, both cigarettes and marijuana, in their bathrooms," Murray said. *** (*The Albuquerque Tribune*, 3-19-96)

Rio Rancho High School Locks Restrooms

[Rio Rancho is north of Albuquerque. This article explains that this new multimillion-dollar school, with 2,100 students, was opened in August, 1997. Already school officials decided to lock restrooms during part of the day because of vandalism.]
(*Albuquerque Journal*, 10-18-97)

There is no way that this school vandalism can be blamed on poverty. Rio Rancho, for example, is a new progressive community. Industry in the area must seek people from out-of-state to fill meaningful jobs of a technical nature. There is plenty of work for anyone with the capability and inclination. This school vandalism is just one more result of children being brought up in a sick society that is fast becoming completely adrift from traditional moral moorings.

Teens who cut classes linked to burglaries

[ALBUQUERQUE] — Four teen-age girls who spent their mornings where they belonged — in high school — skipped their afternoon classes to burglarize at least four homes, police said. The girls were arrested in a series of burglaries dating back to October, police said.

The teens, students at Moriarty High School, stole jewelry, stereos and at least 13 guns, said Roni Sparks, spokeswoman for the Bernalillo County Sheriff's Department.

A 15-year-old charged with 29 felony counts remained at the county's Juvenile Detention Center Wednesday.

A 16-year-old charged with 19 felony counts was released to her parents Tuesday.

Police did not release information on the two other girls.
(*The Albuquerque Tribune*, 3-21-96)

Teen-burglary case grows to 17 defendants of all ages

An investigation into several burglaries thought to be committed by teen-age girls has mushroomed into a case with at least 17 defendants, many of whom are believed to be methamphetamene users, authorities say. ***

From those arrests, "it started mushrooming," said Lt. Louis Sena, an investigator with the Torrance County [New Mexico] Sheriff's Department. "One name led to another." ***

"When we got into the older bunch, every search warrant we did we recovered narcotics," Sena said. ***

(*The Albuquerque Tribune*, 4-4-96)

Guns part of boys' lives

[ALBUQUERQUE —The father, David A. Roemer] of a 13-year-old gang member testified that his son and other neighborhood children posed with rifles, shotguns and handguns for polaroid photographs he found in a closet. ***

Roemer's account of last summer's gang activity came during a children's Court hearing Tuesday for Darren John Bowers, 16.

Bowers, a former La Cueva High student, has admitted stabbing Renee Garcia, an Eldorado High School senior, on Aug. 14, the first day of school.

Bowers said he had to commit a violent crime to get into a gang.

The stabbing occurred in Garcia's driveway. The girl was getting ready for school and went to her sister's car to get a hair tie from the trunk. As she lifted the trunk, she was stabbed in the neck. The knife pierced her spinal cord and she fell, instantly paralyzed.

Her recovery has been miraculous, doctors and therapists have testified, but they said she will not regain full use of an arm, hand and legs. *** (*The Albuquerque Tribune*, 4-17-96)

Four Boys Charged in Molesting

HAGERSTOWN, Md. — Four boys [two were 9, one 8 and one was 7] have been accused of sexually assaulting a 6-year-old girl. ***

(*Albuquerque Journal*, 4-20-96)

At 6, he's the youngest ever in U.S. to be charged
with attempted murder

RICHMOND, Calif. — In school, he couldn't keep still, tripping other children in the aisle. Many families wouldn't allow their children to play with him. Those who did often regretted it.

Now, he's the youngest child in the nation ever charged with attempted murder, a 6-year-old whose legs are too short to reach the floor from a chair in a juvenile courtroom.

The case has confounded juvenile authorities debating whether to punish or help the boy — and how.

On Friday, the boy listened impassively ... to a juvenile prosecutor's chilling account of how he beat a neighbor's month-old baby with his fists, feet and an inch-thick stick.

The attack left tiny Ignacio Bermudez Jr.'s skull fractured in two places, his brain damaged, his survival chances slim.

Prosecutors say the boy recruited two 8-year-old boys to break into the house days after he went to the Bermudez house and was thrown out.

"He entered the house with the idea of doing something," says Ignacio Bermudez Sr. "He had a large stick. I threw him out. I'd never seen him before then."

The boy apparently took deep offense. Prosecutors say he told others he planned to get back at the Bermudez family.

The boy would travel the streets with stick in hand, threatening other children, trying to knock them off bicycles, pointing it at them like a gun, she said.

"He was always getting into trouble," said neighbor Sara Kammer. He liked to sneak into neighbors' homes. He'd steal whatever wasn't tied down — sometimes even tires.

On Monday, April 22, the day of the beating, he hooked up with 8-year-old twin brothers from his elementary school, who have good grades and no history of discipline problems. "Model citizens," said their principal and teacher.

The 6-year-old told them he had a plan to steal a Big Wheel tricycle from the Bermudez home. They went along.

While the baby slept in the bassinet, the sister went to the bathroom. At that moment the three boys slipped in, apparently through an unlocked back door.

They found the Big Wheel. But the 6-year-old had another agenda as well, authorities say. He found the baby in the bassinet and went on a rampage. *** (*The Albuquerque Tribune*, 4-29-96)

Teens Kill Foiler of Arson Plot

FORT MYERS, Fla. — Four teens who plotted to burn down a high school auditorium but were caught by the band director have been charged with fatally shooting him, authorities said Saturday.

They killed Mark Schwebes at home because they feared he would turn them in, the Lee County sheriff's office said.

Charged Friday were Christopher Paul Black, 18; Derek Shields, 18; Kevin Don Foster, 18; and Peter Edward Magnotti, 17.

Black, Shields and Magnotti were enrolled at Riverdale High School. Foster was a former student.

Authorities said the four belonged to a gang called "The Lords of Chaos."

The teens went to the school Tuesday but Schwebes, 32, foiled the attempt, the sheriff's office said. Later that night, they went to Schwebes' home and shot him twice when he came out, the office said. (*Albuquerque Journal*, 5-5-96)

Nightly walk with girlfriend turns deadly

[ALBUQUERQUE] — An Albuquerque man has died of stab wounds suffered while walking his girlfriend home in a Southeast Heights neighborhood, police said.

Samuel Begaye, 41, died Tuesday evening at University Hospital ... .

A 16-year-old was charged Thursday with the death.

Begaye was stabbed just after midnight on April 5 as he and his girlfriend walked along East Central Avenue, police said.

... the couple was approached by two teen-age boys who also were walking.

One of the boys pulled out a knife about 8-inches long and stabbed Begaye ... .

On Thursday, police charged Isidro Ortiz, 16, with murder and evidence tampering, according to court records.

Police arrested Ortiz within a few hours of the stabbing after a witness identified him as the assailant. ***

Police say Ortiz was affiliated with a gang and that known gang members were with him when he was arrested at an apartment [in Albuquerque]. *** (*The Albuquerque Tribune*, 5-11-96)

Girl, 11, Charged in Tot's Death

AUSTIN, Texas — An 11-year-old girl was charged with murder Thursday in the alleged beating death of a 2-year-old at the home of a Baptist deacon.

The older girl, whose name was not released because of her age, could get up to 10 years in custody, including prison.

The victim, Jayla Belton, was one of several children being cared for during the day at the home of the Baptist deacon. The 11-year-old is the deacon's grandchild and adopted daughter.

(*Albuquerque Journal*, 5-31-96)

Belen Woman, 78, Beaten to Death

BELEN [New Mexico] — A 78-year-old woman [Premia Vance] died Tuesday after being bound and beaten by assailants who forced their way into her home as she was finishing breakfast with her daughter.

The adult daughter [Betty Jo Vance] also was bound during the robbery attempt. She told police she was put in a bathroom and could hear the intruders demanding money from her mother during the attack.

Police arrested two teen-agers [Paul Silva, 19, and Toby Gonzales, 18] later Tuesday after following a muddy trail of footprints to two mobile homes on a street about a mile and a half away from the crime scene. Belen Police Chief Lawrence Romero said the two were being hidden by friends. [Police are hunting a third suspect.]

"This was particularly brutal because the woman was so harmless," Romero said. "She was a little 78-year-old woman who presented no threat to anyone." ***

Romero said Silva and Gonzalez are known gang members and had been arrested previously on drug-related charges. Both were scheduled to be arraigned today in Belen Magistrate Court.

Romero said police found Premia Vance still bound and bleeding from the mouth.

"I knew both Mr. and Mrs. Clayton [Vance] as very respectable good people; good Christians," Romero said. ***

Betty Jo Vance said her father and mother were married for almost 60 years. She said her father, who is deceased, was a longtime railroader and her mother was a homemaker and gardener. ***

(*Albuquerque Journal*, 10-30-96)

Truckers Slain Outside Shiprock (New Mexico)

Federal authorities have charged a Navajo teen-ager in connection with the "brutal" slaying of two truckers – a man and his son – who had been hauling candy through New Mexico.

And investigators also expected to arrest and charge a second teen-ager from the Shiprock area. ***

[The victims died of gunshot wounds to their faces.]

(*Albuquerque Journal*, 12-15-96)

[A second article on the incident tells of the arrest of the second boy, a 16-year-old Navajo, and notes that the first one arrested was 14-year-old.] (*Albuquerque Journal*, 12-16-96.)

Young purse snatcher apprehended ... again

A Rio Rancho [N.M.] girl was apprehended by her intended victim at a restaurant on Southern Boulevard Tuesday after trying to steal a cellular phone and $20 out of the woman's purse.

It was the very same girl who had been caught the day before and confessed to six previous purse snatchings. *** (*The Observer*, 1-31-97)

Teacher, Students Face Animal Abuse Charges

BELLPORT, N.Y. — With their teacher in the room, students in a technical high school veterinary class here tortured animals they were supposed to care for and groom, animal-protection officials said.

Instead, officials say the Long Island students locked a dog in a cage to watch him die from starvation, slashed hamsters with razor blades, smashed two ferrets' heads together to kill them, used hamsters as hockey pucks, used mice as hacky sacks to kick around, threw a pregnant guinea pig against the wall and juggled three kittens in the air, dropping one and breaking its leg.

Sworn statements from students who watched the abuse which started as early as September, contend that the teacher looked the other way. Based on statements from students, officials charged the teacher Alan Goldman, 54, with two misdemeanor counts of animal cruelty by the Suffolk County Society for the Prevention of Cruelty to Animals. If convicted, he could face up to two years in prison and $2,000 in fines. Five students were also charged with cruelty to animals. ***

[Detective Adam Gross of the SPCA:] "...The other students were having nightmares. They were threatened with physical harm if they did something about it." (*Albuquerque Journal*, 12-24-96)

Teen 'Vampires' Held in Spree

DALLAS – Four teen-agers claiming to be vampires went on a drug-crazed rampage vandalizing dozens of cars and homes, spray painting racial slurs and burning a church, police say.

The fire early Thursday destroyed the office and fellowship hall at Bethany Lutheran Church. Its outside walls were scrawled with satanic graffiti in hot pink and white paint.

The Dallas Morning News reported that one of the suspects told detectives the teens believe they are vampires and that the teen-agers had marks on their arms from sucking each other's blood. The newspaper said the teens smoked marijuana laced with some kind of substance before the rampage. (*Albuquerque Journal*, 3-7-98)

12-Year-Old Convicted of Murder

ODESSA, Texas — A 12-year-old boy was convicted of capital murder Friday for bludgeoning a man to death with a tire iron for his Social Security check.

Juvenile Judge Jim Bobo, who closed the trial to the public, sentenced the child to 30 years' confinement. He will serve in the Texas Youth Commission until age 17, when a judge will decide whether he will move into the state prison system.

He could have sentenced the boy to 40 years in prison.

The jury took several hours to reach the verdict in the case of Ruben Benavides Hernandez, 45, who was killed at his home in June.

Authorities canvassed the neighborhood after a brother found the body. Benavides Hernandez suffered facial wounds so severe that police on the scene first thought he had been shot.

"The crime scene looked like something out of a violent horror movie." Odessa police spokesman Robert Hammerman said at the time. "The motive to the murder was simply robbery."

Several neighbors reported that the boy had been a frequent visitor to the victim's house, Hammerman said.

After Ector County juvenile authorities detained the boy on a capital murder charge, he confessed to the killing, they said.

The boy may be he youngest person convicted of capital murder in Texas history.

Ward Tisdale of the Texas Attorney General's office and D. August Boto of the Texas District and County Attorneys Association both said they know of no one younger who had been convicted of the charge. (*Albuquerque Journal*, 10-18-97)

However, the murderers are still getting younger.

Boy, 11, convicted of killing elderly woman

NORFOLK , Va. – An 11-year-old boy has been convicted of stabbing a 71-year-old woman to death while he was delivering food to the needy just before Christmas.

The boy, whose identity was withheld because of his age, was working with a subsidized food program operated by his mother. The food he delivered, including a Christmas turkey, was found Dec. 20 on the kitchen floor alongside the body of Dorothy Mae Davis.

The victim was stabbed 18 times with two large kitchen knives. The boy's fingerprint was found in blood on one of the knives, prosecutor Catherine Dodson said.

No motive was established for the killing. ***

(*The Albuquerque Tribune*, 2-27-98).

'Death Rims' Incite Violence—

Robbers Willing To Kill For Custom Car Wheels

DALLAS — Rapper Snoop Doggy Dogg immortalizes the flashy car accessories in song calling them "Danas." One young man says they attract women. A Los Angeles cop, however, calls them "death rims."

Police across the country report that people are being killed by thieves who covet their custom car wheels, the fanciest of which are plated with gold. They can cost $4,500 a set. ***

In Dallas, at least nine people have been killed for their wheels this year, police say. Even in Greenville, Texas, with a population slightly more than 23,000, authorities attribute a slaying this month to the victim's gold wheels.

Albuquerque police have said that the motive in the May carjacking that killed Patricia Tafoya, 15, was robbery of the wire wheel rims and car stereo in the car she was driving.

Tafoya, an honor student from Valley High School, was cruising Central when she was stopped by two men who ordered her out of the car. One of the men shot her in the chest. She died later at University Hospital.

Two 18-year-olds, one with a history of taking wheel rims, have been charged in her death.

Los Angeles police have estimated that 10 deaths a year are connected to carjackings involving fancy rims. ***

Police say that 467 sets of wheels have been stolen this year in Dallas, some at gunpoint. ***

In recent years, many cities have reported that youths are killed or assaulted for their fancy athletic shoes or jackets emblazoned with sports logos.

Now custom wheels have become status symbols. ***

On Tuesday, a Dallas jury sentenced Toronto Patterson to death by injection for murdering his cousin's 3-year-old daughter while stealing a set of gold-plated custom wheels. Patterson, 18, also was accused but not tried in the killing of the girl's 6-year-old sister and their mother. Each was shot once in the head.

Also on Tuesday, three men were charged with killing two men the previous day, apparently to get cash and gold-plated wheel rims, Dallas police said. *** (*Albuquerque Journal*, 11-24-95)

In the *Albuquerque Journal* of May 10, 1995, there was an apropos cartoon relating to current things in the news. It showed a woman talking to a man, who appeared to be probably a middle aged husband and wife, looking at a number of tombstones in a cemetery. The woman says, "**No wonder kids have trouble with a sense of self-worth.**" The following five epitaphs were on five of the tombstones:

KILLED FOR A SET OF WIRE WHEELS
KILLED FOR A TEAM LOGO JACKET
KILLED FOR A PAIR OF SNEAKERS
KILLED FOR A STEREO
KILLED FOR A WRONG LOOK

Teen-age crime is not limited to the United States. General immorality is increasing worldwide. And the violence is neither caused by guns, nor is it limited to guns.

The heinous murder of a 2 year old toddler by the two 10 year olds in England was related above.

In the Volga River town of Togliatti, Russia, a 12 year old boy caught trying to change his grades beat his teacher and the teacher's 7-year-old daughter to death with a hammer, a Moscow newspaper reported. (*Albuquerque Journal*, 11-3-95)

U.S. Craves More Heroin

RESTON, Va. — Columbian drug traffickers are rushing to satisfy a growing U.S. appetite for heroin, federal law enforcement officials said Tuesday.

The supply of heroin on U.S. Streets has doubled over the last decade, and about 60 percent of the heroin seized by authorities comes from South America, mainly Columbia, said Thomas Constantine, head of the Drug Enforcement Administration. Traffickers are catering to a new generation of drug abusers who think the drug is relatively harmless, Constantine said during a meeting of 250 state and local officials from the United States.

The social stigma once attached to heroin use has weakened, said Barry McCaffrey, director of White House Office of Nation Drug Control Policy.

"Heroin is back. It is more potent, and it's more deadly than ever," McCaffrey said. "A new generation of kids has come along and they simply haven't got the message." (*Albuquerque Journal*, 2-5-97)

U.S. will see teen 'blood bath,' experts say

[An Associated Press Article] ATLANTA — The U. S. murder rate, already described by some as an epidemic, will increase sharply and lead to a "blood bath" within the next decade as the number of teen-agers grows, a researcher says.

Murders by children aged 14 to 17 have increased by 165 percent since 1985, said James Alan Fox, dean of the College of Criminal Justice at Northeastern University.

That will surge even more as some 40 million young children mature into their teens, Fox said.

"Unless we act today, I truly believe we'll have a blood bath in 10 years when all these kids grow up." Fox said Friday at the national meeting of the American Association for the Advancement of Science. "I'm not optimistic."

Alfred Blumstein of Carnegie Mellon University called Fox's description "excessive," but agreed that America should brace for a spurt in the national murder rate. ***

Despite billions of dollars spent by the government on social programs, the solution to widespread violence in America is still unknown, even by the experts, Blumstein and Fox said.

Fox said the government's concentration on correcting teen-agers may be too little too late.

"We need to invest in kids at age 6 or 7," he said. "If we wait until high school, then there is little we can do to reach them."
(*The Albuquerque Tribune*, 2-18-95)

Mr. Fox and Mr. Blumstein must surely be modern liberals. They appear to be sufficiently intelligent to prepare statistics, but state that the "solution" "is still unknown." They recognize that the spending of billions of dollars by the government on social programs has not worked, and then contradictorily advocate that we "invest" more. They seem to have no comprehension that government spending programs are not the answer, and, in fact, are usually counter-productive. They seem not to understand at all that this particular problem of murder and violence by young people, is caused by the same thing that has caused, during the same period of time, an increase in teen-age pregnancies, and increase in drug use, an increase in lack of respect for law and authority, generally, a lack of respect for parental authority and parents, and most of our other problems of present day society. Liberals do not comprehend the reason for these problems, because they do not understand the importance of religious beliefs that teach that none of these things are right or acceptable, and the dire consequences of violating these religious tenets.

As the belief in religious moral principles has decreased, the problems in question have proportionately increased, and the reasons are rather simple. A child who follows the teachings of Judaic-Christian religious principles does not engage in such acts. Certainly there have been crimes and immoral acts, even during some of the most religious periods of this country, and there always will be; but as immorality increases, degradation necessarily increases. And more particularly, destructive behavior of children increases, because they are the most impressionable and susceptible to modern ideas. The modern secular humanist movements, including the homosexualists' influences, have visited a terrible destruction on our children.

Almost the entire issue of the February, 1997, *Family Voice*, a publication of Concerned Women for America, was devoted to the terrible and devastating problems with children of this country, with which we are faced today. The following reviews the two primary articles.

Kids Without a Conscience, by Rosaline Bush. pp. 4-12.
What has happened to the American Dream? Did it die in the '60s when responsibility fled the scene—scattered to the four winds by the "flower children"? Was respect for property of others obliterated by the graffiti "artists" in the subways? Who decided to transfer authority from

responsible adults to 10-year-olds brainwashed by situational ethics? When was God's gift of married sex exchanged for pornographic power plays on prime-time TV? Why has the breath of life been reduced to a "choice" in America's abortuaries—and Kevorkiian's van? When was God our Creator demoted to a "higher power"? And how have our children as gifts from God become as disposable as today's newspaper?

Our country was founded by men inspired "by God Himself." And they created a government that was intended to be "of the people, by the people, and for the people." We once had real and worthwhile heroes like George Washington, who proved himself in battle fighting for the freedom for the people of this country; and the other founders of our country, who established a government, unique in the world, that was actually designed to be controlled by and run by its citizens through representative government. And heroes like Booker T. Washington, who was born a slave and became a highly respected educator, writer, and black leader in this country, and was an advisor to two Presidents.

(And what have we now become?) "According to former Education Secretary William Bennett, we boast 'more murders, violent crime, juvenile crime, abortion, ... pornography, and the consumption of ... drugs than any other industrialized country.'"

The following is a quote from Charles Colson, founder of Prison Fellowship:

What chilled me to the bone were the eyes. Some were cold, distant, as if the life had been sucked out; others were seething with rage and anger. All were impenetrable. "Has this place changed?" I asked the assistant warden ... "Changed? Ten years ago I could talk to these kids about right and wrong," he said. "Now they don't know what I am talking about." (p. 5)

According to a three year study by the U.S. Department of Justice, more than 250,000 teens could be arrested for violence in the year 2010. Looking for explanations for soaring juvenile crime, Charles Patrick Ewing analyzed 14 juveniles on death row. He found that 13 of the 14 grew up in violent homes; 12 had been brutally, physically abused; and 5 had been sexually abused by male relatives.

Recently, the American Medical Association revealed that family violence—domestic violence, children's physical abuse and neglect, child sexual abuse, and mistreatment of the elderly—is widespread. And kids are striking back. (p. 5)

The article goes on to explain the destructive forces that have been exerted on our children and youth, and the terrible result.

The seeds of separation and rootlessness were sown in the 1950's, with promiscuity, decline in conventional morality, and permissive parenting espoused by Dr. Benjamin Spock.

The seeds of confusion, permissiveness, adultery, alcoholism, and dependence on big government, were sown in the '60s. The era of free love, drugs, protests, sit-ins, drop-outs, group sex, and acid rock. The birth control pill, and its misuse promoted promiscuity and sexual disease. Patriotism and loyalty to our country "suffered a deadly blow."

With the '80s were planted the seeds of selfishness, divorce, murder and homosexuality. Colson said, "'Feel-good' New Age spirituality permeated the culture as the 'tune-in, turn-on, drop-out' mentality of the '60s was resurrected—this time in designer drugs."

The bad seeds planted for fifty years are resulting in a "bumper crop of bitter fruit."

Living together in sin by unmarried couples, often with children in the house, has become common.

The birth of illegitimate children, and unmarried teen-age mothers, are common-place. Sexual and physical abuse of children is common.

We have a welfare system that encourages illegitimacy and poverty.

"Still, First Lady Hillary Clinton is pushing the U.N. Convention on the Rights of the Child. This 'new' concept proclaims that the government should 'protect children from the power of parents.' Yet 94 percent of registered voters in a nationwide poll by Luntz research agreed that 'parents, not government should be primarily responsible for the welfare of their children,'" Colson said.

Our young people are subjected to "feel-good" education that fails to educate them in the basic academic subjects, promotes immorality, and attacks traditional moral values and a belief in God.

GAY IS GREAT

We also have practicing homosexuals in high government offices and in the clergy. Because of the President's "don't ask; don't tell" policy, gays can remain in the military free from harassment. Currently, homosexuals are trying to infiltrate the Boy Scouts of America. At least one local troop has succumbed. San Francisco Bay Area Boy Scout officials are now forbidden to investigate a member's *or a leader's* sexual orientation. But the homosexual activists' greatest coup was in Hawaii—where, in late 1996, they were granted the right to "marry." [The court order was stayed awaiting review by the Hawaii Supreme Court.]

MONSTER MEDIA
Nowhere has the nation's love affair with homosexuality been greater than in our media—TV, Broadway, movies, and advertising. ...

... We have demonstrated that family ties mean nothing. But more significantly, we have delegated the worship of God to a few religious "fanatics." And the result? Superpredators—kids operating without a conscience.

GANGS: WHEN FAMILIES FAIL,
by Nina George Hacker, Assistant Editor.
THAT WAS THEN Time was, juvenile offenses consisted of truancy, shoplifting "drag" racing, petty vandalism, or underaged drinking and smoking. Occasionally, a fist-fighting "rumble" made the news if one gang member pulled a switchblade knife on another. But killings were rare, and drugs were virtually unknown. Jump ahead to today's generation of adolescents, whom Princeton Scholar John Dilulio, Jr. characterizes as "fatherless, godless, and jobless."

Criminologist James Alan Fox said that we are seeing an epidemic of criminal violence by juveniles, "especially the 'superpredators'—who *kill and maim on impulse*, without any intelligible motive." They "have no fear of justice and absolutely no respect for human life." said Arianna Huffington, chairman of the Center for Effective Compassion.

Between 1983 and 1993 murders committed by 14 to 17 year olds rose 165%. (That is an astounding average increase of 16.5% per year.) During the same period, juvenile arrests doubled. (The carnage by children has continued.) "In 1994, alone, the FBI says, more than 114,000 persons under 18 were charged with *rape, robbery,* and *aggravated assault.*" In 1995, 2.7 million teen-agers were arrested. This article give the following examples of the nature of some of these crimes by children:

- A gang savagely beat, then repeatedly stabbed and raped a jogger in New York's Central Park—leaving her for dead. Later, one of the attackers told prosecutors, "It was fun."
- A 14-year-old gang member was arrested on charges of dousing two 11-year-olds with alcohol and setting them on fire.
- Five boys, aged 13 to 14, brutally tortured another 13-year-old boy for hours in the west coast home of one of the attackers.
- In Virginia, a 13-year-old boy was charged with three counts of extortion and one count of robbery after threatening schoolmates.
- A 16-year-old Washington, D.C. area girl was sentenced to life in prison for the gang-ordered killing of a 14-year-old classmate— she was stabbed more than 40 times.

Children in gangs are regularly engaging in damaging and stealing property of others, robbery, extortion, drug dealing, and various other violent crimes.

Gang members, girls or boys "will kill over trivial matters—a jacket, some sneakers, a dirty look," says James Fox. "For them, murder is just not the taboo it once was," Yancey Griggs, director of Juvenile Hall in Detroit, laments: "Twenty years ago a youngster would shy away from a killer . . . Today kids flock around [him]. He's a big shot, a hero, and he shows no remorse, no sense of wrong."

The plight of our youth is blamed on every conceivable thing, including movies and television.

However, movies, television, video, pornographic publications, and depictions of gratuitous violence, merely reflect what people want. They mirror the decadence and moral decay of our society. The producers are guided by and are slaves to the box-office and the ratings. They give the people what they most desire. If they could not sell their sleazy sorry products, they would be forced to turn to the production of decent material. Our society has become rotten to its very core. Our children only reflect what they have been taught, and the examples set for them, by their parents, in their schools, by the media, and even in many of our modern churches. We have failed them in every important area. They are the unfortunate victims of a sick immoral society.

Another aspect of our country's decay is explained by Suzanne Fields, in **Memoir on Incest Shows Cultural Rot of U.S. Elite,** *Albuquerque Journal,* 2-27-97.

The following reviews that article.

Ms. Fields defines the "cultural rot" of which she writes as about "decay throughout the contemporary culture, high and low, determined by what's deemed significant by the elite, the sophisticated, the trendsetter, the intellectual pacemakers who give their imprimatur and status to the latest sensation."

Older novels such as "Catcher in the Rye" are not sufficiently vulgar as to "hardly raise an eyebrow" now, she says.

"It's difficult for fiction to do that anymore. In fact, the novel is out, the memoir is in. We want the down-and-dirty, not transcendent imagination. No one knows this better than Kathryn Harrison and her publisher, Random House."

Ms. Harrison published three novels, two of which were about incestuous relationships, but they were not particularly successful, from a money standpoint.

Finally Ms. Harrison has real success and acceptance by the media and the elitist element of the public, because of her memoir, "The Kiss," to be published by one of the world's largest publishers, Random House. It is about her willingly entering into a sexual relationship with her father, and becoming his mistress when she was twenty. "She tells how she moved in with him and a later wife and their children to continue their affair."

Now the author has gained acceptance and applause. "Intellectual advance men and women describe the therapeutic value of this memoir for the author."

"Vanity Fair calls the author and her husband Colin, an editor at Harpers, a 'glam couple.' Ms. Harrison has become a literary glitter, if not a luminary, as head fiction judge for the National Book Awards this year. Her husband will do a spin-off of his wife's memoir for Vogue:

What it's like to be married to your father's-in-law incestuous daughter, or, 'I could have been cuckolded by my wife's father if only I met her before he did.' "

The Sunday New York Times Book Review has assigned Ms. Harrison to review Mia Farrow's memoir about her life with Woody Allen. "How clever. Woody, for those who have been enjoying the snooze of Rip Van Winkle, is enjoying an affair with Soon-Yi Previn, an adopted daughter of Mia Farrow, Woody's former 'significant other.' The affair began in 1992 when Soon-Yi was 21 and the catalyst for Mia's memoir."

Mia relates finding photos of a naked Soon-Yi, exposed in a sexually vulgar way, on the mantle in Allen's apartment. Ms. Harrison considers Mia's appraisal of Woody Allen "too consistently 'cold, disturbed and monstrously selfish.'"

Ms. Harrison apparently finds nothing wrong with her sexual relations with her father, or with such actions of Woody Allen.

Our country has become an unbelievable producer of perverted filth, and not all of it is produced or purchased by homosexuals. Theirs is only a part of the evil manure in which this country is now wallowing. The way was paved by erroneous decisions of the United States Supreme Court, which misinterpreted constitutional law preserving free speech and freedom of the press, and turned the law into something that could not have been imagined by our forefathers who wrote and enacted those provisions. Although Presidents Reagan and Bush fought vigorously against the rise in pornography, they could not stem the tide. With our decline in morality came an intense demand for filth, and, with the help of the United States Supreme Court, our country is now engulfed in it.

The following reviews the article, **The Business of Porn**, *U.S. News & World Report*, 2-10-97.

Pornographic publications, music, videos, and movies have become so commonplace that we tend to forget how strictly is was prohibited not long ago. (p. 44) (Prior to United States Supreme Court opinions encouraging it as referred to above.) "The Sociologist Charles Winrick has noted that the sexual content of American culture changed more in two decades than it had in the previous two centuries. Twenty-five years ago, a federal study of pornography estimated that the total retail value of all the hard-core porn in the United States was no more than $10 million, and perhaps less than $5 million." (p. 44)

Attorney General Edwin Meese (under President Ronald Reagan) issued a report that sexually explicit materials were harmful and calling for enforcement of federal obscenity laws. (p. 43)

"The report prompted President Ronald Reagan to launch one of the most far-reaching assaults on porn in the nation's history, a campaign that was continued under President George Bush. Hundreds of producers, distributors, and retailers in the sex industry were indicted and convicted. Many were driven from the business and imprisoned.

"The Reagan-Bush war on pornography coincided, however, with a dramatic increase in America's consumption of sexually explicit materials." ... (p. 43) (It grew at an unprecedented rate under President Clinton, whose administration has done many things to promote pornography which accompanies the general rise of immorality. This article does not describe the pernicious obstructions raised to prohibit the enforcement of laws against obscene pornography, particularly by activist judges, and the length of the article would not permit any comprehensive explanation. Neither will the length of this book be extended to such coverage of that complicated problem, as that subject would, in itself, require a book.)

(The increase in the consumption of pornography also coincided with the homosexual movement, and its acceptance; and the increase in destructive misbehavior of all kinds, the use of drugs, and murder and violence committed by the nation's children.)

The consumption of pornography in this country has risen from the "perhaps less than $5 million, of the estimate twenty-five years ago, at an alarming rate. "According to *Adult Video*, an industry trade publication, the number of hard-core video rentals rose from 75 million in 1985 to 490 million in 1992. The total climbed to 665 million, an all-time high, in 1996. Last year Americans spent more than $8 billion on hard-core videos, peep shows, live sex acts, adult cable programming, sexual devices, computer porn, and sex magazines—an amount much larger than Hollywood's domestic box office receipts and larger than all the revenues generated by rock and country music recordings. Americans now spend more money at strip clubs than at Broadway, off-Broadway, regional, and nonprofit theaters; at the opera, the ballet, and jazz and classical music performances—combined. (p. 44)

"At a factory in Panorama City, near the foothills of the San Gabriel Mountains, shelves are lined with genitalia of famous porn stars. The casts are used to make sexual devices, lifelike reproductions packaged with celebrity endorsements." (p. 45)

"There are gay videos and straight videos; bondage videos and spanking videos; tickling videos, interracial videos, and videos like *Count Footula*, for people whose fetish is feet. There are 'she-male' videos featuring transsexuals and 'cat fighting' videos in which naked women wrestle one another or join forces to beat up naked men. There are hard-core videos for senior citizens, for sadomasochists, for people fond of verbal abuse. The sexual fantasies being sold in this country are far too numerous to list. America's sex industry today offers a textbook example of how a free market can efficiently gear production to meet the consumer demand." (p. 46)

"Men are by far the largest consumers of porn. ... Some American women, however, are consuming a good deal of hard-core material. During the late 1980's, a survey by *Redbook* magazine, famous for its recipes and household tips, found that almost half of its readers regularly watched pornographic movies in the privacy of their homes. And a recent survey by the *Advocate*, a leading gay magazine, found that 54% of its lesbian readers had watched an X-rated video in the previous 12 months." (p. 46)

"Sexually transmitted diseases are one of the industry's occupational hazards. Performers are now required to undergo monthly HIV testing, and their test results serve as a passport for work. A number of producers insist upon the use of condoms during especially high-risk activity; the majority of producers don't. A leading actor with AIDS could in a matter of days spread the virus to many other performers. ..." (p. 47)

(This article presents a gruesome picture of what our American culture has now become.)

What have we reaped from our decline in morality? The destruction is related throughout this book.

A small part of it is the spread of AIDS and other sexually transmitted diseases.

The following are facts about the spread of herpes, for which there is no known cure, gleaned from an article by Joan Beck, **AIDS Isn't the Only Risk Inherent in Sexual Promiscuity**, *Albuquerque Journal*, 10-23-97:

Herpes has increased 30 percent since the end of the 1970's, according to a new report from the Centers for Disease Control and Prevention.

During our period of "sex education" of our young, herpes has quadrupled among white teen-agers, and doubled among whites in their twenties. (Curiously, no figures were given for non-whites, as to these particular increases.) "Forty-five million Americans are now infected with this nasty, chronic, recurring disease—21.9 percent of everybody older than age 12."

"25.6 percent of women and 17.8 percent of men have herpes (17.6 percent of whites and 45.9 percent of blacks.)."

Sexually transmitted diseases, other than AIDS, can also be fatal to newborn babies of infected mothers.

"The herpes epidemic spreading out of control doesn't carry the deadly perils of AIDS. But the uncomfortable, painful, itching infection should be a reminder that millions of people are paying a price for this country's changing attitudes toward extra-marital sex."

There are other very detrimental effects on our culture.

"Premature sexual intimacy distorts what should be a careful getting-to-know-you stage of love that is essential for sound marriage. Sex based on love and commitment can be the mortar that holds a couple together. But when half of American marriages end in divorce sooner or later, young people should be helped to understand this mortar should not be diluted with casual encounters."

The greatest havoc of our moral decline is visited on the children of this country. They follow the examples of their parents, and the destructive teachings to which they are exposed in their schools and in the media. They have not been taught basic religious morality that could help them overcome these destructive influences to which they have been subjected.

The basic problem is aptly described by the title of another article by Suzanne Fields, **"Children have no moral compass,"** *Conservative Chronicle*, 6-28-93. The following are excerpts from that article.

> ... We've got a big problem in the United States: Young men in groups. Increasing numbers of boys at ever younger ages are sexually aggressive, violent, vicious.
>
> Jennifer Ertman, 14, and Elizabeth Pena, 16, of Houston were raped repeatedly and then strangled with a belt and shoe laces. The suspects, six Houston teenagers ranging in age from 14 to 18 years old stomped on the necks of the girls to make sure they were dead.
>
> THE ATROCITIES committed by young men under 18 is epidemic, an increase of 85 percent in five years, according to the FBI. All kinds of crimes are on the increase by teen-age rat-packs. Research suggests that 85 percent of juvenile crime takes place in groups.
>
> Two 14-year-old girls in Montclair, N.J., say they've been gang-raped three times by boys, some of whom were in the seventh grade. Programs for sex offenders include hundreds of children under the age of 10, and in one study of 1,600 children who sexually abused other children, one in every four said they began their abuse before they were 12 years old.
>
> "We're seeing earlier onset of behavior that used to be reserved for late adolescence, then it was early adolescence and now it's late childhood." says Michael D. Resnick, and associate professor of public health and pediatrics at the University of Minnesota who has surveyed 36,000 teen-agers for a study on adolescent violence.

And, as we have seen from information presented in other parts of this book, this phenomena is not limited to boys. Perhaps the increase is at an even greater rate among girls.

The immoral destructive forces that have been unleashed on the children of this country are unforgivable. All of us—even those who have no children—share a part of the blame. We have failed to do what was necessary to stem the tide of evil influences that has engulfed them while we watched in disbelief of what should have been clear to us. It is no wonder that a person of the caliber of Judge Robert Bork has doubts as to whether or not we can now extract ourselves from the mire we have created, and which is now sucking us into its darkest depths. The potential harm to society is exponential. As the children grow up without religion and sound moral guidance, they too have children—many of them illegitimate. What do you think that their children will be like? What have we done to our society?

EMBRACING SODOMY

The embracing and promotion of sodomy during the last forty years has been one of the most sad chapters in the history of America. It has been brought about primarily by news and entertainment media, entertainers and actors, liberal educators, and liberal politicians. It has taken place in our courts. Even many of our churches are at fault. Many of the relevant things along this line are also covered in other chapters of this book.

Acceptance has even grown for such things as homosexual "marriages", and support has been found in the courts of liberal activist judges, as well as from liberal politicians.

Laws have been passed giving "sexual orientation" a special protection under civil rights laws, at state and local levels. Such laws are presently being pushed by liberal politicians at the federal level.

The insidious intrusion by these "sexual orientation" laws on the rights of ordinary citizens to take into consideration the moral character of people with whom they deal, hire, associate with, or have on their premises, or to conduct their life and business according to traditional moral and religious principles, is dealt with at length in Chapter 8. This was a right recognized from the birth of this country until the liberal politicians began taking it away from us during the past several years. Prior to the Clinton administration, good moral character was required for a position as an F.B.I. agent, a special agent or revenue agent of the U.S. Treasury department or Internal Revenue Service, and many other government positions. Homosexuals were not allowed in those positions. They were not allowed in the military. Good moral character was even required for becoming an attorney, but this has become somewhat of a joke in the last several years.

Many of our large corporations, schools, and local governments now give homosexual "partners" the same medical and other fringe benefits that had previously been reserved to lawfully married husbands and wives and their families.

Homosexuals who have acquired AIDS and other sexually transmitted diseases through knowingly engaging in vile acts of sodomy are given tremendously expensive medical care, while many decent deserving poor people cannot afford and do not get adequate medical care.

People get hero treatment by the media and entertainers merely because they are homosexuals dying of AIDS. The same is true of many of them after they die of AIDS. There are continually big articles with photos in newspapers playing up the lives of homosexuals and promoting homosexuality, and even giving favorable portrayals of those who contracted AIDS by their vile and promiscuous acts. This is one more attribute of a sick society—one that can no longer discern what is admirable from what is profane and reprehensible.

The following is a review of the article, **Why Do Media Lionize Louganis, a Self-Made Victim?**, by Reed Irvine and Joseph Goulden of Accuracy in Media, *Lambda Report,* April-June 1995. I share their sentiments.

(The article is about the Olympic diving champion and gold medalist, Greg Louganis, who had justly acquired acclaim for those accomplishments, but whose new rounds of fame and applause are based only upon his acquisition of the HIV (AIDS) virus through his own promiscuous and repulsive homosexual acts. There is no way that this man could not have known of the extreme danger of his acts.)

*** He has been omnipresent, beginning with a clucking Barbara Walters on ABC's "20/20," and continuing through Oprah Winfrey, morning shows, CNN and unaccountable other places.

Now what's our gripe? It's this. Louganis is a grown man, 35 years of age, and apparently intelligent. He has been around long enough to read and hear the warnings about unsafe sex. Nevertheless, he faces death because of his admitted unsafe misconduct.

For these reasons, we have trouble fathoming why this man is treated as a sympathy figure, even a hero, by the media. The message being given to other homosexual men is that AIDS might be deadly — but it is also a badge of honor. Our media are lionizing a man who is dying from a sexually transmitted disease—and remember, not long ago, a person with syphilis or gonorrhea was treated as a pariah, not an icon.

A CNN interviewer praised Louganis for his "courage" in speaking publicly of his condition. In this instance, courage equates with commercialism. Louganis went public to promote a book that rocketed to the *New York Times* best-seller list in less than a month's time, with sales so brisk that stores could not keep it in stock. Louganis came through Washington as a part of his 10-city publicity tour, and sure enough, he showed up at the White House to receive a warm welcome from President Clinton.

At the same time they glorify Louganis, the media are giving short shrift to a more important story: the responsibility of homosexuals for the AIDS epidemic. In February, the *New York Times* ran an opinion section article by gay activist Michelangelo Singnorile, who has made a journalistic career of "outing" homosexuals, regardless of whether or not they want their sexual preference revealed to the public, their friends or families. The shocker in Signorile's article was his admission that he regularly engages in unsafe sex, even though he does not know whether or not he is infected with the HIV virus. His attitude is that he gets so carried away that he ignores the precautions that have been urged on the homosexual community for almost a decade. He is not alone. Signorile cites a recent study from the Center for Disease Control that two-thirds of the homosexual men surveyed had had unsafe sex in the last 18 months. ***

One chore we perform at Accuracy in the Media is monitoring such homosexual newspapers as the *Blade*, a tabloid weekly published in Washington. A recent full page ad invited men to nude dances. A tag line said, "Please don't attend if you're easily shocked."

Must our limited quotient of sympathy be squandered on persons who do the sexual equivalent of running across an eight lane freeway during rush hour?

Louganis admitted contracting AIDS by his homosexual behavior. He also admitted to being a heavy drug user as an adolescent. When diving in the Olympics, he hit his head on the diving board, bled in the water to be used by others, and failed to tell the officials or let the other divers know he was infected with the AIDS virus, although he was aware of it. He publicly and apparently proudly continues and publicly flaunts his homosexuality. (*Newsweek*, 3-6-95) He did not even tell the doctor who stitched his bleeding head without gloves that he was infected with the AIDS virus. (*Albuquerque Journal,* 2-23-95) Our national media indeed pick some strange "heroes" upon which to bestow their admiration.

The media, including The Wall Street Journal, do not need a national figure such as Louganis to make into a hero. It seems that any personable homosexual with AIDS will do. Consider the following information from an article, **The Last Chapter of 'Pedro's Story' Is Drawing to a Close**, by Eric Morgenthaler, *The Wall Street Journal*, 10-21-94:

> MIAMI – It was late afternoon. Pedro Zamora is lying on his side in bed, his head cradled in his arm, when the call comes through. His sister brings him a telephone and, when he doesn't take it, holds it to his ear. "Hello," a familiar voice says. "Hello? Pedro? " Pedro, who is 22 years old, is so sick with an AIDS-related illness that he barely can speak, but he manages a weak, "hello."
> "Hello, Pedro," the caller responds, "Its President Clinton. I'm just calling to tell you I'm thinking about you and praying for you."
> Pedro Zamora was 19 years old in 1991 when The Wall Street Journal published a front page article about him, headlined "Pedro's Story." Now, Pedro's story is drawing to a close, and its final chapters have completeness. ***

When Pedro was 3, his mother died, sending him into an emotional nose dive. He turned to promiscuous sex and, at 17, was found to be infected with the AIDS virus. As a way of coping, he began speaking to groups of young people about AIDS and – with his good looks, easy manner and engaging style – was soon in great demand as a speaker to Miami-area schools. ***

After his story appeared, Pedro went on to become one of the nation's leading AIDS educators. His story was told on NBC's "Today" program and National Public Radio, on the Spanish language networks and even on Japanese television. He testified before the Presidential Commission on AIDS, was appointed to the Florida Governor's public-service ad campaign on AIDS prevention. ***

"I love Pedro," says Donna Shalala, secretary of Health and Human Services. "He is more than an AIDS educator. He has an ability to personalize this brutal illness. And he has reached everybody, across generations." ***

In recent months, Pedro became a TV star— after being chosen to appear in the seven-person cast of "The Real World," one of the most-popular shows on MTV, the top cable network. For several months this year, Pedro lived with the other cast members in a San Francisco house while camera crews taped their goings-on for up to 24 hours a day. The footage was edited into a weekly real-life soap opera, of sorts, that began its current season in June and continues into next month. Pedro's health, homosexuality and AIDS work—became plot strands. POZ, a new magazine for HIV positive people, put Pedro on its cover, with the caption, "MTV's HIV Heartthrob." [Emphasis Added) ***

News of Pedro's illness—because of his MTV renown—has been carried in everything from the Boston Globe to the News Tribune of Tacoma, Wash. He is a topic on several computer networks, including America Online and the Internet, which have "Real World" bulletin boards. And cards and letters are pouring in, more than a thousand a day. ***

The article does not indicate that Pedro ever voiced repentance for the reprehensible life from which he acquired his AIDS. On the contrary, it showed that he continued his homosexual activity after he contracted AIDS. In other parts of this book we have covered details on AIDS "education" conducted by homosexuals. It amounts, to a large degree, to a promotion of the homosexual lifestyle to our impressionable young people.

And I have no reason to believe that Pedro's was different. The news and entertainment media are intensively promoting depraved and destructive behavior. Our media exhibit no morality at all in this area, and in few others, and are at the lowest level of morality in the history of America.

It appears that no one loves the homosexuals and their agenda any more that our current president, William Jefferson Clinton.

Clinton Saturates Bureaucracy With Pro-Gay Edicts

New evidence has emerged demonstrating that the Clinton Administration continues to take powerful governmental action to bring about the legitimization of the militant homosexual agenda. The Clintons have steadily pursued this course since they came to town last January, most notably in their effort to lift the ban against homosexuals in the armed forces. ***

On November 23, the Office of Personnel Management issued formal recognition to a homosexual employees group within the federal government, saying that any future questions about homosexuality in background checks of applicants or employees would be prohibited.

Simultaneously the White House announced that it had revised its "Equal Employment Opportunity Statement" and bestowed protected class status on homosexuals.

These policy changes take place against a backdrop of homosexuals frequently being appointed to important executive branch positions, such as the tapping of radical lesbian activist Roberta Achtenberg to become assistant secretary for fair housing and equal opportunity at the Department of Housing and Urban Development. *** (*Human Events*, 12-18-93, p. 1)

Before the end of 1994. according to the *Register of Opinion*, Winter, 1994, a publication of the Public Advocate, President Clinton had appointed thirty self-proclaimed homosexuals to high federal positions. Such appointments are unprecedented in the history of America.

The Clinton Administration has given the green light to the general debauching of American culture.

Gays Not Denied Clearance

WASHINGTON — Federal agencies appear to have stopped using homosexuality as a basis for denying security clearances, a congressional report says.

The agencies for years denied clearance to homosexuals on the assumption that gay people are at risk of being blackmailed.

In a report released Friday, the General Accounting Office said it reviewed records from eight agencies: the departments of Defense, Energy and State; the Office of Personnel Management; the U.S. Information Agency; the Federal Bureau of Investigation; the Secret Service; and U.S. Customs.

All eight told the GAO that homosexuality is not a criterion in granting security clearances. (*Albuquerque Journal*, 3-25-95)

With a MEMORANDUM from Martin Mawyer, president of Christian Action Network, dated March 13, 1995, was a picture of twenty-six men and women, with their names in the caption, which the memo said was published in the homosexual magazine OUT, of the prior month. The title of the photo was **1995 and Counting**. These were represented to be homosexuals appointed to official positions in the Clinton Administration up to that time. Another disturbing bit of news in the memo was, "Roberta Achtenberg (a lesbian homosexual), the undersecretary of HUD, has issued a policy that allows homosexuals to get <u>preferred</u> promotions. She calls this 'cultural diversity.'"

Child Pornographers Starting National 24 hour TV Network

President Clinton's Attorney General Janet Reno has quietly reversed the prosecution of known child pornographers and even dropped long-term pursuits of major pornographers accused of corrupting children as young as eight years old.

As a result, sexual material distributor Adam and Eve, whose parent company PHE was charged with eleven counts of violating federal child obscenity laws by delivering unsolicited obscene catalogs to children and adults in Utah, has announced a 24 hour a day X-rated television network for airing in 50 states. Public Advocate has dubbed it the "Child Pornography Network" because it will sell many of the materials promoted as "toys" in obscene homosexual, bisexual, and "straight" publications distributed throughout the U.S. Now it will be sold on television 24 hours a day—where children can see it. ***

The owner of the Child Pornography Network was investigated for four years by the federal obscenity prosecutors and last week, under the Clinton administrations lenient non-enforcement of the federal obscenity laws pleaded guilty in Alabama to one count of violating postal regulations, and agreed to pay a fine.

The 11 counts filed against PHE, Inc. in Utah were dropped by the Justice Department "Adam & Eve" promotes sodomy and homosexual acts through videos and books and sick "products". (*Register of Opinion*, Winter, 1994)

Reno Intervenes in Anti-Gay Case

WASHINTON—Attorney General Janet Reno ordered Justice Department mediators into their first case of anti-gay harassment and threats – where residents were trying to close a feminist camp run by two lesbians. *** (*Albuquerque Journal*, 2-19-94)

Persecuted gays can seek asylum

WASHINGTON—Attorney General Janet Reno has issued an order that would allow homosexuals from other countries to seek political asylum in the United States if they can prove that they were victims of government persecution solely because of their sexual preference. *** (*The Albuquerque Tribune*, 6-17-94)

Immigrant given U. S. asylum for sex orientation dies of AIDS

SAN FRANCISCO — The first person granted asylum by a U.S. immigration officer because of sexual orientation has died of AIDS.

The case of Ariel Da Silva prompted Attorney General Janet Reno to declare that persecution based on sexual orientation is grounds for political asylum, a principle now binding in all immigration cases. Da Silva said he was afraid he would be persecuted in his native Mexico because he was a homosexual.

Da Silva, 36, died last week in a Los Angeles hospital, five months after the favorable ruling by an immigration hearings officer, attorney Marc Van Der Hout said Monday.

Da Silva, who entered the United States in the 1980s, was diagnosed with the AIDS virus in November 1991, Van Der Hout said.

He had been working in health education.
(*The Albuquerque Tribune*, 8-3-94)

How many people do you think that Da Silva, directly and indirectly, may have given AIDS? And who do think pays for all of this expense brought about by the catering to homosexuals and the resulting spread in AIDS and other STDs?

This is but another example of liberals and Democrat politicians promulgating regulations and passing laws to get the votes and the backing of special interest groups, to the detriment of the country. Democrats have long been past masters of high taxation, and then using the money taken away from the productive members of society to spend on special-interest groups to buy their votes. Not only do they use our money to buy votes, but they pass outrageous laws and regulations to get the backing of special-interest groups—without regard to how outrageous and damaging to the country the things are that they do. They pass laws for and spend money on every group that they think may furnish them substantial votes or money, including but not limited to homosexuals, labor unions, senior citizens, farmers, working mothers, teachers, welfare recipients, minorities, and the disabled. They have little regard for the harm done to the productive citizens from whom the money is taken, and who bear the unreasonable burden of such laws as the Americans With Disabilities Act (ADA). What they are interested in is elections. Many of the programs such as welfare for able-bodied people, without work requirements, and "affirmative action" for minorities—particularly blacks—have done the people who were supposed to be helped more harm than good. Such things have caused families to be dependent on welfare, generation after generation; and people to lose respect for the true ability of black people and to resent the positions they have acquired by affirmative action. They take away from—and often destroy—an individual's pride and ambition. It also cannot be said that Republicans are entirely innocent of such charges. They have engaged in pork-barrel projects and they have also shown timidity in opposing Democrat actions that they knew were harmful to the country, but currently popular with powerful groups. But there is no question that the Democrats have been the tax and spend party, and have done great harm to the country by running up huge deficits with money they were using to buy votes. Who needs campaign financing when you are that adept at buying votes with money bled from the taxpayers? I was a Democrat for most of my life, but these are the things that finally drove me out of the party.

But the liberal Democrats finally hit the bottom of the pit with their complete embracing of the vile and destructive acts of sodomy by their complete capitulation to and their participation in the homosexual agenda.

Forty years ago, before the morality of this country degenerated to where many, including our present federal administration, even embraced acts as abominable and loathsome as homosexuality, such acts were a felony all over this country, and still are in many of the states. I suppose homosexuals from any country which makes sodomy unlawful could seek asylum, including citizens of Britain.

Elders' support of gay adoptions upsets cardinal

WASHINGTON—The Roman Catholic archbishop [Cardinal James Hickey] of the nation's capital is not happy with recent remarks of Surgeon General Joycelyn Elders advocating acceptance of homosexuality. ***

In this month's issue of The Advocate, Elders endorsed gay and lesbian adoptions and denounced certain sexual attitudes of conservative religious groups.

Sex is "a normal part and healthy part of our being, whether it is homosexual or heterosexual," she told the gay-oriented magazine.

"I think the religious right at times thinks that the only reason for sex is procreation. Well, I feel that God meant sex for more than procreation. Sex is about pleasure as well as about responsibility." *** (*The Albuquerque Tribune*, 3-24-94)

It was also widely reported in the news that Surgeon General Elders advocated the legalization of drugs, sex education and passing out condoms to school children. This country has never had an administration that was so morally corrupt. But the part that discloses a general lack of morality among the people are the polls that show that they care little about these things—the polls continue to show a high approval rating of President Clinton, and the people elected him twice knowing of his immoral stands and immoral behavior. It appears that about the only thing that matters to the majority of the voters now is what the government is likely to do for them in the form of welfare benefits, medical benefits, farm subsidies, benefits for the elderly; and the passing of laws for special-interest groups, such as homosexuals, labor unions, senior citizens, and blacks who have voted solidly for the Democrats and for Clinton and Gore.

ELLEN IN A HANDBASKET

When former Vice President Dan Quayle addressed TV industry elites, he chastised the way they glorified singe parenting in *Murphy Brown*. When Vice President Al Gore addressed the TV honchos in Hollywood in October, he praised the way they forced Americans to "look at sexual orientation in a more open light" in *Ellen*.

Mr. Qualye was pilloried in the media for criticizing TV, though after the election pundits admitted he was right. Mr. Gore ... placed himself solidly in the good graces of homosexual activists and the Hollywood elite, both of whom are big spenders on presidential campaigns. (*WORLD*, 11-1-97)

Vice-president and Mrs. Al Gore have continually supported the homosexual agenda.

The following are excerpts from an article showing the repulsive acts of homosexuals at a party in San Francisco. It was attended by Mayor Willie Brown and his campaign manager, Jack Davis. Brown had to leave and missed part of the party. When it came to light and the Mayor refused to apologize, it nearly killed a bond issue they were supporting.

The limits of tolerance

*** ... prominent liberal political consultant and San Francisco power broker Jack Davis, held an X-rated party attended by Mayor Willie Brown, various elected city supervisors, and many other civic leaders supportive of the proposition.

The party, which featured acts of profound sexual perversion, was a 50th birthday celebration for Mr. Davis, and was organized by some of his friends. There were both male and female strippers dancing at the party, as well as live and simulated sex acts openly performed on a stage throughout the night.

The bacchanalia concluded with a "dominatrix" beating a man in front of the crowd, urinating on him in full view of the audience, and carving a satanic symbol – a pentagram – into the man's bare back with a knife. Finally, the man was publicly sodomized with a whiskey bottle. According to reports, some in attendance walked out in disgust, but many did not.

One of those who left in shock was Barbara Kaufman, president of the San Francisco Board of Supervisors, who was seen leaving during the mutilation part of the man, moaning, "Gross ... gross." ... San Francisco Sheriff Michael Hennessey was among them. He said, "It was like walking into a Mapplethorpe exhibit. It was so disgusting, I thought it was funded by the NEA [National Endowment for the Arts]." *** (*World*, June 14/21, 1997)

The above article merely shows common examples of the homosexuality so praised and promoted by our liberal media.

Gores host 150 homosexual leaders
ASSOCIATED PRESS

Vice President Al Gore and his wife, Tipper, reached out to the homosexual community and entertained 150 of its political activists at a party in their home. ***

"It's a wonderful thing to do what you're doing, and that's devoting your lives to others," Mr. Gore told the guests. "This dedication is an outgrowth of the way you live your entire lives."

"We very deeply share your vision of a society that is fair and free of discrimination for gay and lesbian people, and we want you to know that," Mrs. Gore said.

The vice president took note of what he called "a tremendous victory" Thursday when the House Appropriations Committee voted to restore $36 million that it previously had decided to cut from AIDS programs this year. *** (Information from Dr. Jerry Falwell, Liberty Alliance, Feb. 1996)

We should at this time reconsider the sick and repulsive acts in which homosexuals engage, and by which they get their classification, which were described in detail in Chapter 1. This is the ugly part of their life which they wish to foist upon decent people as natural, good, and acceptable. This is necessarily a part of the life of homosexuals that is being accepted and highly praised by Al and Tipper Gore. And they would like Al Gore to be our next president!

In 1993, the United Nations Gives Official Consultant Status to International Gay and Lesbian Association (ILGA) Which Includes as a member the North American Man/Boy Love Association

ILGA was given official consultative status to the Economic and Social Council of the United Nations. The U.S. delegation voted for the admission. After the matter was aired on the "Larry King Live" show on CNN, homosexual politicians called for NAMBLA to be expelled from ILGA. Congressional sources were demanding that ILGA remove NAMBLA as a condition for not switching its vote. (*CFV Report*, Jan. 1994)

Yet support for NAMBLA persists in the rest of the homosexual "community." Peri Jude Radecie, executive director of the National Gay and Lesbian Task Force called the action " ... a homophobic move on the part of the U.S. Government."

Meanwhile, ILGA representatives have been laboring to downplay any notion that NAMBLA has had meaningful influence in their organization — despite the fact that some of ILGA's past resolutions bear the clear mark of NAMBLA. One such resolution in 1990 is titled "Man/Boy, Woman/Girl love" — copying NAMBLA's terminology exactly.

It's important to remember that regardless of whether NAMBLA remains a member, we are still seeing an activist homosexual organization being recognized by the United Nations. A purging of pedophile associations hardly makes ILGA an acceptable member of the world community. (*CFV Report*, Jan. 1994)

Fortunately for this country and the world we have people with the moral convictions and courage of Senator Jesse Helms. There no longer are many statesmen of his character and quality. He fights for what he believes in. Look at his reaction to the UN's support of pedophiles:

Senate Punishes U.N. $119 Million for Pedophile Ties

WASHINGTON, D.C. — The United States Senate dealt a blow to the International Lesbian and Gay Association (ILGA) January 26 by voting 99-0 to deny $119 million in U.S. contributions to the United Nations until it breaks ties with all groups that promote pedophilia. ***

Sen. Jesse Helms (R-NC) sponsored the amendment to a State Department funding bill. His measure would cut $118,875,000 in U.S. finds for fiscal years 1994 and 1995 to the United Nations until: *the President certifies that: no United Nations agency or United Nations affiliated agency grants any recognition to an organization that condones pedophilia.*

Ever since ILGA's NAMBLA connection received national attention, it and other gay groups have been scrambling to disassociate themselves from the New York based pederasty group and denounce pedophilia in the strongest terms. ***

It appears that the U.S. State Department may allow ILGA to keep its consultative status if the homosexual umbrella group ousts NAMBLA in its June meeting. ...

But Sen. Helms said "nothing could be further from the truth" than allowing his amendment to be negated should ILGA oust NAMBLA. "It has been more than amply documented that ILGA itself is an organization that promotes, condones, or seeks legalization of pedophilia in the language of the amendment. ILGA falls under the purview of the amendment — whether or not NAMBLA is expelled from ILGA — as any honest examination of the record will reveal," he said.

Helms cited the same ILGA resolutions that were reported by *Lambda Report* ... .

... Helms highlighted recent ILGA resolutions recognizing:

- *"that young people have the right to sexual and social self-determination and that the age of consent laws often operated to oppress and not protect."*
- *"the right of every individual, regardless of age, to explore and develop his or her sexuality."* (*Lambda Report*, Spring 1994)

Yet Senator Helms' efforts are not enough to stem the overwhelming tide of the pro-homosexual agenda being forced on our government employees and military members. Here are just a few examples:

DOT to celebrate Gay Pride Month
In an effort to improve relations among its employees, the Department of Transportation has decided to celebrate "gay pride" this month.

And though its scheduled celebration of homosexuality has little, if anything, to do with the Transportation Department's mission, it has made the agency a standout in the Clinton administration.

According to the Department of Transportation Gay, Lesbian or Bisexual Employees (DOT GLOBE), the department is the "first Cabinet level agency to have activities to observe lesbian, gay and bisexual pride." (*The Washington Times*, 6-11-93)

Federal Agency Demands Christian Employee Group Put "Sexual Orientation" in its Charter to Gain Recognition

WASHINGTON — The U.S. Department of Transportation (DOT) is demanding that a Christian group accept language guaranteeing non-discrimination on the basis of "sexual orientation" as a condition for being recognized like other employee groups at the agency. ...

Members of the evangelical group, the DOT Christian Prayer and Fellowship Association, have resisted the "sexual orientation" proviso as a violation of their beliefs. Leaders say that while they encourage everybody, including homosexuals, to attend their meetings, the "sexual orientation" clause could allow unrepentant homosexuals to assume leadership positions in the group. They also say it gives undue recognition to homosexuality, which they consider sinful. ***
(*Lambda Report*, Jan. 1996)

[In the article above, the recognition of DOT GLOBE, and the departments "gay" activities are explained.]

Achtenberg's Conformation Only the Tip of the Iceberg

... Roberta Achtenberg was confirmed by the United States Senate for the number two position at the Department of Housing and Urban Development (HUD) by a vote of 58-31.

Achtenberg is another of President Clinton's choices for high federal office who hold contempt for the Boy Scouts of America, once referring to them as an organization that "harm[s] children."

... She will oversee discrimination cases in both public and private housing based on race, religion, sex, national origin, handicap and family status. Miss Achtneberg has said in the past that she would also like to see sexual orientation as a basis for non-discrimination in housing.

... we sent a copy of the video tape of Achtenberg and her lover Mary Morgan to media outlets in the state of senators who voted to confirm [her]. ***

While a member of the San Francisco Board of Supervisors, Achtneberg urged groups to withhold support of the scouts because they forbid homosexuals from serving as scout leaders.

In June of 1992, Achtenberg introduced resolutions which commended both Levi Strauss and the United Way of the Bay Area for suspending contributions to the Boy Scouts because of their policy of sexual discrimination. *** (*Family Alert*, a publication of the Christian Action Network, June 1993)

'Moral deregulation' in high office

What do you think about two women (one of them Roberta Achtenberg) riding in a convertible with the top down, kissing each other passionately on the mouth, while the 7-year-old son of one of them sits in the back seat, watching in bewilderment? What do you think when you see that the car carries a banner "Celebrating family values"? ***

The photograph of the kissers is a scene from a video of the 1992 San Francisco Gay Pride parade; another scene portrayed a white-haired "God" in anal intercourse with "Uncle Sam." Their sign reads: "One nation under God."

Is this mockery a parade for a 7-year-old boy? Why is there so little concern for protecting a child?

In only a very short time our society has moved from taking pride in appeals to moral righteousness to disdain for anyone who espouses virtue; from believing that public figures ought to display good judgment in public (if not always in private) to "rights" for public figures no matter what character qualities they display; from looking out for what's best for children to condoning if not celebrating, exhibitionistic self-indulgence. ***

Sen. Daniel Patrick Moynihan of New York, a Democrat, describes a contemporary phenomenon called "defining deviancy down." He refers to our capacity for "moral deregulation"—redefining deviant behavior so that it appears to be normal. He specifically refers to the high level of violent crime, the exploding numbers of unwed mothers and single parent families that we all know weaken our social standards. "We are getting used to a lot of behavior that is not good for us." *** (*Conservative Chronicle*, 6-9-93, article by Suzanne Fields)

Navy officers pressured to attend pro-gay seminar

In early September, the armed forces and a number of federal agencies urged their personnel to attend "Diversity Day 1994 Training Event," a sensitivity training program during which activists promoted homosexuality and discussions ranged from cross-dressing to equating homosexual with heterosexual sex.

The daylong event for both federal workers and uniformed military personnel was endorsed by 20 government agencies – among them the Office of the Secretary of Defense, the Air Force, Army, and Navy.

Two officers of the Navy, the branch which appeared to take the lead in promoting the event, felt obliged to remain anonymous when they complained that the seminars amounted to forced indoctrination. The officers supplied two memos from Navy agencies urging attendance and warned that the seminars mark the first time our armed forces have sponsored a program promoting homosexuality and pressured uniformed men and women to attend.

"This is a blatant effort by the Clinton administration to promote homosexuality," said retired Army Colonel Robert Maginnis, an analyst at the Family Research Council. "Do the American people realize that their tax dollars are being used to teach federal employees to accept homosexuality as a legitimate and healthy lifestyle?" ** *

(The reference for the article was: Rowan Scarborough, "Navy officers balk at pro-gay seminar," *The Washington Times*, 8 September 1994) (CFV Report, Nov. 1994)

Gay Spouses Have Congress IDs

WASHINGTON — Despite campaigns on Capitol Hill to outlaw gay marriage, Congress gives some official acknowledgment to the companions of three gay members, a published report says.

The partners of Reps. Gerry Studds, D-Mass., Barney Frank, D-Mass., and Steve Gunderson, R-Wis., all have spouse identification cards, said the July issue of *Washingtonian* magazine.

The card allows the men to park in Capitol Hill garages and move freely in and out of restricted areas, even when security is heightened for events like the State of the Union address.

"This is to certify that the person whose name and photograph appear on the card is the spouse of the above named member of the United States House of Representatives," the cards say.

(*Albuquerque Journal*, 6-22-96)

Clinton Aide Adopts Gay Barbs in Endorsing Pro-gay Bill

Senior presidential advisor George Stephanopoulos gave a passionate endorsement of federal legislation that would ban workplace "discrimination" based on "sexual orientation"—including a characterization of those opposing homosexuality as "bigots and bashers." *** (*Lambda Report*, Oct. 95 - Jan. 96)

The Clintons continually make a show of carrying the Bible and going to and from churches that purportedly believe in the Christian religion. This is pure "show," hypocrisy, and deceit. Their actions prove this. There is no Scriptural or logical way to reconcile the vile acts of homosexuality with the Christian faith which is based entirely on the Old Testament and the New Testament. Without qualification or equivocation, both strongly condemn homosexuality. The sacrilege of the Clintons is not singular. Even their "church" engages in the same sacrilege, as shown by the following article. When even the churches become hotbeds of immorality, homosexuality, and sacrilege, our moral degradation is indeed complete. The entire article is copied because of the significance of the facts disclosed.

Clinton's Church Hosts Gay Activist Event—
Pastor Ponders Whether Jesus Was "Drag Queen"

President Clinton's church hosted an event sponsored by the gay activist group PFLAG in which St. Paul was described as a "bisexual" and a discussion ensues over whether Jesus might have been a "drag queen," according to eye witnesses to the event.

The November 10 all-day "celebration" at Foundry United Methodist Church on 16th Street in the nation's capital, featured the controversial, pro-homosexual Episcopal Bishop John Shelley Spong, who said regarding the Apostle Paul: "Our primary understanding of God's grace came from a self-hating gay man," reports Mark Tooley of the Institute on Religion and Democracy (IRD), who attended the affair.

Foundry is the Washington, D.C. church of the President and First Lady Hilary Clinton, who is a Methodist. Until last year it was also the church of Sen. Bob Dole and his wife, Elizabeth. Several hundred attended the PFLAG (Parents, Families and Friends of Lesbians and Gays) event, which was titled, "Sharing Our Rainbow of Light."

Tooley reports that at the symposium, Spong proudly recalled that the first woman he ordained in 1977 later declared herself a lesbian.

He said supporting homosexuals within the church is "a total justice issue exactly like the civil rights movement" and said he would "sacrifice my career" for this "life and death struggle." Spong said he has 15 openly homosexual priests in his own diocese in New Jersey.

According to Tooley, Foundry pastor J. Philip Wogaman praised Spong's morning remarks as "stimulating," and said, "I'm not sure what to do with Bishop Spong's thoughts on St. Paul being gay ... but I am much touched by the relationships of gay couples in this church." He said he shares Spong's concerns about an overly "literalistic" reading of the Bible.

Wogaman agreed with Spong that King David of the Old Testament may have been bisexual, reports Tooley, who is the Methodist Director at IRD, an organization based in the nation's capital that defends orthodox Christianity.

When someone in the audience asked Wogaman about the possibility that Jesus Christ was a "drag queen," the pastor responded, "I don't condemn it. I just don't know. I'll have to think about it some more."

In October, Foundry's board voted to join the "Reconciling Movement," a movement within the United Methodist Church that rejects the church's teaching proscribing homosexuality and allows openly homosexual people to "fully serve as ministers in the church," the *Washington Blade*, a homosexual newspaper, reported last May. According to Tooley, Foundry is one of under 100 Methodist churches out of the denomination's 37,000 to adopt the pro-homosexual stance.

Tooley reports that during the PFLAG event, homosexual male couples "held each other and kissed in the pews." He said a United Methodist minister named Harry Kieley declared, "Jesus is speaking as a gay man to the church today. The United Methodist Church has been supporting the persecution of human beings."

PFLAG took out a full-page ad for the "Rainbow" event in the October 27 *Blade*, with the headline: "This is one conference Pat Robertson won't attend ... but you should!"

Wogaman's Foundry church is listed regularly in the religion section of the *Blade* as a "Reconciling Congregation, welcoming & affirming to all, including G & L (gay and lesbian) persons. ... [Here reference was made to a "box" with the article which set out the ad.]

In his May interview with the *Blade,* before Foundry voted to become a "Reconciling" church, Wogaman criticized the United

Methodist denomination's edict that forbids ordaining openly homosexual ministers.

"I deeply regret that some fine people have not been able to serve
because of that rule," he said. (*Lambda Report on Homosexuality,* Oct.
95 - Jan. 96)

Homosexuals seem to have an inability to tell the truth, and perhaps
even to recognize it. This is probably because they, in their hearts and
in their subconscious, recognize how heinous the acts are in which they
engage, and by which they acquire their classification. They therefore
have to live in a hideous dream world to convince themselves that what
they are doing is right, and even "beautiful." This is a complete world
of fiction and falsity. In this same vein, they then try to associate themselves with great people—falsely calling everyone from King David to
Abraham Lincoln "gay"—now even Jesus Christ and the apostle Paul.
This is puke vomited from a sick mind. I assure you that the Bible does
not support such statements about the biblical characters, and history
does not support their false claims about George Washington, Abraham
Lincoln, and such others to which history attributes greatness. This is
pure fictional garbage—primarily put out for the swallowing by themselves and gullible liberals, many of whom also seem to have a great
difficulty in recognizing truth and facts. Some of these false claims about
great people of history will be further discussed in Chapter 6, The Homosexual Agenda.

But the Clintons are far from the only liberal politicians who are
working to promote homosexuality and the decline of moral values.

Mayor Dinkins guts foundations of society
(by columnist Cal Thomas)

MARCH 7 — Two foundations in New York City were attacked in
recent days.

One, the World Trade Center, was caused by a bomb. Although
there was tremendous loss of life and property, the structural damage
will be repaired.

The other occurred at the Municipal Building, where 109 couples
showed up to register as "domestic partners." A new city law grants
many rights previously reserved to heterosexual married couples to
people of the same or opposite sex who want to live together without,

as they used to say, benefit of clergy [though there are now sufficient clergy who will do anything, including "marry" homosexuals]. The damage from this assault on the nation's primary social foundation is substantial and may be very difficult to repair. ***

The law fulfills a goal first outlined in 1970 at a homosexual convention in Philadelphia. Delegates called for "the abolition of the nuclear family because it perpetuates the false categories of homosexuality and heterosexuality." A lesbian workshop demanded the "destruction of the nuclear family," which the statement called "a microcosm of the fascist state." ***

Marriage, like law, has its roots in the *Bible*, which says, "A man shall leave his father and his mother, and shall cleave unto his wife; and they shall be one flesh." ***

In his once widely read *Commentaries on the Laws of England* (1765) the great British legal scholar William Blackstone saw law as flowing from a Creator, who not only endowed humans with certain rights, but also established rules for a social order which, if followed, would profit individuals and society.

... Blackstone said the will of Man's Maker is "the law of nature" and "this law of nature, being co-equal with mankind and dictated by God himself, is of course superior in obligation to any other ... no human laws are of any validity, if contrary to this."

SADLY, IN NEW YORK CITY and in increasing numbers of places, people like Mayor David Dinkins in effect have declared themselves God and are busy destroying the foundation of the law of nature and the bedrock principles of history. This can cause destruction far greater and more long-lasting than any single bombing. (*Conservative Chronicle*, 3-17-93)

Giuliani Condones Pro-NAMBLA Parade
(By Peter LaBarbera)

NEW YORK CITY— Mayor Rudoph Giuliani enraged pro-family conservatives here June 28 [1994] by failing to enforce a court order barring an illegal parade by radical gay activists that featured a pedophile contingent and nude men prancing down 5th Avenue as police stood motionless nearby. The unauthorized parade was called in support of the right of the North American Man/Boy Love Association (NAMBLA) to participate in Stonewall commemorations. Organizers of the main Stonewall march had banned NAMBLA as a signal that gays do not support pedophilia. ***

Giuliani, who took a pro-"gay rights" position in his successful campaign for mayor, marched in the honorary position in front of the legal gay march that began at the United Nations. Meanwhile the city's police force ignored a federal court order—which had been issued at the request of city lawyers—banning the illegal "Spirit of Stonewall" parade. Instead the police actually facilitated the pro-NAMBLA event by clearing the parade route and barricading the streets. ***

... The mayor also said he wanted "to show that New York is a city that respects differences in opinion and all differences in terms of sexual orientation. Everyone in this city is entitled to equal protection and equal respect." ***

New York Post columnist Ray Kerrison had some choice words for Giuliani and his gay-accommodating tactics. He wrote:

"Giuliani, the Catholic mayor, not only ignored this blasphemy and abdicated his duty by permitting unlawful acts, but he welcomed these people and their allies to City Hall, congratulated them , praised the cops for failing to uphold the law and patted himself on the back for his brilliant strategy. The inmates truly have taken over the asylum." *** (*Human Events*, 7-8-94)

Seattle gays cut the wedding cake

[A photo with the article shows two men kissing, although one is attired and has a hairdo that makes him appear more as a woman. It is not hard to guess which of these two takes the "butch" and which takes the "femme" part of their "marriage."]

SEATTLE — Carolyn Sue enjoyed a celebratory piece of chocolate raspberry cake with Linda Gonzales outside the city clerk's office after the couple registered as domestic partners under Seattle's new law. ***

They were among about 90 live-in couples, mostly gay or lesbian, who paid $25 to have their relationship recognized under the ordinance that went into effect this week, city clerk Judith Pippin said.

About 25 cities and a growing number of corporations provide for health benefits to their workers' domestic partners, but Seattle's ordinance provides for no legal benefits. *** (*The Albuquerque Tribune*, 9-8-94)

San Francisco recognizes gay marriages

SAN FRANCISCO — Gay and lesbian couples who register with the city as domestic partners would get to tie the knot, symbolically at least, before the country clerk under a new ordinance moving through the Board of Supervisors. ***

"It's a very San Francisco sort of thing," [Supervisor Carole Migden] said. ***

"In San Francisco's mind it's marriage, but in the state of California it's not valid," Migden said. (*The Albuquerque Tribune,* 1-25-96)

Mass. Democrat Gerry Studds To Retire From House
EDGARTOWN, Mass. — ***

"It is time for me ... to move on to other challenges," Studds told about 200 supporters at the Old Whaling Church in this Martha's Vineyard town. ***

... Studds was first elected to Congress in 1972. In 1983, he was censured by the House for having sex with a young man who had served as a congressional page; despite the bad publicity, Studds kept on winning re-election. *** (*Albuquerque Journal,* 10-29-95)

The page boy with whom Gerry Studds admitted to a sexual relationship was 17 years old. (*The Wall Street Journal,* 1-12-96) This tells us something about the morality of typical liberals. Such things seem not to faze them in Martha's Vineyard.

But it even happens in Texas.

Texas County Yields to Pro-Gay Pressure
*** On November 30, [1992], in a 3-to-2 vote, Williamson County commissioners had made national news by rejecting a $750,000 tax abatement for California based Apple Computer to build its U.S. Customer Support Center, because the company extends health benefits to so-called "domestic partners" of its employees, including homosexual live-in-lovers. Commissioners basically sent the message that they weren't going to go out of their way to invite a company with immoral policies into the neighborhood.

[On December 7, the commissioners caved in to the pressure from local citizens who were more interested in money than moral values, and from pressure from liberals around the country.]

[An example of the pressure was a diatribe from the Austin *American-Statesman* criticizing the county's "fear and prejudice," and it "scolded Christians for not keeping their moral beliefs to themselves, behind church walls."] *** (*Human Events*, 12-18-93)

Politicians yielding to the pressure of homosexualists and liberal media has continued throughout the country. Many are reluctant to even express any traditional moral values, and most are far too timid and cowardly to stand up for them under the immense pressures exerted. Our large corporations continually cave in to the same pressure. Forsaking any moral values seems to them to be the path of least resistance — and, at least in the short-run, they avoid expensive lawsuits. The powerful American Civil Liberties Union (ACLU) continually attacks any governmental agency and even private individuals and companies who dare to express and be guided by Judaic-Christian religious tenets; and it fights in behalf of the homosexual movement all over the country with expensive and burdensome lawsuits, that many cannot afford to defend, and many would rather give in to than incur the expense.

The organization bearing the misnomer "American Civil Liberties Union," throughout its entire history, has worked toward the destruction of American principles, and American traditions, that were forged for us by our founders. It has contributed immensely to the decline in morality in this country. The following information is derived from a newsletter of D. James Kennedy, Ph.D., head of Coral Ridge Ministries, and from a pamphlet on the ACLU put out by that organization, with that news letter.

Coral Ridge Ministries explains that the sources used for the information in the pamphlet were, primarily, the ACLU Policy Guide; George Grant, *Trial And Error*; John W. Whitehead, *The Stealing of America*, Crossway Books, Westchester, Il., 1983; William A. Donohue, *The Politics of the American Civil Liberties Union*, Transaction Books, New Brunswick, NJ, 1985; Daniel L. Dreisbach, *Real Threat and Mere Shadow*, Crossway Books, Westchester, Il, 1987.

The actions of the ACLU and the statements of its founder and leader show that its true purpose is to destroy our form of government, and to eliminate all true religion, and religious principles. Its special hate has been Christianity.

Roger Baldwin, the founder and leading force in the ACLU until his death in 1981, asserted the partisan nature of his agenda saying:

I am for Socialism, disarmament, and ultimately for abolishing the state itself as an instrument of violence and compulsion. I seek social ownership of Property . . . Communism is the goal.

Since Roger Baldwin founded the organization in 1917 as the Bureau for Conscientious Objectors of the Americana Union Against Militarism, it underwent several name changes. In October, 1917, the name was changed to National Civil Liberties Bureau, which was raided by the FBI on August 31, 1918, and searched for evidence of subversive materials. On November 11, 1918, Baldwin began serving a sentence in a Federal prison for sedition. After his release in January, 1920, Baldwin renamed the organization to the American Civil Liberties Union, which it still goes by. The most telling information about the organizations is its position taken on specific matters.

The ACLU Supports:	The ACLU Opposes:
• Legalization of child pornography.	• Voluntary school prayer.
• Legalization of drugs.	• Sobriety checkpoints.
• Tax exemption for satanists.	• Tax exemption for churches.
• Legalization of prostitution.	• Religious displays in public.
• Abortion on demand.	• Medical safety regulation and reporting.
• Mandatory Sex education.	• Parental consent laws.
• Busing.	• Educational vouchers and home schooling.
• Ideological testing for court appointees.	• Governmental ethics committee.
• Automatic entitled probation.	• Prison terms for criminal offenses.
• Public demonstrations for Nazis and Communists.	• Public demonstrations for direct action pro-lifers.
• Legalization of polygamy.	• Teaching "monogamous heterosexual intercourse within marriage" in public schools.

The ACLU has always been at the forefront in the promotion of the acceptance of homosexuality. Whenever there is a "homosexual rights" bill or a "hate crimes" bill, you can expect the ACLU to be there lobbying for it. As has been previously explained, any argument that the ACLU supports individual rights, generally, simply is not true. The ABC TV show, Ellen, whose main character is the lesbian, Ellen DeGeneres, is clearly a media promotion for the acceptance of the homosexual lifestyle. The ACLU has now awarded her the "Bill of Rights Award" for advancing "the cause of gay rights 100-fold" (*Albuquerque Journal*, 12-9-97). What a farce! There is no protection in the Bill of Rights of the United States Constitution for acts of sodomy, and never has been. Homosexuals have the same rights as anyone else, without any special laws in their behalf. But all people are legally, and constitutionally, prohibited from certain sex acts that are against the norms of society.

THE MEDIA LEAD

It is the media, however, that leads the nation in embracing sodomy.

In the *Albuquerque Journal*, 1-15-94, we were blasted with three extensive articles on the same day put out by the Associated Press and its writers. They were "HOLLYWOOD - Gay Issues Emerge From The Tinseltown Closet," "Gay Actors Find Acceptance Slow," and "Stereotypes, Exclusions Have Long Film History." The following quote from one of the articles sums up both the purpose of the shows referred to and the purpose of the articles: "What they're bringing is gay life into the main stream." That is the purpose of the articles and it is the purpose of the many movies and television shows referred to in the articles. We have been continually bombarded with their filth. The purpose of all of this is to convince the pubic, including the children of this country, that sodomy is common, acceptable, and that there is nothing wrong with the vile and depraved acts which constitute sodomy and homosexuality, which are one and the same.

The *Oprah Winfrey Show* on January 26, 1996, was one of ABC's contributions to the homosexual movement. It reeked with homosexual bias. It was about parents of "Gays" and support groups. As usual there is no talk about getting help for the homosexuals, and there is no discussion of the repulsive acts in which they engage. It is typical of the current approach of the homosexualists, which is to have us accept that which should never be acceptable in a society with any remaining remnants of decency.

On Sunday, September 29, 1996, the ABC evening news program contained unadulterated propaganda promoting the idea of "gay marriage." On the program was a young man talking about his sodomy and promiscuity — his fear of AIDS because of what he was doing—but he continues to engage in such activity anyway. (This is typical of the homosexual community.) He said that he hopes sometime to get married to another man an "have children." (No one explained how this was to be accomplished.)

In the campaign for homosexual "marriages," the ultimate in immorality, degradation, and corruption, the media and entertainment field lead the charge. ABC News is always on the cutting edge in promoting all forms of homosexuality, including same-sex marriage. A good example was the ABC show, "TURNING POINT—For Better of for Worse—Same-Sex Marriage," narrated by Elizabeth Vargas and Diane Sawyer, 11-7-96. The following are comments on that show.

The write-up for the show in TV Guide was:

> Good Morning America newsanchor Elizabeth Vargas hosts an upbeat report on same-sex couples seeking to formalize their relationships.
>
> Instead of focusing on politics, Vargas sets out to "let the audience meet these people one-on-one" in interviews with intendeds and their families. Some may be surprised by how traditional the couples are, as they cope not only with the usual pre-wedding jitters but also the challenges of dealing with those who disapprove of their sexuality. Included: a divorced mother whose daughter and sister react differently to her lesbian union; a male couple's challenges in registering for gifts, an Episcopal priest who helps plan a same-sex ceremony.

The word, upbeat, in the above description was correct. It was a pure whitewash, a snow job aimed at selling the homosexual agenda. This show displayed a complete lack of any sense of morality. Its sole purpose was the promotion for homosexuality and its complete acceptance—even to formally recognized "weddings."

As in all public promotions of homosexuality, no mention whatsoever is made of the nature of the vile sexual acts in which they engage. No one mentions how they are going to consummate their "marriage."

It is a complete mockery of traditional holy matrimony. And it is a mockery of the Christian religion. This of course is nothing new for ABC or its parent company, The Walt Disney Company, since Walt Disney died and the homosexualists took over.

An attempt is made to show only the best side of the couples. Conventional clothing is worn. The "drag" and "butch" garb is completely absent. The usual obscenities are kept to a minimum.

There was holding of hands and kissing between the same-sex couples.

Everything was staged, planned and produced over a period of time, for the obvious purpose of selling the public on same-sex marriages It was extremely shallow, with no in-depth consideration of the real issues at all. No mention is made of the loathsome and filthy acts of sodomy being foisted upon the public.

The pinnacle of sacrilege was reached with an Episcopal priest officiating one of the weddings, a Jewish father toasting his son's wedding, and the use of the words, "in the name of the Father, the Son, and the Holy Spirit."

It is the same thing that has been going on in the media for the past twenty years. The promoters believe that slowly but surely we will be worn down and desensitized. We will finally accept. The American public will accept the most profane and reprehensible acts in which one can engage as natural and beautiful. We will become brainwashed into believing that right is wrong and wrong is right.

Strangely enough, there are enough star-struck and gullible people, with so little foundation in religious morals, that this and similar homosexual propaganda has been amazingly successful. It is indeed a sad day for America and the world. Our society has never been so sickly corrupt since the advent of Christianity as a major religion.

ABC is of course not the only national network promoting homosexuality and homosexual marriages. Another example was **Friends**, a show on NBC on 1-18-96. This was actually a meaningless show, with nothing of substance to it, about a lesbian wedding. The whole thing is a part of the current insidious attempt to expose us to so many of these things that we become desensitized to the underlying crimes against nature — the details of which are carefully never mentioned.

In this NBC show, they wheel in a baby at the head of the wedding march, the meaning of which escapes me, as I am sure it was not consummated between the two lesbians, and that their marriage was not going to give it any legitimacy. Candice Gingrich, Newt Gingrich's half-sister, served as the minister. I have not heard of, and this show did not present, her credentials to serve as a minister.

> **95 was the year that gay came to stay on prime-time TV**
> (By Kinney Littlefield, Orange County Register)
> Take a sharp look back and TV-95 was edgier and riskier than you might think. Despite the absence of new hit series, despite the excess of really bad new sitcoms, 1995 was the year that Gay Came to Stay on prime-time TV.
> Finally, gayness wasn't just a verboten titillation anymore. Suddenly, gayness was cool. Although gay characters still weren't allowed to connect physically in prime time, homosexuality became a topic deemed safe, sanctioned, and wide open for discussion on series old and new. ***
> [This article lists a large number of shows embracing homosexuality in one way or another, and most are so well known that we will not take up the space to name them. It certainly has become a common theme.] (*Albuquerque Journal*, 1-11-96)

A newsletter of D. James Kennedy, Ph.D., of Coral Ridge Ministries, dated 10-17-97, states in part:

> According to "Broadcasting & Cable" magazine (8/18/97), the Gay & Lesbian Alliance Against Defamation (GLAAD) reports that a record

30 homosexual and bisexual characters are featured in prime-time broadcast TV shows this season.

I believe that all of the major television networks, and most of the major entertainment fields, as well as the majority of the news media, have capitulated to the homosexual movement.

The Walt Disney Company—
From Family Entertainment to Homosexual Filth and Sacrilege

Walt Disney built an empire on decent family entertainment. But it is now clear that those who have taken over since his death are blatant homosexualists. That word is used in this book to include homosexual activists and also those who support homosexuality, whether or not they are homosexuals.

There was substantial news coverage in 1997 in connection with the Southern Baptist Convention voting to boycott Disneyland and The Walt Disney Company. That brought down a general attack against the Baptists from the conventional media. Baptists were called "bigots," "fundamentalists," and "Bible thumpers," terms usually used against those who believe in ordinary decency and the Christian religion. The Baptists as well as any others with any real morality should welcome such attacks from the liberal news media. It shows that the persons being attacked are on the right track. The liberal media, educators, and politicians are always on the opposite side of any aspects of traditional morality, and have no respect whatsoever for Judaic-Christian principles. But they have particular venom for those who dare to stand up for Christian beliefs.

The Baptists and other Christians, and many who truly follow the Jewish faith, have had concerns about the direction of Disney for several years. My sense is that what finally brought this to a head was that Disneyland and Disney World were having special days for homosexuals, and were even refusing to warn people with families of those days. That was exposing families with children to unseemly displays between homosexuals to which no decent family should be exposed. As was shown in the first chapter, when these people get together in groups they seem either unable or unwilling to act with any decency whatsoever, and have no consideration for decent people around them.

In his newsletter of October 27, 1997, D. James Kennedy, Ph.D., of Coral Ridge Ministries, endorsed the Baptist boycott, and called for a general letter-writing campaign to Disney. He recognizes the dramatic effect on our culture that the entertainment industry has, and particularly in the fields that substantially affect young people. With the newsletter was a paper of Coral Ridge Ministries entitled, **Facts to Ponder**, with the leadoff statement: "The Walt Disney Company, once a trusted family-entertainment empire, has taken a tragic turn away from decency and toward immorality." The following are facts and information gleaned from that paper.

According to *Entertainment weekly*, 9-26-97, Disney's ABC Television airs a new series this season, "Nothing Sacred," about a priest "who fights, flirts, and questions the existence of God." A story on the show in *The Wall Street Journal*, 8-18-97, says that he even refuses to counsel a pregnant teenager against abortion; one scene brings the priest, "Father Ray," to a hotel room with an "old flame:" and "the young rebel priest tells parishioners he refuses to hear any more sexual confessions, because sexual sin isn't what the Gospels are all about."

On Halloween Eve last year, a Disney subsidiary, Hollywood Records, released the CD BLACKACIDEVEL, by the rock group, DANZIG. That group put out a music video, *It's Coming Down*, that even MTV and Playboy Channel banned. It reportedly had scenes of "sadomasochism, masturbation, urination and genital mutilation." (*American Family Association Action Alert*, Nov. 96)

Disney World has apparently hosted homosexual and lesbian theme nights with no warning to others that such things were taking place. (*AFA Journal*, Aug. 96)

"A teenager oriented book, *Growing up Gay: From Left Out to Coming Out*, was published through Disney's Hyperion subsidiary, which clearly connects the Walt Disney Company to the promotion of the homosexual agenda." (*Southern Baptist Convention Resolution*, 8/96)

Disney has extended health-care benefits to the partners of its homosexual employees, but denies them to unmarried partners of heterosexual employees. (*The Advocate,* 4-29-97)

Disney employs an open homosexual as vice-president of feature animation, who took his male sexual partner to a company social function, and he said, "I got feedback like 'I can't believe you brought your lover.' But from the people who run the d——— company, there wasn't an ounce of trouble." (*The Advocate,* 6-28-94)

Tom Schumacher, Disney's homosexual producer, says that some were surprised when Disney hired an openly homosexual executive, but he says that Disney has a very supportive environment for homosexuals, and that there were now a lot of gay people at entry level in the company. (*The Advocate,* 6-28-94)

The paper discusses an article in *Business Week,* 8-4-97, about the Ellen show on ABC, and Disney Chairman Michael Eisner defended the homosexual aspects of the show.

In May, a Disney subsidiary, Hyperion, released the book, *The Rile and Fall of Gay Culture,* parts of which have already been serialized in publications such as *The Harvard Gay and Lesbian Review.* (*Publishers Weekly,* 2-24-97)

Disney's subsidiary, Miramax, produced the movie, *Priest,* which "does, in fact, present an uncompromising yet non-stereotypical portrayal of homosexuality—including a depiction of gay sex that by all accounts is one of the most realistic ever filmed outside the world of pornography. ... Certainly the film is one of the gayest the Walt Disney Co. ... has ever released." (*The Advocate,* 4-18-95)

Miramax acquired a movie, *Kids,* which seems to have the theme of teenagers having sex, built around a teenage boy whose specialty is having sex with virgin girls. " ... the boy from the scene's opener turns out to be HIV positive, spreading the deadly AIDS virus to the other youngsters." There was so much heat on Disney because of the immoral content of this film that it has not yet been released. (*Newsweek, 2-20-95,* and *The Wall Street Journal,* 3-30-95.) (But wait until the public is sufficiently desensitized. The film was not acquired to waste money by a company that now appears to worship only immorality, homosexuality and the Almighty Dollar.) Joe Roth, Disney studio chief, praised Miramax cochairmen Harvey and Bob Weinstein, who acquired the film, saying:

"They have a real commitment to quality, and we're lucky to be associated with them." (*The Wall Street Journal,* 3-3-95)

"Disney's Hollywood Pictures released *Chicks in White Satin* about a lesbian couple who decide to stage their 'commitment ceremony.' (*Glamour,* 8-9-94)"

An article, DISNEY DYKE, in *The Advocate,* 3-8-94, contains information about Jan Carr, a lesbian who wrote *Harem Wish,* a "dark and steamy new lesbian novel." Jan Carr "created the novelizations of many Disney animated classics—including *The Little Mermaid, Cinderella,* and *The Jungle Book.*" She is quoted as saying:

> I certainly don't want to give more fuel to the Christian right so that they come down on the lesbian and gay community. ... But I wanted to write about women's sexuality, and about how very powerful lesbian sexuality can be.
>
> I certainly wouldn't be adverse to writing a children's book with gay characters or gay themes.

The description above of the movie, *Priest,* put out by the Disney subsidiary Miramax does not properly inform us of the true filth and sacrilege in the movie. I am sure that this is because the information came from *The Advocate,* a homosexual publication.

The following comes from a review of *Priest* by Tom Fitton in *Lambda Report,* April-June 1995.

The movie begins with the desecration of the cross. A priest who appears to be drunk and disgruntled uses the cross as a battering ram to attack the residence of the local bishop.

One character is a priest who makes left-wing political "sermons" during mass, and carries on an affair with the rectory's housekeeper.

Another priest, Father Gregg, is a practicing homosexual. He takes off his clerical collar and rides his bicycle to a gay bar, where he meets another male homosexual and commits sodomy. "The sex scene is about as explicit as an R rating allows. Interestingly though, this anal sodomy scene is depicted in a 'gentle' manner."

The scenes keep going between Mass and the Holy Eucharist to sodomy scenes, as if to establish some kind of link.

After a tiff with his homosexual partner, the two make up, and Father Gregg pulls over his car while his male lover orally sodomizes him.

"Seeking advice from a disgruntled priest [the same one who attacked the bishop's residence with a cross], Father Gregg says he can't help himself—in fact he's sexually attracted to the crucified Christ. This outrageous blasphemy is part and parcel of the homosexual activist agenda. It seems folks who throw condoms during church are now into movie-making."

(It appears from the review that the characters of the movie have no repentance, morality, or any sense of right or wrong. This is typical of homosexual activists.)

Disney, through Miramax, has put its "resources behind a movie that promotes homosexuality, attacks organized religion, and blasphemes Christ. ... The movie is a blunt attempt to legitimize homosexual activity through its sympathetic depiction on screen."

(It is typical homosexual sewage.)

Peter LaBarbera wrote an informative article, **Major Media Underwrite, Recruit at Gay Journalists Convention**, in the *Lambda Report*, January, 1996. The following is derived from that article.

Major media companies sent recruiters to the National Lesbian and Gay Journalists Association convention in October.

Some of the major supporters and contributors were: Associated Press; Knight-Ridder; The Gannett Foundation; NBC News; CBS News, Radio, and Television Stations; The New York Times; Los Angeles Times; Hearst Newspapers; The Washington Post; Hill & Knowlton; The Miami Herald; Army Times Publishing Co.; St. Petersburg Times; Scripps Howard, Washington Bureau; and a number of others.

The liberal bias of the news media has been long established. A good example is: "The Times-Mirror pollsters found that while 53 percent of the public believes homosexuality should be discouraged, only 4 percent of national media polled hold that view." Another Times-Mirror poll found that zero percent of the national media executives thought homosexuality should be discouraged.

"The group's members hold powerful positions in the media, from producers at National Public Radio to editors and reporter at big-city newspapers. The influential Associated Press sent enough gay staffers to field its own caucus at the NLGIA event, as did Gannett and Knight-Ridder."

"As **LR** reported last issue, the Times Mirror Center for the People and the Press declared in its latest annual survey of media attitudes that, 'Nowhere do press values differ from public values more strikingly than on homosexuality. While the public is split on whether the homosexual lifestyle should be accepted or discouraged . . . the media overwhelmingly said that lifestyle is acceptable.'"

The information about the media being almost entirely controlled by homosexualists points up the reason that the media, including both entertainment and news, has been a predominant contributor to the decline in morality in this country for the past forty years. It has influenced everything from our churches to our courts, as well as the common people. It is truly a wonder that over half of the people still have sufficient common sense to take the opposite position. The only other group that may have been more influential to our moral decadence is the educators.

The onslaught of the homosexual movement in the schools has been one of the most damaging aspects of it. This problem is covered in other chapters of this book, as well as in this one.

AIDS and Your Kids

All over America school boards are accepting misinformation on AIDS promoted by the "comprehensive sex-education" crowd. As dads, I believe we need to know what is being taught in our local schools and be prepared to cut through the misinformation and teach our teens the truth. Condom distribution is certainly not the answer and many teens are insulted by the implication that they are so controlled by animal impulses that they can't wait for sex. Parents should be aware that many of the HIV/AIDS programs are being used to promote homosexuality— a lifestyle that steals decades from the lives of the young men and women who choose to live it. Teens should understand that their lives are very important, too important to be wasted on promiscuity. *** (*Family Voice*, July 1993, by Jim Woodall of CWA, a minister and father of five.)

Author Loulan Leading Lesbian UNM
(University of New Mexico) Workshops

*** Loulan is a licensed marriage family and child counselor and sex therapist in northern California. Her latest book is called "The Lesbian Erotic Dance: Butch, Femme and Other Rhythms."

During the lecture Friday at 8 p.m. Loulan will talk about lesbian sex and relationships. On Saturday, she will offer a day-long workshop for mental health professionals who work with lesbian clients. Another all-day workshop Sunday is geared toward lesbians who want to explore their sexual styles. *** (*Albuquerque Journal*, 6-17-92)

Duke Students Demote Christianity
But Gladly Promote Homosexuality

(By Herbert London, John M. Olin professor of Humanities at New York University)

The Student government at Duke University recently voted against the recognition of a student evangelical group, leading to charges that the university is hostile to certain religious positions. Student leaders denied a charter to this religious group because "its proselytizing would not promote diversity" on campus.

The reasoning is curious to say the least when at the same campus meeting, student representatives urged the university chapel to remove its ban on same-sex weddings. On the face it would appear that diversity for the student government at Duke translates into tolerance for some and intolerance for others. ***

... there is a growing consensus on many campuses that orthodox religion of any kind is anathema, while homosexuality must be tolerated. ***

... At another university campus, activist students argued vehemently for the unexpurgated expression of pornographic material at a public meeting. ***

To apply a standard employed at many institutions to Duke, a crucifix in a bottle of urine is an expression of art that should be discussed and evaluated, but a crucifix on the wall as a religious symbol is a violation of the hallowed separation of church and state. Is it any wonder that evangelism is rejected and same-sex marriages accepted? *** (*Human Events*, 1-19-96)

CU Regents approve pro-gay "diversity plan"

In June, the University of Colorado Board of Regents passed a four-inch thick "diversity plan" containing ominous and far-reaching goals for promoting homosexuality on its campuses. *** (*CFV Report*, Nov. 1994)

Stanford Pays Pro-NAMBLA Poet $1 M

Gay beatnik poet Alan Ginsburg negotiating a deal with Stanford University to receive $1 million for his memorabilia.

The decision by Stanford, which years ago turned away the Reagan presidential library, was controversial enough, but was made more so by Ginsburg's praise for the North American Man/Boy Love Association.

"I'm a member of NAMBLA because I love boys," he said. "Everybody does who has a little humanity."

A Stanford spokesman said the purchase "has nothing to do with the author's purported sexuality." (*Lambda Report*, April-June 1995)

"Discrimination" gets even more absurd at university

In our past discussions of the term "discrimination," we've exposed bizarre ways in which the term has been manipulated for political ends. None rivals the latest example from George Mason University.

In its student handbook, discrimination includes "jumping when a homosexual touches you on the arm." It also includes "keeping a physical distance from someone because they are a known gay or lesbian." (Ref.: Charles Colson, *"Postmodern Power Grab,"* Christianity Today, 20 June 1994, p. 80) (*CFV Report*, Sept. 1994)

It was refreshing to read about one lawmaker that had both the morality and the courage to take a stand against homosexual promotion in his district in Washington State. The following contains excerpts from the article.

Beeksma assails photos of gays

MOUNT VERNON — State Rep. Barney Beeksma (R - Oak Harbor) told the Skagit Valley College trustees last night that an exhibit of gay and lesbian photographs displayed at the college this spring has cost the college support in the area, and may affect its support in the next legislative session. ***

The comments centered on the exhibit of 46 photographs of gay and lesbian individuals in everyday life that was displayed at the Norwood Cole Library at the college in May. The SVC display was funded and sponsored by the SVC Lesbian, Gay and Bisexual Academic Union, a school-sponsored student group. ***

"I have had numerous calls from students and faculty afraid to speak up (against the photo display) for fear of retribution," Beeksma said. ***

Rep. Cheryl Hymes, R - Mount Vernon, said she felt the issue was not primarily the photography display, but about the principle of protecting the rights of the minority as well as the majority. These days she said, Christians such as herself are in the minority.

"Believe me it is not fun to be made fun of for being a Christian, or a conservative," Hymes said. "Being a Christian in this society gets you labeled as a nut case." *** (*Skagit Valley Herald,* 7-9-96)

Dartmouth and Vassar Mired In Homosexual Groupthink
(By Jeffrey Hart)

*** *The Dartmouth Review*, an independent conservative newspaper at Dartmouth College, recently investigated the political allegiance of the liberal arts and social science faculties. The newspaper checked out the voter registration data in the towns around the college and found that 79% of the faculty are registered Democrats, 6% are registered Republicans, and the rest independent. A slight imbalance wouldn't you say? ***

Within that 79% of registered faculty Democrats are professors eager to teach "Guatemalan lesbian poetry," for example, which turns out to be lousy poetry but definitely lesbian.

To the extent that many in the 79% are "Democrats," they derive from the wing of the Democratic Party that split for George McGovern in 1972 and headed off into the fever swamps of Identity Politics, with quotas for delegates and all the rest of it.

By Identity Politics I mean that one's identity is categorically postulated: The most important thing about you is that you are black, or lesbian or whatever. ***

Here are a few passages from a revealing letter to the editor in a recent issue of *Commentary* magazine.

"In August 1993 we drove our daughter to Vassar College to begin her freshmen year. The beauty of the campus reinforced our pleasure in her happy choice of colleges.

"I was surprised that the administration had chosen to leave painted scrawlings on the sidewalks announcing 'We're queer and we're here.'

"In October,, we picked up our daughter for fall break. On the bathroom walls everywhere—even on the inside doors of the toilet stalls—detailed and graphic announcements taught us how to avoid AIDS.

"BIGLA (Bisexual, Gay and Lesbian Association) wanted to be certain that we were all initiated into the mysteries of the dental dam and the finger cot as well as certain formerly arcane sexual practices that might have made Krafft-Ebing blush.

"When our daughter went to consult a female professor concerning a paper, she found the office door covered with slogans and pictures glorifying lesbian sexual encounters."

The daughter, the letter writer reports, has transferred to a smaller relatively obscure college run on more acceptable lines.

There is plenty to observe about homosexual exhibitionism, but one thing is clear: We are deluged with propaganda demanding that we treat homosexuality as normal, just another "sexual orientation." Homosexuals are to be able to marry legally, adopt children, etc. But at the same time many are exhibitionists who recommend bizarre behavior. They do not seem normal at all. *** (*Human Events*, 2-16-96)

Lesbian Teacher Unmercifully Intimidates Christian Student

By the time she was admitted to Children's Hospital on Feb. 7, 1994, Johanna Jenei's heart rate had dropped to 35 and her blood pressure was 80/50. For weeks she had been feeling unwell and coming down with headaches. She was tense to the point of sickness, her face was turning blue, and she kept crying herself to sleep at night.

[This article was written by Jeff Jacoby, a columnist for the Boston Globe. It is about the mistreatment of a Christian student at Brookline High School by Polly Attwood, an openly lesbian teacher openly promoting homosexuality. The location of the school was not given, so I assume that it was in the Boston area.]

[Johanna had disclosed in a essay that she was a Protestant and a member of the Christian church; that she admired her grandfather who had been a Lutheran minister; that she had all of his sermons and often read them.]

[Johanna was made uncomfortable when the lesbian openly advocated homosexuality, and when she had to sit through discussions about lesbian sexuality. In a course on "Ancient Traditions," Attwood pressed the idea that women "could thrive without men." "Many in the class adopted Attwood's view; on one occasion they shouted in derision when Johanna insisted that it is good for men and women to form families and live together." She was consistently and purposefully intimidated and embarrassed.]

[The school would not let Johanna withdraw from the class and change to another more supportive teacher. Her other teachers at Brookline had considered her "alert, eager to learn, and a joy to teach."]

[But Brookline High presented a very hostile environment for Christian students with traditional views on sexual morality.]

The sex education is hard core, the gay rights advocacy relentless. During "Homophobia Awareness Month," $50 prizes are offered to students "whose work best depicts some aspect of homophobia." Pink-triangle stickers with the word "ALLY" are distributed so students can show support for homosexual activism. There is an assembly to mark National Coming-Out Day; posted notices urge students, in giant letters: "TELL SOMEONE." ***

... One March 1, the attending physician at Children's urged that she be transferred to a different school. Johanna withdrew from Brookline High on March 11 and enrolled in Lexington Christian Academy.

... The tolerance of the left, after all, goes only so far. Liberals will defend many things, but the beliefs of a 14-year-old traditional Christian girl aren't among them. (*Human Events*, 4-15-96, p. 15)

School Committee Forbids Boy Scout Recruiting

[North Adams, Mass.] — The Boy Scouts have taught honor, respect and responsibility to young men in North Adams for nearly a century, but the local school committee recently banned scout recruiting in public schools. "It has effectively cut off our recruiting efforts," said the scout leader. The committee's ban came just months after similar action in neighboring Williamstown and Lanesboro schools. In 1992 the local United Way pulled $22,000 in funding from the Scouts because they don't allow homosexuals. *** (*Religious Rights Watch*, an official publication of the Christian Coalition, April 1995)

Transvestite Activist Gives Commencement

[A transvestite is a "person who wears the clothes and often adopts the behavior of the opposite sex." *Franklin Electronic Dictionary & Thesaurus*]

Leslie Feinberg, a lesbian "Transgendered" activist, was invited to give the commencement address at Bradford College in Massachusetts. Feinberg dresses as a man and is a member of the Worker's World Party, which is enamored with North Korean communism, according to communism expert Herb Romerstein.

Students demanded Feinberg as commencement speaker after being required to read her book *Stone Butch Blues* in a required humanities seminar taught by a lesbian professor. Bradford's president, Joseph Short, at first refused, for which he was praised by a local newspaper. Hardly grateful, Short condemned the "intolerance of the local news media for those who live a different life and have alternative views." Soon Short reversed himself and welcomed Feinberg.

A spokesman said Short was unaware of Feinberg's pro-communist beliefs until notified by a reporter for Accuracy in Academia 48 hours before her May 13 speech. (*Lambda Report*, April-June 1995)

Massachusetts Celebrates "Gay Youth Pride"

The Massachusetts government sponsored the nation's first "Gay/Straight Youth Pride March" May 20 as part of its expanding campaign to support self-described "gay" issues. ***

[Republican Governor William Weld] issued an official proclamation supporting "Gay/Straight Youth Pride Month" .... *** (*Lambda Report*, April-June 1995)

Certainly, Massachusetts has become well known for its liberalism and promotion of homosexuality, but it is not alone. It has spread all over this country, and its cancerous grasp seems to have become even more prevalent in Europe.

Gay Calif. Teens Get Own Prom

HAYWARD, Calif. — A prom for gay and lesbian youths in Northern California offered something they couldn't find at their regular schools: a chance to go to the dance without fear. *** (*Albuquerque Journal*, 7-2-95)

Israeli schools to impose nationwide pro-homosexual curriculum

Beginning next school year, Israel's Ministry of Education will begin teaching a new, pro-homosexual curriculum to its students. The ministry has announced that its curriculum will "... help young people develop tolerance toward a different way of life."

As part of the program, homosexuals will visit schools to tell children about the acceptability of the gay lifestyle.

Predictably, homosexual activists hailed the decision and praised a government-funded international gay conference in June, as well as the government's grant of funding to a gay synagogue.

Following a now-familiar pattern, Israel repealed its sodomy law in 1988, and in 1992 passed a law giving homosexuals minority rights in the work place. Last year its military reaffirmed its policy of allowing homosexuals. Could the same be next for America? (Reference: "Schools to get pro-gay curriculum," *The Washington Blade*, 27 May 1994, p. 21) (*CFV Report*, Sept. 1994)

NEA Calls for Celebrating 'Lesbian and Gay History Month'

The National Education Association, the nation's leading teachers' union, passed a resolution calling for the celebration of "Gay and Lesbian History Month" in schools at the annual convention in July.

The resolution joins dozens of other motions already passed by the NEA supporting the affirmation of a homosexual "orientation" in students, pro-gay "diversity" and comprehensive AIDS education programs in schools. *** (*Lambda Report*, Jul. - Sept. 1995)

Other officials, in this country and around the world, contribute the downfall of society.

Judge enforces gay-couple benefits

PORTLAND, Ore. — A judge has ordered the state of Oregon to offer insurance benefits to the partners of gay state employees in a decision that appears to be the first of its kind in the nation. *** [On the ground that denial of such benefits was unconstitutional.]

"What we're really doing is systematically destroying the whole notion of family," said Lon Mabon, director of the Oregon Citizens Alliance. *** (*The Albuquerque Tribune*, 8-10-96)

Judge Rules Hawaii Cannot Deny Marriage Licenses to Gay Couples

HONOLULU — A state judge [Kevin Chang] Tuesday barred Hawaii from denying marriage licenses to gay couples, a decision certain to be appealed. ***

Chang "in a nutshell ruled that the sex-based classification in the State's marriage law is unconstitutional," .... . ***

If the Hawaii ruling is upheld, gay activists would then sue to overturn the national law, called the Defense of Marriage Act, said David Smith, spokesman for the Human Rights Campaign, a gay rights group based in Washington, D.C. (*Albuquerque Journal*, 12-4-96)

Sweden OKs Gay Marriage

STOCKHOLM, Sweden — Sweden followed Denmark and Norway on Tuesday and passed a bill allowing homosexuals to marry — a measure one supporter said was a "contribution to love." ***

The vote makes Scandinavia a leader in gay rights. In 1989, Denmark became the first country in the world to allow marriages between members of the same sex. Norway adopted similar legislation last year. (*Albuquerque Journal*, 6-8-94)

Church supports gay marriages:

The Unitarian Universalist Church voted to support legal recognition of gay marriages, the first major religious denomination in the country to do so. The vote Tuesday at the church's annual assembly in Indianapolis made support of same-sex marriages official policy for 1,040 Unitarian congregations. Individual churches may decide whether to have such weddings. (*The Albuquerque Tribune*, 6-26-96)

As homosexuals gained their power in San Francisco, any semblance of decency seems to have left. Homosexuals have continually fought to open up organizations, such as the Boy Scouts, so that they can more easily prey upon them. The safety of children has become a problem. The following is from an article by Steven A. Chin, San Francisco Examiner, about a part of the people of San Francisco trying to protect their children from the horrible evil.

Pedophiles prey on Asian immigrants

SAN FRANCISCO — Before a classroom of attentive 9-year-olds at the Chinese Education Center, Kingston Lum and Andrea Mar acted out a skit of a baby sitter coercing a child into watching an adult video. ***

The program is the latest offensive by the Chinatown-based Wu Yee Children's Services to combat sexual abuse of Asian children in the streets as well as in the home. ***

As the San Francisco area's Southeast Asian population has grown in the last decade, immigrant boys increasingly have become prey to pedophiles.

The Tenderloin, home to the majority of the Southeast Asian community, "is like a candy store for them," said Officer Pat White of the San Francisco Police Department's Children Sexual Exploitation Unit.

Some pedophiles find Asian boys particularly attractive because they tend to be of smaller stature and have less body hair, White said.

But it is the circumstances surrounding poor immigrant families that make Southeast Asian boys most vulnerable. Parents may work long hours earning survival wages, and speak little or no English, she said. ***

The problem is compounded by the cultural tendency of Southeast Asians to be open and trusting, added Mar. *** (*The Albuquerque Tribune*, 2-12-94)

These things truly show that western civilization, and that most civilized nations in the world, are in a sad state of cultural rot and decay. And America led the way. Can you imagine a "gay synagogue"? The sole basis of the Jewish religion is the Old Testament. The Old Testament as well as the New Testament condemnation of homosexuality was set out in detail in Chapter 3. In the Old Testament, the scripture tells us that God destroyed the cities and the people of Sodom and Gomorrah, and that their primary sin was homosexuality. In no other place in the Bible are we told of an instance, after the Great Flood, when God was so disgusted with the particular sins of a people that he chose to destroy the entire people and their cities. The Old Testament states clearly that homosexuality is an "abomination," and that there shall be no "sodomite of the sons of Israel." Now we have a government funded synagogue for the sodomites of Israel.

Capitulating to the homosexual movement will be the beginning of the end of our religious principles and traditional family values based upon the Bible, which have been the backbone of this country since its inception. There will no longer be any basis for the idea that one man should be married to one woman. Once the idea of same sex marriage is accepted, there is no longer any logical basis for barring bigamy, polygamy, incest, and multiple marriages. The government has no more right to prevent any of these things than it does same-sex marriages. Why should not a bi-sexual have the right to be married to both men and women? If we follow the liberal ideas of "discrimination," the bi-sexual is definitely being discriminated against.

It sometimes seems astonishing that there are still a few people that have the knowledge and moral courage to take a stand against the destructive culture engulfing us. But there are not many left with the will to fight, and the homosexual juggernaut rolls over us.

The following is a quotation attributed to Abraham Lincoln: **"To sin by silence when they should protest makes cowards of men."**

AIDS—AN UNNECESSARY CRISIS

The AIDS epidemic with which this country is now faced need not and should not have happened. It exists because of two things—promiscuity and politics. Both were necessary elements to the calamity.

The promiscuity was caused by two things—lack of morality and lack of willpower. And the two go together.

The politics were caused by two things—lack of morality and stupidity. And the two seem to go together.

When we lose our moral compass of the Christian and Judaic religions, we consistently go the wrong direction. And this is what has happened. There was a time when the AIDS crisis would not have happened in this country. The people once had the morality, the courage, and the strength that would have prevented it. It is merely a natural part of our present day decadence. We removed sodomy laws and gave homosexuals the "rights" that they pressed for. We encouraged their vile and destructive sexual acts, and their binges of promiscuity. Homosexuals responded by giving to their country the AIDS epidemic.

Today there are at least two sexually transmitted diseases (STDs) with no known cure—AIDS and herpes. In this day and time, anyone who would have sex with a stranger, either "protected" or unprotected, thereby putting one's life and health on the line for the sake of a sexual encounter, has a lack of morality, a lack of judgment, and a suicidal complex. And all three seem to go together. Yet every night and every day, our "bathhouses" and other homosexual meeting places, our nightclubs and other heterosexual meeting places, and even our parks and streets, contain large numbers of people who are hunting and eager to do that very thing.

The homosexualists and many of the other liberals do not have the moral base to be able to comprehend that casual sex is not necessary. There have been people that were celibate all of their lives. There have been many others that were celibate for substantial parts of their lives. Would you believe that there are even people who have refrained from sex until they found a person of good character, and of the opposite sex, and got married? These things are possible.

Many will say that these ideas and arguments are "too simplistic." This is a trite phrase often used by liberals to try to avoid facing facts that should be obvious by the use of common sense.

Until the people of this country return to a religious moral foundation, they will never have the judgment, the courage, and the strength to turn this country around. Many of our churches today have become spineless. They are so afraid of criticism of the liberal media and of lawsuits from homosexuals and their liberal ilk that they no longer have the courage to take a stand for what is right on a matter that is as controversial today as homosexuality. And it is this cowardly attitude that is wrecking our country. It not only exists in our churches, but the same cowardice permeates our schools, our government officials, our elected representatives, our entertainment and news media, and our large corporations. It is indeed a destructive cowardice.

We should not blame our elected representatives, because we are the ones that elected them—often knowing their lack of morality and what they stood for. Classic examples of this are the election and re-election of President Clinton; and the continued reelection in Massachusetts of Gerry Studds and Barney Frank as congressional representatives. We, the people, are to blame for our country's moral destruction.

We are also to blame for the physical destruction caused by AIDS reaching its epidemic proportions.

From the outset this country should have done what was necessary to identify those with HIV, the virus that causes AIDS, and protect those who had not acquired it. At one time this country would have even had the sense and courage to use quarantine, if necessary. But what was done was the exact opposite of what should have been done. The homosexualists ruled, and calamity is the result.

As explained in Chapter 1, AIDS was spread by the homosexuals and their promiscuous excesses. They even contaminated blood supplies by their willful and wrongful actions, thereby causing the infection of many men, women, and children who were completely innocent and engaged in no wrongdoing of any kind. It is this latter group that really deserves our sympathy. Now that it has spread to the heterosexual community, it continues to be spread by promiscuous and immoral actions—and they go together.

The homosexuals celebrated their "rights" and immediately began to self-destruct with their perversion. They spread AIDS among themselves by their promiscuity and perversion. They even spread it to other parts of the world. And even worse, they spread it to innocent people and to innocent children by their reckless—and sometimes intentional— acts of giving blood when they knew that they either had AIDS or were at risk for it.

The homosexualists have learned well how to prey on the sympathy of kind-hearted people. They misuse the natural sympathy one holds for a person with a deadly disease, to try to make heroes of homosexuals with AIDS, and to gain further acceptance of homosexuality. They have been amazingly successful.

They misused the AIDS crisis they created to try to get sex education into our schools for the purpose of the prevention of the disease. But their so-called sex education consists, to a large part, of the promotion of homosexuality, and selling it to impressionable adolescents as an acceptable lifestyle—one that is interesting and attractive, according to the false homosexual presentations. Some of their insidious inroads into the schools will also be covered in Chapter 6, The Homosexual Agenda.

The homosexualists have helped spread the AIDS virus by actively promoting laws that prohibited required examinations to determine if a person has the AIDS virus, and prohibitions of disclosure of the identity of those who have the virus. They have knowingly and willfully, by such actions, greatly increased the danger to innocent people, as well as those who unknowingly engage in sex without knowledge that their partner has the virus. That gives any thinking person further insight into the thinking and the morality of the homosexual mind.

The homosexualists gained early influence over the National Commission on AIDS, to the detriment of the country.

AIDS Commission Report Ignores Individual Responsibility
(By Joan Beck, *Chicago Tribune*)

Its hard not to feel some irritation reading that new report by the National Commission on AIDS – no matter how much you care about people with AIDS and HIV infection and how urgent it is to stop this devastating epidemic. ***

... it keeps conveniently quiet about the individual responsibility of people to avoid the high-risk behavior that enables the AIDS virus to keep on spreading so tragically.

The report is careful not to blame drug addicts who share needles and disease with others. Or the gays who refuse to give up high-risk sex. Or the HIV-positive people who won't allow notification of the contacts they are exposing. Or the women with HIV who get pregnant and inflict AIDS on their infants. Or those with high-risk lifestyles who won't even allow themselves to be tested for HIV.

Instead, it lays the responsibility on the government for not tailoring its educational efforts to reach target populations more effectively

"There has been a dominant undercurrent of hostility toward many people with HIV disease, as if they are somehow to blame," says the report. "But no one gets this virus on purpose." ***

But sympathy for those who have AIDS is no reason for a report like this one to gloss over the fact that individual behavior is responsible for most of the continuing spread of the AIDS virus. Stopping high-risk behavior is the surest way to halt the spread of this disease until scientists can solve the unusually difficult problems involved in making a vaccine.

The report makes the outrageous assertion that "the country has responded with indifference" to the AIDS epidemic. And it charges the government with "inertia" ... .

"Inertia"? The response to AIDS has been unprecedented. AIDS has gotten more public attention, more research funding, more media coverage and more educational effort than any other disease in

the last decade – including those that have effects that are just as devastating and take 10 times as many lives. ***
(*Albuquerque Journal*, 10-7-91)

On December 5, 1993, in ABC News, on television, it was disclosed that a little girl in New York was intentionally stabbed with a needle. **She did not have the right to have her attacker examined to find out if the attacker carried the AIDS virus.** Under New York law, according to the news item, only sex offenders can be compelled to be tested.

In 1994, the World Health Organization estimated that by the year 2000 30–40 million people will be HIV–positive. (*The Albuquerque Tribune*, 8-12-94) The current spread of this disease is now due almost entirely to irresponsible sexual behavior. It is a disgrace and a blot on our current civilization, and their is no reasonable excuse for the epidemic in this country. It is one more tragic part of our moral decline, and demonstrates the destructiveness of that decline.

By 1995, the disease had become the top killer of young adults in this country—even surpassing accidents.
(*The Albuquerque Tribune*, 2-2-95)

I thought that an article, "**43 actors died from AIDS, but Live on in 'Philadelphia'**", by Clifford Rothman, *The Albuquerque Tribune,* 1-20-95, to be interesting from several aspects. It reflects the push of the entertainment media to make the disgusting admirable, and with great success. "'Philadelphia' became one of the most successful dramatic films of 1993, earning an Oscar for Tom Hanks and $125 million at the box office worldwide before it was released on video."

Tom Hanks portrayed a homosexual lawyer, Andrew Becket, who had AIDS. I have not read or heard of anything portrayed by the film that amounted to anything great or admirable, or beneficial to society, done by its characters. I, of course, see nothing admirable about being a homosexual and acquiring AIDS by vile homosexual acts. What is interesting is that, according to the article, fifty-three people with AIDS or who were HIV positive played parts in the film, and by the time of the article forty-three of them were dead. It also makes me wonder about how many other people were given AIDS through contacts with those fifty-three, and how many of them were also dead. One must have compassion for someone who contracts such a deadly disease, no matter what wrongful acts brought it on—but, please, deliver me from the admiration part.

From everything I have read about the movie, it has an insidious plot designed to remove the gullible viewer from any sound sense of reason, and leaves one with the sense that there is something good about the vile acts by which the homosexual contracts AIDS, and that the acquisition of the deadly disease thereby makes him some kind of a hero. I suppose that in this day and time there are those with that degree of gullibility. I agree with the following:

> **"Philadelphia:" pro-homosexual indoctrination at a theatre near you.**
> Every performance of the movie "Philadelphia" should begin with the film equivalent of a Surgeon General's warning. "Beware: the images you are about to ingest have been expressly designed to manipulate and reshape your emotions for political ends. Viewers may experience a reduction in logical faculties." ***
> Any victim of AIDS is a human tragedy. However, to idolize the behavior which introduced this deadly disease to America and then by its political power enabled it to become an uncontrollable epidemic, is an even greater tragedy. (*CFV Report*, May 1994)

The public has been continually bombarded with lengthy illustrated articles and programs in our newspapers, magazines, and TV shows trying to brainwash us into thinking that there was something admirable about homosexuals acquiring and living with AIDS. We have marches for those who have AIDS and monuments to those who have died of AIDS, and quilts made in memory of them. But the most disappointing thing is how much of the gullible public has fallen for this illogical and foolish propaganda. This brainwashing has been an integral part of the homosexual movement.

Now AIDS has become a tremendous problem in this country and in the world. It is reaching staggering proportions even among heterosexuals. Immorality often has its natural penalties.

Clinton to reverse foreign-AIDS ban

WASHINGTON — President Clinton will reverse the 6-year-old policy that barred foreigners infected with the AIDS virus from

entering the United States, the White House said today. ...
(*The Albuquerque Tribune*, 2-9-93)

How could inviting those with AIDS to come into this country do anything but harm? What prompts a president to do such destructive things to his own country?

AIDS Grant To Fund Housing

WASHINGTON — New Mexico was awarded $1.1 million Monday by the U.S. Housing and Urban Development Department to provide housing assistance to people with HIV or AIDS, ***
(*Albuquerque Journal*, 11-4-97)

This country spends untold millions throughout the country on people with AIDS and AIDS-related programs. It would be a mammoth job to even try to determine the total amount as there are so many different programs.

AIDS Grove New Landmark

SAN FRANCISCO — A quiet, wooded grove — one of the first public places to grieve AIDS victims — will soon join the ranks of Mount Rushmore, the Vietnam Veterans Memorial and other national landmarks.

... President Clinton is expected to sign the bill including the designation.

The grove was conceived in 1989 by a small group of people who had lost loved ones to AIDS. *** (*Albuquerque Journal*, 10-6-96)

Can you imagine a country becoming so decadent and submissive to the homosexualists that those dying of AIDS—most of whom were homosexuals and acquired AIDS because of their intentional lecherous acts—are honored together with our greatest presidents and war veterans who died in the service of their country? Why do we not have a memorial for those who died of other sexually transmitted diseases? We do not even have memorials for innocent victims of illnesses or diseases such as leprosy, tuberculosis, cancer, and heart disease. Why is this? Should we have a worldwide monument honoring those who spread the AIDS virus and die of it? See the next article.

40% of Paris Men 25-44 Die of AIDS

PARIS —Sounding a new alarm in the European country worst hit by AIDS, government researchers say the disease accounts for 40 percent of deaths among Parisian men age 25 to 44.

Paris' large, AIDS-vulnerable homosexual population, and resistance to AIDS education are cited as reasons why France has had the most AIDS cases and deaths in Europe. ***

(*Albuquerque Journal*, 1-10-93)

Young Gays' AIDS Rate 'Very High'

BALTIMORE — AIDS is spreading fast among males in their teens and early 20s who have homosexual encounters, even though they grew up amid widespread awareness of ways to avoid the lethal virus, a study found.

Preliminary results presented Saturday from the first national survey of young homosexual and bisexual men show that 7 percent are infected with HIV, the virus that causes AIDS.

"HIV prevalence is very high among young men who have sex with men, compared with the general population of youths in the U.S.," said Dr. Linda Valleroy of the U.S. Centers for Disease Control and Prevention.

Her survey found that more than a third of these young men have had anal sex without condoms in the past six months. This is the primary way HIV spreads among homosexuals.

"The prevalence of unprotected anal sex is alarming, given that these young men grew up in an era of HIV awareness," she said.

The study was based on interviews and tests of young men at places where homosexuals often congregate, including bars, beaches and street corners. *** (*Albuquerque Journal*, 2-11-96)

When considering statistics about homosexuality and AIDS, I think we should keep in mind that there is surely a natural reluctance to admit that one is a homosexual or has AIDS, and that such statistics are more likely to be understated than overstated in that regard.

A government report in 1995 announced that AIDS appeared to be leveling off, with about 40,000 new infections every year balanced by about 40,000 annual deaths. (*Albuquerque Journal*, 11-24-95)

The World Health Organization estimated that about 18.5 million people worldwide were infected with the AIDS virus. The United states accounted for about 7 percent of the estimated cases. (*Albuquerque Journal*, 12-16-95) The same organization predicts that there will be 30 million HIV cases worldwide by the year 2000.
(*Christian American*, Feb. 1994)

AIDS PATTERNS SHIFTING

More than half a million AIDS cases have been reported to the Centers for Disease Control and Prevention as of [November, 1996] ... . Some 62 percent, or more than 311,000 of those AIDS patients died.

Men who have sex with men continue to account for the largest proportion of AIDS cases, but that is declining. ... Groups accounting for an increasing portion of AIDS cases include people who use injectable drugs and people infected through heterosexual sex. ...

Although rates of infection with AIDS remain highest in the Northeast, the greatest proportionate increases have occurred in the South and Midwest, CDC officials said.

... The rates for AIDS cases are six times higher among American blacks than among whites, and three times higher among Hispanics. Whites now account for less than half of all AIDS cases in the United States. ...

The World Health Organization estimates that 18 million adults and 1.5 million children have been infected with HIV, the virus that causes AIDS. (*The Washington Post*, 12-12-96)
(*Issues at a Glance*, Feb. 1996)

World AIDS Cases Surpass Estimate

AIDS has struck the world much harder than previously thought, a U.N. agency (UNAIDS) said Wednesday in a report showing that more than 30 million people are infected. ***
(*Albuquerque Journal*, 11-27-97)

The following is from **THE POLITICS OF AIDS**, by Connie Zhu, *Christian American,* October 1993:

*** Why does AIDS, a deadly contagion merit its own billion-dollar federal budget, its own politically correct education programs that push condoms and clean needles, its own activist lobbying groups that bar traditional medical procedures, and its own television specials, while it continues to ravage America and the world largely unchecked?

Author Stanley Monteith, M.D., traces the history of the disease in his 1991 book *AIDS, the Unnecessary Epidemic.* According to Monteith, the Centers of Disease Control quickly located the common threads to the new illness that was killing young male homosexuals in the United States. As early as October, 1981, the CDC knew that most of those contracting killer opportunistic infections had frequented gay bathhouses, for example.

By 1982 the CDC directly or indirectly linked 40 AIDS cases to one French Canadian individual. But "Patient Zero," as they referred to him, refused to stop having sexual relations.

Monteith believes that several steps by the CDC could have halted the epidemic, which had by that point moved out of the gay community and begun infecting IV-drug users and hemophiliacs. They could have deported "Patient Zero," since he was not a U.S. citizen, after his refusal to cooperate. Instead he was allowed to spread HIV infection unchecked for nearly another two years. And they should have closed all gay bathhouses, sex clubs, pornography shops, prostitution rings and IV shooting galleries. ***

And long before 1985, when AIDS researcher Robert Gallo patented the HIV antibody blood test, gay activists and leaders of the AIDS lobby began to demand that the tests only be used to test blood bank specimens rather than used to screen the general population.

Members of the AIDS lobbies then convinced state legislators to enact laws prohibiting identification of those infected with HIV. They convinced lawmakers to make a distinction between HIV infection and AIDS, the end-stage infection.

And this is where problems began. Since HIV infection was not considered an infectious disease, like AIDS, it did not need to be traced or reported to the CDC like AIDS had been since 1981.

Consequently, laws were passed in every state prohibiting doctors without written or informed consent from routinely using HIV blood tests and reporting test results to health officials.

In 1985, California passed a law which fined physicians up to $10,000 plus a year in prison if they violated confidentiality in regards to a patient testing positive for HIV. This meant, for example, that no doctor could alert any of his staff about a patient's HIV status prior to surgery or treatment without breaking the law. ***

Another example of the politics of AIDS came on the opening day of the 1991 VII International Conference on AIDS. The Harvard AIDS Institute, local sponsor of the next year's VIII International Conference, distributed a statement that they "strenuously oppose the listing of HIV on the list of communicable diseases of public health significance, and in fact oppose any restrictions on travel or immigration to the United States by people with AIDS. If HIV is not removed from the list, the VIII International Conference on AIDS may be canceled. If this cancellation occurs, the resulting year's delay in progress against AIDS will be the responsibility of the government of the United States."

The Harvard AIDS Institute and the AIDS Action Council activists also pressured Louis Sullivan, Health and Human Services director. By the time he submitted his list of "communicable diseases of public health significance" to the Federal Register on January 23, 1991, there was only one listed—infectious tuberculosis. But Sullivan's proposal met with such public outcry that he was forced to amend it.

If the public had been as verbal in their opposition to other such public health measures concerning HIV infection today's AIDS epidemic might look much different.

"They neglected being involved because they felt that this was going to be largely a gay disease," said Shepherd Smith founder of Americans for a Sound HIV/AIDS Policy. "They allowed the gay community to dictate policy, which it did."

Smith advocates a return to traditional medical and public health procedures historically used to control other infectious diseases. In this approach the responsibility to diagnose and monitor the spread of HIV infection is again placed on the medical and public health communities.

"In many states today, because we've focused on the rights of people infected and neglected the rights of uninfected people, there are individuals living together, sometimes in marriage, who don't have the benefit of knowing that the person they live with is HIV-positive," stated Smith.

In some of these cases the medical and public health communities have this information. But unless the HIV-positive individual has given written and informed consent for partner notification, others who have had intimate contact with that person may not know that they are at risk of becoming infected. ***

Until all states enact legislation requiring some types of mandatory testing and confidential partner notification, there is little chance of abating the spread of HIV infection. As a result we still have the most deadly disease that by law cannot be tested for, its spread traced and its whereabouts reported. As a result no one really knows the extent of HIV infection. That's why the CDC only estimates the number of infections.

But even while partner notification programs are gaining a toehold in some states, Americans continue to indulge in behavior that may continue to ensure the spread of HIV and AIDS. ***

The article also explains how Jesse Helms and others have tried to get a bill passed for mandatory testing of public health workers and cannot even get that through Congress.

It is abundantly clear that the homosexualists bear the primary responsibility for the spread of AIDS in this country. Yet—consistent with that ilk's propensity to state the opposite of the truth—they blame it on "homophobia." But I have never seen nor heard any logical explanation of this contention. It is typical of the mind of the homosexual activist.

What Really Furthers the Spread of AIDS?
By Don Feder

*** "Irrational prejudices like homophobia have obstructed public health efforts to prevent the spread of AIDS," the [Public Media Center] charges. ***

In 1994, AIDS killed about 42,000 Americans. The same year, more than 730,000 died of heart disease and cancer claimed around 520,000.

Not counting entitlement spending on Medicare and Medicaid, under the president's fiscal 1996 budget, Washington will allocate

$1,134 per heart-disease death, $4,808 for every cancer victim and $71,429 for each individual who died of AIDS last year. Homophobia is not among the factors driving AIDS policy.

AIDS is our first politicized disease—a tribute to the power of the homosexual lobby. There are no cancer activists beating their fists and feet on the floor over "inadequate funding" for their ailment.

At Academy Awards ceremonies, celebrities don't wear miniature insulin bottles to express solidarity with diabetics (even though, each year, diabetes kills more than AIDS). There are no elderly demonstrators lying down in front of traffic to protest the lack of a cure for Alzheimer's disease.

AIDS Funding Safeguarded
To Promote Homosexuality

Activists are intent on safeguarding AIDS funding because much of it goes toward promoting homosexuality. According to an April 6, 1994 article in the *Trentonian*, a $100,000 federal AIDS grant was used to sponsor a "drag-queens' ball," in Newark, NJ.

We homophobes reckon that AIDS is a lifestyle disease. By and large, you get it from doing certain things that everyone knows are highly hazardous. Trouble is, certain people just keep doing them anyway.

In a 1992 feature on gays, *Newsweek* profiled Wally Hansen, who works for a San Francisco gay newspaper and is HIV-positive. Hansen believes pushing condoms in the schools is crucial to stopping the spread of AIDS.

But says *Newsweek*, personally, "Hansen is reckless," despite the risk of acquiring other strains of AIDS and giving his disease to partners. "I only think positively," Wally explains. "I do anything I want. I feel like I'm doing more damage to myself by stressing my system out of worry."

Just over a year ago, *The City Paper*, a Washington, D.C. weekly, reported on doings at an establishment called Men's Massage Parties (less than a mile from the White House) where more than a therapeutic rubdown is available. A journalist who checked it out saw group sex ("three-, four-, or moresome"), often unprotected.

The Washington *Blade*, a gay paper, urges the readers to practice "safer sex," while carrying display ads for those orgies. Since the publication clearly is not homophobic, it couldn't possibly be facilitating the spread of AIDS.

We know what works in combating a sexually transmitted disease—testing and contact tracing. Before penicillin, that's how syphilis was checked. The average AIDS activist will marry the girl next door before dropping his opposition to either approach.

In July, the U.S. Senate rejected an amendment to reauthorization of the Ryan White Act that would have required HIV positive testing for all mothers and newborns. True to form, AIDS activists opposed the amendment as an intolerable intrusion on privacy, never mind that children born with the virus won't get the care they need. For the AIDS lobby, mom's privacy nixes baby's health.

Here another dastardly effort of vile homophobes to spread AIDS through ignorance and prejudice was stopped dead in its tracks by heroic activists. Hurrah, hurrah. (*Human Events*, 1-12-96)

THE CLINTON ADMINISTRATION LEADS US IN DECADENCE AND HYPOCRISY

The promotion of homosexuality by President William Jefferson Clinton continues in high gear. Consider the following excerpts from an article by nationally syndicated columnist Linda Bowles, "With benefit of political doxology," *The Washington Times*, 9-21-97:

For the first time in the history of America, a United States President has appeared as guest speaker before a homosexual group.

President Clinton recently made such an historic appearance before the Human Rights Campaign, a powerful organization of rich and influential homosexuals who had gathered to celebrate themselves and to raise money with which to buy politicians.

Mr. Clinton was a hit. He solidified his legacy as a champion of the underdog. He received whistles, cheers and standing ovations as he confirmed his approval of homosexual behavior and pledged his support of legislation to advance the homosexual agenda. ***

Mr. Clinton announced his intention of sponsoring legislation to protect homosexuals against job discrimination. *****

The president's agenda goes far beyond tolerance for that which is different. He is actively engaged in the business of validating homosexuality, reinforcing and stroking those who practice it and using the punitive power of the law to force it upon American society. *****

I believe that President Clinton has now established himself to be a man who is completely devoid of morals, and the ultimate hypocrite. He still, in 2000, regularly has news photographers on hand to photograph him coming out of church—always carrying a Bible, which obviously has no meaning to him. Carrying his Bible around, he continues to promote homosexuality—and this certainly does not seem to be his only vice. His admitted adultery has now caused him to be impeached, and sex scandal after sex scandal continues to come out about this man. There are unqualified allegations by people who knew Clinton about his illegal and improper behavior of all kinds, both while he was governor of Arkansas and while he was president. More detrimental books have been written and more detrimental videos—containing direct allegations by identified people—have already been published about Clinton than about any president in history. It is hard to believe that all of these people who personally knew Clinton, and had dealings with him, are all liars, and thereby making themselves liable for defamation actions. Also, many of them have now stated their claims under oath, which, if untrue, would make them subject to perjury as well as defamation.

He has been using all of the offices and power of the federal government that he can to not only promote, but to force the acceptance of homosexuality on the people of America.

And he's been successful. A large part of our people, particularly the young, have already forsaken the traditional morals of this country, which were based on Christian and Judaic principles. Many more seem to think that morality is immaterial and irrelevant to the leadership of this country. According to national polls, a majority of those who voted for Clinton did not believe him to have good moral character. His approval ratings are being reported to have climbed during all of this to the seventy percentiles—his highest ever. The same polls show that most of the same people believe that the scandalous allegations are true, that he lied under oath about them, and that he lied to the people.

Our president, still following his hippie, anti-war, anti-American, and anti-Judaic-and-Christian principles, has now led us to the lowest point of immoral degradation in our history. Our forefathers could never have imagined the depth to which we have sunk.

Let us look at another specific example. While I am writing this part of the book, in March, 1998, Clinton has numerous investigations going against him for alleged criminal conduct, including various forms of adultery, perjury, subornation of perjury, and obstruction of justice; and is in danger of impeachment as President. Part of the allegations involve his misconduct with Monica Lewinsky, an intern in the White House, in her early twenties when the alleged affair began. According to taped statements of Miss Lewinsky, that are now widely reported, she had "oral sex" with Clinton, on many occasions, in the Oval Office, and adjoining studies. Such acts are still criminal in some states, and prior to the sixties, were criminal in most of our states. The tapes showed that she was planning to then falsely state under oath, in the pending Paula Jones civil case against Clinton, that she had no sexual relations with Clinton, at the behest of Clinton and his aids. According to the news she then filed such an affidavit. It also came out in the news and television shows that she had a sexual affair before this with a former married teacher in the university to which she went. And that she informed this instructor and his wife of her unnatural affair of oral sex with Clinton. At this point few reasonable people doubt the affair. But the depth of our moral muck is shown by polls reporting that the people care little about these allegations—including the perjury and obstruction of justice—whether or not they are true. The national polls still give Clinton high approval ratings. The following is an example of the convoluted and degenerate morality of our people:

Former Intern Escapes D.C.
MOUNT LAUREL, N.J. – Monica Lewinsky left star-struck admirers in New Jersey last weekend, where she escaped Washington for a visit with a family of a friend of her lawyer.

Lewinsky and lawyer William H. Ginsburg spent about nine hours visiting with Fred and Anni Schall and their children, shopping, dining out, visiting Philadelphia and dropping in on a cheerleading squad.

"She's absolutely beautiful," Mrs. Schall said, "I was completely taken by her. I felt like I was meeting a star. She's perfect. She's gorgeous."

The family said Ginsburg told them they could not ask Lewinsky about the grand jury investigation into whether she had an affair with President Clinton and then denied it in an affidavit.

(*Albuquerque Journal*, 3-21-98)

It is hard to believe that the thinking of people could sink to this level. Not only does it show complete lack of morality—it is also stupid. There has been nothing in the news that could have made Miss Lewinsky such an admired celebrity, except the allegations that she on many occasions had oral sex with an adulterous president. What a wonderful example for the cheerleading squad!

Many people in this country have lost the moral courage to take a stand on anything or make any attempt to stop wrongdoing and violence, even in their presence. There have been many instances in the past thirty years of people standing by and doing nothing while they witnessed various kinds of assaults, robbery, and murder. The following is typical:

Witnesses See Man Beaten (to death)

DENVER – People watched from the safety of their high rise apartments before dawn Sunday as four men beat a taxi driver to death and dumped his body in the trunk of the cab, investigators said.

"Eyewitnesses saw him being beaten and dragged by his feet and thrown in the trunk, but no one called 911," said Detective Virginia Lopes. "It's disgusting." ***

Police were summoned to the area when the victim's friend called police from a nearby store and said the two were being robbed and beaten by four men. Officers searched near the apartments for the driver while neighbors watched, Lopez said. (*Albuquerque Journal*, 3-30-98)

A CBS TV News report, 3-30-98, on this incident. said that over a dozen people watched this incident, yet only one claimed to have called police, and that his call didn't get through.

What kind of people are these that will not even call the police from the safety of their own apartments when they are witnessing such a crime?

We have the same lack of courage, lack of morality, and apathy when it comes to fighting the onslaught on this country by the homosexualists.

If the present trend of immorality continues in this country, we are heading for the same decadence that possessed Nazi Germany; and it is only a matter of time until our country meets its demise, as did Germany and the Roman Empire—and for the same reasons.

CONCLUSION

The facts speak for themselves. This country and the world is in a tragic and unprecedented moral decline. The homosexual movement has flourished because of this, and, moreover, it has been a large contributing factor. That group has spent a terrific amount of time, money, and effort to destroy our traditional values, and replace them with the most vile paganism imaginable. Their great success has occurred because there have not been sufficient decent people who have recognized the danger and had the courage to take a stand against it.

CHAPTER 5

THE CAUSE OF OUR DECLINE IN MORALITY

The fact of the rapid decline in morality in this country and around the world is well established. The fact that it is caused by the turning away from Christian-Judaic principles is also equally established. This should be obvious to anyone. One who is living by those principles does not engage in sodomy, murder, mayhem, adultery, or even in one of the most common sins against those religions, which is heterosexual fornication. But a large question still remains: What caused us to turn away from these traditional principles of morality? That question is more complicated. But I believe that the teaching of modern theories of evolution as proven facts in our universities and places of higher learning has caused us to turn from and disregard the religious principles of Christianity and Judaism; and that this is the initial and most important cause of our decline in traditional morality. Such false teachings have done immense harm to our civilization.

Generally speaking, our churches have failed us. They have not had the will to fight and defend the teachings of the Bible, which is the sole basis of their faith. They impotently compromise and reconcile. Even music now allowed in some of the churches seems modern, strange, and has not the steady strength and character of older religious music.

473

In one respect, we have now gotten to the low point in our history because of cowardice and timidity. We who have moral convictions are afraid to voice them because of the derision and contempt displayed by the "educated elite." Fortunately, though, there are a few left that still have both convictions and courage. I have referred to many in this book. One is syndicated columnist Suzanne Fields, who wrote the article from which parts are quoted below. I consider it exceptional, and I believe that she displays a clear understanding of some of our basic problems, and the solutions to them.

Religious Morality Unwelcome in Political Discourse

Religion, sex and politics have often been disruptive topics at American dinner tables, and hence taboo in some places, but today only religion is the bastard in the family of politically cultured topics. God is not dead in such politics, but He sure is told to shut up.

Of course, this doesn't include the Christian Coalition, the religious right and other orthodox and conservative groups whose members define religion as the major influence on their political thinking. They have become politically savvy inside and outside the Beltway. This observation doesn't extend to the well-wishers of the civil rights movement first led by Martin Luther King. Nor does it stretch to include the left-wing Catholic radicals such as the Berrigan brothers and their socialist brothers in Latin America. ...

... neither God nor religion is allowed to inform sophisticated arguments. Religious people are quickly put on the defensive.

Last month Justice Antonin Scalia of the Supreme Court, a Catholic, speaking to a prayer breakfast at the Mississippi College School of Law, a private Baptist institution, received a standing ovation when he said: "We must pray for the courage to endure the scorn of the sophisticated world." The next day the sophisticated world argued that his remarks were inappropriate for a man in his position.

Last week Justice Clarence Thomas, also Catholic, picked up on the same theme when he spoke to graduates of Liberty University, a Baptist school in Lynchburg, Va. He described the dark days of his soul when he lost faith at college, temporarily succumbing to the pressures of his better-educated peers and rebelling against the rock bottom faith of his grandparents in Pin Point, Ga.

"It is only by God's grace and His mighty shoulders that my wife and I endured the unpleasantness of my confirmation," said the man who has rediscovered the spiritual roots of his family. (Imagine how Anita Hill's defenders heard that?)

I am a Jew, and not a very religious one, but in the cultural turmoil of the last few decades I have grown to appreciate the Catholics who publicly hold a moral line, who offer standards that require others to argue against. I have grown to appreciate the evangelical Christians on the right for raising issues of family values that emanate from their faith and illuminate the standards we once all held to. Many men and women of other faiths and no doubt those of no faith cheer their moral positions but are loath to give them credit.

A moral person need not base his moral beliefs on religion, but religious faith grounds our inalienable rights bestowed by the Creator. A secular society without God-fearing men and women who inform moral judgment is a society with very big problems. Every infant who comes into the world can learn the universal standards of good behavior. But without a society informed by the principles enshrined in ancient faith and belief, whose ethical rules are understood even in the breach, who is there to teach him?
(Fields, Suzanne, *Albuquerque Journal*, 5-16-96)

It appears that some of Justice Scalia's remarks may have been in response to (or prompted by) three stories in the three most popular newsmagazines, *Time, Newsweek,* and *U.S. News and World Report,* all for the week of April 8, 1996, at Easter time. James C. Dobson, Ph.D., in his newsletter, *Focus on the Family,* June 1996, speaks of these magazine cover stories as "each questioning the historic validity of Jesus' resurrection," as stated in the New Testament. It is certainly a sign of the times that top media sources, at Easter time, all and simultaneously denigrate the Christian religion.

Scalia's speech was reported in this manner (Ibid.):

"Devout Christians are destined to be regarded as fools in modern society," Supreme Court Justice Antonin Scalia said Tuesday, offering a rare glimpse of his private views. "We are fools for Christ's sake," the conservative jurist said. "We must pray for courage to endure the scorn of the sophisticated world."
Scalia said intellectuals through history have rejected miracles and the Easter story. "The wise do not investigate such silliness," he said sarcastically. "They do not believe [in the resurrection of the dead.]"

Scalia said it's "irrational" to reject miracles. "One can be sophisticated and believe in God. Reason and intellect are not to be laid aside where matters of religion are concerned."

He [Scalia] took note ... that the word "cretin," or fool, is derived from the French word for "Christian."

"To be honest about it, that is the view of Christians taken by modern society," Mr. Scalia told 650 persons ... "Surely those who adhere to all or most of these traditional Christian beliefs are to be regarded as simpleminded."

"To many Americans," he added sarcastically, "everything from the Easter morning to the Ascension had to be made up by the groveling enthusiasts [the disciples] as part of their plan to get themselves martyred."

"Prominent editorial writers, columnists and cultural elites were appalled at this audacity. They came after the justice with a vengeance, just as he knew they would, and just as they regularly castigate another conservative, notably [Justice] Clarence Thomas." (Ibid.)

Even James C. Dunn, Executive Director of the Baptist Joint Committee on Public Affairs in Washington, D.C., scoffed at Justice Scalia's words (Ibid.), although I think that such an attitude is certainly contrary to the general thinking of the Baptist laity, and their ministers, too. As shown by Dr. Dobson's newsletter (Ibid.), the general thrust of the arguments of the political pundits and Washington insiders is that it is wrong for a Supreme Court Justice to voice his religious faith and concerns about the attacks against religious beliefs, because it breaches the wall separating church and state, and is contrary to our Constitution as enacted by our founding fathers.

Nothing is further from the truth. The First Amendment barring the passing of laws "respecting an establishment of religion, or prohibiting the free exercise thereof," was clearly for the purpose of protecting freedom of religion, and prohibiting the establishment of a federally dictated religion or the establishment of a federally governed church, such as many had fled in coming to this country. The view of our founding fathers as to religion, and the Christian religion in particular, is the exact opposite of what our liberal pundits and politicians of today would have us believe. This is of course entirely consistent with general liberal thought today — invariably, it is the exact opposite of the truth. In

Chapter 8, we will consider in detail what many of the early leaders and later great leaders of this country thought in regard to religion. Without exception, they have all recognized the importance of our government and our leaders being guided by religious principles. Modern deviation from these principles is the direct cause of our moral degradation today, and its resulting damage to our culture and our country. It has brought us to our lowest point in our history.

The following is from Chapter 22—RELIGION AND RELIGIOUS GROUPS IN AMERICA, Great Issues in American Life, Conspectus, Vol. II, *The Annals of America*, Encyclopedia Britannica, Inc., 1968; pp. 418–419:

> Religion has pervaded all aspects of American culture and largely determined its basic political, moral, and social views. It fostered and established the educational institutions out of which the later secular culture evolved. Its book—the Bible, especially the King James Version—has had an enduring effect on the American mind, culture, and literature ... .
>
> The central and pervasive role of religion in the three centuries of American history is not seriously disputed. Most observers have remarked on the strikingly greater religiousness exhibited by Americans in comparison with their European contemporaries in various eras. "There is no country in the world," Alexis de Tocqueville asserted in the 1830s, "where the Christian religion retains a greater influence over the souls of men than in America." Similarly, in 1855, the German–Swiss theologian Philip Schaff estimated that there were in America "more awakened souls, and more individual effort and self-sacrifice for religious purposes, proportionally, than in any other country in the world, Scotland alone perhaps excepted."

Alexis de Tocqueville, the famous 19th century French statesman, historian and social philosopher, also said:

> Religion in America ... must be regarded as the foremost of the political institutions of that country; for if it does not impart a taste for freedom it facilitates the use of it. Indeed, it is this same point of view that the inhabitants of the United States themselves look upon religious belief. (*One Nation Under God*, Christian Defense Fund, U.S. 1997)

Patrick Henry said:

It cannot be emphasized too strongly or too often that this great nation was founded, not by religionists, but by Christians; not on religions, but on the Gospel of Jesus Christ. For this very reason peoples
of other faiths have been afforded asylum, prosperity, and freedom of
worship here. (Ibid.)

At its inception, this country was a bastion of freedom and religion—primarily the Christian religion. It was reflected in our Constitution and in our laws.

The major blot on our history was slavery, and its end came as a
result of Christian influences in this country. "Abolitionism as an organized force began in England in the 1780s, when William Wilberforce
and a group of wealthy evangelical Anglicans began agitating against
the African slave traffic. Their success stimulated further political assaults on slavery itself. Parliament abolished West Indian slavery in
1833." (*Encarta 98 Desk Encyclopedia*) "In the United States, antisla-
very activity began in colonial days. During the 1680s, Quakers in Pennsylvania condemned slavery on moral grounds. In the late 1700s, several
leaders of the American revolutionary movement, including Thomas
Jefferson and Patrick Henry, spoke out against slavery." (*World Book
Encyclopedia*, 1997) President Abraham Lincoln, who ushered in the
end of slavery, often professed his belief in God and the Holy Scripture.
A quotation from him showing his beliefs is included in Chapter 8.

How did it happen that this religious country, in a relatively short
period of time, did a one hundred and eighty degree turn and went the
exact opposite direction?

The deplorable state into which our educational institutions have
sunk was covered in Chapter 4.

Peter LaBarbera, editor of the Lambda Report, whose material I have
previously referred to at length in prior chapters, is now executive director of Accuracy in Academia, Washington, D.C. The purpose of the
organization is to examine, report on and turn around some of the leftist bias, intimidation, unethical behavior, and harassment on campuses
of conservative and religious groups. He has a tremendous job ahead of
him, but I certainly wish him success. Our places of higher learning

have degenerated into hotbeds of radicalism and atheism that are doing untold harm to the minds, and even the bodies, of our young people.

Our professors and teachers, newscasters, journalists, and others of the modern educated went to these colleges and universities. Their liberal bias and atheism was instilled in them by false dogma. It appears that not many were sufficiently equipped to see the fallacies to which they were exposed, nor did they later acquire sufficient knowledge to overcome their instilled delusions.

The general Godless attitudes which have encompassed most of our major universities has been a contributing factor to students being wrongly convinced that Darwinian theories of evolution have been proved, and that it is a proven fact that species have developed into new species, all of which is false. This factor is probably the one greatest contributor to atheism that there is. This misdirection has been devastating to the traditional morality of our culture. We continually see its effects.

As far as morality and religion are concerned, we now have a large number of influential people, looked up to and admired by many, but who may well be considered educated fools. They have been deceived by institutions where they acquired their "knowledge." They have failed to acquire a true moral base, and their work and writings are permeated with the resulting undirected meandering. I have known people who had never been to college and exhibited much more good common sense than some of these more educated people admired by so many.

Consider two articles in the widely read Parade Magazine on the same day, March 10, 1996.

Marilyn vos Savant a Parade columnist is said to be listed in *The Guinness Book of World Records* Hall of Fame for "Highest IQ." In her column that day, Savant was presented the question: "What do you think is the source of moral authority?" Her answer was:

> Most people find the source of moral authority in their religions, but I don't. That's because there would be multiple authorities, many of them in conflict and most of them biased. Speaking only for myself, I find the source of moral authority in the lessons of history—the principles that arise out of the mass of good choices, bad ones and all the rest in between.

History is written by a multitude of narrators, most of them in conflict and all of them biased. But at least we don't see them as authorities—or shouldn't anyway. ***

How do you think that a person supposedly having the "Highest IQ" got into such a state of mental confusion? No sensible person would try to simultaneously follow all religions. The natural result would be confusion from the conflicts. Her misuse of "bias" is an example of how she would also probably misuse "discrimination," "homophobia," and other such buzzwords of the liberal establishment. If a religious person does not believe that he or she is following the true word of God, then that person has no real faith in the religion.

It should be obvious that Ms. Savant's attempted answer was that of a person who had none. I suppose she felt compelled to give it a shot anyway.

What it does establish is that making a high IQ score does not ensure the possession of common sense.

To me, the most saddening thing about it is that a person's moral base should be the most important thing in one's life. Such a vague and meaningless answer by a person who is looked up to by so many is indeed disheartening.

She does correctly recognize that: "History is written by a multitude of narrators, most of them in conflict and all of them biased." What a thing on which to base your moral beliefs!

History purports to be a relation of past events. It continually changes as the events unfold. If we are to base our morals on the interpretation of history, and we are independently thinking individuals, then there will necessarily be as many moral bases as there are people. That is somewhat more "multiple authorities" than there are religions.

Each person's idea on morality would be as valid as the next one's, and none would really have any validity at all.

Now let us consider the article, "In the Valley of the Shadow," by the late Carl Sagan, *Parade Magazine*, 3-10-96. Sagan was a noted astronomer and television personality admired by many. The article is about his being diagnosed with myelodysplasia, a deadly and unusual disease; and about his hope for life after a bone marrow transplant. However, he died not long after the article. It seemed, previously, that he took every opportunity to express his anti-religious, evolutionary, and atheistic beliefs.

One of the interesting things about this article is that Sagan does not seem as adamant about expressing his atheistic views as he once was. This is encouraging. Maybe there was something to what he called his "character-building experience." (I had hoped that this character building would continue, but with an improvement in his health.)

Sagan states: "While I do not think that, if there is a god, his plan for me will be altered by prayer ... ." He does not state that there is no God, although his failure to capitalize the word God continues to show his disrespect for the religious beliefs of most Americans.

It is also noteworthy that he appears to substantially adopt a statement of Albert Einstein that definitely has religious connotations. It was: "I cannot conceive of a god who rewards and punishes his creatures or has a will of the kind that we experience in ourselves. Neither can I—nor would I want to—conceive of an individual that survives his physical death. Let feeble souls, from fear or absurd egotism, cherish such thoughts. I am satisfied with the mystery of the eternity of life and a glimpse of the marvelous structure of the existing world, together with the devoted striving to comprehend a portion, be it ever so tiny, of the Reason that manifests itself in nature." Please note the capitalization of Reason.

I am no authority on Einstein, but I have read statements attributed to him in his later years that rather clearly indicated a definite belief in God, although not of any particular religion. The part quoted seems closer to the Jewish religion than to the Christian, since the Jewish religion does not incorporate the life after death idea of the Christian religion. As I understand it, Einstein was Jewish, so this is no particular surprise. It is surely a shame that a man of his caliber may have died without ever having been able to really make up his mind about so important a subject. It appears that Sagan followed his footsteps in this regard.

There are many agnostics and atheists who are good decent people. However, these are the ones who are always searching and trying to find and exhibit some moral base outside of religion. Some of their ideas are good and many are shared by other good people, but none have any authoritative basis, because one has as much right as the other to think up and decide these things. So then we have a billion sets of morals to guide us in passing our laws and trying to manage our society. We are not quite that bad off yet, but thanks to such "thinkers," we sure have a running start.

I am sure that if he were asked the question under discussion that was asked Ms. vos Savant, Sagan's answer would have been entirely different. He would probably have used science as his moral base. And his answer would be no more nor no less valid than hers.

Both Marilyn vos Savant and Carl Sagan were well-educated people. But they failed to learn the fundamental fact of infinity, and that is that it is impossible for mortals to ever learn the ultimate secret of life by scientific research and study. Even if a person could trace our planet and universe back to some start such as the "big bang" theory, one need only ask: Where did that come from?

Some argue that our source of morality should come from "learned" philosophers. But here we have the same bias and confusion.

So vos Savant would choose history for her source of moral authority, Sagan would choose science, and others would choose the philosophers (who are also in conflict). What a conglomeration of confusion and hopelessly groping minds!

Making up one's own mind as to what is right or wrong based on individual ideas and humanism certainly makes living a proper life simple, particularly for those engaging in particular sins. The part of the Bible that proscribes their particular sins can just be ignored. However, this indeed leads to a dangerous state of affairs, and often to mental illness. It is bad enough for one to sin and do things that are wrong, but to not even realize that wrongs are being committed immensely magnifies the harm to one's self and to society. It is also a form of mental illness.

David, of biblical times, was perhaps the greatest of all kings. But even when King David grievously sinned, it was recognized as sin by both him and his people. He was punished by the Lord. He fled Jerusalem, and almost lost his kingdom when his own son and his people rose up against him. His transgressions were not accepted as righteous and good. How different our thinking has become with our modern day "tolerance," "nondiscrimination," and love for "diversity," in our anything-goes society.

What has happened to us? Why did we lose the moral base of Christianity that was the foundation of this country for its first two hundred years? It appears from history that it was a process that began slowly, and then greatly accelerated in the past thirty years.

The following are some astute observations from **If The Foundations Be Destroyed**, by Josh McDowell:

Crumbling Foundations

Once upon a time, children were raised in an atmosphere that communicated absolute standards for behavior. Certain things were right and certain things were wrong. A child's parents, teachers, ministers, youth workers, and other adults collaborated in an effort to communicate that the former should be heeded and the latter avoided. At one time, our society, by and large, explained the universe, humanity, and the purpose of life from the Judeo-Christian tradition—a belief that truth existed, and everyone could know and understand it.

A clear understanding of what was right and wrong gave society a moral standard by which to measure crime and punishment, business ethics, community values, character and social conduct. It became the lens through which society viewed law, science, art, politics—the whole culture.

That has changed drastically, however. Our children are being raised in a society that has largely rejected the notions of truth and morality—a society that has somewhere lost the ability to decide what is true and what is right. Truth has become a matter of taste. Morality has been replaced by individual preference. ***

The Birth of Modern Culture

*** The acknowledgment of an infinite, immutable God made sense of the whole human experience, and provided a valuable foundation for questions about right and wrong.

But that all began to change during the Renaissance. The Renaissance, which began in Europe in the 1300s, marked a significant shift in human thought. The major theme of art, literature, and philosophy shifted away from glorifying God to exalting man and his abilities. This shift gave birth to the doctrine of humanism.

The Renaissance was followed by the Age of Reason or the Enlightenment. This period began in the 1600s and prompted society to depend upon its own powers of reason to discern truth. Standards of right and wrong were no longer based on the character of God, but upon human reasoning.

Two more historical influences have shaped how modern people—including our own youth—think and act today. The Industrial Revolution of the eighteenth and nineteenth centuries focused on human productivity and advancement. Human accomplishments had made man arrogant and confident in his own abilities to create good and judge evil. Finally, with the publication and increasing acceptance of the theories of Charles Darwin, God became *persona non grata*—unnecessary and unwelcome—leaving man free (in his mind, at least) to judge truth, to reach his own conclusions about right and wrong, independent of God and his decrees. *** (*Family Voice*, Nov./Dec. 1994)

As to the theories of evolution, I am of the strong opinion that if all of the known changes in known kinds of life, from redwood trees, to humans, to germs, were mathematically projected backwards to the estimated beginning of the earth, that the idea that all living things could have developed in that time from a "one-cell amoebae" would prove utterly impossible. And certainly no such thing has ever been proved—nor can it be proved. There has not even been proof in all of known history of one species turning into another species. If the current theories of evolution are correct, from a mathematical standpoint, we should have clear proof of a very large number of such crossovers since recorded history—but we have not one instance.

Let us consider another rather simple problem with the theory of evolution. When the very first living thing crawled out of the "primeval soup," on what did it live and with what did it breed? If there were other plants or animals from which it could get sustenance, from where did they come, and what "accident" accounted for that life? If there were none, how did the plants and trees develop from this first animal? Where did all of these things come from, how, and when did it happen? As a new species developed from another species, was it one animal or plant at a time or more than one at a time? If more than one at a time, how did this occur? If one at a time, what did the new species breed with to continue the new species—or how did it reproduce? Why aren't such things going on now when we have so many species? Did a new species continue without a reproductive system? How did each species develop its particular reproductive system? Why are there different reproductive systems? What caused these different reproductive systems to be developed that appear to be particularly suited to each species? If life began in the sea or some "primeval soup," how did the trees and plants get out of it and develop? How did all of these things develop so early in time from the same source? Why has it stopped? If a completely different form of life develops from another different form and species, as all of these various forms developed then the increases in different forms and species should have increased exponentially, and the development of new species now should be very great in degree and number, and common everywhere. This is not the case. Why? How many accidents were there that resulted in a form of life, and how do you arrive at the number? If there was more than one, how can we really say what developed from what? If there was one "accident" of life, why could not there have been more than one?

Are there not laws or rules of nature that show balance and consistency? Are not mathematics, physics, biology and all natural sciences bound by rules of balance and consistency? Does not this balance and consistency appear to be of an intelligent nature? How did this come about?

If monkeys, baboons, apes, and chimpanzees are our "cousins," why, in all the years they have been in existence, have not the members of one group established a civilized society, written books, composed music, made paintings, invented machines, devised boats or transportation means or systems, or done anything but live as animals? Why are humans the only species to have done such things since the world was created? The Bible clearly explains these things. Where is it explained by science?

Many of Darwin's basic theories have been substantially refuted by later scientists and evolutionists themselves, but our schools keep teaching students that these impossible theories are proven facts, and that they are incompatible with Biblical ideas of God. I base my views on common sense and fundamental mathematics. I am admittedly getting into a field here that is outside of my expertise, and, in any event, proper exploration of such ideas requires complete books on that subject alone, and a number are now coming out. However, for those who are more deeply interested, I would recommend starting on this subject by reading a book by another attorney, who has acquired the necessary expertise in the subject. The book is by law professor Phillip E. Johnson, *Darwin On Trial,* 2d Ed., InterVarsity Press, Downers Grove, Ill., 1993. Of course, as Johnson says, disproving the current theories on origin of the species does not prove creation by God. This cannot be proved, any more than the true origin of the universe and of life can be proved. When one gets back to a place that might be called "the beginning," another need only ask: Where did that come from? The projection backward is infinite, and beyond the comprehension of the human mind. It should not take a scientist to see this. Religious beliefs can only be accepted on faith.

On public television and educational channels, we are bombarded with statements about apes and monkeys being our "ancestors," and about how one species evolved from another, as if these things were proven facts. Such things are not only false and misleading, but they are highly damaging to the impressionable and uninformed. This is a further tragedy because these shows—many of them nature shows—are some of the best types of shows one can watch on television. They do not reek with the smut and gratuitous violence that constitute much of TV today. Except for the evolution tripe, they are some of the most educational shows available.

Theories of evolution ignore creation by God or any higher being as even a possibility. Their position is that such creation is unprovable, and therefore unworthy of scientific study. But the true origin of life, from whatever source, is equally impossible to prove.

Science then tries to prove its unfounded assumption of evolution, because if the possibility of creation is disregarded, no other possibility has been thought of. This is not good science. The unfounded assumption on which the theory is based is equally unprovable.

Nevertheless, it appears to me that it is impossible to reconcile archeological finds of fossils and things of that nature, well recognized scientific dating, and a literal reading of Genesis in the Bible. We could say that if God has the power to create the heavens and the earth, then creating the world with those fossils in place would be no great problem. But is it within our conception of God for him to purposely set up things to confuse and mislead us? I think not. This certainly presents problems with a "fundamentalist" reading of the Bible. There nevertheless can be reasonable reconciliations. We do not really know how time was considered and calculated at that time. Did Methuselah really live 969 years as stated in *Genesis* 5:27 as we now calculate years? Or was a different method of time calculation used? Moreover, were the statements meant to be historical or figurative? We know that the Bible contains stories, poetry, and songs that are not meant to be taken as historical statements of fact, but are a part of its teachings. We know that it contains common use of figurative language that is not meant to be literal history or statements of fact. So what is Genesis and do we really need to know? It is not necessary and it is not possible for us to know everything. We cannot even count to infinity, and our minds cannot comprehend the extent or limits of the universe. Some things we must accept on intuition and faith. All truths cannot be proved.

Nevertheless, to me, the Bible has the ring of truth. It has the holy goodness and balance of the word of God. It is the true anchor of a way of life on which we can always depend, and which will never change with the many whims, fads, and mores contrived by people, which could lead one in any imaginable direction. Real truth and righteousness never changes.

It appears that the yarn from which is woven the theories on evolution, and the origin of life and species, is now unraveling at all four corners. The theories are clearly not established by facts. More importantly, as to origin of life and the universe, many integral parts of the theories are not consistent with known facts.

There have been recent news articles on large conferences of scientists and other interested persons organized by Phillip E. Johnson that are getting international interest.

> Mr. Johnson believes that Darwinism is crumbling. "Those people are already fighting with each other. Sometimes what people say is that we are a major defection or two away from total victory. Once we get some undeniably legitimate figures in the scientific and intellectual communities saying, 'This is a legitimate issue. We can't sweep this under the rug anymore,' that's when the situation will have radically changed."
>
> The ascent of Darwinism brought on a frightening new world, Mr. Johnson says. Naturalistic evolution, by definition, excludes God; the natural conclusion, once evolution became the accepted orthodoxy, was for absolute lines of morality and behavior to become relative, allowing for the flourishing of many elements now seen as harmful: the sexual revolution fueled by easy methods of birth control; feminism; the "right" to abortion; and a consequent devaluation of human life. (World, 11-22-97, p. 13)

The article containing the above-quoted material, "You say you want devolution," *World*, ibid., pp. 12-13, was primarily about Johnson, and his book, *Darwin on Trial*, but the author, Jay Grelen, noted another recent book (among the many writings on the subject) that he considers to be significant in the recognition that Darwinism is not based on fact. That book was *Darwin's Black Box*, by Michael Behe. The article also contained this interesting biographical information about Johnson:

> But grabbing the greatest amount of attention these days is Phillip E. Johnson, the lawyer and professor who is somewhat of a prodigal son. Mr. Johnson grew up in a nominally religious home, majored in English literature at Harvard, went to law school at the University of Chicago, clerked for liberal U.S. Supreme Court Justice Earl Warren, and in 1967 became a professor at the University of California at Berkeley, his academic home to this day.
>
> Mr. Johnson, however, was theologically homeless. He had been an agnostic with a failing marriage. Then he accompanied his 11-year-old daughter to a Vacation Bible School dinner. The pastor's message caught Mr. Johnson's attention, however, and he started down the path to Christ. First, he slowly came to understand Jesus and his need for salvation. Then he started to reevaluate the systems of belief, on issues such as evolution, that he had absorbed during his years apart from God.
>
> The work that now consumes him began when Mr. Johnson visited Charles Darwin's home in England and began to read books about evolution, such as Richard Dawkins's *The Blind Watchmaker*. The more Mr. Johnson read, the more he realized that "mutation and selection can't create, and that there are even more fundamental problems than that with the Darwinian scenario." Six years ago Mr. Johnson published the result of his study, *Darwin on Trial*—and since then he has been a frequent debater and college lecturer on the inadequacies of the evolutionary faith.

The following contains interesting statements from scientists (*Evolution*, Ambassador Publishing, U.S.A., 1995, p. 33):

> Physicist Stephen Hawking concluded his best-selling *A Brief History of Time* with this statement: "If we find the answer to that [why

the universe exists], it would be the ultimate triumph of human reason—for then we would truly know the mind of God."

Hawkins is not the first scientist to include theological-sounding statements or to mention God in popular scientific works. Albert Einstein, questioning the validity of quantum theory, said, "God does not play dice."

Physicist Paul Davies, in *The Mind of God*, acknowledges as well that "among those scientists who are not religious in the conventional sense, many confess to a vague feeling there is 'something' beyond the surface reality of daily experience, some meaning behind existence."

However, in the same material quoted from above is included the cautionary statement that scientists often use *God* as a metaphor for the metaphysical, rather than an acknowledgment of a divine Being worthy of worship.

I consider the following to be aptly stated:

> Mathematician Carl Gauss put it like this: "There are problems to whose solutions I would attach infinitely greater importance than those of mathematics, for example . . . our relation to God, or concerning our destiny and our future, but their solution lies wholly beyond us, and completely outside the province of science." (*The New Story of Science*, page 56) (*Creation or Evolution*, Ambassador Publishing, U.S.A., 1995, pp. 32-34)

The origins of life and the universe are definitely beyond the realm of science.

Gary Parker, Ph.D., a biologist and former evolutionist, states in **"Creation: A Faith That Fits The Facts,"** *Coral Ridge Ministries Impact*, June 1994:

> *** In textbooks you get the impression that evolutionists have found all sorts of things—missing links. They used to know they had the missing link. First, it was Piltdown man. Well, that was a fake that fooled the experts. Then, they knew it was Nebraska man at the Scopes trial. Well, that was the tooth of a single pig. So evolutionists have constantly had to change their stories. ***
>
> Scientists can be extremely dogmatic, not on the basis of the scientific evidence, but on the basis of preference for naturalistic

philosophy. What evolution has done in order to maintain its standing is shift science from an objective search for the truth to science as a search for naturalistic explanations. And so an evolutionist can continue to believe in evolution in spite of the facts because he believes there is no alternative—there is no creator God. ***

Yes, when it comes to science, science is based on observations, things we can see, test, repeat, and so forth. ... And if real scientists would do that, we wouldn't have this evolution—creation controversy at all. That's what we'd really like is to get science back to what it really is, observable and testable, and evolution back to what it really is, simply a faith that denies the existence of God. ***

If science disregards creation by a higher power because it cannot be proved, then it should not teach the theories of evolution on how life evolved, because that is equally impossible to prove. Neither can science determine or prove the origin of the universe. It is impossible and beyond human perception. The things that we are able to determine and understand should be thoroughly explored and studied to the extent to which we are capable. It is a fascinating and dynamic field, and more information is being discovered, and new ideas and writings are being published at a rapid rate. There is nothing dangerous in learning the truth—no matter what it is. But never should theories be presented or accepted as facts.

These are the kinds of truths that should be taught in our schools. And once this is done, I believe that the general acceptance of a balanced religion will naturally follow. But I do not believe that government supported schools should teach the validity of any particular religion. This should be left to the various churches and their schools.

However, this still does not mean that because some cult or form of worship adopts the name of religion that it should be accepted or equally treated either in school or by law. If a cult or belief incorporates such things as terrorism, drugs, suicide, violence, and Satan worship, as many have done and do now, they are not entitled to and were never intended to have the religious protection incorporated in our constitution. We have many freedoms, but none gives us the right to be an active danger to our neighbors, our country, our society, or even to ourselves.

Our schools are the educators of our leaders and the backbone of our society. Their rot and decay commenced slowly with the acceptance of evolutionary theories as established facts. To say that students are fully informed that things such as the origin of species are theory belies the facts. Many students leave these institutions believing them to be true, as do their teachers and professors. The result has been a deviation from the Christian heritage of this country, and its effect was clearly predictable.

During the past forty years, this deviation from the traditional moral principles of Christianity and Judaism led to the acceptance of the radical liberal movements in our schools. Their decadence rapidly increased with the liberal ideas of "tolerance," "diversity," and "nondiscrimination." Their acceptance of homosexuality erases their last semblance of any morality. And so follows our country.

The Christian and Judaic religions when taught to a child by parents and the churches provide a firm and valid moral base. When youths then develop an inquiring mind, and become educated, they are still equipped with sound knowledge to retain their religion. It makes sense and has the ring of truth and goodness. In adulthood, they can then be thankful that they had the ability to sift the wheat from the chaff, on the many things that were taught in the schools and the many writings to which they have been exposed. They realize the limits of their own minds and the limits of the minds of others.

The Christian religion is the only pattern for life that fits my idea of complete justice and mathematical balance. With it, two and two always makes four. It does not change with the whims of individuals. It should be apparent to anyone that justice is not always done as to each person in our courts or on this earth. Many undergo extreme pain and hardships that they have done nothing to deserve. Others have life handed to them on a silver platter, and have done nothing in life to really earn it. Many of us are very fortunate to have been able to discern and believe in a pattern of life that includes ultimate and complete justice, fairness, and balance. The New Testament teaches this. Contrary to what many seem to believe, it does not tell us just how that will be accomplished. But perhaps it is just as well. There is much that we cannot possibly know anyway.

CHAPTER 6

THE HOMOSEXUAL
AGENDA

The term "homosexual agenda" is used to describe the goals and purposes of the activist homosexual movement. The information presented in prior chapters substantially shows the principal aims. The primary goal is the complete acceptance by society of sodomy as a wholesome exemplary way of life.

A further purpose is to recruit others into participating in their destructive lifestyle. Since their sexual acts are not designed for reproduction of the species, as is normal sexual behavior of people and animals, this is the only way that they can get new bodies into their group for participation in their perversions.

Their attack has been well planned and well executed. In the 1970s they began having amazing success in their lobbying efforts to get state sodomy laws repealed. Where they could not get them repealed they attacked them in court. But they did not have much success in their court attacks, at least until recent years.

They successfully usurped the methods of the civil rights movement, making great use of the climate of "nondiscrimination" instilled by that movement. Since the liberal element is easily confused and misled, and with a powerful lobbying and promotional effort, they soon had the liberal establishment—from the politicians to the news and entertainment media—behind them. They carefully avoided discussions of their behavior, by which they acquire their classification as homosexuals, and pushed the idea of nondiscrimination.

The liberals could not seem to discern between voluntary behavior and immutable characteristics. I have been personally acquainted with several ex-homosexuals, and know of many, but I have never known nor heard of an ex-black person.

They have successfully gotten the government to expend tremendously disproportionate amounts on AIDS victims and programs, some of which were merely promoting homosexuality. They cooked up false figures to make the public believe that the spread of HIV in the heterosexual community was greater than it was, for the dual purposes of getting more money and diverting responsibility for the continued spread of AIDS from themselves.

They successfully lobbied, infiltrated, and influenced, our churches, our schools, our social organizations, our corporations and businesses; and government at all levels, from the president of the United States, to the smallest municipalities, such as Aspen, Colorado.

They were successful in getting laws passed at state and local levels, and regulations at schools and universities, prohibiting discrimination against a person based upon "sexual orientation," and providing for punishment of "hate" crimes against people because of their "sexual orientation." They were even successful in getting state supreme courts and state bar associations to adopt ethics rules limiting statements that lawyers could make in court that amounted to disparaging remarks against a person because of his or her sexual orientation. These things are a breach and an elimination of true basic rights enjoyed in this country for its first two hundred years before the homosexual movement. These things will be covered in more detail in other chapters. Many of these matters such as the agenda and its successes are overlapping issues that necessarily relate to other chapters of this book. For example, the following chapter will deal in detail with some of the successes of the movement. Now the homosexualists are engaged in a big push for the recognition and legitimization of homosexual "marriages."

Their North American Man/Boy Love Organization (NAMBLA), as well as other homosexual organizations, continually push for the admittance of homosexuals into and acceptance by youth organizations, and the lowering of the age of legal consent for children to engage in sexual acts, so that they can safely and legally prey on our young people.

As related in Chapter 1, even without legalization homosexuals have had amazing success at infiltrating all kinds of organizations where youths are present, such as the Boy Scouts, churches, and schools. Their abominable attacks on children—from boy scouts to church choir boys—have visited a terrible destruction on our youths, turning many into homosexuals.

Their infiltrations and programs in schools are highly destructive. There are several purposes behind them, including promotion and acceptance of homosexuality, recruiting, and available young prey.

Ten years ago two homosexuals laid out a comprehensive plan for the brainwashing of America into accepting homosexuality, and breaking down our traditional moral values in this regard. It is indeed interesting to look back ten years and see how this very plan has been followed, and how successful it has been with the media and the gullible segment of the public. The article was **THE OVERHAULING OF STRAIGHT AMERICA—WAGING PEACE PART TWO**, by Marshall K. Kirk & and Erastes Pill, *Guide Magazine*, November 1987. The following are excerpts:

> The first order of business is *desensitization* of the American public concerning gays and gay rights. To desensitize the public is to help it view homosexuality with indifference instead of with keen emotion. Ideally, we would have straights register differences in sexual preference the way they register different tastes for ice cream or sports games: she likes strawberry and I like vanilla; he follows baseball and I follow football. No big deal. ***
>
> ... A large-scale media campaign will be required in order to change the image of gays in America. ***
>
> The way to benumb raw sensitivities about homosexuality is to have a lot of people talk a great deal about the subject in a neutral or supportive way. ...
>
> And when we say *talk* about homosexuality, we mean just that. In the early stages of any campaign to reach straight America, the masses should not be shocked and repelled by premature exposure to homosexual behavior itself. Instead, the imagery of sex should be downplayed and gay rights should be reduced to an abstract social

question as much as possible. First let the camel get his nose inside the tent—and only later his unsightly derriere!

Where we talk is important. The visual media, film and television are plainly the most powerful image-makers in Western civilization. ... So far, gay Hollywood has provided our best covert weapon in the battle to desensitize the mainstream. Bit by bit over the past ten years, gay characters and gay themes have been introduced into TV programs and films (though often this has been done to achieve comedic and ridiculous effects). On the whole the impact as been encouraging. ...

... Second, we can undermine the moral authority of homophobic churches by portraying them as antiquated backwaters, badly out of step with the times and with the latest findings of psychology. Against the mighty pull of institutional Religion one must set the mightier draw of Science and Public Opinion (the shield and sword of the accursed "secular humanism"). Such an unholy alliance has worked well against churches before, on such topics as divorce and abortion. With enough open *talk* about the prevalence and acceptability of homosexuality, that alliance can work again here.

... Portray gays as victims, not as aggressive challengers. In any campaign to win over the public, gays must be cast as victims in need of protection so that straights will be inclined by reflex to assume the role of protector. ...

A media campaign to promote the Gay Victim image should make use of symbols which reduce the mainstream's sense of threat, which lower its guard, and which enhance the plausibility of victimization. In practical terms, this means that jaunty mustachioed musclemen would keep very low profile in gay commercials and other public presentations, while sympathetic figures of nice young people, old people, and attractive women would be featured. (It almost goes without saying that groups on the furthest margin of acceptability, such as NAMBLA, must play no part at all in such a campaign: suspected child-molesters will never look like victims.)

Now, there are two different messages about the Gay Victim that are worth communicating. First, the mainstream should be told that gays are *victims of fate*, in the sense that most never had a choice to accept or reject their sexual preference. The message must read: "As far as gays can tell, they were born gay, just as you were born heterosexual or white or black or bright or athletic. Nobody ever tricked or seduced them; they never made a choice, and are not morally blameworthy. What they do isn't willfully contrary—it's only natural for them. This twist of fate could as easily have happened to *you!*"

Straight viewers must be able to *identify* with gays as victims. ...

The second message would portray gays as *victims of society.* ***

Along the same lines, we shouldn't overlook the Celebrity Endorsement. ***

There would be no parallel to such an effort in the history of the gay community in America. ***

So what can be done to crash the gates of the major media? Several things, advanced in several stages. ***

Newspapers and magazines may very well be more hungry for gay advertising dollars than television and radio are. And the cost of ads in print is generally lower. ... So to get more impact for our dollars, we should skip the *New Republic* and *New Left Review* readers and head for *Time, People,* and the *National Enquirer.* ***

... As usual, viewers would be treated to squeaky-clean skits on the importance of family harmony and understanding—but this time the narrator would end by saying, "This message was brought to you by—the National Gay Task Force." ...

The gay community should join forces with other civil liberties groups of respectable cast to promote bland messages about America and the Melting Pot, always ending with an explicit reference to the Task Force or some other gay organization. ***

By this point, our salami tactics will have carved out, slice by slice, a large portion of access to the mainstream media. So what then? It would finally be time to bring gay ads out of the closet. The messages of such ads should directly address lingering public fears about homosexuals as loathsome and contrary aliens. ***

We have sketched out here a blueprint for transforming the social values of straight America. At the core of our program is a media campaign to change the way the average citizens view homosexuality. ***

The above should be considered in conjunction with the diatribe of "Michael Swift" quoted in the first part of Chapter 1.

As their successes piled up, the homosexual movement became more expansive and demanding.

Consider the following from the **PLATFORM OF DEMANDS AND RELATED ITEMS** developed and distributed in connection with the 1993 March on Washington by homosexual activists:

A) We demand passage of a Lesbian, Gay, Bisexual and Transgender civil rights bill and an end to discrimination by state and federal governments including the military; repeal of all sodomy laws and other laws that criminalize private sexual expression between consenting adults.

1. Passage of "The Civil Rights Amendment Act of 1991" (HR 1430 & S574).
2. Repeal of Department of Defense directive 1332.14.
3. Repeal of laws prohibiting sodomy between consenting adults.
4. Repeal of laws prohibiting cross-gender expression (dress codes) between consenting adults.
5. Repeal of laws prohibiting non-coercive sexual behavior between consenting adults.
6. Amendment of Code of Federal Regulations to recognize same-sex relationships.
7. Passage of the Equal Rights Amendment.
8. Implementation of, funding for and enforcement of the Americans with Disabilities Act of 1991.
9. Passage and implementation of graduated age-of-consent laws.

B) We demand massive increase in funding for AIDS education, research, and patient care; universal access to health care including alternative therapies; and an end to sexism in medical research and health care.

10. The provision of responsive, appropriate health care for people with disabilities, deaf and hard of hearing people.
11. Revision of the Centers for Disease Control definition of AIDS to include infections particular to women.
12. Implementation of the recommendation of the National AIDS Commission immediately.
13. A massive increase in funding for AIDS education, research and care—money for AIDS, not for war. This money should come from the defense budget, not existing social services.
14. An increase in funding and research to provide an independent study of HIV infection in women, People of Color, Bisexuals, Heterosexuals, children, and women to women transmission.
15. Access to anonymous testing for HIV.
16. No mandatory HIV testing.
17. A cure for AIDS.

18. The development and legalization of a national needle exchange program.
19. Free substance abuse treatment on demand.
20. The re-definition of sexual re-assignment surgeries as medical, not cosmetic, treatment.
21. The provision of appropriate medical treatment for all transgendered people in prisons and hospitals.
22. An increase in funding and research for chromic illness, including breast, ovarian, and other cancers particular to women.
23. The right of all people with chronic illness, including HIV/AIDS, to choices in medical treatment as well as the right to end such treatment.

C) **We demand legislation to prevent discrimination against Lesbians, Gays, Bisexuals, and Transgendred people in the areas of family diversity, custody, adoption and foster care and that the definition of family includes the full diversity of all family structures.**

24. The recognition and legal protection of whole range of family structures.
25. An end to abuse and exploitation of and discrimination against youth.
26. An end to abuse and exploitation of and discrimination against older/old people.
27. Full implementation of the recommendations contained in the report of the Health and Human Services Task Force on Youth Suicide.
28. Recognition of domestic partnerships.
29. Legalization of same sex marriages.

D) **We demand full and equal inclusion of Lesbians, Gays, Bisexuals and Transgendered people in the educational system, and inclusion of Lesbian, Gay, Bisexual, and Transgender studies in multicultural curricula.**

30. Culturally inclusive Lesbian, Gay, Bisexual and Transgender Studies program at all levels of education.
31. Information on abortion at all levels of education.
32. Information on AIDS/HIV, childcare and sexuality at all levels of education.
33. Establishment of campus offices and programs to address Lesbian, Gay, Bisexual and Transgender students' special needs.
34. The ban of all discriminatory ROTC programs and recruiters from learning institutions.

35. An end to discrimination at all levels of education.

E) **We demand the right to reproductive freedom and choice, to control our own bodies, and an end to sexist discrimination.**

36. The right to control our bodies.
37. Unrestricted, safe and affordable alternative insemination.
38. An end to sterilization abuse.
39. That access to safe and affordable abortion be available to all people on demand, without restriction and regardless of age.
41. That access to unbiased and complete information about the full range of reproductive options be available to all people, regardless of age.

F) **We demand an end to racial and ethnic discrimination in all forms.**

42. Support for non-racist policies.
43. Support for affirmative action.
44. An end to institutionalized racism.
45. Equal economic opportunity and an end to poverty.
46. Full reproductive rights, improvement of pre-natal services, availability of alternative insemination for Lesbians and Bisexual women of color.
47. Repeal all "English Only" laws and restore and enforce bilingual education.
48. Repeal all discriminatory immigration laws based on race and HIV status.
49. A commitment to ending racism, including internalized racism in our communities and in this country.
50. A commitment to ending sexism and all forms of religious and ethnic oppression in our communities and in this country.
51. An end to the genocide of all the indigenous peoples and their cultures.
52. Restoration of the self-determination of all indigenous people of the world.

G) **We demand an end to discrimination and violent oppression based on actual or perceived sexual orientation/identification, race, religion, identity, sex and gender expression, disability, age class, AIDS/HIV infection.**

53. An end to anti-Semitism.
54. An end to sexist oppression.
55. An end to discrimination against people with disabilities, deaf and hard of hearing people.

56. An end to discrimination based on sexual orientation in all programs of the Boy Scouts of America.
57. An end to economic injustice in this country and internationally.
58. An end to discrimination against prisoners with HIV/AIDS.
59. An end to discrimination against people with HIV/AIDS, and those perceived as having HIV/AIDS.
60. An end to consideration of gender dysphoria as a psychiatric disorder.
61. An end to hate crimes including police brutality, rape and bashing.
62. An end to censorship.
(For more details see *Washington Times*, April, 1993)

The above demands and goals are interesting from the standpoint of how well they followed the recommendations of Kirk and Pill in associating with other "civil rights" and "minority" causes. In this document the homosexuals associated themselves with most all of the militant causes in existence, and certainly with all of the more radical ones. Why would homosexuals be so interested in the right to abortion on demand?

In Chapter 4 we discussed the inability of the homosexual activist to recognize and tell the truth in connection with their calling so many great and famous people homosexuals, without any proof or reasonable foundation—even Jesus Christ and the Apostle Paul. In truth, they have a great hate for Jesus and Paul, as well as the Bible, generally, because of the strong condemnation of homosexuality. However, rather than engage in a difficult and unsuccessful frontal attack on the Bible, Judaism, and Christianity, they have chosen an easier method, which is to infiltrate and undermine churches, and, on the basis of sympathy and nondiscrimination, get them to accept homosexuality. In this they have had amazing success, which will be more fully discussed in the next chapter.

NEA Grant Funds Book Claiming St. Augustine, King David, St. Paul, and Eleanor Roosevelt Were "Gay", by Peter LaBarbera

WASHINGTON—The federal National Endowment for the Arts (NEA) gave a $20,000 grant toward the research of a book that claims St. Augustine, the Apostle Paul, First Lady Eleanor Roosevelt and others were homosexuals, LR has learned.

In his book, "The Gay 100: A Ranking of the Most Influential Gay Men and Lesbians, Past and Present," Vassar English professor

Paul Russell thanks the NEA "for a grant that allowed me time to research the material."

Joining Augustine and Eleanor Roosevelt among Russell's "top 100" are King David of the Old Testament, Florence Nightingale, Emily Dickinson, Wila Cather, suffragist Susan B. Anthony and other notables whom homosexual activists have posthumously labeled as "gay." Traditionalist scholars and biographers, including some homosexuals, have disputed these claims as speculative and tendentious in their application of historical evidence. ***

In compiling his "Gay 100," Russell admits that proof is lacking that some of his subjects were homosexual. For St. Augustine, who is ranked as Number 16 in the book, Russell writes, "The presence of Augustine on this list will no doubt provoke some protest. What I am claiming here is that Augustine appears to have indulged, in his early life, in pleasure of the flesh, both with males and females . . . ." Russell writes that had he not included St. Augustine on his list, he "might have included the apostle Paul"—citing a controversial book by the Episcopal Bishop John Spong that asserts that Paul was a repressed homosexual. Spong's book has infuriated Orthodox Christians.

As he did with Spong, Russell frequently relies on the work of other pro-homosexual writers to buttress the contention that his subjects had homosexual tendencies. He ignores scholarship that rebuts these claims.

For example, Russell writes that he included poet Emily Dickinson because, "My position is that we will never know her secrets . . . If the last hundred years have worked fruitlessly to heterosexualize Emily Dickinson, perhaps the next hundred will be more successful in lesbianizing her."

Similarly, in his section on Eleanor Roosevelt, he includes a quotation from a professor who posits that the First Lady had a secret lesbian relationship. No opposing viewpoint is presented.

Duke history professor William H. Chafe has written that the "preponderance of evidence" suggests Roosevelt did not have outside sexual affairs with women, or men. (**Lambda Report** on *Homosexuality*, July - Sept. 1995)

We referred to Bishop Spong in Chapter 4 in connection with his homosexual sacrilege at the Foundry Methodist Church. I would think that this man has even less reliability than Russell, referred to above, if that is possible.

It seems to be an integral part of the homosexual agenda to try to convince the public that a large part of our historically respected individuals were homosexual. There usually is no respected historical basis for these scurrilous allegations, and they usually choose people who are deceased and cannot defend themselves. They make them about everyone from Jesus Christ on down. They are not really even worthy of mention, from the standpoint of truth and validity, and the only reason I waste the time of the reader on them is to demonstrate the vicious nature of certain homosexualists and other scandal mongers.

One example, is the accusation that J. Edgar Hoover, deceased director of the FBI, was "gay" and went to gay orgies dressed as a woman. This accusation was made in a book by an Anthony Summers, and published in articles in the Vanity Fair magazine. The claim was made that the mob had pictures of Hoover. The "evidence" was supposed to be the pictures of Hoover, which the author didn't have; two anonymous informers, whose names the author didn't disclose; and information from "a mobster's fourth wife." "Probably the Hoover-As-Drag-Queen story could have been computer-predicted. After all, it plays both to the modern appetite for juicy scandal and to the revisionist trend of cutting great men and women down to size—perhaps because the mites doing the revising don't like looking up," ("Hoover was nothing if not complex," The Albuquerque Tribune, 3-17-93). Gordon Liddy, who was in the FBI for many years and worked under Hoover said that the homosexual allegations about Hoover were false, and that Hoover despised homosexuals. ("Kennedy Scandal is Worth Researching," by William F. Buckley Jr., Albuquerque Journal, 3-3-93)

Allegations such as those about Hoover by Summers, with such evidence, would insure a substantial judgment against the author and publishers if Hoover were alive to protect himself. This is undoubtedly why such trash is ordinarily published long after the death and availability of those accused. I would also mention that during the time that Hoover was head of the F.B.I. that organization did careful background investigations of applicants for agents' positions, and that homosexuals were considered persons of bad character, and were not allowed to be agents; which was also true of other federal law enforcement agencies, as well as many state agencies.

'Gay Lincoln' Prof Says George Washington Was Homosexual, Too

Charley Shively, the homosexual professor whose allegation that Abraham Lincoln was a homosexual surfaced in the Los Angeles public school district, has further revelations.

Shively, an American Studies professor at the University of Massachusetts at Boston, says George Washington had homosexual liaisons as well.

Boston Globe columnist Alex Beam contacted Shively after seeing LR's story.

Writes Beam: "Shively, a Harvard Ph.D.., has also published a 'sustained piece of historical research' arguing that George Washington had homosexual experiences throughout his life starting as a teenager."

Shively, Beam continues, "is quite resigned to the ridicule heaped upon him by his colleagues: 'People cannot accept this sort of material,' he says."

Shively told LR his Washington "evidence" is found in the anthology "Gay Roots II," under the chapter title, "Was the Father of Our Country a Queen?"

Shively's claim about "gay" Lincoln appeared in his book, "Drumbeats: Walt Whitman's Civil War Boy Lovers," published by Gay Sunshine Press. Several Lincoln Biographers contacted by LR said that they were astounded at Shively's contention. Each said there was nothing to support the notion that "Honest Abe" was anything other than a heterosexual man.

Asked about the universal scorn for his Lincoln thesis, Shively said reaction is clouded by "unreasonable doubts based on prejudice rather than evidence." (**Lambda Report** *on Homosexuality*, Jul.-Sept. 1995)

The following is more information on the Lincoln trash.

L.A. Educator Asserts Lincoln Had Homosexual Affairs
Defends Gay Education Commission Article Claiming Abe Had "Gay"
Sex with Friend (By Peter LaBarbera)

The director of the Gay and Lesbian Commission of the Los Angeles public school system strongly defended an article published by the commission that asserts Abraham Lincoln had a homosexual affair with his best friend, Joshua Fry Speed. ***

The article relies mainly on a book by a gay University of Massachusetts professor Charley Shively, who writes that Lincoln was an "ass man" and that he and his best friend Joshua Speed were homosexual lovers for four years.

In his book, *Drum Beats: Walt Whitman's Civil War Boy Lovers,* Shively asserts that Speed's sharing a bed with Lincoln was a sign of their homosexuality.

Among the other evidence of Lincoln's alleged sexual inclinations, Shively cites a Lincoln poem in which he did letter plays on the words *gingerbread* and *fishing pole*, turning them into *binger-gred* and *pishing-fole*. ***

Such interpretations engendered a shocked and sometimes bemused reaction from Lincoln historians contacted for this story.

"It's just amazing . . . I have never seen anything this wild," said Tim Townsend, an historian with the Lincoln Home National Historic Site in Springfield, Illinois. "The sad thing about this [L.A. school district] article is this guy [Shively] is thrown in with some reputable scholars."

Townsend said Shively had made some "pretty amazing leaps," especially his interpretation of Lincoln and Speed sleeping in the same bed as proof of both men's homosexuality.

"In those days, bed space was at a premium, so this was very common," he said. "Basically what [Shively] is doing is transferring 20th Century views into 19th Century customs."

University of Wisconsin historian Richard Sewell concurred.

"This strikes me as preposterous," Sewell told **LR.** "The standard practice of the day was to put even strangers in the same bed."

Established historical accounts of Lincoln universally hold that he and Speed were merely best friends. In fact Lincoln helped persuade Speed to get over his wedding jitters and marry Fanny, his fiancé, according to the most famous Lincoln biographer, Carl Sandburg. In a letter Lincoln helped persuade Speed that he obviously loved Fanny enough to marry her.

That account was left out of the book by Shively, who instead writes that Lincoln himself married his wife Mary Todd to get over his longing for Speed. ***

Indeed, Shively's allegations about the 16th president add another name to this simmering controversy. In an effort to demonstrate the pervasiveness of homosexuality throughout history, gay activists have posthumously labeled heroes and heroines from Jesus Christ to Anne

Frank as "gay," touching off outraged reactions from their descendants and those involved in upholding their historical legacy.

In 1993, townspeople in Cleburne, Texas were scandalized when the town's namesake, Confederate Maj. General Patrick Cleburne, was included among the alleged homosexual soldiers in Randy Shilts' book, *Conduct Unbecoming: Gays & Lesbians in the U.S. Military.*

The main evidence for including Cleburne in the book was that he had shared a blanket during wartime with his aide, Capt. Irving Buck. Critics said the general was merely being unselfish and that bunking together was common during the war.

Joseph Nicolosi, a psychologist who specializes in treating homosexuals, said gay activists tend to project homosexuality onto others out of their own misunderstanding of same-sex friendships.

"The homosexual worldview cannot include normal healthy friendships," he said. "They can't imagine two males being in non-erotic friendship . . . . because they don't know it." (**Lambda Report** *on Homosexuality*, April-June 1995)

The homosexual "scholars" such as Shively make up horrendous falsifications about others, and then cite each other for authority. Some of them, without doubt, are so mentally disturbed because of what they know about themselves that they actually believe at least a part of what they are saying. However, they are without a moral foundation, and the truth also makes little difference to them. As previously stated, they are out to convince us that wrong is right and that right is wrong – that truth is false and that false is truth.

The gays' advance: implacable, deadly
by Don Feder

The great military theorist Karl von Clausewitz wrote that victory in war lies in eliminating the enemy's will to resist. This, and nothing less, is the objective of the homosexual movement.

It seeks not mere tolerance, but equality with monogamous heterosexuality, by suppressing all objections to the gay lifestyle. "Homophobia"—hatred of gays—is no longer the primary target. Now the enemy is the "heterosexist," a term of opprobrium applied to one who finds heterosexuality in any way preferable to homosexuality. From college campuses to courtrooms to comic book pages, it's a war fought on a thousand fronts.

[Mr. Feder then outlines homosexual picketing of and attacks on the Catholic Church and Cardinal O'Connor, because of opposition to homosexuality; and New York Mayor David Dinkins trying to force the St. Patrick's day parade to include homosexual groups.]

[*Peninsula*, a conservative magazine at Harvard, published an article about "the ethical case against gay sex without acrimony or invective," and homosexual groups posted the names and dorm numbers of the editors, inviting "harassment calls at hours most likely to disturb sleep.]

Our leading centers of open inquiry are closed to dissent from erotic orthodoxy. Over 100 colleges and universities have codes that bar discrimination based on "sexual preference."

Words that homosexuals find offensive can bring a firing squad response. No similar effort is made to protect the sensibilities of heterosexuals. Students at Rutgers report cruising in the library's basement bathroom with males exposing their genitals, a perversion the administration tacitly condones. Says Jason T. Brown, president of the Rutgers College student government, "The university totally caves in to any demand gays make." ***

[Feder relates how a Manhattan judge approved the adoption of a 6-year-old boy by his mother's lesbian lover. The judge said he could see no disadvantage to the child.] The omniscient jurist somehow overlooked a recent study in the Journal of Sex Research indicating that "31 % of lesbians . . . reported being victims of forced sex by their current or most recent partner," with battery frequently employed.

... Marvel Comics introduced the first gay super hero, who battles homophobia and AIDS discrimination. ***

If homosexuality is legitimized, no perversion (sadomasochism, incest, sex with children) can logically be opposed. *** (*CFV Report*, Colorado for Family Values, Sept. 1994)

As noted in Don Feder's article, above, the homosexual agenda is now even trying to brainwash us and our children through comic strips. One example is the Doonesbury comic strip published in The Albuquerque Tribune. I looked at several of the strips that carried the homosexual message. Two homosexual men partners are depicted as riding along in an auto discussing informing the father of one of them as to his being "gay," and making the statement: "...Dad will have to come to terms with his deep-seated bigotry and homophobia." This is the same typical and worn propaganda of the homosexualists. But what is amazing is the number of gullible people that fall for it. However, the most gullible are the media, and this naturally coincides with their lack of morality.

An article, "Kinsey Breakthrough," *Family Research Council Washington Watch* (FRC), 10-27-95, gives one of many examples of the influence of the homosexual movement on public television. FRC published a video raising questions about information relating to child sexuality compiled by Alfred C. Kinsey, and later by the Kinsey Institute, a recipient of taxpayer money. The article states:

> Answering charges raised by FRC's new video, *The Children of Table 34*, Kinsey Institute Director John Bancroft told the *Indianapolis Star* (Sept. 19) that he believes the child sex data in the famous Kinsey Report from the 1940s was the work of one pedophile. This account contradicts that of Alfred C. Kinsey himself, who wrote in *Sexual Behavior in the Human Male* (1948) that explicit sexual data on 317 youngsters was collected by nine pedophiles.
>
> Kinsey's findings continue to be the most influential data on sex research published in this century. Because the data have been used to validate the idea of child sexuality that animates most of sexology and today's sex education, public illumination of Kinsey's ethical swamp may lead to educational, legal and scientific reform. FRC is pressing Congress for an investigation into the Kinsey Institute's child sexuality files, whose existence Dr. Bancroft has now confirmed. First questions: Who were the aforementioned pedophiles and how did they get access to hundreds of children, including infants? Dr. Judith Reisman, who first explored the Kinsey child data in a 1981 monograph, and later in the 1990 book, *Kinsey, Sex and Fraud* with co-author Edward Eichel and editors Dr. J. Gordon Muir and Dr. John H. Court, says she is encouraged that the 50-year-old mystery might finally be solved.
>
> Meanwhile, FRC is appealing the Public Broadcasting Service's rejection of *The Children of Table 34* for airing. PBS designates June as Gay Pride Month and in mid-October, began running a four-part series celebrating homosexual activism. This same PBS says that the FRC video presents a "conflict" because FRC, as a pro-family group, has an interest in the material. Presumably, the "conflict" is that the film accords with FRC's stated aim of protecting children from sexual abuse.

The Kinsey Institute is still a heavy recipient of taxpayer money through its connection with Indiana University. Kinsey's work and continuing influence are long overdue public scrutiny.

We indeed live in a strange world when the Public Broadcasting Service sees a conflict because an organization which produced a video has an interest in protecting children from pedophiles; but pro-homosexual videos produced by homosexualists present no "conflict." Is it the view of those controlling public TV that children should be fair game for homosexual pedophiles?

PBS Flaunts Promiscuous Gays of '70s San Francisco
By Marilyn Duff

Lindsay Law, executive producer of PBS' "American Playhouse" series, may be guilty of the biggest rationalization of the network's liberal bias—ever. When the Public Broadcasting System (PBS) broadcast "Tales of the City" recently, part of the hype was Law's statement, "It's not a heavy dramatic piece—it's a lark." Wrong. It was more like watching a sensitive comedy of 1930s Germany before the Holocaust, only the enemy here is not facists—it's a terrifying, silent virus.

Watching the story of life in San Francisco in the late 1970s was, therefore, painfully discomforting. Armisted Maupin's fiction account ran first as a serial in the San Francisco Chronicle in 1976, the halcyon days of homosexuality.

Bay City homosexuals seemingly had it all back then: style, influence and free-wheeling sex lives. They had their own bars, with mud-wrestling, slave auctions and jockey shorts contests. And along with the unbridled promiscuity, they had political clout, for in San Francisco, gays were the most important single voting bloc and had just elected the first openly gay city councilman, Harvey Milk. ***

The series ran at 9:00 p.m. over three nights in January, easily accessible to teens and young adults.

With glorious beauties of San Francisco as a backdrop, viewers are given the charming affability of a young male homosexual, the frolicsome loyalty of a lesbian twosome—and the smothering repressiveness of two heterosexual marriages. One character is a married man who is a closet gay, another a married, middle-aged business executive who has an affair with the transsexual landlady.

PBS has had skirmishes with its audience over its broadcasts of "Tongue of Flame," an explicit view of homosexuality; "Stop the

Church," a documentary of gay protest in St. Patricks' Cathedral in New York City; and a "P.O.V." documentary of a sex-change by a man who wished to be a woman.

Congressmen, most notably GOP Senators Robert Dole (Kan.) and Jesse Helms (N.C.), have waged valiant but futile campaigns to defund PBS' parent company, the Corporation for Public Broadcasting (CPB)— or to reduce or freeze its stipend of tax monies. But to no avail. Last year CPB received an increase in funding of $19.36 million from the Democrat-controlled Congress, which was heavily lobbied by its liberal constituents including the vocally and financially still strong gay lobby.

Meanwhile PBS has steadfastly refused to respond to complaints of straight America that it's pushing a homosexual agenda at a time when the AIDS epidemic is taking far more lives of homosexuals than any other group. Though "Tales" was well written (Maupin is a master of observation and an entertaining social commentator) the question remains: When is PBS going to spend anything like equal money to push a return to heterosexual marriage and family values as an antidote to many of society's ills? Or offer viewers opposing views such as a thoughtful documentary based on Michael Fumento's *The Myth of Heterosexual AIDS?* (*Human Events*, 2-16-94)

It is a disgrace that taxpayer supported public television is used as a tool to destroy the moral foundation of this country. It is even more disgraceful that our apathetic citizens, and their elected representatives, allow it to happen. The left would use its worn and invalid argument of censorship to counter my statements. The truth is that those who control public television, like those who control commercial television, must and do have the right to choose their programs. The problem is that for the past thirty years, all of them have consistently chosen programs that are destructive to traditional morality—and it is intentionally and systematically done.

Another of my pet peeves is that the creation of public television appears to have been the creation of a self-sustaining monster feeding on taxpayers. It uses taxpayer money to run pure promotion ads against budget cuts, and to get more tax money. Taxpaying citizens are having their money forcefully taken from them, and then used to propagandize themselves—along with the nonproductive segment of the public—into being further bled.

Private corporations operating television stations are controlled by their boards of directors, which are elected by their stockholders. Their stockholders have been more interested in profit than in the moral destruction of this country. And management of many of them, such as the Disney company, has obviously been infiltrated by homosexualists. The ultimate control of public television should be by the taxpaying citizens who make it possible, and their elected representatives. But the citizens have been extremely unconcerned about the moral destruction occurring, and many of their representatives are homosexualists.

The media, generally, have become lackeys of the homosexual movement.

On October 5, 1995, Richard Rodriguez who often reads his essays on the MacNeil-Lehrer News Hour, was on that program criticizing Pope John Paul II and the Catholic church regarding policies against homosexuality. He admitted he was a homosexual. Not too long before, on the same program, a panel of regular news editors all supported the homosexual "rights" movement. This is typical of the media in this day and time.

The homosexualists have devised many ingenious and unique ways to brainwash the American public through the natural sympathy one has for the oppressed. The early scheme to use that as the homosexualist main theme was followed with great success. One of the most insidious of the homosexual schemes has been the adoption and infiltration of remembrance and memorial events relating to the Nazi holocaust. They deceitfully dwell only on the fact that some homosexuals were among those put in concentration camps. They never mention that the greatest persecution of homosexuals was the persecution of the "femme" group by the "butch" group of homosexuals in Germany, and that the cause was their political differences and alliances. Nor do they mention that the driving forces of the Nazi party were to a large degree controlled by homosexuals. And they do not mention the moving parts that homosexuals played in the Nazi movement and the concentration and death camps. These were the things that *The Pink Swastika* was about, which was referred to at length in Chapter 1.

In a letter in behalf of *Lively Communications Inc.*, Salem, Or., dated January 1, 1996, Scott Lively, one of the authors of The Pink Swastika, states in part:

During my research for *The Pink Swastika* I learned how tremendously important the "gay" Holocaust myth is to the "gay rights" movement. All across the nation this arrogant revision of history is being used to propagandize a generation of Americans who do not remember that the Nazi Party was at the core a homo-erotic brotherhood. For example, the highly organized and well-funded "Anne Frank" exhibit was most recently in New Mexico where it featured blatant pro-homosexual events and themes over an entire month. Tens of thousands of New Mexicans were taught that opposition to "gay rights" is equivalent to supporting the Holocaust. Much more harmful are the permanent Holocaust memorials that present "gay" victim mythology in somber surroundings that lend it instant credibility.

The pink flyer included with this letter is about one of several new Holocaust memorials going up around the nation. New England homosexuals have pledged over $1,000,000.00 for the Boston memorial. My friend Dr. Howard Hurwitz of New York City, warns of another pro-homosexual Holocaust memorial going up there. I personally believe that all of these, the Anne Frank exhibit, the memorials, and similar "educational" and political projects promoting "diversity," are a part of a single plan conceived and orchestrated by the national "gay rights" power structure. Once these institutions are in place and fully functional they will provide the homosexualists a nearly invulnerable position from which to denounce their adversaries. They finally have the one thing they have lacked in their decades-long battle to defeat the Christian church—"moral" authority. The key to this strategy is the "gay" Holocaust myth.

The pink flyer referred to in Scott Lively's letter was published over the name, Gay and Lesbian Committee of the New England Holocaust Memorial Committee. It contained the following:

Lest we forget:

"HOMOPHOBIA
and ANTISEMITISM

ARE PART OF THE SAME
DISEASE."
— Rabbi Bernard H. Mehlman

In a small park near the Freedom Trail, a monument is being built in memory of the six million Jews exterminated by the Third Reich. To be dedicated on October 22nd, the **New England Holocaust Memorial** will encourage millions of visitors to recall the Shoah — the Holocaust — and consider the many bitter lessons. Carved in the Memorial's black granite path, alongside six haunting towers of steel and glass, is this horrible reminder of near-history:

"German homosexuals were early victims of Nazi persecution. Many were imprisoned, some were castrated or used in medical experiments. Thousands died in concentration camps." **New England's Gay and Lesbian Community** proudly joins a select group of generous corporations and civic leaders as a **Cornerstone Benefactor** of Boston's newest addition to the Freedom Trail.

Thank you to all who contributed.

NEW ENGLAND HOLOCAUST MEMORIAL

***

REMEMBER
GAY AND LESBIAN COMMITTEE OF THE NEW ENGLAND HOLOCAUST
MEMORIAL COMMITTEE

The Truth About Homosexuals and the Holocaust
By Howard L. Hurwitz

*** Yet another obscenity will mar the opening, (in New York) of the Battery Park Holocaust museum. It will perpetuate the myth that homosexuals were "victims" of the Nazis. This false history is encased in an exhibit in the Washington museum where a professed homosexual Karl Muller has directed "research."

A few thousand homosexuals were sent to camps for crimes against the Third Reich. None were herded into cattle cars or gassed. They were given privileged status. Elie Wiesel, a survivor reports in his classic *Night* that homosexuals preyed on children in the camps.

Homosexuals were founders of the Nazi Party. Ernst Roehm, a notorious homosexual, was one of the founders and a close friend of Hitler. *** (*Human Events*, 8-29-97 and 9-5-97)

It certainly appears to me that the homosexualists have made suckers out of a large part of the Jewish community. And that those Jewish people have abandoned the teachings of the base of their religion, the Hebrew scriptures, which in substance is the same as the Old Testament of the King James Version of the Bible, which I have used for Bible references in this book. Sodomy is clearly and unequivocally condemned. So, according to the homosexualists, all Jews and all Christians who believe the teachings of their Bibles, the bases of their religions, have the "disease" of "homophobia." The acceptance of homosexuality cannot be reconciled with the Bible. Neither can the vile acts of sodomy be reconciled with common decency and virtue.

At times it seems that the homosexual activists have been successful in infiltrating and associating themselves with all activist and minority groups, but as disclosed by the following news item, there is one activist group that they strongly oppose—that is the group of animal rights activists. The homosexualists are all for the killing of and experimenting with animals, as long as it is for the purposes of AIDS patients. And, as usual with the homosexual activists, they try to prevent those with different views from even expressing them.

AIDS Activists Protest Animal Rights
9 ACT UP Members Arrested
WASHINGTON — The MAN WHO MADE HISTORY LAST YEAR BY RECEIVING AN experimental AIDS treatment using a baboon's

bone marrow was picked up by authorities Thursday for blocking traffic at an animal rights rally.

Jeff Getty of San Francisco said he and eight others were released after paying a $15 fine for obstructing traffic outside the US Air Arena, where the rally took place.

Maryland National Capital Park Police spokesman, Lt. James Johnson, said that about 25 demonstrators from the AIDS activist group, ACT UP blocked the entrance to the arena. He said the nine were removed after they refused to clear the roadway.

"I was there to demonstrate and educate America that, when you give money to animal rights activists, you're giving money for them to stop AIDS, Alzheimers' and cancer research," Getty said.

All week, animal rights activists and AIDS patients have been clashing over whether doctors need to use animals.

Thousands of animal rights activists are in Washington as part of an annual visit to lobby Congress to strengthen laws protecting animals used in scientific research.

Animal rights activists have frequently targeted Getty for acts of protest because, last year, he received bone marrow from a baboon that was killed so doctors could first check it for disease-causing organisms. (*Albuquerque Journal,* 6-21-96.)

There is an error in the above article. ACT UP is a homosexual group that participates in extremist acts of protest in behalf of the homosexual movement, generally—it is not just an AIDS group. It is similar to the Lesbian Avengers group on the women's side of the homosexual movement. Also, it is interesting that, according to this news item, they still managed to try to align themselves with two other groups, "Alzheimers' and cancer research."

NOW Rally Draws 15,000

SAN FRANCISCO — Marchers cheered for affirmative action, women's reproductive freedom and gay rights Sunday while protesting "ultra-right wing" politicians.

About 15,000 people attended the National Organization for Women rally, which was intended to bring together minority and women's groups that organizers said should work in tandem, rather that at cross purposes as they often do. (*Albuquerque Journal,* 4-15-96)

An article in *The Albuquerque Tribune*, 4-15-96, "'Fight the Right' rally is held in San Francisco," discloses that author Gloria Steinem and Rev. Jesse Jackson took part in the rally and marches referred to in the above article.

A Black Conservative's Cry

Emanuel McLittle left a career as a psychologist nine years ago to become a publisher, and when he looked at magazines put out by fellow blacks, he was appalled at their shallowness and reflexive acceptance of liberal myths. His own philosophy of independence and self-reliance is a hallmark of his magazine., *Destiny*, published from Grants Pass, Oregon. McLittle was our Saturday luncheon speaker, on "The Growing Conservative Underclass."

McLittle contended that liberals consistently emulate the civil rights movement's approach towards blacks in mobilizing various constituencies. Homosexuals, for instance, "know skillfully how to become victims, know how to make you as a heterosexual, to be abnormal, whereas they are normal." *** (*AIM REPORT*, May-A, 1996)

Some of the worst destruction done to the country and to themselves was the pressure brought to bear by homosexuals on the American Psychological Association and the American Psychiatric Association and getting these organizations to delete homosexuality as one of their diagnosed mental or pathological abnormalities, and to declare it as a "normal status." This debacle was covered at length in Chapter 2.

The ongoing homosexual attacks on our culture and morality are relentless. California always leads the way. In 1997, a bill passed both houses of the California legislature that was the ultimate of depravity. "It prohibited virtually every organization in the state from refusing to hire openly gay and lesbian individuals, including Bible bookstores, Christian businesses, and even churches. This bill required schools to teach gay and lesbian propaganda to children by defining homosexuality as a civil right. Finally, organizations and individuals that did not comply were to be fined up to $50,000 and forced to pay unlimited civil court penalties." Fortunately for California and the rest of the country, Governor Pete Wilson vetoed it, and it didn't become law. (*Family News From Dr. James Dobson*, Focus on the Family, Jan. 1998)

THE TEN-PERCENT PROPAGANDA

From the outset of the homosexual movement, its members have consistently and falsely tried to convince the public that 10 percent of the population are homosexual. Even after the falsity of this claim was clearly shown, the same statements and propaganda continued. Such false statements are of course typical of the homosexualists. The basis of the original homosexual claims seems to have been the original Kinsey data, a large part of which was shown to have been based on research with prisoners and other suspect classes, which itself shows that the data are not from general population sources, and therefore could not be reflective of the general population. It is also well established that prisoners have a much higher rate of homosexual activity than the general population.

In their book *Kinsey, Sex and Fraud* (Lochinvar-Huntington House Pub., 1990), Reisman and Eichel point out that Kinsey's data base was clearly skewed by his choice to include a high percentage of prison inmates and known sex offenders. Both practice homosexual behavior much more frequently than individuals in the general population. ...

Tom W. Smith's much more recent study, *Adult Sexual Behavior in 1989: Numbers of Partners, Frequency and Risk*, conducted among a full probability sample of the adult U.S. household population, reported that "Overall . . . less than 1% [of the study population] has been exclusively homosexual." (The Homosexual Deception: Making Sin A Civil Right, *Concerned Women for America*, 1991 - 1992)

How Many Gays Are There?

For years the gay-rights movement has sought safety in numbers. Its leaders have long claimed that homosexuals constitute 10 percent of the American population. They cited Alfred Kinsey, who interviewed thousands of men and women for landmark studies on human sexuality in the 1940s and 1950s. Activists seized on the double digits to strengthen their political message—that millions of citizens are excluded from the mainstream by anti-gay discrimination. Policymakers and the press (including Newsweek) adopted the estimate—despite protests from skeptical conservatives—citing it time and again.

But new evidence suggests that ideology, not sound science, has perpetuated a 1-in-10 myth. In the nearly half century since Kinsey, no survey has come close to duplicating his findings. ... Some gay activists now concede that they exploited the Kinsey estimates for its tactical value, not its accuracy. ***

... Between 1989 and 1992, the National Opinion Research Center (NORC) at the University of Chicago added two sex questions to its annual General Social Survey. The results have been consistent. Among men, 2.8 percent reported exclusive homosexual activity in the preceding year; women registered 2.5 percent. NORC is still tabulating the results of a full-scale, 3000-person study, but experts don't expect the numbers to be appreciably different.

... Child-pornography researcher Judith Reisman argues in her 1990 book, "Kinsey, Sex and Fraud," that homosexuals constitute perhaps as little as 1 percent of the population. *** *Newsweek*, 2-15-93)

The following is from a comprehensive article in *The Wall Street Journal*, 3-31-93, by J. Gordon Muir, M.D., a former medical researcher and contributing author, editor and co-publisher of *Kinsey, Sex and Fraud*. Robert H. Knight of the Family Research Council contributed to the article:

Homosexuals and the 10% Fallacy

*** The 10% estimate also has been extensively used by activists lobbying for gay-affirmation programs and extensions of family benefits to homosexual employees of major corporations, as well as seen as evidence of gays' voting clout.

But there long has been much evidence that the 10% estimate is far too high. Surveys with large samples from the U.S., Canada, Great Britain, France, Norway, Denmark and other nations give a picture of homosexuality experience rates of 6% or less, with exclusive homosexuality prevalence of 1% or less.

The most comprehensive example is the continuing survey conducted by the U.S. Census Bureau since 1988 for the National Center for Health Statistics of the Centers for Disease Control. The survey, which polls about 10,000 subjects quarterly on "AIDS Knowledge and Attitudes," asks confidentially if any of several statements is true, including this one: "you are a man who has had sex with another man at some time since 1977, even one time." No more than 2% to 3% of the more than 50,000 men surveyed have answered "yes to at least one statement." Since some yes answers were given to the four other questions (blood transfusions, intravenous drug use, etc.), the data strongly suggest that the prevalence of even incidental homosexual behavior is less than 2% for men. Most studies report that women have about half of the male prevalence rate, so a general population estimate of homosexuality would fall below 1.5%. A national poll showed 2.4% of voters in the 1992 election described themselves as homosexual.

Abundance of Evidence

Numerous other surveys reveal similar percentages. Father-son researchers Paul and Kirk Cameron have compiled a new report, "The Prevalence of Homosexuality" (scheduled to be published in Psychological Reports), that summarizes more than 30 surveys with "large, plausibly unbiased samples." Here are a few of them:

- *France*: A 1991-92 Government survey of 20,055 adults reports that 1.4% of men and 0.4% of women had had homosexual intercourse in the five years preceding the survey. The exclusive lifetime homosexual rates were 0.7% for men and 0.6% for women; lifetime homosexuality experience was 4.1% for men and 2% for women.

- *Britain*: A 1990-91 nationwide survey of 18,876 adults aged 16 to 59 reports that 1.4% of men had had homosexual contact in the five years preceding the survey. Only 6.1% of men had any lifetime homosexual experience.

- *U.S.*: A nationwide 1989 household sample of 1,537 adults conducted by the National Opinion Research Center at the University of Chicago finds that of sexually active adults over 18, 1.2% of males and 1.2% of females reported homosexual activity in the year preceding the survey; 4.9% to 5.6% of both sexes reported since age 18 having had partners of both genders, and 0.6% to 0.7% exclusively homosexual partners.

- *U.S.*: A stratified cluster sample from the Minnesota Adolescent Health Survey (1986-87) of 36,741 public school students in seventh through 12th grade found that 0.6% of the boys and 0.2% of the girls identified themselves as "most or 100% homosexual"; 0.7% of the boys and 0.8% of the girls identified themselves as "bisexual"; and 10.1% of males and 11.3% of females were unsure.

- *Canada*: A nationwide cluster random sample of 5,514 first year college students under age 25 finds 98% heterosexual, 1% bisexual, 1% homosexual.
- *Norway*: A 1987 random national mail sample of 6,155 adults age 18-60 finds that 0.9% of males and 0.9% of females had homosexual experiences within three years of the survey, and 3.5% of males and 3% of females had ever had any homosexual experience.
- *Denmark*: A 1989 stratified random sample of 3,178 adults 18-59 finds homosexual intercourse reported by 2.7% of sexually experienced males. Less that 1% of men were exclusively homosexual.

Many other studies also vary greatly from the Kinsey research, which in retrospect has little validity. ***

Other Kinsey Myths

Now that the mythology surrounding Kinsey's homosexuality statistics is being laid to rest, perhaps it's time to examine some other Kinsey conclusions. A good place to start would be his findings on childhood sexuality.

Kinsey's research contains the only body of experimental data purporting to demonstrate that children from a very young age are sexual and have sexual needs. This wisdom is part of the "scientific" foundation of modern sex education, allowing Lester Kirkendall, a sex education pioneer and Kinsey colleague, to predict in a professional journal in 1985, that once our sense of guilt diminishes, cross-generational (adult-child) sex and other forms of sexual expression "will become legitimate."

But the Kinsey "findings" are based on criminal experiments conducted by pedophiles who sexually stimulated infants (as young as two months) and children against their will, without parental consent (obviously), for up to 24 hours at a time. Kinsey compiled these data in a series of tables illustrating normal childhood sexual response and orgasmic capability. A Lance reviewer has called for an explanation from Kinsey's surviving co-workers. (None has been offered.) The National Institutes of Health's fraud specialist Walter Stewart has called for an investigation. It's about time.

The report, **Homosexuality: The 10% Lie**, *The Family Report,* Family Research Institute, Inc., 1992, was referred to at the beginning of

Chapter 2. The substance of the report was given in statements in Chapter 2 and in the above article of The Wall Street Journal. This report also gives publication references for research data described. An interesting thing in the report is information about how the American Psychological Association has misrepresented the 10 percent homosexuality figure even long after it knew or should have known that the figures had no validity. The article states that the APA even "lied about homosexuality to the United States Supreme Court."

Homosexuals continually and systematically present false information to the public in an effort to convince people of things considered beneficial to their agenda, as is shown in many places in this book. They also have tried to falsely convince us that a large part of our population over the years have been homosexuals, including many great people of this country.

For many years, reputable researchers have long suspected and heard rumors that Alfred Kinsey was a homosexual and a masochist. There has now been a published verification, by Dr. James H. Jones, who served on the scientific board of advisors of the Kinsey Institute for Sex Research, that Alfred Kinsey was indeed a homosexual, a masochist, an exhibitionist, and had other sexual perversions. ("Kinsey—A Homosexual!", *Family Research Report*, Family Research Institute, Sept. - Oct. 1997; referring to Jones, J.H. Dr. Yes. *New Yorker*, August 25 - September 1, 1997, 98-113) The nature of some of Kinsey's perverted acts were covered in Chapter 1. The Family Research Report states that Kinsey "was a homosexual masochist who managed to [mis]use the scientific axe to chop down the Christian scaffolding of American society."

DAMAGE TO AMERICA BY THE POLITICIZING OF AIDS

A vital part of the homosexual agenda is the politicization of the AIDS crisis despite the many innocent men, women, and children who have died from this deadly disease because of the lies of the homosexual movement.

The homosexual activists, fearing that people might wake up and demand effective protective measures to combat AIDS such as mandatory testing and tracing, have destructively opposed the determination of how contagious the HIV virus is and how it may be transmitted. We covered this question in part in Chapter 1, including information in Dr. Lorraine Day's book, *AIDS—WHAT THE GOVERNMENT ISN'T TELL-ING YOU.* Dr. Day related at length on the problems caused by the homosexualists successfully opposing taking of proper precautions to protect health care workers. She stated:

> I personally knew of 17 surgeons who are infected with the AIDS virus from occupational exposure, eight of whom are orthopedic surgeons.
>
> I know of five non-surgeon doctors who are positive from needlesticks, not sustained in the operating room, but from routine patient care on the hospital wards. (p. 201)

It appears that the politicizing of the AIDS issue has even prevented us from learning how the AIDS/HIV virus is transmitted.

THE NEW AIDS MYSTERY,
by Peter Korn, *Redbook Magazine,* July 1994:

No one wants to discuss them, but 688 people in the U.S. — some of them children — claim to have contracted AIDS without knowing how. No sex. No needles. No blood transfusions. Could there really be means of infection we don't know about yet?

*** [Bruce Williams], 42 an insurance salesman and his wife, Anita, 31, a nurse's aide, moved [to Chicago] in 1984. Their daughter Whitney was 2, and Bret, the second of their five children, was a newborn. ... [In March, 1992], Whitney, now 12 was diagnosed with full-blown AIDS.

... Doctors have no idea how the girl was infected. Both parents have tested negative for HIV, and Whitney has never received a blood transfusion. ...

In February 1990 Jim Sharpe looked at his doctor and tried to control his temper. For months the 47-year-old former deli owner from Northampton, Massachusetts, had been feeling run-down. Doctors took repeated throat cultures and blood tests. Then one day Jim's wife, Jeanne, 60, was asked to leave the room. The doctor told Jim he was HIV-positive. He asked Sharpe to be honest. Had he had an affair? Sharpe didn't know whether to laugh or shout. No, he said, he'd never cheated on Jeannne. Had he ever used intravenous drugs? No again. Despite Jim's denial, the doctor said an exhaustive body search would be done to look for concealed needle marks. None were found.

... Sharpe has AIDS but no apparent source of infection. Not sex, needles, or transfusion. The doctors are mystified. Sharpe is bewildered. "This is the first time in my life I've faced something I can't handle," he says.

THE LATEST ESTIMATE PUTS THE number of HIV-positive Americans at one million. Almost all of them contracted AIDS through one of four established means of transmission: unprotected sex, contaminated needles, a transfusion with tainted blood, or from an infected mother. *Almost* all. Despite efforts by public health officials to attribute every AIDS case to one of these factors, there are still those that cannot be explained.

Jim Sharpe and Whitney Williams are two of 688 listed by the Centers for Disease Control and Prevention (CDC) as NIR—No Identified Risk factor. Forty-nine of the cases are children under 13. The number dates back to 1981, when the CDC first started tracking AIDS. Its not known how many of the 688 are still alive, and some of them died before their cases could be fully investigated. Of those still living, some were infected so long ago that tracking the source is impossible. Many more are probably hiding the truth.

Conversely, there could be thousands more who belong in the NIR category. Why? Because when health officials examine an AIDS patient they try to identify a risk factor. If a patient admits he once had unprotected sex with another man, that becomes his factor, though there's no proof that that's how he was infected.

At least that's what David Lewis, Ph.D., a microbiologist at the Environmental Protection Agency in Athens, Georgia, believes. After years of research, he's convinced that there are other means of HIV transmission., and he's critical of the CDC's method of classifying cases. Adds Ronald Mitsuysu, M.D., director of the UCLA Center for Clinical AIDS Research and Education, "We can't guarantee that people won't be infected with HIV by as yet unidentified routes of transmission. You can't say it's not possible. We learn as we go."

But Harold Jaffe, M.D., director of the CDC's HIV/AIDS division, maintains that there are no documented cases that prove alternative means of HIV transmission. ...

Some believe that Dr. Jaffe and other CDC scientists are just reluctant to divert attention from the proven, preventable causes of transmission because they know only too well how easily public panic can be triggered. ...

The article goes on to relate other recent NIR cases. One was of two children (siblings), and all investigators know is that the HIV carrier had frequent nosebleeds, and the child he infected had an open skin rash through which the virus may have entered his system. Another was two hemophiliac brothers, and CDC speculates one somehow passed HIV between them by "a shared razor—which has channels that stay moist and dark."

In 1993, Walter Kyle, a New Hampshire lawyer, published a paper in *The Lancet*, the leading British medical journal, proposing that a few people may have been infected with HIV through contaminated polio vaccines. He had found government documents that mentioned simian viruses that might be infectious to humans, and for years there had been theories that a virus resembling HIV had made its way into polio vaccines made from African green monkeys. The CDC refused to test batches of suspected vaccines after repeated requests from Kyle and other researchers. (Ibid.)

There has been testimony before both Congress and the CDC about the need for testing healthcare workers who perform invasive medical procedures and patients who undergo them. One person who testified on this need was Sanford Kuvin, M.D., a Florida infectious-disease specialist, and vice chairman of the National Foundation for Disease. (Ibid.) As yet this is not done, because of the opposition of homosexualists. Homosexual activists continue to endanger innocent people in this country in many ways—many of which are not at all evident—and the homosexualists want to keep them covered up as much as possible.

> According to the CDC, there are 39 documented cases of healthcare workers who have contracted HIV through contact with patients' blood: an additional 81 cases are still under investigation. Dr. Kuvin believes that's just a fraction of the actual numbers. He estimates there may be more than 50,000 healthcare workers infected with HIV, and that those numbers are at least part of the explanation for the existing NIR cases. "In my opinion there's been an attempt to whitewash this."
>
> A recent example is a case in Australia, the first documented example of patient-to-patient HIV transmission in a healthcare setting.

Investigators there reported a cluster of five infected patients who each visited the same surgeon on the same day in November 1989. The doctor removed skin lesions first from a man who later died of AIDS, then from four women. So far, investigators aren't sure how the virus was transmitted from the man to the women, though the likely route was the surgeon's instruments or anesthetic solution. (Ibid.)

The article goes on to explain how the HIV virus may be transmitted by other medical and dental procedures. It relates to the case of the Florida dentist, David Acer, who died of AIDS, and to six of his patients getting AIDS, three of whom were then dead from it, which was covered earlier in the book.

When such cases come to light, consideration should be given to suing doctors who are HIV positive and treat patients without informing them of the condition and the risk.

There is no question that if were it not for political pressures, much could, and would, have been done to prevent the transmission of this deadly and terrible disease. Many have died and will die because of homosexual politics.

It also rather conclusively appears that the CDC, the homosexual activists, and the media cooperated to falsely convince the public that there was a much greater danger of people getting AIDS through heterosexual sex than actually existed. The purpose was to get more government money for AIDS programs, and a large part of the money was not used at all for AIDS prevention in any effective manner—instead much of it was used for the promotion of homosexuality among government employees, in the military, and much worse—in our schools. This promotion of sodomy has been thoroughly covered in other parts of this book.

A number of articles, news programs, and at least one book have been published on this exaggerated and false propaganda.

The Wall Street Journal of May 1, 1996, had an article entitled **AIDS Fight Is Skewed By Federal Campaign Exaggerating Risks**. The article stated in part:

> *** In the U.S., the disease was, and remains, largely the scourge of gay men, intravenous drug users, their sex partners and their newborn children. ***

The emphasis on the broad reach of the disease has virtually ensured that precious funds won't go where they are most needed. For instance, though homosexuals and intravenous drug users now account for 83% of all AIDS cases reported in the U.S., the federal AIDS-prevention budget includes no specific allocation for programs for homosexual and bisexual men. ***

The article goes on to explain how the CDC and AIDS groups then settled on a campaign to alarm the public and to convince the public of a false and exaggerated danger to people generally. The article ends:

Even back in the 1980s, Stephen C. Joseph, who was commissioner of public health for New York City from 1986 to 1990, blasted the notion that AIDS was making major inroads into the general population.

Today Dr. Joseph, who is assistant secretary of defense for health affairs at the Pentagon, says: "Political correctness has prevented us from looking at the issue squarely in the eye and dealing with it. It is the responsibility of the public-health department to tell the truth."

Sensible people would think that homosexuals and their groups should want the truth known, and efforts directed so that the most good would be done with available resources to eradicate the disease. Instead, the disclosure of the false propaganda about the spread and danger of AIDS enraged them. Homosexuals seem to have the inability to arrive at correct answers to anything that reflects on the dangers of their destructive lifestyle.

News Media Collaborated in Lethal AIDS Fraud
By David R. Boldt, *Philadelphia Inquirer*

The Wall Street Journal has just blown the whistle on the biggest, best intentioned, and possibly most lethal fraud ever perpetrated by the U.S. government. ***

The article talks about whether this official deception will further erode trust in the government, but bypasses a comparably crucial aspect: the complicity of the media.

And let's not make any excuses about it. We all knew what was going on (or should have). I can remember hearing from other journalists that the danger was being exaggerated very early on. Oddly, there seemed to be "less" discussion of the deception as time passed. ***

The emotion-charged nature of the AIDS story undoubtedly discouraged rational analysis. Even today, alluding to the fact that AIDS is not a disease one can pick up in a crowd is often seen as a defamation of gays.

All this was reflected in the reaction to Michael Fumento's book, "The Myth of Heterosexual AIDS," which contains the same medical information as the Journal article, but which lacks the CDC's admission of a conscious conspiracy.

Its publication set off a barrage of protest from ACT UP and other gay activist groups. Fumento says that despite brisk sales, the publisher stopped printing the book and declined to bring out a paperback edition. Forbes magazine retracted a story on the furor the book had caused among both conservatives and liberals.

Fumento himself was fired from his job as an editorial writer for the Rocky Mountain News and pilloried in publications ranging from the Village Voice to Science. No First Amendment advocacy groups rushed to his side. *** (*Albuquerque Journal*, 5-7-96)

The article went on to say that some "gay" writers were now praising Fumento's book. How they have concluded that they could now use it to their advantage was not explained.

We see that homosexual activists have no regard for what is true or what is just, nor have they any regard for what is good for the country. The policies they support even harms them. The things that could help eradicate AIDS and benefit the society, such as testing, tracing, and warning people who may be exposed to those with AIDS, they always vigorously fight. They do not even want patients to be protected from infected healthcare providers, and they do not want health care providers to be protected from patients. They want the fact that a person is an HIV carrier to be kept in strict secrecy. And the fact that we allow these things to go on shows the degeneracy of our society.

CORPORATIONS AND BUSINESSES

Many of the large corporations and businesses in this country have succumbed to the pressures and threats of homosexual activists. They have adopted company rules against discrimination because of "sexual orientations," and have even afforded medical and other benefits for "partners" of homosexuals, the same as they afford medical benefits for dependent family members of workers. Threats and infiltrations have taken many forms, including lawsuits and threats thereof, and boycotts and threats of boycotts. The success has been amazing, and it appears that many of these businesses have been much more interested in profits and avoiding trouble that in any form of morality.

Also, the passing of a number of laws in various states preventing discrimination because of "sexual orientation," has certainly helped nudge large corporations to adopt such laws on a national basis, even in states they operate in where they do not have such laws. It allows them to have corporate rules and procedures that are uniform throughout their operations.

They are also following the lead of the federal government during the Clinton administration.

On this subject, and all others in this chapter, the issues and factual matters are intertwined with other chapters. This is particularly true with the issues in the following chapter, which deals with the successes of the homosexual agenda. The successes show the agenda of homosexual activists by their accomplishments in the political, business and other arenas. The homosexualists also want "'Buycotts' to celebrate and promote businesses that have positive human relations records" and "diversity training for businesses." (*CityBeat*, Feb. 2-8, 1995) This is a local article of a Cincinnati publication about homosexual activists working to overcome what the voters did in Cincinnati in repealing a local ordinance adopted by the city which gave special protection for "gays" against discrimination in work, housing, and other things. As we have seen, "positive human relations records" means the acceptance of sodomy as a commendable practice, and diversity training means brainwashing workers into believing this.

Many actions brought have no legal or factual basis, and are done for the sole purpose of trying to prevent people from exercising a real constitutional right—which is freedom of speech under the First Amendment to the United States Constitution—in criticizing homosexuality and its destructive effects. I believe that when such actions are defeated, whether they are criminal or civil, counter actions of abuse of process, and malicious prosecution of a civil or criminal matter, should be considered by the victims of the homosexualists. An example of what may well be such an action or attempted action is the following:

TV host may be charged

DENVER — Criminal investigators are studying a rarely used libel law to see whether it applies to a TV talk-show host who broadcast an AIDS victim's obituary and told viewers, "Don't be a homo."

The investigation weighs Bob Enyart's free-speech rights against the right of James Bybee to not have his memory "blackened," Arapahoe County District Attorney Bob Gallagher said.

Enyart, 36, is a conservative host on Christian-run KWHD in Greenwood Village south of Denver. (*The Albuquerque Tribune*, 2-22-95)

I do not know whether or not the deceased victim was a homosexual, but I do know that during 1995, in Colorado, homosexuality and AIDS were certainly matters of public concern and they still are. If the victim was a homosexual there is no question whatsoever that the comment was a constitutionally protected comment. Even if the victim was not a homosexual, the comment was constitutionally protected, because homosexual conduct was then and is now the most common way of contracting AIDS, and this is a fair comment on a public problem. Also, the homosexual community tells us that there is nothing wrong with homosexuality, so why should an implication that someone is homosexual be defamatory?

In the early days of the homosexual movement, well-known singer Anita Bryant was forced out of her work advertising orange juice on national TV because she stuck by her Christian views and publicly opposed the homosexual movement for special rights to keep people from discriminating against homosexuals for their immoral character and vile acts of sodomy. A lucrative career was destroyed because Bryant had the courage and morality to take a stand for the moral good of America, and for her Christian beliefs. It is certainly a shameful thing that there weren't more in the country like her, and that she did not get the public support that could have saved her career. It was one more step downward toward Sodom and Gomorrah for this country.

It seems that most of the large corporations have capitulated to the homosexual onslaught.

Microsoft offers health-care benefits to same-sex partners of its employees, and eligible dependents. The policy is modeled after those of several companies, including software rival Lotus Development Corp., in Cambridge, Mass., that began offering benefits to gay partners in September 1991. (*Albuquerque Journal*, 4-23-93)

An article in *The Albuquerque Journal*, 12-3-93, discussed the fact that Apple Computer was denied a special tax break to open a plant in Williamson County Texas, because of Apple's benefits for same sex partners. However, money finally won out, and the Williamson County commissioners later gave in. The article also noted that Levi Strauss & Co. adopted a "domestic partners benefits program" in 1992. The article also stated that : "One high-technology company considered a 'straggler' by gay and lesbian rights advocates is Dell Computer Corp., an Austin, Texas, company with 6,000 employees. Dell does not offer health benefits to partners of gay and lesbian employees ... ."

Blue Cross Worker's Plan to Cover Unmarried Pairs

BOSTON — In an unusual move for a health insurance company, Blue Cross and Blue Shield of Massachusetts has announced it would expand its employee medical benefits to also include unmarried couples.

The policy, to begin Jan. 1, will extend benefits to couples whether they are same sex or opposite sex. *** (*Albuquerque Journal*, 11-10-93)

Fifteen Florida lawmakers are condemning Walt Disney Co., for extending health insurance benefits to partners of gay employees. The lawmakers said in a letter sent last week that the move was "a big mistake both morally and financially" that would alienate families. (*Albuquerque Journal*, 10-19-95)

Partners' Benefits Trouble Airline
San Franciscans Pressure United

SAN FRANCISCO — Disney's done it. So have Levi Strauss, IBM and American Express.

All offer benefits to employees with domestic partners, many whom are homosexual. Companies and employees alike say the policy improves morale and can sharpen the recruiting edge.

But nobody forced the decisions; no David aimed a slingshot at a corporate Goliath. Then San Francisco told United Airlines it had to obey an ordinance requiring companies doing business with the city to offer spousal benefits to their workers' unmarried and same-sex partners.

"We're surprised. ... We're disappointed," said Mary Jo Holland, a United spokeswoman in Chicago.

Holland said that if United offered benefits in San Francisco, it would have to offer them worldwide. United had no estimate of what such compliance might cost. ***

In Israel, a 1994 lawsuit forced El Al to offer domestic partner benefits. And Air Canada has offered domestic partner benefits to its 18,000 Canadian employees since early last year. ***
(*Albuquerque Journal*, 1-27-97)

There are a few that are fighting against some of this corporate moral degradation.

Family Alert, Christian Action Network, August 1995, carries an advertisement attacking AT&T for promotion of homosexuality, including such things as: "AT&T indoctrinates their employees to accept homosexuality using the video 'On Being Gay' by homosexual activist Brian McNaught." The ad offers a program to adopt Lifeline Long Distance Service as a long distance carrier, and "10% of your long distance billing is donated to Christian Action Network." A number of other Christian organizations are joining in such programs.

However, it appears that there are fewer and fewer people with the moral courage to continue to fight the homosexual movement. Consequently, the morality of our society continues its downward plunge.

GOVERNMENTAL CORRUPTION

The homosexual agenda has had a tremendous impact on local, state, and federal governments and agencies; and also on activist court actions.

A large part of the corruption has been brought about by our president, Bill Clinton. It commenced as soon as he got in office with his attempt to overturn regulations and allow homosexuals into the military. The homosexual groups contributed greatly, in funds and support, to the election of Clinton. And as soon as he became president he lost no time in trying to make good on his commitments to their agenda. However, he at once met great opposition, both from the people and from congress. In 1993 and 1994, the papers were full of news about the fight on this matter.

Conservative columnist Cal Thomas said in **Gays won't stop making demands:**

> If homosexuals are officially welcomed into the military, it won't stop there. The argument will then be that if homosexuals can fight and die for their country, the state should sanction same-sex marriages. And after that? The pedophiles are knocking on the cultural door, asking for legitimacy. The *New York Times* Book Review last Sunday published a favorable review of a book that praises adult-child sexual relations.
>
> Too far out? Not when you consider how far down the moral ladder we have slipped these last 30 years. Once the standard that measures right and wrong has been removed, anything becomes possible, even probable. And the decline of a moral universe brings with it an inevitable decline in the relatively human political universe it supports. As political scientist Glenn Tinder has written, without a moral order founded on the principles of the Judeo-Christian tradition, "The kind of political order we are used to . . . becomes indefensible." (*Conservative Chronicle*, 2-10-93)

It seemed to make little difference to Clinton that he was greatly overstepping his authority in ordering the elimination of the military ban on homosexuals. The Uniform Code of Military Justice, which is passed by Congress, had long made sodomy a crime, as did the laws of many states. The president has no authority to change the Code.

However Clinton went stubbornly on his way, attempting to lift the ban on homosexuals in the military by the mere signing of an Executive Order. (*The Albuquerque Tribune*, 1-21-93)

He at first stood firm and told the military that it was a done deal and that the "gay ban is history." (*The Albuquerque Tribune*, 1-25-93; *Albuquerque Journal*, 1-26-93)

There was immediately tremendous opposition from the military. Having dodged the draft in the Vietnam War, and never having served in the military, Clinton's actions were indeed considered rash and destructive. Those with military experience strongly objected to the action.

The Pentagon and the Joint Chiefs of Staff openly opposed allowing homosexuals in the military. This included the Chairman of the Joint Chiefs of Staff, General Colin Powell. "Feelings are so strong that one senior officer was telling colleagues about his horror at seeing two men dancing together at an inaugural ball Wednesday night. The military people who were there left the dance floor in disgust, the officer said." (*The Albuquerque Tribune*, 1-22-93)

Clinton then sends his "top gun," Defense Secretary Les Aspin, to try to break down opposition in both the military and in Congress. (*The Albuquerque Tribune*, 1-27-93, 6-5-93)

However, the military Chiefs continued to defy the wishes of their Commander in Chief. "The Joint Chiefs of Staff, emboldened by pleadings from congressional backers, are standing firm in their opposition to President Clinton's effort to end the ban on homosexuals in the military." (*The Albuquerque Tribune*, 7-9-93)

Retired General H. Norman Schwarzkopf, hero and commander of the armed forces in the Gulf War against Iraq, was opposed to the lifting of the military's gay ban. However, by this time President Clinton's ratings in the polls were plummeting due to this issue (*The Albuquerque Tribune*, 1-28-93), and he then began shifting his position to one of not asking recruits about their sexual orientation, but not allowing open homosexuality. The following Associated Press article typifies military opposition to allowing homosexuals in the military:

Schwarzkopf opposes lifting military's gay ban

WASHINGTON — Retired Army Gen. H. Norman Schwarzkopf today said he accepts the current policy of not asking recruits about their sexual orientation but remains opposed to gays serving openly in the military.

"I have no objection to leaving the situation exactly where it is now," Schwarzkopf, who commanded U. S. Forces in the Persian Gulf War, told the Senate Armed Services Committee.

Swarzkopf said lifting the ban would hurt morale and the cohesion of military units.

"The armed services' principal mission is not to be social experimentation," he said.

While Schwarzkopf was willing to accept the current policy, the three other witnesses on the panel were steadfastly opposed to any change in the prohibition.

Marine Corps Col. Fred Peck, who had just returned after five months in Somalia, said he would counsel his three sons against joining the military if the ban is lifted.

Peck said he would strongly oppose it in the case of his oldest son, Scott, a senior at the University of Maryland, because he feared for the boy, who he said is homosexual.

"I'm a father of a homosexual and I don't think he should serve in the military," Peck told the panel.

On Monday, members of the panel traveled to Norfolk, Va., where they visited several ships to sound out sailors who would have to serve with homosexuals if the ban is lifted.

The message from most of the sailors was clear: Keep the ban.

Most of their testimony was critical of the idea that the Pentagon's stand against homosexuals is similar to past discrimination against African-Americans and women.

"It is not comparable to being Black. It is not comparable to being a woman," said Cmdr. Lin Hutton, the Atlantic Fleet's first woman aircraft squadron commander. "It defines a lifestyle."
(*The Albuquerque Tribune*, 5-11-93)

The moral conviction and courage of the military officers opposing the ban must be admired. They had to know that opposing their Commander in Chief and the Secretary of Defense could be detrimental to their promotions and military career.

General Colin Powell announced he wanted to take early retirement and resign as Chairman of the Joint Chiefs of Staff. Although a New York Times article reported that his desire to retire early was reinforced by disagreements with Clinton's homosexual policy, Powell denied this, stating he was not unhappy and "crosswise with the administration."
(*Albuquerque Journal*, 2-11-93)

Although Democrat Senator Sam Nunn of Georgia, with a few of the other Democrats, and most of the Republican members of Congress, opposed allowing homosexuals in the military, they began giving in to the compromise policy called "Don't ask, don't tell." The idea was summarized as follows:

"The bipartisan plan would end the military's efforts at unmasking homosexuals but would continue to bar gay men and lesbian women from serving if they are open about their sexuality.

If adopted, the policy would mean that the military would not ask new recruits about their sexual orientation or conduct investigations meant to ferret out homosexuals.

But it would also impose a strict code of conduct that would address such questions as harassment, holding hands on base and same-sex dancing. Homosexuals would not be allowed to serve openly.

The Clinton administration and homosexual-rights groups oppose the plan, which would essentially make permanent an interim Defense Department policy hammered out by President Clinton and Sen. Sam Nunn in January." *** (*The Albuquerque Tribune*, 5-12-93)

This eventually became the policy in the military. And it is a shame that Congress compromised its principles to this extent. In addition, wide dissension on both sides continues until now.

Enlistees Oppose Lifting of Gay Ban

WASHINGTON — An overwhelming number of enlisted personnel in the U.S. military oppose President Clinton's plan to lift a ban on homosexuals in the services and predict widespread violence if openly gay men and lesbians are admitted to their ranks, according to an unprecedented poll of enlisted men and women conducted by the Los Angeles Times. *** (*Albuquerque Journal*, 2-28-93)

The **Non-Commisioned Officers Association** strongly opposed allowing homosexuals in the military. (*NCOA Journal*, Feb. 1993) It countered the "discrimination" argument as follows:

In the face of discrimination of equal opportunity arguments, NCOA suggested to the Committee that the recruitment and retention of homosexuals in the military should not be confused with racial integration. It was pointed out that skin color, an inert, benign characteristic, must not be compared to a behavioral characteristic when attempting to justify action.

Despite the pressures and retributions from the top, military members and ex-military members continued to speak out. The controversy continued, and I have no doubt that the administration supplied some of the witnesses.

Witnesses speak out on gay ban

WASHINGTON — The House Armed Services Committee has taken up the issue of homosexuals in the military, with witness calling the idea everything from a high moral challenge to an embrace of deviance and perversion.

Retired Marine Corps Brigadier General William Weise likened gay sailors aboard a ship to "putting a hungry dog in a meat shop."

Retire Army Col. Lucian Truscott III, who led infantry troops in the Korean and Vietnam wars, said "I have never heard of any trouble in any unit because of gays."

Another retired Army colonel who is homosexual and who also led combat troops in Vietnam, Karl Cropsey, said the military ban "rests on prejudice not fact."

But retired Marine Corps Col. John Ripley, also a decorated Vietnam combat veteran, predicted that lifting the ban would turn the military into a place of "deviants."

Ripley said that "decent, God-fearing people do not consider homosexuality decent, normal or acceptable," and will not permit their children to join a military that condones it.

Ripley maintained that admitting open homosexuals would ruin unit cohesion and morale because, he asserted, homosexuals "constantly focus on themselves, their so-called needs, what they want, their entitlements, their rights.

"They never talk about the good of the unit. It is this constant focus on themselves and their inability to subordinate their own personal desire for the good of the unit (that is) an instant indicator of trouble."

Ripley and Weise also maintained that fear of contracting AIDS would be ruinous in battle situations where soldiers are frequently covered with each others blood.

Cropsey countered that the military "winks at" and even encourages adultery among heterosexual soldiers. He said sailors from ships docking Bangkok frequent "brothels where 80 percent of the prostitutes are infected" with AIDS and other sexually transmissible diseases.

Cropsey and former Army captain Tanya Domi, a lesbian, also denied charges that lifting the ban would lead to homosexual demands for "special rights," including hiring quotas and other "affirmative action," spousal benefits and homosexual marriage.

"All we want is equal treatment," said Cropsey.

But California Republican Robert Dornan shot back that live televised coverage of the gay march on Washington earlier this month proved otherwise. "That bizarre scene on that platform" Dornan said, "told Americans a lot about the agenda you say doesn't exist."
(*The Albuquerque Tribune*, 5-5-93)

Military Retirees Launch Campaign To Keep Gay Ban

WASHINGTON – A group of retired military officers will try to persuade Congress to write into law the ban on homosexuals in the military that President Clinton seeks to overturn.

The creation of the Defense Readiness Council was announced at a news conference Monday. Its purpose is "to stop a political effort bent on forcing the armed services to admit and accommodate homosexuals contrary to professional military judgment and experience."

The existing ban on homosexuals in the military is contained in a Defense Department directive issued in 1982. Before that each service had rules providing dishonorable discharges for anyone caught engaging in homosexual conduct. Those dated from World War II.

"The American people do not fund the American military for the purpose of social engineering," said retired Rear Adm. Clarence A. Hill Jr. "From a military and moral standpoint, we think it's wrong."

The retired officers said they have started a grassroots campaign to persuade Clinton to withdraw his plan to allow homosexuals to serve openly in the armed services. They said they are attempting to raise money from veterans groups and others to lobby Congress to make the military ban on gays a federal law.

"I think Clinton is a pragmatic politician, and we hope he will face up to the fact that most Americans don't support him on this," said retired Marine Lt. Gen. Charles G. Cooper.

Among 21 members of the council's board of advisers is retired Adm. Thomas Moorer, who was chairman of the Joint Chiefs of Staff from 1970 to 1974. Others include retired Gens. Alfred M. Gray Jr. and Robert H. Barrow, both former Marine Corps commandants, and retired Gen. Charles L. Donnelly Jr., former commander of U.S. Air Forces in Europe. *** (*Albuquerque Journal*, 5-4-93)

Marine Still Opposed to Gays

WASHINGTON — Most people underestimate the possible harm from homosexuals serving openly in the military, the Marine Corps' top officer said Thursday. He and other military leaders remain opposed, he said.

Gen. Carl Mundy, commandant of the Marine Corps. said he thinks a compromise will be worked out that will be acceptable to the service chiefs, but he indicated the debate is continuing at the Pentagon.

As for himself, he said, "It's better just to have a clear-cut policy that says: "This is the way it is—if you must talk about your homosexuality then you probably are better served in another profession than the military."

He told reporters there is wide agreement among military leaders. (*Albuquerque Journal*, 7-2-93)

Opposition to Clinton's proposal continued around the country. Some opposition got quite flagrant.

General's Remarks Spark Probe

WASHINGTON — The Air Force considers allegations that one of its generals ridiculed President Clinton at an official function a serious matter that must be investigated, a Pentagon spokesman said Tuesday

Pentagon spokesman Bob Hall said Maj. Gen. Harold Campbell allegedly made derogatory comments about Clinton at a May 24 dinner in the Netherlands attended by 200 people.

The Washington Post reported Tuesday that Campbell (a decorated combat pilot) described Clinton as a "draft-dodging, pot-smoking, womanizing" commander-in-chief, and that the general also referred to the president as "gay-loving" in a speech before an awards banquet at Soesterburg Air Base.

Hall said the service was conducting an informal investigation but said the matter will proceed up the chain of command.

"There are specific guidelines in the UCMJ [Uniform Code of Military Justice] in terms of behavior" towards elected officials Hall said. Those include barring "contemptuous words" against the president, vice president, members of Congress, the secretary of defense and other officials. (*Albuquerque Journal*, 6-9-93)

Certainly such statements amount to a violation of military code, but I cannot help but sympathize with the outspoken general. Clinton is trying to severely damage and demoralize the military service. Also, I consider his criticism of Clinton's bad character to be a gross understatement, which has been born out by later events. I consider him to have the worst character of any person who has ever been president of the United States—and a person who is completely unfit.

The military policy and regulations that resulted from the compromise of the Clinton administration and Congress is the "don't ask don't tell policy," and it presently exists as of this writing. However, it as well as the prior complete restriction has continually been attacked by homosexuals in court in numerous cases that are so many and diverse it would serve no useful purpose to cover them here. Different judges and courts have ruled in opposite ways. There have been a large number of homosexuals convicted of sodomy, and a large number who "came out" in the service were successfully discharged. But some activist judges have ruled that a few should be reinstated. In some cases it seemed that the administration was not making any all out effort to enforce the new regulations. At least one appeal from a judge's ruling that barring homosexuals was unlawful discrimination was dropped (*The Albuquerque Tribune*, 11-29-94). It was certainly not a policy that Clinton had wanted. The administration dropped the appeal to the U.S. Supreme Court in the Meinhold case, referred to below, after the 9th Circuit U.S. Court of Appeals ruled that Meinhold could not be discharged merely for saying he was homosexual. The Administration claimed that a favorable ruling obtained in another case "would have the effect of limiting any damage done to the military policy done in the Meinhold case." (Ibid.)

An activist federal judge in California, Terry Hatter Jr., attempted to prohibit the military from enforcing the policy generally, ruling that the ban was unconstitutional, and threatening to impose a fine of $10,000 per day for failure to abide by his ruling. (*The Albuquerque Tribune*, 10-2-93 and 10-12-93) The United States Supreme Court entered an order limiting Hatter's order only to the homosexual in the case before him, Navy Petty Officer Keith Meinhold, and allowing the administration to continue with its "don't ask don't tell policy" during the appeal. (*Albuquerque Journal*, 10-30-93)

The cases continue, but for now it seems that the "don't ask don't tell" policy remains in effect. However, this matter will finally be decided by the United States Supreme Court. And although the policy is clearly constitutional under present law, as are laws against sodomy generally, for the reasons explained in Chapter 8, this can change, and will change if Clinton, or some other liberal president, is successful in getting more liberal judges appointed to the Supreme Court.

Although Clinton was prevented from having open homosexuals in the military, and sodomy remained a crime under the Uniform Code of Military of Justice, he nevertheless continued his promotion of the homosexual agenda—even in the military.

An article in *The Wall Street Journal*, 4-27-94, tells about Karl Mertz, who was a senior Equal Opportunity Manager at the Agriculture Department in Atlanta. Mertz said he was "stripped of a title, stripped of support staff, stripped of working in the field of my expertise," because, as a private citizen, when asked about the gay-rights policy in the Agriculture Department, he said that the department should be headed "toward Camelot, not Sodom and Gomorrah." He had dared to exercise his constitutional right of freedom of speech and say what he thought of what was termed by the article as "Agriculture Secretary Mike Epsy's gay-rights agenda, part of the Clintonites' kowtowing to a key group." The article states, in part:

> At a Washington meeting of the department's affirmative-action administrators on Feb. 25, Mr. Mertz listened to a report by the head of the department's gay employees group. An outline distributed by the gay activist during her presentation states: "Until our relationships are recognized and respected and benefits are available to our partners and families, we are not full members of Team USDA." Top executives pledged to hold "sensitivity training" to spread this message among the ranks and to punish those who don't toe the line.
>
> In other words, homosexual employees aren't just asking to be left alone—Mr. Mertz is in favor of that. They want other employees to actively approve of their lifestyle. And Mr. Epsy is backing the gay rights agenda with taxpayer-funded indoctrination courses for the department's workers. "I was pushed as far as I could go," Mr. Mertz says.

Again we can be thankful for the courageous Senator Jesse Helms.

Helms Faces Down Homosexual Lobby

Dr. Karl Mertz won an important victory last week when soon-to-be-homeward-bound Secretary of Agriculture Mike Epsy agreed to reinstate him conditionally to his position as equal opportunity manager for the 10-state Southeastern region ... .

Before he violated the political correctness agenda, the 49-year-old Mertz had compiled an exemplary record throughout nearly two decades of government employment and has, indeed, espoused liberal positions on most political issues.

Without the steadfast help of Sen. Jesse Helms (R.-N.C.), Mertz would at best still be languishing in the post to which he was transferred by Epsy after he criticized coercive government programs that championed the homosexual agenda. ***

A greatly relieved Mertz told Human Events last week, "Epsy and Clinton knew that unless there were to be a veto of the crop insurance bill, the legal requirement for a public hearing in my case would come into play. Above all, they feared the consequences of this."

He added, "What I've gone through might give pause to others who are considering objecting to the constant government promotion of the homosexual agenda. Without Helms, Dole and the Becket Fund for Religious Liberty, I could be on the street without a job. They all deserve a lot of credit, as do Human Events, the *Wall Street Journal* and the Washington *Times*. The USDA E-mail, which goes to all executives, cited your articles and they knew you were paying attention. The press was my only shield."

If so, it was Helms who was Mertz's sword. From the Senate floor, as he announced news of Epsy's agreement, Helms explained, "I am confident that the homosexual lobby is displeased and I am sure their disapproval of Secretary Epsy's action will be heard loud and clear."

"But regardless of who stands in the way, the defense of our citizens' constitutional right to express freely their opinions when it comes to moral and spiritual convictions is a defense well worth the fight. When the federal government decides that this right is no longer valid, the miracle of America will be in grave jeopardy."
(*Human Events*, 10-14-94)

The homosexual lobby, and liberal senators and congressman, often led by Senator Edward (Ted) Kennedy, D-Mass., have continually pushed for and had introduced various bills "that would ban discrimination on the basis of sexual orientation in hiring, firing, promotion and pay." So far no such bill has ever been successful. But the Clinton administration has nevertheless continually supported the agenda, and appointed a large number of open homosexuals to government posts. Even the Republicans have not shown much moral courage in opposing these appointments.

Similar things have happened in state and local governments around the country. In most of the states, so far, the homosexualists have continually tried to get bills passed by state legislatures that would bar such discrimination, as well as in many other areas such as forcing people to rent to homosexuals and have them on their property, and would even force them into non-governmental organizations, such as the Boy Scouts and religious organizations. They are continually trying to force the acceptance and even the "celebration" of homosexuality on all of us. When they fail at the state level, they nevertheless go against the wishes of the people and find small-time politicians that will carry their agenda, and force such regulations on the people through local governments and agencies, and in many of the schools.

There is certainly one thing for which we must give credit to the homosexual activists—they vigorously, continually, and systematically work for their agenda. That is more than can be generally be said for the churches, Christians, orthodox Jews, other groups, and citizens that oppose them. For these reasons, we who are against the acceptance of sodomy, and various other kinds of immorality, are fast losing ground. It is a war against the most worthwhile things in our society, but we lack soldiers in the trenches that are needed to stem the assault upon us, our culture, and our basic liberties.

In, New Mexico, where the homosexualists have failed, so far, on the state level, they have nevertheless been successful in Albuquerque, our largest city, Santa Fe, our Capital, The University of New Mexico, our largest university, Technical Vocational Institute, our largest vocational school; and in many other colleges, schools, agencies, and organizations around the state. Their success at this level is phenomenal.

And it is primarily with Democratic politicians, although there are also some defecting Republicans.

New Mexico is not unique, it is happening all over the country. Much of the successes of the homosexual agenda will be covered in the next chapter, which is particularly on these successes at all levels of government. In addition, the accomplishments tell us much about the agenda.

Another front is the continual lobbying of officials, from the President on the national level to school board members and teachers, at the local level. They are continually and successfully pressing for all kinds of laws and regulations such as provisions against discrimination on the basis of "sexual orientation," "hate crimes" because of sexual orientation, sensitivity training to brainwash people into accepting homosexuality as natural and good—and convincing us that we who oppose such things are the ones who are abnormal. The same approach is made at the corporate level. They have even gotten state supreme courts and state bar associations to accept such rules.

Staff writer Marian Wallace in an article, **Homosexuals are moving into the Main Stream**, *Family Voice*, Concerned Women for America, November/December, 1993, makes the summary observation: "The homosexual community is growing more powerful—not because society has chosen to accept the homosexual lifestyle as 'normal,' but because society has grown afraid of opposing the movement." The article reports that many police departments in the country, including Boston, New York City, San Francisco, and the Los Angeles County Sheriff's Department, have actively recruited homosexuals for their offices. Many other departments have had to deal with the question because of various kinds of court actions brought. "Both the Maryland State Police and Dallas Police forces were ordered by the courts to admit homosexuals to their ranks when two lesbians each brought a lawsuit against the departments for violating their 'rights of privacy.'" (Presumably by questions or application investigations.) Some police agencies, however, have not capitulated. "In Virginia, both the Virginia State Police and the Fairfax County police have gone on record as not hiring homosexuals, citing that Virginia's anti-sodomy law prevents them from hiring people who might break the law. But as more states overturn their sodomy laws, it is easy to see that these laws are losing their effectiveness." (Ibid.)

There have been some limited successes in the country by people rising up against the homosexual onslaught. The people of Colorado, led by the campaign of Colorado for Family Values, and Focus on the Family, voted against special rights for homosexuals by a substantial majority. However, the will of the people has now been overturned by the United States Supreme Court. The legality of this decision, and what can be done about it, is covered in the last chapter.

The people of the city of Cincinnati, Ohio, led by the organization, Equal Rights Not Special Rights, Inc., overturned a city ordinance barring discrimination because of sexual orientation. So far, this action has been upheld on appeal, and I would think that there would be no question about its legality. It is not general legislation aimed at any "special group." It merely overturned a particular ordinance that was passed. If a particular piece of legislation can be passed, certainly the people, who have ultimate control, can overturn it.

But there has been nothing that even comes close to the homosexual assault carried on by the Clinton administration. Our regular news media seem to have been very quiet on these matters. It is also amazing that a Republican-controlled Congress has not had the moral courage to put a stop to what has amounted to the most shameful promotion of destructive filth that has ever occurred in the history of our government.

The most comprehensive study I have found on this matter is reflected in an article, **Federal Government Promotes Homosexuality Using "Diversity" Cover**, distributed in May, 1996, by The Liberty Alliance, founded by Dr. Jerry Falwell. Rev. Falwell is one of the "most hated" individuals in the country by the homosexualists. The article was written by Col. Robert Maginnis, a distinguished Policy Analyst with the Family Research Council in Washington, D.C. Gary L. Bauer is president of that organization. This well documented article has over fifty references (consisting of various government publications, orders, memorandums, and news items) which are omitted for purposes of brevity. The following contains some of the factual statements from the article:

FEDERAL GOVERNMENT GRANTS HOMOSEXUALS OFFICIAL STATUS
During the first two years of the Clinton Administration, most federal agencies have amended their equal employment opportunity and civil rights policies to include the term "sexual orientation."

... Carol Browner, Administrator of the Environmental Protection Agency, sent a memo to all EPA employees on October 14, 1994 stating, "Today the EPA joins the growing list of public and private sector employers which have added 'sexual orientation' to our equal employment opportunity policy."

[The article states that Secretary Federico Pena, Department of Transportation, adopted the policy in 1993, and Secretary Henry Cisneros, Housing and Urban Development, took similar action in August, 1994]

... director Louis Freeh [Federal Bureau of Investigation] [stated that] "homosexual conduct is not per se misconduct," and adopted a new policy to admit homosexuals to the ... Bureau. Several homosexuals are now being trained to become FBI agents. [The FBI is under the Department of Justice, headed by Janet Reno as Attorney General.]

... Attorney General Janet Reno (in 1993) declared that the Department of Justice will not discriminate on the basis of sexual orientation when conducting security clearances. ... Reno removed any reference to sexual orientation from application forms. Congressman Barney Frank (D-MA), an open homosexual, stated, "The clear implication is that, outside the uniformed military services, being gay will not be a relevant factor."

... Reno ruled that a foreigner, who claimed he was persecuted by his government for being homosexual, may be eligible to immigrate to the U.S. In 1994 [she] waived immigration laws so that avowed HIV-infected homosexuals could participate in New York's "Gay Olympics." ***

... Office of Personnel Management Director James King sent a memo to all OPM employees in January, 1994 announcing the formal recognition of the Gay, Lesbian and Bisexual Employees (GLOBE) as a professional association. ... GLOBE can now use government facilities, communication systems, bulletin boards, and have official representation at personnel meetings. ***

... famous people alleged to be homosexual were displayed on bulletin boards [of the Department of Transportation]. The posters were made at government expense and identified Eleanor Roosevelt, Virginia Woolf, Errol Flynn, and Walt Whitman as homosexuals.

Federal Aviation Administration employee Anthony Venchieri complained when he received a DOT voice mail message inviting him to "celebrate with us the diversity of the gay and lesbian community." The message was broadcast to all 4,100 DOT voice-mail users. He was removed from the system after complaining but was later reinstated. ...

GLOBE also uses government facilities to promote homosexuality. During June 1994, many federal agencies permitted GLOBE chapters to use space to host homosexual programs. ...

THE DIVERSITY AGENDA

[In July 1994, the U.S. Fish and Wildlife Service put out a memo] entitled, "Stepping Stones to Diversity: an Action Plan," the service proclaims, "Managing diversity needs to be a top service priority. The service must also recognize that the differences among people are important."

... In a policy statement (DOT's Secretary Pena defines "diversity") as "inclusion — hiring, developing, promoting and retaining employees of all races, ethnic groups, sexual orientations, and cultural backgrounds."

[Memo of Region 5 Forester Ronald E. Stewart to all Region 5 employees]: "We cannot allow our personal beliefs to be transformed into behaviors that would discriminate against another employee." The recommended policy:

- Prohibits discrimination based on sexual orientation.
- Empowers homosexuals to serve as mentors and network coordinators.
- Incorporates sexual orientation awareness training.
- Establishes a computerized network for isolated homosexual employees.
- Awards pro-gay work settings.
- Encourages local "multicultural awareness celebrations" like gay pride month.
- Directs supervisors to consider an employee's domestic partner when assigning schedules.
- Prohibit private permittees and concessionaires from discriminating against domestic partners.
- Mandates unions to become proactive in the "sexual diversity" movement.
- Requires that contracts include domestic partner services.

- Guarantees government child care for children of an employee's domestic partner.
- Considers gay and lesbian owned businesses when arranging local purchase agreements.

The proposals encourage Forest Service employees to lobby for the following:
- Amend federal travel regulations to incorporate needs of domestic partners.
- Adopt this definition of a family: "A unit of interdependent and interacting persons, related together over time by strong social and emotional bonds and/or by ties of marriage, birth, and adoption, whose central purpose is to create, maintain, and promote the social, mental, physical and emotional development and well being of each of its members."
- Advocate to the Small Business Administration the inclusion of gay- and lesbian-owned businesses eligible for minority set-aside contracts.
- Advocate that retirement benefits include domestic partners.
- Add non-discrimination provisions to all private sector contracts prohibiting discrimination based on sexual orientation except for bona fide religious and youth groups.

DIVERSITY TRAINING MANDATORY

[This part of the article details various examples of "diversity" training of a number of U.S. departments and agencies, including the Labor Department, U.S. Postal Service, Forest Service, U.S. Health and Human Services.]

[A Forest Service training booklet contained such statements as:] "Fact: Psychological and social influences alone cannot cause homosexuality. . . Fact: A biological (genetic, hormonal, neurological, other) predisposition toward homosexual, bisexual, or heterosexual orientation is present at birth in all boys and girls." No source for these "facts" is provided. ***

Possibly the largest diversity event was hosted by the U.S. Navy on September 8, 1994 near the Pentagon. Diversity Day '94 included an opening ceremony with a welcome by a three-star admiral who stated, "The federal and private sector must make diversity part of business." ***

The activities included a seminar entitled "Another Color of the Rainbow: Sexual Minorities in the Workplace" taught by an acknowledged lesbian, and a videotape, "On Being Gay," which promotes homosexuality as the moral equivalent of heterosexuality. ***

AIDS AWARENESS OR MORE DIVERSITY TRAINING?

President Clinton announced on September 30, 1993 to all heads of executive departments his HIV/AIDS policy. The policy requires each secretary to designate a senior staff member to implement [the workplace policies].

... Federal employees have called the Family Research Council to complain that they found the training offensive.

... An FCC employee stated, "The classes are basically an adult version of high school sex ed, with the modern day sensitivity training thrown in."

[Department of Energy:] "All employees are required to complete this training."

... There is a discussion of needle sharing and sexual contact. Federal employees are told to reduce their HIV contraction risk by practicing "safer sex" by using barriers like condoms, dental dams, Plastic wrap, and latex gloves. The Manual states, "A dental dam (a small, square piece of latex) or plastic wrap may be used for an oral-vaginal or oral-anal contact. ***

... Probably the most outrageous example of government-sponsored AIDS training was done for the ... Forest Service's Tahoe Region on May 6, 1994 and was conducted by a local health official with degrees in sexology, a self-described homosexual phlebotomist (individual who draws blood), and an HIV-positive woman from the community.

... The phlebotomist was an ex-convict who tried to debunk "homophobic" misconceptions. He speculates that many husbands were involved in homosexual affairs. He showed a variety of condoms and how to apply them to a life-size replica of erect male genitalia. He even explained a technique for using one's mouth to apply the condom. He also explained the proper cleaning techniques when sharing hypodermic needles.

One of the workers in the audience later complained, "There seems to be no logic or equity in penalizing one employee for repeatedly bringing up 'Christmas' at work, during December because he or she believes in God, yet other employees are instructing how to use intravenous drugs or engage in anal sex."

FEDERAL MONEY FUNDS "GAY SCIENCE"

[This part of the article describes the tremendous amount of money spent by the government on AIDS "research" and research on sexual behavior, including funding of homosexual genetic research by Dr. Dean Hamer. Dr. Hamer's research was criticized in Chapter 2. Studies include such things as "homosexual men who are purportedly unable to avoid unsafe sexual behavior," and a "study designed to analyze behavioral data about HIV transmission among bisexual men in Mexico."]

FEDERAL EMPLOYEES ON THE GAY AGENDA FRONT

U.S, Patent and Trademark Commissioner Bruce Lehman is a self-described homosexual who promotes Commissioner Ron Brown's "Diversity Policy." For those who object, Lehman states, "As far as I'm concerned, it's got to be forced down their throats. If they want to be bigots, they can go work for someone else's department. The agency's director of human resources created a "diversity recruitment support team" to spend up to 15 days of diversity recruiting in 1995.

[Here the views of former Surgeon General Joycelyn Elders are outlined, which have already been discussed in other chapters.]

Roberta Achtenberg is HUD's assistant secretary for Fair Housing and Equal Opportunity. She appeared in San Francisco's 1992 gay pride parade riding in the back seat of a convertible next to her "partner" (Mary Morgan, a San Francisco municipal court judge) and "their" child. The sign on the car said "Celebrating Family Values."

While a member of the San Francisco Board of Supervisors and a member of a United Way chapter in that area, Achtenberg helped to defund the Boy Scouts for their moral standards. She has continued her activism in the federal government.

In February 1994 Achtenberg signed a diversity policy that requires managers to "participate as active members of minority, feminist or other cultural organizations to qualify for an 'outstanding' rating."

Some federal agencies have appointed homosexual watchdogs to ensure employee compliance with pro-gay diversity policies. [And employment programs.] ***

DISCOURAGING DISSENT

... U.S. Merit Systems Protection board Chairman Ben Erdreich has embraced diversity. The MSPB is the agency that rules on federal employee appeals of personnel actions. Erdreich told his employees on November 19, 1994: "I have a strong commitment to diversity and equitable treatment in the workplace ... Managers will be graded on respect for diversity in the workplace and (the extent to which they) perform responsibilities without regard to the differences of race, color ... sexual orientation. ..."

[Here the article discusses the problems of EEO manager Karl Mertz, which were discussed above.] ***

A part of the "sensitivity" training in the government finally got some attention of Congress.

Federal Workers Tell Congress of Abuse in Sensitivity Training

WASHINGTON — Congress heard a litany of harassment and abuse Thursday as government workers described training that included shouted obscenities, physical groping, religion-bashing and intimidation.

"The training consisted of three days of psychological abuse," Marie E. Birnbaum, retired Transportation Department staffer, told House Appropriations transportation subcommittee.

For air traffic controller James Ferguson, the intimidation went beyond the verbal. He told of being forced to walk a gantlet of women who rubbed his chest, groped his buttocks and tried to undo his belt.

And Frances Wirtanen said she suffered depression and required hospital treatment after a session in which she said women were required to relate incidents of past sexual abuse and harassment.

The problems occurred in courses intended to make Federal Aviation Administration and other Department of Transportation managers more sensitive to women and minorities. Subcommittee Chairman Frank Wolf, R-Va., said similar programs have been held in other government agencies including the Internal Revenue Service. ***

Wolf said the training included staring at candles for hours, being tied to co-workers and being required to take an oath of secrecy.

People were forced to reveal intimate details of their lives and then subjected to verbal abuse, Birnbaum said. Participants were called "jerks" and "jerkettes" and one overweight woman was called a "muffin queen."

Charles Smith, former FAA director of operational analysis, told the subcommittee he walked out of a training session after being amazed by the approach of verbally attacking participants.

And Charles Fluet of the Office of Aviation Safety said he found the training "unsettling," particularly in being told that all religion was fear-inducing and repressive. (*Albuquerque Journal*, 3-11-95)

Peter LaBarbera, writer and editor of *Lambda Report*, has continually investigated and written about the homosexual movement, and is one of the foremost authorities on it in America. He sheds further light on the homosexual indoctrination of the government and the armed forces in his article, **DIVERSITY "Daze,"** *Family Voice*, Concerned Women for America, November/December, 1994:

A pro-homosexual "diversity" workshop sponsored by the Pentagon featured a video lecture by a gay activist who spent 17 minutes attacking orthodox biblical teachings that proscribe homosexual behavior. Federal workers attended the seminar on government (i.e., taxpayer) time and received official diversity training credits for being there.

The "Diversity Day 1994" workshops were sponsored by the "Partners for Diversity" that included the Departments of the Air Force, Army, Navy and the Office of the Secretary of Defense, as well as private groups. But the Navy took the lead in pushing the conference, with Vice Admiral George Sterner, commander of Naval Sea Systems Command, urging attendance in a memo to all naval personnel. ***

"The federal government is simply crossing the line when it recruits and employs homosexual activists in order to instruct employees about the 'normality' of homosexual behavior—a behavior that the vast majority of our country finds morally offensive, and that is still illegal in many states," wrote Rep. Robert K. Dornan (R-CA) in a letter to President Clinton.

In the video, "On Being Gay," which was shown during the workshop, renegade Catholic writer Brian McNaught systematically attempts to rebut orthodox biblical scriptures cited by Christians as condemning homosexual behavior. ***

"Gay people were called by God to stand tall" as homosexuals, McNaught says, adding that gays must realize that God sees their sexual "love" for others of the same gender as "a very special love." He says people should "take a critical approach to the Bible," which is "continuing to be written" today. ***

McNaught's 1986 video also cites pro-homosexual statistics, such as a claim by 1950s sex researcher Alfred Kinsey, that have since been widely discredited. For example, McNaught uses Kinsey to assert "that at least 10 percent" of one of his high school senior classes "probably was gay" and repeats Kinsey's claim that "37 percent of men will have a homosexual experience to the point of orgasm." ***

The McNaught claims are but another example that shows the homosexualist to be either completely unable to recognize the truth or to have no regard whatsoever for facts. People like him certainly are trying today to rewrite the Bible, but for those who consider the Bible to be the word of God, it has not been disclosed how or when God gave him and his ilk the authority and power to either rewrite or change its passages, which condemns homosexuality in the clearest and strongest terms possible.

It is truly intolerable that such false brainwashing and blasphemy should not only be condoned by our government, but forced upon military personnel and government workers. It also shows a great lack of courage of many in our military, and of our Defense Secretary, William S. Cohen. They are simply kowtowing to the evil wishes of their Commander in Chief, who obviously prefers homosexuality to the armed forces, and to any decency in the government; and who is willfully trying to destroy any semblance of morality remaining in this country.

Clinton Says Yes to Gay Refugees, No to Chinese

Under the Clinton Administration, the Justice Department and Immigration and Naturalization Services (INS) has denied political-refugee asylum status to numerous Chinese families fleeing their government's forced abortion and sterilization policies, while at the same time using homosexuality and HIV-infection as a basis for granting political refugee status to others. ***

But in the case of HIV-positive refugees none of the traditional criteria seems to be applicable, no matter how they are construed. In one instance, a judge granted asylum to a man from the West African nation of Togo on the basis of AIDS-related illnesses because of a lack of adequate medical care in his home country. Applying such a rubric across-the-board could result in a massive influx of HIV-positive refugees. There are currently 26 million persons suffering with AIDS worldwide—many of them in Third World countries where health care is substandard.

Has asylum law typically been limited only to politically correct groups? "On the contrary," says Jim Jatras, policy analyst at the Senate Republican Policy Committee, "the previous assumption has always been that the law was applicable especially to universal persecution." ***

Unless Congress can call the administration to account, however, it is clear that the Clinton immigration policy will continue to favor gays and AIDS over families and children, regardless of what the law says. (*Human Events*, 1-10-97)

Prior to the Clinton administration, venereal diseases of all kinds were a bar to immigration, as was homosexuality. It appears that this administration strikes down, by administrative fiat, certain laws that were set up to protect the people and welfare of this country. This is indeed perplexing—and it is even more perplexing that Congress allows such things. As to homosexuals being persecuted, many states in this country still make homosexual sodomy a felony. How can we say that homosexuals are persecuted by other countries that make homosexuality a criminal act? We have an administration that is merely doing everything it possibly can to promote homosexuality—not only here but in other countries, too. And by unlawful acts that are contrary to the health and welfare of the citizens of this country.

SAME SEX MARRIAGES AND HOMOSEXUAL ADOPTIONS

I believe that there are few homosexuals who really believe in marriage or legal adoptions of children—at least for any good purpose. In any event, one thing is sure, the homosexualists are making an all out attack on the sacred institution of marriage. And as usual they are being aided by the liberal media and politicians. It appears that the real purpose is to destroy our basic traditional and religious values.

In 1996, the homosexuals made another push for admission into churches as ministers. This is a vital component in the promotion of same sex marriages and adoption of children by homosexuals. All of our major American churches have the Bible as the basis of their religions, and how they could accept homosexuality without forsaking the sole basis of their religion is beyond me. I therefore must believe that the real agenda here is to destroy the churches from within, because their frontal attacks have had little success. Highly publicized fights took place again in both the Methodist and Presbyterian churches. On a national and official basis the homosexuals lost and, at least for now, Christianity prevailed. But, as we see from other material in this book, on an individual basis, homosexuals have made inroads into particular churches. An article, "Church meeting renews gay debate, and neither side will give up fight," *The Albuquerque Tribune*, 4-22-96, about the upcoming general conference of the United Methodist Church states in part:

> The United Church of Christ is the only major Protestant denomination to permit the ordination of homosexuals. Opinion polls show a majority of people in the pews oppose ordination of homosexuals.
> But the issue continues to convulse mainline Protestantism.

The following from *CFV Report*, Colorado for Family Values, Jan. 1995, gives us a glimpse of some true homosexual thinking on this matter:

> **"A middle ground might be to fight for same-sex marriage and its benefits and then, once granted, redefine the institution of marriage completely . . . to debunk a myth and radically alter an archaic institution that as it now stands keeps us down. The most subversive action lesbian and gay men can undertake . . . is to transform the notion of family entirely."**
> ... (Leading homosexual writer Michelangelo Signorile, "Bridal Wave," *Out*, December/January, 1994, p. 161)

On May 5, 1993, the Supreme Court of Hawaii ruled in a 3 to 1 opinion that the state's ban on same-sex marriages may be unconstitutional because it amounts to sex discrimination, which is illegal there. The court also invited the state to offer compelling reasons to keep the ban. (*Albuquerque Journal*, 5-17-93) There was then quite a groundswell against such "marriages" by concerned people in Hawaii. Legislative action was initiated, and the matter has not yet been put to rest in that state. But the Hawaii ruling caused considerable concern all over the country because of the "full faith and credit" clause of the Constitution of the United States. This problem will be fully discussed in the last chapter.

The idea that there is a constitutional right to same-sex marriage is indeed ludicrous to any true student of the law. This is one more erroneous decision of an activist liberal court. The rights of states to regulate marriage was recognized before the United States was a country, and, except for the early federal prohibition against polygamy, that recognition has continued until now.

When the Mormon religion came into being and acquired a substantial following and influence in the west, the officials of the United States became concerned about the practice of polygamy. In 1857, United States troops were sent to Utah to discourage polygamy among the Mormons. In 1890, the Mormon church officially declared an end to that practice, but the United States was still concerned about admitting territories to statehood because some of the people there continued the unofficial practice of polygamy. (*Encarta 98 Desk Encyclopedia*) Five western states, Arizona, Idaho, Oklahoma, New Mexico, and Utah, as a requirement for admission to statehood, had to have in their constitutions that "Perfect toleration of religious sentiment shall be secured ..." and "Polygamous or plural marriages and polygamous cohabitation are forever prohibited." These provisions could not be amended without permission of the United States Congress. Religion, freedom of religion, and the sacred sacrament of marriage were of critical importance to the founders of this country, and to all sincere officials who were elected to represent our country, for its first 200 years. These people, and even the early Mormons, could never have imagined the vile and vicious attacks on these institutions today.

If people have a right to form same-sex marriages, there is no logical reason why there should not be the same right for incestuous marriages, for polygamy, bigamy, group marriages, or even marriage to animals. But laws defining marriage and prohibiting such things have been based on Judaic-Christian principles, and if the homosexualists and atheists can destroy these principles, then anything is possible. The depths to which we can sink will only be limited by the imagination of the perverts.

As in the rest of their agenda, the assault on American sensibilities for the purpose of the acceptance of same-sex marriages is on a number of fronts.

The media, both entertainment and news, are in the forefront with news articles, movies, and television programs that subtly and consistently put "gay" couples and "gay" marriages before us—and always in a manner that shows the best side of homosexuals—and never showing or discussing the vile acts in which they engage.

San Francisco Ceremony Weds 200 Gay Couples

SAN FRANCISCO — With the words, "I hereby pronounce you lawfully recognized domestic partners," more than 200 gay couples— some in drag, some in traditional white dresses and tuxedos—tied the knot Monday under a new and largely symbolic city ordinance.

"As usual, we are first, and by virtue of your participation in this ceremony, you are a part of history," Mayor Willie Brown said at the start of the ceremony in a theater across from City Hall. ***

The unions are strictly ceremonial and not recognized by state law. Under the city's 1991 domestic partnership ordinance, couples already have visitation rights in hospitals, shared health plans for city employees, and bereavement leave for city workers when a partner dies. *** (*Albuquerque Journal*, 3-26-96)

Colorado Gov. Vetoes Gay Marriage Ban

DENVER — Gov. Roy Romer vetoed a bill banning same-sex marriages Monday, saying such unions may deserve recognition. ***

Will Perkins, chairman for Colorado For Family Values, condemned the veto.

"The governor is absolutely unaccountable to the electorate," he said. "He is in the pocket of pro-homosexual interests and is attempting to hold the state hostage." (*Albuquerque Journal*, 3-26-96)

Let us consider the following on use of the courts to gain recognition of same-sex marriage:

Into The Courts, Away From Congress

*** The vote in Congress against same-sex marriages and equality for gays in the workplace, ironically enough, came on the same day that the women's lawsuit was being heard in a Hawaii courtroom against a legal backdrop far more favorable to gay rights. The two women want the state to recognize their marriage.

And predictably enough, gay rights advocates in Washington late Tuesday said they would go to federal court to challenge the constitutionality of the law passed by Congress. It defines marriage as the union of a man and a woman.

Why the well-worn path toward the courts and away from elected bodies? One reason is that judges, immune from electoral politics, are sometimes more willing than legislators to buck public opinion. The latest poll data suggest the public still overwhelmingly opposes legal recognition of gay marriages.

A recent USA Today/CNN/Gallup Poll found 67% opposed and 28% in favor. ***

"What you're seeing now is a building process," says William Rubenstein, a Stanford University law professor who formerly spearheaded the ACLU'S legal efforts on gay rights "Slowly (court decisions) will build to national consensus ... But it's got to be bottom up, not top down." *** (*USA Today*, 9-11-96, p. 4A)

The homosexualists and their allies, the liberal media and politicians, well know what they are about, and how to get it done. Consider the following thoughts from an article in the homosexual magazine, *The Advocate*, 12-12-95, p. 96:

*** We need to lobby local churches and unions and other organizations to endorse the Marriage Resolution. ***

Ultimately, same-sex marriage will not be won in the law courts, no matter how the Hawaii case or any other case turns out. It will be won – or lost – in the court of public opinion, when we convince the majority in this society that same-sex marriage is morally right. ... We'll have to change the hearts and minds of the majority. ***

Announcement Campaign Begins

The Boston-based Forum on the Right to Marriage (FORM) has announced a formal campaign encouraging newspapers across the country to publish photos and wedding announcements of homosexual couples. FORM sees this as "an excellent way to educate the public both about gay couples, as well as raise consciousness about the unfairness of being denied this most basic human right."

Jeff Nickel, FORM's founder and president, writes that "in the process of getting local newspapers to recognize our unions, even if we don't at first succeed, we will be helping the public understand that marital discrimination against us is an issue we take very seriously. If newspapers refuse, we have an issue to rally around; one that really has the power to energize people, to get them talking. And if they agree, we'll see the simple, everyday message that gay people form families, too." (*SPHA Bulletin, Jan./Feb. 1996*)

The homosexualists certainly have not failed. They have gained the help of most all of the media of all kinds, including news and entertainment. The American people are being subjected to the greatest and most destructive brainwashing program in American history. The changing of our minds to believing the exact opposite of what is true and what is good is well under way, and having great success.

The following are excerpts from **Lawfully wedded**, *Family Voice*, April 1996:

MOVED BY THE MEDIA

Already the mainstream media has made the gay agenda its focal point. And television producers are pushing it with all the zeal of crusaders.

USA Today noted that this year brought us the "gayest TV-season in memory"—probably in history. Examples of the gay friendly themes abound. "Mad About You" features an episode where the lead character's sister announces she is lesbian. On "Wings" we learn that the unpalatable character Roy has a long-lost homosexual son. And on "Party of Five," a teenage girl's best friend announces that she wants to be "more than just friends."

Perhaps the culmination of this gay-friendly season occurred on the NBC sitcom "Friends." The episode featured a lesbian wedding, officiated by none other than Candace Gingrich—homosexual activist and half-sister of Speaker of the House Newt Gingrich. Speaking as *clergy*, Gingrich said, "God is pleased when any two people come together in love." ...

Clearly Hollywood media moguls are pushing an agenda on society. And it was no coincidence that the "gayest TV-season in
memory" would air only months before Hawaii rules on legalizing
same-sex marriage.

NATURE AND NORMALCY

Gay activists don't want to just live their lives and be left alone.
They are not asking to be seen simply as equals. They want everyone
in America to believe that homosexuality is normal. And gay marriage is the best vehicle for them to win the coveted title of "normalcy."

'The most obvious advantage [to gay marriage] is the hope that
society, including, but not limited to, our families, schools and
churches, will not only accept our relationships, but our homosexuality as normal," wrote one gay activist in *Quest.* ***

The newspapers and magazines around the nation have dutifully
followed suit in promoting homosexual marriage by full page and multi-
page articles, with large photographs, featuring "homosexual weddings."
And always presenting homosexuals in their best possible light, showing them well dressed in tuxedos and dresses, and, as a rule, never showing them in "drag." A classic example that included all of these elements
was an article in *The Albuquerque Tribune*, 2-18-93, about a "wedding"
in Albuquerque, New Mexico, in a state which does not legally allow
homosexual marriages. It was conducted like an ordinary marriage between a man and a woman, and officiated by Rev. Stanley Hadsell, "a gay
Catholic Priest from Texas." They had a large reception in the La Posada
de Albuquerque, a landmark hotel in Albuquerque. I am sure that New
Mexico Catholic priests would be rather cautious about such things,
because so many of them have been caught up in both criminal and civil
actions for commission of homosexual pedophilia, and the Catholic
church has been out many millions of dollars in the last several years
because of such actions.

The rights of homosexuals to have custody of and adopt children
has also been pushed hard in the courts, and with considerable success.

In Virginia, a trial court had ruled that a lesbian mother was an unfit
parent because of her relationship with her live-in lover. The Virginia
Court of Appeals overruled the decision, and granted custody to the
lesbian. (*The Albuquerque Tribune*, 6-21-94)

A homosexual couple, Michael Galluccio, 35, and Jon Holden, 34, were allowed by a New Jersey court to adopt a foster child , a 2 year old boy, that they had been caring for since he was 3 months old. (*Albuquerque Journal*, 12-18-97)

The danger of having homosexuals in care of young people is well established—and is twofold.

First, a child is brought up in an extremely immoral environment, which is something to which no child should be subjected. Secondly, it is well established that, as a class, homosexuals sexually abuse children at a much higher rate, based on their percentage of the population, than do heterosexuals. This book is full of examples and statistics that fully support this statement.

One more recent and typical example of the danger is the following:

Appeals Court Rules Lesbian Fit Parent

RICHMOND, Va. — A lesbian regained custody of her son Tuesday when a state appeals court ruled that the woman's sex life — though illegal under Virginia law — does not make her an unfit parent. [This reversed the decision of the trial court that heard the case.] ***

In the case closely watched by gay rights groups, Circuit Judge Buford M. Parsons last year awarded custody of 2-year-old Tyler Doustou to Sharon Bottoms' mother, Kay Bottoms. The judge said Sharon Bottoms was an unfit mother because she and her live-in-lover engaged in oral sex, a "crime against nature" in Virginia. ***

... Sharon Bottoms testified that she occasionally hugged and kissed her lover in front of Tyler but did not have sex in his presence. (*Albuquerque Journal*, 6-22-94)

The Virginia Supreme Court showed more wisdom and reversed the Appeals Court in the Bottoms case, leaving stand the trial judge's decision. However, it was a 4 to 3 decision. The fact that so many people, including judges seem to be able to find nothing wrong with sodomy, and particularly around children, only further shows the rot in our society. (*The Albuquerque Tribune*, 4-21-95)

Unheeded Red Flags Let Foster Dad's Dark Side Flourish

*** CYFD, the [New Mexico] agency that licensed [Scott] Neff's foster home, has denied prior knowledge of his criminal activities.

The state faces a federal lawsuit filed by two of Neff's victims. A third claim was settled out of court for an undisclosed amount.

Neff's pedophilia came to light after a 16-year-old foster son known as E.M. moved out of the home in May 1994 and alerted a friend's stepmother.

Neff would show up in the boy's room around midnight, the boy told police.

"He would tell me, 'You know that you're gay and you want this.'"

Police determined Neff also molested E.M.'s younger brother at least once.

E.M. said Neff told him that he would be sent to an out-of-town boys home if he told anyone.

"No one wants teen-age boys," E.M. quoted Neff as saying.

Neff, 38, was charged with multiple counts of sexual penetration of a minor. He pleaded no contest to contributing to the delinquency of a minor and sexual exploitation and is serving 7 years in prison.

A Roswell mental health counselor contends she alerted E.M.'s caseworker about Neff's sexual interest in the boy two years before E.M. reported Neff court records show.

Neff took E.M. to counseling starting in 1991, saying the boy wouldn't communicate with him.

During several counseling sessions in early 1992, Neff expressed interest in E.M.'s penis size and said he had written a letter asking the boy if he'd consider having sex with him, the counselor said in September 1994 letter to CYFD. ***

CYFD officials say homosexuals and bisexuals are allowed to serve as foster parents. *** (*Albuquerque Journal*, 2-20-97)

Certainly New Mexico, and any other state or organization, has little concern about the proper upbringing of children, and protecting them from molestation, when there is a policy allowing children to be placed in the care of homosexuals and bisexuals. And as long as such policies continue, we will continue to have such cases as the one with Neff. In New Mexico, alone, we have had so many such cases that it is nigh unto impossible to keep count of all of them. Yet, due to the homosexual power and influence, such policies continue, and, naturally, such cases continue.

THE HOMOSEXUALIST ATTACK ON OUR
CHILDREN AND SCHOOLS

The media, both news and, in particular, entertainment have been enlisted as major contributors to the agenda to indoctrinate children in this country, as well as the general public, with the idea that homosexuality is natural, good, and acceptable to be engaged in by young people. Other areas of infiltration for the same purposes have been our churches and our schools. The heaviest attacks, and the most successful, have probably been within the schools—particularly universities and public schools.

Children, above all should be protected from the homosexual activists and their perverted propaganda promoting sodomy. Our youths have enough difficulty, particularly in puberty, without the onslaught of immorality from all angles to which they are now subjected. It certainly is no wonder that our young people engage in some of the terrible deeds previously reported in this book. And it is no wonder that many are in a state of confusion about many things.

Unfortunately, we have steadily lost ground in our schools, which are at least as important as our churches in this war against our institutions by homosexuals.

The attack on our schools and young people has been insidious and destructive. Another sad aspect of this is that many of our school teachers were parties to the homosexual indoctrination of the children they taught.

In The Wall Street Journal article referred to above, on the 10% Fallacy, Dr. Muir referred to a study by the Minnesota Adolescent Health Survey, in which students in grades seven through twelve were surveyed, and 10.1% of the boys and 11.3% of the girls didn't even know whether or not they were homosexual, bisexual, or heterosexual. With what we know about causes of and development of homosexuality, there is no doubt whatsoever that the homosexual brainwashing, to which many of our school children have been subjected could be a proximate cause of many of them experimenting in and turning to homosexuality. There also is no doubt in my mind that the homosexual activists pushing these programs know this and purposefully are trying to recruit young people into homosexuality. Since their vile activity does not result in reproduction, they want to increase their number by recruiting our children and youths into their destructive society.

The Nazi type militancy, deceit, disrespect for Christian principles, lack of morality, and design to corrupt the children of this country disclosed in the following article is so typical of the mind of the homosexual activist, that I believe the interested reader should have the benefit of its entire corrupt contents. It discloses the thinking of the psychotic mind that has lost its ability to distinguish what is clean and decent from what is filthy and destructive; and what is true from what is false. It is FRIENDLY FIRE, by Donna Minkowitz, published in the homosexual magazine, *The Advocate*, 12-29-92.

Recruit, recruit, recruit!

"Next, we'll hear from a gay woman who says it's all about recruiting," Montel Williams announced.

That gay woman was me. I was about to go on Williams's show and talk about children, sexual choices, and the reasons we need pro-gay curricula in our public schools.

I was ambivalent about the provocative line I intended to take. I've been in the strange position lately of saying things about homosexuality that piss off many, if not most, of the lesbian and gay activists I know. How to respond to far-right depictions of our movement is a question we are all increasingly tense about, me included. With the Christian right maneuvering to pass more laws like Colorado's Amendment 2, no wonder we're tempted to turn tail and run from some of the riskier implications of our lives.

Since Anita Bryant's day, 'phobes' have claimed that we "recruit" children. Of course we don't—if the phrase is taken to mean we sexually abuse the young in order to make converts for our community. But I am increasingly impatient with the old chestnut that our movement for public acceptance has not increased and will not increase the number of gay men and lesbians in existence. "There are more of us than there used to be," historian John D'Emilio has written. Firmly believing this, I wanted to go on the show to argue the morality of teaching kids that gay is OK even if it means that some will join our ranks.

Other right-wing aspersions also have grains of truth in them. As a community, we are a sexually adventurous, gender-defying bunch. We have also come up with configurations for relationships and families that go a long way toward solving the problem that has kept heterosexuals sad for centuries—how to combine emotional fidelity with sexual freedom. One of the right wing's goals in making these attributes into smears is to force lesbians and gay men to abandon the most defiant, least heterosexual aspects of our lives. If we become the straightest gays in world history, they've already won half their battle. And if we are pushed into denying any smidgen of our own truth, we have allowed the Right to dictate our agenda.

We have been on the defensive far too long. It's time to affirm that the Right is correct in some of its pronouncements about our movement. Pat Buchanan said there was a "cultural war" going on "for the soul of America" and that gay and lesbian rights were the principal battleground. He was right. Similarly, 'phobes' like Pat Robertson are right when they say that we threaten the family, male domination, and the Calvinist ethic of work and grimness that has paralyzed most Americans' search for pleasure.

Indeed, instead of proclaiming our innocuousness, we ought to advertise our potential to change straight society in radical, beneficial ways. Hets have much to learn from us: first and foremost, the fact that pleasure is possible (and desirable) beyond the sanctions of the state. Another fact gleaned from gay experince—that gender is for all intents and purposes a fiction—also has the potential to revolutionize straight lives.

For some straight people, our movement will simply help them to live out hetero desires to the fullest. Others, living on strawberry for years, will finally taste the pineapple almond fudge.

Let's take the offensive for a change, whether the issue is promiscuity or recruiting the previously straight. Remember that most of the line about homosex being one's nature, not a choice, was articulated as a response to brutal repression. "It's not our fault!" gay activists began to declaim a century ago, when queers first began to organize in Germany and England. "We didn't choose this, so don't punish us for it!" One hundred years later, it's time for us to abandon this defensive posture and walk upright on the earth. Maybe you didn't choose to be gay—that's fine. But I did.

Months before the presidential election, Robert Bray, public information director of the National Gay and Lesbian Task Force, told me something that shocked me. "We want to provoke the Republicans to show their homophobic hand," he said.

I couldn't believe it. Why on earth would we want them to show it? Didn't we want them to hide their homophobia? It was much too scary, I thought, to prod George Bush into running an openly homophobic campaign.

Then the Republican convention happened, and Republican fortunes began to erode. Homophobia, it turned out, wasn't a wining ticket with most Americans. Lying low, pandering to it, asking Barbara Walters to stop raising the issue with candidates would have hurt our movement, not helped it.

What we need to give the Christian right is a solid sock to the jaw—not a whiny plea for forgiveness. The best gay and lesbian demo I ever saw was the zap of a speech Jerry Falwell gave to Virginia delegates to the Republican convention. Outside, Queer Nationals from around the country chanted. "Ten percent is not enough! Recruit, recruit, recruit!" Inside tactics were even bolder: Whenever Falwell said anything negative about homosexuality, air sirens would go off and ACT UP members in Christian garb would start yelling things like "We are your families, and you are killing us!" These young men and women would be promptly beaten by Falwell followers and police, but they kept coming forward until it was impossible for all but the morally deaf not to hear their statement of resistance.

Tell America how much it can gain by emulating us. How much, like Madonna, it already envies us. Be guided by the dream of liberation, not by fear. Provoke the right.

A picture of the author accompanied this article, and the woman certainly looks her part of a militant lesbian—"butch" type. Her hair was short and sticking up like a shaggy butch haircut of a man. And her picture looked more like a man than a woman—purposefully I am sure.

The most amazing thing is that such things as the above prattling of a sick mind have actually been effective. But only because of the timidity and cowardice of our politicians, media, schools, and church members who have not had the morality and courage to take a real stand against the depravity being thrust upon us.

There is an interlocking relationship between pedophelia and the homosexual agenda for indoctrinating children. This goes back probably as far as there have been homosexual movements, and at least back to Alfred C. Kinsey's time. And Kinsey and his work have been worshipped and continually referred to by the homosexual activists. The world should be deeply grateful to researchers like Dr. Judith Reisman who have done sufficient work to expose the falsity of the Kinsey homosexual propaganda.

The following is from the book, *Kinsey, Sex and Fraud*—The Indoctrination of a People—(An Investigation into the Human Sexuality Research of Alfred C. Kinsey, Wardell B. Pomeroy, Clyde E. Martin and Paul H. Gebhard), Authors: Dr. Judith A. Reisman and Edward W. Eichel, Editors: Dr. J. Gordon Muir and Dr. John H. Court, Lochinvar-Huntington House, 1990:

> The overwhelming conclusion is that Kinsey knowingly presented a criminally biased model of sexual behavior to the world as "normal." The atypical sexual behavior of prisoners and other biased groups was used to convince people that the normal population engaged in a higher percentage of aberrant sexual behavior (particularly homosexual relations) than was actually the case. Far from being an objective scientist, Kinsey intentionally weighted his data, attempted to obscure the bias and promoted a preset agenda. *** (p.203)
>
> It is quite clear, for example, that, without any factual foundation upon which to base his case, Kinsey was advocating pedophilia. *** (p. 204)
>
> In addition to his interest in sex experiments with children, Kinsey was an avid collector of pornography (and maker of sex films)—an elemental feature of the pedophile syndrome. *** (p. 205)
>
> The classification of pedophilia as normal sexual orientation is not the final step of the Kinseyesque agenda. Another sex theorist has attempted to advance the status of the pedophile to that of Good Samaritan, dedicated to helping children learn about, and develop, their sexuality. In other words, pedophiles could be viewed as natural helpers of children, with special gifts—much as John Money views homosexuals as special People ... . (p. 206)
>
> In her article "Intergenerational Sexual Contact: A Continuum Model of Participants and Experience" (*Journal of Sex Education & Therapy* 15(1):3-12, 1989), Joan A. Nelson, Ed.D., advocates a model of adult-child sexuality in which sex acts with children are to be viewed as acceptable and even essential to the healthy development of the child. She minimizes the harmful effect of what has generally been perceived as child sexual abuse; and she emphasizes the harmful effect of "society's condemnation" of adult-child sex—an approach straight out of the pages of Kinsey *et al.* *** (p. 206-7)

From some of the foregoing it will be obvious that the agendas of gays and pedophiles are closely connected. There is a commonality of research sources used for "scientific" support, an overlap of objectives and a similarity of language, clichés and tactics, particularly in the pursuit of "rights." In addition, a number of activists share both agendas. *** (p. 212)

Other peculiarities of the psychotic minds of many homosexuals are their obsessions with voyeurism and pornography. The following is an example of this, and a further demonstration of the psychosis of homosexuals.

Priest Accused of Sex Crimes Kept Videotapes, Source Says

PHOENIX — A Roman Catholic priest arrested last week and accused of sex crimes with a minor kept a detailed log—card files and hundreds of videotapes—of nearly 2,000 sex acts he performed with youths and men, The Arizona Republic has learned.

The tapes, which police seized last week in a search of the St. Benedict Catholic Church rectory in Chandler, show the Rev. Wilputte Alanson "Lan" Sherwood, 47, taking part in sex acts, but it is unknown whether his partners knew they were being taped, a source close to the investigation said.

Sherwood, founding priest and pastor of St. Benedict, was arrested by Chandler police on March 11 and booked on suspicion of two felonies—furnishing obscene materials to a minor and public indecency with a minor—a misdemeanor count of indecent exposure.

A Judge ordered Sherwood released on his own recognizance a day after his arrest. Church officials say he has resigned as pastor of St. Benedict.

The priest was arrested after a 12-year-old hitchhiker from Tucson told police Sherwood picked him up along Interstate 10 south of Phoenix and took him back to the church rectory in Chandler, where Sherwood lives alone.

The teen-ager whom police have not identified, said Sherwood exposed himself and showed him pornographic films. The youth notified police after leaving the rectory. ***

A source said the tapes show the priest participated in both oral and anal sex and that the tapes appeared to have been made at the rectory.

"He's definitely a homosexual who kept detailed reports on all his sexual exploits," the source said. "You wouldn't believe the records he kept." *** (*Albuquerque Journal*, 3-19-93)

The writing of homosexuals for their own consumption gives us one of the best insights into true homosexual thinking. Consider the following from *CFV Report*, Colorado for Family Values, Jan. 1995:

" ... **Thailand is a paradise for gay men and Bangkok – the filthiest, smelliest, dirtiest and most exciting city in the world—has hundreds of pubs, clubs, discos and gay guesthouses.**"

> From an article of homosexual travel suggestions. Remember that Thailand is notorious for its profusion of under age boy prostitutes—indeed, a naked Asian teenager is frontally displayed above the headline question, "Which is the best ticket to buy if I want to see the world and every boy in it?" Mind you this is not an explicit pedophilic publication: it's Australia's leading gay tabloid. "Around the world with only gays," *Sydney Star Observer*, 22 September 1994, p. 8

Who but a homosexual or other pervert would think that there was anything attractive about "the filthiest, smelliest, dirtiest" city in the world? However all of this, including the pedophilic implications, completely coincides with many other things presented in this book on the minds of homosexuals.

One of the earliest of the recently known plans to indoctrinate the children of this country through the schools was known as **Project 10**. The following information about the project came from a tape of a lecture, "Gay & Lesbian Youth in America," of Dr. Virginia Uribe, a lesbian who claims to have developed the model for Project 10. A brochure and the tape of the lecture, for local teachers, was furnished to me by a local concerned citizen. The lecture was at the University of New Mexico on October 28, 1992.

The brochure states that her work, commencing in 1984, led to the creation of Project 10, "the first dropout-prevention program that targeted gay and lesbian youth through self-esteem promotion and homophobia reduction." In recognition of her efforts, the National Education Association awarded Dr. Uribe with their 1992 "Award for Creative Leadership in Human Rights."

(As shown by a number of places in this book, the National Education Association [NEA] has been infiltrated with and taken over by homosexualists to the extent that they have long supported the homosexual agenda and laws favoring homosexuals, and has even supported the agenda in its platform. The homosexuals call teaching young children that sodomy is a good and acceptable activity "homophobia reduction." What it really is, is brainwashing children, far too young to know better, that vile and depraved things are commendable. It is also "Recruit, Recruit, Recruit!")

Dr. Uribe stated that people, and children at an early age, should be taught that the homosexual lifestyle is a good acceptable way of life. This should be strongly promoted in the schools. Ideas based upon the Bible must be rejected. People who do not believe that homosexuality is right are bigots. Organizations like the Boy Scouts of America, and all other such organizations that are against homosexuality, must be eliminated from the campuses.

She developed the model for Project 10 in 1984 in the Los Angeles School District. She started at Fairfax High School.

The teachers' union (NEA) has a gay and lesbian group that works on the project. They have a monitoring commission called the Gay and Lesbian Education Commission that makes recommendations to the local school boards.

The indoctrination programs should be presented to children at an early age—in headstart programs and in kindergarten, and in the early grades.

She wants comprehensive programs in the high schools promoting the homosexual lifestyle by teaching that it is acceptable; and comprehensive AIDS education, starting in kindergarten, and AIDS education in high school which includes the distribution of condoms.

There should be legislation and regulations supporting courses in our colleges and universities including ant-bias courses on homosexuality and courses on homophobia.

There should be legislation against discrimination in employment, so that gay and lesbian school teachers are protected in their jobs.

There should be legislation to support health benefits for unmarried gay and lesbian partners.

Policies should not be based upon the Bible, but "good science and social justice."

She refers to promises made to the homosexual community by presidential candidate Bill Clinton.

She makes continual derogatory remarks against Senator Jesse Helms and Anita Bryant.

"**PROJECT 10** – What Schools teach children about gay sex," was an article by Manley Witten, Editor, *Valley Magazine*, August 1988, pp. 27-31, about the controversy caused when Virginia Uribe introduced her Project 10 in the San Fernando High School (California). Mr. Witten gives the following description of the program:

> A controversial program sponsored by the Los Angeles United School District pits parents and legislators against principals and board members in a battle likely to have nationwide impact. At issue is whether morality and life-style should be taught at home or in the school.

The introduction at San Fernando High School was on February 22, 1988. Children were brought into the library without notice to them or their parents. "There, according to a number of students, they heard Virginia Uribe, a lesbian teacher tell them she practices 'safe sex,' that it is OK for them to have sexual feelings for other people of the same sex and, based on research, that 10 percent of them probably are gay." The article explains that two of the books that were made available to students through Project 10 were *One Teenager in 10* and *Changing Bodies Changing Lives*. (The latter is explained below in an article by Karen Jo

Gounaud.) This Valley Magazine article gives the following excerpt from
One Teenager in 10: Testimony by Gay and Lesbian Youth:

> "I am a sixteen-year-old lesbian. I have been a lesbian since I was
> twelve. I had known my dance teacher for three years before I was
> asked to give a special dance presentation in another city.
> "... 'I want to make love to you. Let's go to bed,' (my teacher
> said) ... She positioned me on the bed, with my head on a pillow and
> my legs spread as wide as she could get them. . . Before long she was
> getting her face closer to me and kissing me; using her mouth and
> tongue on my c———, giving me a feeling I had never felt before. . . .
> We continued that night, all weekend and for almost three years until
> I had to move with my family. I became a lesbian and a woman that
> weekend! . . . Since I moved, my teacher and I talk occasionally on the
> phone, and we write each other. . . . My present lover and I have been
> together for almost a year. . . . She is fifteen and will be in the ninth
> grade next year."

The two books referred to above were removed (apparently from
both the San Fernando and Fairfax school libraries) after protests by
citizens. The objecting citizens were assisted by the Rev. Lou Sheldon,
chairman of the Traditional Values Coalition.

To me, only the sick mind of a homosexual could prompt a person
to foist such destructive pornographic trash on the young people of this
nation, but it has been successfully done around the nation.

The Eagle Forum and its president, Phyllis Schafly, have been tireless in fighting against the homosexual degradation in our schools. In
an *Eagle Forum* newsletter, October, 1990, the following article from
the *Education Reporter*, September 1990, was reprinted. Eagle Forum
states that the article, which is a list of ways to infiltrate schools and
brainwash children, was distributed by the National Education
Association's Gay and Lesbian Caucus at the NEA national convention
in Kansas City in 1990.

Recommendations for Addressing the Concerns of Gays and Lesbians in Education—Managing Heterosexism and Homophobia

1. Enactment of anti-discrimination policies which address the issue of sexual orientation.
2. School administrations should keep accurate [sic] of "bias-related" and "hate-violence" incidents on each school campus that involve the *perceived* sexual orientation of victims.
3. Enactment of an anti-slur policy which includes sexual orientation.
4. Interrupt anti-gay or lesbian comments by staff and students alike. State that assaultive and/or derogatory jokes, behaviors, or other actions against anyone because of perceived minority sexual orientation is unfair, offensive and harmful to others and to themselves.
5. Implement lesson plans for managing homophobic name calling.
6. Enactment of policies which ensure and encourage classroom presentation of controversial issues, in a prejudice-free, discrimination-free atmosphere.
7. Encouragement of teacher utilization of gay and lesbian people, or parents of gays and lesbians as speakers in classes as part of their material on the diversity of sexual orientation.
8. Inclusion of sexual orientation in clauses of teacher contracts. Be supportive of the presence of openly lesbian, gay, and bisexual staff at all levels.
9. Inclusion of benefits for the domestic partners of educational personnel.
10. Do not make any assumptions regarding the sexual orientation of students, clients, parents, or colleagues. Use non-gender specific language consistently whenever possible (e.g. partner, lover, person).
11. Inclusion of information, discussion, and recognition of gay and lesbian issues (heterosexism, homophobia, homosexuality) into curriculum, lesson plans/syllabus, and course work in various disciplines at various grade levels.
12. Include readings which address lesbian and gay issues on required and recommended reading lists.

13. Include gay and lesbian issues on a list of possible and required topics for written assignments or class presentations.
14. Encourage all students to think about, write about and discuss the ways in which homophobia have impacted on their lives (has or will hurt them personally).
15. With your students, discover and plan ways to participate in local and national gay pride month/week activities as a way to celebrate, learn about, and better understand lesbian, gay, and bisexual culture.
16. Acknowledge lesbian and gay people who have made significant contributions to society by discussing and avowing their sexual orientation as it relates to their contributions to society. Educate yourself about lesbian and gay people like Jane Addams, James Baldwin. Gertude Stein, Walt Whitman, and many others.
17. Familiarize yourself with local gay and lesbian resources (social/political organizations, health care agencies, counseling services, clubs, youth group, readings and file materials) and use them in your class.
18. Requirement of comprehensive human relations/sex education instruction within the health curriculum framework which include information of the diversity of sexual orientation.
19. Requirement of instruction in sex education courses on Acquired Immune Deficiency Syndrome at all levels using accurate, nonjudgmental and current information.
20. Inclusion of age appropriate gay-sensitive literature in school libraries and have them accessible to students.

As has been described in many places in this book, the homosexual destruction in our schools has been extensive—and it is amazing and unbelievable that this country could have allowed such assaults on its children.

In Chapters 1 and 4 details were given on some of the homosexual filth that has been filtered into our schools. Indoctrinating school children, even as young as those in kindergarten, has long been a part of the homosexual agenda.

It didn't take long for the homosexual assault on this country's children to have its desired effect—moral destruction.

Tune In, Come Out—Generations: Spurred by media images and a new climate of acceptance, teenagers are experimenting more openly with gay and bi-sexuality. This was the title of an article in *Newsweek*, 11-8-93, and the title gives a good indication of the contents. (Although the authors seem pro-homosexualist and unaware of the impact of the information, it clearly shows the moral destruction of young people. One thing that it shows without question is that the homosexualist indoctrination of students is making that lifestyle acceptable to a large part of them.)

The article is about "COMING-OUT DAY" at Cambridge Rindge and Latin, an "elite Massachusetts high school." (The fact that there would be such a celebration in a school shows the depravity into which the community has sunk.) "'They're open to everything': Cambridge students adopt the pink triangle in support of gay rights." One 1993 survey of students by a task force set up by Massachusetts Gov. William Weld found that 64 percent of all students (78 percent of female students) condemned discrimination against homosexuals. Sixty percent favored gay support groups. (Gov. Weld has consistently supported the homosexual movement.) A 16-year-old student was "coming out" and felt it her responsibility to tell other students that "'straight' wasn't the only possibility."

Rindge and Latin was the first public school to join Boston's Gay Pride parade, two years ago, with two students. "Now the contingent has grown big enough to carry the huge pink and black banner of Project 10 East, the school's formally recognized gay-straight alliance." Student "gay" organizations now exist in Chicago, Berkeley, Miami, Minneapolis, and New York. There are more than a hundred in Massachusetts, alone.

The article relates a Boston teen-ager stating her sexual confusion, saying that she thought she was a lesbian until she found herself enjoying a relationship with a man. "Teens' eagerness to experiment has made bisexuality almost "cool" in some schools." At Newton (Mass.) North high school, students say that one female couple is constantly 'making out' in the hallways and the cafeteria." One group member says "The truth is, they're open to everything."

(The article does note that there has developed a "backlash" among parents who are concerned about the kind of "education" their children are getting.) One concerned parent complained: "They have gay assemblies, with speakers extolling the virtues of gayhood. The kids are sick of it."

As to the Newsweek article referred to above, one of the reasons I consider the writers to be biased in favor of the homosexual agenda is the following statement made in support of the activities of the homosexual groups in the schools: "Clearly, changes are in order. The task force was established after Weld saw a little-advertised 1989 Department of Health and Human Services report that said 30 percent of youth suicides occur among gays and lesbians." This is often used homosexual propaganda to help get footholds in the schools.

Any person with any conscience at all would naturally be depressed from a guilty conscience when engaged in the loathsome and repulsive acts of practicing homosexuals. The suicide rate would naturally be greater among such people. Many more are committing suicide by intentionally engaging in acts from which they contract AIDS.

Now the homosexualists want us to remove the problems of conscience by making us devoid of any conscience—by completely destroying our morality—starting with our school children, as young as those in the kindergarten. To me, it is utterly stupid—but then I am of course not one of the entertainment, media, or liberal elite. And when I see this kind of destruction to children, I thank God that I am not.

The article shows how this homosexual brainwashing can remove from young people any sense of morality and any ability to determine right from wrong. How could this happen in a country that was once considered a bastion of religious morality?

The factual material excerpted from the following article shows early results from the acceptance of the homosexual agenda. It will get worse.

Homosexuality is an invitation to disaster

... "Being bisexual seems to be the thing. I just wish they wouldn't push it on everybody else." So says a Washington area 18-year-old who just finished high school. She's referring not to the National Gay and Lesbian Task Force or ACT UP. She's talking about her own high school classmates. According to the *Washington Post*, bisexuality and homosexuality have become the "in" thing among the high school and junior high school set. They sport pink ribbons, kiss members of the same sex in the hallways ["to see what people will say"] and tell reporters that "Everyone is bisexual, if you ask me."

... But is there a risk that by acquiescing to demands for acceptance and equality, we will miss the mark and wind up encouraging homosexuality as a fashion?

THE ACCOUNT BY THE *Washington Post* of the burgeoning number of teen-agers who are now calling themselves "gay" or "bi" suggests the overwhelming power of fashion in human affairs — particularly when the humans are between the ages of 13 and 20. Confused and overwhelmed by sex in any case, and now bombarded by talk of homosexuality in the press, in school sex-education classes and in entertainment, lots of kids are calling themselves "gay" to be trendy or rebellious. *** [I would add that they are also acting out the part.]

Key to the argument of homosexual activists is the idea that homosexuality is an innate, immutable characteristic. ...

... Whether our society in fact fits that description is now debatable, as these high school kids demonstrate. But neither is it clear that homosexuals are born, not made. There is a great deal of evidence that many people who have no difficulty describing themselves as heterosexual can be tempted into homosexuality. Look at the behavior of men in prison. They engage in homosexual conduct because women are unavailable. Do gay activists insist that their fundamental natures have changed? [And I would ask: Do they change back and forth, as many such as those in prison have done? This could not be genetic. What about the homosexual acts of bisexuals? Do you really believe that their "orientation" changes back and forth? Do you really believe that they are genetically both ways?]

BESIDES, TO SAY THAT no one would willingly choose to be homosexual, in light of the difficulties attending that life, is to interpret the word "choose" much too narrowly. Most people make decisions based upon partly or even largely unconscious motivations, fears and needs. A peeping Tom doesn't rationally weigh all the sexual options available and "choose" voyeurism the way one chooses chicken salad at a cafeteria. He feels driven to it by his history and his upbringing.

The young man who told the *Post* that, having thought it over, he could "go either way" probably speaks for thousands, if not millions. Sexuality is not fixed and permanent, like eye color. It is influenced by emotion, age, experience and, yes, culture. When I was a student at Columbia University in the mid-and late 1970s, the homosexual and lesbian group was a tiny fringe. By 1990, according to the report of a recent graduate, a substantial number of women students were experimenting with lesbianism as "a political act." In the space of a decade, a taboo had fallen, a new fad was born and people acted accordingly. *** (By Mona Charen, *Conservative Chronicle*, 6-28-93)

The information and ideas from the above article should also be considered, compared and weighed with the information submitted in Chapter 2, CAUSES OF AND CURES FOR HOMOSEXUALITY. The article contains some interesting additional facts and ideas.

One of the moving factors has been the teachers' union called the National Education Association (NEA).

The NEA Proves Itself Extremist Again

... the National Education Association's annual Convention approved the usual list of extremist resolutions presented by the professionals who run this very political union. ***

The NEA is obsequious in catering to its own very visible NEA Gay and Lesbian Caucus . The Convention passed at least 15 resolutions addressing sexual orientation.

The NEA demands "awareness" instruction about diverse sexual orientation "whenever sexuality and/or tolerance of diversity is taught." This means the NEA wants teaching about homosexuality always to be part of sex education, and uses "diversity" as a code word for gay-lesbian teaching.

The NEA supports "ongoing training programs" to identify and eliminate "sexual orientation stereotyping." The NEA demands a "Lesbian and Gay History Month as a means of acknowledging the contributions of lesbians, gays, and bisexuals throughout history."

The NEA demands that gay-lesbian teaching be part of Family Life education, sex education, and AIDS education. The NEA supports the right of teachers who have tested positive for HIV or have been diagnosed as having AIDS to be retained in the classroom and not transferred.

The NEA even wants public school training of pre-kindergartners to include "diversity-based curricula" with "bias-free screening devices." Pre-kindergarteners in school? Yes, the NEA wants the taxpayers to take on baby-sitting "in the public schools for children from birth through age eight" culminating in "mandatory kindergarten with compulsory attendance." *** (*The Phyllis Schafly Report*, August 1996)

(This article explains many more of the radical and outrageous demands of the NEA. It was a typical convention for the union of the teachers in our schools.)

As noted above, the article claiming that Abraham Lincoln was a homosexual was published in a newsletter by The Gay and Lesbian Commission of the Los Angeles public school system. This is the kind of trash the homosexualists want children to be taught all over the country, along with how wonderful it is to engage in sodomy.

In **Lambda Report** *on Homosexuality*, April-June 1995, was a large full page article, **Out of the Closet—Into Young Minds**, by Karen Joe Gounaud. Peter LaBarbera praises the author and states: "Karen Jo Gounaud represents a unique phenomenon in the controversy of 'gay rights' in our culture: the mother-turned-activist. Like thousands of other moms across America, Karen became engrossed in this issue when confronted with the promotion of homosexuality by educators—in her case libraries, who allowed their library foyers to become weekly hosts to stacks of the *Washington Blade* a homosexual newspaper."

In the above referred to article, Ms. Gounaud states:

> The ALA (American Library Association) was originally conceived during the wartime forties by the nation's libraries, who united in a sincere, protective response to Adolf Hitler's infamous book burning. There was originally no intent to undermine traditional family values. Adult books on sexuality, particularly those with explicit illustrations and instructions, were normally kept in places away from kids. Library personnel tended to be as protective of children's sensibilities as their parents.
>
> Unfortunately, the ALA's founders were, within two decades, replaced by radical leaders with a bold agenda. Local controls were overshadowed by ALA demands. ***

Ms. Gounaud then explains that in the last few decades, children have been exposed to the same "anything goes" publications as adults. She tells of the "gay" influence, and how traditionally essential books on history, literature and science were becoming hard to find, but homosexual publications were becoming plentiful and prominent. Examples given of this latter are the *Washington Blade, Daddy's Roommate* and *Heather Has Two Mommies*. The *Daddy's Roommate* book is about a father living with his "gay" lover. "Illustrations include a picture of two men in bed. The boy's mother assures him that 'being gay is just one more kind of love.'" The article also states:

> Both books are published by Alyson Publications. What the libraries don't tell you is that the same people also publish adult pornography such as *Macho Sluts* that includes a story about "a lesbian who performs sadomasochistic sex on her 13-year-old daughter." (*Lambda Report*, February 1993) Another popular Alyson work, *Gay Sex: A Manual for Men Who Love Men*, by Jack Hart, includes helpful hints (courtesy of NAMBLA) for pedophiles on how "to avoid problems with parents or police."

(The *Gay Sex* book by Jack Hart was explained in Chapter 1, above. It is hard to imagine anything more filthy.) Ms. Gounaud then explains the difficulty she had getting some offsetting kinds of books into the Fairfax County, Virginia, library. But Gounaud and a citizen's group did get into the library several books, including Jeff Konrad's *You Don't Have to Be Gay*, Dr. Joseph Nicolosi's fine volume on *Reparative Therapy of Male Homosexuals*, and *Alfie's Home*, a children's book about healing from homosexuality ... based on author Richard A. Cohen's own life experience. The article tells of the criticism about the latter book:

> Will Manley, liberal columnist for the *American Libraries* magazine. He called the book "the homophobe's answers to *Daddy's Roommate*." Manley even questions whether such "misguided propaganda" belongs in the library!

NEA Teacher Handbook Reveals Far-Reaching Pro-Gay Agenda
by Peter LaBarbera
(Lambda Report on *Homosexuality*, April-June 1995):

The NEA now has a manual for training educators that was "created by the NEA's Gay and Lesbian Caucus." The following are just a few of the things from the article showing the radical pro-homosexual ideas with which teachers and students are to be indoctrinated:

HOMOSEXUALITY: Sexual attraction to and/or behavior with the same sex. It is normal, has no known cause, and is not an illness.
HOMOPHOBIA: "The fear and intolerance of homosexuality ... Homophobia is the disease, not homosexuality ..."

* * *

STRATEGIES FOR TEACHERS

3. Change language that assumes everyone is or should be heterosexual (use "partner" rather than boyfriend, "permanent relationship" rather than marriage.
4. Identify gay/lesbian contributions throughout the curriculum (history, literature, art, science, religion, etc.) ...
6. Submit requests to improve library holdings (both fiction and nonfiction) related to sexual diversity ...

Source: *Institute for Sexual Inclusiveness Through Training and Education (INSITE)*

RECOMMENDATIONS FOR PUBLIC SCHOOLS

2. Change heterosexual language ...
4. Conduct in-service "sensitivity" training for all school personnel.
6. Introduce gay/lesbian issues into all curriculum areas ...

Source: *INSITE*

It is truly a national disgrace and a terrible tragedy that many schools, and the parents of the children attending them, have allowed such homosexual excrement to be foisted upon teachers and schoolchildren under them. This is a major contributing factor to the disgraceful condition of our public schools, and to the lack of morality of young people.

Young people are assailed by the homosexual brainwashing from all sides – the government, schools, schoolteachers, the media (both entertainment and news), and even our libraries join in the assault. Is it any wonder that children show the confusion and immorality disclosed by the article above on the Boston school children?

Karen Jo Gounaud had another article, "You Really Can't Judge a Book by its Cover," in the July-September 1995 *Lambda Report on Homosexuality*. The article is interesting from two standpoints. It gives information about books made available for children—but it also gives us further insight into the minds of homosexuals and perverts. The following information was given about the ALA:

> *** The original organization from which today's American Library Association (ALA) evolved was founded in 1876 ... .
>
> ... the Library Bill of Rights, which the ALA uses as its central philosophical document, was adopted in 1939 out of a concern for perceived problems of censorship, fears that were heightened by Hitler's book burning and book banning. That bill was last amended in 1967, and adopted by the entire ALA in 1972, with the support of the ACLU, to allow any child of any age access to all materials in the library without prior parental approval.

The article gives more information about some of the books thereby available to children:

> *** Some sexuality books broadcast their position loud and clear. "Understanding Sexual Identity: A Book for Gay Teens and Their Friends" by Janice E. Reach ... . it is helpful for parents to read a book like this to more fully educate themselves on what misinformation and propaganda rolls of gay-friendly presses to target young minds. ***
>
> ... some innocuous titles like "Changing Bodies, Changing Lives" for teens contain some of the most sexually explicit, left-leaning and age-inappropriate fare that's ever hit print. Chapters include "Exploring Sex With Yourself" and "Exploring Sex with Someone of Your Own Sex." Instructions are specific, including for oral sex, and kids share their personal experiences in great detail with language to match. ...
>
> "It's Perfectly Normal," an innocent looking sexuality book for children by Robbie H. Harris, goes a step further in conditioning kids

to leave traditional sexual mores in the dust ... . Artist Michael Emberly explicitly illustrates many styles of sexual activity and nude bodies, complete with a variety of nipples, pubic hair and other genital details. Kids are shown in so many nude settings, one could conclude that modesty is a thing of the past. Masturbation is given its own illustrated chapter, orgasms and fantasizing are encouraged, but virginity is not listed. ... The chapter on homosexuality never mentions relevant diseases, but it does provide an historic endorsement: The ancient Greeks thought that love between two men was the highest form . . . it was hoped that male lovers would be in the same army regiment . . . The Spartan army was one of the most powerful and feared armies in ancient Greece." (p. 17) (That civilization's demise through moral decay is forgotten.) Those who disapprove of homosexuality are dismissed with the explanation that "Usually these people know little or nothing about homosexuals, and their views are often based on fears or misinformation, not on facts."

... Some organizations like Dr. James Dobson's Focus on the Family produce consistently high quality materials. But other familiar names like Dr. Ruth Westheimer write almost entirely within today's liberal agenda. "Dr. Ruth Talks to Kids" is an attractive looking tome with a smiling, grandmotherly Dr. Ruth on the cover. Inside, her support of homosexuality is clear. For example, accompanying a nice line drawing of a friendly looking pair of teen boys holding hands, her segment on homosexuality states, "A long time ago, there was a lot of prejudice against homosexuals. Much prejudice still exists, and some gays feel that they have to keep their sexual preference a secret. But more and more people now understand that homosexuals are healthy and normal and, except for their sexual preference, exactly like everybody else."

A famous professional reputation doesn't even guide you safely away from pedophile books. Dr. Wardell B. Pomeroy, for example, is touted as a "nationally renowned author," and is listed in seven consecutive editions of "Who's Who." But Pomeroy's work with sex researcher Alfred Kinsey included the infamous "Table 34" ... , which lists sexual responses in babies as young as four months old—data that could only have come from child molesters, or people lying about it.

Pomeroy's books for children "ten and up," "Boys and Sex" (henceforth, BAS) and "Girls and Sex," consistently encourage kids to experiment with sex and ignore parental teaching. Incredibly, each includes a section on bestiality. On page 163, BAS mentions "case histories of boys who build up a strong emotional attachment to a particular animal and have intercourse with it whenever possible." Pomeroy warns that " . . . you would be best advised to keep any knowledge of [this behavior] to yourself so you can avoid either ridicule or punishment, or both. You can feel secure in your knowledge that you're not a monster, no matter what society may think about it."

Pomeroy also writes positively about sadomasochism and questions the validity of negative research on incest ... . He devotes supportive chapters to "Sex for Yourself" (masturbation) and "What Being Gay is All About." Here's one of the thoughts from the latter: "In many states boys who have sex with each other can be prosecuted as juvenile delinquents and sent to institutions. Fortunately its virtually impossible to enforce such laws; otherwise, there would not be enough jails to hold all the offenders" (BAS, p. 143).

"It's Perfectly Normal" has impressive jacket endorsements from renowned baby doctor T. Berry Brazelton and columnist "Dear Abby." When some of our country's thousands of outspoken successful former homosexuals wrote to contest her position that being "gay" is irreversible and should be accepted and tolerated, she refused even to print their letters. So Abby's endorsement on books for children and teens should serve as a warning, not reassurance.

The best answer for parents, as always, is to remain very involved in your children's lives, including their sex education. The homosexual agenda encroaches at all levels, hiding in many unexpected places. Protect your children by staying informed and scrutinizing carefully what is sent their way, even between the covers of a friendly-looking book. And remember, when it comes to this issue, don't trust the "experts."

Let us consider what the factual information in the above referenced article discloses about the thinking of the homosexualist mind—particularly that in Pomeroy's book—with the sexual acts of homosexuals listed in Chapter 1. Is there any sexual act imaginable that is so low and filthy that it would be considered as unacceptable by such demented minds? On this question, an interesting statement was made by conservative columnist, Cal Thomas, in an article, "Gay rights would open the door," *Conservative Chronicle*, 5-12-93:

> A decade ago, I was a guest on Merv Griffin's show. Another guest was a woman who said she was a lesbian.

I listed for her sexual behavior I felt was unwise, even immoral, and asked her to stop me when she felt I had gone too far. When I got to necrophilia and she did not protest, the audience gasped.

For those of us who are not as worldly, a definition for necrophilia, given in *The American Heritage Dictionary*, 3rd Ed., is: "Erotic attraction to or sexual contact with corpses." So, the conclusion is, that at least for some homosexuals, there is no sexual act of any kind so gross as to be any longer taboo.

From time to time, when it suits their purposes, as when they are trying to get homosexual representation or influence in the United Nations, or when they are trying to get "gay rights" legislation passed, the homosexual groups try to make the public believe that some of their organizations are distancing themselves from NAMBLA and pedophilia advocates. The truth is that the homosexual activists are continually promoting pedophilia and trying to get the age that youngsters can consent to sex lowered. They also continually promote it in their literature and film presentations. The following is only one example of many referred to in this book.

Pedophilia Film in UNM [University of New Mexico] Festival Raises Disputes About Pornography

A group of University of New Mexico students and teachers say a university film committee is breaking the law by showing a film depicting sexual relations between a soldier and a 12-year-old boy.

But District Attorney Robert Schwartz disagrees, as does the chairman of the Associated Students film committee.

"For a Lost Soldier" was shown Friday evening and is scheduled to be shown again at 2:45 p.m. today in the Student Union Building theater.

It is based on a novel by Rudi van Dantzig and follows a choreographer who reminisces about his childhood in newly liberated Holland.

At a news conference Friday afternoon, members of the ad hoc group said they support the Southwest Film Center's lesbian, bisexual and gay film festival, of which the movie is a part. ***

Jerry Barron, director of the Southwest Film Center and the chairman of the Associated Students film committee, said the film is "relevant to the times" and that it is not pornographic. (*Albuquerque Journal*, 10-23-93)

I have not seen the film referred to above, but I have my doubts if D. A. Robert Schwartz was correct even from a present-day legal standpoint. I do know that activist judges have given great leeway for showing filth and pornography. I also personally know that D. A. Robert Schwartz has continually supported the homosexual movement by supporting various "gay rights" bills, ordinances and regulations.

Colorado for Family Values gave a less guarded description of "For a Lost Soldier." Its report states:

> It's " . . . the kind of film NAMBLA might drag out to justify its existence." Robert Julian, critic for the homosexual Bay Area Reporter, is referring to "For a Lost Soldier," ... . (Bay Area Reporter, 17 June 1993)
>
> It's about a young boy discovering his "sexuality" at the hands of an adult soldier. According to Julian, this soldier, whom he calls, "the young boy's liberator (in every sense of the word) . . ." actually "manages to make the soldier's attentions seem natural and compassionate. This is no small feat, when you see them naked in bed together, with the young boy on the bottom." (CFV Report, May 1994)

I consider it rather clear that the film is one more promotion of pedophilia by a homosexual group. I also agree with Schwartz that the subject, at least, is "relevant to the times." Pedophilia is not only being promoted by homosexuals, but is being engaged in by them to an unbelievable degree. That is why organizations, such as the Boy Scouts and other youth organizations, should prevent homosexuals from getting the opportunity to indoctrinate young people with their evil and sordid ideas, and from abusing and attacking young people. The following is only one more of the numerous examples detailed in this book as proof of this.

Boy Scout leader faces sex charges

PORTALES [New Mexico] — A Boy Scout troop leader was in a Portales jail Wednesday, accused of photographing a nude 14-year-old boy who had been tied to a bed at the troop leader's residence.

John Charles Roberts, a 28-year-old graduate student at Eastern New Mexico University, was charged with sexual exploitation of a child and seven counts of contributing to the delinquency of a minor, all felony charges.

Authorities said the 14-year-old apparently was not a member of Robert's Scout troop.

According to police, the alleged incident involving the teen-ager occurred during a party at Roberts' residence on May 15. Authorities said beer was provided minors at the party.

Investigators found several photographs of young nude males, several sets of handcuffs and other items considered to be sexual paraphernalia, according to court documents.
(*The Albuquerque Tribune*, 5-27-93)

"The national organization [Boy Scouts of America] removed 1,800 Scoutmasters suspected of molesting between 1971 and 1991, according to files that attorney Michael Rothschild obtained for a lawsuit." (*The Albuquerque Tribune*, 10-15-93) A screening program to keep out child abusers is explained in the article. The homosexual community vehemently opposes such screening. An example is the following:

Gay ex-Scout's suit advances

LOS ANGELES — A judge's ruling has cleared the way for a homosexual man to proceed with a discrimination lawsuit against the Boy Scouts of America and its national policy banning homosexuals as poor role models.

Timothy Curran, 19, was asked to leave the Scouts in 1980 when he took a young man to his senior prom. He filed his lawsuit in 1981 when his bid to return as an adult leader was rejected.

Superior Court Judge Sally Disco ruled late Tuesday that the Mount Diablo Council in the San Francisco Bay area is subject to California's Unruh Civil Rights Act. (*Albuquerque Journal*, 11-9-90)

Fortunately for the country and for the Boy Scouts, the ruling of the judge that the organization did not have the right to bar such people as scout leaders was overturned by a higher court. But the homosexual attack still comes from all sides, and in all forms.

Now the ACLU is handling an appeal of the Curran case to the California Supreme Court. It is also handling an appeal to that court, against the Boy Scouts for Michael and William Randall, twin brothers who refuse to recite the Boy Scout oath to God. Action was brought under the same California "civil rights" law.("Boy Scouts Under Attack," by Cathleen Al Cleaver, Esq., and Crystal M. Roberts, *Washington Watch*, Vol. 9, No. 4, Family Research Council, Feb. 1998) I believe that the real object of the ACLU is to do everything it can to destroy religious morality in this country, to instill atheism and the belief in sodomy in the people, and to either change or destroy organizations that hold to traditional morality.

Santa Fe Boy Scouts to lose United Way funding for barring gays

SANTA FE [New Mexico] — The Boy Scouts of America's national policy of excluding homosexuals will apparently prevent its Santa Fe organization from receiving funding from United Way of Santa Fe County. ***

Under the new policy, only those agencies that provide services without discrimination "on the basis of age, gender, race, religion or national origin, sexual orientation or disability" will be funded. *** (*The Albuquerque Tribune*, 9-22-94)

Strangely enough such policies allow funding of homosexual organizations that promote sodomy as a proper way of life, and the United Way has contributed to such organizations. The above referred to article did point out that the United Way in different localities does have different rules. Nevertheless, many people who believe in traditional moral values no longer contribute to the United Fund. Certainly more deserving charitable organizations can be found.

Boy Scouts Under Siege

The Boy Scouts attempt to provide moral instruction, male role models, and promote boy-man companionship. It is often the last opportunity for a fatherless boy to experience male bonding. Yet this venerable institution is under attack:

- New Jersey: Lambda Legal Defense and Education Fund filed suit against the Boy Scouts under the states' new gay civil rights law. It is expected to go to trial late this year. (*Washington Blade* 4-23-93) ***

- Of the 102 homosexuals court martialed in the Army over the past four years, four involved Scout leaders. The Office of the Judge Advocate General wrote that Sergeant Stephen Ahern used "leather restraints and dog collars, [and] he viciously assaulted many scouts aged 9 to 12. He anally assaulted the boys, often jamming a dildo-tipped nightstick into their anuses as he video-taped the screaming children."

An organized cadre of homosexuals—the very people who commit these unspeakable acts against boy scouts—are demanding further access to leadership positions in the Scouts through the courts.

Homosexuals' presence in the Scouts causes the same kinds of sexual problems as their presence in the military—only the victims are younger. (*Family Research Report*, May-June 1993)

It is quite clear that activist homosexuals and their supporters want homosexuals to have access to children. Time and space will not permit covering all of the articles on homosexual attacks on children and young people when this wanted access is successful. The following is just one more typical example:

Priest created a boys club for sex

WHITE PLAINS, N.Y. — A veteran Roman Catholic priest has pleaded guilty to taking at least 11 boys from his parishes to a condominium at a New Jersey beach and at motels on Cape Cod and engaging in a variety of sexual acts with them over the last 10 years.

... Pope John Paul II and the leaders of the American Catholic Church have been struggling with how to deal with priests who have sexually abused children and teen-agers in their trust. ***

In federal court, [Rev. Edward] Pipala, a priest for 27 years, admitted that he organized a parish boys club called "the Hole" in which he would provide liquor and beer to boys as young as 12 and engage them in anal and oral sex and mutual masturbation.

Law-enforcement authorities said he swore the 30 to 50 boys who belonged to the club to an oath of secrecy, and for years no one revealed the activities of the club.

The club was named the Hole after a basement room at the Monroe church. At first, the Hole was to be a club that would help troubled boys. *** (*The Albuquerque Tribune*, 7-10-93)

Sex offender pleads guilty to knowing he had AIDS

LOS ANGELES—A police officer has pleaded guilty in a case involving a rarely used law that increases the penalty for sex offenders who know they are carrying the AIDS virus, prosecutors said.

Marvin Anthony Jackson, 35, faces up to seven years and eight months in prison for engaging in sex with a former police Explorer Scout who worked at the Los Angeles Police Department's Southeast Division, where the officer was assigned.

Jackson pleaded guilty Wednesday to two felony sex counts, and admitted two special allegations that he committed the crimes knowing he had tested HIV positive, said Deputy District Attorney Richard Goul.

The allegations can enhance a sentence by up to three years. ***

No information was available on whether the victim has tested positive for the HIV virus. (*The Albuquerque Tribune*, 10-6-94)

Prostitute Regains Teaching Job

TORONTO — A part-time journalism instructor, suspended after admitting he moonlights as a gay prostitute, will be allowed back at his job, his university announced Wednesday.

The instructor, Gerald Hannon, also has drawn criticism for contending that sex between adults and adolescents is not necessarily wrong. A report released Wednesday by Ryerson Polytechnical University clears Hannon 51, of allegations he used his writing class as a platform for his views on sex between children and adults.

However, the Toronto university reprimanded Hannon for admitting to a newspaper reporter that he was a part-time prostitute. Prostitution is not illegal in Canada. (*Albuquerque Journal*, 12-21-95)

As we have seen from many sources, Hannon's view on adult-child sex is a common one among homosexuals. It is another example of a university which has no interest in the moral character of its teaching staff, and is undoubtedly promoting homosexuality.

The so-called sex education in our schools is covered in various places in this book, because of its relevance to other subjects, too. It is a national disgrace.

Sex in Sacramento—
And other adventures in the sensitivity sweepstakes
By George Will (Columnist)

"Here's a cute one," said the professor, according to one of her students. The professor was commenting on one of the slides of female genitalia that she used together with a catalogue of sex toys, in her lecture on female masturbation. ...

But why does the professor, Joanne Marrow of California State University in Sacramento, need a lawyer? Because she and CSUS are being sued by a male student who says the lecture made him feel "raped." ...

... Rogers remembered it in a description he recorded two days later. What he says he found "sickening" and "horrifying" and made him want to "vomit" included: "She told us about buying dildos for her family for Christmas, and how one sister didn't like the present she got because it wasn't the right size . . . She was showing us all the nooks and crannies and nuances of women's genitalia . . . All the wisecracks about using a wine bottle, wrapping a wine bottle in a towel and . . ." You get the idea.

Among the 18 ideas that Marrow, a lesbian, hoped listeners would get from her lecture and the slides projected on a large screen (including slides of the genitals of pregnant and post-partum women, and of 9- and 11-year-old girls) were that women can "use genital self-examination as an exercise in self-acceptance," that "the sole function of the clitoris is to provide physical pleasure to the woman" and "that women have a right to enjoy their clitoris through masturbation." ***
(*Newsweek,* April 3, 1995)

Sex Education Norms Criticized—
Promiscuity Touted, House Panel Told

WASHINGTON—Educators are going too far in their discussions of birth control, homosexuality and AIDS in the nation's classrooms, implying that it's OK to be promiscuous, three parents told a House subcommittee Wednesday. ***

... some instructors cross the line and advocate homosexuality and premarital sex while "denigrating the strongly held contrary views and beliefs, religious or otherwise, of students and staff members alike,"

said Grantham, father of two St. Paul, Minn., public school students.
*** (*Albuquerque Journal*, 12-7-95)

The following is from an article by columnist Jeffrey Hart about a conservative independent student newspaper at Dartmouth College, which has tried to stem the tide of the promotion of homosexuality and immorality generally in the college:

The importance of the Dartmouth Review
*** The Review is a permanent threat to whatever wild scheme the Dartmouth administration or faculty might dream up.

Would you believe condoms—condoms in flavors!—are made available to Dartmouth freshmen at registration? And still worse, literature and equipment dealing with sex acts I had never heard of—and am sorry I now have heard of. Do you know what "water sports" are? The term has nothing to do with the swimming team. Have you heard of "rimming"?

Would you believe that hard-core pornographic movies are required viewing for students in the film studies program? Or that freshmen are treated to skits praising homosexuality?

Without the weekly presence of the *Dartmouth Review*, things could be much worse. If the *Review* cannot block such vulgar nonsense, it can call attention to it and prevent further degradation. ...

Of course the Dartmouth administration has relentlessly smeared the students involved with the *Review*.

The administration has called them racists, anti-Semites, sexists, homophobes. Such smears are brazen lies. When the newspaper was called racist, for example, the editor in chief was a black student named Kevin Pritchett, now with the *Wall Street Journal*.

Among its previous editors were two from the Indian subcontinent, including the now famous Dinesh D'Souza, author of the bestselling *Illiberal Education: The Politics of Race and Sex on Campus*.

Three women have been *Review* editors. The current editor, Ken Weissman, is Jewish, as is the next editor, Oron Strauss. ***
(*Conservative Chronicle*, 3-24-93)

School counseling programs—Newt: Gays recruiting
WASHINGTON—School programs that deal with gays and lesbians may be thinly veiled efforts to recruit new homosexuals, according to House Speaker Newt Gingrich.

"You have had, clearly, examples, of what is, in effect recruitment in so-called counseling programs," Gingrich, R-Ga., said Tuesday at his daily news conference. "So I'm very cautious about the idea that you want to have active homosexuals in junior high school and high school explaining to young people that they have all these various wonderful options."

Gingrich referred to children's books used with grade schoolers such as "Heather Has Two Mommies," as evidence that education programs are going beyond tolerance into promotion of homosexuality. (*The Albuquerque Tribune*, 3-9-95)

A number of religious and conservative organizations, including the Christian Coalition, Focus on the Family, Traditional Values Coalition, Concerned Women for America, various writers and organizations cited herein, and others, are fighting to stem the tidal wave of immorality engulfing schools and young people in the country. But it is often discouraging and seems that moral decency continues to decrease at a rapid rate. Another such organization is the Alliance Defense Fund (ADF) which is active in bringing and financing court cases to try to protect religious rights and the rights of parents to prevent the corrupting of their children. The following is excerpted from an article in the news publication of the ADF:

Parents Fight for Right to Protect Their Children ...
Now pending in the United States Supreme Court on a petition for certiorari: *Brown, et al, v. Hot, Sexy, and Safer Production, Inc.*

<u>Facts of the Case</u>: In Chelmsford, Massachusetts, public high school students—with no warning, no opportunity to "opt out," no chance to confer with their parents, and without parental permission, were forced to attend the 90-minute performance entitled *Hot, Sexy, and Safer*. The performance—in detailed explicit, and vulgar language and illustrations—contained references to various sexual acts, genitals, excretory functions, and advocated homosexual and premarital sexual conduct. ***

The following is stated to be from the transcript of the case showing the actual record of part of what took place:

"I guarantee you, if you cannot talk during a sexual experience, you won't even get to the moment. If you can't look your partner in the eye and say, 'Listen, I want to take all of your clothes off, and then I want to run my tongue on the back of your neck and work my way down.' If I can't say that to my partner, I'm not ready to do it,"

* * *

"Okay, you know what bisexual means? That means you go 'either-or,' men or women, right? Now think about that. That's a very, sort of interesting, um. situation, because I think you get a lot more people to choose from, right? . . . Hey, I'll take your brother or sister. It doesn't matter to me. I don't care. (Giggle) Alright? So, that's a bisexual, alright?"

* * *

The female performer goaded a male student to join her on stage in the act of licking a candy-flavored condom while he knelt in front of the audience: [Performer displays several condoms.] "Heavy Duty. This is a latex condom . . . . You know what this is? It's a condom that comes with its own applicator . . . but this one is for oral sex. So if I have to put this on a [male genital] and put it in my mouth. I'm not asking you [to male student] to put a [male genital] in your mouth. I'm asking you to take the condom to be a good sport for me. [Student licks condom] What is it, is it sweet?"

* * *

"Do you know that most young men, the very first orgasm they will have will be with another guy? Think about that. Does that mean they're gay? Of course not. It means that it's easier to experiment with someone that has the same equipment that you have because it's less pressure."
(**ADF Briefing**, Alliance Defense Fund, January 1996)

The article referred to above states that after the showing for the 9th and 10th graders, the school officials directed another mandatory assembly for showing it to the 11th and 12 graders.

Other organizations doing similar work to the ADF are the American Center for Law and Justice, founded by Rev. Pat Robertson, who also founded the Christian Coalition, and the Rutherford Institute. These organizations seem to be kept busy with the many available cases such as the one explained. I presume that they are limited only by time and money.

Political agenda, not AIDS, fuels condom battle
(By George Will, noted columnist and author)
*New York City's school condom-distribution program is at bottom a plot to promote alternative lifestyles.

WASHINGTON—The Gaderene descent of society was slightly reversed recently in an unlikely place, New York City. A state court struck down a particularly offensive facet of that city's condom crusade.

... (Some parents) objected not to AIDS education but that the program contained neither a requirement for prior parental consent, nor even a provision for parents to make their children ineligible for school-dispensed condoms.

... the court held that the condom program ... violates the parents' constitutional rights—14th Amendment due process rights construed to concern the rearing of their children. ***

Condom distribution is the latest chapter in a long story of cultural clashes as old as American schooling. The [United States Supreme Court] recognized the liberty interests of parents in directing the education of their children in 1923, overturning a Nebraska statute prohibiting the teaching, even in private schools, of foreign languages to children before ninth grade. The desire of Nebraska was to foster American homogeneity, especially by preventing the teaching of German. The court said this did not justify overriding more fundamental values. ***

This campaign (on AIDS and condom distribution), misleading about the demographics and mechanics of the epidemic, has had the intended effect of making AIDS a spectacularly privileged disease. AIDS receives a share of research resources disproportionate to the resources allocated to diseases more costly in lives and less driven by behavior known to be risky.

It is difficult to doubt that the public school condom crusade appeals to some proponents precisely because it derogates parental authority and expands that of government. These are twin components of a political agenda.

The agenda is to assert equal legitimacy for all "lifestyles" or "preferences" and to reduce personal responsibility, under a therapeutic state, for the consequences of choices. In short, this is the 1960s coloring the 1990s. (*The Albuquerque Tribune*, 1-6-94)

Although lawsuits to protect religious and parental freedoms have had some success, schools seem to be more afraid of actions brought by homosexual activists. I am sure, however, that a lot of this purported "fright" is because of infiltration of the homosexual element. But there is some real fear of lawsuits—and I have also run into some of it over a church-supported school being pressed to adopt policies prohibiting discrimination against teachers because of "sexual orientation."

The new homophobia: Schools fear lawsuits, by Roy Maynard of Omaha, Texas, *World,* 1-16-96. pp. 17-18, is an article about parents of children in an Omaha elementary school being threatened with a lawsuit by the Texas State Teachers Association. The complaint of the parents was the announcement by a sixth-grade music teacher, in class, that he was a homosexual. Some parents then objected to the school about having their students under that particular teacher. The article states:

> *** Schools are the newest focal point in homosexuals' fight to legitimize their lifestyle. *Education Week* admits: "Public schools are [becoming] a battleground for gay-rights issues." Announces gay activist Donna Redwing, "We're here, we're queer, we're in the classroom."
>
> At the fore is a group calling itself the Gay, Lesbian and Straight Teachers Network (GLSTN). Holding national conferences and winning the ear of President Clinton, the group is quietly effective in the broaching of the subject of homosexuality in the classroom. ***

The article gives incidents of "coming out" and homosexual propaganda in various schools around the country, including areas of St. Louis, San Diego, Dedham, Mass., and St. Paul. "GLSTN is seeing slow but steady progress." "Five states and numerous school districts have changed their education codes to bar discrimination based on sexual orientation." It gives instances of lawsuits brought by teachers and homosexual students, stating:

> Perhaps here, finally, is a legitimate use of the word "homophobia." School districts see a minefield of potential litigation. The National Education Association has a long standing policy of providing free legal counsel to teachers who feel they've been discriminated against because of their homosexuality. The Lambda Legal Defense and Education Fund is representing (for free) a number of teachers who make such claims. One homosexual teacher, who feels the school didn't do enough for him when students taunted him because of his homosexuality, is suing for discrimination and also filing a worker's compensation claim. And in three separate cases, homosexual youths are suing because they were bullied.

The article also tells how the Rutherford Institute attorneys were then working with "the lawsuit-threatened parents." Mr. Stewart (the homosexual teacher who "came out" in the elementary school classroom) will be leaving in December (he's told students he's going to Mexico). And some of the offended children were going to school in a nearby district.

The country can be thankful for a few people in the country, like the Texas parents and the Rutherford Institute who backed them, who stood their ground and refused, for the sake of their children, to allow the indoctrination of homosexual filth. The coming-out incident was, without doubt, only the commencement of the full scale press for acceptance of the homosexual "lifestyle" and the accompanying vile indoctrinations. It appears that the Omaha, Texas, parents, at least for the time, stopped it in its tracks.

Parents should not be misled by organizations with moralistic or patriotic sounding names, such as the American Civil Liberties Union (ACLU), and People For the American Way (PAW). At various places in this book, information has been referred to that shows how the ACLU continually supports the homosexual movement.

Coral Ridge Ministries Media, Inc., a respected Christian-oriented organization, put out an information bulletin referring to sources dated in 1994 and 1995, about the PAW organization, entitled: **PEOPLE FOR THE AMERICAN WAY—Another ACLU—behind an even more deceptive mask!** The bulletin also explains how PAW supports and brings lawsuits, similar to those in which the ACLU engages. It also states:

> *** When parents express concern about reading materials their children are being exposed to in public schools, [PAW] calls it "censorship," a common ACLU-style attack. ... They complained about citizens objecting to "sexual content, objectionable language, and religion" as well as materials related to homosexuality. [PAW] took exception to schools moving objectionable books to "less accessible sections" of school libraries as a blow to "academic freedom." ***
>
> Former PAW board member Ted Field is president of Interscope Records, a producer of violent and profane "gangsta rap" music. ... From 1988 to 1991, the record mogul contributed $470,000 to PAW. ...
>
> PAW is closely aligned with Time Warner, the media giant responsible for rock star Madonna's pornographic book *SEX*, gangsta-rap

songs like *Cop Killer*, and so on. Some former PAW board members are serving or have served in high-level positions with Time Warner and/or its subsidiaries. PAW gets overwhelming support from Hollywood. Playboy Enterprises and the Playboy Foundation have contributed $342,000 to PAW in the past 15 years. ***

Under the pretense of "programs" such as sex education, AIDS education, diversity, and nondiscrimination, it seems that the homosexualists have gained substantial control of a large part of our universities and public schools. Conservative organizations and writers are continually publishing articles on this, and certainly time and space prohibit referring to more than samples of them. Unfortunately, it seems that much of the news media are so liberal and homosexualist-oriented themselves that they try to keep these matters from public attention. Therefore much of the general public has no idea as to the extent to which our educational institutions have capitulated to the homosexual activists. Students are forced to attend these programs, and many are humiliated and embarrassed.

In connection with the material covered in this chapter, material presented in Chapter 1 should be considered—particularly the pornographic material promoting "fisting" and other destructive and heinous practices. If these programs reach the success that is intended, all ideas of decency and morals will be removed from the schools, and in their place will be paganism, sodomy, and all forms of perversion.

The onslaught is on all fronts. Many schools will not allow ROTC programs. On the public television *News Hour With Jim Lehrer*, 1-15-96, it was stated that many schools bar armed forces recruiters from their campuses because the military discriminates against homosexuals.

We have seen various examples of subtle and ruthless programs for brainwashing young people. However, homosexuals also have well-laid plans and ideas to directly and physically assault them, as many continually have done since there has been homosexuality. They continually try to figure out more effective ways of carrying out their corruption. The following is an example:

NAMBLA Essay Teaches Pederasts How to Seduce Young Boys
The following is taken from an essay that appeared in the January/ February 1993 edition of NAMBLA Bulletin ... . The essay is titled,

"Letter to a Young Boy Lover," and was written by "A.Z.," a man nearly thirty years of age. The 6 page essay gives advice on how a "young boy lover" can seduce boys aged 9-13—evidently the age of boys A.Z. seduced years before.

If there were ever any doubts that NAMBLA seeks the entrapment and exploitation of young boys, these passages should put them to rest:

"You can tell a lot about a boy with a few well-placed sexual jokes and comments. . . The reaction you are looking for is relaxed receptiveness. . . Eventually you want to joke about masturbation. . . Communicate that you fully approve of masturbation. . . From there, you might make other suggestions to which you feel your partner is receptive. Move one step at a time."

"Leave a pornographic magazine someplace where he's [the boy] sure to find it, but where discovery can still be considered accidental. Once he notices it, you'll know some things you need to know. . . if he wants to see more pornography, you could be in business."

"If possible don't introduce one boy you're having sex with to another. . . You'll do yourself a world of good by performing oral sex on your boys. . . By giving him this pleasure, you increase the chance he'll keep your secret to himself in our homophobic and pedophobic culture. You also give him an excellent reason to come back for more. You build his desire for your company, which is what you want." (*Lambda Report*, Spring 1994)

With a newsletter in May, 1996, Concerned Women for America included an excerpt from *NEA Today*, September 1995, showing the adoption by the National Education Association of a Resolution for "The acceptance of diverse sexual orientation and the awareness of sexual stereotyping whenever sexuality and/or tolerance of diversity is taught" and "Support for the celebration of a Lesbian and Gay History Month." The following includes excerpts from a news release of CWA with the newsletter:

Teachers Call for Lesbian/Gay History Month in Public Schools
*** Homosexual and lesbian activists, an extremely powerful faction in the NEA, declared, "This is an important milestone. The NEA represents 2.2 million teachers throughout the United States and is a leader in educating our society about sexual orientation." ***

CWA president Beverly LaHaye said, "The NEA has a long track record of trying to take over every aspect of education in our country, and force the values and morals of the home out of our schools. I believe every Christian parent in America will view this official promotion of homosexuality as a direct assault on innocent unsuspecting children." ...

The power, wealth, and influence of the NEA has recently been exposed, not only by pro-family organizations like CWA, but also by national publications. *Forbes* magazine has called the NEA America's "largest and richest . . . brass-knuckled labor union." With over 2.2 million members in the U.S., the NEA rakes in more than $785 million in revenues annually. NEA members exert incredible power over the U.S. Congress and the White House

President Clinton tapped former NEA members for key roles in government. He even appointed an NEA member to organize the Democratic National Convention. Speaking before one NEA conference, the President told the delegates, "I believe . . . we have had the partnership I promised. . . . You and I are joined in a common cause, and I believe we will succeed." Gay and lesbian coalitions, including homosexual NEA activists, contributed large amounts of money to Mr. Clinton's 1992 presidential campaign.

CWA's LaHaye responded, "The President is surrendering the moral authority of his office to the radical homosexual political agenda. Concerned Women for America is not going to retreat one iota from its position that the nationwide surge for gay rights is destructive to our country, society, and families." ...

CWA is urging concerned citizens across the nation to stand firm against this pro-homosexual NEA resolution. ...

[Dr. LaHaye:] "We are fighting to protect the innocence and purity of our children and grandchildren. Our schools have our children and grandchildren. Our schools have absolutely no business implementing programs and curricula that 'teach' homosexuality. In this battle, I pray each and every Christian who CWA reaches with this vital information will stand with me." ...

The Arrogance of the Public School Establishment

*** The trendy liberals have placed one of their own as chancellor of New York's public schools, Joseph A. Fernandez, who has implemented a 445-page "multicultural" curriculum called *Children of the Rainbow*. It requires first-grade teachers to "include references to lesbians/gay people in all curricular areas" and insists that same-sex "parents" deserve the same dignity as a married mother and father.

When the nine-member local school board of District 24, which was elected from a multi-ethnic, working-class neighborhood in Queens, superseded the two offending pages, Fenandez just "fired" the board and appointed three of his own employees to run the district! ***

One of the first-grade readers recommended by the rainbow curriculum, *Heather Has Two Mommies*, describes how two lesbians became mommies: one of them was artificially inseminated by a "special doctor." To the liberal oligarchy that runs the public schools, any parent who tries to protect first graders from the information deserves to be attacked with the epithets "censor," "right-wing fundamentalist," and "enemy of the public schools."

Daddy's Roommate, which pictures Daddy and his male roommate in bed together, is another book sanctioned as a first-grade reader. A third reader in the rainbow collections is *Gloria Goes to Gay Pride*.

Before this flap, Fernandez was principally known as the man who started condom distribution in the public schools. ... thumbing his nose at parents who protested. After all, why should parents have anything to say about it! Big Daddy Fernandez is the expert," and he refused to let parents opt-out their children ...! He has similar contempt for members of the city-wide school board who disagree with him, calling Ninga Segarra, the board's Bronx representative, "a political prostitute" when he didn't like her vote on condom distribution. ***

... Fernandez's autobiography published by Little, Brown and just released to the press, describes how he regularly snorted and injected heroin for years as a teenage dropout on the streets of Harlem, more than once passing out from a near overdose. He certainly is a man from the streets of New York, and his foul language, ungrammatical English, and what some call his "abusive temper" have stayed with him.

Fernandez's own New York school board finally realized that he had gone too far and voted 6-to-0 (with one abstention) on December 9 to reinstate the nine-member board in District 24. The *New York Times*, which had editorialized that Fernandez "was right to act decisively" in firing the Queens school board and that he "stands tall" in his battle against parents, reported as "surprising" that even the mayor's own appointees would not back Fenandez in this dispute. (*The Phyllis Schlafly Report*, Jan. 1993)

Amazingly, the brainwashing of our school children is even more than some homosexuals can stomach—at least when funds designated for AIDS education are being misused.

Lesbian Blasts Promiscuous Gay Sex Indoctrination in Public Schools
"Promotion of Homosexuality" in School Hearings Disappoint Pro-Family Groups
WASHINGTON — Open lesbian Clair Connelly told Congress in December that billions of federal dollars designated for AIDS education are being misused "to espouse homosexuality and promiscuity" in public school classrooms. ***

Even before Connelly and other conservative speakers testified, the homosexual lobby group Human Rights Campaign had distributed a press advisory denigrating them and attacking their credibility. *** (**Lambda Report** *on Homosexuality*, October '95 - January '96)

The extent of the attacks, and the sources from which they come, to corrupt the schools and young people in this country, indeed prove the old adage: "Truth is stranger than fiction." The attacks come from our own government; from various unions and homosexual organizations; from feminist and abortion groups; from churches that have prostituted themselves before the homosexual movement and abandoned the very base of their religion; from liberal politicians; and even from private business corporations.

Concerned Women for America, launched a national campaign to expose the "SIECUS scandal"—an organization organized for the purpose of corrupting the morals of this country—and particularly of the young and the schools. The following is from a fact brochure distributed by CWA with its newsletter of July, 1996:

EXPOSING THE "SIECUS SCANDAL"
The facts you need to know about the Sexuality Information and Education Council of the United States (SIECUS)
SIECUS, PLAYBOY, And KINSEY
With an initial grant from the Playboy Foundation, SEICUS was founded in New York in 1964 as the sex education arm of the Kinsey Institute. Alfred Kinsey's research on human sexuality shocked the nation with its contention that many people engage in deviant sexual

behavior. The promotion of Kinsey's views by SIECUS has been a major factor in shaping the sexual norms of two generations of Americans and igniting the sexual revolution.

It has been learned, however, that much of Kinsey's research was fraudulent and based on studies of a disproportionate number of prison inmates, homosexuals, and child molesters, among others. Infants may even have been molested as part of the "research."

How SIECUS Operates

SIECUS works closely with the U.S. Departments of Education and Health and Human Services. Materials written by SIECUS sexologists are published widely through other organizations and form the basis for sex education curriculum in many schools.

SIECUS identified five policy areas for the Clinton Administration to act upon:

1. Support for comprehensive sexuality education.
2. Implementation of straightforward and explicit HIV/AIDS prevention education.
3. Support for reproductive rights—including the freedom to choose abortion and access to family planning information—and services for all, regardless of gender, age, or ability to pay.
4. Elimination of bias based on sexual orientation.
5. Opposition to censorship of art and sexually explicit materials.

What SIECUS Believes

Here are actual words from SIECUS's own materials about "Sexual Orientation and Identity":

"SIECUS believes that an individual's sexual orientation—whether bisexual, homosexual, or heterosexual—is an essential part of sexual health and personality. SIECUS supports the right of each individual to accept, acknowledge, and live in accordance with his or her orientation. SIECUS advocates laws guaranteeing civil rights and protection to all people of all sexual orientation and deplores all forms of prejudice and discrimination against people based on sexual orientation."

SIECUS publishes and distributes a wide variety of literature to school children. Here's a sample of the contents of one illustrated SIECUS booklet, Talk about Sex:

"A non-lubricated condom may be cut lengthwise up the side, opened up, and used to cover the female sexual parts (the vulva) during oral sex to protect both people" (pp. 12–13)

"Transsexual: a person who feels he or she is really the other sex or gender trapped in the wrong body and may have had an operation to change his or her gender" (p. 16)

"Transvestite: a person who dresses in clothes of the other gender, often as a turn-on; called dressed in 'drag'" (p. 16)

"Our sexual orientation—or who we are attracted to—is not a choice we make. . . . For many young people, exploring their sexuality with someone of the same gender is a natural part of growing up. These normal feelings may continue through young adult lives" (pp. 18–19)

"Touching yourself sexually, or masturbation, is something you may enjoy and feel good about. It is a perfectly healthy thing for boys and girls, men and women to do as a way of releasing tension and having physical pleasure." (p.27)

How SIECUS Plans to Advance its Agenda

In his book An End to Shame: Shaping our Next Sexual Revolution, Ira Reiss states that promoting the beliefs espoused by SIECUS will require totalitarian measures:

"To build [sexual] pluralism, we must firmly root-out the narrow thinking about sex that exists in all of our basic institutions—family, political, economic, religious, and educational. We need to change our whole basic social institutional structure . . . . We don't need a majority of the nation in order to make significant changes in our society. We need only a small percentage of the population who are dedicated to promoting all of our sexual rights."

The People behind SIECUS

Here are some of the founding members of SIECUS:

Mary Calderone left her position at Planned Parenthood to become the first director of SIECUS.

Harriet Pilpel was vice chairman of the national board of directors of the ACLU

Lester Kirkendall was the 1966 director of the American Humanist Association, a staff member of Sexology magazine, and active in Planned Parenthood.

Wardell Pomeroy was coauthor of the 1948 Kinsey male sexuality study.

Deryk Calderwood was a prohomosexual consultant to committees establishing sex education programs in public schools.

Who Endorses SIECUS?

Some of the organizations that endorse all or part of the SEICUS agenda may surprise you—others won't. Here's a sampling:

- AIDS Action Council
- American Association of Sex Educators,Counselors, and Thera-pists
- American Association of University Women
- American Association on Mental Retardation
- American Medical Association
- American School Health Association
- Catholics for a Free Choice
- Child Welfare League of America
- Girls Incorporated
- Human Rights Campaign Fund
- National Abortion Federation
- National Abortion Rights Action League
- National Association of School Psychologists
- National Council of the Churches of Christ, Commission on Fam-ily Ministries and Human Sexuality
- National Education Association Health Information Network
- National Lesbian and Gay Health Association
- Parents, Families, and Friends of Lesbians and Gays
- Planned Parenthood Federation of America
- Society for Adolescent Medicine
- Society for the Scientific Study of Sex
- Unitarian Universalist Association
- Y.W.C.A. of the U.S.A.

The above article should give one some idea of the tremendous in-roads that the homosexual movement has made into the mainstream of our society. The organizations backing the immoral trash put out by SEICUS are astounding. It also should give a person some understand-ing why many conservatives, such as Judge Robert Bork, refer to the "liberal elite" as a primary force in the demoralizing of America. Has this country indeed sunk so far into the mire that we cannot recover?

Following are excerpts from **The Homosexual Agenda:** *How the Gay Lobby is Targeting America's Children,* Americans for Truth About Homosexuality, A Division of the Christian Defense Fund, Washing-ton. D.C., 1997:

Universities Defend Profs Linked to Pedophile Journal

Two professors who sit on the editorial board of "PAIDIKA: The Journal of Pedophilia" received the backing of their employers.

On December 9, 1993, in response to a reporter's inquiry, Hunter College of the City University of New York released a statement in defense of Professor Wayne Dynes, who teaches art history at the college. Dynes had told Focus on the Family magazine Citizen (November 16, 1992) that he was "not sure that a 7 year old can give informed consent. That doesn't mean that one should necessarily exclude sexual relations with them."

"An intergenerational sexual relationship could be and should be character building," said Dynes citing a male friend in Thailand who has a 17 year old boyfriend.

The Hunter College statement said Dynes, who has taught at the school since 1972, "has an unblemished record of classroom performance and conduct. Professor Dynes has never been charged with inappropriate conduct of any kind by any student or colleague during his tenure at this institution."

The statement goes on to say that "the opinions of faculty members, like those of all Americans, are constitutionally protected."

It says that as long as professors fulfill their obligations to the university and refrain from illegal conduct, "the extracurricular expression of ideas has no bearing on a faculty member's status."

At San Francisco State, university officials offered a more detailed response defending psychology professor John DeCecco's involvement with PAIDIKA, which is published in Amsterdam. The Dutch Pedophile journal exchanges ads with the NAMBLA Bulletin, the mouthpiece of the North American Man/Boy Love Association. Its founding statement of purpose in 1987 states that the "oppression of pedophilia is part of the larger repression of sexuality ... Through publication of scholarly studies ... we intend to demonstrate that pedophilia has been, and remains, a legitimate and productive part of the totality of human experience."

DeCecco came under attack by a group of child abuse survivors after a college newspaper reported his involvement with PAIDIKA. San Francisco State's public relations office released a letter on DeCecco's behalf by Joseph Julian, Dean of the School of Behavioral and Social Science—to which DeCecco belongs. Julian said after reviewing PAIDIKA that it is a "bona fide scholarly publication."

Julian said published interviews in the Journal of Pedophilia have been both critical and supportive of pedophilia. "Under the circumstances," he wrote, "Dr. DeCecco's involvement with the journal PAIDIKA is in keeping with the academic enterprise ... The principle of academic freedom must be preserved."

Another professor at San Francisco State who is also on PAIDIKA's editorial board, Hubert Kennedy, writes for the NAMBLA Bulletin. In the Bulletin's September 1995 issue, Kennedy penned an essay about Robert Turner, a.k.a. "Rob the Artist," a fellow NAMBLA enthusiast whose etched drawings of young boys were popular among pedophiles. Turner recently committed suicide at age 35. (pp. 16–17)

Pro-Homosexual Propaganda in the Schools

America's schools—public and private—have become the new frontier of homosexual activism. Homosexual teachers, aided by the ACLU, the National Education Association, and other left-leaning groups, demand the "right" to be openly homosexual in the classroom. A new group called the Gay, Lesbian and Straight Teachers Network (GLSTN) promotes homosexual-affirming policies in schools, using the argument that "gay kids" will kill themselves or drop out if their homosexual "identity" is not validated. ('Gay' activists routinely use a bogus statistic—that "one third" of all youth suicides are by "gay youth"—as part of their efforts to promote the victimization of alleged homosexuals in the schools. A leading expert on youth suicide has criticized the 30 percent figure as arising from "hocus pocus math.") A new video, It's Elementary, documents the efforts of homosexuals and their allies to indoctrinate young children with pro-"gay" messages. Views opposed to homosexuality are not presented; worse, they are caricatured by pro-homosexual educators as "bigotry" or "hatred." For the next decade and beyond, it is clear that schools will be the major battlefield in the culture war over homosexuality in America.

Head of Homosexual Teachers Group Lays Out
Victim Strategy for Schools

The leader of a growing homosexual teachers groups said that the key to passing a landmark student "gay rights" law in Massachusetts was framing the issue around "child safety" and "safe schools"—a strategy which had pro-family critics "backpedaling from day one."

Kevin Jennings, the executive director of the Gay, Lesbian & Straight Teachers Network (GLSTN), based in New York City, said in a 1995 speech that the "safe schools" strategy paved the way for quick passage of Massachusetts' precedent-setting "gay rights" law for public schools in 1994. Other states and localities are now trying to pass similar measures.

"We immediately seized upon the opponents' calling card—safety—explained how homophobia represents a threat to students' safety by creating a climate where violence, name-calling, health problems, and suicide are common," Jennings said in a speech to the homosexual activist group Human Rights Campaign last year. ... (pp. 28–29)

As we saw in Chapter 1, a large percentage of homosexuals have engaged in sex with under-aged young people. It appears that pedophilia is an integral part of homosexuality. We also see that, for purposes of public acceptance, some of the mainstream homosexual organizations have tried to make it appear that they do not subscribe to pedophilia. From my own studies, I consider it clear beyond any reasonable doubt that this is a deception and a false front put on for political purposes. What they do and say among themselves, and write for homosexual publications, gives us a better perspective of where the truth lies.

As I have previously indicated, it is indeed sickening to me the way homosexuals use the word, love, when speaking of filthy homosexual sex acts. This in itself shows a serious psychosis and sickness of mind.

In March, 1994, Colorado for Family Values, submitted a position analysis on pedophilia with its news letter. (*CFV Report*, March 1994) The following is information from the analysis, entitled: **Pedophilia—the Part of Homosexuality They Don't Want You to See.**

- Some quotations were included. One was from the writing of "Michael Swift," which I quoted at the beginning of Chapter 1.
- **The following are others:**
- **"The love between men and boys is at the foundation of homosexuality. For the gay community to imply that boy-love is not homosexual love is ridiculous."**

- "No Place for Homo-Homophobia," letter to the editor, *San Francisco Sentinel*, March 26, 1992.

"**The age of consent is just one of many ways in which adults impose their system of control on children.**" NAMBLA quoted in Shirley J. O'Brien's article "The Child Molester," *National Federation for Decency Journal*, May/June 1987, pp. 9–11.

"**How many gay men, I wonder, would have missed out on a valuable, liberating experience — one that initiated them into their sexuality — if it weren't for so-called molestation?**"

—Carl Maves, "Getting Over It," *The Advocate*, 5 May 1992, p. 85.

"**Boy-lovers and the lesbians who have young lovers . . . are not child molesters. The child abusers are priests, teachers, therapists, cops and parents who force their staid morality onto the young people in their custody.**"

—Pat Califia's essay, "Man/Boy Love and the Lesbian/Gay Movement," *The Age Taboo: Gay Male Sexuality, Power and Consent* (Boston and London: Alyson Publications/Gay Men's Press, 1981), p. 144.

The following are other excerpts from the position analysis:

The facts

Evidence showing that pedophilia is in fact a common part of the homosexual lifestyle is staggering. Ironically, most of it comes from homosexuals themselves. In *Gay Report*, for instance, a survey of gay attitudes and behavior by homosexual researchers Jay and Young, revealed data showing that 73% of homosexuals surveyed had at some time had sex with boys sixteen to nineteen years of age or younger. (K. Jay and A. Young, *The Gay Report* [New York Summit Books, 1979], p. 275)

The Journal *Psychological Reports* revealed that homosexuals, while representing perhaps 2% of the population perpetrate more than one-third of all reported child molestations. (*Psychological Reports*, 1986, vol. 58, pp. 327–337)

[Here this CFV Analysis cites statistics covered in Chapter 1 in this book about the many attacks by homosexual scout leaders against boy scouts.] ...The Boy Scouts spend nearly $50,000 per month in litigation against their attackers — in case you were wondering why they are so adamant on the subject.

[Here the CFV Analysis covers statistics compiled by Dr. Judith Reisman, and on a study of Canadians imprisoned for pedophilia;

showing the disproportionately big percentage of attacks by homosexuals on young people—particularly boys. These statistics were also covered in Chapter 1.]

In a desperate attempt to counter these numbers, many homosexual proponents claim that homosexuals are less of a threat to the innocence of the young than heterosexuals, because "heterosexuals commit a majority of child molestations." Many people fail to recall that since heterosexuals make up nearly 98% of society, it would be incredibly surprising if they did not commit a majority of child molestations. What is extraordinary is the disproportionate amount of child molestations committed by homosexuals, *relative to their presence* in the general population. ***

In fact, noted sex researchers Masters and Johnson describe the process of establishing "homophile orientation" as follows:

"In most cases, homophile interests developed in the early midteens . . . There was no history of overt heterosexual experience prior to homophile orientation. Recruitment usually was accomplished by an older male, frequently in his twenties, but occasionally men in their thirties were the initiator. When the homosexual commitment was terminated, in most instances, the relationship was broken by the elder partner. With termination, the teenager was left with the concept that whether or not he continued as an active homosexual, he would always be homophile-oriented." (C. Masters and O. Johnson. *Human Sexual Inadequacy*, [Boston: Little, Brown and Company, 1970], p. 180)

The cover-up

Realizing the incredible public relations disaster pedophiles represent to their cause, homosexual leaders have consistently tried to keep NAMBLA "out of sight" of middle America and to play down their historical association with child abuse.

David Thorstad made this very clear when he complained that pedophilia was being swept under the rug by the gay right movement, which " . . . seeks to sanitize the image of homosexuality to facilitate its entrance into the social mainstream." Thorstad also writes that "The issue of man-boy love has intersected the gay movement since the late nineteenth century." ("Man-Boy Love and the American Gay Movement," *The Journal of Homosexuality*, 1990, vol. 20, pp. 251–252)

[In part of the Position Analysis omitted here, material is quoted from *The Overhauling of Straight America*, which was referred to in the first part of this chapter.]

The point is clear: homosexual activists know full well how prevalent pedophilia is in their midst. They merely want to hide it until public acceptance is high enough to safely acknowledge it.

The Push for "Pedophile Rights"

It should come as no surprise, then, that militant homosexual manifestos, such as "The 1972 Gay Rights Platform," have consistently called upon governments to: (1) "Repeal all state laws prohibiting private sexual acts involving consenting persons [not consenting adults]," and (2) "Repeal all laws governing the age of sexual consent." ...

On May 27, 1993, *Washington Times* reported that the University of Massachusetts at Amherst had revised its non-discrimination policy to protect "persons whose sexual orientation includes minor children as the sex object." (PC 101, *Washington Times*, 27 May 1992, p. B-1)

Dr. John Money, a retired professor of medical psychology and pediatrics at Johns Hopkins University, was quoted as saying, " . . . pedophilia should be viewed as a sexual orientation, not a disease or disorder." (Michael Ebert, "Pedophilia Steps into the Daylight," *Focus on the Family Citizen*, 16 November 1992, vol. 6, no. 11, pp. 6–8)

The same article quotes John DeCecco, head of the Human Sexuality Program at San Francisco State University, as telling his students that "adult-child sex" is a legitimate expression of sexuality.
The 31st Annual Conference of the Society of the Scientific Study of Sex featured an "expert" on sex offenders and child sex abuse who argued that pedophilia may be an "orientation," not a perversion. She also suggested that pedophiles, too, have sexual rights. (*New York Post*, 20 October 1990)

Humm, a leading gay activist and "outreach coordinator" for the Hetrick Martin Institute, an organization for gay youth that runs the Harvey Milk school, a public school in New York City for "homosexual youth," says the following: ". . . I led the fight to draft what is known as the lesbian and gay rights bill in the [New York] City Council to remove limiting definitions from the term sexual orientation that we hope to add to the list of protected statuses. No one should be denied basic civil rights because of his or her orientation, whether the person be homosexual, heterosexual, transsexual, transvestite, pedophile, sadist, masochist, asexual — whatever one can imagine." (Andy Humm, "National Variations" letter to the editor, *New York Times*, 1–4 August 1983)

As these statements prove, pedophilia is not only a basic part of the homosexual lifestyle, it's also one of the most frightening aspects of their political agenda.

We see the exact same arguments being made for the acceptance of pedophilia as for homosexuality generally. If our downward trend in morality continues, it is only a matter of time until the public is indoctrinated and desensitized into its acceptance.

The homosexual agenda is to convince society that homosexual perversion is acceptable, and to make it legally safe for homosexuals to practice their perversions of all kinds—including child molestation. A direct and, unfortunately for our society, a highly successful attack has been launched against our schools, at all levels, from pre-kindergarten to the universities.

Time and space will not allow a complete coverage of just the material available on the poisonous infiltration of our schools with homosexuals and their propaganda. Because it is in the schools, the backbone of our society, it is extremely devastating and destructive.

Not only does the propaganda have its desired effect of convincing students that homosexuality is acceptable, and desirable, but it recruits young people into that vile and destructive perversion. This is an integral part of the homosexual movement. A good example is the Newsweek magazine article referred to above about the "Coming Out Day" in a Massachusetts school. The ideas presented that these programs are merely to help children recognize their "identity" is insidious and false.

The great battleground in the war against the homosexual movement is in the schools. The students are the future leaders who will shape this country. If we lose the battle here, we will see the ultimate completion of the destruction of the moral base of this country. And I believe it will literally destroy our American civilization—just as surely as homosexuality and its related decadence led to the destruction of the Third Reich and the Roman Empire.

In addition, the public in general is now being subjected to the greatest brainwashing in American history—by the government and by the media. The most insidious and subversive is by the media—both news and entertainment. A recent example, in June, 1998, was the ballet **Swan Lake** on public television. The ballet—the redoing of an old and well-known Russian ballet—treated us to scenes of half-clad men dancing together and embracing. It was shown on prime-time television, with no warning to the public or parents of the filthy content. Such onslaughts have been continuous. Sadly, we are becoming desensitized to the hideous aspects of homosexuality.

There was much in the news in 1996 and 1997 about the legacy of President Clinton. I respectfully submit that his primary legacy—if not his only legacy—will be the destruction done to America by his promotion of sodomy.

CHAPTER 7

THE AMAZING SUCCESS OF THE HOMOSEXUAL MOVEMENT

P rior chapters, particularly the ones on our decline in morality and on the homosexual agenda, necessarily show the great success of the movement. Nevertheless, a few things will be added in this chapter to help show the true extent of that success.

It was amazing, from material in the prior chapter, to see the list of the organizations that support the radical, immoral, and harmful SEICUS organization. The greatest destruction to our society is the pervasive and controlling immorality in so many of our schools, and particularly in the institutions of higher learning. The federal government has become our largest single promoter of sodomy. State and local governments, and quasi-government organizations, of all kinds and at all levels, have been infiltrated and influenced.

However, the homosexual devastation that has occurred to this country is not just the fault of the homosexual activists, President Clinton, and his government officials. They had to have either the help or the apathy of Congress, and of state and local legislators, politicians, and officials. And what is the most disheartening, they had either the help or the apathy of a great part of the people. Some have been fooled by the propaganda on discrimination and equal treatment. Some seem not to care about our moral destruction, as long as they have a job and the economy seems in good shape. Others are so devoid of morality, that they either see nothing wrong with sodomy, or they take the attitude that "what a person does in private is his own business." Such an attitude is not supported by logic—most immoral acts are done in private. And some, such as sodomy, incest. and adultery should never be condoned, and have been considered unacceptable throughout civilized history. Others of us just do not have the moral courage to stand up against the onslaught.

Let me give you an example of how smoothly and efficiently the homosexualists have operated, in just one small area—the almost unnoticed infiltrating of the New Mexico State Bar, and the changing of the rules of conduct for attorneys.

Sodomy was made a felony, by statute, in New Mexico in the Laws of 1876, soon after New Mexico became a territory of the United States, and before it became a state. Sodomy remained a felony in New Mexico after statehood, and until the statute then making it a felony was repealed in 1975. This repeal was a result of the lobbying and influence of the homosexual activists. The homosexualists in the late 1980s began trying to get "gay rights" bills passed, but the citizens of the state were not yet too demoralized to object, and a number of them made known their opposition; and so far, no such bill has been passed in New Mexico. But the skirting activities of the homosexualists, and their successes at the local levels, and in various schools, have been described. They never stop.

I am licensed to practice law in both New Mexico and Texas. Pursuant to a recommendation of the New Mexico State Bar Association, the New Mexico Supreme Court unanimously approved, in December 1993, the following Rule to become effective January 1, 1994:

16-300 Prohibition against invidious discrimination.
In the course of any judicial or quasi-judicial proceeding before a tribunal, a lawyer shall refrain from intentionally manifesting, by words or conduct, bias or prejudice based on race, gender, religion, national origin, disability, age, or sexual orientation against the judge, court personnel, parties, witnesses, counsel or others. This rule does not preclude legitimate advocacy when race, gender, religion, national origin, disability, age or sexual orientation is material to the issues in the proceeding.

[In the State Bar Commentary on the rule, the following was included: "For purposes of this rule, the term 'sexual orientation' shall mean heterosexuality, bisexuality or homosexuality."]

It had puzzled me how such a thing would have been recommended by the State Bar Association, and then approved by the New Mexico Supreme Court. I had no idea that the homosexualists had infiltrated our bar and gained this kind of influence.

On May 5, 1994, a small article appeared in the *New Mexico State Bar Bulletin*, entitled, "Conference on Legal Issues Affecting Lesbian, Gay Men and Families." I then realized what must have been going on within the New Mexico Bar Association. We who were apathetic and depended on our elected State Bar directors to look after our interests soon learned the error of our ways and got what we deserved. The article stated in part:

> The State Bar's Family Law Section and the National Lesbian and Gay Law Association are sponsoring the Southwest Regional Conference on Legal Issues Affecting Lesbians, Gay Men, and Their Families .... The conference will be held at the La Posada Hotel in Albuquerque.
>
> An impressive list of local and national featured speakers includes Paula Ettelbrick, attorney and director of Public Policy for the National Center for Lesbian Rights in New York City; Abby Abinanti, attorney and legal director for the National Center for Lesbian Rights in San Francisco; Mauro Montoya, attorney and advisor to the Legislation Clinic, in Washington, D.C.; Suzanne Goldberg, attorney with the Lambda Legal Defense and Educational Fund in New York City; and Jeanne Winer, lead counsel in the challenge of Colorado's Amendment 2. These and other speakers will discuss issues relating to family law (domestic relations including custody and adoption), employment, mediation, estate planing policy, constitutional, AIDS, and ant-gay initiatives. ***

All of these things together made it quite obvious that while most good decent members of the bar were attending to their caseloads, and trying to take care of their law practices and their families, the homosexualists had infiltrated and influenced our organization for some time.

In April 1994 a similar provision was proposed to the Texas Bar, and the most disheartening thing is that it was approved by a vote of the membership.

For over a hundred years, lawyers had been practicing in Texas and New Mexico, and never before was there such a provision. For many years, both federal and state civil rights acts had been in place—although not yet has there been one including "sexual orientation" in either state. There is no doubt whatsoever that the same thing was either happening or being attempted in other states along about the same time. Never before had there been such provisions restricting and making "politically correct" the conduct of attorneys. Of course there is no doubt that, as always, the homosexuals would have enlisted the help of all of the civil rights groups, minority groups, and unions that they could get to support them.

It is indeed frightening that the homosexual brainwashing of America is even going on in our courts and in our attorney bar associations. These are, above all, organizations that should be guarding our freedom of religion and freedom of speech, and not trying to eliminate such rights by these insidious actions.

Things like these rules may seem unimportant, when the effect of just one provision is viewed alone—but even one such freedom destroyed is highly detrimental to our society. And the real purpose—and the big thing that is being accomplished—is that we are having sodomy crammed down our throat by those practicing it—with the help of those in official positions who succumb to their influence.

For most of the history of our country, homosexuality was a felony, almost universally, and certainly it was universally considered immoral conduct. It would have been grounds for refusal to admit an applicant to the bar, and could have resulted in disbarment. In New Mexico, as in the other states, one of the requirements for being admitted to and remaining in the attorneys' bar is the requirement that the applicant "is a person of good moral character." However, as previously stated, in our modern time, this has largely become a joke; and this has been helped along by decisions of the courts, including the United States Supreme Court, holding that qualification requirements must have a rational connection with the applicants fitness to practice law. Such a decision leaves the field wide open for most any liberal interpretation a court or an organization may wish to adopt.

Liberal courts have for the last thirty years continually trampled reason, logic, and the rights of the people of this country to govern themselves. Consider the following from an article by James J. Kilpatrick, in the *Albuquerque Journal*, 1-12-89:

Humpty-Dumpty Decision Shatters Logic

WASHINGTON—There is mighty little difference, when you come to think about it, between Humpty-Dumpty on the wall and a federal judge upon the bench. The resemblance was remarkably illustrated last month in a case involving Congress, the District of Columbia and U.S. District Judge Royce C. Lamberth. The case has meaning beyond the Potomac.

These were the circumstances. In 1977, the D.C. City Council, which is perhaps the most liberal legislative body this side of Sweden, adopted a Human Rights Act. The law undertakes to prohibit discrimination on every conceivable ground including "sexual orientation." Because Georgetown University benefits from public funds, the university was caught within the law's embrace.

But Georgetown is an institution closely affiliated with the Roman Catholic Church. The church's teaching on the matter of homosexuality is explicit: Homosexuality is a mortal sin, condemned by God's commandments. Nevertheless, a Gay Rights Coalition sprang up at Georgetown. Citing the Human Rights Act, the group demanded the same recognition, facilities and support the university accords to other student groups.

The university understandably refused ... .

[The students sued and won in the district court and the court of appeals.]

Colorado's Sen. Bill Armstrong found the decision outrageous. He successfully introduced an amendment to the D.C. Appropriations Act. His amendment directed the District to adopt a further law providing that religious institutions could not be required to accommodate any group organized to promote a homosexual lifestyle. Failure to adopt this further law would cost the district its $3.2 billion federal appropriation.

[All thirteen Members of the D.C. Council sued.]

[Judge Lamberth held that the council had a constitutional right to vote freely. That decision was on appeal at the time of the article.]

You will recall Humpty-Dumpty's magisterial assertion in "Through the Looking Glass": "When I use a word it means what I choose it to mean – neither more nor less." The colloquy continued:

"The question is," said Alice, "whether you can make words mean so many different things."

"The question is," said Humpty-Dumpty, "which is to be master—that's all." ***

There is no such thing as a constitutional right for the council of the District of Columbia to "vote freely," contrary to the wishes of Congress, which has control over that district; and have Congress forced to appropriate money to be used in whatever wrongful manner the council wishes. And it is the judge's decision that is clearly beyond his constitutional powers. For many years, it has been well established that Congress can pass appropriations with requirements attached as a prerequisite for its use. It is continually done with the states and with the District of Columbia. Such actions by a liberal court are exactly why so many homosexualists resort to them, and, as they did in this case, they have had many successes.

By the end of March 1995, homosexualists (including President Clinton) had substantial control of the executive branch of our federal government. As shown by publications referred to in Chapter 4, by March 13, 1995, twenty-six homosexuals had been appointed to the Clinton administration, and more such appointments were expected. Federal agencies adopted programs to brainwash federal employees and military personnel into accepting sodomy as morally equal to heterosexuality.

The U.S. Senate, in many instances, capitulated to the homosexual agenda. It even approved the appointment of Roberta Achtenberg as assistant secretary for fair housing in the Department of Housing and Urban Development. Her blatant lesbianism, and her attacks on the Boy Scouts in California seemed to meet the approval of the majority. This was even though Republican Senators Jesse Helms of North Carolina, Trent Lott of Mississippi, and Malcolm Wallop of Wyoming spoke against her on the Senate floor, depicting her as an intolerant, radical homosexual rights extremist bent on foisting her views on others (*The Albuquerque Tribune*, 5-20-93).

It appears that two of the most important elements of modern liberalism are lack of morals and lack of courage. Its complete capitulation to the homosexual movement conclusively establish these two elements. Not only has this been evident with the successes of homosexuals in the Clinton administration, and in the Democratic Party, it is equally true in the entertainment media, and in the news media.

Gay and lesbian journalists: Quota favorites (by Brent Bozell)

... The National Lesbian and Gay Journalists Association (NLGJA) held their second convention in New York recently, touting the fact that 20 major media organizations sent recruiting agents forth to hire their quota of homosexual journalists. The list included ABC, NBC, Associated Press (print and broadcast), the Los Angeles Times, the Washington Post, the New York Times, Newsday, the Philadelphia Inquirer and Gannett, the owner of USA Today. Almost all the heavy-weights—Dan Rather, Tom Brokaw, Robert MacNeil, Judy Woodruff—turned out to pay homage to their cause.

MAKE NO MISTAKE: Gay journalists are being hired precisely because they are gay. *Washington Post* media reporter Howard Kurtz suggested, "The brisk traffic (at the job fair) suggested that being gay is now a plus for newsroom managers who previously limited their minority outreach efforts to blacks, Hispanics, and Asians. *** (*Conservative Chronicle*, 1-6-93)

Unmarried couples get legal status

NEW YORK CITY — Six weeks after Mayor David N. Dinkins signed an executive order enabling heterosexual and homosexual couples to register as unmarried "domestic partners" and receive some of the rights of married couples, the City Clerk's office Monday began conducting the registration.

In a short process in the Municipal Building, couples filled out a few forms, presented identification and received a certificate similar to a marriage license.

Under the mayor's executive order, registered domestic partners employed by the city are entitled to the same unpaid leave that has been available to city workers who are married and wish to care for a new child. Also, registered domestic partners will have the same rights as married spouses in visiting partners at municipal hospitals and city jails.

In addition, registered domestic partners will be entitled to the same standing as married couples in qualifying for apartments and in inheriting a lease in residential buildings owned or overseen by city housing agencies, including rent-controlled and rent-stabilized apartments. (*The Albuquerque Tribune*, 3-2-93)

On January 29, 1993, in the *MacNeil-Lehrer Newshour*, on public television, there was a panel discussion with four of their regular newspaper editors from around the country about lifting the ban against homosexuals in the military. All were for lifting the ban. This contrasted with polls of the American people at that time, all of which showed that public opinion was strongly against allowing homosexuals in the military, as were members of the military. This has been typical of all of the liberal media—which is most of the media. They have been well sodomized from the start by the homosexual movement.

Lt. Col. Robert L. Maginnis (U.S. Army, retired) was a policy analyst for the Family Research Council and served on the 1993 Army study group that investigated the issue of homosexuals in the military and advised the Pentagon's task force that wrote the present "don't ask, don't tell" policy on homosexuals in the military. He also testified in the case of Army Col. Margarethe Cammermeyer, who was discharged in 1992 for telling a security investigator that she was a lesbian. Col. Maginnis wrote the article, **NBC Offers Aid and Comfort To Subverters of Civilization**, which is an article criticizing NBC for its pro-homosexual show, **"Serving in Silence: The Margarethe Cammermeyer Story."** Ms. Cammermeyer is a lesbian Army colonel, who was serving in the National Guard as a nurse. She deserted her husband and children to pursue her homosexuality and lesbian activism.

A federal judge labeled the colonel's discharge "grounded solely on prejudice." (This is the kind of statement that a liberal judge constantly uses in place of valid legal reasoning. Sodomy remains a criminal offense in the Uniform Code of Military Justice, because those who have the authority to make the law consider such acts sufficiently reprehensible and destructive to military life. A judge has only the authority to interpret the law—he has no authority to change the law because he may think it is based on prejudice.)

The show amounts to only one more instance of the media trying to sell us the homosexual political agenda and it is a frontal attack on pro-family truth and morality.

The article details the following falsities and distortions:

- *The military's ban is portrayed as being based on prejudice and having little support.* In fact, Congress affirmed the ban's rational basis and so do most Americans and soldiers.

- *"Experts" and Pentagon reports are alleged to contradict the policy.* The "experts" are sympathetic gay activists and the "reports" have either been debunked or misrepresented.

- *Homosexuality is portrayed as a harmless quirk of nature and homosexuals are said to make up 10% of the military*—a totally discredited estimate.

"NBC has used a biased movie to promote the homosexual political agenda."

The following were the advertisers that supported the airing of the movie: **AT&T, Block Drug Co.** (X-14 cleaner), **British Aerospace** (Land Rover), **Burlington Coat Factory, Cosmair, Inc.** (L'Oreal hair products), **Dow Chemical, Duracell, Foulds, Inc.**, (No-yolk egg noodles), **General Motors, Grand Metropolitan, Inc.**, (Pillsbury foods), **Honda, Isuzu, La-Z-Boy Furniture, Miles, Inc.** (Alka-Seltzer), **National Dairy Board, PepsiCo.** (Mountain Dew), **Phillip Morris Companies** (Kraft and Tombstone pizza), **Revlon, Scott's Liquid Gold, Inc.** (Alpha Hydrox), **Sears, Roebouck and Co., Slimfast Foods Co., Unilever United States, Inc.** (Calvin Klein cosmetics), **Warner-Lambert Co.** (Halls cough drops), **Whirlpool Corp.** (*Human Events*, 2-17-95)

Since the movement, the homosexualists have continually gotten newspapers and magazines to publish lengthy stories about homosexuals, young "gay" people, AIDS, and sex education. The regular line used is one hundred percent consistent with the agenda. It either praises homosexuals or continually gets the matters before the public in a neutral manner. They exactly follow the brainwashing plan of propaganda. Let us consider a very few of the many examples of the continual barrage.

In the 1990s, the homosexuals gained the all-out assistance of national media in the spreading and promotion of their agenda of propaganda. A good example is the Associated Press article, **A Social Shift Occurring On Playing Field,** by Steve Wilstein, published in the *Albuquerque Journal*, on 6-21-95. Please note all of the homosexual buzzwords in the italicized leadoff paragraph:

> **A TV commentator's reported remarks about lesbians in the LPGA ignites a storm of controversy. A gay major leaguer's death from AIDS revives allegations of homophobia in baseball. Homosexuality in sports is gaining acceptance, albeit more slowly than in the fields of entertainment and politics. Amid gay pride celebrations in New York this week, the issue still evokes passion, fear and ignorance among athletes, spectators and sponsors.**

A leadoff subheading states: **Homosexuality Is Now Part of Sports**. This is repeated on the second page. The article takes up most of two newspaper pages, and has four color pictures of sports figures, and a black-and-white picture of the diver Greg Louganis. The color pictures are of Martina Navratilova, the lesbian tennis player; Beth Daniels, the golfer, who "refuses to answer questions about her sexual preference;" the baseball player Glenn Burke, who came out in the 1970s; and "Spain's Conchita Martinez," "whose relationship with fellow player Gigi Fernandez is an 'open secret' on the women's (tennis) tour." The following leading paragraphs aptly reflect the homosexual degradation into which we have fallen, and which is considered laudable by the national media:

> EAST LANSING, MICH.—Two young women lay languidly in the sun along the 18th fairway, T-shirts rolled up above their bellies, arms and legs braided in a casual embrace.
>
> Beth Daniels, and the gallery that followed her at this LPGA tournament, paid no attention to the couple. On a Sunday when about half of the 27,000 spectators were lesbians, walking around together, holding hands, hugging and kissing, nothing about this couple seemed unusual. ***

The gist of the article is that breaking the "homosexual barrier" is similar to breaking the "color barrier" earlier in sports. All of the usual homosexualist sales words, "passion, fear, ignorance, and homophobia," are used for the purpose of convincing us that the deviants should be considered normal, and their acts of sodomy commendable; and that if we who are normal think otherwise, then we are the ones who are abnormal.

We have continuously been subjected to this false propaganda from all of the media—both news and entertainment. It takes intelligence and a deep moral base to withstand it. And, unfortunately, not many of our young people are so equipped.

It appears to me that the false propaganda war to which we are being subjected is very similar in nature to the sale of the Nazi movement in Germany in the 1930s. The same methods are being used, and it is every bit as insidious, false, and destructive.

Knight-Ridder Newspapers, another nationwide news source for newspapers, was once considered a dependable purveyor of the news. But since the homosexual movement, it has become one of the foremost organizations for propagandizing the public with the homosexual agenda. An example is an article by Lori Teresa Yearwood of that organization, **"Finding a home in A HOUSE—Alienated gay youths discover acceptance, sense of family in nontraditional community of support."** According to the article, it is about a "family" of thirty-four "gay" teen-agers and young adults, both male and female, who live in a townhouse known as "The House of Lords." These are excerpts from the article:

> *** Together they offer one alternative of family life in the '90s. ***
>
> "The kids in the house scene have created a completely supportive culture for gay youths," says Freddy Gonzales, an outreach educator for the Health Crisis Network in Miami ... . ***
>
> The 1991 movie "Paris is Burning," which documented the daily lives of a group of house drag queens in New York, was a breakthrough vehicle. ...
>
> The first South Florida house was formed four years ago. Today there are six, all in Dade: the House of Lords, the House of Infiniti, the House of Xcentricka, the House of Righteous Shade, the House of Elegance, the House of Independence.

The houses have their own lingo, their own fund-raisers (often for local AIDS groups)—and their own brand of entertainment, the dance competitions that Salt-N-Pepa sing about.

These are the height of house culture.

"You get to prance around, you get to be cute and everybody adores you," says [Alexis] Rodrigues. ***

[Relating to their big attractions, the "balls":]

Men dress like women. Women dress like men. They dance like Madonna and walk down a runway like Iman. ***

There is a price for the unconditional acceptance: Heroin is an admitted problem among some kids, as is unprotected sex.

Rodrigues sees his tolerance of dangerous behaviors as a trade-off for keeping the kids off the streets. He knows he can't make them stop. "I'm their father, but I'm not really their father." So he does what he can, he says. He makes sure for instance, that a bowl full of condoms sits to the right of his townhouse's front door.

When he senses things are getting out of hand, he threatens to "chop" his kids—housespeak for kicking them out. But pressed to mention a single name of someone he axed, he couldn't.

"We're family," he says. *** (*Albuquerque Journal*, 1-17-97)

The above article took up most of two pages of the newspaper, with pictures of drag queens. It has previously been stated that we have videos of things going on in cities in this country that are worse than anything depicted in the Bible relating to Sodom and Gomorrah. Consider the group sodomy that you know goes on in the "houses" described. It seems to me that they are similar to the "bathhouses" previously discussed, only of a more permanent nature. Yet it appears that they have become tolerated in the communities involved—if not completely accepted. And the obvious purpose of such articles is desensitizing us into complete acceptance. It is certainly our doorway to Sodom and Gomorrah. How much lower can we sink? And more importantly, how many of us are fighting against these things?

We are bombarded with the same kind of tripe in stories in our national news magazines and on television—including public television.

The power of the "gay" community grows. Money talks. Companies engaging in national advertising of their products reach out to the homosexuals. They try to please them and sell products to them. In

October 1994, Associated Press articles were published in both Albuquerque newspapers, and I am sure in newspapers around the country, with titles such as : **Advertisers reaching out to gay consumers.**

Even *The Wall Street Journal*, 5-1-95, had an article: **Big Business Boosts Effort to Win Share of Gay Market.**

The power of the homosexual lobby grows.

> **Senate rejects AIDS law:** The U.S. Senate voted without debate Tuesday to overturn a month-old law that requires the mandatory discharge of members of the armed forces who test positive for the virus that causes AIDS. (*The Albuquerque Tribune*, 3-20-96)

President Clinton had threatened a veto when the bill was first passed. (*Albuquerque Journal*, 12-19-95) He later signed it because it was attached to an appropriations bill. (*Albuquerque Journal*, 2-10-96)

At one time, the armed services could discipline or discharge a person who acquired a venereal disease. But to accommodate the homosexualists, changes have been made that subject other servicemen to the deadliest sexually transmitted disease known. It could be transmitted by the blood of an HIV positive person in the battlefield and elsewhere. It has also been established that the virus can be in other body fluids, such as tears and saliva. As has previously been noted, all of the ways of contracting AIDS are not yet known. This lack of knowledge, I believe, can also be attributed in part to the same homosexualists who do not want others protected from those who have AIDS, by use of disclosure and tracing.

In many localities, and in many instances, not only have we lost the right to take moral character into consideration when determining with whom we associate, and with whom we deal; but where homosexuals and AIDS are involved, we have lost the right to refuse to handle, associate with, and treat a person who poses a danger to us. In the case of doctors and dentists—their rights to refuse treatment to persons who may be a danger to them or to their other patients have been taken away.

Dentist Pays for Discrimination

> WASHINGTON — A dentist who refused to treat two HIV-positive patients will pay $120,000 in damages under a settlement worked out Tuesday by the Justice Department.

Dr. Drew Morvant of New Orleans will pay $60,000 to Russell Hodgkinson and $60,00 to the family of Ismael Pena, who died from AIDS in 1993, the department announced.

On March 23, the U.S. District Court in New Orleans found Morvant had violated the Americans with Disabilities Act by discriminating against people with the HIV virus or with AIDS, which the virus causes, by refusing to treat them or referring them to other dentists because of their HIV-positive status. (*Albuquerque Journal*, 6-14-95)

We are slowly but surely losing our once cherished freedoms – of speech, of religion, freedom of association, and even the right to protect ourselves from disease. The homosexualists even want to give us training to eliminate our "homophobia" and "heterosexualism"—we must have sensitivity training to instill in us the knowledge that sodomy is indeed a respected and good thing—that it should even be celebrated. Are we just before having the "thought police" to enforce these thoughts upon us, until we fully have them in mind sufficiently to please the homosexuals?

TEACHER'S BIBLICAL OPINION CENSURED, by Peter LaBarbera

When Owen O'Malley, a teacher at the prestigious Boston Latin School, took seriously a student newspaper's request for comment on Massachusetts' new Gay and Lesbian Students Rights law, he could not have anticipated the firestorm that would follow.

O'Malley, 56, dispatched a quick letter to the February edition of the *Argo*, the student-run newspaper at Boston Latin, which held a forum on the law banning discrimination in public schools on the basis of "sexual orientation." He wrote that homosexuality is a "great weakness and a sickness" and chastised Republican Gov. William Weld for "promoting homosexual propaganda in the public schools." [The letter also asserted that "adults who engage in homosexual acts are perverse and wicked and extremely dangerous to any society," and also that, "The glory of being a human is that we can change our conduct and overcome our weakness and sins."]

The letter was published in a small corner of the newspaper's letters page, surrounded by others that were hostile (including one that, in the sophomoric fashion typical of student papers, was already "reacting" to O'Malley's words even though they were only then being printed).

... David LaFontaine, a leading homosexual activist in Massachusetts and the outspoken chairman of Gov. Weld's novel Commission on Gay and Lesbian Youth, called a news conference which he said the Boston Latin teacher should be "harshly disciplined for his letter attacking homosexuality. ... and called for O'Mally's dismissal." ***

Pro-family groups in Massachusetts—beleaguered by Gov. Weld's pro-gay and liberal social agenda—rushed to O'Malley's defense. D. J. Doyle, operations director for the Catholic League for Religious and Civil Rights, said the campaign against the Latin reader was "one more example of homosexual intolerance toward the opinions and constitutional rights of the majority." O'Malley, he said, was "merely exercising his First Amendment right to express his moral judgment."

Critics of pro-homosexual legislation say the O'Malley incident is only the latest example of the conflict between the gay political agenda and free speech and association rights. In Canada, a "human rights" ordinance that allows homosexuals to complain to the government about anti-gay speech has had a chilling effect on ministers who preach against homosexuality. And on college campuses across the United States, "sexual orientation" laws are being used to prohibit students assigned a homosexual roommate from finding new dormitory arrangements. ***

After some negotiations between the school district and the teachers' union that represents him, O'Malley said he is awaiting word on a scaled back "reprimand" [for distributing literature it was claimed he distributed about homosexuality) that would expire in a year if there are no further incidents. *** (*Christian American*, July/August, 1994)

This article also related the indoctrination of the students with pro-homosexual propaganda by an event sponsored by the Massachusetts Department of Education and Gov. Weld's Commission on Gay and Lesbian Youth. (In the prior chapter there was discussed similar brainwashing of Massachusetts schoolchildren by these agencies.)

It would appear that our constitutional rights of freedom of speech and freedom of religion are becoming meaningless in Massachusetts—unless you believe in sodomy.

Along with some Protestant churches, it appears that the Reform Jewish religious organizations are capitulating to the homosexual movement, both here and in Israel. As I understand it, all of them have either the Bible, the Hebrew Bible, the Old Testament, or the New Testament, or both the Old Testament and the New Testament, as the basis of their respective religions. And the base of each is considered to be the word of God. Each one contains clear, unequivocal, and unconditional strong condemnation of homosexuality. It is unclear to me how certain "reformers" and "enlightened" mortals acquired the authority to change or disregard this word of God as a part of their religion. This, in itself, is a large part of and one of the reasons for the decline in morality suffered by this country, and by Israel. The capitulation to the homosexual agenda—which is a capitulation to sodomy—allows a terrible desecration of both the religion and the church that succumbs to it. The following is just one example.

Seder for Jewish Gays, Lesbians, Bisexuals

[ALBUQUERQUE] A special Seder for the Jewish lesbian, gay and bisexual community, friends and family members, will be held at 6 p.m. April 16, the third night of Passover, at Congregation Albert ... .

Rabbi Paul Citrin and Cantor Don Croil will read and sing from an "egalitarian" Haggadah at the Seder. *** (*Albuquerque Journal*, 4-1-95)

Instead of capitulating to the homosexual agenda, all churches should be offering help to homosexuals who want to escape their horrible lifestyle, and churches should encourage them to change and lead a decent and constructive life. That would help build our American and traditional values—and it would help enhance our civilization, instead of adding to its ruin.

Israeli Gays Win One in Court

TEL AVIV, Israel — The Supreme Court handed Israel's gay community a major victory Wednesday in a landmark ruling recognizing same-sex couples.

The 50-page decision forces the national airline El Al to grant the boyfriend of flight attendant Jonathan Danielevitz the annual free tickets and other benefits for heterosexual partners of its workers. *** (*Albuquerque Journal*, 12-1-94)

Church To OK Gay Marriages

COPENHAGEN, Denmark — The State Lutheran Church in Denmark, the first country to allow civil marriages of homosexuals, is expected to approve same sex religious marriages, a Christian newspaper reported Friday.

The Kristelig Dagblad, and independent paper which is close to the church, said the church's 12 bishops will be presented with a report by a church-appointed committee on the question next week.

The bishops are expected to approve the report, which recommends allowing homosexual weddings, the newspaper said without citing its sources. (*Albuquerque Journal*, 5-17-97)

Churches Defy Ban On Gays (Santa Fe Presbytery Among Dissenters)

WASHINGTON — Representatives from nine area Presbyterian Church (USA) congregations gathered at a downtown church here recently—on the evening of Pentecost—and vowed to defy a recently approved denominational rule that bars gays and lesbians from holding ordained offices in the church. *** (*Albuquerque Journal*, 5-24-97)

Fuss over anti-gay resolution —
OLYMPIC SITE IS SWITCHED

ATLANTA — After months of controversy over an anti-gay resolution the Atlanta Committee for the Olympic Games today pulled the 1996 volleyball competition out of suburban Cobb County.

Committee officials said the preliminary volleyball rounds instead will be held at the University of Georgia in Athens.

The move came after months of public debate over Cobb County's anti-gay resolution, passed last year, which says the gay lifestyle is incompatible with community standards. Gay activists and some athletes, including former Olympic diving gold-medalist Greg Louganis, had urged ACOG to switch to another venue.
(*The Albuquerque Tribune*, 7-29-94)

Olympic torch will hide its light as a protest of anti-gay stand

COLUMBIA, S.C. — The Olympic flame that has blazed through thousands of communities across the country will be shrouded for part of the journey tonight because of Greenville County's anti-gay resolution.

Organizers decided Monday to carry the torch inside a van from the county line to the city of Greenville, where runners will take it out into the open again to carry it to the city's center. The most vociferous opponents to this resolution are based in the city.

The decision came after the Greenville County Council reaffirmed a resolution passed on May 21 saying homosexuality was incompatible with community standards. *** (*The Albuquerque Tribune*, 6-25-96)

To comply with the agenda, we must now accept sodomy as a community standard.

Seattle church offers job to gay couple

One of Seattle's Protestant churches has voted to hire a gay couple to share a job as associate minister.

After almost two hours of debate at a meeting open only to members of the University Congregational Church, it was announced that 76% of the 624 members who cast ballots voted to hire the two men.

Peter Ilgenfritz, 32, and David Shull, 35, of Chicago, conducted the morning worship service Sunday and waited afterward at the home of a church member as the vote took place at the church. ***

The couple met at Yale Divinity School, where both earned master's degrees. *** (*The Albuquerque Tribune*, 6-12-94)

METHODIST REBELS (About same-sex marriages)

- Trustees of UMC [United Methodist Church] affiliated Emory University in Atlanta recently ruled that same-sex weddings can occur in campus chapels if they involve clergy, faculty, and students from denominations that approve. Emory chaplain Susan Henry-Crowe told reporters that of the two dozen faith groups represented on campus, only the United Church of Christ and the Reform Jewish synagogue now perform such ceremonies. Eight UMC bishops are trustees, and the school's charter places it under the jurisdiction of the denomination.

- Pastor Jimmy Creech of 1,900-member First United Methodist Church, Omaha, Neb., was placed on 60 days suspension with full pay and benefits last month by Nebraska Area Bishop Joel Martinez and a regional ministerial board. Mr. Creech had conducted a lesbian wedding at the church earlier, prompting an outcry among many members and official complaints to the bishop. The United Methodist Book of Discipline prohibits clergy from holding services of union for homosexual couples. ...

- At Princeton University, UMC chaplain Sue Ann Morrow conducted a wedding ceremony at a campus chapel for two homosexuals who were professed atheists. Her bishop, Pittsburgh-based George Bashore, has spoken with her but has taken no administrative action against her. Ms. Morrow has said publicly that she plans to conduct future same-sex ceremonies. ...

- A new caucus group, "Covenant Relationships Network (COR-NET)," has formed to lobby for same-sex marriage in the UMC. It has called on churches to open their facilities to same-sex couples and called on clergy to officiate at same-sex ceremonies as an "essential form of pastoral support." (*World*, 12-20-97)

(However, some Methodist lay leaders and clergy are insisting that the Church take strong action against the blatant defiance of Church and Biblical doctrine.)

The United Methodist Church takes another step downward:

Minister Innocent In Lesbian Ritual

KEARNEY, Neb. — A jury of Methodist ministers ruled Friday that a reverend who performed a lesbian unity ceremony was innocent of disobeying church rules.

Had he been found guilty, the Rev. Jimmy Creech could have lost his position as a senior pastor of Omaha's largest United Methodist Church and be stripped of his ministerial credentials.

The Case was the first challenge to United Methodist policy on homosexual marriage, and the jury's decision could shape how the 9.5 million-member denomination interprets rules governing its treatment of gays. (*Albuquerque Journal*, 3-14-98)

The capitulation of the entertainment media and the "arts" has reached the ultimate of base filth. Consider the following:

No Sensitivity Issues Arise in Artistic Christian Bashing
By John Leo

Coming soon to Broadway or off-Broadway: a play about a homosexual Jesus character named Joshua who has sex with his disciples and is crucified as "king of the queers." The play, not yet finished, is "Corpus Christi" by Terrance McNally, who has won three Tony awards for his other work. ***

... The draft ends with the frank admission: "If we have offended, so be it. He belongs to us as well as you." ***

Michelle Malking of The Seattle Times wrote a recent column about a Seattle art show that drew no media criticism, even though the paintings feature Jesus on an obscene cross, a pope apparently engaged in a sex act and pages of a Bible defaced with Satanic marks.

What would have happened, she asked, if the art had featured a lascivious rabbi or a black slave woman performing oral sex on Thomas Jefferson? "There is no question the city's civility police would be out in full force," she wrote.

The paintings are close to the vicious images of 19th-century Nativists, who were among our most famous bigots. Assaults of the sensibilities of Christians in general and Catholics in particular are now going mainstream with nary a peep out of those who concern themselves so deeply with "hate speech." ***

In the art world, blasphemous art intended to debase Christianity, much of it coming from gay artists, routinely features fellatio involving Jesus, or the pope, or priests. Colorful things are done to the Virgin Mary, too. Gay parades often feature swishy-looking Jesus figures and hairy guys dressed as nuns. Its a continuing theater of propaganda, much of it under the guise of art.

Question: In our age of hypersensitivity, what other group in America has put up with vilification like this? No religion should expect immunity from critics. But these aren't arguments about sexual norms or dogma. They are attempts to degrade and enrage. The technical term for this is bigotry. Sensitivity-mongers, please note. (*Albuquerque Journal*, 6-9-89)

De-Christianized Dartmouth, by R. Albert Mohler Jr.
Now the naturalists have come to convert the Christians

"We must confront the ghosts of the past, said James O. Freedman, president of the new Roth Center of Jewish life at the college. Freedman used the occasion to look back to Dartmouth's past and a legacy of "bigotry" the college had long since repudiated. ***

... Eleazar Wheelock, a leading light of the first Great Awakening, founded the school with the purpose of evangelizing American Indians. "Moor's Indian Charity School" began operations in 1750, but Wheelock quickly determined to see the school become a full-scale college to rank with Harvard and Yale. The school was to retain its evangelistic mission and to accept liberal-arts students, with the goal of training them as missionaries. ***

This is the great tragedy of American higher education. All of the colleges and universities founded before the Revolution were established for the training and educating of Christian ministers and for the evangelization of the Nation. Harvard, Yale, Princeton, and even the Anglican "College of William and Mary" were essentially religious institutions. This pattern remained true through most of the 19th century.

The radical secularization of American higher education began with a broadening of the schools' missions and purposes. Eventually this led to a denial of Christianity as normative for the institutions. Now, as President Freedman's comments show clearly, the very Christian roots of the schools are cause for head-hanging shame inside the ivy-covered walls of the elite academy. *** (*World*, 12-27-97)

In other parts of this book, information was presented showing the complete demoralization of these "Ivy League" schools, and the indoctrination of the homosexual agenda. Their bedrocks of Christianity have been destroyed—in its place we have radicalism and promotion of homosexuality. And these are some of the most respected universities in the country. It also appears that a form of paganism and homosexuality have now spread to most of the major colleges and universities in the country. We have the teaching of filth.

Teaching Homosexuality in Schools

On *60 Minutes*, CBS TV, with Mike Wallace, 3-22-98, was a segment covering the homosexual trash and filth being taught in a large number of our major colleges and universities. It shows some of the extent to which this cancer has spread in our society.

This segment of the program opened up with Mike Wallace saying:

"The time was, not too long ago, when the hot studies on campus were Black studies, Chicano studies, and women studies.

"Now its what many people call queer studies. It's about gays, lesbians, and trans-genders, and their history.

"It's about studies that explore sexual identities, sexual ambiguities. And today it's being taught at some of the top universities in the country."

The first part was about the State University of New York at New Paltz.

Wallace said that at the State University of New York the women's studies department had an academic conference called "Revolting

Behavior—Re: Challenges of Women's Sexual Freedom," and, he said, revolting it was to some that were there.

A woman came on the screen, identified as Candice Derusy, a trustee of the college. She said: "This conference was a travesty of academic standards and a travesty of academic leadership." She was at the conference, and she said it was embarrassing to describe how lurid this conference was. "It was a platform for lesbian sex—for public sado-masochism—for anal sex—bisexuality—and masturbation." "It even included disposing of one's razor blades after blood-letting sexual activities." "It featured the sale and free distribution of pornographic material—bisexuality—masturbation."

Mike Wallace then introduced the college president, Dr. Roger Bowen, who then acted as an apologist for the studies, saying that if students were interested in such things they should be studied in a safe academic environment.

Wallace read to Bowen from a pamphlet: "For safe penetration use a slippery lubed up latex glove —." Then he said: "Needless to say we cannot read all of this." Then he read further: "To safely rock her into a frenzy." (Obviously this part was about fisting, and the material was the same or similar to the pamphlet on lesbian fisting previously referred to in this book.)

Dr. Bowen came back, still defending this offensive kind of trash, and said the larger issue is protecting first amendment rights and academic freedom in the academy. He said the same topics are being explored in the University of Minnesota, the University of Iowa, the University of Virginia, Yale, and Brown, in N.Y.U., and the top quality colleges in the country.

Wallace then said that with those comments they decided to check out some of those top colleges and universities. The scenes then shifted to various colleges.

They found that students were discussing in class sexual practices and pleasures.

Dartmouth for example was offering: English 69: Queer Theories, Queer Texts.

At Brown University, Unnatural Acts: Lesbian and Gay Literary and Cultural Studies.

At Stanford University: Homosexuals, Heretics, Witches, and Werewolves—Deviants in Medieval Society.

A professor George Chancey was shown who teaches a "gay history course." He admitted that not long ago professors would not have been allowed to explore such things on campus. He said that they take a look at some of America's greatest heroes, like Abraham Lincoln. He said that before Lincoln was married he shared a bed with his friend, Joshua Speed, for 3 1/2 years. And their correspondence indicates that they had a very close intimate relationship. (The professor of course read from no correspondence that indicated any such "intimacy" as was here being implied, and according to more respected Lincoln historians there is none.) He then says: "Some claim that Lincoln was a homosexual, but I don't call him a homosexual, but at the same time I don't think we can call him a heterosexual either." (Here the clear but false implication is that history shows that Lincoln was a bisexual. These are clearly the same homosexual lies that we have covered elsewhere in this book, and that reputable historians have debunked.)

Then a woman comes on that Wallace says is a candidate for a Ph.D. at Columbia, and runs her own Queer Studies course.

Then Wallace goes to courses at Duke University. There are courses being taught entitled: Perspectives in Lesbian, Gay, and Bisexual Studies. A man who appears to be a professor discusses his classes. He talked about Butch - Femme Lesbian relationships, and Sadomasochism including whips and chains. Then he talks about apparently lesbian activities, top, bottom, penetrator, penetratee. There were a bunch of odd-looking students in the class.

The scene then shifts to Rutgers University. An instructor calls himself a pioneer in what he calls queer studies. He puts on a big defense for the teaching of sadomasochism.

Mike Wallace then says that it's his understanding that a large part of these gay studies are being driven by people who are themselves gay. The instructor says well that's true. He says that needs to be because they're the ones that need to overcome the stigma of homosexuality.

Then the scene shifts to the University of California, Santa Cruz, and the studies there. Here they have an academic conference organized by the Gay, Lesbian, Bisexual, and Transgender Association. They showed a section on this called "Latex Lovers Workshop on Queer

Women's Safe Sex." They showed various "toys." One girl was holding what appeared to be an artificial penis with a wide base, which was apparently for fastening on another woman. (I have seen such thing in some of the homosexual sex catalogs—some of the "toys" are harnesses that various varieties and sizes of artificial "penises" may be fastened in. Such things as this were probably what the lady trustee of State University of New York was complaining about at the beginning of the show.)

A man appeared whom Wallace identified as Roger Kimbal, Managing Editor of the New Criterion, which Wallace said was one of the most outspoken critics of this trend on campuses. He gave examples of how disastrous the actual education was in these places. He said that the things they should be learning they weren't learning, that many of the students wouldn't even know who Winston Churchill was. He said that what students are being taught is total politicization. (I would add that it amounts to total immorality, too.)

(I will say this for this program: It did not appear that Mike Wallace was promoting these programs, and I think that bringing out how such homosexual filth is taking over in our colleges and universities was beneficial to the country. It was a refreshing change from the usual homosexual brainwashing by the media.)

From our colleges and universities come the future leaders of this country. Is it still possible for this country to go any direction but down?

The Association of American Law Schools requires members to pledge a willingness to hire homosexuals. (Justice Scalia's dissent in Romer v. Evans. See Chapter 8.)

'Gay' Benefits Endanger Country's Social Structure
By Ray Kerrison, writer for the New York Post

NYNEX, the $13 billion-a-year telephone and communications giant, is laying off thousands of employees to boost the bottomline profits.

At the same time, it has decided to spend an unspecified portion of its revenues to provide homosexual and lesbian employees and their partners with the benefits and privileges of married employees.

The company's priorities are revealing. Less money for workers and plenty of funds to subsidize aberrant relationships.

The NYNEX policy is the latest misguided thrust in the cultural war that is afflicting modern American life and threatening to overwhelm it. ***

Homosexual Benefits Today, Legal Marriage Tomorrow

It is only the beginning. Gay-partnership benefits and adoption privileges are preliminary skirmishes leading to the main event: the legalization of homosexual "marriage." ***

Marriage between man and woman is the sheer anchor of civilization; it is the institution, divinely ordained, to procreate and protect children and ensure the survival of the human race. ***

There is no future for a country that cannot distinguish between right and wrong. Not even Sodom and Gomorrah did what our governments, courts and corporations are now doing in the social arena. *** [Emphasis added]

Today's Sages Promote Illegitimacy, Violence

... In 1995, politicians, judges, TV anchors and corporate chieftains claim to be the source of all wisdom—which probably explains why the country is spinning into cultural decay.

The perils are becoming evident to some. Senator Robert Dole attacked the Hollywood establishment for its sleaze. Bill Bennett put the ax to TV talk trash with all its corruptive exploitation. Gen. Colin Powell's parting presidential shot was a wistful wish to "restore a sense of shame in society."

We are struggling through an age of cultural chaos in which the old guiding lights have been junked, institutional authority dismissed, and respect for law, life and civility devalued.

The harvest is rampant illegitimacy, drugs, violence, crime, perversion, pornography, human alienation.

Conferring marriage's special rights and entitlements on homosexual partnerships is a dagger thrust at the institution of marriage. It implies that they are equal, that homosexual practices are acceptable alternatives to conjugal love.

So NYNEX—like Disney, Time Warner, Microsoft and Sprint before it—is contributing to the dismantling of the values and standards that have served this country so well for more than 200 years. ***
(*Human Events*, 12-15-95)

There was an article, "**Gay Employees Win Benefits for Partners** at **More Corporations**," in *The Wall Street Journal*, 3-18-94, about the push of the homosexualists to obtain same-sex partner benefits for homosexual employees. The only thing considered noteworthy about the article is that it shows that it is a nationwide push in most all of the major corporations in the country.

The capitulation of our major industries is great indeed, and it is not considered worthwhile to try to detail all of them, nor do I have all of the information. And the capitulation continually grows. Without question, there are not many large corporations that have had the moral courage and integrity to withstand the assault, and one after another they give in to the homosexualists. There is no question about it—the Sodomites have gained a firm foothold in the large corporations of this country. It surely seems that morality in business has been trampled into the ground on all fronts.

Not only are the homosexuals gaining acceptance in the corporate world, but they are successfully pushing for special benefits for those with AIDS. And, as in all of their agenda, they are assisted by the media. In *The Albuquerque Tribune*, 3-10-94, was a full page article: **Working With Aids**—*Employers begin to face their responsibilities to workers with the disease*. The article was obviously written by, and the information furnished by homosexuals. How AIDS became the responsibility of employers is, of course, not explained. Heretofore, injuries on the job were usually covered by workmen's compensation, but illnesses not acquired on the job, as a result of work, were never considered an "employers responsibility to the workers." The article tells of corporate workshops conducted by the Northwest AIDS Foundation, and I am sure that some such organization furnished the information for the article. The object of this particular push is to have companies take "steps to educate their work force and guard against discrimination" against those with AIDS; and to get medical and health benefits for those with AIDS.

I never see articles telling people who do not have AIDS how to protect themselves against those who have AIDS, nor cautioning those that have the disease about measures they should take to protect fellow workers or those with whom they come in contact. In truth, laws have been passed which are specifically designed to prevent people from protecting themselves and avoiding contact with those who have AIDS.

Helen Mathews Smith, the former editor of MD magazine, was writing a book on the HIV/AIDS epidemic. She wrote the following article, published in *The Wall Street Journal*, 10-25-95:

The Deadly Politics of AIDS

Even though it was clear by the early 1980s that gay bathhouses were deadly breeding ground for AIDS, Mervyn Silverman, director of the San Francisco Department of Public Health, took three years to decide whether to regulate or close down the bathhouses. ***

For more than a decade, bowing to narrow interests, American public health officials have ignored the central tenet of plague control: routine testing, tracking the path of the disease, and warnings to those at risk. Because HIV infection has been given a unique legal and medical status, says Denver's director of public health, Franklyn Judson, "we have gotten off track" with a national strategy that is "irrational, erroneous and unethical." ***

How did the nation's public health system fail? An early preview of the coming crisis occurred at the Atlanta meeting held by the Centers for Disease Control and Prevention in February 1987 to examine the future role of HIV testing. The two-day conference was attended by 800 people, including health officials and representatives of the American Civil Liberties Union, the Gay Men's Health Crisis, the National Gay and Lesbian Task Force, and the American Association of Physicians for Human Rights.

To track the path of the epidemic nationwide, the CDC proposed testing new groups, including pregnant women, marriage license applicants and hospital patients. AIDS activists strongly opposed the new strategy as a slippery slope toward detention camps. They argued that wider testing was unnecessary, expensive, and raised civil rights issues that would have to be resolved. They advocated instead more counseling and a mass-education campaign targeted to the general public. For teenagers, they recommended candid discussions of sex and condoms; for drug addicts, needle exchange programs.

In the end, the medical establishment voted for individual rights over public health. "The need for legislation to protect the rights of AIDS victims was endorsed by everyone present," wrote a New York Times reporter, "from dark-suited federal officials to jeans-clad advocates of homosexual rights." This was a radical departure from public health principles. Exactly 50 years earlier, President Roosevelt's surgeon general began a campaign against syphilis that advocated the opposite strategy. He organized an aggressive testing and partner notification system—before the discovery of penicillin—that brought that infant and adult epidemic under control. ***

The director of research at the Pediatric Aids Foundation in Novato, Calif., Arthur Ammanna, says that "once treatment for HIV-infected babies was available in the late 1980s, anonymous testing by the CDC should have been abandoned immediately, and those infected identified." ***

Would routine or mandatory testing nationwide bring an end to the epidemic? No one can know. But at the very least, thousands of lives would be saved. The nation has a moral duty to care for those who are infected, but the infected also have a responsibility to those with whom they share their lives—and bodies. Public health officials once enforced that responsibility. They need to do so again.

Although the proper way to deal with an infectious disease like AIDS was known from the outset, it is still handled in the political way that the homosexual groups and their ally, the ACLU, have wanted it to be. Only the rights of homosexuals and the advancement of their agenda has prevailed. The rights of others, including adults, children, and infants, to be protected from the carriers of HIV have been ignored. Great and unnecessary harm has been done to the country, to the people, and even to the homosexuals themselves. Their "education" programs have progressed, with the help of the Clinton administration, in just the way they wanted. It has been an indoctrination of the people, the military, government employees, corporate employees, and worse yet, our school children, with the acceptance of homosexuality as a good and healthy lifestyle. The success has been phenomenal.

The ACLU has become so radicalized and entwined with the homosexual movement that one of its top members could no longer stand the harm being done to the country. Even liberals apparently have a gag reflex.

Nat Hentoff Quits ACLU Over HIV 'Privacy' Case

Nat Hentoff, who served as a board member of the New York arm of the American Civil Liberties Union (ACLU) is resigning from the organization after 35 years as a "card carrying" member. "I can no longer continue to be associated with an organization," Hentoff wrote in the April 18 *Village Voice*, " . . . that sacrifices the lives of children and diminishes the life expectancy of their mothers to a rigid principle grounded in willful ignorance of medical facts.

A lawsuit filed by Gretchen Buchenholtz, executive director of the Association to Benefit Children, prompted Hentoff's decision. Buchenholz is fighting for mandatory diagnostic testing and identification of all HIV-infected infants in the state of New York, and is being opposed by the ACLU...

Results of tests for syphilis, sickle cell anemia and other conditions are given to parents, but HIV is hidden, Hentoff wrote, in part because it would subsequently identify the source of the mother's infection. *** [Organizations in league with the ACLU on this issue are the Gay Men's Health Crisis, the National Organization for Women (NOW) and the National Abortion and Reproductive Rights Action League.] (Human Events, 5-5-95)

Because of absurd policies supported by these radical organizations and supported by various laws which they got enacted, not only do those responsible for healthcare fail to see that proper testing is done to protect even newborn babies from HIV, but when "anonymous" testing is done of newborns, on a "purely voluntary basis," by the CDC, parents or guardians are not informed of the test results, and proper treatment does not result. An article, Sacrificing Babies on the Altar of Privacy, was published on this in The Wall Street Journal, 8-4-95, concludes with the statement:

With all of the talk from this administration—notably from the first lady—about protecting children, this dreadful policy should have been changed long ago. Further delay will only sentence additional thousands of infants to a terrible death and deprive their mothers of a chance for a longer and healthier life.

The homosexuals are gaining ground in most countries of the world. One thing they have is ingenuity. The AIDS epidemic should have demonstrated to society one of the many destructive elements of homosexuality, but in another reversal of reason, homosexuals have successfully used it to their advantage. However, in the politicization of AIDS, the homosexuals did great harm to themselves by causing the AIDS epidemic. But much worse, great harm was done to innocent people around the world.

Russia Repeals Law Barring Homosexuality

MOSCOW—Male homosexuality is no longer a crime in Russia, and gay activists hope the repeal of the Soviet-era law will improve Russia's ability to combat AIDS.

A decree repealing Article 121, which made consensual sex between men punishable by up to five years in prison, was signed by President Boris Yeltsin and approved by lawmakers April 29. It took effect last week. *** (*Albuquerque Journal*, 5-30-93)

Our media not only sanitize the news—they give us homosexual propaganda while purporting to give us the news. A good example was *ABC World News*, on Sunday evening, 6-3-96. A portion of the news was on the "Gay Pride" parade and celebration in New York. As to the parade, they showed only the more favorable and respectable parts—although the term "respectable" is a misnomer when applied to any of it. They kept away from the filth and obscenity which was rampant everywhere—and they kept away from the NAMBLA parts of the celebration and parades. They showed two older respectable-looking homosexuals, claiming they had been together for forty-seven years. If true this must indeed be a record—but proves nothing but an enduring love of sodomy. It was pure propaganda for the homosexual agenda, and it purposefully omitted the part that would have given us an accurate picture of the proceedings. We have to go to Christian and conservative publications to get the truth about any of these things. ABC and its liberal anchor Peter Jennings have long been at the forefront of promoting the homosexual agenda—trying to insidiously brainwash us while presenting what is supposed to be a newscast—and applying such words as "bigotry" and "homophobia" to those who do not consider homosexuality acceptable.

Even when the citizens have been able to prevent "gay rights" and "hate crime" laws, ingenious lawyers, with the help of liberal activist judges and jurors imbued with modern liberalism, still find ways to twist the law to benefit homosexuals. Consider the following:

On CBS National Television, March 3, 1998, there was a guest, James Dale, a clean-cut but openly homosexual young man who had attained the rank of Eagle Scout. He had become an assistant scoutmaster, but was banned upon his admission that he was a homosexual. The court ruling that was allowing him to continue in the Boy Scouts was the subject of discussion. This was clearly a selling job by the media to convince the public that this was wrongful "discrimination." No question was brought up about how many attacks there had been on Boy Scouts by homosexual leaders who infiltrated them. No question was brought up about the vile acts in which Dale would have engaged to acquire his homosexual classification. No question was brought up about whether the Boy Scouts, a non-governmental organization, should have a right to determine its qualifications for membership. Certainly, no question was brought up about whether or not the Boy Scouts have the right to require that their leaders have good moral character—and whether or not we are required to accept the homosexual view that those who engage in sodomy are of good moral character. This part of the program was purely and simply one more selling job to the public of the homosexual agenda—and it is indeed the most reprehensible part of it. It is the forcing of the acceptance of homosexuality on our youths, and putting homosexuals in a position to prey on young people. It has been reported that there are already reported over 1,800 known cases of homosexual attacks on boy scouts. In an article, **Some Fired Scoutmasters Still Abuse Boys**, *Albuquerque Journal,* 10-15-93, are the statements:

> The Boy Scouts of America dismissed about 1,800 scoutmasters suspected of molesting boys between 1971 and 1991, but some moved on to other troops and continued to abuse Scouts, organization files show. ***
> The organization asks applicants about criminal convictions and suggest local troops check references, but doesn't specifically urge them to perform background checks through law enforcement agencies [Richard Walker, a spokesman for the Scouts] said.

I am sure that there are many homosexual attacks on Boy Scouts that we don't know about. In fact, the Boys Scouts have been accused of covering up some of the cases for purposes of self defense and avoiding adverse publicity. Also, I am sure that some of the boys would be so ashamed of being engaged in such acts, even if completely against their will, that some would keep it to themselves.

I got more information about the boy scout case in a news article and an editorial in *U.S. News & World Report*, 3-16-98. The news article:

Scouts' honor includes gays

Must the Boy Scouts of America accept gay members and leaders because the group is a place of "public accommodation," like a hotel or restaurant? Last week, a New Jersey appeals court said yes, rejecting what it called the Scouts' "stereotypical notions" about homosexuality. ***

The Boy Scouts, which calls itself a voluntary association with a "right to establish standards," rejects the decision—and the notion that it should be regulated under the same laws that were used to desegregate lunch counters.

Critics of the New Jersey ruling contend that if it is upheld, it could lead to limitations on the moral teachings of charitable groups. While the Scouts take their arguments to the New Jersey Supreme Court, a California court will decide whether boys who refuse to recite the Scout's religious oath have the right to be a member. (p. 28)

An editorial by John Leo:

The lawyers are at it again

*** The third interesting case of the week was a gay-rights case in New Jersey. A three member Superior Court appellate panel ruled 2 to 1 that the Boy Scouts cannot exclude homosexuals from membership because they are a public accommodation covered by state antidiscrimination law. Normally, a public accommodation is a place or structural facility open to all, like a hotel or a diner. The Scouts may be right or wrong in banning gays, but converting a private membership group into a public facility in order to defend gays is exactly the kind of tortured, result-oriented logic that brings so much disrepute onto the courts. The categories of "inclusion" and "bias" so dominate the thinking of our elites that they often can't think through the positions they take or the lines they cross—in this case, overriding freedom of association and casually declaring a long moral tradition inoperable in a private group. *** (*U.S. News & World Report*, 3-16-98, p. 10)

Such decisions as these in the Boy Scout cases are blatant judicial legislation at its worst. And the fact that it goes on, and its allowance by the people, are part and parcel of the moral degradation in this country. It would indeed be shocking to the great thinkers who formed this country and provided us with a Constitution designed to prevent such things. But our decline in morality has been accompanied by an equal decline in reason. And the liberal activists seem to have lost any ability to reason, and they certainly have lost any semblance of honesty and integrity.

We have, however, had some encouraging decisions. The following is one of the more important:

Scouts can bar non-believers

WASHINGTON — The Supreme Court today refused to require the Boy Scouts of America to let in boys who won't acknowledge a duty to God.

The court, acting without comment on the appeal of an 11-year-old boy from Illinois, left intact a ruling that said the Scouts organization is not subject to a federal anti-bias law. ...

Today's action is not a ruling on the merits of the Scout's policy, and carries no direct impact for other legal fights over it.

Cub Scouts and Boy Scouts must promise to "do my duty to God and my country."

A U.S. District Judge in Illinois and the 7th U.S. Circuit Court of Appeals ruled that the Boy Scouts of America, unlike restaurants, hotels and places of entertainment, is not a public accommodation covered by Title II of the Civil Rights Act of 1964.

The law bars discrimination based on race, color, religion or national origin. (*The Albuquerque Tribune*, 12-6-93)

Yet for every positive step, homosexualists manage to advance their perverted agenda two steps. Overturning the long-standing ban on same-sex marriages is just one example:

Judge rules against same-sex marriage ban

JUNEAU, Alaska — A state judge hearing a challenge to Alaska's ban on same-sex marriage says choosing a partner is a fundamental right that could result in "non-traditional" choice. Anchorage Superior Court Judge Peter Micalski said Friday that the state must show

why it should be able to regulate who people marry. ***
(*The Albuquerque Tribune*, 2-28-98)

So now we even have a liberal judge trying to impose the homosexual agenda in the last frontier of this country. Can you imagine how far such an idea would have gotten in our early frontier days?

When a liberal activist judge, as Alaskan Judge Peter Micalski obviously is, says that homosexuals have a "fundamental right" to engage in a sodomite relationship, he is attempting to take a fundamental right away from the people and their representative, and give it to the courts—and that is what is fundamentally wrong. It is the people and their representatives in the government who have the right to determine the public policy of the state, and the laws that should govern the health and welfare of the state and its people. The only prerogative of the courts is to interpret the meaning of those laws, and no interpretation is even proper if the law is clear and unambiguous on its face, as are the laws on qualifications for the issuance of marriage licenses by the states. This ruling was also against established precedent that should have been followed.

It is up to the people to determine public policy and what acts are so fundamentally wrong and against nature that they should be prohibited. Thus the people, from the inception of our country and of our federal and state constitutions, have had the right to make sodomy, incest, bigamy, polygamy, adultery, fornication, and many other things not only unlawful, but a criminal offense. Likewise, the people have always had the right to determine to whom the state can issue a marriage license, and the requirements for marriage, even to the extent of requiring blood tests and health certificates. They have and always have had the right to prohibit bigamy, polygamy, incestuous marriages, sodomite (same-sex) marriages, and marriages to animals.

From a legal standpoint, decisions of liberal activist judges such as the Alaskan judge and the Hawaiian judges have no legal basis and are completely asinine. It is one more blatant attempt to violate our tripartite forms of state and federal governments, and to take from the people and give to the courts the rights to make our laws. And if the people do not have the backbone to put a stop to such liberal and judicial activism, then they are certainly deserving of what they get.

We are in dire danger of losing basic freedoms which our forefathers tried to give us permanently through our Constitution. The people are losing their rights to govern themselves, and to determine who they have on their property, and with whom they associate. There are those who wish to take away basic freedoms bestowed upon us by our Bill of Rights. They wish to take away our right to bear arms, our freedom to practice our religion, and even our freedom of speech and freedom of press.

Gay Employee Can Sue Employer Over Firing

An employee who was fired because he was gay can sue under a state statute that prohibits companies from firing employees for their "lawful activity" outside of work, say the Colorado Court of Appeals in upholding a jury award of over $90,000, including $40,000 in punitive damages.

Most states have similar statutes, according to Cliff Palefsky, an employment law expert in San Francisco.

The Colorado statute was enacted in 1990 as a "smokers' rights" law, but the court said it applied to homosexual activity.

The employer [a law firm] argued that the firing was based on the plaintiff's *status* as a homosexual, so there was no "lawful activity" at issue.

But the court disagreed, and cited testimony by one of the firm's partners that he was aware that the plaintiff "was a homosexual man who had been engaged in a sexual relationship."

A U.S. District Court in New York recently allowed a suit under a similar New York statute where a company fired a sales manager and then demoted a sales assistant who had been living with him. The court found that the sales assistant's cohabitation was a "recreational activity" under the statute. *** (*Lawyers Weekly USA*, 11-20-95)

Girl Scouts Can Personalize Pledge
(Group Leaving God Behind, Critics Say)

MINNEAPOLIS — Promising to serve the "Creator" instead of "God," or simply to serve, is now OK for Girl Scouts, but the decision to allow the choice was not universally cheered Sunday by people outside the scouts. *** (*Albuquerque Journal*, 10-25-93)

In Chapter 4, it was noted that the Girl Scouts removed the bar to homosexuals. One by one, our Judaic-Christian principles fall around us under the liberal and homosexual onslaught.

Same-sex partners of Tucson employees eligible for benefits

TUCSON — The Tucson City Council has agreed to extend medical insurance benefits to homosexual "domestic partners" of city employees but refused to do the same for unmarried heterosexual couples.

The council voted 6-0 to approve the measure earlier this week, which is expected to cost about $7,000. ***

(*The Albuquerque Tribune*, 5-1-97)

Going the gay way, eh?—
Homosexual activists make big inroads in Canada's schools

*** The push to promote homosexuality in the public schools began in Ontario five years ago when the Toronto Board of Education published a "resource guide" called "Sexual Orientation: Homosexuality, Lesbianism, and Homophobia." It is now a part of the board's official curriculum even though psychiatrist Joseph Berger, a member of the Toronto board's advisory committee, condemned it as blatant homosexual propaganda filled with "unacceptable prejudice." ***

In March, the homosexual agenda was advanced again when the British Columbia Teachers' Federation endorsed a resolution to "develop recommendations and strategies for achieving the elimination of homophobia and heterosexism in the public school system." ***

(*World*, May 3-10-97)

We are heading in the same direction as our liberal neighbor to the north, Canada, whose people have basically lost those rights. It seems that they have now substantially capitulated to the whims of their liberal legislators and judges. There they have long been severely restricted in owning and using firearms—and now it appears that any remaining freedom of press, freedom of speech, and freedom of religion are on their way out. It is a sad day, for there are many fine people in Canada. But when people become so dependent on and subjugated to their government that they no longer have the courage to fight for their rights—those rights will be taken from them. It is only a matter of time. And the United States is heading in the same direction. Consider the following statements and thoughts.

Family News From Dr. James Dobson, Focus on the Family, June 1998, contained substantial and important information on the success of the homosexual movement in Canada. The following relates to information contained in that newsletter.

Homosexualists have made great advances, both on the legislative front and in the courts. And as we see from the information in the *Family Research Report*, cited below, unbelievable things are taking place in other areas of society and religion.

In Canada, it is becoming illegal to oppose or even criticize the homosexual movement. Several provinces have passed legislation that prohibits publications of any statements considered as discriminatory toward homosexuality. The Canadian Radio-Television and Telecommunications Commission monitors programming that portrays homosexuality in a negative light. The newsletter states: "Even Focus on the Family Canada is muzzled on this topic. So much for free speech north of the border."

In 1997, the British Columbia College of Teachers refused to accredit a teacher education program offered by Trinity Western University, a Christian school, because the university requires its students to sign a code of conduct that, among other things, prohibits homosexual behavior among the students. A Christian school, King's College in Edmonton, dismissed a lab instructor because of openly homosexual conduct. The instructor brought suit and the Supreme Court of Canada ruled that legal protection, amounting to a preference, must be extended immediately, and that protection because of sexual orientation must be made a part of Alberta's Human Rights Code. Alberta had chosen not to enact such a preference. This clearly takes away any right of the people to pass their laws themselves on the subject. A Supreme Court Justice said:

I believe that judicial intervention is warranted to correct a democratic process that has acted improperly.

Dr. Ted Morton, a professor of political science at the University of Calgary, said:

> There will be strong pressures to define and isolate any private—especially religion-based—educational institutions that do not embrace 'gay positive' policies. The argument has already been made before the courts in Canada that 'equal rights' are more important than freedom of religion and freedom of association."

In Ontario, the highest provincial court ruled that the traditional definition of "spouse" is unconstitutional and that the federal income tax law must be rewritten to include same-sex partners.

The age of consent in Ontario is fourteen, and pro-family groups have not been successful in getting it raised to sixteen. As I have detailed in this book, homosexual activists work hard to lower the age of consent so that they will have more leeway to abuse youngsters.

Success of the homosexual movement in the Netherlands is also stated. "In the Netherlands, where prostitution, pornography and pedophilia are already rampant—and in many cases, legal—the Dutch government recently allowed homosexual couples to form legal unions, with the same inheritance and tax rights as heterosexual married couples." Homosexual couples have gained the right to adopt children. Homosexualists in the Netherlands are now working to lower the legal age of consent for sexual acts from fourteen to *twelve* years of age. (The efforts of homosexual activists to get the legal right to prey on children, who are not old enough to really realize the nature and consequences of such vile and degrading acts, is clearly apparent.)

"Truly, the homosexual movement has become a steamroller in nations around the world." Lyndon Bowring, head of the Care for the Family ministry in the United Kingdom wrote to Dr. Dobson:

> We are up to our eyes here in London with the rampant advances of the militant gay lobby. Our Parliament is planning to reduce the age of consent for homosexual intercourse between 'adult' males from 18 to 16. Apart from a sovereign miracle of grace, we will not succeed in persuading them not to do so. We are doing everything in our power to prevent it and calling on His divine power to intervene on behalf of our young boys.

Dr. Dobson observes:

There is hardly a place on the globe where similar struggles are not occurring, except where no fight remains in discouraged or outnumbered Christians.

There have been two principal impediments to the homosexual juggernaut. One is the repulsive nature of the vile and despicable sexual acts in which homosexuals engage. They have had great success in steering public thinking around and away from those things, and getting people to concentrate on ideas of equality and discrimination to a degree that belies common sense. The other primary impediment is the religious belief of the people—particularly the Christian and traditional Jewish religions. But the homosexualists also have the answer to this latter problem. It is rather simple. They plan to rewrite the Bible so as to eliminate the many condemnations of homosexuality. And the gullible liberal element appears ready and willing to even accept this absurdity. And, as one would expect, Canada is in the forefront, as shown by the following referenced article.

Homosexual Marriage: Scriptural Debate, *Family Research Report*, Family Research Institute, May-June, 1998, contains a four-page article relating to the move in progress to change the many passages of the Bible that constitute a general condemnation of homosexuality. The current idea is to change the meaning to, at most, only condemn "male prostitution, heterosexuals who engage in occasional homosexuality and sexual relations between men and boys." (However, I am sure that the homosexual activists will eventually even want those condemnations removed, and the Bible rewritten to praise all homosexuality—including sexual relations between men and boys—as the leaders of the activist movement now do.)

How is this to be accomplished? It is very simple. They just go back to the ancient Greek and Hebrew words, which few people are capable of understanding, and place the new and desired interpretation on them. For those that are more interested in an agenda than in truth and veracity, this is really no problem at all.

And who is one of the leaders of this movement toward change? Vancouver's Bishop Michael Ingram of Canada's Anglican Church. He is an advocate of "gay and lesbian Christians," and wants to "reverse [the ban of the church] on the ordination of practicing homosexuals and the blessing of same-sex marriages."

Including my computer Bibles, I have five versions and translations of the Holy Bible: King James Version, New King James Version, New International Version, American Standard Version, and American translation. There are no material differences in any of them regarding the many passages condemning homosexual acts.

Now we suddenly have "scholars" that tell us that all of these translations are wrong—that the work done over the centuries by all of the many unbiased scholars was in error—and that the homosexualists now have the right answer. Homosexuals never allow themselves to be burdened by facts—truth and facts are whatever conforms with their agenda. This "scholarly work" is in the exact same vein, with the same degree of veracity, as the false writings calling Jesus Christ, the Apostle Paul, George Washington, Abraham Lincoln, and many others, homosexuals.

To a knowledgable person, these things would be amusingly ludicrous. But the effects of them are indeed sobering—their success has been unbelievable. And Bishop Michael Ingham is now confident that the Anglican Church of Canada will soon be blessing same-sex marriages and ordaining practicing homosexuals as ministers. He sees no problem in rewriting the Bible, the basis of the Anglican religion, so that its teachings will conform to the wishes of the activist homosexuals.

George Washington, John Adams, Thomas Jefferson, James Madison, and Patrick Henry will be looking down upon us wondering how we could have drifted into to such utter stupidity.

CHAPTER 8

BRINGING MORALITY BACK TO AMERICA

"Freedom prospers when religion is vibrant and the rule of law under God is acknowledged." (President Ronald W. Reagan, 1983, *The Columbia Dictionary of Quotations*)

The Constitution of the United States provides for its amendment in Article V, as follows:

> The Congress, whenever two thirds of both Houses shall deem it necessary, shall propose Amendments to this constitution, or, on the Application of the Legislatures of two thirds of the several States, shall call a Convention for proposing Amendments, which, in either Case, shall be valid to all Intents and Purposes, as part of this Constitution, when ratified by the Legislatures of three fourths of the several States, or by Conventions in three fourths thereof, as the one or the other Mode of Ratification may be proposed by the Congress ... .

Article I, Section 1, of our Constitution provides:

> All legislative Powers herein granted shall be vested in a Congress of the United States, which shall consist of a Senate and House of Representatives.

Article II provides that the executive power shall be vested in the President of the United States, and Article III provides that the judicial power of the United States shall be vested in the Supreme Court.

Our Constitution was a great document, formed by some highly intelligent and thoughtful men. Had it been properly followed, I believe it would be the greatest document of that kind in all history. It provided for a tripartite system of checks and balances. But some of the greatest damage has been done to our country by what is termed as "judicial legislation." Some of our appointed federal judges, and more importantly, justices of the United States Supreme Court, have unlawfully taken it on themselves to change the law and even our Constitution to fit their own particular political views. By doing this they violate not only their oaths of office, they violate the three basic and most important parts of the Constitution they had all sworn to uphold. These judges and justices were appointed for life, and have no responsibility to the people insofar as being subject to removal by election. They unlawfully usurp both the constitutional powers bestowed on the executive branch and the legislative branch of our government.

A great harm to our country has occurred from this leftist onslaught of modern liberalism. This is one of the greatest dangers of electing a liberal president. He has the authority to appoint federal judges and justices. And it is liberals who violate our Constitution and engage in judicial legislation, instead of merely interpreting the provisions of our laws and Constitution, which is the only power given them. They change our laws, and more importantly, our Constitution, to provide for things that could not possibly become law in the proper manners provided by our Constitution. Sometimes this is done by five to four decisions. It is indeed a travesty that five unelected officials, none of whom have ever been omnipotent, violate their oaths of office and unlawfully change our Constitution to fit their own particular political views. And this same body, the United States Supreme Court, has declared its decisions to be the supreme law of the land, overriding all acts of our elected officials, including those of Congress and the president. Some of the destruction done was described in Chapter 4, in reviewing the book, *Slouching Towards Gomorrah*. We will cover more here.

Some of the most flagrant judicial legislation has taken place in the area of capital punishment (death sentences), although this certainly is not the only field of the law that has been so violated.

The United States Constitution specifically provides for and recognizes capital punishment in four different places.

Amendment V, adopted in 1791, provides:

> No person shall be held to answer for a *capital,* or otherwise infamous crime, unless on a presentment or indictment of a Grand Jury, except in cases arising in the land or naval forces, or in the Militia, when in actual service in time of War or public danger; nor shall any person be subject for the same offence to be twice put in jeopardy of *life* or limb; nor shall be compelled in any criminal case to be a witness against himself, nor be deprived of *life,* liberty, or property, without due process of law; nor shall private property be taken for public use, without just compensation. [Emphasis added]

Amendment XIV, Section 1, adopted in 1868, provides in part:

> ...No State shall make or enforce any law which shall abridge the privileges or immunities of citizens of the United States; nor shall any State deprive any person of "life," liberty, or property, without due process of law; nor deny to any person within its jurisdiction the equal protection of the laws. [Emphasis added]

Some of the most liberal members of the United States Supreme Court, in modern times, have been Chief Justice Earl Warren, and Justices William O. Douglas, William J. Brennan, Jr., and Thurgood Marshall. All of them truly had an obsession for changing the law and the Constitution to fit their own particular political and moral views of what was right and wrong. Fortunately for the country, the attacks on capital punishment by the liberal element came after Earl Warren had retired, in 1969. Had a case come before the court when all four of these gentlemen were there (1967-1969), capital punishment would undoubtedly have been declared unconstitutional. This would have been the ultimate of judicial legislation, going directly against the then existing provisions of the Constitution of the United States. Fortunately, the big case on the subject did not come until 1972, but even so, this totally confused decision remains an example of liberal and even some moderate judges injecting their own political views as constitutional law, and thereby changing the Constitution. The death penalty still exists in this country, although the cases in which it can be applied, and the way in which it can be applied, are restricted by the 1972 decision of the United States Supreme Court, *Furman v. Georgia*, 408 U.S. 238, 92 S.Ct. 2726 (1972). This decision created such a sense of confusion in our law that it appeared for awhile that the death penalty was unconstitutional. In the *Furman v. Georgia* case, the Supreme Court reviewed decisions of the Supreme Court of Georgia affirming imposition of the death penalty on two defendants convicted of murder and rape and a decision of the Texas Court of Criminal Appeals affirming imposition of the death penalty on a defendant convicted of rape. In a five to four decision, the United States Supreme Court reversed the decisions, holding that in these cases the imposition of the death penalty would constitute cruel and unusual punishment in violation of the Eighth and Fourteenth Amendments to the United States Constitution. This was a most unusual case in several ways; one of them being that nine separate opinions were written. The justices supporting the decision were Douglas, Brennan, Stewart, White, and Marshall. Those opposing it were Chief Justice Burger, and Justices Blackmun, Powell, and Rehnquist.

Justice Douglas went through a long discussion, and at the end stated: "Whether a mandatory death penalty would otherwise be constitutional is a question I do not reach." The only thing that I could find in his opinion that amounted to any reason for overturning the death penalty in these cases was his statement (92 S.Ct.):

> ...we deal with a system of law and of justice that leaves the uncontrolled discretion of judges or juries the determination whether defendants committing these crimes should die or be imprisoned. Under these laws no standards govern the selection of the penalty. People live or die, dependent on the whim of one man or of 12. (p. 2734)
>
> ***
>
> Thus these discretionary statutes are unconstitutional in their operation. They are pregnant with discrimination and discrimination is an ingredient not compatible with the idea of equal protection of the laws that is implicit in the ban on 'cruel and unusual' punishments. (p. 2735)

This reasoning of Douglas is typical of a liberal approach—it is illogical and not supported by sound constitutional law. He does not explain how this makes the punishment "cruel and unusual." He does not explain how it differed from the way such punishment had been meted out for the past 200 years. He does not explain how the laws in question here in Georgia and Texas differed from the other 38 states that then had capital punishment. (The opinion shows that at that time 40 states had capital punishment.) This kind of inapplicable language is the necessary cloak for covering up the unspoken truth—the injection of personal political views. Five unelected and unaccountable judges, appointed for life, are here overruling the United States Constitution, the constitutions of all of the states, together with the laws passed by the legislatures of the states, who represent the people in passing these laws.

Justice Brennan gets even more wordy and obfuscating. He states that all capital punishment is now unconstitutional as "cruel and unusual punishment." He states (92 S.Ct.):

> The question under this principle then, is whether there are objective indicators from which a court can conclude that contemporary society considers a severe punishment unacceptable. ... (p. 2746)
>
> ***
>
> ...I will analyze the punishment of death in terms of the principles set out above and the cumulative test to which they lead: It is a denial of human dignity for the State arbitrarily to subject a person to an unusually severe punishment that society has indicated it does not regard as acceptable, and that cannot be shown to serve any penal purpose more effectively than a significantly less drastic punishment. Under these principles and this test, death is today a 'cruel and unusual' punishment. (p. 2750)

Justice Brennan sets up his own tests, which are not at all supported by acceptable principles of constitutional law, and then comes to his own personal conclusion. Not only that, he makes fallacious factual statements. This is the cancer of judicial legislation at its terminal stage. There is no better example of a judge ignoring the clear provisions of the Constitution relating to capital punishment, usurping the duties of the legislative bodies, and enacting his own law. The things he considers are what it is the duty of the legislative representatives of the people to consider, and to enact our laws accordingly.

Justice Thurgood Marshall, as does Justice Brennan, forsakes any semblance of interpreting the Constitution according to the intent of its framers, or of any kind of logical or judicial construction of the document.

They completely ignore the basic rules of logic and of legal construction, which are that a document should be construed according to its plain wording, if there is no ambiguity; and according to the intent of its framers, if there is an ambiguity. Words should be construed according to their plain meaning, and all parts of the document should be construed together, in such a way that meaning will be given to all parts; and no part should be construed in such a way that other parts would be rendered superfluous or meaningless. Each and every one of these principles are clearly violated by both Brennan and Marshall to arrive at their own personal political views of what they consider to now be right or wrong. There is no more blatant example of judicial legislation, by which such judges violate their oaths of office and do irreparable harm to our country. The other three justices who voted with the majority in this case did little better. This includes even Justice White, from whom many would have expected a much higher level of judicial integrity.

The excuses used by liberals for disregarding the Constitution, and the ways of changing and amending it which are plainly set forth therein, are that the Constitution is a "living document" that should be interpreted according to our changing times, ideas, and mores. But this, according to our Constitution, is clearly the prerogative of our elected legislative bodies, and of the states and the people—not nine (or in many instances five) unelected judges, appointed for life, who are not accountable to the people. The people and their periodically elected representatives are the ones who should decide whether or not conditions and mores have changed to the extent that our Constitution and laws should be accordingly changed; and it is unconstitutional and unlawful, and a violation of their oaths of office, for these appointed judges to usurp that authority. Such flagrant violations should be impeachable offenses.

Marshall goes into the history of the death penalty, the ideas of those who oppose it, the changing mores of society, whether or not it has a detrimental effect on crime, and concludes that "the death penalty is an excessive and unnecessary punishment that violates the Eighth Amendment. Not one place in his opinion does he consider the elements of interpretation and construction that he validly could and should consider. The fact that many people consider this man to have been a great jurist is one more example of modern liberal thought that has forsaken basic reason.

Justice Stewart concluded that "the constitutionality of capital punishment in the abstract is not, however, before us in these cases." He simply concluded that the sentences were unconstitutional in these particular cases because (92 S.Ct.):

> These death sentences are cruel and unusual in the same way that being struck by lightening is cruel and unusual. For, of all the people convicted of rapes and murders in 1967, and 1968, many just as reprehensible as these, the petitioners are among a capriciously selected random handful upon whom the sentences of death has in fact been imposed. ... (p. 2762)

Justice White's explanation for his concurrence in overturning these death sentences was (92 S.Ct.):

> In this respect, I add only that past and present legislative judgment with respect to the death penalty loses much of its force when viewed in light of the recurring practices of delegating sentencing authority to the jury and the fact that a jury, in its own discretion and without violating its trust or any statutory policy, may refuse to impose the death penalty no matter what the circumstances of the crime. Legislative "policy" is thus necessarily defined not by what is legislatively authorized but by what juries and judges do in exercising the discretion so regularly conferred upon them. ... (pp. 2764–65)

Chief Justice Burger clearly recognized both the confusion of the decision, and that it exceeded the powers of the court (92 S.Ct.):

> Since there is no majority of the Court on the ultimate issue presented in these cases, the future of capital punishment in this country has been left in an uncertain limbo. ... (p. 2811)
>
> ***
>
> ...If legislatures come to doubt the efficacy of capital punishment, they can abolish it, either completely or on a selective basis. ... (p. 2811)

***

The highest judicial duty is to recognize the limits on judicial power and to permit the democratic processes to deal with matters falling outside of those limits. ... (p. 2812)

Justice Blackmun recognizes the overreaching of the majority, stating (92 S.Ct. 2816):

Although personally I may rejoice at the Court's result, I find it difficult to accept or justify as a matter of history, of law, or of constitutional pronouncement. I fear the Court has overstepped. It has sought and has achieved an end.

Justice Powell wrote an excellent dissenting opinion in which he applied the proper and appropriate judicial reasoning to this case. He recognized the several places in the Constitution explicitly recognizing capital punishment as appropriate and consistent with due process of law. He writes (92 S.Ct.):

Although determining the range of available punishments for a particular crime is a legislative function, the very presence of the Cruel and Unusual Punishments Clause within the Bill of Rights requires, in the context of a specific case, that courts decide whether particular acts of the Congress offend that Amendment. The Due Process Clause of the Fourteenth Amendment imposes on the judiciary a similar obligation to scrutinize state legislation. But the proper exercise of the constitutional obligation in the cases before us today must be founded on a full recognition of the several considerations set forth above— the affirmative references to capital punishment in the Constitution, the prevailing precedents of this Court, the limitations on the exercise of our power imposed by tested principles of judicial self-restraint, and the duty to avoid encroachment on the powers conferred upon state and federal legislatures. ... (p. 2826)

***

...In a democracy the first indicator of the public's attitude must always be found in the legislative judgments of the people's chosen representatives. ...(p. 2827)

***

...This Court is not empowered to sit as a court of sentencing review, implementing the personal views of its members on the proper role of penology. To do so is to usurp a function committed to Legislative Branch and beyond the power and competency of this Court.

Justice Rehnquist's dissent is succinct and clear in spelling out the overreaching of the majority (92 S.Ct.):

...Sovereignty resides ultimately in the people as a whole and, by adopting through their States a written Constitution for the Nation and subsequently adding amendments to that instrument, they have both granted certain powers to the National Government, and denied other powers to the National and the State Governments. Courts are exercising no more than the judicial function conferred upon them by Art. III of the Constitution.... (p. 2842)

***

Rigorous attention to the limits of this Court's authority is likewise enjoined because of the natural desire that beguiles judges along with other human beings into imposing their own views of goodness, truth, and justice upon others. ... (p. 2843)

***

...The Framers were well aware of the natural desire of office holders as well as others to seek to expand the scope and authority of their particular office at the expense of others. They sought to provide against success in such efforts by erecting adequate checks and balances in the form of grants of authority to each branch of the government in order to counteract and prevent usurpation on the part of the others.

***

... It is for this reason that judicial self-restraint is surely an implied, if not an expressed, condition of the grant of authority of judicial review. The Court's holding in these cases has been reached, I believe, in complete disregard of that implied condition.

There was a great outcry throughout the country, and by many legal scholars, about the usurping of the authority of the legislative branches of the government, and of the people, as a result of the Furman v. Georgia case. Fortunately, on the matter of capital punishment, a solid majority of the United States Supreme Court came back to its senses. In addition, Georgia and many other states amended their laws on capital punishment, and sentencing procedure in an effort to try to comply with what was conceived to be possible tenets of the Furman decision that might still support capital punishment.

In 1976, the United States Supreme Court again granted certiorari and heard three capital cases, *Gregg v. Georgia*, 96 S.Ct. 2909 (1976), *Jurek v. Texas*, 96 S.Ct. 2950 (1976), and *Proffitt v. Florida*, 96 S.Ct. 2960 (1976). In the Georgia case the defendant was convicted of armed robbery and murder, and in the Texas and Florida cases the defendants were convicted of murder; and all were sentenced to death. The convictions and sentences were affirmed by a seven to two decision by the United States Supreme Court. Brennan and Marshall dissented, holding to their same view that capital punishment should be declared unconstitutional, and adhering to their own personal and irrelevant views. There were concurring opinions by several justices, and concurring statements by Chief Justice Burger and Justice Blackmun, but the death penalty was solidly affirmed, and we were now, as to capital punishment, substantially back to the law as set forth in the Constitution, and as intended by its framers and the states that had adopted it. In the Georgia case, the state procedure had been amended and was separated into two stages—first the determination of guilt—secondly the determination of the sentence, by the jury; with the jury being instructed on statutory factors of aggravation and mitigation. Under the Texas procedure, the jury first determined the guilt, and then, in the sentencing phase, relevant evidence was presented and the jury determined certain factors bearing on aggravation and mitigation, and on a continuing threat to society. On a finding against the defendant on these factors, the judge then sentenced the defendant to death in accordance with the statute. In the Florida case, the guilt was determined by the jury, and the judge had the sentencing authority, which required him to take into consideration a number of aggravating and mitigating circumstances that might exist, and to consider the character of the defendant. When the cases are looked at together, there is really not that much difference in them and the prior *Furman* group of cases. The important thing was that a majority of the Court had decided to uphold the Constitution.

We now move ahead twenty years to a case that is more directly relevant to the main theme of this book, which is *Romer v. Evans*, 116 S.Ct. 1620 (1996). Here we have a majority of the United States

Supreme Court again engaging in flagrant and improper judicial legislation. This case resulted from the people of Colorado attempting to protect themselves from the intrusion of the homosexual agenda upon the rights of the people to take into consideration the character of a person in deciding with whom they would associate, and in deciding who they would hire, serve or have on their private property. Under ordinances being passed, people were being deprived of this important right, which they had for more than two hundred years. Under these ordinances, people were either denied the right take into consideration the moral character of a person with whom they chose to deal or to associate, or they had to accept the premise of the homosexualists that sodomy is an acceptable lifestyle, and that the persons engaging in it are of good moral character. Such things also prevented people from practicing their religion and going by their own religious moral values. One's religion means nothing if it must be practiced in a vacuum, and not used to determine how a person conducts his or her day-to-day life. In this sense, I believe that these ordinances themselves, when, on an individual basis, force one to go against one's religious beliefs, are a violation of the First Amendment to the United States Constitution, which provides in part: "Congress shall make no law respecting an establishment of religion, or prohibiting the free exercise thereof;... ." This part of the Bill of Rights, along with at least the other first eight amendments which make up the Bill of Rights, were made applicable to the States by the Fourteenth Amendment.

To try to protect themselves from this intrusion, the people of Colorado voted on and enacted an amendment to the Colorado Constitution, referred to as "Amendment II." It was at once attacked in the courts by certain homosexuals and municipalities involved. The modern liberals have learned well that the will of the people, no matter how well founded on a constitutional basis, can often be overturned by liberal judges engaging in judicial legislation. This is a sad case that is a concrete example of that very thing.

The majority opinion was written by Justice Kennedy, and joined in by Justices Stevens, O'Connor, Souter, Ginsburg, and Breyer. What should have been the decision is well explained in the dissenting opinion of Justice Scalia, joined in by Chief Justice Rehnquist and Justice Thomas.

The Colorado Amendment provided:

No Protected Status Based on Homosexual, Lesbian, or Bisexual Orientation.

Neither the State of Colorado, through any of its branches or departments, nor any of its agencies, political subdivisions, municipalities or school districts, shall enact, adopt or enforce any statute, regulation, ordinance or policy whereby homosexual, lesbian or bisexual orientation, conduct, practices or relationships shall constitute or otherwise be the basis of or entitle any person or class of persons to have or claim any minority status, quota preferences, protected status or claim of discrimination. This Section of the Constitution shall be in all respects self-executing.

As was contemplated by some, the Colorado Amendment was attacked on the basis that it discriminated against a particular group of people and was unconstitutional under the Fourteenth Amendment to the United States Constitution in that it unlawfully denied equal protection of the laws to this group. It was on this basis that the majority opinion struck it down. The majority opinion recognized long-standing principles of constitutional law under the Fourteenth Amendment, which merely amount to a necessary and reasonable construction. The opinion even sets out these principles, referring to the many Supreme Court cases that established them, as follows (citations to the many cases are omitted):

The Fourteenth Amendment's promise that no person shall be denied the equal protection of the laws must co-exist with the practical necessity that most legislation classifies for one purpose or another, with resulting disadvantage to various groups or persons. ... We have attempted to reconcile the principle with the reality by stating that, if a law neither burdens a fundamental right, nor targets a suspect class, we will uphold the legislative classification so long as it bears a rational relation to some legitimate end. ...

***

...In the ordinary case a law will be sustained if it can be said to advance a legitimate government interest, even if the law seems unwise or works to the disadvantage of a particular group, or if the rationale for it seems tenuous. ...

After stating the correct principles of law, the opinion then violates them by injecting the personal views of the majority justices.

In my opinion, the one arguable point of legitimacy about the majority decision was: "Homosexuals, by state decree, are put in a solitary class with respect to transactions and relations in both the private and governmental spheres." This amendment was arguably against a class of people. However the class of persons is determined by acts in which such persons engage. It is not an immutable and involuntary class, such as one's race. I have met a number of ex-homosexuals, but I have never met an ex-black nor an ex-white. Homosexuals are no more an immutable class than are alcoholics or drug addicts. Such classes may be lawfully discriminated against when its comes to hiring, renting of property, and other dealings. This is a matter of common sense as well as law. It is also well established that some people are born with genetic defects, which may increase their probability of becoming such things as alcoholics, or even criminals, but even this does not prohibit discrimination against them. There are some acts that are too vile and base to be accepted by a reasonable society, regardless of the cause.

However, even if it were true, as the majority concluded, that homosexuals constituted a class that could be given special protection, this is not the end of the question, as shown by the law quoted above. This law did not burden a fundamental right, and it did advance a legitimate government interest. No one has a fundamental right to engage in homosexual conduct. And there is no constitutional requirement that homosexuals should have any more rights against discrimination than any other person. Anyone who does not have special minority protection may be generally discriminated against. It is also a complete fallacy for the majority to conclude that the law did not advance a legitimate government interest. The right of a person to abide by one's religious views, and to take moral character into consideration in deciding whether or not to associate or deal with a particular person should certainly be considered a legitimate interest subject to protection if the people or their government so desire.

The opinion also makes the fallacious statement that "the disadvantage imposed is born of animosity toward the class of persons affected," and fallaciously adopts the statement that there was a "desire to harm a politically unpopular group" as applicable to this case.

The following is from Justice Scalia's scathing and appropriate dissenting opinion:

> In holding that homosexuality cannot be singled out for disfavorable treatment, the Court contradicts a decision, unchallenged here, pronounced only 10 years ago, see *Bowers v. Hardwick*, 478 U.S. 186, 106 S.CT. 2841, 92 L.Ed.2d 140 (1986), and places the prestige of this institution behind the proposition that opposition to homosexuality is as reprehensible as racial or religious bias. ...
>
> ***
>
> ...In *Bowers v. Hardwick*, ... we held that the Constitution does not prohibit what virtually all States had done from the founding of the Republic until very recent years—making homosexual conduct a crime. That holding is unassailable, except by those who think that the Constitution changes to suit current fashions. ...If it is constitutionally permissible for a State to make homosexual conduct criminal, surely it is constitutionally permissible for a State to enact other laws merely *disfavoring* homosexual conduct. ... '...After all, there can hardly be more palpable discrimination against a class than making the conduct that defines the class criminal.'... And *a fortiori* it is constitutionally permissible for a State to adopt a provision *not even* disfavoring homosexual conduct, but merely prohibiting all levels of state government from bestowing *special protection* upon homosexual conduct. ...
>
> ***
>
> As Justice Kennedy wrote, when he was in the Court of Appeals, in a case involving discharge of homosexuals from the Navy; 'Nearly any statute which classifies people may be irrational as applied in particular cases. Discharge of the particular plaintiffs before us would be rational, under minimal scrutiny, not because their particular cases present the dangers which justify Navy policy, but instead because the general policy of discharging all homosexuals is rational.' *Beller v. Middendorf*, 632 F.2d 788, 808 - 809, n. 20 (C.A.9 1980). ...
>
> ***
>
> First, as to eminent reasonableness. The Court's opinion contains grim, disapproving hints that Coloradans have been guilty of 'animus' or 'animosity' toward homosexuality, as though that has been established as unAmerican. Of course it is our moral heritage that one should not hate any human being or class of human beings. But I had thought that one could consider certain conduct reprehensible—

murder for example, or polygamy, or cruelty to animals—and could exhibit even 'animus' toward such conduct. Surely that is the only sort of 'animus' at issue here: moral disapproval of homosexual conduct, the same sort of moral disapproval that produced the centuries-old criminal laws that we held constitutional in *Bowers*. The Colorado amendment does not, to speak entirely precisely, prohibit giving favored status to people who are *homosexuals*; they can be favored for many reasons—for example, because they are senior citizens or members of racial minorities. But it prohibits giving them favored status *because of their homosexual conduct*—that is, it prohibits favored status *for homosexuality*.

***

...See , *e.g.,* Jacobs, The Rhetorical Construction of Rights: The Case of the Gay Rights Movement, 1969-1991, 72 Neb. L.Rev. 723, 724 (1993) ('[T]he task of gay rights proponents is to move the center of public discourse along a continuum from the rhetoric of disapprobation, to rhetoric of tolerance, and finally to affirmation.').

By the time Coloradans were asked to vote on Amendment 2, their exposure to homosexuals' quest for social endorsement was not limited to newspaper accounts of happenings in places such as New York, Los Angeles, San Francisco, and Key West. Three Colorado cities— Aspen, Boulder, and Denver—had enacted ordinances that listed 'sexual orientation' as an impermissible ground for discrimination, equating the moral disapproval of homosexual conduct with racial and religious bigotry. ...

***

But the proposition that polygamy can be criminalized, and those engaging in that crime deprived of the vote, remains good law. ...

...Has the Court concluded that the perceived social harm of polygamy is a 'legitimate concern of government,' but the perceived social harm of homosexuality is not?

I strongly suspect that the answer to the last question is yes, which leads me to the last point I wish to make: The Court today, announcing that Amendment 2 'defies ... conventional [constitutional] inquiry,' ... employs a constitutional theory heretofore unknown to frustrate Colorado's reasonable effort to preserve traditional American moral values. The Court's stern disapproval of 'animosity' towards homosexuality might be compared with what an earlier Court (including the revered Justices Harlan and Bradley) said in *Murphy v. Ramsey,* 14 U.S. 15, 5 S.Ct. 747, 29 L.Ed. 47 (1885), rejecting a constitutional challenge to a United States statute that denied the franchise in federal territories to those who engaged in polygamous cohabitation:

> [C]ertainly no legislation can be supposed more wholesome and necessary in the founding of a free, self-governing commonwealth, fit to take rank as one of the coordinate States of the Union, than that which seeks to establish it on the basis of the idea of family, as consisting in and springing from the union for life of one man and one woman in the holy estate of matrimony; the sure foundation of all that is stable and noble in our civilization; the best guaranty of that reverent morality which is the source of all beneficent progress in social and political improvement.

***

When the Court takes sides in the culture wars, it tends to be with the knights rather than the villains—and more specifically with the Templars, reflecting the views and values of the lawyer class from which the Court's Members are drawn. How that class feels about homosexuality will be evident to anyone who wishes to interview job applicants at virtually any of the Nation's law schools. The interviewer may refuse to offer a job because the applicant is a Republican; because he is an adulterer; because he went to the wrong prep school or belongs to the wrong country club; because he eats snails; because he is a womanizer; because she wears real-animal fur; or even because he hates the Chicago Cubs. But if the interviewer should wish not to be an associate or partner of an applicant because he disapproves of the applicant's homosexuality, *then* he will have violated the pledge which the Association of American Law Schools requires all its member-schools to exact from job interviewers: 'assurance of the employer's willingness' to hire homosexuals. By-laws of the Association of American Law Schools.... This law school view of what 'prejudices' must be stamped out may be contrasted with the more plebeian attitudes that apparently still prevail in the United States Congress, which has been unresponsive to repeated attempts to extend to homosexuals the protections of federal civil rights laws. ...

***

Today's opinion has no foundation in American constitutional law, and barely pretends to. The people of Colorado have adopted an entirely reasonable provision which does not even disfavor homosexuals in any substantive sense, but merely denies them preferential treatment. Amendment 2 is designed to prevent piecemeal deterioration of the sexual morality favored by a majority of Coloradans, and is not only an appropriate means to that legitimate end, but a means that Americans have employed before. Striking it down is an act, not of judicial judgment, but of political will. I dissent.

Judge Bork states: "There is no logical or constitutional foundation for the majority's decision in *Romer v. Evans*. The decision is an unsupported victory for homosexual activists, with whom the Court evidently sympathizes." Commenting on the statement of the dissenters that the decision was not judicial judgment, but political will, he states: "That is just what the dissent said of the majority in *Roe v. Wade* (the case creating the right to abortion), and the condemnation was correct in both cases, as it would be in dozens of other decisions in which the Court, without authority in the Constitution or any law, has forced Americans to adopt the Court's view of morality rather than their own. (*Slouching Towards Gomorrah*, p. 114)

Because of this decision on the Colorado Amendment, we need to reconsider *Bowers v. Hardwick*. That case was a five-to-four decision, and now is in danger of being overruled. The only justices remaining on the Court who were in the majority in the *Bowers* case are Rehnquist and O'Connor; and the only one who was a dissenter is Stevens. Both O'Connor and Stevens were in the majority in the Colorado case. It is quite obvious from the Colorado case that six of the justices have somewhat of a liberal bent. The primary reason for the dissent in the Bowers case was the view of the minority that the "constitutional right to privacy" was violated in prosecuting homosexual sodomy.

One of the things that has happened with our liberal courts is that they have invented and are now building on what they call a "Constitutional Right of Privacy" under the United States Constitution. Since they invented it, no one knows what it includes or excludes, until they decide. There is no right of privacy set forth in the Constitution — it is something that has merely been invented from the general wording of the Bill of Rights. This has been a great vehicle for their judicial legislation. Limitations in the size of this book prohibit an extensive discussion of the "right of privacy," and the way it has been used in unlawful judicial legislation by both federal and state judges.

Judge Bork states: "Radical individualism is the only explanation for the Supreme Court's creation, out of thin air, a general and undefined right of privacy." He explains that the Court has used the invented right to strike down laws against the use of contraceptives, restricting access to contraceptives by single persons, and against abortion. (*Slouching Towards Gomorrah*, supra, p. 103)

Judge Bork said the following about Bowers v. Hardwick:

> ...The majority, which ruled against Hardwick, tried to limit the reach of the limit of the right of privacy by saying that the cases decided under that heading had related to the protection of the family. The dissenters made an astonishing response: 'We protect those rights not because they contribute, in some direct and material way, to the general public welfare, but because they form so central a part of an individual's life.' So much for the family as the basic unit of society. The family's value is measured by its contribution to individual gratification. That is a major theme of modern liberalism, particularly of its feminist component, which views the family as oppressive to individuals. (*Slouching Towards Gomorrah*, p. 104)

Judge Bork quotes Lino Graglia, a professor of law at the University of Texas: "the thing to know to fully understand contemporary constitutional law is that, almost without exception, the effect of rulings of unconstitutionality over the past four decades has been to enact the policy preferences of the cultural elite on the far left of the American political spectrum." (*Slouching Towards Gomorrah*, p, 114)

It has become quite clear in the last half of this century that liberal members of the federal courts, and more importantly, the United States Supreme Court, have joined in and contributed to the moral decline of this country. While tearing down religious and moral values, they have supported pornography, abortion, and now homosexuality, under pseudo constitutional theories.

Family News From Dr. James Dobson, Focus on the Family, November 1996, states:

> Today's generation has been bombarded with more evil and more dangerous ideology than any comparable age group in the history of

Western nations. Dogging the young like hungry wolves are those who would exploit them for financial gain, including drug pushers, movie and television producers, sex abusers, abortion providers and rock music junkies. They are also pursued by those who would use them to revolutionize the culture, including homosexual activists, New Age gurus, Planned Parenthood types, and the more radical leaders of the National Education Association.

A Classic example of this manipulation hit my desk a few days ago in the form of an article published in *The Weekly Standard*. It is entitled "Gay-Ed for Tots," which describes a pro-homosexual curriculum for kindergartners and first-graders in the San Francisco Unified School District. It is called "My family," and is promoted via the district's Support Services for Gay, Lesbian and Bisexual Youth Department. This is the convoluted world in which we are raising our children. Whereas the Supreme Court has ruled that the Ten Commandments can't be posted in public schools (*Stone v. Graham*, 449 U.S. 39 [1980]), it is entirely legal to teach perverse lifestyles to babies at taxpayers' expense. No wonder so many of our kids are in such trouble.

Two instances of recent judicial legislation are the Hawaii case in which a state judge ruled that under the Hawaii constitution same-sex marriages must be allowed; and in California where the people passed Proposition 209, which merely required that no one would be discriminated against or given preferences over others because of one's race—a liberal judge struck down this law of the people.

The decision in the Hawaii case was based on an equal rights amendment that had been made part of the Constitution of Hawaii, and provided that no person should be discriminated against on the basis of sex. When this type of amendment to our United States Constitution was being promoted unsuccessfully by the liberals, some conservative writers predicted that such an amendment would be used by liberal judges in just this way, which was then denied. This is a common tack with liberals. Such use of deceit is common with them. Nevertheless, this decision by the Hawaiian judge is pure judicial legislation, and a clear usurpation of the rights of the people and their representatives. So far in this country only two sexes have been recognized: male and female. We do not have some kind of a third sex. Either can enter into a proper lawful marriage with the opposite sex, and this has been the law in this country prior to its independence, and at all times since then. No judge has the authority to change this.

The California decision on Proposition 209 is even more flagrant. This liberal judge, according to The Wall Street Journal, was a former member on the local board of the ACLU. This decision is certainly typical of that ilk. Equal treatment under the law for all persons, regardless of race, was the primary purpose of the Fourteenth Amendment to the United States Constitution. Equal treatment certainly is not giving one person preference over another because of race. This has also been the express purpose of every valid civil rights law that has been passed. To try to find some law to support his decision, the judge invalidly relied on *Romer v. Evans*. He had to have enough sense to know that, as bad as that decision was, the Colorado Amendment could at least be arguably (although invalidly) construed as to be against a particular class of people. This does not exist in the California case. This is a classic example of a liberal judge imposing his own personal political will, contrary to the law. Now the Clinton administration is following suit, and filing briefs taking the same view as the judge. This is the one way that liberals have found that they can overturn the democratic rule of the people provided for in our constitutions, both state and federal. They do it with liberal judges who are not bound by traditional morals of fairness and decency, and continually violate their oaths of office.

An editorial on these cases in *The Wall Street Journal*, 12-20-96, states in summary:

> We certainly hope that the California and Hawaii cases may be a turning point for the many Americans who are growing frustrated by a judiciary so unrestrained that it badly flouts voters and common sense. Courts are not, and were never intended to be, our governing bodies. Judge Henderson and Judge Chang aren't the boss. In a democracy we are.

However, the harder and more important question is whether or not the American people have now become so regulated, beaten down, demeaned by government handouts for their vote, numb, and apathetic, that they no longer have the will to do anything but submit. This is the legacy of government succor. As it has been more crudely, but perhaps more aptly, put: Have we been on that government tit too long to ever become weaned? Will we merely squeal and run back if someone tries to pull us off? Have we been succored into permanent submission? Has our will and our spirit now been removed from us?

Or could it be that the homosexual movement has resulted in an unexpected blessing? Having shown us the gates of hell, has it pushed us so far that we are now willing to throw off our shackles and avoid entering those gates? Are we now ready to stand up and reclaim our traditional morality, and with it reclaim control of our government?

If we are ever going to return to the democratic form of government provided by our Constitution, we are going to have to do something to stem this tide of judicial legislation. Judge Bork's suggested solution is:

> There appears to be only one means by which the federal courts, including the Supreme Court, can be brought back to constitutional legitimacy. That would be a constitutional amendment making any federal or state court decision subject to being overruled by a majority vote of each House of Congress. The mere suggestion of such a remedy is certain to bring down cries that this would endanger our freedoms. To the contrary, as already noted, it is the courts that are not merely endangering our freedoms but actually depriving us of them, particularly our most precious freedom, the freedom to govern ourselves democratically unless the Constitution actually says otherwise. The United Kingdom has developed and retained freedom without judicial review. (*Slouching Towards Gomorrah*, p. 117)

Such drastic changes would need to be given very careful consideration, and much thought by a number of people. But if our system is not to disintegrate, something must be done. Perhaps a two-thirds majority of each House of Congress would be better than mere majorities, with particular rules on the use of this overriding authority, and, of course, no court review.

Another thing that should be considered is more frequent use of the impeachment process, particularly where there is serious usurping of legislative powers by United States Supreme Court justices. However this is a cumbersome, lengthy, and seldom used procedure. Article III of the Constitution provides that judges of both the Supreme Court and the federal inferior courts will hold office during good behavior. Surely knowing failure to do their duty and overstepping their authority by unauthorized changes to the United States Constitution should constitute sufficient misbehavior for impeachment. Using such words as the Constitution being a living document, and that it must be interpreted according to changing times and conditions, is no excuse for changing the Constitution by judicial decree. This prerogative lies only with the people and their elected representatives who are accountable to them. In fact, the very use of such language shows that a judge is overstepping his authority. Otherwise, legal precedent and the wording of the Constitution could be given as authority for the decision. Likewise the inventing of such things as a "right of privacy" should not be tolerated.

Procedure requires that the impeachment charges be initiated in the House of Representatives, and then tried in the Senate. If this were done a few times, it would be much easier for judges to keep in mind what their duties are and the extent of their authority. It probably would not then be needed too often. Also, consideration should be given to streamlining and making more efficient the impeachment process. Nevertheless, we have now gotten to a point where something needs to be done about this serious situation that prohibits the proper working of our democratic and republican form of government. This judicial legislation by the courts has done such harm that there are certain things that should be done as soon as possible to alleviate past transgressions, and to protect further eroding of some of our basic rights that are in immediate danger.

It is respectfully proposed that the people of this country, and their representatives, consider working toward the passage of an amendment to the United States Constitution, such as the following:

Amendment XXVII.

(1) Every person and entity shall have the right to refuse to associate with, work for, hire, retain, promote, have as a member, rent to, rent from, contract with, deal with, or have on his, her, or its premises, any other person or entity, based upon the moral character of such other person or entity, as perceived by the person or entity making the determination and refusal. This right shall not be denied or abridged by the United States or by any State or local government, nor by any existing federal, state, or local laws or regulations.

(2) For purposes of this amendment, entity shall be defined as including, but not limited to, any church, business, corporation,

company, organization, school, or institution, and including any federal, state, or local government, governmental body, or agency.

(3) This amendment shall not be construed as changing in any respect the prohibitions and rights relating to religion set forth in Amendment I of this Constitution, nor rights of a government to condemn property in eminent domain proceedings, nor shall it be construed as changing any rights or duties of persons claiming exemption from military service as conscientious objectors.

It is also proposed that the people and their state representatives work toward passing such an amendment in each state, as getting this done at the federal level would be certain to be long and tedious, even if successful. However, with the people behind it, it certainly could be done. An amendment for state constitutions would necessarily need to be worded so as not to place any prohibitions on federal power, for purposes of legality. Also, the part relating to conscientious objectors would be inappropriate for state constitutions, and other wording in Part (3) would need to be changed to fit particular state constitutions, but such things as this can easily be done on a state by state basis.

We need to consider the purpose of such an amendment, and what it would do, and what it would not do.

It would stop the primary problems we are having with the homosexuals and their movement, and their trying to push acceptance of themselves and their way of life on people and organizations who consider sodomy to be immoral.

It could not be used to discriminate against anyone because of race, as this is something that one has no control over, and no one could reasonably argue that one is immoral because of his race. There are obviously moral and immoral people of every race and color.

Since the amendment would only recognize and insure a right that the people in this country had for two hundred years, and still have in most states, it still probably would not be used to discriminate against anyone because of any true sexual "orientation," if a person is actually born with such, as no one is forced to engage in any unnatural behavior or sexual act, and certainly not in the immoral act of sodomy. Except in rape situations, no one is forced to engage in any sexual act, whether moral or immoral. People are ordinarily discriminated against on a moral basis because of their behavior.

Certain religious groups, such as the Jewish community, may have concern about such an amendment in that one might consider another's religion as a factor of moral character. However, prior to the civil rights movements and the leftist onslaughts which were coincidental with it, our people were free to decide such things for themselves, without the dictation of government. Some governments have now taken it on themselves to decide such things for the people who are apparently considered by these governments as not having sufficient intelligence to make their own decisions.

Certainly in the past and even now there are religious groups that show preference for those of their own religion in determining with whom they associate and with whom they enter into marriage. People should not be prohibited from considering such things in other areas, if they so desire.

Insofar as discrimination in the marketplace, in hiring, in renting and other such things is concerned, little discrimination because of one's religion was exhibited in this country prior to the civil rights movements or any of our drastic movements to the left. Without question, the morality of this country was at a much, and in fact an incomparably higher level at that time. Our market economy and the basic intelligence of our people are sufficient to discourage any unreasonable discrimination based upon religion, rather than the actual morality of the person being considered.

Such an amendment would also help alleviate another growing problem based upon the insupportable and highly illogical idea that in no case should one person be free to discriminate against another in anyway. Even in religious matters, one should have the freedom to use his own judgment in deciding whether or not another's conduct is sufficiently destructive or repressive as to be immoral, even though such conduct may be in connection with or pursuant to some peculiar religion.

Today we have murder and terrorism being committed in the name of certain religions, and even pursuant to orders of those in the hierarchies of such religions. We have Satanic worship, snakes used in worship, and religious claims of rights to use drugs. We all know that recently many people, including women and children, were killed, and apparently some murdered, in connection with and as a part of a radical religious movement. Several years ago another radical religious movement involved the use of drugs, and members of the group committed mass suicide and murders. Some of us are still of the belief that such things are wrong, immoral, and should be discriminated against, even if done in the name of religion. Each of us should have the right to make our own decisions as to whether or not such acts are moral or immoral.

The Pink Swastika, supra, vividly describes the extent to which homosexuality has been a part of many pagan religions. "In pagan cultures homosexuals often hold an elevated position in religion and society." (p. 46) Another reference in this book explains homosexual rites and orgies as a part of religious worship. (pp. 46–47)

Although any vile and destructive belief can be called a religion, we should never be put in the position of having to define religion in a statute or constitutional provision. Likewise, no civil rights law or constitutional provision should ever prevent discrimination on the basis of one's religion. Such things should be left to the conscience of the individual making the determination. That policy served us well under our Constitution for two hundred years.

Such an amendment would make a broad statement that we not only still have a right to have moral beliefs, even if based on our religious views, but that we also still have a right to follow those beliefs in meeting the problems that we face in our day to day life. It would reinforce our right to freedom of speech, and help put an end to some of the ideas of "political correctness" and political oppressiveness taking place in some of our colleges and universities today by the use of official regulation and through campus committees and organizations. Many are trying to force other campus organizations to adopt nondiscrimination policies as to homosexuals, and even to adopt affirmative action programs and brainwashing programs in behalf of them.

It would protect organizations such as the Boy Scouts and Girl Scouts of America and insure their right to determine their own moral standards, instead of having those of the homosexuals forced upon them.

A constitutional amendment such as the above would also bring back some meaning to one's right to practice his own religion as provided by the Constitution, as long as such practice is not unreasonably destructive to one's self, to others, or to society.

The very first clause of the First Amendment to the United States Constitution provides: "Congress shall enact no law respecting an

establishment of religion, or prohibiting the free exercise thereof; ... ."
This was considered a very important right by our forefathers who forged
our bill of rights for us.

This provision is rendered impotent and largely meaningless when
we may have only religious thoughts, but are prevented from exercising
our religious beliefs in any meaningful way in our day to day living. This
is exactly what is happening when a government tells us that we must
consider those who commit sodomy, and other such vile and depraved
acts, on the same basis as those who we consider as having good moral
character and with whom we would be proud to work or associate.

The Bill of Rights in the United States Constitution has been largely
applied to the states, and the First Amendment, in particular, has been
so applied. These laws that make homosexuals a special class that cannot be discriminated against, and forcing them on people whose religious beliefs are strongly opposed to sodomy, violate the First
Amendment, in my opinion. If the matter comes before a conservative
Supreme Court of the United States, which believes that the Court should
interpret the law rather than engage in social legislation, such laws should
be held to be unconstitutional, when forced upon people contrary to
their religious beliefs.

The first part of the clause of the First Amendment on religion, which
merely provides that "Congress shall make no law respecting an establishment of religion," has been applied in an extremely broad manner.
It has been applied to the states, when by its plain wording it applies
only to Congress, and the states are not even mentioned. And although
by its clear wording it prohibits only laws respecting an establishment
of religion, it has been stretched and twisted to the extent that it has
been interpreted to require a complete separation of church and state,
and to the still further extent that people are prohibited from having
Christmas plays in school, and are prohibited from having anyone lead
a prayer in school in situations where it had long and historically been
done. Moreover, public schools are now being prevented from teaching
any meaningful moral values to children, and, instead, schoolchildren
are being taught immorality.

If the prohibition against laws denying one the free exercise of religion is applied even slightly as broadly as the other half of the prohibition, there is no question that a person whose religious beliefs are

offended by the practice of sodomy, cannot be made to accept practicing homosexuals on the same basis as persons who are considered by them to have good moral character. The exercise of one's religion is meaningless if it must be done in a vacuum, in thought only—but can never be applied to how one conducts his or her own business and life.

The proposed amendment would restore the rights that were enjoyed by citizens of this country for over two hundred years, until taken away from some of us by the liberal element in the past 30 years. It would also restore the rights to organizations and governmental bodies to which these rights have been recently denied. We would again have freedom of religion, freedom of association, and the right to take moral character into consideration in determining with whom we deal and have on our premises.

Certainly this proposed amendment, if enacted by a state, could not be reasonably attacked on the basis that it discriminates against a group of people, or that anyone is denied equal protection of the laws under the Fourteenth Amendment. It would guarantee a basic right to every person, and one to which all of us are entitled.

In 1996, the federal Defense of Marriage act was enacted. This act does not prevent a state from recognizing homosexual marriages. It merely provides that a state does not have to recognize such marriage because of the acts of another state under the full faith and credit clause of the United States Constitution. However, there is some doubt about the validity of this act.

Article IV, Section 1, of the United States Constitution provides:

> Full Faith and Credit shall be given in each State to the public Acts, Records, and judicial Proceedings of every other State. And the Congress may by general Laws prescribe the Manner in which such Acts, Records and Proceedings shall be proved and the Effect thereof.

Any authority of Congress for the Defense of Marriage Act must be based on the wording that it may prescribe the manner in which such acts may be proved, "and the Effect thereof." Such acts may not be disregarded, and liberal judges who want to promote homosexual marriages will be tempted to say that such acts must be recognized, and that Congress may only prescribe the procedures, and not allow states to disregard the full faith and credit clause. On the other hand we are fortunate to have strong legal precedent for the proposition that a state is not required to subvert its own public policy to that of another state under this clause. In any case, neither federal nor state law prevents a state from allowing homosexual marriages. It is therefore recommended that both federal and state constitutional provisions be enacted to take care of this matter.

The following is a proposed amendment that is being circulated in New Mexico, by the New Mexico Christian Coalition, which is expected to be presented at the next general legislative session.

A JOINT RESOLUTION

PROPOSING AN AMENDMENT TO ARTICLE XX OF THE CONSTI-TUTION OF NEW MEXICO TO PROHIBIT THE VALIDITY OR REC-OGNITION IN NEW MEXICO OF ANY MARRIAGE EXCEPT A MARRIAGE BETWEEN ONE MAN AND ONE WOMAN.

BE IT RESOLVED BY THE LEGISLATURE OF THE STATE OF NEW MEXICO:

Section 1. It is proposed to amend Article XX of the constitution of New Mexico by adding a new section to read:

"The only marriage that is recognized, or valid, in the State of New Mexico, whether performed or entered into in New Mexico or elsewhere, is a marriage between one man and one woman; and any other marriage is against the public policy of New Mexico."

Section 2. The amendment proposed by this resolution shall be submitted to the people for approval or rejection at the next general election or at any special election prior to that date which may be called for that purpose.

I would certainly recommend that such an amendment be enacted in all of the states, and that consideration also be given to amending the United States Constitution by appropriate wording to accomplish this same thing.

States which do not now have sodomy laws would also do well to reenact laws making homosexual sodomy a criminal offense. Such laws do several things which are helpful to bringing traditional morality back to our society. First they send a message to the community, including the young and impressionable, that sodomy is wrong and unacceptable. They discourage the kind of promiscuity among homosexuals that was so instrumental in bringing the AIDS epidemic to this country, and in spreading all kinds of venereal diseases. And one of the greatest things that sodomy laws do is send a message to homosexuals that what they are doing is considered wrong, and it thereby encourages them to seek help in leaving this destructive lifestyle. They make the strong statement that our society places a value on our morality and Christian–Judaic principles.

Western civilization has always outlawed sodomy

To do away with sodomy laws goes against the accumulated wisdom of centuries of known civilization. In sixteenth-century England, Henry VIII made sodomy a felony and imposed the death penalty for the "detestable and abominable vice of buggery." Sir Edward Coke and Blackstone, the legal authority even of the American colonies, concurred. The death penalty remained there until 1861 when the Offenses Against the Person Act reduced the punishment to a maximum of ten years' imprisonment. (Bayer, R., *Homosexuality and American Psychiatry*, Basic Books, 1981, p. 17)

Since the founding of this country, and even before the colonies became a country, sodomy has always been recognized as a detestable crime against nature, and punished as a crime. It has proved to be a grave error on the part of some of the states that capitulated to the homosexualists and repealed such laws in the last thirty years.

The Founders of this nation also advocated strict sodomy laws. Thomas Jefferson, in his revision of the criminal code of Virginia during the Revolution, prescribed penalties for rape and sodomy. For the male he prescribed castration and for the female a hole, no less than one-quarter inch in diameter, bored through the cartilage of the nose. (Jaffa, H.V., "Sodomy and the Future of the Academy," *The Proposition*, April 1989; Jaffa, H.V., "The Right To Be Queer: A Very Queer Right," *The Proposition*, March 1987.)
(*The Colorado Model*, Colorado for Family Values, supra, pp. 3–6 to 3–11)

From a practical standpoint, I think that a statement of U.S. Supreme Court Justice Clarence Thomas is applicable here, although made in a different context:

> A society that does not hold someone accountable for harmful behavior can be viewed as condoning it—or even worse, endorsing—such conduct. (From a speech by Justice Clarence Thomas, reported in *Human Events*, 6-10-94)

In a state where sodomy laws are enforced, you do not have the bathhouses or clubs where the vile, heinous, and despicable acts of homosexuals are engaged in. You would not have the unbelievably depraved activity now planned in San Francisco, where these things are planned to be openly licensed and condoned. Our parks and public places would also be much safer for young people.

Homosexuals should be given sympathy and help. But homosexuality should never be condoned in any way. It was strongly and criminally condemned in this country when its people had high moral values. Before we can lift our society from the depravity into which it has fallen, we must regain our religious and moral values. This is the only way that we can win the cultural war in which we are presently engaged— not just as to homosexuality, but also as to teenage murder, drug use, illicit pregnancies, illegitimate children, abortion as a form of birth control, pornography, rampant divorce, theft and robbery, and violence in general. Until we regain those values, we will make little progress in any of these areas.

The leadership of our conventional churches has failed us in this cultural war—particularly on the national level. A number of leaders on the national level have chosen the opposite of morality. They have even sided with the homosexual movement on such issues as allowing homosexuals in the military; and forcing them on private citizens, thereby violating their rights to practice their religion, follow their moral values, and to follow traditional values of decency.

We need to do what is necessary to eliminate the effect of various special rights laws enacted in behalf of homosexuals, including the non-discrimination laws based on sexual orientation, "hate-crime laws," and all such laws that in any way promote sodomy. The only way that this can be done from a long range standpoint is by enacting the necessary constitutional amendments at both federal and state levels.

In 1993, Jeremiah Films, Inc., produced the Video, **GAY RIGHTS— SPECIAL RIGHTS**, which is an excellent documentation of dangers of these "rights" laws being foisted on us by the activist homosexuals, and the need to combat them. A number of informed speakers appeared in the film, including Ed Meese, former Attorney General of the United States, Ralph Reed of the Christian Coalition, Dr. Joseph Nicolosi, Senator Trent Lott, and William Bennett, former Secretary of Education. William Bennett said:

> Twenty years ago, they stated their goals, and now, these goals, twenty years, later have become a reality. We are on the very verge of our civilization and our culture being totally overhauled by the homosexual agenda. You need to be that person who takes the stand, either in your school district or in your city or county, or state or on the national level, saying 'enough is enough.'

Senator Trent Lott:

> It's important that people in America rise up and express their indignation and make it clear they're not going to follow it, because what is at stake is the future of our boys and girls, but also what is at stake is the future of America.

Until, as a country, and as a society, we sufficiently regain those traditional moral values, there will be no substantial progress toward accomplishing the things recommended in this book.

Religious people must take an active part in politics, and they must actively and monetarily support organizations that are fighting in the trenches on the moral side of this cultural war. Merely building their church membership, their inner church organizations, and participating in their building projects is not getting the job done.

When testifying before New Mexico legislative bodies and school organizations against the homosexual bills and regulations, I have noticed few churches and ministers up there carrying their share of the load. The great amount of work was done by such organizations as the New Mexico Christian Coalition, headed by Tony Olmi; Family Watch; Col. Dick Toliver (Ret.), with the Reform Party, formerly United We Stand; and a number of interested professionals and other individuals. There were, as I recall, a Baptist church, and perhaps one other church represented. However, there were also several purported churches and church organizations appearing in behalf of the homosexuals. The American Civil Liberties Union was always there representing the homosexual movement, and have continually promoted homosexual and atheist agendas all over the country.

From my observations over the years, the two churches that have best withstood the various onslaughts from the left, including the homosexual movement, have been the Mormons (The Church of Jesus Christ of Latter-Day Saints) and the Southern Baptist Church. There have even been some isolated defections in the Baptist church, but as a church, it has firmly stood its ground. I wish my own church, United Methodist, had done as well. In 1993, the Southern Baptist Convention amended its constitution to give the church the power to oust congregations that condone homosexuality. One church had already been expelled for blessing a union of "gay" men. (*Albuquerque Journal*, 6-14-93)

The 1996 Southern Baptist Convention also voted overwhelmingly for a boycott of Disney films and parks, because of the granting of benefits to homosexual employees and catering to homosexuals in its other activities, and homosexual-themed events at its parks. (*The Albuquerque Tribune*, 6-12-96) Notre Dame, a Catholic university, refused to recognize a campus gay and lesbian group because it would have appeared to have been sanctioning a lifestyle the church opposes. (*The Albuquerque Tribune*, 9-22-95) We should be very thankful that there are still a few universities with such morality and courage.

Christian Islanders resist the imposition of immorality from homosexual-themed Caribbean cruises. Grand Cayman, a territory of Great Britain, informed the agents of Atlantis Events, a tour operator that caters to homosexuals, that it would not be welcome. "Members of homosexual advocacy groups in the United States and Great Britain are furious." The island also has a law against allowing homosexuals to migrate there. "There are similar laws in other Caribbean countries, though the British government is now being urged to sanction its satellites for their intolerance." (*World*, March 7, 1998) It is refreshing to see such morality and courage in this day and time.

Other encouraging things occurred in 1998. By a vote of the people, Maine citizens overturned a "homosexual rights" law enacted by their legislature which had added "sexual orientation" to the civil rights law. (*World*, 2-21-98) It was widely reported that the citizens of Washington state voted down a similar "homosexual rights" law. These actions were widely supported by Christian groups.

I agree with Judge Bork that our best chance—if not now our only chance—to regain our values, is by "a moral regeneration and an intellectual understanding capable of defeating modern liberalism." "Perhaps the most promising development in our time is the rise of an energetic, optimistic, and politically sophisticated religious conservatism. It may be more powerful than merely political or economic conservatism because religious conservatism's objectives are cultural and moral as well." (*Slouching Towards Gomorrah*, p. 336) I believe that the religious conservative movement is the only thing that can turn this country around, and that it definitely has the power to do it, if we who are involved in it do not lose our faith and courage.

Judge Bork further states (*Slouching Towards Gomorrah*, pp. 336–37):

> We may be witnessing a religious revival, another awakening. Not only are the evangelicals stronger than ever in their various denominations but other organizations are likely to bring fresh spiritual forces to our culture and, ultimately, to our politics. The Christian Coalition, the Catholic Campaign for America, and the resurgence of interest among the young in Orthodox Judaism are all signs that religion is gaining strength. If so, religious precepts will eventually influence political action.

> Promise Keepers, like earlier religious awakenings that benefited America, adds an emotional fervor to churches that too often lacked it. It may be a crucial question for the culture whether the Roman church can be restored to its former strength and orthodoxy. Because it is America's largest denomination, and the only one with strong central authority, the Catholic Church can be a major opponent of the

nihilism of modern liberal culture. Pope John Paul II has been attempting to lead an intellectual and spiritual reinvigoration, but there is resistance within the church. Modern liberal culture has made inroads with some of the hierarchy as well as the laity. ...

Liberals of the modern variety are hostile to religious conservatism in any denomination. They realize, quite correctly, that it is a threat to their agenda. For that reason, they regularly refer to the "religious right," using the term as a pejorative to suggest that anything conservative is extreme. ...

It is long past time for all churches that purport to have the Bible as the basis of their religion, and for their members, to begin to shoulder their share of this cultural war. When something is as directly against their religion and is threatening to tear it into shreds as is the homosexual agenda, it is high time that the churches and their members take a political stand, and fight against this planned destruction of our religious moral structure.

There are several organizations that have been carrying this burden for us, and they have been doing it without sufficient help from us. We should give them the needed help with our manpower, with membership, and with finances. We will not win this cultural war without soldiers in the trenches, equipment and supplies for them, and the needed financial support.

The Christian Coalition, formed by the Reverend Pat Robertson, has been at the forefront of this fight, both on a local and on a national basis. Traditional Values Coalition, headed by Rev. Louis P. Sheldon, is another. Colorado For Family Values, formed and headed by Will Perkins of Colorado Springs, did a wonderful job in fighting the homosexual movement in Colorado and in educating the people so that Amendment 2 was passed. Kevin Tebido was director of the organization during the time it was promoting Amendment 2, and during the litigation, and certainly did a commendable job of both working and writing. This organization is now showing a national interest in the fight. Focus on the Family, in Colorado Springs, headed by Dr. James Dobson, and Family Research Council, Gary L. Bauer, President, in Washington, D.C., have been a great benefit to the country in this regard. Dr. James Kennedy and his organization, Coral Ridge Ministries, have constantly and vigorously fought against the homosexual agenda. Christian Action Network, headed by Martin Mawyer, is a similar ministry. The Liberty Alliance and its founder, Dr. Jerry Falwell, continually fight the homosexual movement. The Family Research Institute, headed by Dr. Paul Cameron, has long been in the forefront in the fight against the homosexual agenda. Besides all of his writing, much of which has been used in this book, Dr. Cameron has testified and submitted information around the country, in everything from legislative hearings to court adoption proceedings, and other court cases. He testified in the Colorado case, and was recently on a media program in Britain. Material was previously used at length in this book from the Lambda Report, headed by Peter LaBarbera, Washington D.C. Mr. LaBarbera has long been a tireless fighter against the homosexual movement. He has written extensively and debated issues on the matter around the country, and in the media. There has been a group, Equal Rights Not Special Rights, in Cincinnati, and Stop Promoting Homosexuality, in Hawaii, that have fought the homosexual agenda in their local areas, and are now working to some extent on a national basis. Tony Olmi, head of the New Mexico Christian Coalition, and various members of that organization in New Mexico, have worked tirelessly against that agenda—and for principles of Christianity. I know that there are other individuals and groups that have courageously stood by their religious principles in this war against forcing sodomy upon us, but space and my limited knowledge does not allow me to name and give credit to all of them. But that does not mean that their work has been less valuable—and certainly not in the eyes of the One who counts. Had it not been for people and organizations such as these, this country would be far worse off than it is now. We all owe them a deep debt of gratitude, instead of the denigration they have received from the homosexualists and the liberal media. We owe them our support in the future.

This country was founded on, and our laws have been based on, religious moral principles, until the modern liberal element cut into these principles in recent years. Our Constitution was not formed to keep these principles out of government, but to insure freedom of religion to the people. That is the purpose of the First Amendment to our Constitution, which is the first article of the Bill of Rights. The part that states "Congress will pass no law respecting an establishment of religion" was for the purpose of protecting religion against government encroachment, and for the purpose of further insuring freedom of religion by prohibiting the establishment of government prescribed religion to the exclusion or detriment of other religions. It was not to remove religion or religious principles from our government, from our schools, or from our lives, as the atheistic American Civil Liberties Union would have us believe.

We seem to have forgotten and we need to review some history of this country. It was religiously oriented from the beginning.

The forefathers of this country were the Pilgrims and the Puritans. Both were religious groups who were at odds with the Church of England and its hierarchy. The following is from *The Rebirth of America*, supra.

"When Americans look back to their beginnings, they usually point to the little band of sea weary pioneers that landed in 1620 at Plymouth Rock. Of the more than one hundred pilgrims aboard the Mayflower, the majority were devout Christians. They were Separatists bent on shaking the Church of England and building a new life in an unknown wilderness, where they could worship the Lord in the way they believed the Scripture taught." (p. 27)

"The very purpose of the Pilgrims in 1620 was to establish a government based on the Bible. The New England Charter, signed by King James I, confirmed this goal: '...to advance the enlargement of Christian religion, to the glory of God Almighty... .'

"Governor Bradford, in writing of the Pilgrims' landing, describes their first act: 'being thus arrived in good harbor and brought safe to land, they fell upon their knees and blessed the God of heaven... .'" (p. 31)

It was thought that the reason King Charles granted the Puritans a charter for the Massachusetts Bay Company in 1629 was so that he could get rid of some of his sharpest critics on England's religious policies. (p. 28)

"The goal of government based on Scripture was further reaffirmed by individual colonies such as The Rhode Island Charter of 1683 which begins: 'We submit our persons, lives, and estates, unto our Lord Jesus

Christ, the King of kings, and Lord of lords and to all those perfect and most absolute laws of His given us in His Holy Word.' Those 'absolute laws' became the basis of our Declaration of Independence, which includes in its first paragraph an appeal to the laws of nature and of nature's God. Our national Constitution established a republic upon the 'absolute laws' of the Bible, not a democracy based on the changing whims of the people." (pp. 31–32)

(It should also be noted that the last sentence of the Declaration of Independence was: "And for the support of this Declaration, with a firm reliance on the protection of divine Providence, we mutually pledge to each other our Lives, our Fortunes and our sacred Honor.")

"In the summer of 1787, representatives met in Philadelphia to write the Constitution of the United States. After they had struggled for several weeks, eighty-one-year-old Benjamin Franklin rose and addressed the troubled and disagreeing convention that was about to adjourn in confusion.

" '... I have lived, Sir, a long time, and the longer I live, the more convincing proofs I see of this truth: that God governs the affairs of man. And if a sparrow cannot fall to the ground without His notice, is it probable that an empire can rise without His aid? We have been assured, Sir, in the Sacred Writings that except the Lord build the house, they labor in vain that build it. I firmly believe this....

"'I therefore beg leave to move that henceforth, prayers imploring the assistance of Heaven and its blessing on our deliberation be held in this assembly every morning.'" (p. 31)

Our Constitution was then formed by the representatives.

Daniel Webster later stated: "Lastly, our ancestors established their system of government on morality and religious sentiment. Moral habits, they believed, cannot safely be trusted on any other foundation than religious principle, nor any government be secure which is not supported by moral habits." (p. 29)

"Continuing through the decades of history, we find in the inaugural addresses of all the Presidents, and in the Constitution of all fifty of our states, without exception, references to the Almighty God of the universe, the Author and Sustainer of our liberty." (p. 32)

"One of George Washington's early official acts was the first Thanksgiving Proclamation, which reads, 'Whereas it is the duty of all nations to acknowledge the providence of Almighty God, to obey his will, to be grateful for his benefits, and humbly implore His protection and favor....' It goes on to call the nation to thankfulness to Almighty God." (p. 32)

Abraham Lincoln said:

> It is the duty of nations of men, to own their dependence upon the overruling power of God and to recognize the sublime truth announced in the Holy Scriptures and proven by all history, that those nations only are blessed whose God is the Lord. (p. 32)

All of our Ivy League schools, Harvard, Yale, Princeton, and Dartmouth, owe their origins to the Christian Gospel. Harvard was formed by the Puritans in 1638, Yale was formed in 1701, Princeton in 1746, and Dartmouth in 1754. Evangelical religion was the common base of all of them. Columbia, William and Mary, and a number of other Christian colleges and universities were later formed. The Ivy League schools later became secular. (pp. 41–42) (The fact that many have now in fact become anti-religious is certainly one of the critical moving factors in the decline of moral and religious values that has now reached the greatest degree of decadence in our history.)

(Noah Webster lived from 1758 to 1853, and was highly respected as both a statesman and an educator. His name also became synonymous with "dictionary." [*Encyclopedia Britannica*, 1973, Vol. 23, pp. 360–361]) He stated:

> The moral principles and precepts contained in the Scriptures ought to form the basis of all our civil constitutions and laws. All the miseries and evils which men suffer from vice, crime, ambition, injustice, oppression, slavery, and war, proceed from their despising or neglecting the precepts contained in the Bible. (p. 33)

In the case of *Rector, etc., of Holy Trinity Church v. United States*, 12 S.Ct. 511 (1892), the Supreme Court of the United States reviewed the religious history of this country. The case involved the church bringing over a person from England to be its rector and pastor. It was claimed that this was a violation of the immigration law that prohibited the bringing in of aliens who had contracted to do labor. The Court held that the acts in question were outside the purpose of the law, and that any other construction would be against the right of the church to practice its religion, and that congress could not reasonably have intended such a construction. The Court stated:

> But, beyond all these matters, no purpose of action against religion can be imputed to any legislation, state or national, because this is a religious people. This is historically true. From the discovery of this continent to the present hour, there is a single voice making this affirmation. ... (p. 514)
>
> ***
>
> The fundamental orders of Connecticut, under which a provisional government was instituted in 1638-39, commence with: "For as much as it has pleased the Almighty God ... there should be an orderly and decent Government established ... ." (p. 514)
>
> In the charter of privileges granted by William Penn to the province of Pennsylvania, in 1701, it is recited: "Because no People can be truly happy, though under the greatest Enjoyment of Civil Liberties, if abridged of Freedom of their Consciences, as to their Religious Profession and Worship; And Almighty God being the only Lord of Conscience, Father of Lights and Spirits; and the Author as well as Object of all divine Knowledge, Faith, and Worship, who only doth enlighten the Minds and persuade and convince the Understandings of People, I do hereby grant and declare ... ." (p. 515)
>
> Coming nearer to the present time, the declaration of independence recognizes the presence of the Divine in human affairs ... .
>
> If we examine the constitutions of the various states, we find in them a constant recognition of religious obligations. Every constitution of every one of the 44 states contains language which either directly or by clear implication, recognizes a profound reverence of religion, and an assumption that its influence in all human affairs is essential to the well-being of the community. ... (p. 515)
>
> ***
>
> There is no dissonance in these declarations. There is a universal language pervading them all, having one meaning. They affirm and reaffirm that this is a religious nation. These are not individual

sayings, declarations of private persons. They are organic utterances. They speak the voice of the entire people... .

...These, and many other matters which might be noticed, add a volume of unofficial declarations to the mass of organic utterances that this is a Christian nation. (p. 516)

Imagine the harsh criticism today if one in public, in other than a church, should utter the religious sentiments such as those expressed above by the forefathers of this country. The liberal media would call such things the hateful and bigoted utterances of the radical right and religious fundamentalists.

Imagine the uproar if the United States Supreme Court made statements today, such as those made in 1892 in *Holy Trinity Church v. U. S.* Compare those statements to the Court's anti-religious statements of modern times. Compare them to the religiously devoid and morally devoid statements of the majority opinion in *Romer v. Evans*.

The newsletter of James C. Dobson, Ph.D., *Focus on the Family*, Colorado Springs, Colo., June 1996, is a rich source of quotations on the subject of religion from prior leaders and great men of this country, from which we get the following:

Honorable John Jay, the first Chief Justice of the United States Supreme court, who had also served as governor of New York:

Providence has given to our people the choice of their rulers, and it is the duty . . . of our Christian nation to select and prefer Christians for their rulers.
—1816. (Johnston, Henry P., ed., *The Correspondence and Public Papers of John Jay*, [New York: G. P. Putnam & Sons, 1893], vol. 4, p.393)

(Dr. Dobson also quoted a part of the opinion of the *Church of the Holy Trinity vs. the United States*, referred to above, noting that Justice David Brewer wrote for the majority, in 1892)

Justice William O. Douglas (who, incidentally, was one of the most liberal justices of our time) wrote:

We are a religious people whose institutions presuppose a Supreme Being. — 1952 (*Zorach vs. Clauson*, 343 U.S. 306 at 313. 1952)

"One of our more liberal Supreme Court chief justices, Earl Warren, left no doubt about what he believed in a 1954 speech reported in *Time* magazine. I consider this quote to be breathtaking, considering how recently it was made and that it was uttered by a chief justice who is not remembered as a conservative jurist. This is what he said:

I believe no one can read the history of our country without realizing that the Good Book and the spirit of the Savior have from the beginning been our guiding geniuses . . . Whether we look to the first Charter of Virginia . . . or to the Charter of New England . . or to the Charter of Massachusetts Bay . . or to the Fundamental Orders of Connecticut . . the same objective is present . . . a Christian land governed by Christian principles. I believe the entire Bill of Rights came into being because of the knowledge our forefathers had of the Bible and their belief in it: freedom of belief, of expression, of assembly, of petition, the dignity of the individual, the sanctity of the home, equal justice under law, and the reservation of powers to the people . . . I like to believe we are living today in the spirit of Christian religion. I like also to believe that as long as we do so no great harm can come to our country.
      —1954 ("Breakfast at Washington," *Time*, Feb. 14, 1954, p. 49)"

George Washington, our first and perhaps our most revered president, wrote a prayer addressed to "O most glorious God, in Jesus Christ." He concluded with these words:

      . . . Let me live according to those holy rules which Thou has this day prescribed in Thy holy word . . . Direct me to the true object, Jesus Christ the way, the truth and the life. Bless, O Lord, all the people of this land." — 1752 (Burk, W. Herbert, *Washington's Papers*, [Norristown, Pa.: Published for the benefit of the Washington Memorial Chapel, 1907], pp. 87–95)

John Adams, our first vice-president and second president, wrote:

Our Constitution was made only for a moral and religious people. It is wholly inadequate to the government of any other. — 1798 (Adams,

Charles Francis, ed., *The Works of John Adams, Second President of the United States*, [Boston: Little, Brown, and Co., 1954], IX, p. 229)

Thomas Jefferson, our third president, and the principle framer of our Declaration of Independence, wrote:

Can the liberties of a nation be thought secure when we have removed their only firm basis, a conviction in the minds of the people that these liberties are of the gift of God? — 1781 (Padover, Saul K, ed., *The Complete Jefferson*, Query XVII [New York: Tudor Publishing, 1943], p. 677)

James Madison, our fourth president and one of the founders of this country, said:

[T]o suppose that any form of government will secure liberty and happiness without virtue in the people is a chimerical idea. (*Human Events*, 9-20-96)

Our sixth president, John Quincy Adams, said:

No book in the world deserves to be so unceasingly studied and so profoundly meditated upon as the Bible. — 1812 (*Letters of John Quincy Adams to his Son on the Bible and its Teachings*, [Auburn N. Y.: James M. Alden, 1850], p. 119)

Is it not that the Declaration of Independence first organized the social compact on the Foundation of the Redeemer's mission upon earth? That it laid the cornerstone of human government upon the first precepts of Christianity? — 1837 (Adams, John Quincy, *An Oration Delivered Before the Inhabitants of the Town of Newburyport, at their request on the Sixty-First Anniversary of the Declaration of Independence, July 4, 1837* [Newburyport: Morass and Brewster, 1837])

Benjamin Franklin, one of the highly respected founding fathers, stated:

Only a virtuous people are capable of freedom. As nations become corrupt and vicious, they have more need of masters. (*Human Events*, 9-20-96)

Another quote from Abraham Lincoln, our 16th president:

...we have forgotten God. We have forgotten the gracious hand which preserved us in peace and multiplied and enriched and strengthened us; and we have vainly imagined, in the deceitfulness of our hearts, that all these blessings were produced by some superior wisdom and virtue of our own. Intoxicated with unbroken success, we have become too self-sufficient to feel the necessity of redeeming and preserving grace, too proud to pray to the God that made us. It behooves us, then, to humble ourselves before the offended Power, to confess our national sins, and to pray for clemency and forgiveness. — 1863 (Stokes, Anson Phelps, (*Church and State in the United States*, [New York: Harper and Brothers, 1950], vol. III, p. 186)

Theodore Roosevelt, 26th president:

In this actual world, a churchless community, a community where men have abandoned and scoffed at, or ignored their religious needs, is a community on the rapid down-grade. — 1917 (*Ladies Home Journal*, October 1917, p. 12, as cited in Albert Bushnell Hart and Herbert Ronald Ferleger, *Theodore Roosevelt Cyclepedia*, [New York: Roosevelt Memorial Association, 1941], p, 77)

Woodrow Wilson, 28th president and Governor of New Jersey:

America was born a Christian nation. America was born to exemplify the devotion to the elements of righteousness which are derived from the revelations of the Holy Scripture. — 1911 (Lundin, Roger and Mark A. Noll, eds., *Voices from the Heart: Four Centuries of American Piety,* [Grand Rapids: Eerdmans, 1987], p. 235)

Calvin Coolidge, our 30th president, said about America's founding fathers:

They were intent upon establishing a Christian commonwealth in accordance with the principles of self-government. They were an inspired body of men. It has been said that God sifted the nations that He might send choice grain into the wilderness . . . who can fail to see it in the hand of Destiny? Who can doubt that it has been guided by a Divine Providence? — 1923 (Coolidge, Calvin, *The Price of Freedom: Speeches and Addresses*, [New York: Charles Scribner's Sons, 1924], pp. 351-353, as cited in *The Annals of America* [Chicago: Encyclopedia Brittanica, 1976], vol. 14, pp. 410–411)

From Franklin Roosevelt's prayer on a national radio hookup on D-Day, June 6, 1944, as our troops stormed the beaches of Normandy, France:

Almighty God . . . with Thy blessing we shall prevail over the unholy forces of our enemy. Help us to conquer the apostles of greed and racial arrogance. Lead us to the saving of our country. Thy will be done, Almighty God. Amen. — 1944 (Cassette Recording, Franklin Delano Roosevelt Presidential Library, Hyde Park, N.Y., June 6, 1944)

Harry Truman, our 33rd president:

If men and nations would but live by the precepts of the ancient prophets and the teachings of the Sermon on the Mount, problems which now seem so difficult would soon disappear . . . That is a supreme opportunity for the church to continue to fulfill its mission on earth. The Protestant church, the Catholic church, and the Jewish synagogue—bound together in the American unity of brotherhood—must provide the shock forces to accomplish this moral and spiritual awakening. No other agency can do it. Unless it is done, we are headed for the disaster we would deserve. Oh, for an Isaiah or a St. Paul to reawaken a sick world to its moral responsibilities. — 1946 (Stokes, *op. cit.* vol. III, pp. 712–713)

Gerald Ford, 38th president, quoting from a speech by Dwight D. Eisenhower (34th president):

Without God there could be no American form of government, nor an American way of life. Recognition of the Supreme Being is the first—the most basic—expression of Americanism. Thus, the founding fathers of America saw it, and thus with God's help, it will continue to be. — 1974 (Ford, Gerald R., "National Day of Prayer, 1974," Proclamation 4338, December 5, 1974)

Ronald Reagan, our 40th president, (and former governor of California):

> The frustrating thing is that those who are attacking religion claim they are doing it in the name of tolerance, freedom and open-mindedness. Question: Isn't the real truth that they are intolerant of religion? They refuse to tolerate its importance in our lives. — 1984 (*New York Times*, "Remarks by President at Prayer Breakfast," Aug. 24, 1984, p. A11)

The founders of our freedom, our American government, and our Constitution were always clear and emphatic about the importance of religion to all of these principles.

After George Washington decided not to run for a third term as president, he wrote a long farewell address, containing some important things that he wanted to say to the people of the country. This was so important to him that he sent a draft to Alexander Hamilton, asking him to rework it, which Hamilton did. Washington then reworked it again, and it was published as his farewell address in the American Daily Advertiser, Philadelphia, September 19, 1796. The following are some of the thoughts contained in it:

> Of all the dispositions and habits which lead to political prosperity, religion and morality are indispensable supports. In vain would that man claim the tribute of patriotism who should labor to subvert these great pillars of human happiness, these firmest props of the duties of men and citizens. The mere politician, equally with the pious man, ought to respect and cherish them. A volume could not trace all their connections with private and public felicity.
>
> Let it be simply stated—Where is the security for property, for reputation, for life, if the sense of religious obligation desert the oaths, which are the instruments of investigation in courts of justice? And let us with caution indulge the supposition that morality can be maintained without religion. Whatever may be conceded to the influence of refined education on minds of peculiar structure, reason and experience both forbid us to expect that national morality can prevail in exclusion of religious principle.

It is substantially true that virtue or morality is a necessary spring of popular government. The rule indeed extends with more or less force to every species of free government. Who that is a sincere friend to it can look with indifference upon attempts to shake the foundation of the fabric? (*The Annals of America,* Vol. 3, p. 612, Encyclopedia Britannia, Inc., 1968)

Patrick Henry, one of the founders of this country, a Revolutionary leader, an orator, and five times Governor of Virginia always supported religious and Christian principles. He said:

The Bible is worth all other books that have ever been printed. (*Our Nation Under God*, Christian Defense Fund, U.S. 1997)

On his death bed, Patrick Henry said:

Doctor, I wish you to observe how real and beneficial the religion of Christ is to a man about to die ... . I am, however, much consoled by reflecting that the religion of Christ has, from its first appearance in the world been attacked in vain by all the wits, philosophers, and wise ones, aided by every power of man, and its triumphs have been complete. (Ibid.)

Justice Scalia, as detailed in Chapter 5, was recently severely criticized by the media for even bringing up his belief in God in a speech he made that was not in court and had nothing to do with any particular court decision. How times have changed!

Therein lies the basic and only reason for our current lack of morals and degradation in this country. We have forsaken the religious morals of our forefathers, and we are now reaping the results of our immoral ways—and it will only get worse unless we, as a nation, turn back to those teachings.

Please consider what George Washington said, and what John Adams said, referred to above, that "our Constitution was made for a moral and religious people." Because we have torn loose from our religious and moral moorings, that document has been effectively torn asunder, and we are now faced with the great problem of getting it back to what it actually was in the first place before liberals with their judicial legislation changed it to their own invalid views.

This part of the book is written during the second term of President William Jefferson Clinton. It is my assessment that this is by far the most immoral and destructive administration in the history of this country, and that President Clinton, and his wife, Hillary Clinton, are the most immoral pair to ever disgrace the White House. Due to Clinton's lecherous and perverted sexual appetites, along with his continuous wrongful acts, and false and perjurious statements, he is presently in danger of impeachment. And I would consider his impeachment and removal from office as immensely uplifting to the morality of the country.

The most disheartening thing is that the people elected him to two terms knowing of his immorality and serious character flaws. This came about because various factions and special interest groups, and many individuals, felt that they would gain something—either in money passed out in the form of welfare programs or subsidies—or in the passing of laws for the benefit of special interest groups. And this they got—along with the greatest moral decline in any six years of our history.

One of the great thinkers among the forefathers of this country was Noah Webster. Of all of our historical writings, I have found none that more aptly fits our present situation than the following passage from **Value of the Bible and Excellence of the Christian Religion**, by Noah Webster, 1834. The subtitle is my own:

The Necessity of Morality in Government

When you become entitled to exercise the right of voting for public officers, let it be impressed on your mind that God commands you to choose for rulers *just men who will rule in the fear of God*. The preservation of a republican government depends on the faithful discharge of this duty; if the citizens neglect their duty, and place unprincipled men in office, the government will soon be corrupted; laws will be made, not for the public good, so much as for selfish or local purposes; corrupt or incompetent men will be appointed to execute the laws; the public revenues will be squandered on unworthy men; and the rights of the citizens will be violated or disregarded. If a republican government fails to secure public prosperity and happiness, it must be because the citizens neglect the divine commands, and elect bad men to make and administer the laws. Intriguing men can never be safely trusted. (Bennett, William J., *Our Sacred Honor*, pp. 396-397)

And so we get what we deserve!

Our Constitution and our laws have been decimated by modern liberalism. We have forsaken the religious moral tenets upon which our country was founded, and our society is on its way to becoming worse than Sodom and Gomorrah. We first, with the help of God, must regain our moral principles. Until we do, we will never have the courage and the energy to turn our country around, and regain the decent and worthwhile quality of life that once existed.

However, I believe that there still remains a great amount of decency in this world. We have the ability, with God's help, to turn our country back in the right direction. Its future is in our hands.

TABLE OF CITATIONS

(This table contains what are considered
major citations – including some citations within citations.)

Kennedy, D. James, Ph.D., Coral Ridge Ministries, newsletter of
  October 27, 1997 439
Kerrison, Ray, writer for the New York Post. "'Gay' Benefits Endanger
  Country's Social Structure." *Human Events*, 12-15-95 636
Kilpatrick, James J. "Humpty-Dumpty Decision Shatters Logic."
  Albuquerque Journal, 1-12-89 617
Kilpatrick, James J. Radicals Are Ruining American Universities.
  Albuquerque Journal, 11-40-90 236
King James Version of the Holy Bible 211-218, 514, 652
King, M. and McDonald, E. "Homosexuals who are twins: a study
  of 46 probands." *British Journal of Psychiatry*, 1992, 160: 407-409 162
Kinsey – A Homosexual! *Family Research Report*, Family Research
  Institute, Sept. - Oct. 1997, referring to an article (Jones, J.H.,
  Dr. Yes., *New Yorker*, August 25-Sept. 1, 1997, 98-113) 37, 521
Kinsey Breakthrough. *Family Research Council Washington Watch*,
  10-27-95 508
Kirk, Marshall K., and Pill, Erastes. "THE OVERHAULING OF
  STRAIGHT AMERICA—WAGING PEACE—PART TWO." *Guide*
  Magazine, November 1987, a large part of which was reprinted in
  The Colorado Model, Colorado for Family Values, 1993 . . . . 22, 77, 495
Kirk, Marshall, and Madsen, Hunter. *After the Ball*. Penguin Books
  USA, Inc., New York, c/o Doubleday, New York, 1990 . . . . 33-36, 66, 68, 69
Korn, Peter. "THE NEW AIDS MYSTERY." *Redbook Magazine*,
  July 1994 522
Krauthammer, Charles (Columnist). "Polls Suggest Voters Don't
  Care if Clinton is Dishonest." *Albuquerque Journal*, 7-7-96 275
Kuchta, John C., Ph.D. "Homosexuality, Psychiatry &
  Amendment 2: The Whole Story." *Tri-Lakes Times*, March 3, 1993,
  reprinted in *The Colorado Model*, Colorado for Family Values,
  Colorado Springs, Co. 1993 195
LaBarbera, Peter. "Giuliani Condones Pro-NAMBLA Parade." *Human*
  Events, 7-8-94 431
LaBarbera, Peter. "L.A. Educator Asserts Lincoln Had Homosexual
  Affairs." *Lambda Report on Homosexuality*, April-June 1995 504
LaBarbera, Peter. "Major Media Underwrite, Recruit at Gay
  Journalists Convention." *Lambda Report*, January, 1996 444
LaBarbera, Peter. "NEA Teacher Handbook Reveals Far-Reaching
  Pro-Gay Agenda." *Lambda Report on Homosexuality*, April-June 1995 . . . 580
LaBarbera, Peter. "TEACHER'S BIBLICAL OPINION CENSORED."
  Christian American, July/August, 1994 626

LaBarbera, Peter. "What the Media Didn't Show You – SADO-MASOCHISTS HOLD 'S/M-FETISH' CONFERENCE AS PART OF GAY MARCH ON WASHINGTON." *CFV Report,* June, 1993 61

LaBarbera, Peter. DIVERSITY "Daze." *Family Voice,* Concerned Women for America, November/December, 1994 551

LaBarbera, Peter. Louganis Said To Typify "Made" Homosexual. *Lambda Report,* April-June 1995 164

LaBarbera, Peter. NEA Grant Funds Book Claiming St. Augustine, King David, St. Paul and Eleanor Roosevelt Were "Gay". *Lambda Report on Homosexuality,* July - Sept. 1995 501

Langer, Walter C. *"The Mind of Adolf Hitle": The Secret Wartime Report.* New York: Basic Books, Inc.,1972 . . . . 135, 136, 137, 138

Lawfully wedded. *Family Voice,* April 1996 558

Leo, John. "Recent Research Exposes Myth of Victimized Homelessness." *Albuquerque Journal,* 11-293 291

Leo, John. "Television Still Pushing Envelope of Public Coarseness." *Albuquerque Journal,* 4-15-96 286

Leo, John. "Time Warner Corners Popular Market on Cultural Degradation." *Albuquerque Journal,* 3-21-95 292

Leo, John. The lawyers are at it again. *U.S. News & World Report,* 3-16-98 644

Leo, John."No Sensitivity Issues Arise in Artistic Christian Bashing." *Albuquerqu Journal,* 6-9-89 631

Lesbian Blasts Promiscuous Gay Sex Indoctrination in Public Schools. *Lambda Report on Homosexuality,* October '95 - January '96 601

Lesbian faces life in taped slayings. *Albuquerque Journal,* 5-23-96 133

Lesbian Teacher Unmercifully Intimidates Christian Student. *Human Events,* 4-15-96 449

Littlefield, Kinney. "95 was year that gay came to stay on prime-time TV." *Albuquerque Journal,* 1-11-96 439

Lively, Scott, and Abrams, Kevin. *The Pink Swastika.* Keizer, Oregon: Founders Publishing Corporation, 1995 . . . .
. . . . 22, 113, 114, 117, 128, 135, 136, 139, 140-145, 154, 227, 511, 677

Lively, Scott. *The Poisoned Stream -"Gay" Influence in Human History.* Vol. 1. Keizer, Or.: Founders Publishing Corp., 1997 137

London, Herbert. "Yale Won't Make Concessions to Religious Students." *Human Events,* 10-10-97 334

Look Who's Teaching Our Children! *The Phyllis Schafly Report,* Sept. 1994 329

Lundin, Roger and Mark A. Noll, eds. *Voices from the Heart: Four Centuries of American Piety.* Grand Rapids: Eerdmans, 1987 695

Maginnis, Lt. Col. Robert L. (Retd.). "NBC Offers Aid and Comfort To Subverters of Civilization." *Human Events*, 2-17-95 620

Manligit, G.M., and Talpaz, M., etal. "Chronic Immune Stimulation by Sperm Allonantigens." *Journal of American Medical Association*, 1984, 251)2), pp. 237-241 . . . . 24, 26

Marine Still Opposed to Gays. *Albuquerque Journal*, 7-2-93 538

Marmor, Dr. Judd. *Homosexual Behavior: A Modern Reappraisal.* New York: Basic Books, 1982 160

Marshall, W. L., et. al. "Early onset and deviant sexuality in child molesters." *Journal of Interpersonal Violence*, 1991, 6, 323-336) 74, 78

Massachusetts Celebrates "Gay Youth Pride". *Lambda Report*, April-June 1995 451

Masters, C. and Johnson, O. *Human Sexual Inadequacy.* Boston: Little, Brown and Co. 1979 . . . . 78, 609

Maves, Carl. "Getting Over It." *The Advocate*, 5 May 1992, p. 85 76

Maynard, Roy. "The new homophobia: Schools fear lawsuits." *World*, 1-16-96 90

McDowell, Josh. IF THE FOUNDATIONS BE DESTROYED. *Family Voice*, Nov./Dec. 1994 484

McIlhenny, Chuck & Donna, and York, Frank. *When the Wicked Seize a City.* Lafayette, La.: Huntington House Publishers, 1993 148

McKusick, L., etal. "AIDS and Sexual Behavior Reported by Gay Men in San Francisco." *American Journal of Public Health*, 1985 . . . 24, 26, 27

Media and Homosexuals. *Aim Report*, Accuracy in Media, Inc., May-A 1996 116

Medical Consequences of What Homosexuals Do. Family Research Institute, 1993 . . . . 65, 112, 223

Mehlman, Rabbi Bernard H. "Lest We Forget: 'Homophobia' and Anti-Semitism are the Same Disease." (Undated Pink Flyer advertising New England Holocaust Memorial project) 512

METHODIST REBELS (About same-sex marriages). *World*, 12-20-97 630

Military Retirees Launch Campaign To Keep Gay Ban. *Albuquerque Journal*, 5-4-93 537

Minkowitz, Donna. "FRIENDLY FIRE." *The Advocate*, 12-29-92 563

Mohler, R. Albert Jr. "De-Christianized Dartmouth." *World*, 12-27-97 632

Morgenthaler, Eric. "The Last Chapter of 'Pedro's Story' Is Drawing to a close." *The Wall Street Journal*, 10-21-94 414

Sodomy Laws. *The Colorado Model*, Colorado for Family Values, Colorado Springs, Co., 1993 (pp. 3-6 to 3-11) 26, 43, 68, 69, 113

Some Fired Scoutmasters Sill Abuse Boys. *Albuquerque Journal*, 10-15-93 643

Sowell, Thomas W. "Americans are sick of liberals and criminals." *The Albuquerque Tribune*, 12-17-93 284

State v. Lamure, N.M. Court of Appeals, 12-21-92 82

Stewart, S. A. *USA Today*, November 21, 1984 26

Stokes, Anson Phelps. *Church and State in the United States*. [New York: Harper and Brothers, 1950], vol. III, p. 186 695

STONEWALL -- 25 YEARS OF DECEPTION. VCR, The Report, 1994 63

Students' study sessions turned into sex parties. *The Albuquerque Tribune*, 11-6-95 330

Survey of Homosexuals in the Military. Family Research Institute (FRI), then in Washington D.C., 1992 94

Survey on the Constitutional Right to Privacy in the Context of Homosexual Activity. 40 *U of Miami L Rev* 521, 525 (1986). 219

Swift, Michael. "For The Homoerotic Order." *Gay Community News* (Boston), Feb. 15-21, 1987; reprinted in *The Congressional Record*; reprinted in *The Colorado Model*, Colorado for Family Values, Colorado Springs, Co. 1993 21

Teacher, Students Face Animal Abuse Charges. *Albuquerque Journal*, 12-24-96 395

Teachers Call for Lesbian/Gay History Month in Public Schools. *The Phyllis Schlafly Report*, Jan. 1993 598

Teen 'Vampires' Held in Spree. *Albuquerque Journal*, 3-7-98 395

Teen-agers laugh while they watch Mister Softee die. *The Albuquerque Tribune*, 6-17-94 376

Teen-burglary case grows to 17 defendants of all ages. *The Albuquerque Tribune*, 4-4-96 390

Texas County Yields to Pro-Gay Pressure. *Human Events*, 12-18-93 433

The Annals of America, Vol. 3, p. 612, Encyclopaedia Britannia, Inc., 1968 698

The Business of Porn. *U.S. News & World Report*, 2-10-97 406

The Columbus of AIDS. *National Review*, November 6, 1987 135

The Gay Agenda - The March on Washington. The Report, 1993, a VCR tape 60

The Gay Agenda, by The Report, a VCR tape, published in 1992 . . . . 25, 28, 29, 30, 31, 32, 52, 57, 67, 73, 98, 160, 164, 172

The Homosexual Agenda: How the Gay Lobby is Targeting America's Children. Americans for Truth About Homosexuality, A Division of the Christian Defense Fund, Washington. D.C., 1997 604

The Homosexual Deception: Making Sin A Civil Right. Concerned Women for America, 1991 and 1992 . . . . . 25, 41, 43, 67, 72, 73, 105, 135, 157, 517

The limits of tolerance. *World*, June 14/21, 1997 421

The NEA Proves Itself Extremist Again. *The Phyllis Schafly Report*, August 1996 578

THE NEW TESTAMENT 213

THE OLD TESTAMENT 211

The Psychology of Homosexuality. Institute for the Scientific Investigation of Sexuality. ISIS, 1984 27

The Rebirth of America. Nancy Leigh DeMoss, Editor, Arthur S. DeMoss Foundation, 1986 . . . . 229, 238, 244, 688

Thomas, Cal. "Gay Conversion: A reality psychologists ignore." *Christian American*, Jan/Feb 1998 206

Thomas, Cal. "Gay rights would open the door." *Conservative Chronicle*, 5-12-93 583

Thomas, Cal. "Gays won't stop making demands." *Conservative Chronicle*, 2-10-93 532

Thomas, Cal. "Mayor Dinkins guts foundations of society." *Conservative Chronicle*, 3-17-93 430

Thorstad, David. "Man-Boy Love and the American Gay Movement." *The Journal of Homosexuality*, 1990, vol. 20, pp. 251-252 . . . . 77, 609

Thorstad, David. "The Death of Gay Liberation?" *NAMBLA Bulletin*, June 1994, vol. 14, no. 4, pp. 8-9 77

Transvestite Activist Gives Commencement. *Lambda Report*, April-June 1995 450

Trout, T.J. "No reason to be surprised at Pius buckle incident." *The Albuquerque Tribune*, 10-25-96 304

Tune In, Come Out—Generations: Spurred by media images and a new climate of acceptance, teenagers are experimenting more openly with gay and bi-sexuality. *Newsweek*, 11-8-93 574

TV host may be charged (For saying "Don't be a homo.") *The Albuqurque Tribune*, 10-25-96 529

Two boys, 11 and 13, arrested—2-year-old raped, beaten. *The Albuquerque Tribune*, 7-22-95 382

U.S. Craves More Heroin. *Albuquerque Journal*, 2-5-97 398

U.S. will see teen 'blood bath,' experts say. *The Albuquerque Tribune*, 2-18-95 399

Unheeded Red Flags Let Foster Dad's Dark Side Flourish.
   Albuquerque Journal, 2-20-97 560

Unmarried couples get legal status. *The Albuquerque Tribune*, 3-2-93 619

Uribe, Dr. Virginia. "Gay & Lesbian Youth in America." AudioTape
   of Lecture at University Of New Mexico, 10-28-92 568

Vaginal 'Fisting' as a Cause of Death. *American Journal of Forensic
   Medicine and Pathology*, 1989 45

Victim of Prison Rape Devotes Life to Battle. *Albuquerque Journal*,
   July 9, 1995, previously in the Chicago Tribune 83

vos Savant, Marilyn. "Ask Marilyn." *Parade Magazine*, 3-10-96 480

Voyages. U.S.A., 1994 55

Waite, Robert G. L., *The Psychopathic God Adolf Hitler*, New York:
   Signet Books, 1977 138

Wallace, Marian. "Homosexuals are moving into the Main Stream."
   Family Voice, Concerned Women for America, Novemer/December,
   1993 543

Webster's New Twentieth Century Dictionary – Unabridged,
   Second Ed., 1964, The World Publishing Co., Cleveland and
   New York 209

Webster, Noah. *Value of the Bible and Excellence of the Christian
   Religion*. 1834 699

Western civilization has always outlawed sodomy. (Bayer, R.,
   Homosexuality and American Psychiatry, Basic Books, 1981, p. 27) 681

What Causes Homosexual Desires and Can It Be Changed. The Family
   Research Report, Family Research Institute, Inc., 1992 . . . . 75, 160, 166

What Homosexuals Do. Institute for the Scientific Investigation of
   Sexuality, 1987 26

White, M. *AIDS and The Positive Alternatives*. Marshal Pickering, 1987 27

Whitehead, John W.. *The Stealing of America*. Westchester, Il.:
   Crossway Books, 1983 434

wilde. San Francisco, 1995 53

Will, George. "Political agenda, not AIDS, fuels condom battle."
   The Albuquerque Tribune, 1-6-94 593

Will, George. "Sex in Sacramento – And other adventures in the
   sensitivity sweepstakes." *Newsweek*, April 3, 1995 590

Wilstein, Steve. "A Social Shift Occurring On Playing Field."
   Albuquerque Journal, on 6-21-95 622

Witnesses See Man Beaten (to death). *Albuquerque Journal*, 3-30-98) 471

Witnesses speak out on gay ban. *The Albuquerque Tribune*, 5-5-93 536

Witten, Manley, Editor. "PROJECT 10—What Schools teach children about gay sex." *Valley Magazine*, August 1988 570

Woodall, Jim. "AIDS and Your Kids." *Family Voice*, July 1993 445

Yearwood, Lori Teresa, of Knight-Ridder Newspapers. "Finding a home in A HOUSE—Alienated gay youths discover acceptance, sense of family in nontraditional community of support." *Albuquerque Journal*, 1-17-97 623

You say you want devolution. *World*, 11-22-97 489

Zhu, Connie. "THE POLITICS OF AIDS." *Christian American*, October 1993 463

INDEX

To order additional copies of

AS WE SODOMIZE
AMERICA

Have your credit card ready and call

(877) 421-READ (7323)

or send

$24.95 Softcover each
or $29.95 Hardcover each

+ $5.95* S&H to

WinePress Publishing
PO Box 428
Enumclaw, WA 98022

Online orders: www.winepresspub.com

*add $2.00 S&H for each additional book ordered